T0328171

Storage and Commodity Markets is primarily a work of economic
theory, concerned with how the capability to store a surplus affects
the prices and production of commodities. Its focus on the behavior,
over time, of aggregate stockpiles provides insights into such questions as how much a country should store out of its current supply
of food considering the uncertainty in future harvests. Related topics
covered include whether storage or international trade is a more effective buffer and whether stockpiles are more useful in raw or processed form. Several chapters are devoted to analyzing such government programs as price bands, buffer stocks, and strategic reserves –
material in the domain of applied welfare analysis within public
finance. Other chapters deal with the statistical properties imparted by
storage.

Storage and commodity markets

Storage and commodity markets

JEFFREY C. WILLIAMS
Stanford University

and

BRIAN D. WRIGHT
University of California–Berkeley

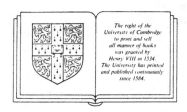

The right of the
University of Cambridge
to print and sell
all manner of books
was granted by
Henry VIII in 1534.
The University has printed
and published continuously
since 1584.

CAMBRIDGE UNIVERSITY PRESS

Cambridge
New York Port Chester Melbourne Sydney

CAMBRIDGE UNIVERSITY PRESS
Cambridge, New York, Melbourne, Madrid, Cape Town, Singapore, São Paulo

Cambridge University Press
The Edinburgh Building, Cambridge CB2 2RU, UK

Published in the United States of America by Cambridge University Press, New York

www.cambridge.org
Information on this title: www.cambridge.org/9780521326162

First published 1991
This digitally printed first paperback version 2005

A catalogue record for this publication is available from the British Library

Library of Congress Cataloguing in Publication data
Williams, Jeffrey C.
Storage and commodity markets / Jeffrey C. Williams and Brian D. Wright
   p. cm.
Includes bibliographical references.
Includes indexes.
ISBN 0-521-32616-8
1. Farm produce – Storage – Econometric models.
2. Petroleum – Storage – Econometric models.
3. Metals – Storage – Econometric models.
4. Commercial products – Econometric models.
I. Wright, Brian. II. Title
HD9000.5.W47   1991
338.1′8 – dc20   90–20063

ISBN-13 978-0-521-32616-2 hardback
ISBN-10 0-521-32616-8 hardback

ISBN-13 978-0-521-02339-9 paperback
ISBN-10 0-521-02339-4 paperback

Contents

v

viii   Contents

Preface

Had this book been written some centuries ago, it would have carried one of those leisurely titles that made authors' prefaces unnecessary. Someone might well have called it *The Stockpiler's Preceptor: or, A Compleat Theory of Rational, Aggregate, Interperiod Storage. Containing a true Account of the Effects of Storage upon the Sequence of Prices & Production of Commodities. To which are added, divers & useful Applications of the aforesaid Theory to Inventories of raw Material, Monopoly, Interactions with Trade, publick Interventions, &c. &c.* But brevity in book titles has since become a virtue, so a word to the reader about our intentions seems advisable here. Our focus is on a multiperiod model of the competitive equilibrium resulting from risk-neutral, forward-looking storers. Although our stylized commodity is most obviously identified with agricultural products, the theory is sufficiently general to offer insights into metals and petroleum as well. We emphasize the behavior of marketwide inventories, at which level price and new production are also endogenous. Our model presents the "first-best" reaction to the continual social uncertainty of unalterable, unpredictable weather or similar exogenous shocks. Rational storage cannot eliminate the effects of these periodic shocks but it can modify them.

We believe it necessary to understand the allocative and welfare effects of idealized competitive storage for an idealized commodity in an idealized market that clears every period before one attempts an analysis of more realistic and more complex situations. Specifically, the dynamic sequence of equilibria must be understood before one can analyze possible disequilibria. By the same token, the behavior of risk-neutral participants should be understood before one attempts to identify the additional effect of risk aversion. Rational competitive storers, who collectively are equivalent to a benevolent planner, provide the level of social welfare against which one can measure market failures or policy distortions.

Readers impatient with the microeconomic theory of competitive industries should nonetheless have several further reasons for reading this book. To those interested in the inventory decisions of individual firms – the domain of back orders, production smoothing, (S, s) models, warehouse placement, and so forth – we can point out that even simple inventory decisions at the individual level lead to complex behavior at the aggregate level. For example, the mere fact that inventories collectively cannot be below zero introduces a profound nonlinearity into the system, which is manifest, among other places, in price series characterized by long periods of busts with occasional sharp peaks. In addition, many theories of a single firm's inventory behavior, notably the production-smoothing model, are themselves tested on aggregate data. The implicit assumption is that the industry behaves as one firm, whereas the feedback effects of collective behavior may not create that result at all.

To those who are primarily interested in econometric study of commodity markets, we make the bold claim that they should not proceed to statistical work before having understood the theory presented here. For example, many econometric systems representing commodity markets posit a demand for inventories as a structural equation along with those for consumption demand and new production. But such a demand for inventories is not a structural equation; rather it is implicitly a function of the characteristics of the true structural equations. Storage may also be influencing econometric testing even when it is not explicit in the problem. Rational storage induces serial correlation in prices and rational forward-looking production. It may be the source of what is taken to be irrational cobweb planting decisions. The same induced serial correlation, which is a direct consequence of the smoothing properties of storage, biases statistical tests of futures prices. Thus, conventional econometric procedures may be giving misleading results because no account is taken of the effects of storage.

To those who focus on the actual policies of countries producing and consuming commodities, we can offer two arguments for reading about this first-best world of an undistorted competitive industry. Admittedly, most policy analysis considers whether the public intervention moves the situation up from the fourteenth- to the thirteenth-best outcome or down to the fifteenth-best. In that setting, an understanding of the first-best world helps to identify counterbalancing distortions. Although much welfare and policy analysis is done in an "open" setting, in which the welfare of some group – say, foreign exporters – is not considered, the "closed" (i.e., worldwide) model developed here is the more inclusive approach, because it can show the effects of the policy on the outsiders.

Although this book presumes a good grounding in the principles of a competitive equilibrium, it is intended to be accessible to the nonspecialist. There are, for example, no long mathematical derivations and, indeed, because the storage model is solved numerically, there is little scope for them. Instead, many graphs and tables present the numerical solutions for specific combinations of parameters.

Despite good intentions, we admit that our text cannot be described as light reading. It presents a new theory, and therefore deprives the reader of the convenience of a familiar conceptual framework. We have tried to make the journey through this new territory less arduous by distinguishing, in separate chapters, the modeling strategy from the solution technique and from the model's lessons. But the three are intertwined to the extent that the solution methodology is helpful for thinking systematically about ways in which the uncertain future influences the present and to the extent that one of the model's lessons is the importance of a multiperiod approach to storage.

Acknowledgments

This book was conceived as a way of expanding several papers that we had written on various aspects of storage into a single work presenting a comprehensive theory of this subject, along with many new applications. Although there remains scarcely a line from our published papers in this text, the ideas and analysis are important in about half of the chapters. For example, our first paper, "The Economic Role of Commodity Storage" (1982a), is the heart of Chapter 4. Our two papers emphasizing welfare effects, "The Welfare Effects of the Introduction of Storage" and "The Incidence of Market-Stabilizing Price-Support Schemes" (1984b, 1988a), are the basis of the arguments of Chapters 5, 12, and 13. Our paper, "The Roles of Public and Private Storage in Managing Oil Import Disruptions" (1982b), appears much expanded in Chapter 15, while "A Theory of Negative Prices for Storage" (1989) is presented in a different form in Chapter 9. Chapter 11 on monopoly traces back to part of our article, "Anti-hoarding Laws: A Stock Condemnation Reconsidered" (1984a). Other material is entirely new, specifically Chapters 6 and 7 on statistical implications of storage, Chapter 8 on the market's reaction to news, Chapter 9 on trade and storage, Chapter 10 on inventories of raw materials and finished goods, and Chapter 14 on price-band schemes. Jeffrey Williams, who between the two of us was responsible for the computer runs, also drafted the new material in Chapters 6–11. With his long-standing interest in the welfare effects of stabilization, Brian Wright took the lead in drafting Chapter 12. The final product, as with our papers, is entirely joint.

Our interest in storage stemmed naturally from our prior interests in futures markets and in the welfare effects of market stabilization. Bruce Gardner's *Optimal Storage of Grain* (1979) and David Newbery and Joseph Stiglitz's *Commodity Price Stabilization* (1981) stand as important contributions to the study of commodity storage and provided the starting point for our work. Bruce Gardner very kindly provided the computer program that served as the point of departure for our routines. Mary Anderson, on the technical support staff at the Department of Agricultural and Resource Economics, Berkeley, and Timothy Richards, a graduate student at the Food Research Institute, Stanford, helped considerably to improve the description of those routines, now in the Appendix to Chapter 3. Doug Christian, a graduate student in the Department of Agricultural and Resource Economics, Berkeley, provided help in assembling the bibliography and reading the various drafts. Brooke Isham, a graduate student at the Food Research Institute, Stanford, helped edit several chapters and improve several graphs. Stephen DeCanio noticed some of the implications of our model for time-series behavior and also made a number of helpful suggestions concerning the introduction and conclusion. Anne Peck, Peter Timmer, and Angus Deaton were most conscientious in reading the entire manuscript. We owe them special thanks. Lorraine Nelson was responsible for the more than one hundred graphs that are key to this volume. She and Anne Hoddinott, both of whom are on the support staff at the Food Research Institute, Stanford, conscientiously retyped the many revisions. Michael Gnat with his copyediting and page layout brought the entire volume together. Our original work on storage was supported by grants from the National Science Foundation in 1979 and 1983, the first at Yale in collaboration with Paul MacAvoy, for which we are most thankful. Brian Wright also received funds in 1987 from the Giannini Foundation for the research that appears here in Chapters 9 and 10. Jeffrey Williams received support from an Alfred P. Sloan Research Fellowship during 1985-7.

CHAPTER 1

Introduction

Anyone with even a passing exposure to the literature on commodity markets and agricultural policy knows the dominant place of issues of price supports and market stabilization. Important ways of supporting prices include marketing quotas, as in many national agricultural policies and international commodity agreements, and purchases by a public authority. The traditional analysis of such programs, such as by Wallace (1962), is a simple supply–demand snapshot of current effects on participants. The differences among the implications of surplus disposal, buffer stocks, or supply controls for the market outcomes in subsequent periods are typically ignored or estimated with an educated guess (e.g., Gardner 1987). Their differential effects on previous storage now part of the current supply–demand picture go unrecognized.

Similarly, in the huge theoretical literature on market stabilization, the means of stabilization is generally neglected. Even though lip service is often given to storage as the source of the stabilization, typically the mechanism is represented as a *deus ex machina,* who suddenly removes some or all of the uncertainty in a commodity market. Even when the subject is a public buffer-stock scheme, and when the actual behavior of storage would seem to be an unavoidable topic, the public buffer stock is commonly assumed to operate in a world without private storage. In this literature, the effects of stabilization and storage are deduced in the style of long-run comparative statics.

In this book storage takes center stage. The models developed here consider explicitly how and to what extent industrywide storage stabilizes a commodity's price over time. Whenever public interventions like buffer-stock schemes are considered, private storage and its interaction with public storage enter conspicuously into the analysis. The models are multiperiod with infinite horizon and allow for a sequence of equilibria as the uncertain weather buffets the market.

A close look at storage in its own right reveals many features at odds with

1

the simple characterizations in the literature. In a scheme already in operation, apparent current boosts in rent to producers may be less than the negative effects of previous public or private stock increases carried into the current period. In the first period of a new scheme, although producers' rents may be increased, the gain may be less than the expected depressing effects on future revenue caused by the scheme's larger carryovers. Because of the interperiod connections forged by storage, the initial conditions at the introduction of a price-support scheme or public buffer stock have more than a trivial effect on the incidence of the policies. To put it emphatically, conventional comparative-statics analysis may well get the incidence all wrong, implying that a program hurts producers when in fact it benefits existing landholders while leaving later entrants unaffected.

Moreover, storage has a noticeably asymmetric effect on price: If without storage the probability distribution of a commodity's price is more or less symmetric, with storage it is skewed, the long tail being toward high prices. At one level this property calls into question those models content to make stabilization simply a question of variance. At a deeper level this asymmetry calls into question the common notion of how storage stabilizes price. Although private storers are motivated by hopes of a great shortfall, they store when there is a surplus. Because, collectively, the market can always store whereas it cannot borrow from the future, storage is much more effective at supporting what would otherwise be very low prices than at reducing what would otherwise be very high prices.

Another example of what is revealed by a close look at storage itself is the time-series behavior of a storable commodity. Because storage spreads the shock of a good or bad harvest across a number of periods, price and planned production are serially correlated. Also, because storage is a more effective buffer the larger the cumulative stockpile, the variance of price movements period to period decreases with the amount in store. These interesting time-series properties are ignored entirely in the standard long-run comparative-statics analysis.

Additional attention to the interaction of public and private storage also pays off. At one level, some insight emerges into questions such as the extent to which the response of private storers offsets the Strategic Petroleum Reserve. At another level, the analysis challenges widely held beliefs about public programs. Here are some examples of the lessons learned from our model:

1. Destruction of excess supply can be more efficient than public stock-piling as a mechanism for supporting prices.
2. The existence of a price floor may cause average producer surplus to be lower.
3. Price-band schemes – in which a public agency tries to defend a floor price symmetric with a ceiling, even around the long-run mean

free-market price – can be inherently explosive, causing (in expectation) a boundless accumulation of stocks. Even when not explosive, price-band schemes not only have a higher social deadweight loss but to producers are less beneficial than straightforward floor-price schemes.

4. Private storage accompanied by speculative attack – which happens when stocks shift suddenly between private and public hands and is taken to epitomize destabilizing behavior – is actually stabilizing.
5. Some seemingly ill-advised public interventions, such as antihoarding laws, may be justified because they compensate for other distortions in the commodity market.
6. Seemingly optimal policies for management of public stockpiles may not increase social welfare.

Modeling strategies

An explicit storage model of any sophistication cannot be expressed with simple two-dimensional graphs, as can single-period supply and demand curves. Nor is such a model algebraically tractable. In addition to the usual feedback on the market price of the collective decisions of atomistic price-takers, anticipations of future storage decisions also affect current ones. These intertemporal links are made more complex by a fundamental constraint on aggregate storage. For the market as a whole, total storage cannot be below zero. The self-evident restriction that the market as a whole can save but it cannot borrow from the future introduces a profound discontinuity in marketwide behavior in reaction to the vagaries of the collective harvest. For all these reasons, the functions determining equilibrium storage must be derived numerically, for a specific set of parameters.

The need for numerical methods may go far to explain why storage is left implicit in most of the literature on stabilization. Specifically, among economists the preference for closed-form analytical solutions is strong. But this preference represents a lagged reaction to the improvement of computers, which can solve such problems as our storage model in a matter of minutes.[1] A solution is a solution no matter whether analytical or numerical, for numerical methods can be made as accurate as one might wish. Economists' preference for analytical solutions also introduces a subtle bias, directing investigation toward those few formulations with closed-form solutions, even though there is no reason why the world should exhibit convenient functional forms. Analytical solutions are often less general than they seem, depending, for example, on the convenient assumption of linear or log-linear functions.

---

[1] Programs now becoming available may take even analytical solutions into the province of computers.

Analytical derivatives of what is, in truth, a special case may be of much less use than a careful sensitivity analysis done with numerical methods for many combinations of parameters. Also the value of an analysis achieved with an analytical approximation that misrepresents important features of storage is far from obvious. Models are intrinsically simplifications, but they are of little use if they simplify out the essential, such as the nonnegativity constraint on inventories.

The methodological tension here has a parallel with branches of engineering. Closed-form solutions to differential equations are something an engineer desires, but if he must, he solves the problem numerically and simulates the equation, for his purpose is to understand its properties, not to prove a theorem. If anything, the problem is more interesting if it is highly nonlinear, if the solution is not immediate, and if the range of specifications covered is more general.

As these comments suggest, the emphasis in this book is on the complex, nonlinear storage behavior of an entire market. This book is not about the optimal inventory models of the operations research literature, which examine the decisions of a single firm. Indeed, to those schooled in the advanced models of management science, the assumptions made here – Gaussian errors, no fixed costs to orders, no backorders – will seem simplistic. Yet the main point of this book is that trivially simple storage behavior at the individual level results in complex relations at the aggregate level. This book will help those concerned with firm-level inventory management to extend their understanding to the behavior of a whole industry's inventories. Also, careful inspection of some of the models of operations research, including the venerable (S, s) inventory model, which addresses the firm's optimal ordering strategy given a fixed cost to the order, reveals an implicit assumption of a monopolistic firm that constrains itself, at considerable lost revenue, not to alter the price of its output. More generally, these models of a single firm take prices of inputs of raw materials as given. Although this assumption is reasonable for a single firm, for many firms together, prices are endogenous.

In the economics literature, the standard microeconomic model supposes a competitive market with many identical firms and consumers, all under conditions of certainty in a single period. This book expands that model to a multiperiod setting under conditions of uncertainty (such as weather variability) while keeping the focus on the aggregate behavior of an industry of identical firms. As with the standard microeconomic model, the first area of study is allocative efficiency, specifically how storage absorbs and disperses the exogenous shocks to the market.

Unlike models of insurance, in which the pooling of individual idiosyncratic risk may leave little social risk, and unlike models of ideal stabilization, in which the underlying cause of fluctuations is removed, here the social risk is unavoidable. The question is how the risk is best distributed throughout the economy. If there are two (or more) regions each with independent weather, trade is one way to dampen any inherent uncertainty. Storage is another, because it transfers some of the good weather to a period with bad weather. (Obviously, trade between and storage within each region is yet another response – one studied here in Chapter 9.) Storage can be used with planting (or production with a one-period lag more generally) should there be some price responsiveness. If the current weather is poor, the shock can be partly dispersed by drawing down stocks and increasing plantings to be harvested the next period. If the weather is unusually good, the carryover is increased while plantings are reduced. Similar reactions occur among inventories of raw materials, goods being processed, and inventories of finished goods, depending on the nature of shocks to that group of industries.

Keynes (1938, p. 449) has written: "It is the outstanding fault of the competitive system that there is no sufficient incentive to the individual enterprise to store surplus stocks of materials, so as to maintain continuity of output and to average, as far as possible, periods of high and low demand." MacBean and Nguyen (1987) take Keynes's statement one step further and argue that the considerable variability of actual commodity prices must be due to inadequate or irrational private storage and is a *prima facie* case for government intervention. But it is a basic error to presume that price movements are necessarily wrong. Stabilization should not be complete, not least because there is a cost to storage. As Burmeister (1978) reiterates by following up a point made by Samuelson (1972), even under certainty it may be optimal for prices to oscillate, depending on the technology of supply and the seasonality of demand. More to the point, under uncertainty private storers will inevitably have stored too little from the *ex post* perspective of a period marked by bad weather or have carried in too much from the perspective of a period with good weather. The government would not necessarily have predicted the weather any better nor accomplished the storage at lower cost. Given the inevitable forecasting errors whoever does the storing, price movements are a proper response. Prices would be even less stable, however, if *ex ante* rational storage were not a viable response to the uncertainty.

Storage is a useful response to social risk even if all market participants are risk neutral, in which case the analysis is of a first-best world. Moreover, a benevolent planner maximizing social welfare would direct storage in the manner of a risk-neutral competitive industry. Thus, with the understanding of the allocative properties of undistorted private storage comes the opportunity for studying the welfare effects of various public interventions into the market.

As an exercise in pure theory, a multiperiod model of storage presents many challenges. The competitive equilibrium is difficult to deduce even for the most basic formulation, as will be explained in Chapters 2 and 3. Because the sequential equilibria of a multiperiod model, once deduced, are not immediately intuitive, Chapters 4–7 are also devoted to various facets of the basic model of a market for a storable commodity. In later chapters, the basic model is extended to include elements such as serial correlation in the weather (Chapter 8) or to cover storage in two regions that can trade at a shipping cost (Chapter 9). This discussion of storage and trade leads naturally to a discussion in Chapter 10 of raw material inventories versus finished goods or goods in process. Chapter 11 is on monopoly. In Part IV of the book, comprising Chapters 12–15, public interventions such as storage subsidies or buffer-stock schemes are investigated. These extensions are not new models specifically designed to illuminate a particular problem (with the risk that the particular model would be inconsistent with arguments made elsewhere); rather, the emphasis is on presenting a unified theory and respecting its discipline.

No effort is made to build a multiequation econometric model of an actual commodity, to "test" the theory as it were. The book is long enough without a huge empirical section, which in any case would be more concerned with specification of demand and supply curves than with storage. In any event, every effort is made to let the theory inform some empirical issue. For example, Chapter 5 illuminates the economics behind the patterns found empirically in futures prices, as does Chapter 6 the time-series behavior of spot prices. In Chapter 9 we offer a new interpretation of the empirical patterns that were named supply-of-storage curves by Working (1948).

Because the theory reveals a number of problems with accepted empirical techniques, it seems pointless to proceed to empirical work with those techniques. A great advantage of models investigated in this book is that they can generate any number of time series where the underlying parameters are known. These synthetic time series permit a check of the accuracy and power of many common statistical procedures. For example, in Chapter 7 the standard regression test for bias in futures prices is applied to futures prices unbiased by construction. The test suggests that the unbiased futures prices are biased, which is not a reassuring result for the test itself. Also in Chapter 7 three standard techniques for supply estimation, including the famous cobweb model and modern "rational expectations" methods, are applied to many synthetic time series. Although all appear to "work" by accepted diagnostic checks, all underestimate the true supply elasticity by a large margin on average. Standard econometric techniques may not be uncovering much truth about actual commodity markets.

Most economists have a working model in their heads of how a commodity market reacts to an increase in input costs or a harvest failure in one region. From this working model they will directly reason about prospective public policies or about possible market failures. For simplicity's sake, the model has a single period. The purpose of this book is to expand that working model so that it includes time and the intertemporal connections of storage. A multiperiod model, beside increasing the understanding of storage specifically, should improve the understanding of how the uncertain future affects the present. When it neglects the implications of storage, most economists' working model of commodity markets does not perform too well.

1.1 Outline of the basic model

A single model serves as the basis for several chapters, whereas the models that appear in later chapters are extensions of it. The basic model corresponds most closely to an annual agricultural crop whose planting intensity can be adjusted except for the lag of one period, that is, one cropyear. Its yield is at the mercy of the weather, which can be broadly interpreted as a shock to production unknown in advance of the harvest except for its density function.[2] The weather in one cropyear is independent of weather in previous cropyears; that is, the weather and yields are pure white noise. Storage across cropyears helps smooth out these fluctuations in yields.

The groups included

The basic model encompasses the entire market for this crop, not just one component such as warehousemen. In the market are three distinct groups: consumers, producers, and storers. All take prices as given and are risk neutral with respect to income. The producers, who must plant in advance of the harvest, and the storers, who hope to profit from their activity, must form expectations about the price to prevail at the next harvest. Both groups hold rational expectations, although this implies not that they can guess the size of the forthcoming crop, but only that they make objective calculations, based on currently available information, about the probability distribution of yields and about the price response to the inevitable production shocks.

The assumptions concerning consumption demand and new production are intended to keep the basic model simple in those areas. The consumers' demand curve for current consumption and the producers' supply curve for planned production are stationary functions from cropyear to cropyear; they do not depend on past levels of consumption or production, and there are no trends. It is also assumed that consumers spend a small share of their budget on this crop. Further, producers plant on a particular type of land, which is in fixed quantity and can be used only for that one commodity. Production can be increased through more intensive use of factors of production beside land,

---

2 The fundamental uncertainty in the model is exogenous and does not arise from lack of knowledge about how others will act – "behavioral uncertainty" in the terminology of Pesaran (1987, chap. 2). Also, no investments in weather forecasting will reduce this uncertainty.

although these have diminishing marginal productivities. Because this crop is assumed to require only a small portion of the economywide quantity of these other factors of production, their prices do not change with movements in planned production. (Accordingly, the only input price studied is the price of land specific to the commodity crop.)

Another assumption about producers is that they experience the same weather. Unless a substantial portion of producers were to have randomness in common, their great number would admit no collective uncertainty. For the same reason, an idiosyncratic component to each farmer's production does not affect aggregate behavior, and so is omitted from the model.

The nature of storage

The role of consumers and producers in the basic model is intentionally kept simplistic to highlight storage. Even given the center of attention, the model's storage industry is nevertheless a mundane one of constant marginal costs over the whole range of positive amounts stored. Complexities such as fixed costs of ordering, capacity constraints, or locations of warehouses in a transportation network are not considered.

For most bulk commodities, including "nonperishable" food commodities such as grains, the unit cost of storage per period (physical protection, insurance, spoilage, and the like) is roughly independent of the size of stocks for all levels of stocks. For example, cotton can be stored outside covered by a tarpaulin. As long as tarpaulins are available, the amount of cotton stored can be as large as desired. Temporary on-farm facilities for storing corn or wheat can be built or dismantled relatively quickly, especially from the perspective of cropyears. For commodities like cocoa that suffer some spoilage, the loss is proportional to the quantity stored.[3] Some other commodities such as water have a marginal storage cost of about zero up to the capacity of the storage facilities, at which quantity the marginal cost jumps sharply higher. Investment in reservoirs takes too long to adjust to current conditions and is virtually irreversible.[4] The theory of stocks for such commodities as water is distinct from the subject here.

The storage considered is primarily that which occurs between cropyears. The model could include continuous storage and consumption through the cropyear, but that complication would add little. As it stands, the model sup-

[3]   The loss may not, however, be proportional to the time between periods.
[4]   Where long-lived, capital-intensive storage facilities such as grain export terminals are involved, one commodity sometimes competes for storage space against others that may have a different annual production time. Thus, for an individual commodity there may always be ample storage space. (This insight about competition for warehouse space is due to Paul [1970], who used it to study grain storage rates implicit in futures prices.)

poses an infinitely long sequence of discrete periods in which a random disturbance determines the size of a harvest. Virgin production is indistinguishable physically from what was previously stored. The economic problem is to allocate the total amount available from the carryin plus new production between current consumption and a carryover to the following period, and simultaneously to select a level of planting for the following period's harvest. The carryout and planned production are equilibrium quantities; the market clears each period.

Frankly, the model is interesting only at the aggregate level, given that decisions are usually uncomplicated at the individual level. To put it another way, individual behavior is kept simple in the model in order to make unambiguous that the model's complexity is due to the feedback effects of collective behavior. Even the collective behavior is obvious if storage and planting decisions are made in an atmosphere of certainty. The randomness in the harvest's size is the main impetus to store and the main source of the complexity in behavior. To be more precise, the main reason the model is interesting is the interaction among the uncertainty, the constraint that aggregate storage cannot be negative, and the essential role of time in production. The nonnegativity constraint on storage makes aggregate behavior highly nonlinear.

The nature of storage becomes more complex in the extensions introduced in the later chapters. For example, Chapter 9 considers storage behavior when the crop is produced in two locations and can be shipped between them at a cost. This two-location model is comparable to storage at one location with an in-and-out charge. Chapter 10 investigates the interactions among inventories of raw materials, goods in process, and finished goods. Chapter 11 considers the behavior of a storage monopolist.

The basic model conceives of a crop harvested during a few days of each year, but by shrinking the time covered by each period, the model can be made to resemble commodities continuously produced, such as copper and crude oil. Most of the specific examples given are calibrated to an agricultural crop, in large part because the source for a shock in the market seems more obvious. The main insights into storage, however, extend to commodities continuously produced, as long as the assumptions regarding storage technology remain appropriate.

1.2   The notion of a system

In any one period the unforeseeable influence on price is the weather affecting that period's harvest. Although prices in the storage model are serially correlated as a result of storage, such that high prices tend to follow high prices and low prices tend to follow low prices, the probability of any particular sequence of prices immediately repeating itself is negligible. Also, the cycles that seem to come from the serial correlation are not true cycles.

They have no set periodicity, nor set amplitude. Thus, from a short series of prices, it is difficult to comprehend the mechanism determining the prices.

Just behind the surface chaos is considerable order. The system is in fact coherent. By *system* is meant a closed model, in contrast to an open model. In a *closed* model all the behavioral relationships are included, whereas in an *open* model some of the values for the principal variables are determined externally.[5] Given particular parameters about technical matters such as supply elasticity, marginal storage costs, and the curvature of the demand curve, the basic storage model has all the information to solve for price, consumption, storage, and planned production (the four principal endogenous variables) each period – in other words to evolve on its own in response to the realizations of the disturbances. A system can be thought of as an entity in its own right. As a system the basic storage model displays order in several complementary ways.

Stable properties

The basic storage model has a steady state, albeit a stochastic one. (Equivalently, the model displays an invariant probability distribution.) To observe this property, consider two fairly long sequences of, say, price. Although period by period the two sequences will have little in common, the frequency distribution of price in those two samples will look similar. The longer both of those two sequences are, the more the distributions of their prices would have similar means, variances, and skewnesses. Any other sequence will have much the same distribution, and not only for price but for any other variable of note, including storage, planned production, and consumption. From the perspective of the current period, another way of saying this is that the probability distribution of, say, price many periods ahead is well defined. These stable distributions characterize the stochastic steady state.

If the current value for one of the variables, such as price, is far from the mean of the infinitely long sequence, the expected path for that variable returns to the steady-state mean. For example, if because of a huge harvest the current price is very low, the expectation is for prices the next few periods to be higher. That is not to say the price invariably increases – the harvest the next period might be even larger – but that the system represented by the storage model regresses toward its mean. The system is ergodic.

The storage model is also time invariant, in the sense that if price in period 614 is by chance the same as in period 35, the expected path back to the steady-state mean is identical. (This property would not apply if the prospec-

---

5   A closed model may be part of a yet larger system, just as the basic model of a commodity market is embedded in a larger general equilibrium model.

tive number of periods were finite.) More fundamentally, if by chance the system has on hand the same amount of the commodity, whether from the current harvest or previous storage, the endogenous variables will have the same values.

Of course, such duplications of conditions are not likely if the weather is drawn from a continuous distribution. On the other hand, one could deduce the relationship between the amount stored and any conceivable value of the quantity of the commodity on hand. This relationship is a *storage rule*. The storage rule, which is also the reduced-form equation for equilibrium storage, suffices to determine the evolution of all the variables. Although the particular amount stored varies from period to period, the reduced-form equation itself is stable. There is a unique storage rule for a given combination of demand elasticity, storage costs, and other parameters. Related reduced-form equations (which it also may be impossible to represent analytically) describe the other endogenous variables as functions of the exogenous parameters and predetermined variables.

As a stochastic system, in short, the storage model behaves in an identifiable way for each set of underlying parameters. It has a distinctive storage rule, distinctive probability distributions for endogenous variables, distinctive univariate time-series properties, and part and parcel a distinctive speed in its tendency to regress toward steady-state means. All this suggests it is instructive to compare systems, for the same reasons one compares the equilibrium values in simple supply–demand models under certainty for different underlying parameters.

In this book one natural comparison is between a system with the commodity storable and a system with the commodity not storable with all other parameters the same. This technique of comparing systems' storage rules and steady-state distributions is also instructive in such areas as the effect of public price support programs, as in Chapter 13, and public price-band schemes, as in Chapter 14. In that setting, one can think of the public program, which will not be directly applicable each and every period, as a regime. A natural comparison is with a regime where there is no such program, namely, the free market.

1.3 The central role of collective behavior

A system or regime is interesting in large part because of the way in which it feeds back on itself. The basic storage model is what is known as a *closed-loop feedback system:* Storage in a particular period depends on the total quantity available in that period, which is a function of the history of the weather. Storage in a particular period also depends on the price that can be expected for the following period; yet that price will depend on aggregate storage at that time, which, in turn, will depend upon the amount stored collectively in yet more distant periods. As a result, current storage depends in part on the relationship between the amount on hand in some future period and aggregate storage in that future period. This feedback of future storage behavior on current aggregate storage first of all makes solving for the competitive equilibrium difficult; the technique called *stochastic dynamic programming* is required. The feedback of aggregate storage on itself also implies that any change in the underlying parameters of the system, such as a lowering of physical storage costs, or even the prospect of such a change, can be instantly reflected in the equilibrium for the current period.

One could also classify as a feedback effect the endogeneity of price. Although for individual decision makers price is exogenous, collectively it is endogenous. This may seem commonplace until it is appreciated that most of the literature on price stabilization ignores it. Price stabilized at its mean, the common analytical conception of stabilization in that literature, is collectively impossible (for all but a linear demand curve and supply with an additive disturbance) without a change in mean consumption. The basic storage model allows for these endogenous responses to degrees of price variability.

Some collective responses are physically impossible. At the level of the whole market the profound restriction on collective behavior is the nonnegativity constraint on total storage. Individuals may appear to be borrowing from the future, but in fact they are borrowing from others in the same period. Collectively they cannot borrow the commodity from the future, not even with the help of financial assets. Grain that will not be ready for harvest until tomorrow cannot be made into grain ready for delivery today. No similar constraint exists in transforming grain available today into grain available tomorrow, for it can be stored. The ability of storage to work in only one direction introduces a nonlinearity into the system. The feedback of this nonlinearity is the primary source of complex behavior in the basic storage model.

Although private storers hope for bad weather and high prices for some future period, the storage they do undertake occurs in the periods with a surplus. Storage thus has an asymmetric effect, even if its overall effect is to stabilize price and consumption. By its nature rational storage is a shock absorber, the shock being the unpredictable weather. It spreads an extreme surplus over several subsequent periods. If a drought strikes during one of them, it is mitigated by consumption of the carryin. But storage inevitably requires a calculated risk. If the carryin is consumed in one drought, it can be of no help if another drought immediately follows. (In other words, their return would have been higher still if the storers had waited to release their holdings.)

Welfare effects

Because storage stabilizes consumption, its primary effect on the average long-run welfare of consumers depends on the curvature of the consumption demand curve. Among demand curves with the same inelastic point elasticity, a linear shape causes consumers to fare better under consumption instability, whereas a highly curved demand curve (e.g., constant elasticity) causes consumers to be better off with stability. Thus, as for analytical constructs like "ideal stabilization," there are for storage no universal conclusions about welfare and incidence.

More important, the interperiod connections forged by storage present two crucial implications previously almost always neglected in welfare analysis. First, producers' benefits from storage are capitalized in land values, with the result that only those producers who own land or the commodity at the time of a regime change benefit from the change. Second, the comparative-statics effects on long-run stability are not the whole story about welfare effects. The welfare effects of such programs as public price-floor schemes depend a great deal on the particular conditions at the time of the announcement of the scheme. The complication of initial conditions makes general propositions about welfare even more difficult, but it does underscore the importance of a dynamic analysis. Chapter 12 is devoted to demonstrating the importance of the initial conditions, and the welfare analysis in other chapters on public interventions (specifically Chapters 13–15) applies the proper dynamic analysis. Generally speaking, the dynamic component of total welfare effects, which depends on the initial conditions, favors producers. For that reason, programs judged to be harmful to producers by conventional long-run comparative statics may actually be beneficial.

In this synopsis of the welfare effects associated with storage, no mention was made of storers. Because storage is assumed to be performed by a risk-neutral industry with constant marginal and average costs, no rents accrue to the storage industry in expectation. Even though their effect on stability and the connection between periods is central, storers themselves are immaterial to the welfare analysis in the model in the case of global risk neutrality. For that matter they are not even integral to the model itself. The same prices, storage, and planned production would emerge even if the storage function was taken over by producers or if there were consumer-storers. Indeed, consumers and producers could be one entity, from the perspective of market-level behavior. The basic storage model (with no distortions like price ceilings) corresponds to a planner's problem, where that planner's objective is to maximize the expected present value of social welfare.

The place of risk aversion in the analysis

The welfare effects derived or considered here have nothing to do with conventional risk aversion with respect to income. Although it may seem strange that the actors in a model concerned with stability and uncertainty are assumed to be risk neutral with respect to income, this approach is sensible for several reasons. First and foremost, the collective responses in the market create substantial welfare effects, even under risk neutrality, and these could easily be misattributed to risk aversion. These welfare effects need to be understood before the complication of risk aversion with respect to income is added. Second, if the commodity of interest is a small share of consumers' budgets, their risk aversion with respect to their incomes, spent on the many possible commodities and services, is essentially immaterial and the effects we report are dominant – a point we have demonstrated (Wright and Williams 1988b).

Of course, the comparable assumption of a small revenue share is much less plausible for highly specialized producers. Yet the basic storage model raises a number of disturbing questions regarding the representation of producers' risk aversion. For instance, are producers risk averse over income or wealth? This distinction, which is not made in the standard single-period models, is important in any situation with a lag between input decisions and output. Are producers more averse to a bad year if it follows a string of bad years? This question is especially important in the context of storage, for public buffer stocks increase the serial correlation between periods. If the answer is yes, producers' utility functions are not additively separable, an implicit requirement of most conventional analyses based on expected utility. Do the producers not have endogenous responses to the risk, such as savings or greater effort following poor harvests? Also, are there no capital markets for producers to use? Or, for that matter, why have they not diversified away their risk in holding a specific plot of land? Thus, the difficulties of analyzing risk aversion in a multiperiod setting are the third reason to accept the simpler assumption of risk neutrality.

Once these issues about the representation of risk aversion in a multiperiod setting are broached, one can also note that the price of land would reflect the riskiness of the revenue stream. Purchasers of land are compensated for risk with a lower price. Accordingly, the market value of any change in stability through a storage program would accrue to those owning land at the time of the policy change. Especially risk-averse producers would have an additional gain, but more risk-neutral producers a corresponding loss. Later entrants with average risk preferences would neither gain nor lose from the program.

1.4   The assumption of rational expectations

In the outline of the basic storage model in Section 1.1, passing mention was made of the assumption of rational expectations. Because it is a central assumption, perhaps it is best to discuss it here at the beginning of the book. Of course, a model of storage requires some assumption about expectations, because storage by its nature is concerned with the uncertain future. Even so, few assumptions in the economics literature are more controversial than that of rational expectations, especially when applied to macroeconomics. Many economists, especially those skeptical of the assumption, instinctively react to the phrase "rational expectations." They point to the weak evidence for the hypothesis in surveys of businessmen's expectations of inflation, interest rates, or sales. (See the reviews in Sheffrin [1983] and Pesaran [1987].) Indeed, it does seem dubious to assume that farmers and warehousemen are as sophisticated in lag operators, ARMA processes, and forecasting techniques as a Ph.D. in statistics.[6]

One response to this skepticism about rational expectations could be to point out economists' split mind. Economists are willing to assume rationality on the part of consumers allocating their budgets or on the part of farmers selecting inputs to grow a particular crop, even though neither of those assumptions can be expected to hold precisely. Economists should extend the same simplification of reality to expectations formation, for the purposes of modeling. Another response, which opens the door to the large debate on the validation of models, is to argue that the test of the assumption of rational expectations is in the performance, perhaps as measured by predictive ability, of the whole storage model. Actually, a third response may be the most effective: The assumption of rational expectations can be restated in ways far less controversial. These other versions have the same implications for the operation and insights of the storage model.

Internally consistent expectations

Most if not all users of models, whether they be economists, physicists, or statisticians, would view with some suspicion a model that was internally inconsistent. More strongly, we hope that most would agree internal consistency is a necessary condition for an adequate model. What about a model could be more dissatisfying to a theoretical physicist than to begin a derivation by supposing that objects of a particular type do not emit electromagnetic waves, then building on that base, and finally deducing from the model that such objects do omit electromagnetic waves? In the context of the storage model, rational expectations might be better called "internally consistent" expectations. To assume anything but rational expectations is to create an internal inconsistency.[7]

The storage model could also be recast without loss of generality to have

6   One complexity of the assumption of rational expectations is irrelevant here, fortunately. Because the uncertainty is public – a mutual disturbance in the weather – the many private agents do not need to deduce from public prices the private information each one knows.

7   For example, if producers and storers extrapolated from the current price– the style of expectations behind the cobweb model – their expectations would not be self-fulfilling. If current price were high, the large quantity planted along with the large carryover would lead to a much lower price than expected.

explicit futures prices and to include a fourth group, professional speculators. Under that formulation storage involves no uncertainty: The storage industry contracts to deliver the commodity the next period at a price set in advance; storers' expectations are immaterial. The assumption that risk-neutral professional speculators make no systematic mistakes, and that through their competition the futures price equals the expected spot price for that delivery date, seems at least plausible. Yet as far as the endogenous variables in the storage model are concerned, this formulation is the same as the one requiring farmers and storers to have rational expectations.

In the same vein, those who doubt the forecasting ability of private producers and storers or speculators are likely to admit that a manager of a public storage scheme cannot do any better. If private expectations are not rational, as is implicitly assumed in many models about storage, even relatively primitive public interventions may be deduced as a way to increase social welfare. This happens because of an implicit assumption of superior expectations embedded in the public policy.

Perhaps this last argument can be made from another direction. One use of something like our storage model is to measure the change in social welfare from policies like the Strategic Petroleum Reserve. If the welfare effects of such a policy are confused with the loss in welfare due to assumed irrational expectations, it is hard to evaluate such a policy properly; it will tend to be valued too highly.

Empirical formulations and tests of rational expectations

It is also important to disassociate the rational expectations assumed in the storage model from what goes by the same name in the empirical literature. The needs of theory and empirical work can be very different. Many, including Eckstein (1984), Ravallion (1985), Thurman (1988), and Holt and Johnson (1989), have constructed so-called rational expectations models of commodity prices, agricultural supply, or commodity storage. Strictly speaking, these empirical studies are intrinsically (if not explicitly) linear models, which dwell on the time-series properties of the various series (and do not use futures prices if available). The postulated expectations are deduced by assuming that the structure remains constant over the sample. In the setting of theory, this approach would predict no reaction in storage or price if the possibility arose for a public intervention into the market. The expectations of the basic storage model, in contrast, are truly forward-looking. Indeed, a premise of the welfare analysis throughout this book is that any anticipations of public policies are instantaneously reflected in prices, storage, and plantings.[8]

---

[8] Some of the literature on storage, or on stabilization policy more broadly, uses the methodology and mindset of stochastic control, a subject of considerable importance

Finally, in several ways this controversial issue of the validity of the rational expectations hypothesis can be turned to advantage. By construction, the prices, consumption, storage, and production from the basic model are subject to the discipline that makes them consistent with rational expectations. This allows one to study arrays of futures prices while controlling some of their properties. Of particular interest, these constructed futures prices are shown to display the "backwardation" and "convenience yield" found in reality. These topics are discussed, among other places, in Chapter 5. The subject also offers the opportunity to study so-called speculative attack, which can arise in a system with both private and public storage and is often accused of destabilizing the market. Salant (1983) has demonstrated that speculative attack can be consistent with rational expectations. Section 13.4 extends his analysis, showing that private storage, including speculative attack, in a system with public storage is unambiguously stabilizing in this kind of model.

Prices rational by construction also allow a check on a number of tests used in the empirical literature to investigate rationality. In Chapter 7, a main theme is how poorly these tests perform, all giving the suggestion of irrationality. By conventional empirical tests, the constructed futures prices appear to be biased downward. By conventional tests, land values appear to be too volatile. By conventional techniques for supply estimation, cobweb models, so often ridiculed as irrational, would seem to fit well. In other words, because the effects of storage on the distribution and time-series properties of price are not acknowledged, common empirical techniques appear to be biased toward finding irrationality in expectations. Inasmuch as empirical work with such techniques provides the primary evidence for doubting the plausibility of including rational expectations in the model in the first place, the issue has come full circle.

1.5 Relationship to other literature

Naturally this book and our earlier work from which it evolved depends on many other contributions to the theory of storage or the theory of stabilization. This book is most closely related to Bruce Gardner's *Optimal Stockpiling of Grain* (1979). The first chapters in particular cover much the same ground as his book, with the hope of building on his contribution in the later chapters.

Gardner's book in turn owed much to the pioneering articles by Gustafson

in engineering. Yet those with an engineering background may not appreciate the additional complexity caused by human actors who can anticipate the stochastic control. Holly and Hughes Hallet (1989) discuss the restrictions placed on a benevolent planner because of the anticipations of his control.

(1958a,b), which were the first to use dynamic programming to solve for rational storage behavior. Gustafson's work was truly pathbreaking, and it remains unfortunate that these articles are not more widely known.[9] Samuelson (1971) related competitive storage behavior to the planner's problem. In this same tradition of rational, forward-looking storage have been articles by Johnson and Sumner (1976), Helmberger and Weaver (1977), Helmberger and Akinyosoye (1984), Lowry et al. (1987), and Helmberger and Miranda (1988). Scheinkman and Schechtman (1983) have explored analytically as far as possible the basic storage model. Miranda (1985) has incorporated public buffer-stock schemes, and Salant (1983) has examined the interaction of private and public storage. All these papers constitute an important literature but one accessible only to a few specialists. We hope this book will offer the insights of this literature to a wider audience while making the notation more consistent and avoiding the repetition of independent articles.

Ghosh et al. (1987) have emphasized public price-band schemes in the context of private storage. Their private storage, not deduced from the dynamic programming approach, is not truly rational. They sought an empirically oriented model, fit to the copper market in the 1970s and early 1980s. Bigman (1985a) also does not have truly rational forward-looking storage. His algorithm iterates on the time-series properties of his system to deduce consistent storage behavior. Bigman does emphasize the interaction of storage and trade, especially restrictions on trade, and we try to build on his insights in some of the later chapters here.

Because Ghosh et al. and Bigman make storage behavior explicit, their books are more closely related to this book than is the analytical literature on price stabilization epitomized by Newbery and Stiglitz (1981). The analytical literature on price stabilization was begun by Waugh (1944) and developed by Oi (1961), Massell (1969), Turnovsky (1976), and many others in the 1970s. (We review this literature in more detail in Chapter 12.) Its discovery of the importance of functional form, especially the curvature of the demand curve, is central to much of the welfare analysis here. Newbery and Stiglitz's book emphasizes the importance of analyzing collective endogenous responses, that is, the market-level equilibrium. This book, like our earlier papers, is an attempt to convey their message in a multiperiod setting.

Recently, models of the industry-level equilibrium where inventories are important have become a hot topic in the macroeconomic literature. Reagan (1982) and Reagan and Weitzman (1982) have approached the problem of inventories in general terms, and have produced very general propositions about the interaction of inventories and production. Motivated by a desire to have specific hypotheses, Blinder (1981) and Blinder and Fischer (1981) have modeled the inventory behavior of a monopolist, with some extensions

---

[9]   Gustafson's work had an origin in Arrow et al. (1951) and Dvoretzky et al. (1952a,b).

to a competitive industry. To get analytical results they have ignored the non-negativity constraint on storage, assuming that unfilled orders are negative inventories. Other papers, such as those by Weitzman (1974) and Eckalbar (1985a), have modeled the interaction between adjustments in quantities and adjustments in prices. The related question of inventory levels and labor demand is considered by Eichenbaum (1984) and Haltiwanger and Maccini (1988). Imrohoroglu (1989) studies the macroeconomic equilibrium when individuals who can save but not borrow are subject to probabilities of unemployment varying over the business cycle.

This large macroeconomic literature, of which these references are only a sample, reveals a widespread interest in models of market-level inventory behavior. A key question of macroeconomics is, after all, how the economy responds to random shocks. Indeed, a specific question is the proportion of the shock absorbed through price moves rather than employment. As Plosser (1989, p. 52) has observed, this "growing body of research in macroeconomics . . . begins with the idea that in order to understand business cycles, it is important and necessary to understand the characteristics of a perfectly working dynamic economic system." This macroeconomic literature has been developed independently of the material on optimal storage of grain, although at the level of theory, the two perspectives produce essentially the same model. Thus, even though this book uses examples calibrated to grains, oil, and other commodities, it should add to the broader understanding of dynamic economic systems.

Outline of remaining chapters

The remaining chapters are grouped into four parts. Part I, comprising Chapters 2–5, is concerned with what has been referred to in this introductory chapter as the basic storage model. Specifically, Chapter 2 sets out the model in more detail, whereas Chapter 3 is concerned with the solution of the model, particularly from the perspective of a benevolent planner. Those readers conversant with numerical dynamic programming may find the discussion of the routines in the Appendix to Chapter 3 especially interesting; most others will be content with the briefer discussion within Chapter 3. For those for whom Chapter 3 is tough going, it should be stressed that the subject of solving for the storage equilibrium is quite distinct from understanding the effect of storage on the market. That subject begins with Chapter 4 and concludes in Chapter 5 with a discussion of the mean-reverting properties of the system.

Part II is shorter, containing two chapters on the time-series properties of a storable commodity. A somewhat arbitrary line is drawn between properties classified as univariate, autoregressive, moving-average (so-called ARMA) stochastic processes (Chapter 6), and those involving combinations of random variables, such as comparisons of futures prices with realized spot prices, or supply estimation (Chapter 7).

Chapters 8–11, constituting Part III, are loosely grouped extensions of the basic model. Part IV, on welfare and policy analysis, proceeds by degree of difficulty. Chapter 12 is concerned with welfare analysis when there are no distortions. Chapter 13 investigates the relatively simple intervention of a price floor supported by a public stockpile. Chapter 14 investigates price-band schemes on which the public stockpile is released only when price rises to some ceiling. Chapter 15 addresses public policies designed to supplement private storage while accounting for the effect of the public policy on the private storage. The final chapter, Chapter 16, offers some general comments on the methodology of studying storage.

PART I

The basic model

CHAPTER 2

Competitive equilibrium with storage

The general simplicity of the storage technology for bulk commodities means that it offers no notable economies of scale and requires no special technical skills. Because of the minimal fixed costs and ease of entry and exit, it is reasonable to assume the number of firms in the storage industry is sufficient for each to be a price-taker. In contrast to some mining activities where large firms dominate, size is not necessarily an advantage in storage operations. In contrast to many types of agricultural production where single-family farms are the dominant form, there are no great advantages to owner operation of storage facilities. Monitoring of managerial agents by owners is relatively easy since unsatisfactory management of the physical stocks cannot be obscured by the vagaries of the natural environment. Hence, it is reasonable to assume that ownership of stocks can be sufficiently diversified for their managers to be taken to behave in a risk-neutral fashion. Thus, in this chapter we specify the competitive equilibrium resulting from the decisions of many risk-neutral, price-taking storers.

Exercises concerned with deducing and studying competitive equilibria are the bread and butter of economists. With storage, however, a four-course banquet is a better analogy:

1. Aggregate storage cannot be negative: As a result, in any particular period the whole storage industry may not be in operation.
2. Because the problem involves uncertainty, the way in which expectations are generated is important; in equilibrium, "rational" expectations would be forward-looking, internally consistent expectations.
3. With no possibility of borrowing from the future (that is, no negative aggregate storage) and forward-looking expectations, stochastic dynamic programming or a related recursive method must be used to deduce the competitive equilibrium.
4. Even with dynamic programming, only in a few special cases can

the equilibrium be solved analytically or graphically; numerical methods are necessary.

Each of these four subjects offers its own challenge. In Chapter 3, we discuss the conceptual methods for solving for the competitive equilibrium, with the focus on stochastic dynamic programming and proposed alternatives to it. (The discussion of the numerical methods for implementing stochastic dynamic programming is left to the Appendix to Chapter 3.) One message of Chapter 3 is that the competitive equilibrium can be deduced more easily if recast as a planner's problem where the planner is trying to maximize social welfare. In this chapter we want to build up and motivate the model from the perspective of the behavior of individual price-taking firms resulting in an industry-level equilibrium. Section 2.4 illustrates the competitive equilibrium with a specific example.

2.1   Storers' arbitrage relationships

Commodity storage is really a type of production with particularly simple technology. Like most production processes, it takes time to change "goods available now" into "goods available later." Unlike other production, the transformation is over time alone; the physical nature of those goods is preserved. Because of the element of time, storage of a commodity is an investment. Nevertheless, it is an especially simple investment, with a minimal planning horizon of one period, even if storage for more than one period is sometimes observed, and with the feature of being fully reversible the next period. A carryout from this period can always be consumed the next period if new circumstances dictate. And a commitment does not have to be made to store for more than one period, in any case.

For an individual firm i in the storage industry, its total physical cost of storing an amount s_t from period t to period $t + 1$ is the simple linear function of the quantity it stores:[1]

$$K^i[s_t] = ks_t \tag{2.1}$$

where $k > 0$ is the constant marginal and average physical storage cost.[2] All firms have the same technology, and that technology does not change with time. With this specification, the aggregation to the industry-level carryout $S_t = \Sigma_{\text{all } i} s_t^i$ is straightforward:

$$K[S_t] = kS_t \tag{2.2}$$

The number of firms in the storage industry is not the main issue; nor is their

---

[1]   Square brackets [ ] will contain exclusively the arguments of general functions or of the expectations operator E.

[2]   Warehousing fees and other components of the cost function K are due and payable in period t.

vertical integration with production or processing. For the market as a whole, the main issue is collective storage S_t. (To reiterate: S_t represents the aggregate of competitive storers' decisions, during period t, about the carryout provided to period $t + 1$. Period t's carryin is S_{t-1}.)

The important decisions of a storer are neither technical nor managerial but entrepreneurial. The criterion is easy to describe: Store until the expected gain on the last unit put into store just matches the current loss from buying it – or not selling it – now. If storers are risk averse, the gains and losses are changes in their expected utility. If risk neutral, storers measure their net gain as discounted expected profits. Because a competitive storage firm (as well as the industry as a whole) need not view a decision to store in the current period as an irreversible commitment of resources for many periods – as it would construction of a steel mill or a freighter – the storer need not look farther ahead than the next period, even if expectations over many future periods are embedded into the prices for the next period. The storage firm can act as if it plans to sell its entire stockpile to the market next period and then decide on any repurchase of stocks.[3]

Profits earned on average by firm i from storage of quantity s_t^i from period t to period $t + 1$ are, as of period t, the difference between revenue in period $t + 1$ and the cost of purchasing s_t^i in the spot market in period t while covering physical storage costs:

$$E_t[\Pi_{t+1}^i] = E_t[P_{t+1}]s_t^i / (1+r) - P_t s_t^i - k s_t^i \tag{2.3}$$

In (2.3) r is the rate of interest per period (assumed constant across periods) and $E_t[P_{t+1}]$ denotes the mean of the distribution as of period t of the prices that firm i anticipates could be realized in period $t + 1$. As of period t, P_{t+1} is a random variable because it will depend on how the weather affects the harvest maturing in period $t + 1$. Because each firm by assumption shares the same rational expectations with other storers, the expectation of the price for period $t + 1$ need not be indexed by the firm. For this price-taking firm, its first-order condition for maximization of expected profits is

$$\partial E_t[\Pi_{t+1}^i] / \partial s_t^i = 0 = E_t[P_{t+1}] / (1+r) - P_t - k \tag{2.4}$$

Note that the firm treats $E_t[P_{t+1}]$ and the current spot price P_t as unaffected by its choice of the quantity to store (whereas at the industry level, a larger carryout reduces price the next period and raises the current spot price, *ceteris paribus*). That is, the firm is a "price-taker."

Market-level relationships

An individual firm would want to expand its storage to a huge amount if it concluded that expected price for period $t + 1$ was above P_t by

---

[3] This formulation supposes no charges for moving stocks into or out of the stockpile.

more than its costs of physical storage and interest.[4] Also, if $E_t[P_{t+1}]$ were below the current price, allowing for storage costs, and if some stocks were being held, an individual firm might consider storing a negative amount. This could be done by borrowing the commodity from other storers for one period, selling the commodity in the spot market, and arranging for yet another party to deliver the commodity the next period, on its behalf, to the lenders.[5]

Neither of these situations is possible for the market as a whole. As a result, equation (2.4) is more properly described as the condition for market equilibrium rather than the first-order condition for an individual firm's maximization exercise. The fact that storers will take any deal that at least breaks even, measured in expected dollars discounted to the present, means that, in equilibrium, no such deals are available; that is, the net expected profit from a marginal unit of storage cannot be positive in any period.[6] Nor can it be negative if some stocks are being held. Profit-seeking stockholders eliminate these types of disequilibria by adjusting their stocks. If the average price for next period is too high relative to the current period's spot price, storers buy stocks and thereby collectively raise the current spot price. The extra aggregate stocks come from a reduction in current consumption. If the expected price is below the current spot price, aggregate stocks are zero, so there is nothing to be borrowed. Intertemporal arbitrage can run only in a forward direction, so when stocks are at zero a signal to store even less cannot be obeyed.

The possible relationships between the amount of collective storage and the expected net profit from it can be summarized by the following complementary inequalities:

$$P_t + k - E_t[P_{t+1}]/(1+r) = 0, \qquad S_t > 0$$
$$P_t + k - E_t[P_{t+1}]/(1+r) \geq 0, \qquad S_t = 0 \tag{2.5}$$

Equation (2.5) is the central condition for a competitive equilibrium with storage.

Arbitrage relationships from the perspective of futures prices

The arbitrage equation (2.4) for an individual private storer can be recast in terms of futures prices. Suppose $F_{t+1,t}$ is an explicit futures price, recorded on an organized exchange, for delivery of the commodity in period

---

4 This possibility of seemingly limitless profits for an individual firm is the result of the second-order conditions not ensuring an internal maximum. The objective function (2.3) is linear in the decision variable.

5 The first two steps – borrowing and then selling spot – are a "shorting" operation, which leaves the firm with a commitment to deliver the commodity the next period.

6 Throughout this book, the term "profits" excludes the value of inputs in alternative uses, which is also the opportunity cost of attracting inputs into this use; thus, it is net of "normal profits."

$t + 1$ as of period t. Because the amount stored involves no uncertainty (any spoilage is at a fixed rate), unlike the harvest in period $t + 1$, an individual storer could make riskless profits if prices do not satisfy[7]

$$P_t + k = F_{t+1,t} / (1+r), \quad S_t > 0$$

$$P_t + k \geq F_{t+1,t} / (1+r), \quad S_t = 0$$
(2.6)

$F_{t+1,t}$ and futures prices as of period t for yet later delivery dates, such as $F_{t+3,t}$, are related to expected prices through the actions of professional speculators who ensure that

$$F_{t+1,t} = E_t[P_{t+1}], \quad F_{t+2,t} = E_t[P_{t+2}], \quad \ldots$$
(2.7)

That the futures prices equal expected prices as in (2.7) presumes speculators who have rational expectations and who are risk neutral.[8]

---

[7] Since (2.6) involves no risk, it is a true arbitrage relationship. The application of the term "arbitrage" to relationships involving expectations is, strictly speaking, invalid.

[8] Futures markets have traditionally been considered markets for risk transfer between hedgers and the speculators who assume the hedgers' risks in return for a risk premium, although Working (1953, 1962) steadfastly argued against this view. There are a number of reasons to doubt substantial risk premia in futures markets.

According to modern finance theory, any risk premium in the price of a tradeable asset should arise only from that part of the price risk that is correlated with the market portfolio (in the case of the Capital Asset Pricing Model) or with the market factors (in the case of the Arbitrage Pricing Theory). Dusak (1973) found that excess returns above a risk-free (Treasury-bill) rate for wheat, corn, and soybean futures for 15 years (1952–67) were generally insignificant, in contrast to a substantial return on the Standard and Poor Index, which exhibited comparable variability over the sample period. In regressions of semimonthly excess returns for various commodities on the excess returns of the market portfolio, the estimated slope coefficients (the β values of the CAPM) were very small and with standard errors of similar magnitudes, indications of negligible systematic risk to positions in commodities. Further, the estimated values of the intercept terms were also tiny and frequently negative, indicating that the substantial nonsystematic risk of these contracts obtained no risk premium but was diversified away in conformance with the theory. Dusak's method and results were questioned by Carter et al. (1983), but recent work by Marcus (1984) and Baxter et al. (1985) with longer sample periods and better definitions of the market portfolio confirms Dusak's findings.

More traditional studies of market efficiency have searched for the "risk premium" identified by Keynes, with very mixed results. Typically, the price at maturity is regressed on the futures price at earlier dates with null hypothesis of zero intercept and unit slope. The bias in such studies toward rejecting the null hypothesis and finding a risk premium will be exposed in Chapter 7. Still, the many studies show at best inconclusive results regarding positive premia for futures market risk. Even in cases that detect statistically significant premia, their economic significance is generally negligible. One should not forget that Keynes (1930, p. 144) reckoned a typical risk premium at 10% per annum. Finally, an empirical study by Hartzmark (1987) of daily trades of large traders, using a $4\frac{1}{2}$-year sample period for seven commodities plus Treasury bonds and Treasury bills, shows that "noncommercial" (i.e., speculative) traders earn nonpositive average returns, contrary to the Keynesian theory of a risk premium.

(cont.)

This formulation of the problem with futures prices and speculators leads to the same market-level equilibrium as when storers themselves bear the uncertainty of price in period $t + 1$. Obviously, a mixture of speculators who sometimes store and some storers who speculate also leads to the same market-level behavior in this model. Hence, the extent to which various parties combine roles is not a central issue in the model. What is important is that whoever is forming expectations does so rationally. If some speculators are risk neutral, have no capital constraints, and have rational expectations, the risk attitudes of storers will not affect their storage decisions.[9]

2.2   Market-level prices and quantities

Thus far, the focus has been on the response of competitive storers to current and anticipated prices and the qualitative price relationships consistent with profit maximization by such storers. But how are prices and amounts of storage and consumption determined in the market?

As in the storage industry, consumers and producers are assumed to be price-takers. The quantity q_t consumed collectively by the many identical consumers in period t is related to aggregate realized production h_t and storage through the identity

$$q_t = h_t + S_{t-1} - S_t = A_t - S_t \tag{2.8}$$

where A_t denotes marketwide "availability," that is, the amount on hand in period t, furnished from production or previous storage.[10] (A notational challenge arises because, unfortunately, both "storage" and "supply" begin with s, while p begins both "production" and "price"; h for "harvest" seems a good compromise.)

Consumption is related to price via the consumption demand curve, which, written in inverse form, is

$$P_t = P[q_t], \quad \partial P / \partial q < 0 \tag{2.9}$$

Note that income variation of consumers is suppressed for simplicity. The same function applies in each period, which is not the same as saying price is

---

One conclusion regarding storage and speculation seems justified. Given the current state of finance theory and empirical results regarding commodity markets in the United States, our assumption of risk-neutral speculation is the most reasonable maintained hypothesis. Whether alternative assumptions are preferable in some markets is obviously an open question. Some commodities may perhaps have more systematic risk and, in some less-developed countries, price risk may be much less easily diversified.

[9] Storers' risk attitudes will affect only their positions in the futures market, not their storage behavior. This insight was originally derived for producers facing price uncertainty by Holthausen (1979) and Feder et al. (1980).

[10] It is assumed that there is no difficulty measuring A_t, whether it arises from new production or a carryin.

the same in every period. More important, consumption is intertemporally separable: Current consumption is not also a function of the prices, as of period t, for delivery in later periods.

In the absence of intertemporal variation in supply or demand, there would never be any storage in the model, because the net marginal cost of storage is positive. Storage here stems from a random disturbance – weather variation v_t – in yields with a mean of zero. The weather, good or bad, is shared by all producers. All parties know the distribution of v_t, and in each period its value is an independent draw from that distribution. Thus, the realized harvest is

$$h_t = \bar{h}_t(1 + v_t) \tag{2.10}$$

where $\bar{h}_t$ is production collectively planned for period t as of the previous period, that is, $E_{t-1}[h_t]$. For now, assume that $\bar{h}_t$ is constant; there is no supply response.

These relationships for consumption and the harvest complete the model and make it possible to deduce the level of current storage (and, by extension, current price). The arguments in the conditions for intertemporal arbitrage in (2.5) can be expanded to

$$\begin{aligned} P[A_t - S_t] + k &= E_t[P[h_{t+1} + S_t - S_{t+1}]]/(1+r) && S_t > 0 \\ P[A_t - S_t] + k &> E_t[P[h_{t+1} + S_t - S_{t+1}]]/(1+r) && S_t = 0 \end{aligned} \tag{2.11}$$

Here both h_{t+1} and S_{t+1} are random variables, depending on the realization of v_{t+1}. If one knew S_{t+1} conditional on A_{t+1}, the relationship between A_t and S_t could be calculated from (2.11).

An example with two periods

In a problem with merely two periods, t and $t+1$, S_{t+1} must be fixed from outside the model. For example, since any carryout from the last period could be said to have no value, reasonably S_{t+1} could be specified to be zero regardless of h_{t+1}. Under these special circumstances with S_{t+1} known, it is possible to solve for S_t immediately from (2.11). Such a two-period problem is worth working out in detail because it illustrates the nature of an equilibrium under rational expectations.

Consider a specific functional form for the inverse consumption demand curve, applicable in both periods: $P[q] = \beta/q^5$ with the constant β calibrated to have the curve pass through the point (100 units, $100). (The demand curve thus has a constant elasticity of –0.2.) Suppose that h_{t+1} has a three-point distribution of 80, 100, and 120 units, each with a one-third probability. Let marginal physical storage costs $k = \$3/$unit and $r = .02$ (2%), and, no matter why, let the current availability A_t be 110 units. What is the equilibrium storage S_t^* given that particular A_t? Given that the equations of the model are known, S_t^* can be found by trial and error. Try guess A at 5.00 units of stor-

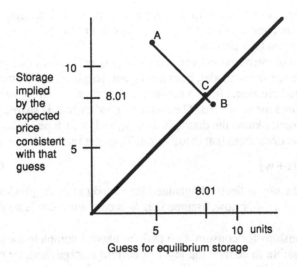

Figure 2.1. Fixed-point solution for equilibrium storage.

age, which should not be far wrong because it is half of the surplus of A_t over $\bar{h}_{t+1}$. If S_t is 5.00, A_{t+1}, which is also consumption q_{t+1}, is 85, 105, or 125, with corresponding prices of \$225.38, \$78.35, or \$32.77. Given S_t is 5.00 units, the expected price, $E_t[P_{t+1}|S_t = 5.00]$, is \$112.17, which is $\frac{1}{3}(225.38 + 78.35 + 32.77)$. Now, were $E_t[P_{t+1}]$ equal to \$112.17, private storers would bid up the current price until it equaled $((112.17/1.02) - 3.00)$, which is \$106.97. The amount of storage consistent with P_t equal to \$106.97 is 11.34.[11] But the presumed value of S_t was 5.00.

The equilibrium storage must be consistent with itself. It must be on the 45° line in Figure 2.1. Because 11.34 units is above 5.00, guess A is not the equilibrium value. A guess halfway in between, namely 8.17 units, might be better. This second guess, marked as B, is also off the 45° line in Figure 2.1, although only slightly. A third guess of 8.01, marked as C, reproduces itself to an accuracy of two decimal points. It is the equilibrium S_t^* when A_t is 110.00 units. With S_t equal to 8.01, P_t is \$90.62 and $E_t[P_{t+1}]$ is \$95.50, which is above \$90.62 by exactly the marginal physical costs of storage plus interest. The arbitrage relationship (2.5) holds for each storer individually and collectively. The value \$95.50 is also the average price in period $t + 1$ should q_{t+1} have a one-third chance of being either 88.01, 108.01, or 128.01 units.[12] This expected price $E_t[P_{t+1}|S_t = 8.01]$ is therefore consistent with

---

[11] $106.97 = \beta/(110 - 11.34)^5$.
[12]   Note how the calculated average $\bar{P}_{t+1}$ changed with a different guess for S_t, specifically, declining with a higher carryover. For that reason $E_t[P_{t+1}]$ is a function of S_t.

the amount of collective storage dictated by that expected price. In that sense of internal consistency the storers' expectations are rational.

Equilibrium relationships as reduced-form equations

In more general problems involving more than two periods, the goal is also to find the rational expectations equilibrium. But, especially in a setting with an infinite horizon, the solution is not so easily found because the complication of knowing S_{t+1} given A_{t+1} cannot be assumed away. The trouble is that, if one knew how S_{t+1} depended on A_{t+1}, one would already have the solution to the relationship between storage and availability in this stationary model. Seemingly, one must know collective storage behavior to deduce collective storage behavior. As explained in Chapter 3, recursive methods such as stochastic dynamic programming permit the equilibrium S_t to be deduced.

A few points can be made about the solution to the general problem, even without dynamic programming. In the two-period example, the equilibrium S_t was found for a particular A_t. Similar calculations could be done for any other A_t. This suggests there is a unique relationship between S_t and A_t. In the case of an infinite horizon, the relationship does not change from period to period, since the nature of the problem does not change. We write this stationary relationship as

$$S_t = f^S[A_t] \tag{2.12}$$

The relationship between S_t and A_t is known as a *storage rule* because it tells how much is stored collectively for any given current circumstance, summarized in the current availability A_t. In the present setting of emphasizing the competitive equilibrium, a better name for (2.12) is that of a *reduced-form equation*. Analogously with large macroeconomic models, the demand curve (2.9) and the storage arbitrage condition (2.5) are the underlying behavioral relationships, (2.8) is an identity, and (2.12) is the reduced-form equation for an endogenous variable, the quantity stored. In a rational expectations macro model, the counterpart to (2.12) is the savings function.

If the reduced-form equation (2.12) could be written explicitly, in addition to A_t, it would be a function of various underlying parameters such as the physical storage cost k, the consumption demand elasticity η^d, and the variance of yields σ_v^2, which specify the physical storage cost function, the demand function, and so on. (An analytical example is given in Chapter 3.) But among these exogenous and predetermined variables, current availability A_t alone changes from period to period, with the vagaries of the harvest. That is why it is singled out for special attention in (2.12). The influences on this relationship of the various fixed parameters (and the functions they represent more generally) are studied in Chapter 4.

The reduced-form equation for S_t would not, however, be a function of variables such as current price P_t, or storage in some future period, say, S_{t+8}. These variables are endogenous and are, in fact, indirectly determined by the relationship between S_t and A_t. One could reexpress the relationship between storage and availability as a reduced-form equation for consumption, $q_t = f^q[A_t]$, or a reduced-form equation for price, $P_t = f^p[A_t]$. For some expository purposes (e.g., Figure 2.6 below) these alternative formulations are useful.

2.3   Market equilibrium with elastic supply

In modeling supply, the issue of a time lag between input commitment and output response is crucial. For the demand side of the model, we have already assumed an instantaneous response of consumption to price. When the consumers choose a level of consumption, they are completely certain of the price. Issues of expectations formation do not arise. We have also assumed that the short-run demand curve is the same as the long-run demand curve.

The realism of instant and full demand responsiveness depends on the commodity. For an intermediate input, its short-run flexibility in use depends on the flexibility of complementary factors. Thus, the demand for natural gas is constrained in the short run by the stock of gas-burning equipment; the demand for cattle feed is constrained by the responsiveness of the stock of feeder cattle. Furthermore, habit formation has been shown to be important for some consumer goods. For foods such as wheat that have been the focus of much of the discussion about stabilization schemes, the assumption of a fully instantaneous (i.e., within-period) consumption response is more acceptable, although habit formation is mentioned in discussions of the effects of foreign aid in countries like Brazil, where the taste for wheat is said to have risen since the United States began sending wheat as a regular form of food aid.

On the supply side, the assumption that all response is instantaneous would clearly be unrealistic for commodities. All commodity production involves commitment of inputs before the output price is known, so that the formation of price expectations is of major concern to producers. In agricultural production, for example, major inputs must be chosen by planting time, usually months before harvest.[13] In mining the delay is usually longer though the labor input may, at least in principle, be more flexible in the short run since work requirements are less susceptible to seasonal constraints.[14] (In practice,

---

[13] For a thorough exploration of the implications of such a situation, with several stages of input commitment as information about the weather unfolds, see Fafchamps (1989).

[14] If there is one instantaneously variable factor, "labor," as well as one quasi-fixed factor, "land," responses to price uncertainty by risk-neutral profit-maximizing firms in their choice of expected output and factor proportions resemble what one might ex-

union contracts or political pressure may severely limit the flexibility of the labor input.) In this book, to represent the delay between "planting" and "harvest," we assume a one-period lag in production response. There is no short-run (within-harvest) response at all. The lag between input and response in production means that producers' expectations have relevance for supply.

When new production is responsive to expected profit opportunities, the market equilibrium is even more complicated. Producers, like storers, are price-taking competitors who are assumed to hold rational expectations. That is, they do not consider the effect of their own individual actions on prices, but their price expectations are consistent with the distribution of prices that will be generated by their collective behavior, given those expectations.

For producer i, expected profit from planned production $\bar{h}_t^i$ is

$$E_{t-1}[\Pi_t^i] = E_{t-1}[h_t^i P_t] - H^i[\bar{h}_t^i] \tag{2.13}$$

where H^i is the total cost to producer i of inputs to production of $\bar{h}_t^i$ which must be chosen in period $t-1$, and $h_t^i P_t$ is the resulting revenue. No revisions can be made at the time of harvesting; within-period supply elasticity is zero. The first-order condition for expected profit maximization is

$$\partial E_{t-1}[h_t^i P_t] / \partial \bar{h}_t^i = \partial H^i[\bar{h}_t^i] / \partial \bar{h}_t^i \tag{2.14}$$

P_t depends on aggregate consumption q_t, that is, $P_t[q_t]$. Since the price-taking producer by definition ignores the response of q_t to his own planned output h_t^i, the left-hand side of (2.14) is the expected increase in revenue from an increase in planned output, which we define to be P_t^r. P_t^r is the producers' incentive price (also known as the action certainty equivalent price) for production planned in period $t-1$ to be realized in period t. (P_{t+1}^r is the planting incentive for the harvest in period $t+1$.) Producers, being identical, have the same incentive price.

In the left-hand side of (2.14), h_t^i can be restated in terms of planned production and the disturbance v_t, and q_t in terms of the harvest and the carryin and carryout:

$$
\begin{aligned}
P_t^r &= \partial E_{t-1}[(1+v_t)\bar{h}_t^i P_t] / \partial \bar{h}_t^i \\
&= E_{t-1}[(1+v_t)P_t] \\
&= E_{t-1}[(1+v_t)P[(1+v_t)\bar{h}_t + S_{t-1} - S_t]] \\
&= E_{t-1}[h_t^i P_t] / \bar{h}_t^i \tag{2.15}
\end{aligned}
$$

The producer, although a price-taker, recognizes that the yield disturbance has the same proportional effect on h_t^i as on realized aggregate output h_t. In

---

pect from risk aversion. See Stigler (1939), Hart (1942), Hartman (1976), and Wright (1984).

general, the producer incentive price P_t^r differs from $E_{t-1}[P_t]$. The third line of (2.15) implies that a term in the second moment of v_t, $E_{t-1}[v_t^2]$, appears in this expression when all the functions are expressed explicitly.[15] For inelastic demand curves, P_t^r is below the corresponding $E_{t-1}[P_t]$. Although for a number of major crops Marcus and Modest (1984) have computed the difference to be within 5 percent, such differences can be important in determining the incidence of stabilization schemes, as we show in Chapter 12.

In all the systems investigated in the book, $\bar{h}_t$ is a simple linear (and stationary) function of P_t^r. Different values for $\bar{h}_t$ can be thought of most simply as adjustments in acres planted. Nevertheless, the more cumbersome notion of changes in "planting intensity" on a fixed number of acres – as when more care is taken in soil preparation or planting – is the terminology used in later chapters. Response of the number of acres planted as the planting incentive changes implies that land is not homogeneous. That heterogeneity complicates the calculation and discussion of the price of land. With homogeneous land and the same expectations about the future, individual producers do not need to be distinguished. Accordingly, $\bar{h}_t$ without the superscript i represents the market-level "planned production," appropriately scaled, planted in period $t-1$.

The producers' incentive price without storage

The producers' incentive price is an unfamiliar concept; many experienced economists have puzzled over it. First of all, it presumes that each producer accounts for the effect of his own yield disturbance on price even though he is a price-taker. Because all producers experience the same yield disturbance, the realized market price covaries with each producer's realized output. Even a price-taker will recognize this covariance and set his planned output accordingly.

Second, the equilibrium producers' incentive price P_t^r for production planned in period $t-1$ to be realized in period t is an endogenous variable at the level of the market. More precisely, it is the fixed-point solution, one that, should the producers all recognize it as their incentive, is consistent with itself. Perhaps an example, in a setting without storage, can make this clear. Suppose the demand curve, which passes through the point (100 units, $100), has a constant elasticity of demand of -0.2. Suppose the supply curve is $\bar{h}_t = 40 + 0.6P_t^r$ (a supply elasticity $\eta^s = 0.6$ at (100 units, $100)), and let the weather have a two-point distribution of $+.25$ and $-.25$ as a proportion of $\bar{h}_t$, both with a probability of 0.5. What are the equilibrium P_t^{r*} and $\bar{h}_t^*$? The

---

15 The distinction between the producer incentive price and the expected price has been drawn by Wright (1979), Newbery and Stiglitz (1979), and Scandizzo et al. (1984). Note that if the disturbance is additive, P_t^r equals $E_{t-1}[P_t]$, the expected price. The first line of the right-hand side of (2.15) would be $\partial E_{t-1}(v_t \bar{h}_t^i) P_t / \partial \bar{h}_t^i$.

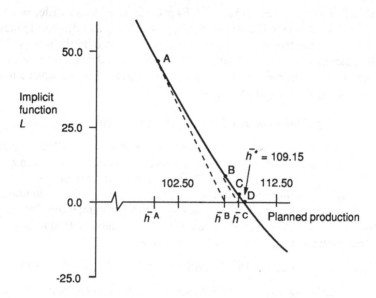

Figure 2.2. Numerical solution for equilibrium planned production.

problem can be approached from either variable; here use $\bar{h}_t$. Define L as the implicit function,

$$L \equiv 40 + 0.6(P_t^r | \bar{h}^{guess}) - \bar{h}^{guess} \qquad (2.16)$$

If an $\bar{h}^{guess}$ is the correct value $\bar{h}_t^*$, L equals 0.0. Figure 2.2 plots L as a function of $\bar{h}$. For these parameters, $\bar{h}_t^*$ can be found by numerical methods. Start with a guess $\bar{h}^A$, of 100 units, which is where the supply and demand curves cross under certainty. If planned production is 100 units, realized production is either 75 units or 125 units, in which case price is either $421.40 or $32.77, and

$$\begin{aligned}(P_t^r | \bar{h} = 100) &= 0.5 \times 421.40 \times 75/100 + 0.5 \times 32.77 \times 125/100 \\ &= \$178.50 \end{aligned} \qquad (2.17)$$

If P_t^r were $178.50, $\bar{h}_t$ would be at 147.10 units, not the 100 units guessed. Point A in Figure 2.2 measures the internal inconsistency when the guess is 100 units. A second guess $\bar{h}^B = 107.42$ is found by linear extrapolation along the function L, as shown in Figure 2.2.[16] The internal inconsistency between $\bar{h}^B$ and $P_t^r | \bar{h} = 107.42$ is smaller; L is 7.54, the vertical coordinate of point B. The discrepancy at a guess $\bar{h}^C$ of 109.08 is smaller still. On the fourth iteration, L is effectively 0.00; the equilibrium $\bar{h}_t^*$ is found to be

[16]   The derivative $dL/d\bar{h}$ is also found numerically, by finding the value of L with planned production 0.001 less than the guess under consideration.

109.15 and P_t^{r*} to be \$115.24.[17] Expected price, meanwhile, is \$125.45 $= .5 \times P[(1 - .25) \times 109.08] + .5 \times P[(1 + .25) \times 109.08]$. It is higher than P_t^r because the two possible prices are not weighted by the size of the harvest, the small harvest weighting the higher price and the larger harvest weighting the lower price.[18] These numerical methods are an economist's tools for ascertaining the competitive equilibrium.

Equilibrium planned production with storage

In a setting with storage, in any one period the collective behavior of producers and storers allocates the current availability between q_t and S_t while setting the amount being planted for harvesting in period $t+1$. Fixed-point solutions must be found together for S_t and $\bar{h}_{t+1}$. The simultaneity of the decisions can be seen in this expansion of the arbitrage condition (2.5) for positive S_t, in which the functions are given time subscripts to make clear the relationships among the endogenous variables:

$$P_t[A_t - S_t] + k = E_t[P_{t+1}[\bar{h}_{t+1}[P_{t+1}^r[S_t]](1 + v_{t+1}) + S_t - S_{t+1}]] / (1 + r) \quad (2.18)$$

This equation (2.18) implicitly contains the relationship between equilibrium storage in period t and exogenous and predetermined variables. Because planned production is a function of S_t and the parameters, the reduced-form equation is still simply the function,

$$S_t = f^S[A_t] \quad (2.19)$$

Obviously, the precise nature of that relationship is affected by the supply function. Also, there is now an associated "planned production rule," which is the reduced-form equation giving a unique amount planted to be harvested the next period for each value of current availability:

$$\bar{h}_{t+1} = f^{\bar{h}}[A_t] \quad (2.20)$$

(The timing is such that $\bar{h}_{t+1}$ is in equilibrium with S_t, because S_t refers to the carryout from period t and the carryin for period $t + 1$. Both $\bar{h}_{t+1}$ and S_t are committed in period t.) The reduced-form equation for storage (2.19) and for planned production (2.20) are simultaneously determined; one supposes the other; f^S and $f^{\bar{h}}$ are different functions, of course.

2.4   Equilibrium for a specific example

A specific example may clarify the simultaneous equilibrium between storage and planned production, for given current circumstances. As the wea-

---

17   The market need not follow such an iterative process, although an auction might well do exactly that.

18   If the weather disturbance were additive rather than multiplicative (and $E_{t-1}[P_t]$ equal to P_t^r), the equilibrium $E_{t-1}[P_t]$ would not, of course, be \$125.45.

ther evolves through time, the prevailing circumstances change. Thus, the interaction between storage and planned production might be better described as a sequence of equilibria, covering eleven periods such as the one at the end of this section. The terminology of a "sequence" of equilibria is used instead of that of "temporary" equilibria, because the latter has been used to connote a revision of prevailing prices in an incomplete set of markets when some aspect of the economic environment is better understood. (See Grandmont [1977] for a review of the literature on temporary general equilibrium theory.) Here it is impossible to improve on the forecast of the weather. There is some irreducible uncertainty, which becomes manifest only with each period's realized weather. The sequence of equilibria is the rational and complete response to that inherent uncertainty.

Both for understanding the model and for making comparisons among systems, a base set of parameters is needed. The point where the demand and supply curves would cross under certainty is an important reference; designate P^N and q^N as this nonstochastic equilibrium. Under certainty q^N equals h^N; there is never any storage. Rather than denominate P^N and q^N with values reminiscent of a specific crop, such as \$3.00/bushel and 2,000,000,000 bushels, let $P^N = \$100$/unit and $q^N = 100$ units. Then deviations from this point can also be read as percentage deviations.

Other than the calibration of the certainty equilibrium, the base case is set to represent a primary food grain in the United States. The consumption demand curve (which, recall, is stable from period to period) should be price inelastic, both to mimic food-grain demand and to allow a significant role for storage. When the demand elasticity is higher, adjustments in current consumption absorb more of the harvest disturbances, so that the price spreads necessary to support storage occur less frequently. Specifically, let the demand curve be linear and have an elasticity $\eta^d = -0.2$ at the nonstochastic equilibrium.[19]

Let planned production be a linear function of the producers' incentive P_t^r, with an elasticity $\eta^s = 0.5$ at the nonstochastic equilibrium.[20] Let the yield disturbance v_t be normally distributed with a mean of 0.00 and a standard deviation of 0.10 (as a proportion of planned production).[21] If supply were perfectly inelastic (or if the comparable disturbance were additive), this yield disturbance would translate into a standard deviation of harvests σ_h of 10 units (and coefficient of variation of 10%). Here, with a disturbance to yields, σ_h fluctuates around 10.00, as the planting intensity changes. In contrast, σ_v is exogenous and constant. Finally, the marginal physical storage cost k is set

---

[19] Thus, the precise form of equation (2.9) is $P[q_t] = 600 - 5q_t$.

[20] Thus, the specific supply function is $h_t = 50 + 0.5P_t^r$. Linearity of this function is not crucial. The range of movement of h_t is small relative to the range of h_t.

[21] The yield disturbance in one period is independent of those in other periods.

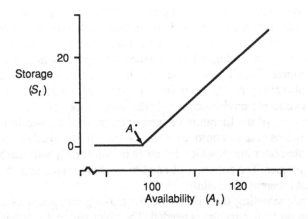

Figure 2.3. Equilibrium storage as a function of current availability.

at $2.00 per period (2% of P^N) and the interest rate r at 5 percent per period. These various parameters do not change with time, and the horizon is infinite.

Reduced-form equations for these parameters

The implications of this system's parameters can be expressed in two reduced-form equations. These are

1. the relationship between the amount stored in any period and the current availability, and
2. the relationship between the amount planted for the next harvest (i.e., planned production) and the current availability.

These two equations imply the relationships between other endogenous variables and current availability. Because the problem has an infinite horizon, these relationships are time invariant.

The relationship between the equilibrium storage and current availability, deduced through numerical methods, explained in the Appendix to Chapter 3, is shown in Figure 2.3. It is the exact relationship, for this group of parameters, represented in general form by equation (2.19). For any current availability A_t, which comprises the current harvest h_t and the carryin S_{t-1}, the storage rule gives the equilibrium carryout S_t.[22] Figure 2.4 plots the equilibrium planned production as a function of the current availability. The availability A^*, below which the equilibrium storage is zero, marks an important

[22] The generic subscript t is meant to emphasize that the reduced-form equation is the same for all periods; otherwise, in (2.19) the function f itself would have a time subscript. The function f would be time-dependent were the system one with a finite horizon.

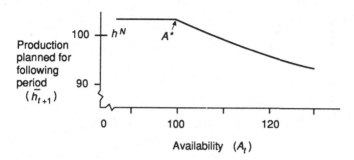

Figure 2.4. Equilibrium planned production as a function of current availability.

transition in the shapes of the reduced-form equations. This kink point $A*$ is marked in both figures. (The asterisk no longer denotes an equilibrium value. All values graphed for S_t and $\bar{h}_{t+1}$ are equilibrium values for particular A_t's.)

From these reduced-form equations for equilibrium planned production and storage can be derived the companion reduced-form equations for other endogenous variables as functions of A_t. For consumption, the transformation is direct. Out of current availability, what is not stored is consumed. Thus,

$$q_t = f^q[A_t] = A_t - f^S[A_t] \tag{2.21}$$

From the inverse consumption demand function given in (2.9) and the reduced-form equation for storage (2.19) comes the inverse demand function for storage:

$$P_t = P[A_t - S_t] = P[\{f^S\}^{-1}[S_t] - S_t] \equiv \phi[S_t] \tag{2.22}$$

$\phi[S_t]$ expresses the current price corresponding to each quantity in store. More precisely, $\phi[S_t]$ is the inverse derived demand for the input of the commodity into the storage production process. Like other input demand curves, it is a function of the costs of the other inputs into that process, including in this case the costs of physical storage and capital. It is not possible, however, to write down this function explicitly. For this system it must be deduced numerically since f^S must be deduced numerically.

Many econometric models emphasizing inventories of commodities, such as the early study of flaxseed by Allen (1954) (Labys [1987] has catalogued others), proceed directly to an explicit "demand curve for inventories" as a function of the current conditions, usually the current price.[23] This inventory

---

[23] These models are distinct from the empirical models exemplified by Weymar (1968) in which inventories are posited to be functions of price spreads, namely the nearby futures price minus the spot price. In essence our model is in this latter tradition as it posits zero inventories at less than full carrying charges and any desired quantity in store at full carrying charges.

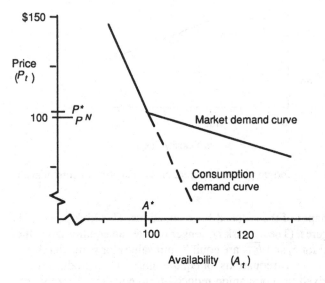

Figure 2.5. Market demand with storage.

demand is treated as a structural equation along with consumption demand and new supply. Depending on the rest of the model, this demand curve for inventories is usually specified as linear or log-linear. Similarly, many empirical models, such as Lovell's (1961), suppose that firms adjust inventories slowly toward some "desired" level. Bivin (1986) rightly criticizes these accelerator models for not being deduced from any standard of optimizing (e.g., profit-maximizing) behavior. Our modeling approach, in contrast, derives the demand curve for inventories from first principles (one conclusion being that the functional form is almost surely not linear). The demand curve for inventories as a function of current price is not a true structural equation, on par with the supply and consumption demand curves. Rather it derives from those very supply and consumption demand curves (and the interest rate, weather uncertainty, etc.). Although a relationship, not a variable, it is endogenous.[24]

Figure 2.5 adds the endogenous inverse derived demand curve for storage ϕ horizontally to the consumption demand curve, which also is a function of the current price. Figure 2.5, therefore, is the information necessary to determine for a given availability the spot price and the breakdown of that availability between consumption and storage. For example, for $A_t = 110$, reading up, one encounters the market demand curve at $P_t = \$93.12$. Along a horizontal line at that price, the consumption demand curve dictates $q_t = 101.38$ units, which implies that $S_t = 8.62$ units.

[24]   The endogenous nature of the demand-for-inventories function is also ignored in the strand of the macroeconomic literature represented by Clower and Bushaw (1954).

All other endogenous variables can be expressed as functions of current availability. One example is the futures price for delivery the next period $F_{t+1,t}$. The reduced-form equation for this variable has the same basic shape as that for planned production shown in Figure 2.4 above.[25] As with P_t, the reduced-form equation for the equilibrium $F_{t+1,t}$ as a function of A_t does not require its own exercise in numerical dynamic programming but can be derived fairly simply from the reduced-form equation for equilibrium storage.

Sequential equilibria in this system

Although the reduced-form relations for equilibrium storage and planned production as functions of current availability, which are the heart of the system, appear simple enough, how they interact through time is far from obvious. Since they cannot be represented analytically, numerical results are particularly helpful at adding insight. This subsection illustrates the interactions in the system over a relatively short time of eleven periods. The "weather" each period is drawn from a random number generator and is plotted in Figure 2.6(a). As it happens, most shocks over these eleven periods are negative (bad weather), which reduces realized compared to planned production, although one of the bigger yield disturbances (in absolute value) is positive. Because the behavior of the system is time invariant, the illustrated series of storage, prices, and planned production would have evolved in the same way had the first date of the period been period 1162 or period 173, provided the situation in the first period and the subsequent drawings of weather were the same.[26] For convenience the first period in this segment is called period 0.

Figure 2.6(b) begins in period 0 with an availability A_0 of 97.73 units because the weather was poor and the carryin small. Although 97.73 is not especially low, it is below the kink point A^* of Figure 2.3, namely 99.62 units. The equilibrium S_0, shown in Figure 2.6(c), is zero (all of the 97.73 units are consumed), and the simultaneously determined equilibrium $\bar{h}_1$ in Figure 2.6(e) is 103.35 units, which can be read from the relationship between equilibrium planned production and current availability in Figure 2.4. Figure 2.6(d) shows that $P_0 = \$111.35$ is the spot price in period 0 at which the market clears.

In period 1 the weather turns out to be a little below average, as can be seen in Figure 2.6(a). The realized harvest h_1 proves to be 101.44 instead of the expected 103.35 units. Because there is no carryin, A_1 is this 101.44 units. The new equilibrium is again read off the (numerically deduced) reduced-form equations for storage and planned production at that value for the cur-

---

[25] Planned production is a linear function of P_t^r, and P_t^r is closely related to $E_t[P_{t+1}]$, which is $F_{t+1,t}$.

[26] The same weather sequence, however, has virtually no chance (zero probability) of occurring twice in a finite series, given that the probability distribution is continuous.

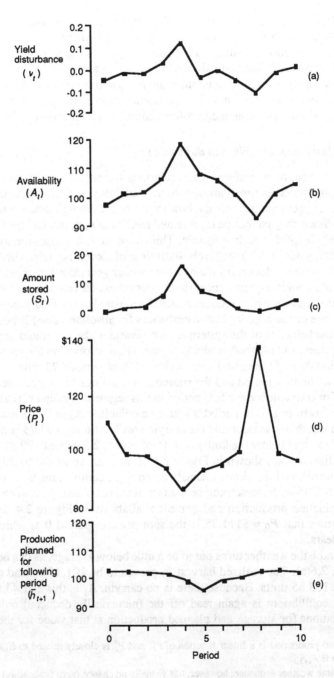

Figure 2.6. Sequential equilibria in a system with storage.

rent availability. According to Figure 2.3, the equilibrium carryout S_1 is 1.45 units, while according to Figure 2.4, equilibrium planned production $\bar{h}_2$ for period 2's harvest is 102.59 units.

If the full 101.44 units of A_1 were consumed, P_1 would be $92.80, given the production planned in period 0.[27] In equilibrium there is storage of 1.45 units and consumption of only 99.99 units, however; thus P_1 = $100.05. From this perspective, storage can be said to support the price. Also, it can be said that, because of storage, price alone does not absorb the exogenous shock.[28]

The availability in period 2 turns out to be nearly the same as in period 1, although this time it includes some carryin (1.45 units to be precise) as well as virgin production. The equilibrium carryout in period 2 S_2 is 1.81 units. This carryout turns out to be a poor investment for private storers, because the yield disturbance in period 3 is positive. The price at which the storers sell their carryin in period 3 ($95.59) is below the price ($99.66) at which they acquired their stocks in period 2 – quite apart from the physical storage costs of $2 per unit and the capital costs of 5 percent of $99.66. Nevertheless, the storers' decisions should not be judged *ex post* for they could not have foreseen the exact weather. After all, the weather could have been poor and P_3 high. Viewed *ex ante,* the decision in period 2 was rational. The equilibrium price P_2 = $99.66 and the equilibrium storage, 1.85 units, are such that the mean profit expected (after expenses) from storage in period 2 is $0.00.

The weather v_4 is the one instance in the eleven-period sequence in Figure 2.6(a) of a large positive disturbance. A_4 is 118.80 units as a result. As can be found on Figure 2.3, the reduced-form equation indicates storage of 16.24 units for that availability. Although this storage can be thought of as supporting prices, perhaps a better way of looking at storage is to see that it absorbs the shock of the weather. For a nonstorable commodity, all that abundance would have to be consumed in period 4. Storage spreads the disturbance out over several periods so that consumption in each of those later periods is slightly higher than otherwise. Both q_5 and q_6 are above 100 units (which

---

[27] Without prospects for storage in period 1, less would have been planted in period 0 to be harvested in period 1. Thus, realized production would have been lower than 101.44 units.

[28] A number of authors, notably Blinder (1982), have thus seen a parallel between the operation of storage and the Keynesian notion of prices sticky downward. In fact, storage does keep prices from adjusting downward (recall the shape of the market demand curve in Figure 2.5). Yet, this process surely violates the spirit of Keynesian sticky prices, which are supposedly sticky downward because of some institutional constraint on renegotiating prices, wages especially. The resulting combination of price and quantity (of wages and labor hired) is a disequilibrium. Because the market does not clear, there is some involuntary unemployment. In the storage model, markets clear by construction.

can be inferred from P_5 and P_6 being below \$100). The decision to store a substantial fraction of the extra availability in period 4 ends up looking exceptionally intelligent because the weather the next three periods is below average, periods 5 and 7 in particular. The cumulative result is a carryout $S_7 = 0.84$ units compared to $S_4 = 16.24$ units.

Cutbacks in planned production also help absorb the shock of the exceptionally good weather in period 4. The equilibrium $\bar{h}_5$ is 96.32 units, 7.03 units less than when the contemporaneous carryout is zero. More stocks can be carried over, and hence more of the current shock absorbed, because planned production can be adjusted so that the carryover does not flood the market the next period. A planned production substantially above the nonstochastic equilibrium production h^N, which occurs when $S_t = 0.0$ (e.g., in period 0), can also be classified as helping to absorb a negative shock, although there is a limit to such positive response (see Figure 2.4). Extra planned production for the next period allows current stocks to be drawn down. Or, as Reagan and Weitzman (1982) observe, the flexibility of storage makes it as if there were instantaneously adjustable supply. Storage and planned production, by moving in opposite directions, together absorb much of the disturbances in yields.

Unfortunately, the weather in period 8 is especially poor; worse weather would occur only 13.7 percent of the periods. The decision to run stocks down to merely 0.84 units as the carryout from period 7 looks foolish once period 8's weather is known. Again, *ex ante*, that carryover was the most intelligent possible, for the bad harvest could not have been forecast. An especially good harvest, better than all but 13.7 percent of all periods, was just as likely from the vantage point of period 7. Private storers (or the professional speculators determining the futures price) must account for both those possibilities. Because storage is costly, it makes no sense to store for the rare sequence in which several poor harvests follow one another.[29]

Over the run of periods in which the large harvest of period 4 is worked off, the current availability, say A_6, is clearly a function of past decisions, specifically storage and planned production. Therefore, availability is a predetermined variable rather than a true exogenous variable. When the harvest is very poor and the carryout zero, as in period 8, that link with the past is essentially broken. The availability in period 9 is not a function of the carryin. Period 8 wipes the slate clean, in the same way that period 0 did. Yet in a larger sense, the slate is always clean: Current decisions are solely functions of current availability since any carryin is physically indistinguishable from new production. In other words, the basic storage model is "Markovian."

Periods 9 and 10 start anew an accumulation of a stockpile, much as peri-

---

29 In fact, no matter how much is stored, a finite stockpile can never insure against a stockout after a sufficiently long string of bad harvests.

ods 1 and 2. Two points are worth attention, nonetheless. First, even though the weather in period 9 is slightly below average, the equilibrium storage is positive. Because the equilibrium planned production as of period 8 for harvesting in period 9 was at its maximum, the resulting availability is above A^*, the level indicating positive storage. Second, the variability in the harvest is endogenous because the disturbance is multiplicative. Although the proportional deviation in yields is exogenous, the planned production that it influences is a decision variable within the system. Thus, the observed deviations from expected production in periods 9 and 10 would be slightly different if the supply elasticity had been other than 0.5.

2.5 Key features of the equilibrium

As this stretch of eleven periods has illustrated, a system with storage is a sequence of equilibria. Of course, the same is true for a nonstorable commodity, but in that situation, it is possible to consider all possible outcomes in a model for a single period in the absence of other interperiod linkages such as serial correlation in the weather. A model with storage cannot be so compressed without losing the important connection from one period to the next. The collective storage in a particular current period affects the possible equilibria in the following periods, and those effects are taken into account in the equilibrium for the current period.

That the prices for a storable commodity follow a sequence of equilibria does not suggest that those equilibria improve with time, that something was wrong with the first ones in the sequence. Rather, with each period comes the collective shock of the weather. With its new information comes the need for a new equilibrium. This period-by-period adjustment also does not indicate irrationality or a market failure. The "forecast error" is unavoidable because it is not possible to anticipate the exact weather.

Throughout the sequence of equilibria, the reduced-form equation for equilibrium storage as a function of current conditions remains stable because the underlying parameters, such as the demand elasticity and the degree of uncertainty in the weather, remain constant. In other words, the collective level of inventories is an endogenous variable. This treatment of storage contrasts sharply with that of MacAvoy (1988), who treats inventories as a variable explaining price. Yes, high inventories occur when prices are low and low inventories when prices are high; but both variables respond endogenously to the exogenous shocks in supply or demand.

The key behavioral features of the sequential intertemporal competitive equilibria are easy to describe:

1. Each period farmers plant up to the point where the marginal expected net revenue from their next harvest equals their marginal planting costs.

2. Each period storers increase or decrease their storage to the point where the difference between the current price and the rational expected price for the next period covers interest expenses and warehousing charges.
3. In any period storage cannot be negative.

These three conditions impose surprising structure on the time path of price, which would otherwise follow the pure white noise of the weather.

Similarities to equilibrium for natural resources

This model of a collective equilibrium has a number of similarities with other broad classes of models. These are worth brief attention as a way of clarifying the features of the basic storage model. The closest connection is to the literature on natural resources. Just as in the theory of finite resources under certainty the value of the resource rises at the rate of interest, the complementary inequalities (2.5) defining the equilibrium for storage imply that the expected increase in the value of stocks put into store in period t is r times $(P_t + k)$ by period $t + 1$. This rate of price increase is not expected to persist, however, as it does with finite resources. That is,

$$E_t[P_{t+j+1}] < (1+r)E_t[P_{t+j} + k], \qquad \text{for all } j > 0 \qquad (2.23)$$

There is a chance of a stockout in period $t + j$. If it occurs, then the expected rate of price increase to the next period may be low or negative (replace t with $t + j$ in the second line of (2.5)). Since the maximum expected rate of price increase is r, the expected rate, anticipated as of period t, is less than r, as in (2.23).[30] This is like the equilibrium condition for a finite resource with a backstop technology, or closer yet, for a renewable resource like timber. Here the new production is the renewable resource and it comes every period. All are in the same class of dynamic models.

We could consider an extension to the basic model that would encompass a nonrenewable resource buffeted by random shocks to demand or discovered reserves. Likewise, we could introduce long-run trends, such as those in the stochastic growth models emphasized by Stokey and Lucas (1989). Such models of stochastic depletion or growth are themselves extensions of models with no uncertainty. In conditions of certainty, depletion and growth are prominent ways of obtaining interesting dynamics in the model. Similarly, the literature on renewable resources (e.g., Mangel [1985] or Clark [1990]) is likely to emphasize biological growth rates or cycles. It does not follow, however, that depletion or growth is a requirement for interesting dynamics in a stochastic setting. To us it seems advisable first to understand the effects of randomness in an otherwise stationary model.

---

[30] This argument is made in detail by Helmberger et al. (1982), who correct an error in Helmberger and Weaver (1977). Also see Bresnahan and Spiller (1986).

Similarities to models of money demand

Cash is an inventory, and many articles on commodities recount the reasons for holding inventories given by so many models of the demand for money: a transactions demand, a precautionary demand, and a speculative demand. All three are supposedly motives for the individual holding of inventories. Our basic storage model does not contain anything like the transactions demand for cash, because such a demand fundamentally derives from nonconstant average storage costs – in-and-out charges, fixed expenses for specialized equipment, and so on. For intercropyear storage of bulk commodities, these elements of fixed costs are relatively unimportant, at least compared to the inconvenience of daily trips to the bank as a motive for holding cash.

Our basic storage model does, however, place great emphasis on the "precautionary" motive for holding inventories. Because of the uncertainty in the next harvest, some of the current period's abundance is held over. But this precautionary demand is not the result of uncertainty in an individual farmer's harvest or in an individual consumer's access to the commodity: It is because of the common shock to the weather. In the basic storage model, if there were individual uncertainty without social uncertainty, trading among the farmers and consumers through costless markets would reallocate the stable collective supplies. Price would be the same every period. Insurance and similar mechanisms may be the dominant response to the uncertainty, but there would be no need for inventories.[31]

The formulation of the basic storage model has storers buying their stocks at the spot price and holding for sale at the uncertain price the next period. Under the formulation with explicit futures prices, those with positions in futures contracts are speculating. From either perspective the basic storage model encompasses a speculative demand for inventories. Yet this is not precisely the equivalent of the speculative demand for cash. Supposedly some people hold different amounts of cash because they have very different views from the market about the value of money the next period (i.e., about the intervening inflation). Similarly, individual farmers who believe the price of their commodity will rise may speculate by holding inventories. Because of a dispersion of speculative expectations, some inventories may be held.

Under close inspection, this motive for inventories does not hold up. By the argument of Holthausen (1979) and Feder et al. (1980), each agent's allocative decision involving inventories can be separated from the decision about

[31] This perspective of the whole market also makes clear that the individualistic precautionary demand for cash has no effect on the market interest rate without the cost constraints behind the so-called transactions demand for cash. If currency could be redirected costlessly to those who needed it just at that precise moment, no one would hold cash.

speculation. One need not hold inventories to speculate, and hence speculation should not dictate the level of inventories. The force of the argument can be seen in a setting like soybeans in the summer of 1989, when the price of old-crop beans commanded a premium over new-crop beans. Even for a farmer who believed new-crop beans would appreciate by harvest time, it was irrational for him (taxes and transportation bottlenecks aside) to speculate by retaining his old-crop beans in store. He should have released his old-crop beans to the market, to obtain the premium, and speculated to his heart's content through long positions in the futures markets.

Similarities to disequilibrium models

In the macroeconomic literature a number of papers have posited inventories as a result of a disequilibrium. As in Green and Laffont (1981) and Eckalbar (1985a), firms are presumed to set, one period in advance, their production runs and list prices. If demand at their list price is lower than expected, the firms absorb the shock by accumulating inventories; if demand is higher, they draw down inventories (to the extent that they have them). The changes in inventories are primarily a result of the disequilibrium price.[32] If price could adjust within the period, there would be no role for inventories.

These disequilibrium models – which can be used, as in Amihud and Mendelson (1982) and Flood and Hodrick (1985), to study the effects of shocks in the money supply – are fundamentally different from our basic model, which concerns the equilibrium reaction to current and future uncertainty. Indeed, as Laroque (1989) has shown, uncertainty itself is not a necessary feature of a disequilibrium model of inventories. And as Blinder (1980, n. 9) has mentioned, some imperfection like market power is also needed, for otherwise it is hard to imagine the firms as setting their individual prices. Finally, many of these models, such as Honkapohja and Ito (1980), assume some arbitrary relationship for desired inventories, say, that it is a linear function of sales, rather than deriving it as a reduced-form relationship.

These models in the macroeconomic literature of explicit disequilibria are closely related to many models of inventory and ordering policy found in the operations research literature. The famous (S,s) inventory model, for example, posits a list price for retail sales and considers the strategy for reordering given a fixed cost to the order. Thus, it imposes the constraint that price cannot adjust within the period. It and related models also emphasize a single firm and so do not investigate the feedback effects of many firms' placement of an order at the same time. These models will be taken up in Chapter 10

---

[32]   In Eckalbar (1985b), the sticky price is in the labor market, which constrains maximum production.

and especially in Chapter 11, where the lost revenue due to the implicit inflexibility in price is compared to the advantage of the flexibility of storage.

Similarities with literature on optimal storage

Finally, the theory of inventories is discussed in the large literature about what food reserves a country should keep because of uncertain harvests. Much of this research dates from the period after the sharp price increases of 1972–4. The emphasis was on public reserves, with private storage generally ignored. Some early papers investigated arbitrary buffer-stock schemes, but eventually others, preeminently Gardner (1979), asked how the sole public agency should store optimally, in order to maximize social welfare.

Fundamentally, our basic storage model of a competitive equilibrium is the same as the approach concerned with socially optimal storage of grain. (The correspondence ceases if there are distortions such as price ceilings while public and private stockpiles coexist.) In a world of no distortions, rational (risk-neutral) competitive storage maximizes social welfare. The beneficent planner running a public stockpile can do no better. Thus, whether the storage is set up as a competitive equilibrium or as a planner's problem makes no difference to the reduced-form equation for storage as a function of current circumstances. We have chosen to emphasize the perspective of an industry of private storers (what would variously be called a merchant regime or a *laissez-faire* regime), in part because several extensions are more natural from the perspective of the competitive equilibrium. In fact, the correspondence between the planner's problem and the competitive equilibrium allows the analyst to solve for the reduced-form equation for equilibrium private storage. This approach is the theme of the next chapter.

CHAPTER 3

Solving for the storage equilibrium

It is unfortunate for an intuitive understanding of the competitive equilibrium with storage that numerical stochastic dynamic programming must be invoked. Much the same obstacle arises for economists studying the equilibrium among a set of spatially integrated markets. The conditions for spatial equilibrium are easy to describe: The price in one city should never be above or below the prices in the other cities by more than the price of transportation. For the many competitive shippers whose vigilance for any opportunity of extra profit keeps prices in line, the relevant calculations are simple. They look at pairs of prices and transport costs, taking them as given, and act when the differentials are large enough. For an analyst trying to model that equilibrium, the problem is a complex exercise in linear or quadratic programming. First of all, at that level of analysis the prices are endogenous. Second, the model must encompass even those cities from or to which no transportation takes place, while allowing for the possible entry of those cities on the transportation among the others.

For the analyst of spatial equilibrium, a conceptual advance comes from recognizing that the myriad decisions made within a competitive industry are like the decisions of a single entity, the "invisible hand." The next step is to personify the invisible hand as an active intelligence, the benevolent planner. From the perspective of a technocratic planner who must allocate supplies among locations, it is natural to conduct thought experiments of the form: "Suppose I direct the shipment of 18 tons from location A to location B and 7 tons from C to D; have I maximized net social welfare?" or "Well, if that plan wouldn't be good, what about 17 from A to B and 8 from C to D?" The analyst can reason in the same manner. The technocrat's superiors can reasonably judge whether the technocrat's thought experiments find the social optimum and how quickly the technocrat's revisions converge. They might also ask whether some rule of thumb might work nearly as well. In the same manner, an analyst's algorithm can be judged for whether it duplicates the

50

competitive spatial equilibrium and how cleverly it minimizes computations.

The simplest storage problem is like the spatial equilibrium problem, with an index of time replacing the index of location. The arbitrage is intertemporal rather than spatial. Although the equilibrium relationship involves expectations, it too is easy to state. Price in the current period should never be below the price expected for next period by more than cost of storage; nor above it unless the total amount stored is zero. As in the case of spatial equilibrium, the trouble for the analyst modeling the equilibrium comes from prices being endogenous at the level of the market, and from the amount stored sometimes being zero when equilibrium price differentials are below storage costs.

As for spatial equilibrium, a fruitful approach to deriving the reduced-form equation for equilibrium storage is to recast competitive storage as a social planner's problem. From the perspective of a single decision maker, an obvious solution technique is that of stochastic dynamic programming. Accordingly, the next section discusses storage as a planner's problem and introduces the terminology of optimal control. Section 3.2 illustrates these solution techniques with an analytical example. Section 3.3 discusses some issues raised when the horizon is infinite or when something like a tax or price ceiling distorts the competitive equilibrium. In Section 3.4 are discussed various approximations, such as "certainty equivalence," intended to come close to solving the planner's problem while avoiding much computational effort.

3.1 Reformulation as a social planner's problem

Actually, the analyst of competitive storage can go one step beyond a reformulation as a planner's problem to picture Robinson Crusoe deciding whether to save food from today in case he finds little tomorrow.[1] Clearly, Robinson Crusoe is a single intelligence, actively making decisions, with every incentive to consider his storage decisions carefully. From his position it is all too obvious that his decision today influences his position tomorrow; hence, an intelligent decision today should take into account the circumstances possible tomorrow. Also, he can foresee that he will have a similar decision to make tomorrow. The good side of this is that he need not be bound by decisions made today: He can revise his plans if his new state so indicates. The bad side is that he must decide yet again: A single, systematic approach to the multistage decision-making would obviously be helpful. To take account of the effect of today's decision on tomorrow's state, he must already have done the calculations necessary for tomorrow's decision for any possible harvest

---

[1] More prosaically, this formulation is known as one with a "representative consumer." Schechtman and Escudero (1977) consider the theory of optimal storage behavior from this perspective of a single, isolated consumer.

outcome.[2] Tomorrow's circumstances are influenced by tomorrow's decision, after all, and tomorrow's decision should take account of the states possible for the day after tomorrow. Stochastic dynamic programming is what Robinson Crusoe or the planner needs.

As noted by Jacobs (1967, p. 1), "'dynamic programming' is a slightly misleading name for what is really a mathematical theory of multistage decision processes." The name was coined by Bellman (1957) because high-speed computers, with their ability to perform a series of similar calculations, are a natural tool for implementing the theory. In brief, dynamic programming solves Robinson Crusoe's problem by induction, working backward from decisions in the distant future to the present period's decision. This inductive approach is sensible because of what Bellman (1957, p. 83) calls the principle of optimality: "An optimal policy has the property that whatever the initial state and initial decision are, the remaining decisions must constitute an optimal policy with regard to the state resulting from the first decision." Cooper and Cooper's rendition (1981, p. 9) shows the intuition behind this principle more clearly: "Every optimal policy consists only of optimal sub-policies."[3] Consequently, it is possible to deduce the optimal policy by building up from the best decisions for subproblems. Decisions in the distant future are such subproblems.

Backward induction through dynamic programming

The best way to understand the inductive logic of dynamic programming applied to storage problems is to consider the case of zero supply elasticity and a finite horizon, in which the world ends in some future period T. (Gardner [1979, chap. 2] presents a good intuitive description of the problem in such a setting.) The planner's (or Robinson Crusoe's) problem in the current period, period t, is to select the current storage that will maximize the discounted stream of expected future surplus; that is,

Maximize with respect to S_t

$$V_t = \sum_{j=t}^{T} E_t \left[\int_0^{A_j - S_j} P[q]dq - kS_j \right] / (1 + r)^{j-t}$$

(3.1)

subject to $S_j \geq 0$

---

2   That the basic problem recurs each period is the origin of "recursive" in Stokey and Lucas's (1989) book *Recursive Methods in Economic Dynamics*, which provides a mathematical underpinning for the application of dynamic programming to many problems in economics.

3   For example, if it is best to drive from Chicago to New York City by way of Cleveland and Buffalo, it cannot be sensible that the best way to go from Cleveland to New York City (a subproblem) is by way of Pittsburgh.

Here surplus each period is measured by the area under the consumption demand curve.[4] The current decision S_t is the primary decision variable, but all future S's (namely, S_{t+1} through S_T), must be considered too. The process works by backward induction from the final period.[5]

In the final period, the planner might as well recommend consumption of everything available. The decision rule is simple. Whatever is A_T, $S_T = 0$. The optimal decision rule for period $T - 1$, the previous period, is slightly more complicated. In period $T - 1$, an abbreviated version of (3.1) applies:

Maximize with respect to S_{T-1}

$$V_{T-1} = \int_0^{A_{T-1} - S_{T-1}} P[q]dq - kS_{T-1}$$
$$+ E_{T-1}\left[\int_0^{h_T + S_{T-1}} P[h_T + S_{T-1}]dq\right] / (1+r) \tag{3.2}$$

As of the period $T - 1$, current storage will not depend on future storage because there will be none. The problem is one of allocating the availability A_{T-1} between consumption in period $T - 1$ and period T. The optimal storage is clearly where the expected marginal consumption value in period T equals the marginal consumption value in period $T - 1$, apart from marginal storage costs and interest:

$$\partial V_{T-1} / \partial S_{T-1} = 0 = -P[A_{T-1} - S_{T-1}] - k$$
$$+ E_{T-1}[P[h_T + S_{T-1}]] / (1+r), \qquad S_{T-1} > 0 \tag{3.3}$$

From this equation, the planner can solve, at least conceptually, for S_{T-1} as a function of A_{T-1}.

Given this decision rule for S_{T-1} for any A_{T-1} for period $T - 1$, the planner can solve, conceptually at least, for the analogous decision rule for period $T - 2$, and so on back to the present period t. The optimal storage for the current period, which is the only irrevocable decision, is thus implied by the cumulative effect, working backward in time, of similar storage decisions. Each subproblem contains an additional period. The backward induction does not, however, expand the number of decision variables at all. Whatever the stage in the backward induction, that period's optimal storage alone is sought. For example, in period $T - 2$, the planner does not solve simultaneously for S_{T-2}, S_{T-1}, and S_T. Rather he exploits this previous solution via equation (3.3) for S_{T-1} as a function of A_{T-1}. (A_{T-1}, from the perspective of period $T - 2$, now includes S_{T-2}.) Dynamic programming is a method of substituting

---

4   Recall our assumption, for simplicity, of zero income elasticity, in which case the Marshallian surplus is identical to the Hicksian compensating and equivalent variations each period.

5   Here the intertemporal separability of consumption demand becomes important. If the objective function is not separable, the problem cannot be broken into the easier subproblems.

out for all but one decision variable. Thus, the subproblems have the general form:

Maximize with respect to S_j

$$V_j[A_j] = \int_0^{A_j - S_j} P[q]dq - kS_j + E_j\left[V_{j+1}^*[h_{j+1} + S_j]\right]/(1+r) \qquad (3.4)$$

The expectation on the right-hand side is over h_{j+1}, the only random variable, as of period j, in this expression. V_{j+1}^* represents the discounted present value as of period $j+1$ of social welfare provided the planner selects storage in period $j+1$ through period T optimally. The optimal S_j dictated by (3.4) specifies V_j^*, which can be used to deduce the optimal S_{j-1}. This compression of future decisions into the function V^* is a corollary to the principle of optimality. This *value function* V^* is central to mathematical representations of dynamic programming algorithms.

The connection between the planner's problem and competitive equilibrium

Just as the value function in (3.4) is a generalization of the planner's problem for period $T-1$ represented by equation (3.2), it is possible to write a general version of the first-order condition for S_{T-1} in equation (3.3) (see Kennedy 1986, chap. 5). The planner's optimal storage in the jth period is the solution to the equation:

$$\partial V_j / \partial S_j = 0 = -P[A_j - S_j] - k + E_j\left[\partial V_{j+1} / \partial S_j\right]/(1+r) , \quad S_j > 0 \qquad (3.5)$$

As in (3.3) for period $T-1$, the generalization of the marginal condition defining the planner's optimal choice of storage in period j can be rewritten as:

$$\partial V_j / \partial S_j = 0 = -P_j - k + E_j[P_{j+1}]/(1+r) \qquad S_j > 0 \qquad (3.6)$$

When j equals t, the first period in the sequence $t, \dots, j, \dots, T$, (3.6) is none other than the equilibrium condition for competitive storage, the "arbitrage equation" (2.5) for situations where storage is positive.[6]

The planner in period t selects optimal storage by weighing the marginal unit of the commodity between current consumption and a bequest to the next period. When the private market suffers no distortions, the marginal value of current consumption is measured by price. In the following period, period $t+1$, the planner again balances the amount on hand between immediate consumption and a bequest to period $t+2$. Should he make that and subsequent decisions optimally, the marginal value of an inheritance from period t is the

---

6   Gustafson (1958a, appendix n. 6) was the first to prove the equivalence of the marginal value as a function of optimal storage to the equilibrium condition for competitive storage.

same whether measured by the marginal value of consumption in period $t+1$ or by the present value of yet later consumption. That equality is dictated by the generic first-order condition (3.5). Because the marginal value of a carry-in from period t, however the planner chooses to use it, can be summarized by the expected price, the planner's condition for optimal storage is the same as the private arbitrage condition.

The identity between the planner's first-order condition and the arbitrage equation for competitive storage (without any distortions) has a number of important implications:

1. Undistorted competitive storage must be socially optimal. A planner, consciously selecting a level of storage to maximize social welfare, should behave like a competitive industry with rational expectations. This result is yet another example of the general proposition that an undistorted competitive equilibrium is a Pareto optimum.
2. It is possible to compute the present value of social welfare by integrating over the argument S_t the arbitrage equation for private storage, since $E_t [P_{t+1}[S_t]]$ is also the derivative of the value function.
3. Of most immediate importance, through dynamic programming the planner's decision rule for optimal storage S_t for any given value of availability A_t is the same function as the reduced-form equation for equilibrium competitive storage, represented symbolically before as equation (2.19).

Strictly speaking, these arguments have been made for a setting with a finite horizon. They generalize to the setting of an infinite horizon (provided some other conditions, such as a positive interest rate, apply). In period t, if period T is sufficiently far in the future, the influence of the anticipation that storage will stop in period T becomes negligible, and the relation derived between current values of S and A is the same as for the previous period, $t-1$ or for the following period, $t+1$. This stable decision rule is thus the reduced-form equation for equilibrium storage when the time horizon is infinite.

The terminology of optimal control

The formulation as a planner's problem naturally describes the storage amount as a *decision variable* because a single intelligence is allocating the current availability between consumption and storage. More broadly, because the planner cannot foresee the precise size of future harvests, he must instead anticipate his strategy for future storage conditional on future availability. He needs a decision rule. That is, the relationship between current storage and current availability – the reduced-form equation for equilibrium competitive storage – can also be called a *storage rule*. In future chapters we use these two expressions interchangeably.

The perspective of a planner's problem brings with it the useful terminology of optimal control theory. The planner, given the current situation or *state* summarized by current availability A_t, can control one or more variables. With the intrusion of the random harvest, the planner's steering cannot be precise. Nevertheless, with his active decision about the current level of storage he has some control over the time path of consumption.

Several more points about the storage problem emerge from the perspective of optimal control. Here the carryout is a *control variable* and the current availability is the *state variable*. Because of the time invariance of the storage rule with an infinite horizon, the same choice is made whenever the state variable happens to be the same value. The planner has a steady policy rule, in other words, but the particular result of that policy rule – the specific amount in store – will change from period to period. An adjustment from one period to the next in the amount in store neither indicates a fundamental shift in policy nor indicts the previous amount as being suboptimal. Because of the vagaries of the weather, the optimal policy rule should lead to some variation in the control variable. (The same will be true, of course, about the competitive equilibrium.)

More important, the choice for the amount stored depends only on the one state variable, current availability. All the relevant past is summarized therein. As the basic storage problem is formulated with the carryin physically indistinguishable from virgin production, it makes no difference whether the current availability arose from a small current harvest and a large carryin or from a large current harvest and a small carryin. Nor does it matter that the carryin arose principally from a large harvest in period $t - 1$, one in period $t - 2$, or one in period $t - 3$. This is not to say that those past harvests do not influence the current storage decision, only that their current implications are completely summarized by the current state variable.

In the current period the planner can adjust the amount stored whereas he cannot alter the current availability. It is wrong, however, to classify current availability as an exogenous variable; it is a "predetermined" variable. The only truly exogenous random variable in the system is the weather. The current availability is partly a result of past storage and planting decisions, which are endogenous. This endogeneity is obvious from the current period, where future storage and production decisions are under the influence of the current storage decision. Yet, by the time those future periods arrive, this period's storage will be unalterable. Clearly, the current storage decision should account for its affect on the subsequent state variables. This interaction makes the evolution of the system endogenous.

From the perspective of optimal control, it is natural to emphasize the carryout as a control variable. The planner's problem is to select the amount of storage out of the amount available. The control variable could instead be the amount consumed, although consumption and storage are not both simultaneously controlled, since the planner determines one exactly through his decision about the other. For that matter, if the problem were formulated such that the planner had full control over availability but sold to consumers on an open market, price could be specified as a control variable. But in any formulation there is only one control, whether price, consumption, or storage.

When supply is elastic the planner does have a second control variable to worry about: the amount to plant for harvesting the next period. The optimal $\bar{h}_{t+1}$ is also a function of the state variable, current availability. The planner's specific decision rule for planned production – the "planned production rule" – is the same as the reduced-form equation for equilibrium planned production, expressed before as equation (2.20). A planner selects simultaneously the amount to store and the amount to plant, for a given value of the state variable.[7] In terms of a competitive market, the amount planted and the amount stored, for a given amount available, is the simultaneous equilibrium resulting from the independent decisions of the many storers and producers.

In short, the basic storage model involves one state variable and two control variables. The extensions to the model made in later chapters add control variables and state variables in various combinations. Indeed, one way of organizing those models is by the nature and number of their state and control variables. Of the two categories by far the more relevant is the number of state variables. The calculations necessary to solve the planner's problem numerically through the routines described in the Appendix increase exponentially with the number of state variables.

The terminology of game theory

The storage rule gives the equilibrium storage for any current availability. The exact amount stored in any one period depends on the specific availability that period. This distinction can perhaps be made clearer with the terminology of noncooperative game theory.[8] A storage rule is a "strategy" played by the "invisible hand" against "nature": For any given situation, how should the invisible hand play? The actual amount stored in any period, once the situation is known, is an "action."[9] Nature uses the "mixed" strategy of the randomness in the weather. Of course, the private storers and producers are not playing against nature with a single mind. Rather, a system with competitive storers and producers acts as if it were one entity playing against nature.

---

[7] Planting may, in fact, be after the storage decision. In the basic model no new information arrives in the meantime. For practical purposes, the two decisions might as well be made at the same time. Most important, they need to account for each other.

[8] See Basar and Olsder (1982) for definitions of this terminology.

[9] Because the weather and amounts stored are continuous variables, the "action set" is infinite, which means from the perspective of game theory the storage problem is very difficult to analyze.

From the perspective of game theory, storage is a "delayed commitment" game because the strategy can incorporate information as it arrives. The strategy expressed in the storage rule anticipates that, although the future weather is unknown in the current period, the future storage actions will take into account the realizations of the weather to that date. The strategy is "feedback" or *closed-loop*. The contrast is with a storage problem where nothing is learned about the weather after the first period. In that setting, the strategy for storage is set for the indefinite period, say, by some unalterable policy such as: Spread a current surplus equally across the next 10 periods. Note that in that *open-loop* type of storage problem, a unique storage strategy in some future period can be written solely as a function of the initial availability, whereas in the type of system proposed in Chapter 2, the rule for that distant period is also implicitly a function of the intervening weather and so is determined by the availability current in that distant period.

3.2   An analytical example

Except in very special cases,[10] an analytical solution for the storage rule is no more possible with the formulation as a planner's decision than with the formulation as a competitive equilibrium. Numerical methods for deducing the storage rule from the perspective of the planner's problem have been available since Gustafson (1958a) for the case with zero supply elasticity. Our numerical methods, employing polynomial approximations to the function relating expected price and current storage, are able to handle elastic supply and any number of distortions such as price ceilings or subsidies to storage. A detailed discussion of the computer routines is left to the Appendix; but because several important insights into storage are gained via understanding at least the logic of the solution techniques, a specific, relatively simple example that can be solved analytically is worth working through step by step.

The example has three periods, and so has a finite horizon. To emphasize the backward induction used in dynamic programming, the third and last period is called period T; the second period, period $T-1$; and the first period, $T-2$. Period T has no carryout for the obvious reason that time ends. The inverse consumption demand curve is linear in the amount consumed, $P_t = \alpha + \beta q_t$, with $\alpha > 0$ and $\beta < 0$. The stationary supply is perfectly inelastic with mean $\bar{h}$. The density function of the random additive disturbance has the simple form of a uniform distribution with mean zero and standard deviation σ. The probability of a particular v_t is $1/2\sqrt{3}\sigma$ from $-\sqrt{3}\sigma$ to $+\sqrt{3}\sigma$ and zero elsewhere. The marginal physical storage cost is k and for simplicity the interest rate is set at zero.

[10]   See Newbery and Stiglitz (1981, pp. 437–8) or Aiyagari et al. (1989).

In this system, the main question to ask is: What is equilibrium competitive storage in the initial period? That is, what is the equation for S_{T-2} as a function of the various parameters such as k and σ? The point of the previous section is that the answer can be obtained more easily by a change of perspective to a planner's problem. What is the planner's decision rule for optimal storage in period $T-2$?

Derivation of the storage rule for period $T-2$

The planner would approach the problem with the inductive logic of dynamic programming. His first step would be to solve for a decision rule in period $T-1$, because the decision in period $T-2$ depends on the prospect for storage in period $T-1$. The planner could write down his objective function to be maximized with respect to S_{T-1}, as in equation (3.2); but he might as well proceed to the first-order condition (3.3), and indeed to its version without the marginal value function. That is, his choice for storage in period $T-1$ is implicitly determined by (3.6), which is also the arbitrage equation (2.5) for competitive storers, with the particular parameters of the example:

$$P_{T-1} + k = E_{T-1}[P_T]$$

$$\alpha + \beta(A_{T-1} - S_{T-1}) + k = \left(1/2\sqrt{3}\sigma\right) \int_{-\sqrt{3}\sigma}^{\sqrt{3}\sigma} (\alpha + \beta(\bar{h} + v_T + S_{T-1}))\, dv \tag{3.7}$$

The planner can manipulate (3.7) to solve for S_{T-1}. His decision rule for the amount of storage in period $T-1$ as a function of the amount available in that period and the various parameters has a simple analytic form, specifically,

$$S_{T-1} = (A_{T-1} - \bar{h})/2 + (k/2\beta), \qquad S_{T-1} > 0$$
$$S_{T-1} = 0, \qquad\qquad\qquad\quad \text{otherwise} \tag{3.8}$$

(If k were equal to zero, any amount above the normal harvest would be shared equally between the last and next-to-last periods.)

The derivation of the planner's decision rule for S_{T-2} applicable in period $T-2$ is far more complex. The possibility of storage in $T-1$ complicates his calculation of the term $E_{T-2}[P_{T-1}]$ in the first-order condition for optimal storage in period $T-2$,

$$P_{T-2} + k = E_{T-2}[P_{T-1}], \qquad S_{T-2} > 0 \tag{3.9}$$

The amount he will be storing in period $T-1$ will depend on the amount available in that period. The amount on hand in $T-1$ will be $\bar{h} + v_{T-1} + S_{T-2}$. The uncertain weather is v_{T-1}, so depending on the weather he will be storing a positive amount or not. He can find the weather where he will make that transition by setting S_{T-1} equal to zero in equation (3.8) and solving for v_{T-1}.

$$0 = (\bar{h} + v_{T-1} + S_{T-2} - \bar{h})/2 + (k/2\beta) \tag{3.10}$$

That crucial v_{T-1} is where

$$v_{T-1} = -S_{T-2} - k/\beta \tag{3.11}$$

Whenever v_{T-1} is less than $-S_{T-2} - k/\beta$, the planner's rule is for no storage in period $T-1$, whereas whenever v_{T-1} is greater than $-S_{T-2} - k/\beta$, he will store a positive amount. As a result, the point of that change in the planner's anticipated behavior depends on S_{T-2}. The planner's first-order condition (3.9) applied in period $T-2$ requires the weighted average of the circumstances without and with storage in $T-1$. It becomes

$$P_{T-2} + k = E_{T-2}[P_{T-1}]$$

$$\alpha + \beta(A_{T-2} - S_{T-2}) + k = (1/2\sqrt{3}\sigma)\left(\int_{-\sqrt{3}\sigma}^{-S_{T-2}-k/\beta} (\alpha + \beta(\bar{h} + v_{T-1} + S_{T-2})) \, dv \right.$$
$$\left. + \int_{-S_{T-2}-k/\beta}^{\sqrt{3}\sigma} (\alpha + \beta(\bar{h} + v_{T-1} + S_{T-2} - S_{T-1})) \, dv \right) \tag{3.12}$$

Despite the complication of S_{T-2} appearing in the limits of integration, the planner can solve explicitly for S_{T-2}. He first substitutes out S_{T-1} with equation (3.8), integrates (3.12) with respect to v_{T-1}, and, finding squared terms in S_{T-2}, invokes the formula for a quadratic. His decision rule for the optimal amount of storage in the initial period is

$$S_{T-2} = 7\sqrt{3}\sigma - k/\beta - \sqrt{144\sigma^2 - 8\sqrt{3}\sigma(A_{T-2} - \bar{h}) - 24\sqrt{3}\sigma k/\beta},$$
$$S_{T-2} > 0 \tag{3.13}$$
$$S_{T-2} = 0, \qquad \text{otherwise}$$

Equation (3.13) is an analytical example of a planner's storage rule. It is also an example of an analytical reduced-form equation for the competitive equilibrium. For any amount available in period $T-2$, that is, for any A_{T-2}, (3.13) gives the equilibrium amount of collective storage (including $S_{T-2} = 0.0$) if the individual private storers behave rationally. The equation contains only exogenous parameters or predetermined endogenous variables.

Lessons from the derivation

This storage rule and its derivation from the planner's perspective establish several points. First, the storage rule, which is illustrated in Figure 3.1 for $\sqrt{3}\sigma = 15$ units, $k = 2$, $\beta = -5$, and $\bar{h} = 100$ units, is a highly discontinuous function. The main nonlinearity is at the break $A_{T-2} = 98.62$ units, where positive storage begins. Optimal storage rules have a kink. Even over the range of positive storage itself, the function is much more nonlinear than what one might infer from the figure; the slope at $A_{T-2} = 100$ is 0.57, where-

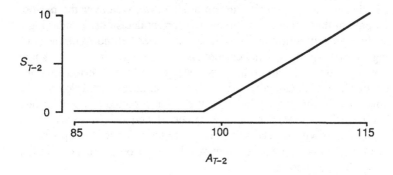

Figure 3.1. Storage rule in first of three periods.

as at $A_{T-2} = 120$ it is 0.65. (The rule for S_{T-1} [equation (3.8)], in contrast, is strictly linear over the range $S_{T-1} > 0$ with slope 0.50).[11]

A second point is that the amount to store in the first period, period $T-2$, is influenced by the prospect of storage in period $T-1$. In the simple two-period example solved in Section 2.2, there was storage only in the first of the two periods. In that problem, solving for storage in that first period involved simply looking at the various possible prices with all the availability in the second period being consumed. Here too storage in period $T-2$, S_{T-2}, depends on the expected price in the next period. But price in period $T-1$ depends on storage S_{T-1}. More generally, the demand for storage on the part of the competitive storage industry in an early (or current) period derives in part from the industry's demand for storage in subsequent periods. These connections and the complication that storage is not always positive are what make deducing the competitive equilibrium difficult.

The third point is the nature of the planner's solution algorithm. Because dynamic programming conceptually moves backward in time, it might seem to be taking account of the past; on the contrary, backward induction takes account of the future.[12] To solve for S_{T-2} the planner's first step was to solve for storage in period $T-1$, which is a period in the future from the perspective of period $T-2$.

[11] Even if slight, this nonlinearity over the range of positive storage in period $T-2$ is an important result. This example intentionally involves a linear demand curve and a linear probability distribution. If there were any chance of a linear storage rule, one would expect it to be found under these circumstances. Market demand curves, those encompassing storage and consumption, in general must be nonlinear over the range of positive storage. Empirical models of commodity markets using linear market demand curves over the range of positive storage – and there are many – are in general misspecified from the outset, even if they rightly recognize the kink in market demand where storage becomes positive.

[12] For more on the logic of dynamic programming, especially how it compares to other solution techniques for deterministic problems, see Bertsekas (1987).

The past is summarized in the current availability, whatever the period. The exact path to that value is immaterial for current decisions. Similar logic works in the other direction and provides the power behind dynamic programming. In making the optimal current choice, the planner needs to know only the next period's decision rule, provided decisions next period are optimally made. The full details about the future are unnecessary. Likewise, in the formulation as a competitive industry, if price next period can be expected to be high, it does not matter to the current period's equilibrium why it will be high, only that it will be. The reason could be the prospect for a poor harvest three periods hence, or a surge in demand two periods hence, or a fall in storage costs the next period.

The whole future can be compressed into the behavior the next period because the equilibrium storage and planned production are recomputed each period. The storage behavior envisioned in this book allows for recomputation of the exact amount stored depending on the conditions in the particular period. Indeed, that amount is given by the storage rule with an infinite horizon, which is stationary and does not depend on previous plans for storage. Moreover, it makes no sense to commit plans for storage beyond one period ahead, for those plans will surely have to change with the realized harvests. Although some quantity may stay in store, say, for four periods, nothing requires a four-period-long commitment to storage. Recognition of this future flexibility is, however, incorporated into the initial decision to store.[13]

Fourth and last, a general analytical derivation of storage rules is all but impossible. Consider just this example if it were extended backward to a fourth (and prior) period, period $T-3$. For the storage rule as of period $T-2$, equation (3.13) is itself not a simple expression. The first-order condition for optimal storage behavior in period $T-3$, analogous to (3.12), will not be simple either, once again because of the nonnegativity constraint on storage. Integration of a radical will be required, and the intermediate limit of integration, analogous to $-S_{T-2} - k/\beta$ will be more complicated. As a result, an explicit solution for S_{T-3} is beyond analytical manipulation. Thus, as few as three periods backward from the finite horizon, even a deliberately simple storage model becomes analytically intractable.

3.3   Further considerations with an infinite horizon

The specific example of the previous section covered three periods including a terminal period T. The basic model put forth in Chapter 2 envi-

---

[13] Note that in the derivation of S_{T-2} in the analytical three-period model, the entire function for S_{T-1}, which summarizes the flexibility in the strategy for S_{T-1}, was used.

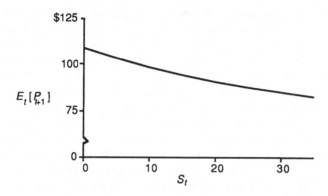

Figure 3.2. Self-replicating relationship between expected price and amount stored.

sions an infinite horizon. The solution for the rational expectations competitive equilibrium in that setting has several special features.

Self-replication as a solution technique

When the horizon is infinite, for our basic model, which has no growth or seasonality, the storage rule is stationary. Part and parcel, the relationship between the average price the next period and current storage, namely $E_t[P_{t+1}[S_t]]$, is stationary. It is also self-replicating. If private storers believe $E_t[P_{t+1}[S_t]]$ to be a particular function, through their collective actions $E_t[P_{t+1}[S_t]]$ should in fact be that function. In other words, their expectations should be self-fulfilling, that is, "rational."

The function $E_t[P_{t+1}[S_t]]$ is plotted in Figure 3.2, for the system of parameters studied in Chapter 2 (the one with the storage and planned production rules shown earlier in Figures 2.3 and 2.4). The function does not extend into the range of negative storage, but then that range is irrelevant. The function $E_t[P_{t+1}[S_t]]$ is used to solve for equilibrium storage in period t. If A_t is low, all is consumed and $E_t[P_{t+1}]$ does not matter. If A_t is high, the relationship in Figure 3.2 determines, in conjunction with the arbitrage equation, the value of S_t and hence P_t. In other words, the function in Figure 3.2 contains the information necessary for the storage rule while being a much smoother relationship, and a smoother relationship is much easier to find through numerical methods. Our technique represents $E_t[P_{t+1}[S_t]]$ with a polynomial in the powers of S_t. Obviously a low-order polynomial describes Figure 3.2 efficiently and completely.

The self-replicating feature of the competitive equilibrium suggests another method for solving for the reduced-form equation. Conceptually, at least, all one need do is find some function of S_t representing $E_t[P_{t+1}]$ that replicates itself. One could guess some function (not blindly, of course) and see what the average price would be if storers used it as their expectations. The guess would not replicate itself, but the discrepancy would suggest an improved guess because the problem is concave. Throughout this refinement process, time remains periods t and $t+1$. The exercise for equilibrium planned production without storage in Section 2.3 worked by a similar refinement of guesses. The difference here is the need to find a whole function rather than a self-replicating point. This approach based on a recursive refinement requires neither dynamic programming nor the reformulation as a planner's problem. That does not suggest the whole discussion in Section 3.1 was unnecessary, because the possibility of such a recursive approach can be grasped only with the perspective of dynamic programming. The backward induction of dynamic programming is, after all, a recursive technique. In any case, if the updating of the refinement method is simply to replace the old guess with the function based on that old guess (a natural method), the refinement method and the backward induction of dynamic programming are essentially the same.

Planner's problem with distortions

When there is some distortion, the approach of recursive refinement has an advantage over the formulation as a planner's problem. Consider the case of a competitive storage equilibrium when a permanent regime of price ceilings restricts the maximum price storers receive should the next harvest be small. Under such circumstances, the private arbitrage condition still holds, only the price expectation $E_t[P_{t+1}]$ includes the possibility of the ceiling being in effect.

It is very difficult to reformulate this competitive equilibrium as a planner's problem. Some constraint would need to be added to the maximization problem (3.4), but it is not obvious how the effect of the price ceilings can be formulated as a constraint. The planner's control variable is storage not price, and even then the marginal consumption value can be above the price ceiling because it is solely the return to storage that is distorted.

Yet, using recursive refinements of $E_t[P_{t+1}[S_t]]$, the solution is hardly more difficult to achieve than before. Still the requirement is for a function that is self-replicating. Private storers' expectations are affected by the prospect of price ceilings, but they remain internally consistent.

The perspective of the planner does have one thing to offer when the problem is a distorted competitive equilibrium. It suggests immediately that the competitive storage behavior deduced by refinements until self-replicating behavior is achieved can then be applied by backward induction to provide the welfare consequences of the regime of price ceilings. Thus, the perspective of the planner's selection of optimal storage and the perspective of the self-replicating expectations of competitive storers are both key insights into the nature of the storage equilibrium.

Transversality conditions

The fundamental difficulty in solving for storage rules is that current storage behavior, if modeled as rational behavior, depends on future storage behavior. More precisely, current storage behavior depends on prices expected to prevail in future periods. If there is some chance, however small, of a complete harvest failure in the next period, the effective price would be infinite. The weighted average price $E_t[P_{t+1}]$ would also be infinite, and no amount of current storage would be an equilibrium. Some restriction is therefore necessary.[14] As Scheinkman and Schechtman (1983) prove, an adequate transversality condition is one that assumes that the discounted value of the current period's carryover plus the next period's harvest goes to zero with probability 1. Salant (1983) invokes a finite "choke price" as the maximum price a consumer would pay. Under either assumption, the solution to the infinite-horizon planner's problem and to the competitive equilibrium exists and is unique.[15]

3.4   Some "shortcut" solution strategies

Whether equilibrium storage is found through refinement of a function representing expectations until it is self-replicating or through the full specification as a planner's problem with stochastic dynamic programming, the solution is internally consistent. Many of the other approaches to deriving the reduced-form equation – the storage rule – involve some simplification of the problem. Hence their solution is not, strictly speaking, internally consistent and rational, nor from the planner's perspective, optimal. A brief discussion of them may elucidate the properties of the solution technique we use.

Disregarding distant future periods

An extreme example of a simplification is the approach of Gislason (1960, p. 579). He argues that

> It does not make sense to accumulate stocks this year if next year's anticipated price is too low to give an expectation of profit from selling them.

---

[14]   Samuelson (1971) simply assumes a transversality condition such that:
$\lim_{T \to \infty} E_t[P_T]/(1+r)^{T-t} = 0$.

[15]   Kollintzas (1989) discusses more extensively the necessary and sufficient conditions for existence of equilibrium with rational expectations, in a linear model. Also see the treatment in Stokey and Lucas (1989) and Deaton and Laroque (1990).

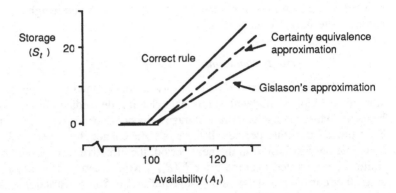

Figure 3.3. Approximations to storage rules.

Rather one would hold off buying until next year, or until anticipated profits exist. Hence, in storing to take advantage of an expected change in price, grain will be accumulated only in those years when next year's anticipated price is so much higher than the present price that all storage stocks will be sold for a profit. In other words, speculators will adjust their carry-over holdings to such a level that anticipated next year's carryout is zero.

By this reasoning, a multiperiod problem reduces to a series of two-period problems, each of which is much simpler. Apart from storage costs and interest, the resulting rule is simple: Store one-half of all availability above the average harvest. Gislason's version of the storage rule is plotted in Figure 3.3 alongside the optimal rule for the three-period example covered in Section 3.2, but with k set equal to $0, to make the computations even easier.

Gislason's rule is far from the mark. He makes no mistake in arguing that private storage will not occur if the resulting expected price would be consistent with expected losses. That is precisely the arbitrage equation behind the correct storage rule. Rather, his mistake is in the argument that all storage stocks must be sold at a profit. All that is required is that expected profits be zero. If next period's harvest is small, profits from this period's storage are high, and the new carryout is zero. If next period's harvest is large, profits from this period's storage are negative, and the new carryout is above zero. This period's storers can and should anticipate that possible outcome. The average outcome for price is what is relevant to this period's storage. Unfortunately, the possibility of future storage complicates the mathematics for solving for this period's storage. Yet, the matter can be put more positively. Part of the need for storage this period is to have supplies for future storage to alleviate some future shortfall in a harvest. Ignoring those more distant needs leads to too little storage, as in Gislason's rule in Figure 3.3.

Disregarding future uncertainty and reactions to it

A related simplification is the idea of *certainty equivalence,* used by, for example, Monke et al. (1987) in their plans for disposal of a surplus of Egyptian cotton. Much of the complexity in stochastic dynamic programming arises from the random component. Certainty equivalence replaces all the future random disturbances by their mean values.[16] For a system with inelastic supply that amounts to saying that subsequent harvests are the mean $\bar{h}$. The problem then is allocating A_t, which is somehow away from $\bar{h}$, between consumption and storage, given that subsequent harvests are known to be $\bar{h}$. That problem for the planner is considerably simpler than if the future harvests are uncertain.[17] A moment's reflection reveals that the planner's solution (or the competitive equilibrium) in this case is to share any surplus so that its discounted marginal value is constant over the subsequent periods until price is above the certainty price P^N, specifically $100. The rule derived through certainty equivalence is also shown in Figure 3.3. Certainty equivalence yields a poor approximation of the correct rule.[18]

The flaw with the simplification achieved by certainty equivalence is that, by ignoring the uncertainty, it ignores a major reason for storing. More precisely, the flaw arises because of the interaction between the randomness and the nonnegativity constraint on storage. Theil (1957) among others has demonstrated that certainty equivalence is reasonably accurate if the functions involved are relatively smooth over the range of the random outcomes. This condition does not hold for storage because of the sharp break at the point where storage is first appropriate. Certainty equivalence should be suspect from the outset as a valid technique for a problem involving collective storage.

Telser (1978, chap. 5) solves for storage behavior where storage and production in future periods are committed in advance. He calls this open-loop strategy *ex ante* storage behavior. This simplification yields a storage rule very similar to that derived with certainty equivalence. Without being able to make adjustments after the harvests in future periods are known, the best

---

16 Rausser and Hochman (1979, chap. 4) describe the technique of certainty equivalence in more detail.

17 A certainty equivalence problem can be solved through dynamic programming but, unlike a stochastic problem, it can also be solved through so-called multiperiod programming, that is, a technique like linear programming in which the values for the various periods are found simultaneously. This is the approach to storage problems put forth by Takayama and Judge (1964, 1971). Their approach is appropriate only for the allocation of a surplus under certainty.

18 Zeldes (1989) argues similarly that the certainty equivalence approach to deducing the consumption function, which is a central macroeconomic relationship, is substantially misleading. Indeed, three puzzles about consumption patterns observed empirically may simply be a result of the error from an analysis with certainty equivalence.

course is to distribute any current surplus more or less equally among the periods.[19] He contrasts this *ex ante* storage plan with *ex post* storage behavior, which allows for an adjustment of storage plans after the next harvest is realized. But in his *ex post* storage behavior, Telser looks only at revisions for the very next period and supposes that in that period plans are made for following periods where the storage is precommitted.[20] This is a crucial, albeit subtle, error. Clearly, the amount stored in the initial period, if initial plans must be followed regardless of subsequent conditions, will be different from the amount stored in the initial period if plans can be revised once in the next period. But the amount stored initially will be different if plans can be revised yet again two, three, four, or more periods ahead. By the nature of storage, which is a reversible investment, plans can be revised each period.

Disregarding the nonnegativity constraint

A seemingly intermediate step between the approach of certainty equivalence and the full problem, with all its complexities, is the approach of ignoring the nonnegativity constraint. This approach is taken directly in a number of influential articles, such as Muth (1961), where storage is not the center of attention as much as is price expectations. With a quadratic loss from back orders symmetric with positive storage costs, Blinder (1982), for example, takes this approach indirectly. But the true cost of borrowing from the future is infinite because it is impossible. Ignoring the nonnegativity constraint implicitly minimizes the discomfort from an exceptionally poor harvest; famines are impossible. With an infinite horizon, any current deficit can be worked off eventually. The storage problem then revolves around the physical storage costs and interest rate; it is relatively uninteresting. More to the point, ignoring the nonnegativity constraint gives the wrong storage rule. Furthermore, from the perspective of understanding commodities markets, the system behaves over time in a markedly different manner.

Another problem with assuming away the nonnegativity constraint is what it does to the prospective price path. If the current period can borrow what it needs from the next period, the equilibrium should always find P_t below $E_t[P_{t-1}]$ by full carrying charges (of which the interest rate is of particular concern). From the perspective of an earlier period, no matter what is the weather in period t, this relationship should hold, as it also would between periods $t+1$ and $t+2$, $t+2$ and $t+3$, and so on. In other words, the price should

---

19   In the three-period model of Section 3.2, the *ex ante* behavioral rule is the same as under complete certainty.

20   Telser's *ex post* storage rule is much like the technique of "updated certainty equivalence," described by Rausser and Hochman (1979, pp. 85–6). Plans made now that cannot be altered later as some of the uncertainty is resolved will be much like those devised under conditions of no uncertainty.

be expected to increase forever, in the case of an infinite horizon. Such a system does not have a long-run average price or average equilibrium. Put another way, it violates the normal transversality conditions. By implication, conventional comparative statics may be inappropriate.

Using backward-looking expectations

The simplifications of certainty equivalence, ignoring future storage, ignoring the nonnegativity constraint, and *ex ante* storage all at least consider storage in the context of forward-looking expectations. They all contrast sharply with the storage models of Taylor and Talpaz (1979) and Bigman (1985a), who use backward-looking expectations.[21] In the context of public wheat reserves based on forward-looking expectations, Taylor and Talpaz specify expectations for private storers and producers as a function of the previous period's price. Among the many objections to this approach is that private storage is rendered as predetermined in every period. Not surprisingly, in their model there is a role for rational public storage when private behavior is specified to be suboptimal.

Bigman uses a much more complicated scheme, making private storers' expected price an average of the prices in the previous nine periods. By iterating on his model (by positing a particular process for price), calculating the storage behavior based on those prices, and checking that the prices would follow from that storage behavior, he achieves a form of internal consistency. Accordingly, he calls the storers' expectations "rational." Nevertheless, they are not actually rational expectations. The reason they are not truly rational can be seen most readily by imagining his storers' response to an announcement of a tax on storage commencing in the next period. Forward-looking expectations would both see this tax coming and calculate its impact. Current storage behavior would adjust. Bigman's storers, in contrast, would not react. Indeed, they would not react fully until nine periods after the tax had gone into effect.[22]

Bigman's use of the term "rational expectations" is explicable to the extent that some empirical models, such as Eckstein (1984) and Ravallion (1985), exploit the time-series properties of prices. For such empirical models, especially where there are no futures markets, those wanting to construct rational expectations estimates may have no alternative but to extrapolate from past prices. A theoretical model with completely specified parameters has no such constraints. Also, it should be emphasized that these empirical rational expec-

---

[21] Taylor and Talpaz also employ certainty equivalence.
[22] Also with an average of nine prices, the more is stored in the current period – which raises the price – the higher will be the storers' expected price for the next period. That is to say, Bigman's model has $\partial E_t[P_{t+1}] / \partial S_t > 0$, whereas reasonably a large carryover would otherwise depress the price expected the next period.

tations models are valid only if the structure of the system is linear, but one knows from the outset that a system with storage has a profound nonlinearity. Also backward-looking empirical models are valid only if the structure of the system does not change; however, many of the questions one wants to ask, such as the incidence of the introduction of a public buffer stock scheme, involve changes in structure. The theoretical model should have forward-looking expectations.

Making direct approximations

A whole other class of approaches to deriving storage rules is to approximate them directly. Rosenblatt (1954) proposed a linear approximation to the storage rule so that, whatever is A_t, some fixed portion is stored. The obvious objection to the approach is that a linear function is a singularly poor approximation because the correct storage rule has a marked kink.

In this same class is the approximation to the storage rule first devised by Gustafson (1958a) and refined by Newbery and Stiglitz (1982) and most recently by Gilbert (1988).[23] This approximation is a piecewise linear function that includes the requisite sharp break at zero storage. It has the advantage of an analytical representation, but the disadvantage of requiring semilog demand and supply curves and storage costs proportional to price (as is the interest expense in our basic model). Gilbert presents a table comparing the kink point and slope of his approximation to those of the correct rules, for a variety of combinations of demand elasticities, supply elasticities, and inherent uncertainty. He claims that his approximation is sufficiently close to the correct rule. Yet, what he takes to be small differences in slope and intercepts are actually substantial. Because storage feeds on itself, a system with his rule will have different average storage and consumption variability. In any case, much more accurate computer routines described in the Appendix can solve in under thirty seconds for a basic storage rule for any desired demand curve, supply elasticity, storage costs, or weather distribution. Strictly speaking, these routines too can provide only an approximation to the storage rule. Yet the approximation can be made arbitrarily accurate at low cost.

Comparison of techniques

Whether these various shortcuts are too far from the correct answer is, of course, more relevant than their theoretical properties. Although estimates of skewness, percentage of periods with storage, and so on might be

---

23 Gustafson used his approximation principally as the starting point for his stochastic dynamic programming algorithm. Without a computer with the power of those in the 1990s, he wanted good starting values for his more refined but more laborious technique.

Table 3.1. *Standard deviation of consumption according to various shortcuts to deriving storage*

	σ_q
No storage possible	10.00
Stochastic dynamic programming	4.62
Shortcut technique	
Gislason's two-period approximation	7.12
Certainty equivalence	6.42
Negative storage possible	approaching 0.00
Rosenblatt's direct approximation	6.53
Ideal stabilization	0.00

interesting comparisons, presumably, the standard deviation of consumption would be of particular interest in any study of stabilization. Table 3.1 shows it according to various techniques for representing storage. This specific set of parameters includes a constant-elasticity consumption demand curve with $\eta^d = -0.2$, zero supply elasticity, $k = \$0$, and $r = 5$ percent.

With optimal storage behavior, in the sense of the stochastic dynamic programming solution to the planner's problem, the long-run standard deviation of consumption in this system is 4.62 units compared to the underlying variability of the harvest of 10.00 units. That is, optimal storage reduces the standard deviation of consumption about half. The other characterizations of storage suggest a substantially different proportion. Gislason's two-period approximation, Rosenblatt's direct approximation, and certainty equivalence all underestimate the reduction in the stabilization achieved. (Rosenblatt's approximation is taken as $S_t = .4 \, (A_t - 80.00)$, $S_t > 0.00$.) They would also considerably overestimate the (excess) profits from storage, which should be zero for a competitive equilibrium. Thus, they would be particularly unreliable for any study of welfare effects.

For its part, the analytical construct of "ideal stabilization" assumes all the uncertainty disappears; it overestimates the stability achieved by storage. The convenient assumption of negative storage being possible also suggests a standard deviation of consumption close to 0.00, the only difference being an effect from discounting. The entry in Table 3.1 for the "negative storage possible" is not the result of a simulation. Rather it follows from the argument given by Muth (1961, Fig. 4.2). If able to borrow the commodity from the future, risk-neutral storers should achieve nearly complete stabilization.

3.5 Solutions versus simulations

Four stages to studying competitive storage in a setting with an infinite horizon can be distinguished:

1. Specification of the conditions for a competitive equilibrium; the derivation of the arbitrage equation was the purpose of Chapter 2.
2. Conceptual reformulation of the conditions for a competitive equilibrium in order to deduce the reduced-form equation for equilibrium storage; various approaches to this task have been mentioned in this chapter.
3. Development of numerical methods necessary to put the conceptual reformulation into practice, since a general analytical solution remains elusive; the Appendix to this chapter discusses and compares three different numerical techniques.
4. Study of the reduced-form equation in action; such simulations are central features of the next two chapters. In that setting of repeated calculations it is obvious why solving for the reduced-form equation once and for all is especially helpful.

Simulations generated the short time series subjected to scrutiny in Section 2.4. Given the storage rule and planned production rule, a system involving a specific set of parameters was followed for eleven periods as it reacted to the random weather. The random weather was easily drawn from a computer's random number generator. Thus, for that short simulation and most definitely for any longer one the computer has a large role. But a high-speed computer is also the appropriate implement for the numerical methods necessary to solve for the storage. Unfortunately, the common role of a computer can cause confusion about the differences between numerical solutions and simulations.

Many authors skip the first three stages entirely, arbitrarily specifying some form of storage behavior. For example, someone might investigate the behavior of a system in which two-thirds of any availability above average production is stored. The research is then the exercise of simulating this storage behavior, to deduce such properties as average storage, average producer revenue, and so forth. This approach, so rightly criticized, gives simulations a bad name. The specified storage rule is one of an infinity of arbitrary rules; "results" are likely to be sensitive to the assumed rule. Also the specified rule is not grounded in any behavioral relationship, such as competitive equilibrium or the planner's effort to maximize social welfare. Consequently, the welfare effects of simulated interventions are untrustworthy. Nevertheless, the fault is not with the use of simulations per se: They are a necessary and useful tool for any multiperiod problem with uncertainty.

Finally, some defense needs to be offered for the numerical solutions, the third stage, because they too are often viewed with suspicion by those used to analytical representations. A general explicit analytical reduced-form equation for equilibrium storage would be nice but it is by no means a necessity. The solution is the solution whether found analytically or numerically. Given the speed of modern computers it is often cost effective to solve numerically those problems that could be solved analytically although laboriously. Sensitivity analysis can illuminate the roles of various parameters.

Appendix: Numerical solution of the storage model

For solving the storage model, several numerical approaches are possible, all based on the recursive logic of dynamic programming. In this Appendix we describe three of them, each in a separate section. The first approach entails a full enumeration of the possible future harvests; this might be called a branching approach. The second approach uses the principle of polynomial approximations and is the technique used throughout this book. The third approach, the type Gardner (1979) uses, employs a large array of cells to tabulate the amount stored for all possible availabilities.[1]

In contrast to the various techniques discussed in Section 3.4, such as using certainty equivalence or ignoring the nonnegativity constraint on storage, all three approaches considered here can solve for the storage rule to a negligibly small degree of inaccuracy. (Accuracy tests constitute Section A3.4.) The three numerical techniques here differ by the amount of computer time they require and the types of problems they can solve.[2] The technique of full enumeration requires by far the most computer time and is not suitable for a problem with an infinite horizon. The cell technique has trouble with elastic supply and cannot readily be adapted to problems with distortions such as price ceilings. Our polynomial technique is the most flexible and fastest, but perhaps at the cost of any intuitive understanding of the computer routines.

Naturally, the emphasis in this Appendix is on the polynomial technique.[3] It is discussed in Section 3A.2 at the detailed level of the loops in the computer program. Gardner's cell technique is discussed in Section 3A.3 at a

---

[1]   Gardner's name is associated here with what is a more general technique, because he applied that technique to optimal storage problems. In other areas, such as the emerging macroeconomic literature on numerically solved optimal growth problems, similar methods have been developed, for example, by Christiano (1990) and Coleman (1990). With much duplication of effort, each specialty in economics and operations research has developed numerical methods independently. Judd (1990) has attempted a general treatment to avoid this repetition.

[2]   See Taylor and Uhlig (1990) for a contest between techniques when applied to a problem with stochastic growth.

[3]   A brief description of the technique, first used in Wright and Williams (1982a), was included in Wright and Williams (1984b). It was a substantial departure from numerical methods for stochastic dynamic programming available at the time for storage problems, although Harvey's (1974) computer system for the solution of dynamic problems was similar. Others, notably Lowry et al. (1987), Miranda and Helmberger (1988), and Bizer and Judd (1989), have subsequently adopted fairly similar approaches. The idea of polynomial approximations (although most often in regard to the "decision rule") dates from the first applications of dynamic programming in the early 1960s.

much more general level. The branching approach is considered in Section 3A.1 primarily as an example, with the description of the actual numerical algorithm left cursory. Instead, we demonstrate how the solution can be achieved much more economically using approximations similar to our algorithm. Readers familiar with numerical solution of stochastic dynamic programming models might skip Section 3A.1 and go straight to the description of our computer routines in Section 3A.2.

3A.1   The technique of full enumeration

The numerical method called here the "branching approach" requires too many calculations for widespread use. But it can be made as accurate as desired for problems with finite horizons, and so is an excellent check on other numerical methods (as it will be so used in Section 3A.4). Also the nature of the calculations involved suggests approximations that are essentially as accurate with orders of magnitude fewer computations.

Whereas the example in Section 3.2 was constructed to have three periods, a continuous probability distribution, no complications from elastic supply, and an analytical solution, the example here has four periods, a discrete probability distribution, elastic supply, and no analytical solution. The consumption demand curve has a constant elasticity $\eta^d = -0.25$; thus $P_t = \beta / q_t^4$, with the coefficient β calibrated to have the curve pass through the point ($100, 100 units). The one-period-lagged supply function is $\bar{h}_{t+1} = a + bP_{t+1}^r$, with the coefficients a and b calibrated so that the supply elasticity is 0.3 at the point ($100, 100 units). The multiplicative disturbance v_t has a two-point distribution with probabilities .2 and .8 of a proportional random disturbance of $-.2$ and $+.05$, respectively. This skewed distribution, with its small chance of a very poor harvest, is a major inducement for storage. Last of all, the interest rate r is 4 percent and the marginal physical storage cost k is $1 per unit per period.

In this system the four periods cover period $T - 3$ through period T. The carryout from period T is zero under all circumstances. Thus, from any condition in the initial period, namely period $T - 3$, it is possible to list all possible sequences of the harvests, the availabilities, the amounts stored, and the amounts planted. After three periods, that is, by period T, eight (2^3) different branches could have been followed. The solution methodology considers the nodes on these branches explicitly.

Solution for a specific initial condition

Consider a specific initial condition, in which availability A_{T-3} is 115.00 units. The question is: How much is stored and how much production is planned in period $T - 3$, given the current availability of 115 units?

An arbitrarily exact answer to this question can be worked out numerically. To understand the nature of the problem, and how it can be solved, it may be helpful to peek at the ultimate "solution tree," which is illustrated in Figure 3A.1. As shown at the top of the tree, 13.35 of the initial 115 units available are stored to accompany 98.97 units planted for harvesting in period $T-2$.[4] These quantities simultaneously satisfy the equilibrium conditions (2.5) and (2.16), namely, that positive storage just cover carrying charges and that the planned production be consistent with the producers' incentive price it implies.[5]

Behind this answer are fourteen other equilibria along the branches of the tree. For example, follow the leftmost nodes. If the yield is high in $T-2$, availability A_{T-2} is 117.27 (the harvest, 98.97 × 1.05, plus storage, 13.35). Storage of 14.31 units makes $P[117.27 - 14.31] + k = E_{T-2}[P_{T-1}] / (1+r)$. If the weather is good again, availability in $T-1$ is 116.58 units, of which 11.62 is stored in equilibrium. If the weather is good for a third time running, A_T is 111.11, all of which must be consumed in period T.

Figure 3A.1 gives no clue, however, about how these sequential equilibria were deduced. All are obviously intertwined. The storage of 14.31 units in period $T-2$ depends on the carryout of 11.62 if the weather is good the next period. It also depends on the carryin of 13.35 from period $T-3$, which is the answer to the main question. It seems that searching for the answer by working forward will not serve because future storage is then unknown, whereas working backward will not work because the precise carryin is unknown.

The sequential equilibria cannot be deduced simultaneously (in the manner of multiperiod programming) because it is not known in period $T-3$ which branch will transpire.[6] The trick is to recognize that, because period T has no carryout, the equilibrium in period $T-1$ can be deduced for any given T_{T-1}. That solution for period $T-1$ in turn allows the equilibrium in period $T-2$ to be found, and so on by backward induction to the initial period.

This backward induction is the standard procedure for dynamic programming. In the analytical example of Section 3.2, S_{T-1} was found as an analyt-

---

4   Actually, the numerical methods were set to yield answers accurate to five decimal places.

5   Specifically, $(93.67 + 1.00) \times 1.04 = 98.46 = .8 \times 88.97 + .2 \times 136.48$. $P^r_{f-2} = .8 \times 88.97 \times 1.05 + .2 \times 136.43 \times .8 = 96.57$; $\bar{h}_{T-2} = 70 + .3 \times 96.57 = 98.97$.

6   The solution for storage and planned production in period $T-3$ (given A_{T-3} is 115 units) is not the weighted average over all the possible sample paths solved under the assumption of perfect foresight. Although the market as a whole can foresee the possible harvests in period $T-2$ (not to mention subsequent ones) and their probabilities of occurrence, it cannot know for sure which harvest will occur. That uncertainty gives rise to different choices in period $T-3$ than the average of the perfect foresight rules for S_{T-3} and h_{T-2}. To put the matter more positively, plans do not need to be made in period $T-3$ for the exact amount stored and planted in distant periods. It suffices to compute those values once the weather in those periods is known. The behavior in those future equilibria does, however, influence the equilibrium in period $T-3$.

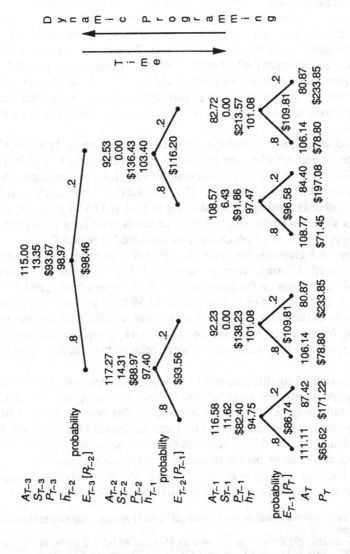

Figure 3A.1. Sequential equilibria from initial condition of $A_{T-3} = 115$; $S_T = 0$.

ical function of A_{T-1}. When S_{T-1} was substituted out of the problem, it was possible to solve for S_{T-2} as a function of A_{T-2}. The complication for the problem here is that S_{T-1} cannot be represented as an analytical function; rather S_{T-1} (and its companion $\bar{h}_T$) can only be found numerically, with each set of calculations applicable only for a particular A_{T-1}. That is, S_{T-1} can only be substituted out for a single A_{T-1}.

Thus, the numerical methods accomplishing the branching approach start with guesses for S_{T-3} and $\bar{h}_{T-2}$. These guesses imply two provisional values for A_{T-2} (depending on the weather). In turn, initial guesses are made for the two equilibrium values of S_{T-2} and $\bar{h}_{T-1}$, which imply four provisional values for A_{T-1}. The exact equilibrium can be found for each of these four provisional values.

For each of these four A_{T-1}'s, the arbitrage equation for planned production requires the implicit function (2.16) be zero:

$$0 = \bar{h}\left[P_T^f\right] - \bar{h}_T \equiv L$$

$$0 = a + b(0.2(\beta / (\bar{h}_T(1.0 - 0.2) + S_{T-1})^4)(1.0 - 0.2) \qquad (3A.1)$$
$$+ 0.8(\beta / (\bar{h}_T(1.0 + 0.05) + S_{T-1})^4)(1.0 + 0.05)) - \bar{h}_T$$

while the equilibrium condition (2.5) for positive storage S_{T-1} requires

$$0 = P_{T-1} + k - E_{T-1}[P_T] / (1 + r) \equiv M$$
$$0 = (1 + r)(\beta / (A_{T-1} - S_{T-1})^4 + k) \qquad (3A.2)$$
$$- (0.2\beta / (\bar{h}_T(1.0 - 0.2) + S_{T-1})^4 + 0.8\beta / (\bar{h}_T(1.0 + 0.05) + S_{T-1})^4)$$

This pair of simultaneous equations (3A.1) and (3A.2) cannot be solved analytically for $\bar{h}_T$ and S_{T-1}, principally because of the exponent 4. Rather the pair of implicit functions must be solved by trial and error, by trying plausible values for $\bar{h}_T$ and S_{T-1} and by paying attention to the derivatives of L and M with respect to the two endogenous variables. (That approach was the logic behind the iterations in Figure 2.2 in the simpler problem in Section 2.3 of determining equilibrium planned production without storage.)

Given these provisional equilibrium values of S_{T-1} for each of the four provisional A_{T-1}'s, it is possible to solve numerically the comparable pair of implicit functions for each of the two provisional values of A_{T-2}. If the provisional values for S_{T-2} and $\bar{h}_{T-1}$ are not correct and must be adjusted, the four values of A_{T-1} change and, consequently, the simultaneous equations (3A.1) and (3A.2) must be resolved for each. Eventually, for the provisional A_{T-2}'s, the computer will find the sequence of equilibria having internal consistency. With that accomplished, the provisional S_{T-3} and $\bar{h}_{T-2}$ are checked for whether they are consistent with the average price in period $T-2$ given the storage behavior in period $T-2$ (and, in turn, period $T-1$). If not, when they are adjusted in the direction of the equilibrium values, the implied A_{T-2}'s will be different. Each equilibrium farther down the branches must be found again numerically. The updating cycle repeats, until equilibrium values of S and $\bar{h}$ at each node along all the branches are accurate to the desired number of decimal places.

To deduce Figure 3A.1 to an accuracy of five decimal places from reasonable starting values, it took about five adjustments of S_{T-3} and $\bar{h}_{T-2}$. For each of the resulting A_{T-2}'s, it also took about five adjustments, and about four adjustments for each of the resulting A_{T-1}'s. Because the derivatives of the implicit functions of L and M in the final stage, as well as the two earlier stages, were deduced numerically, equations (3A.1) and (3A.2) were each evaluated on the order of 25,000 times.

Reductions in calculations

The equilibrium carryout and planned production in period $T-3$ can be similarly calculated for any availability in period $T-3$, such as 105 units. Yet for each the computer time is considerable since the whole model must be re-solved. If the possible outcomes of the harvest each period are more numerous or if the number of periods is much larger, the computer time required is prohibitive.

Fortunately, the number of computations can be reduced. For any particular initial condition, among the many branches some computations are unnecessary and others duplicative. If along some branch, A_{T-1} is very low, S_{T-1} will surely be zero. The equilibrium value for $\bar{h}_T$ does not affect price in period $T-1$ without the connector storage. Because P_{T-1} is what matters to the two arbitrage relationships in period $T-2$, calculations can stop once an equilibrium S_{T-1} is recognized as being zero. And repetitive calculations occur when two branches have the same availability in, say, period $T-2$. It does not matter that A_{T-2} is 116.83 units because a provisional value of S_{T-3} was small and a provisional value of h_{T-2} was big or because the provisional S_{T-3} was large and the provisional $\bar{h}_{T-2}$ was small; the equilibrium S_{T-2} and $\bar{h}_{T-1}$ are the same. If the calculations made the first time A_{T-2} is 116.83 could be preserved, they could be reused. For that matter, the answer for $A_{T-2} = 116.82$ should not be too different; judicious interpolation might suffice.

Indeed, all the calculations beyond period $T-2$ could be dispensed with if there were a way for representing S_{T-2} as a continuous function of A_{T-2}. In the full enumeration method, the derivative of expected next-period price with respect to current storage was used in finding the equilibrium, whichever the period. This suggests that one might use the paired values of $(E_{T-2}[P_{T-1}], S_{T-2})$ from "trees" already worked out to guess the relationship between $E_{T-2}[P_{T-1}]$ and S_{T-2}. In Figure 3A.1, which begins from $A_{T-3} = 115$, the branch with positive storage in period $T-2$ has $S_{T-2} = 14.31$. A tree like Figure 3A.1 for $A_{T-3} = 105$ shows that, if the yield is high, A_{T-2} is 112.81

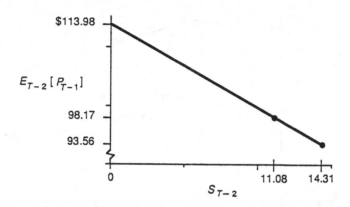

Figure 3A.2. Apparent linear relationship between S_{T-2} and $E_{T-2}[P_{T-1}]$.

and equilibrium storage S_{T-2} is 11.08. (If the yield is low – the other branch – then S_{T-2} is 0.00.)

A reasonable guess for $E_{T-2}[P_{T-1}]$ for any S_{T-2} can be constructed by fitting a linear relation through the points (14.31, \$93.56) and (11.08, \$98.17), as in Figure 3A.2. This relation is

$$E_{T-2}[P_{T-1}[S_{T-2}]] \approx 113.98 - 1.43 S_{T-2} \qquad (3A.3)$$

With equation (3A.3) as an approximation, it is possible to avoid the many recomputations of A_{T-1} and the resulting S_{T-1}'s and $\bar{h}_T$'s necessary to finding the S_{T-2} for a given A_{T-2}. The total number of calculations drops to around 300 from around 25,000, yet the shortcut is virtually as accurate. For $A_{T-3} = 110$, for example, it yields an estimate of 9.64 for S_{T-3}, the same value to three significant figures as the "exact" calculation through full enumeration of the tree analogous to Figure 3A.1.

The usefulness of the linear interpolation in Figure 3A.2 for the S_{T-2} following from $A_{T-3} = 110$ does not depend on the fact that 11.08 and 14.38 are possible values of S_{T-2} after A_{T-3} of 105 and 115, respectively. Very similar interpolations would be obtained from arbitrarily choosing say 11.00 and 14.00 for S_{T-2}, and finding associated equilibrium values of $E_{T-2}[P_{T-1}]$ via enumeration of the shorter branches from $T-1$ to T. For that matter, the relationship between initial-period storage S_{T-3} and $E_{T-3}[P_{T-2}]$ could be estimated from two or three A_{T-3}'s, virtually dispensing with calculations for any other A_{T-3}.

Different terminal conditions

A final point can be made with this numerical, four-period example. The equilibrium in period $T-3$ envisions no carryout from period T. Suppose

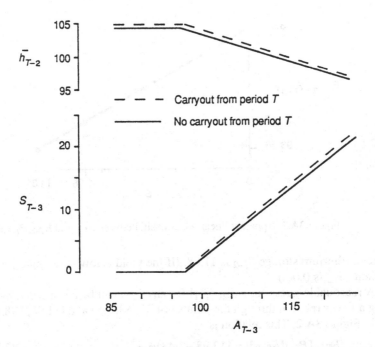

Figure 3A.3. Storage and planned production rules for period $T-3$ derived from different terminal conditions.

instead that 75 percent of any A_T above 100 units is stored. This terminal condition requires a substantial carryout and is radically different compared to S_T equaling zero. With this new terminal condition, P_T will be greater than or equal to the price with the other terminal condition whatever is A_T. These higher prices in period T feed back up the branches, increasing the equilibrium S_{T-1} (if positive) for any A_{T-1} and the equilibrium S_{T-2} (if positive) for any A_{T-2}.

The new terminal condition's effect on S_{T-3} and $\bar{h}_{T-2}$ as functions of A_{T-3} is shown in Figure 3A.3. Also shown in Figure 3A.3 are the storage and planned production rules with the terminal condition of $S_T = 0$. Two points on those rules are the equilibrium values deduced for $A_{T-3} = 115$ and 105. (The full branching approach was applied to all other integer values of A_{T-3}, and the intervening points were drawn as linear interpolations.)

The reduced-form relationship for equilibrium storage for period $T-3$ with substantial storage in period T is not all that different from the relationship with $S_T = 0$. In other words, the terminal condition is relatively unimportant for the equilibrium in period $T-3$, at least compared to its influence on period $T-1$ or $T-2$. More generally, the influence of the terminal condition on the equilibrium in an earlier period $T-j$ attenuates quickly as j increases.

In period $T-8$, say, the influence of wide variation in conditions in period T would be barely discernible in the current storage behavior. The rule that emerges regardless of the terminal conditions is the stationary rule for an infinite horizon.[7]

This observation about the attenuated influence of the terminal condition suggests that the stationary storage rule for an infinite horizon can be found by starting with a reasonable guess for the relationship between $E_t[P_{t+1}]$ and S_t as in Figure 3A.2. Then with this guess, one can fit updated estimates of the relationship $E_t[P_{t+1}[S_t]]$, until the fitted function in one iteration is sufficiently similar to its predecessor to be accepted as a stationary function. This is the approach we use in our numerical algorithm.

3A.2 The technique of polynomial approximations

Our computer routine finds a low-order polynomial in storage $\psi[S_t]$ such that, if ψ represents storers' expectations of next period's price $E_t[P_{t+1}]$ should they store S_t, ψ is consistent with itself. Admittedly, it is by no means obvious why $E_t[P_{t+1}]$ is a function of current storage S_t, or why it is amenable to approximation by a polynomial, or why the storage rule (i.e., the reduced-form equation for equilibrium storage) is not itself approximated. As regards why the expected price can be written as $E_t[P_{t+1}[S_t]]$: Although P_{t+1} is directly determined by the quantity consumed in period $t+1$, consumption in period P_{t+1} is a function of that period's carryin S_t. Moreover, that function should be smooth. Regardless of the weather in period $t+1$, price in period $t+1$ has to be lower the larger is the carryin S_t. Even as $E_t[P_{t+1}[S_t]]$ declines with S_t, it most likely does so at a declining rate. Such a smooth relationship, whatever its precise form, should be well represented by a polynomial.[8] (See Judd [1990] for a more rigorous defense of the use of polynomials.) As regards the focus on $E_t[P_{t+1}]$ rather than the storage rule: Over the observed range of storage, namely $S_t \geq 0$, $E_t[P_{t+1}]$ should be a smoother function than the storage rule itself is, because the relationship between S_t and current availability A_t has a sharp kink.[9]

---

[7]   See Bertsekas (1987, chap. 5) for a formal proof of the convergence to a stationary rule.

[8]   Our idea of a polynomial approximation is closely related to what Gal (1989) has developed more recently under the name "parameter iteration method" of dynamic programming. (Also see Gavish and Johnson, 1990.) Gal argues that a simple approximation, perhaps linear or quadratic, can represent the value function (V^* in equation (3.4)) as a function of state variables. His approximation is designed for problems with many, perhaps a hundred, state variables. The main difference from our approach is that we use a polynomial in a control variable to approximate the derivative of the value function, because this is the smoothest relationship within the storage problem.

[9]   In any case, because $E_t[P_{t+1}]$ can be represented as a function of S_t, the storage rule is but one small step away, since the storage rule is implicit in the equation $P_t[A_t - S_t] + k = E_t[P_{t+1}[S_t]]/(1 + r)$.

In brief, our computer routine follows the logic of

1. supposing future storage S_{t+1} follows a signal ψ representing the expected price for period $t+2$, no matter why;
2. supposing current storage S_t is in turn each of a set of integer values, no matter why;
3. calculating the average price in period $t+1$ under those circumstances;
4. using the implied relationship between that average price for period $t+1$ and storage in period t to revise the signal for future storage; and
5. iterating until ψ reproduces itself.

This section considers first the derivation of the self-replicating polynomial ψ approximating $E_t[P_{t+1}[S_t]]$ for the case where supply is perfectly inelastic, and then the more complicated elastic-supply equilibrium. The many lines of FORTRAN code are not listed; the point is to understand the logic of the embedded iterations. An example is then given of the computer routine in action.

The computer algorithm without supply elasticity

First, consider the steps in the polynomial technique when supply is perfectly inelastic with mean $\bar{h}$. The computer program has already been fed values for $\bar{h}$, the parameters of the consumption demand function, the marginal storage cost, the interest rate, and the probability distribution of the harvest. This probability distribution is time invariant, discrete, and finite, but can be designed to represent closely any continuous distribution such as a normal distribution.

Computer programs have their comparative advantage in "looping" over similar calculations. For the computer routine to find a polynomial ψ consistent with itself requires four loops imbedded one within the other. They are indicated by the vertical lines to the left of the following steps. The description of the steps uses the time subscripts t and $t+1$, but these subscripts are simply aids in understanding the progress of the calculations. The routine does not move backward in time, recomputing relations for period $t-1$, $t-2$, and so on, while saving its calculations for period t and $t+1$. Instead it writes over its previous calculations, refining them as it were. Thus, it is conceptually clearer to think of the outer loop beginning after step (1) as an iteration rather than as a different period.

(1)   Choose a first guess $\psi[S]$ for $E_t[P_{t+1}[S_t]]$, where $\psi[S_t]$ is a low-order (say third-order) polynomial in S_t. The coefficients in ψ are selected so that $\partial\psi/\partial S < 0$ and $\partial^2\psi/\partial S^2 \geq 0$.

THE LOOP FOR POLYNOMIAL Ψ

(2)   Choose a vector $\tilde{S}_t$ of discrete values $S_t^i = 1, \ldots, N$. By the nature of loops in computer programs, the elements of $\tilde{S}_t$ are equally spaced; integers

are also natural. N should be at least 10 or 12 and S_t^N should be close to the maximum storage seen in relatively long simulations. Inasmuch as this long-run maximum depends on the solution for the storage rule, it must be guessed initially. If the selection for S_t^N proves to be markedly off, it must be changed and the routine begun again.[10]

_____ THE LOOP FOR S_t^i

(3)   Multiply $\bar{h}$ by $(1 + v^j)$, $j = 1, \ldots, M$, each v having probability prob[v^j]. Again by the nature of loops in computer programs, the elements of $\tilde{v}$ are equally spaced.

(4)   Add S_t^i to each of the realized values of production generated in step (3) to produce a vector $\tilde{A}_{t+1}^i$, M elements long, of amounts available in the next period.

_____ THE LOOP OVER EACH STATE A_{t+1}^{ij} IN PERIOD $t+1$

_____ THE LOOP FOR FINDING THE EQUILIBRIUM S_{t+1}^{ij}

(5)   For each element A_{t+1}^{ij} of $\tilde{A}_{t+1}^i$ numerically solve the implicit function

$$P[A_{t+1}^{ij} - S_{t+1}^{ij}] + k - \psi[S_{t+1}^{ij}] / (1+r) = 0 \qquad (3A.4)$$

for S_{t+1}^{ij}. This implicit function is the arbitrage equation (2.5) for positive storage, with ψ taking the place of $E_{t+1}[P_{t+2}]$. If the solution is negative, set S_{t+1}^{ij} equal to zero in accordance with the nonnegativity constraint on storage. From the perspective of computer programming, the search for the solution S_{t+1}^{ij} can be thought of as another loop, searching over possible values. Because this loop is repeated many, many times, careful computer programming of this numerical derivation is especially valuable. The loop could be written as a crude grid search, but we make use of the much faster Newton's method. Combined with judicious selection of the starting guess for S_{t+1}^{ij}, this approach usually requires no more than three or four iterations to achieve an accuracy of five significant figures.

(6)   For each pair A_{t+1}^{ij}, S_{t+1}^{ij} that solve the arbitrage equation (3A.4) calculate the associated price $P[q_{t+1}] = P[A_{t+1}^{ij} - S_{t+1}^{ij}]$ from the inverse consumption demand function.

(7)   Using the vector of these prices, calculate the expected price

$$E_t[P_{t+1}|S_t^i] = \sum_{j=1}^{M} P[A_{t+1}^{ij} - S_{t+1}^{ij}] prob[v^j] \qquad (3A.5)$$

[10]   For some extensions of the storage model covered in later chapters this vector $\tilde{S}_t$ is altered from one iteration over ψ to the next. For the basic model, it stays the same.

This is the expected price, from the perspective of period t, given that the carryout from period t is S_t and that storage in period $t+1$ uses ψ as its estimate of $E_{t+1}[P_{t+2}]$.[11]

(8)   When steps (3)–(7) have been repeated for each of the elements of $\tilde{S}_t$, fit the associated values of $E_t[P_{t+1}|S_t^i]$, $i = 1,\ldots,N$, by regression techniques (ordinary least squares) to a polynomial $\psi^*[S]$, where low-order powers of S_t^i are the independent variables.

(9)   If the fitted values of this regression differ by less than a certain chosen small amount from the values using the guess $\psi[S_t]$ from step (1),[12] adopt $\psi^*[S]$ as the function approximating the equilibrium $E_t[P_{t+1}|S_t]$. If the criteria for convergence are not satisfied, adopt $\psi^*[S]$ as the new guess, replacing $\psi[S]$, and repeat steps (2)–(9).

The initial guess for ψ in this procedure is not consistent with rational storage. Only when a revised ψ reproduces itself are the expectations of future storage behavior consistent with current storage. Thus, although the storage in all but the last iteration is suboptimal, the program deduces the rational (i.e., optimal) behavior.

The algorithm with elastic supply

With elastic supply and multiplicative disturbances, the computer routine must find a consistent set among S_t^i, $E_t[P_{t+1}]$, $\bar{h}_{t+1}^i$, and P_{t+1}^r. Given ψ and S_t^i, a search is organized over possible values for planned production to find one consistent with the incentive P_{t+1}^r implied by it, ψ, and S_t^i. This requires a fifth loop, inserted between the second and third loops without elastic supply, that is, between steps (2) and (3). The following additions (designated by "a") and adjustments (designated by a prime) are made:

(2a)   For each component S_t^i of $\tilde{S}_t$, choose a guess χ for the equilibrium value of planned production $\bar{h}_{t+1}^i$ associated with S_t^i.

(3´)   Multiply χ rather than $\bar{h}$ by $(1+v^j)$ to create the vector of realized values of production the next period.

(7a)   Along with the calculation of expected price, calculate $P_{t+1}^r|S_t^i$, the rational producers' incentive price:

---

11   Judd (1990) notes that, because the computation is mathematically a problem in integration, specialized techniques in numerical integration can speed the calculation of $E_t[P_{t+1}[S_t^i]]$ for some probability distributions, especally a normal distribution. Specifically, looping over all M elements in the grid may not be necessary. In problems with more than one state variable, this approach may offer substantial savings in computer time.

12   Because the function ψ determines storage behavior, movements in points spaced along the whole function and not just movements in individual coefficients are used to judge whether the function has changed appreciably.

$$P^r_{t+1}|S^i_t = \sum_{j=1}^{M}(1 + v^j)P[A^{ij}_{t+1} - S^{ij}_{t+1}]prob[v^j]\tag{3A.6}$$

The producers' incentive price is different from the expected price $E_t[P_{t+1}]$ because of the effect of the weighting factor $(1+w^j)$.

(7b)   Substitute $P^r_{t+1}|S^i_t$ in the function for planned production:

$$\bar{h}_{t+1} = \bar{h}[P^r_{t+1}]\tag{3A.7}$$

Check whether this planned production is consistent with the guess χ. If $|\bar{h}_{t+1} - \chi| > \varepsilon$, where ε is set at a small number, choose a new guess for χ, higher or lower as appropriate, and repeat steps (3′)–(7b). If $|\bar{h}_{t+1} - \chi| < \varepsilon$, then the set S^i_t, $\bar{h}^i_{t+1}$, and $E_t[P_{t+1}|S^i_t]$ is internally consistent, at least to the chosen degree of accuracy.

This search for the $\bar{h}_{t+1}$ consistent with S^i_t and ψ is best organized as a grid search over χ in order to find the closest integer and then as successive refinements by means of Newton's method. The internal consistency among ψ, determined by the first and slowest moving loop, S^i_t determined by the next loop, and $\bar{h}_{t+1}$ allows for the convergence of the whole set. Once the larger loop has converged on a stable function for ψ^*, the resulting stationary function representing $E_t[P_{t+1}[S_t]]$ is consistent with the profit-maximizing arbitrage condition for positive storage and with the profit-maximizing condition for planned production. That is to say, the expected price and producers' incentive price resulting from storage and planned production are the incentives used in deciding how much to store and to plant; storers' and producers' expectations are internally consistent.

The problem is sufficiently well behaved that the routine converges for any reasonable starting value of ψ, including that of $\psi[S] = 0$. When $\psi[S] = 0$ is chosen, the iterations are those followed in moving back in time from a terminal period with no carryout. The final self-replicating ψ contains the information necessary for plotting the stationary storage rule. The N pairs $P^r_{t+1}|S^i_t$, S^i_t can be used to fit, through a regression, a polynomial $\theta[S_t]$ to represent the continuous relationship between equilibrium planned production and equilibrium storage.

An example

As an example of our computer routines, consider more closely the set of parameters used for the first numerically deduced storage rule, the one introduced in Section 2.4. That system included elastic supply; specifically $\bar{h}_{t+1} = 50 + 0.5P^r_{t+1}$. Other parameters were a linear consumption demand curve with $\eta^d = -0.2$, an interest rate $r = 5$ percent, and marginal physical storage costs $k = \$2$. Let the continuous normal distribution of yields, which has a standard deviation of 0.10, be approximated by a discrete symmetric distribution with nine points. Also suppose the initial guess for the polynomial is $\psi = \$80\text{-}1.5S$, which is much below the mark. Let ψ in subsequent iterations have four terms: a constant, S, S^2, and S^3.[13]

From this initial guess for ψ, the routine requires ten iterations to find a ψ^* effectively unchanged from the previous iteration. For each of these iterations many other calculations must be performed. A sense of some of the calculations involved is provided by Table 3A.1. This table has three parts, each with a different message about the search for self-replicating behavior.

The first panel of Table 3A.1 asks the question: Supposing that $S_t = 0$, that planned production for period $t + 1$ is 109 units, and that storage in period $t + 1$ follows the incentive $\$80 - 1.5 S_{t+1}$, what are $E_t[P_{t+1}]$ and P^r_{t+1}? Table 3A.1 shows the nine possible harvests in period $t + 1$, given planting of 109 units, and their associated probabilities. For each of these harvests the innermost loop of the routine (step (5)) solves numerically for S_{t+1}, given that ψ. The weighted average of the resulting prices is such that $P^r_{t+1} = \$77.78$. This producers' incentive price, given the supply function, indicates a planned production of 88.89 units, not the 109.00 units supposed. This discrepancy suggests to the routine to try a lower value for planned production. Eventually it finds that a planned production of 100.64 units, still supposing $S_t = 0$ and $\psi = \$80 - 1.5S$, leads to a P^r_{t+1} of $\$101.28$, which dictates the same 100.64 units. The calculations behind this first achievement of internal consistency are shown in the second panel of Table 3A.1. But note that the expected price is $\$104.88$ if $S_t = 0.00$, not the $\$80$ supposed. Another internal inconsistency remains to be resolved.

This point, 0.00 units of storage and an expected price of $\$104.88$, is one datum for the refinement of ψ. It is illustrated as the leftmost dot on the curve in Figure 3A.4 marked "Iteration 1." The other seven dots indicated on that curve are the result of calculations like those in the second panel of Table 3A.1 for values of S_t equal to 5.0, 10.0, 15.0, and so on. A third-order polynomial describes these eight points well; ψ^* after the first iteration is $104.88 - 1.357S + 0.0000623S^2 + 0.00013336S^3$. This polynomial is plotted continuously in Figure 3A.4 as the curve for the first iteration. This revised equation for ψ gives rise to the eight dots on the curve marked "Iteration 2" in Figure 3A.4. When fit by ordinary least squares, they indicate a new polynomial $107.91 - 1.283S + 0.01228S^2 - 0.00004834S^3$. This new polynomial has changed much less.

By the tenth iteration the polynomial essentially duplicates itself. Part and parcel, the remaining internal inconsistencies are negligible. The degree of the final internal consistency can be seen in the third panel of Table 3A.1.

---

[13] For Section 2.4, the polynomial was fourth-order and the probability distribution was finer. Hence the solution was slightly different.

Table 3A.1. *Examples of search for internal consistency*

j	Prob[w^j]	$(1+w^j)$	A_{t+1}	$S_{t+1}|\psi$	$P[q_{t+1}]$	$(1+w^j)P_{t+1}$

1. First iteration, given initial guess for ψ and χ
$\psi = 80 - 1.50\ S;\ S_t = 0.00,\ \chi = 109.00$

1	.0401	0.80	87.20	0.00	$164.00	131.20
2	.0659	0.85	92.65	0.00	136.75	116.24
3	.1212	0.90	98.10	0.00	109.50	98.55
4	.1745	0.95	103.55	0.00	82.25	78.14
5	.1966	1.00	109.00	2.99	69.95	69.95
6	.1745	1.05	114.45	7.22	63.85	67.04
7	.1212	1.10	119.90	11.46	57.80	63.58
8	.0659	1.15	125.35	15.70	51.75	59.51
9	.0401	1.20	130.80	19.94	<u>45.70</u>	<u>54.84</u>

$E_t[P_{t+1}] = 80.35 \quad P^r_{t+1} = 77.78$
$\bar{h}[77.78] = 88.89$

2. Consistency of $\bar{h}_{t+1}$ with latest guess for χ, for given guess for ψ
$\psi = 80 - 1.50\ S;\ S_t = 0.00,\ \chi = 100.64$

1	.0401	0.80	80.51	0.00	$197.44	157.95
2	.0659	0.85	85.54	0.00	172.28	146.44
3	.1212	0.90	90.58	0.00	147.12	132.41
4	.1745	0.95	95.61	0.00	121.96	115.86
5	.1966	1.00	100.64	0.00	96.80	96.80
6	.1745	1.05	105.67	0.40	73.64	77.32
7	.1212	1.10	110.70	4.31	68.03	74.83
8	.0659	1.15	115.73	8.23	62.47	71.84
9	.0401	1.20	120.77	12.14	<u>56.85</u>	<u>68.22</u>

$E_t[P_{t+1}] = 104.88 \quad P^r_{t+1} = 101.28$
$\bar{h}[101.28] = 100.64$

3. Consistency of $E_t[P_{t+1}]$ with latest guess for ψ and $\bar{h}_{t+1}$ with χ
$\psi = 109.13 - 1.207S + 0.01593S^2 - 0.00007118S^3;\ S_t = 0.00,\ \chi = 103.45$

1	.0401	0.80	82.76	0.00	$186.20	148.96
2	.0659	0.85	87.93	0.00	160.34	136.29
3	.1212	0.90	93.10	0.00	134.48	121.03
4	.1745	0.95	98.28	0.00	108.60	103.17
5	.1966	1.00	103.45	3.15	98.50	98.50
6	.1745	1.05	108.62	7.46	94.19	98.90
7	.1212	1.10	113.80	11.87	90.38	99.41
8	.0659	1.15	118.97	16.35	86.91	99.94
9	.0401	1.20	124.14	20.93	<u>83.95</u>	<u>100.74</u>

$E_t[P_{t+1}] = 109.12 \quad P^r_{t+1} = 106.90$
$\bar{h}[106.90] = 103.45$

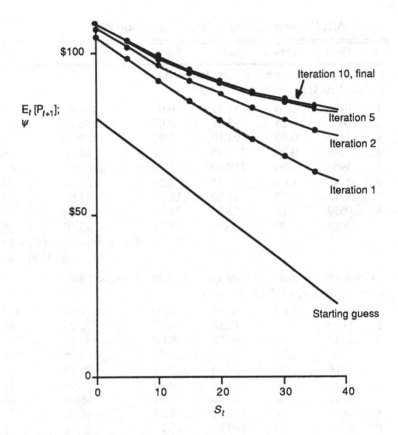

Figure 3A.4. Iterations on polynomial approximation ψ.

For $S_t = 0$, if $\bar{h}_{t+1}$ equals 103.45 units and ψ equals $\$109.13 - 1.207S + 0.01593S^2 - 0.00007118S^3$, the calculated P^r_{t+1} equals \$106.90 (equivalent to planned production of 103.45 units) and $E_t[P_{t+1}]$ equals \$109.12 (within \$0.01 of the polynomial's intercept).

Other candidates for polynomials

As can be seen in Figure 3A.4, the central iteration concerns a polynomial representing expected price. At first glance it might have seemed more natural to use one of two other functions instead. As will be explained in the next section, Gardner's technique uses the future worth of an amount stored. However, when deducing how much to store, it is the marginal future worth, not total, that is crucial. For storage undistorted by price ceilings or monopoly, that marginal future worth is none other than the expected price. It seems

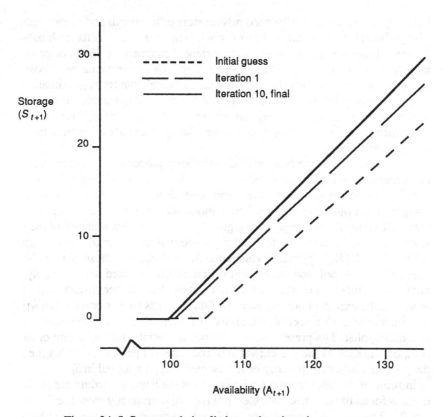

Figure 3A.5. Storage rule implied at various iterations.

more direct, therefore, to use the function representing the marginal valuation from the beginning. Adhering to the logic of directness, it might seem preferable to apply the technique of polynomial approximation to the storage rule itself, which, after all, is the main item of interest. As noted before, there is a direct correspondence between iterations on expected price and on the storage rule. Figure 3A.5 shows how the storage rule changes with some of the new polynomials based on Figure 3A.4.[14] The functions in Figure 3A.5 are much less smooth compared to those in Figure 3A.4 because of the kink where positive storage begins.

The principal challenge of iterating on the storage rule itself would be locating that level of availability at which positive storage begins; beyond that

[14] Although these rules may not seem all that different, a vertical distance of 4 units of storage translates into a difference of $20 in price. Moreover, a 4-unit discrepancy would feed back into the horizontal axis the next period; the difference in average storage in the steady state is much larger than 4 units.

kink point the rule for undistorted private storage is smooth and monotonic. The problem is more difficult, however, when there is occasion for both public and private storage, as when the government supports a price floor or establishes a strategic reserve. The private storage rules over the range of positive total storage can have sharp discontinuities unsuitable for approximation by a polynomial. Fortunately, even under those more complex circumstances, expected price and related marginal valuations remain smooth.[15] Recursive refinements seem most likely to converge when performed on the smoothest available relationships.

Other calculations can be appended to the basic procedure. One example is the calculation of the expected consumption value $E_t[\hat{P}_{t+1}]$ when a price ceiling distorts the market price storers and producers receive. As discussed in Chapter 15, a public storage authority might reasonably use this expected marginal value of consumption as a guide. A guess for this function of total storage can be made in the form of a polynomial Ψ, as for ψ. Along with $E_t[P_{t+1}|S_t^i]$, $E_t[\hat{P}_{t+1}|S_t^i]$ can be calculated for each S_t^i, and those N pairs be used to fit a new polynomial Ψ^*, and the procedure repeated until that polynomial does not change from iteration to iteration. Yet another polynomial can represent the expected present value of future profits from storage $E_t[\Pi[S_t]]$ = $\omega[S_t]$, a relationship needed in Chapter 11 for deriving the storage behavior of a monopolist. The present value of expected social welfare, or any of its components such as the present value of the expected producer surplus (i.e., the price of land), can similarly be represented as a polynomial in S_t.

In some of the later chapters, adaptations of the basic procedure are made to allow for additional state variables. For the two-commodity model of Chapters 9, 10, and 15, the expected price of each commodity is represented by a polynomial in storage of both commodities, including low-order interaction terms. In a seasonal model, such as that in Chapter 8, a different polynomial represents each month or quarter of the cropyear. In the two-hemisphere problem, also in Chapter 8, $E_t[P_t]$ is represented as a polynomial in storage and in the crop already in the ground in the other hemisphere.

3A.3   The cell technique

Gardner's cell technique works directly with the value function of the planner's problem, equation (3.4):

---

[15]   An exception is a price floor that binds much of the time. It may be that for several of the highest values of S_t^i, the distribution of availabilities the next period is such that, for all A_{t+1}^{ij}, the associated price is the price floor. That is to say, the calculated values for $E_t[P_{t+1}|S_t]$, otherwise decreasing as S_t^i increases, level off abruptly at a value equal to the price floor. The computer program ignores these observations when fitting the polynomial. Besides the disruption in continuity they cause, they are never relevant to a rule for private storers, who would never store with $E_t[P_{t+1}]$ equal to the price floor, as will be explained in Chapter 13.

$$V_t = \int_0^{q_t} P[A_t - S_t]dq - kS_t + E_t[V_{t+1}[S_t]] / (1+r) \tag{3A.8}$$

The problem is to find some function V, giving the worth of future uses of current storage, that reproduces itself if (3A.8) is applied. This function V is not represented analytically but as an array of cells, each cell corresponding to the expected worth of a particular amount in store. These cells must be finite in number. For this reason, the cell technique could also be called the grid technique. Gardner restricts storage to a set of nonnegative integers. At the completion of the numerical procedure, therefore, the cell technique provides an array of optimal (integer) storage for any availability, this relationship being a step-function version of the storage rule.

Gardner's numerical procedure for finding the array that tabulates V operates, like ours, as an iterative process of backward induction.[16] The first step postulates some function, represented by elements in the cells, for the expected worth of storage in period $T-1$ carried into a final period, period T. This function is sensibly selected so that it increases in the total amount stored but at a decreasing rate. Because of the restriction imposed by the finite number of cells, the natural unit of storage is 1.0, with the other parameters scaled appropriately. Suppose, for example, that there are 100 cells, covering storage in integer amounts ranging from 0.0 to 99.0, each with a sensible value of the future worth of storage it represents.

With this guess for the values in the cells, the second step moves to one period earlier, seeking to construct a new array of cells for the expected future worth of storage initiated in that earlier period. Take the cell for 10.0 as an example. That 10.0 in store in period $T-2$ will be an addition to any outcome of the harvest in period $T-1$. Suppose, for example, the harvest is 107.5. The total quantity available in period $T-1$, 117.5, can be allotted between consumption and storage by finding the amount of storage in $T-1$, rounded to an integer, that provides the maximum worth.[17] In practice, that maximum is found by searching over the range of storage from 0.0 to 99.0, with the total value being the worth of current consumption plus the expected worth of future storage read off from the appropriate cell. Say the maximum worth is at S_{T-1} equal to 18.0. The worth for the component going into store is read from the cell for 18.0, and the value from consuming the remaining 99.5 is calculated as the area under the consumption demand curve. The sum of these two entries – namely, the maximum worth from the 117.5 units – is

---

[16] Gardner's method, along with Gustafson's (1958a) original numerical approach on which it was based, is described in more detail in Plato and Gordon (1983).

[17] If storage must be in whole units, the cell technique uncovers the definitive storage rule, which would be a step function if it were expressible analytically. In other circumstances, the rounding introduces a small inaccuracy, which feeds on itself through each iteration.

reserved momentarily while the same procedure is applied to the other possible harvests. The expected worth of the 10.0 in store in period $T-2$ is the weighted average of these calculations, the weights being the probability of a particular harvest in period $T-2$. That expected worth becomes the entry for the cell corresponding to 10.0 in the new array of cells for period $T-2$. Similar calculations fill the other cells. The resulting array for $T-2$ can then be used to fill the cells for storage in period $T-3$, that new array to construct the one for period $T-4$, and so on.

Central to this whole approach is that in filling an array of cells the routine need look no farther than one period ahead. The previously calculated array summarizes all possible paths into the yet more distant future (i.e., the results from previous iterations). In effect, the routine does not need to know whether quantities available two periods ahead are consumed or stored (i.e., it does not need to have preserved the details of the most recent iteration). It need only know that future availability is used optimally. This is another illustration of the more general principle of optimality. It is to exploit the power of this principle that the solution technique, whether analytical or numerical, moves by backward induction.

In practice, therefore, only two arrays are necessary: one representing the next period and one representing the current period. Because the creation of a new array for each period would strain the capacity of the computer's memory, once the computer routine has finished filling in all the cells for the current period it can replace the values in the array for the next period. Recalculation followed by replacement amounts to going ever farther backward in time from a starting period.

There is no necessary limit to the number of iterations replacing the array. In all actual applications, after a small number of iterations – generally as few as five or ten depending on the interest rate, the initial guess, and the convergence criteria – the two arrays are essentially identical. Further iterations are pointless. For that matter, the same stable array emerges eventually from any reasonable starting values. That stable array is accordingly the solution to an infinite horizon problem.

Limitations on the cell technique

Although the approach of a large array indexed by an integer amount of storage is adequate for many cases, it works poorly when supply is elastic. The source of the problem is the discontinuity in the storage rule, inevitable in a step function.[18] At some point in the computations, the iterations cease converging and start to diverge.

---

[18] Consider what happens as the routine searches for the equilibrium amount of planned production for a given amount in store in the current period. Suppose the routine has

Several corrections to the routine suggest themselves. The problem could be avoided if only integer amounts of planned production are allowed. Unfortunately, changes in availability (or more generally, changes in parameters such as physical storage costs) have a relatively small effect on planned production. Thus, the scaling appropriate to storage and realized production may preclude reasonable movement in planned production. Another possible improvement is to interpolate between the cells associated with integer amounts of storage. The most obvious interpolation is linear; yet this interpolation still leaves discontinuities in behavior at the cells, and the routine still eventually explodes.

By their nature, the polynomials used throughout this book avoid any discontinuities in behavior. Were it possible to derive analytically the relationship between marginal value and the amount stored, it would surely be relatively smooth. It is well known that such functions can be approximated well by a low-order polynomial.

In addition to the essential advantage of the relationship being smooth and covering values other than integers, the representation of the function as a polynomial is compact. The information about V, the relationship between future worth and storage, contained in the 100 cells can be compressed to four or five numbers – the coefficients in the polynomial – without much information being lost. In fact, in a regression of the numbers in the cells (i.e., the future worth of particular amounts of storage) on a third-order polynomial in the amount stored, the R^2 is above 0.999.

3A.4   Accuracy of the polynomial technique

Despite its advantages, the technique of low-order polynomials does provide only an approximation. Moreover, some discrete representation must replace the continuous probability function for the random component of the harvest, and a particular order and range for the polynomial must be select-

tried as its first guess an amount for planned production that is too low. The resulting distribution of amounts available the next period lead to an expected price (or similar marginal valuation) that would be consistent with higher average output. Accordingly, the routine tries a slightly higher value for planned production. It may be that the integer amount stored is the same as on the previous attempt. Without more storage, price will be lower for any future harvest, as will expected price. So far it would seem that the equilibrium is being approached from both directions. Suppose another small increase is made in the guess for planned production, one deduced from the previous changes to bring the guess very close to the correct value. Perhaps for several of the realized values for production, the point is crossed where one more unit is put into store. Despite the greater availability, price will actually be higher. If this happens to enough of the realized values for production, expected price could actually be calculated as being higher when planned production is higher. Unable to find an equilibrium, the routine explodes.

ed. Could the resulting storage rule be far from the proper relationship? This section provides some sensitivity analysis to allay this worry. The calculated storage rule is robust to the inevitable choices about range, order of the polynomial, and representation of the probability distribution. Even more important, it gives every indication of being sufficiently close to the elusive exact rule that the computer routines can be relied on in general.

Polynomials compared to full enumeration

For a few combinations of parameters, exact storage rules (to the precision constraining numerical methods of any form) can be derived for problems with infinite horizons, and used to test the polynomial technique. As was seen in Figure 3A.3, several periods backward from a terminal period, the storage rule calculated through the branching approach of Section 3A.1 begins to look much the same regardless of the terminal conditions. This property suggests an experiment with carefully chosen terminal conditions. If the terminal condition is taken to be no storage at all, the storage rule in period $T-5$ is a lower bound on the rule for an infinite horizon. If the terminal condition is taken to be substantial storage, the storage rule in period $T-5$ is an upper bound on the rule for an infinite horizon. For that matter, if the "lower" and "upper" terminal conditions are made much like rules in period $T-5$, the upper and lower bounds on the infinite horizon will be very close.

For a practical example, therefore, the polynomial technique can be compared to the lower and upper bounds from the branching approach. Because the branching approach is especially impractical with many possible outcomes for the harvest, let the yield have the three-point probability distribution with probabilities 0.2, 0.6, and 0.2 of disturbances –0.15, 0.0, and +0.15 as proportions of planned production. The variance of this three-point distribution is comparable to the degree of uncertainty used in examples in many chapters. Let the other parameters also be those regularly used: constant-elasticity demand $\eta^d = -0.2$, $\eta^s = 0.5$, $r = 5$ percent, and $k = \$2$. With the branching approach, derive the precise rules for storage and planned production in period $T-5$. Let in one case the arbitrary rule for the carryout in period T have (positive) storage be just slightly less than what appears to be storage behavior in period $T-5$, and in another instance let the carryout in period T be just higher.

Ideally, the rule computed for an infinite horizon using the polynomial technique falls squarely between the upper and lower bounds calculated through the branching approach. Table 3A.2 gives this comparison, for both storage and planned production, for four different availabilities. First, notice that the bounds are tight, so the test is very demanding. Second, notice that the majority of the entries for storage and planned production deduced with the polynomial fall between the upper and lower bounds: Those that do not are very

Table 3A.2. *Accuracy of polynomial approximations*

Availability (A_t)	Storage (S_t)			Planned production $(\bar{h}_{t+1})$		
	Upper bound	Lower bound	Polynomial approach	Upper bound	Lower bound	Polynomial approach
100.00	0.83	0.80	0.82	104.51	104.86	104.43
110.00	8.97	8.91	8.89	100.18	100.00	99.97
120.00	17.16	17.06	17.19	96.37	96.11	96.34
130.00	26.08	25.85	25.87	94.11	93.61	93.68

close, without any tendency to be below or over. Measured from the midpoint of the upper and lower bounds, the technique of polynomial approximation causes a discrepancy of 0.08 units at most. Rules for storage and planned production move about that much with a change in, say, marginal physical storage costs of $0.1. The sensitivity analysis of marginal physical storage costs, to be done in Chapter 4, will use k's of $16, $8, $4, $2, and $0. The polynomial technique is more than accurate enough for such comparisons.

Polynomials compared to the cell technique

Table 3A.3 contrasts the cell technique and the polynomial technique as the solution for the storage rule for a case of a linear demand curve with η^d = −0.2 at the point ($100, 100 units), an interest rate of 5 percent, physical storage costs of $2, perfectly inelastic supply, and a normal distribution for the random component of the harvest with a standard deviation of 5.0 percent of mean production. In all but the first column, the probability distribution is approximated by a nine-point discrete distribution ranging in equal intervals from −10.0 to +10.0 percent (of mean production). The first column has a discrete distribution five times finer, which ranges from −17.0 to +17.0 percent. The maximum storage observed in long simulations proves to be on the order of 23 units; accordingly, the polynomials (with one exception) are fit with S_t^i ranging in integer values from 0.0 to 23.0. The exception is the column marked "smaller range," which has S_t^i ranging from 0.0 only to 10.0. This indicates the sensitivity of the calculated storage rule to the selection of the range.[19] Among these polynomials, the one corresponding to the second column is the one that would normally be used.

[19] Results not reported here show that there is little effect from decreasing the interval between the discrete amounts stored, a direct consequence of the regularity of the function.

Table 3A.3. *Comparison of numerical techniques*

	3rd-order, finer probability function	3rd-order poly-nomial	2nd-order poly-nomial	1st-order poly-nomial	3rd-order, smaller range	Cell technique
1. Expected price with:						
0.0 in store	$105.99	105.87	104.76	100.40	106.04	105.39
5.0 in store	92.74	92.52	93.37	93.64	92.36	91.54
10.0 in store	83.89	83.65	84.25	86.88	83.71	82.76
R^2 in regression of expected price on polynomial in storage	.99987	.99989	.99720	.96189	.99997	—
2. Storage at availability of:						
105.0	3.11	3.08	3.14	2.96	3.06	2.94
110.0	6.64	6.60	6.73	6.94	6.59	6.45
115.0	10.46	10.42	10.50	10.91	10.43	10.27
120.0	14.53	14.49	14.46	14.89	14.49	14.31
3. For 100,000 periods:						
Average storage	2.35	2.32	2.38	2.27	2.30	2.20
% with no storage	36.13	36.45	37.71	44.58	35.01	38.19
4. Average profit from storage when spot price in range:						
$96.0–97.0	–$0.63	–0.43	0.43	1.81	–0.49	0.53
89.0–90.0	–0.22	–0.02	–0.75	0.21	–0.06	0.27
73.0–78.0	0.22	0.30	0.35	–1.04	0.17	0.53

The final column shows the results from the cell technique, made much finer than would be customary. Cells were provided for each 0.1 amount of storage instead of each 1.0; some 300 cells were used. Also, storage was not rounded to the nearest 0.1 but interpolated linearly, which improves the accuracy of the procedure. Even so, the column with the cell technique should not be credited with the most accurate storage rule, for two reasons: First, the linear interpolation between cells is not exact, and there is no telling how that inaccuracy compounds through successive iterations. Second, and more important, the cell technique has an unfortunate interaction with the need to use a discrete approximation for the normally distributed density function. The small change from one cell to the next may coincide with the shift of a major point in that discrete probability distribution moving from no storage to storage. (All elements of the vector $\tilde{A}_{t+1}$ shift up by 0.1 with each cell.) In that new range, the marginal valuation is sharply different, and as a result the final storage rule has discontinuities in its slope. The same problem infects the polynomial technique, but to a lesser extent. The polynomial, by its very nature, smooths the marginal propensity to store.[20]

The first panel of Table 3A.3 gives the calculated values for $E_t[P_{t+1}]$ for three different S_t^i. In the second panel, much the same information is expressed in a related way in the numbers for storage at four different levels of availability. From either perspective the differences are not very large, with the possible exception of the first-order polynomial. One can conclude that the polynomial technique is robust.

A more telling comparison emerges from the third panel of Table 3A.3, showing the performance of the storage rules over a very long simulation of 100,000 periods, during which differences in the storage rules should feed on themselves. Here the differences among the columns are larger. The percentage of times there is no storage is appreciably higher for the cell technique and the first-order polynomial. They both impart too little storage on average.

If a calculated storage rule is optimal, there should be no possible systematic operations for making profits. Although the number of possible procedures is legion (witness all the distinct approaches to technical analysis of stock prices), three variants of one technique are tried here. If whenever price fell in a particular range a speculator routinely bought one unit of the commodity (an amount too small compared to the aggregate quantity to change price) and sold it (with no transactions costs) at the market price next period, his average profit would indicate whether the marketwide storage rule was optimal. The three ranges of prices in the final panel of Table 3A.3 were selected to correspond to the low, middle, and high regions of the storage rule and to provide on the order of 2,000 instances out of the 100,000 periods in the simulation. Roughly speaking, given the variances of profits (which are not shown), any observation for average profit outside the range ±0.40 would be judged statistically significant at the 5 percent level. By that statistical standard, every one of the six attempts at the storage rule is flawed: the first-order polynomial and the cell technique more than the others, and the third-order polynomial the least.[21]

Whatever the verdict by a statistical standard, by an economic standard the mistakes in the storage rules are small. An average profit of 0.50 would be eliminated with an increased storage in that range of prices on the order of 0.07 (surmising how the alteration of the storage rule would feed back on it-

20 That the third-order polynomial is not a perfect fit (with R^2 of 1.00000) mainly reflects the cumulative effect of the discontinuities introduced by the discrete representation of the probability distribution.

21 On the other hand, the interdependence of the three tests for each column complicates that interpretation. For that matter, the average production over the sample of 100,000 periods was minutely above its population mean, and hence the series was slightly biased in favor of finding losses.

self). This is much the same level of accuracy suggested by the comparison with the branching technique. Hence, almost surely conclusions about the response of storage rules to large changes in the underlying parameters are not a reflection of inaccuracies in the derivation of the storage rules. Furthermore, there is even less reason to believe the calculated storage rule for one physical storage cost, say, underestimates the true rule, while the calculated rule for another physical storage cost is an overestimate. That is to say, there can be even more confidence in the comparison of storage rules calculated for different sets of parameters.

CHAPTER 4

The effects of storage on production, consumption, and prices

Prices, consumption, and production are all profoundly affected by the presence of competitive storage, both at one moment in time and over time. The "equilibrium rules" for competitive storage and planned production reveal how the various endogenous variables are related at one moment in time, whereas the long-run probability distributions of the endogenous variables characteristic of the stochastic steady state reveal much about the implications of these rules over time. The first two sections of this chapter consider these two subjects in detail for the "base case" set of parameters introduced above in Section 2.4. Implicit in the discussion of long-run distributions are the characteristics of the sequential equilibria emphasized in that section. Also investigated in this chapter, in the final three sections, is the sensitivity of these aspects of storage behavior to the shapes of the underlying supply and demand curves, storage cost function, and the probability distribution of the weather. In a sense, the numerical sensitivity analysis amounts to examining the reduced-form equations as functions of the parameters representing these underlying functions, in lieu of any analytical representation.

4.1   Characteristics of storage rules

In Figure 4.1 are plotted the relationships between equilibrium storage or planned production and current availability, seen previously as Figures 2.3 and 2.4. Here they are shown on one diagram to emphasize their connections. The specific parameters were a linear demand curve with elasticity η^d = –0.2, a supply elasticity η^s = 0.5, marginal physical storage costs k = $2, a per-period interest rate r = 5 percent, and a standard deviation of normally distributed yields equal to 10 percent of planned production. Although the equilibrium rules in Figure 4.1 are exact only for this specific set of parameters, they display a number of general characteristics common to all systems with storage.

99

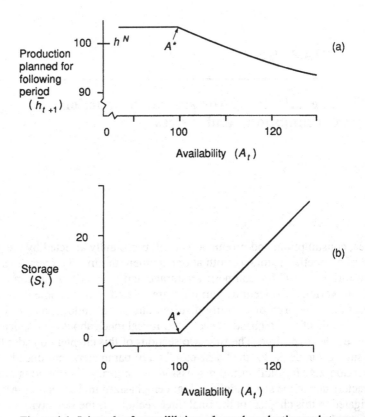

Figure 4.1. Joint rules for equilibrium planned production and storage.

Nonlinearities in the storage rule

The specific storage rule in Figure 4.1(b) has a marked nonlinearity because of the kink. Below kink point A^*, equilibrium storage is zero regardless of A_t, since a negative amount cannot be stored. The exact current availability corresponding to positive storage depends on the specific parameters, but all storage rules have a discontinuity. In this system $A^* = 99.62$ units.

The second characteristic feature exemplified in Figure 4.1(b) is the smooth relation between storage and availability over the range of positive storage. The slope of the storage rule is the marginal propensity to store out of current availability. (Unity minus the slope is the marginal propensity to consume.) Although there are no abrupt changes, except at A^*, in the marginal propensity to store, it in fact increases slowly over the range of positive storage. It is 0.82 at $A_t = 100$ and 0.91 at $A_t = 130$. Equilibrium storage is not a linear function of current availability. Viewed from the perspective of the marginal propensity to consume – namely, 0.18 at $A_t = 100$ and 0.09 at $A_t = 130$ – the nonlinearity in behavior is much more pronounced. Most important, the marginal propensity to store is everywhere between 0.00 and 1.00; the positively sloped part of Figure 4.1(b) is below a 45° line through the kink point.

Like the storage rule, the rule for planned production as a function of current availability is strongly discontinuous. The kink is at the same A^*. According to Figure 4.1(a), planned production $\bar{h}_{t+1}$ is 103.34 units whenever A_t is less than A^*, whatever is the precise A_t. Whenever the market next period is disconnected from the current period's market because the current carryout is zero, the rational planned production for next period's market is the same.

When current availability is such that equilibrium storage is positive, the exact current availability matters to planned production very much. All other things equal, the higher is the carryout, the lower will be price the next period, whatever the weather. Consequently, to the right of A^*, the marginal propensity to plant is negative. (The marginal propensity to plant is always in the range 0.00 to –1.00.) The less is planted for the next period's harvest, the more opportunity there is for storage, or vice versa. The equilibrium rules in Figure 4.1 are the result of this contest between storage and planned production. Each reduced-form equation supposes the other.

Nonlinearities in market demand curves

These characteristic features of the reduced-form equations are manifest in the relationships for the other endogenous variables, especially price. The striking feature of the market demand curve is, once again, that storage causes a kink. (The market demand for the base case was illustrated as Figure 2.5 and can also be seen as part of Figure 4.3 below.) For these parameters the discontinuity is precisely at the P^*, $101.90, corresponding to A^*. Just to the left of A^*, the price elasticity of demand is –0.205, and to the right of A^*, –1.075.

The form of the augmentation of consumption demand below P^* by storage demand is supported by the (admittedly tentative) conclusion of Hillman et al. (1975) that the demand curve for corn is highly nonlinear, being much less elastic at high prices than at low prices. Unfortunately, because actual consumption cannot be measured, grain statistics show "disappearance," a residual concept that includes some stocks. Their measurements, relating price changes to such changes in availability, may reflect the change in the market demand curve's slope caused by the demand for storage apart from any nonlinearity in the underlying consumption demand curve.[1]

---

[1] As shown in Chapter 12, the welfare effects – whether producers gain or consumers gain – are crucially dependent on the curvature of the consumption demand curve, which has no kink, not of the market demand curve. Unfortunately, Hillman et al. fail to draw this distinction, as do several studies of price stabilization that quote their conclusion, including Reutlinger (1976) and Just et al. (1978).

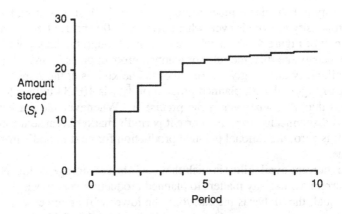

Figure 4.2. Buildup of stocks in a string of good harvests.

Storage during a sequence of good harvests

Another feature of storage rules can be seen in how the system absorbs a series of positive shocks. Consider a sequence of ten periods with weather exactly one standard deviation above the average disturbance of 0.00. Mind, the storers and producers do not know this sequence is coming, or they would react differently. Suppose that in the period before this contrived sequence begins – which we shall call period 0 – the availability is low. With $S_0 = 0.00$, the slate is clean. Figure 4.2 shows the resulting progression in the amount stored through period 10.

Far from causing an explosion in the amount stored, this contrived sequence of the same good weather causes progressively smaller increases. The amount stored plateaus at about 23.60 units. Part and parcel, current availability plateaus at 127.00 units and planned production at 94.00 units. This stability is an important result. Because optimal storage rules have a marginal propensity to store below 1.0, a point is reached where the carryin plus the new harvest dictates a carryout equal to the carryin and consumption equal to the harvest. The value at the plateau and the speed of reaching that plateau depend on the specific sequence of the weather and on the parameters of the system. The value at the plateau, for a contrived sequence of weather, can be used alongside the kink point A^* and differences in marginal propensity to store to compare succinctly various systems with storage.

4.2   Long-run distributions

Even in short series, such as the one in Section 2.4 covering 11 periods, patterns are evident, among them recurrence of equilibrium storage equaling zero and the asymmetry in the number of high and low prices. If the time series covers 1,000 periods instead of 100, these patterns will be much the same, only more evident. In short, as the length of the sample increases, the frequency distributions of the various endogenous variables converge to stable distributions. These stable frequency distributions are probability distributions. The joint probability distribution for the various endogenous variables is distinct for each set of parameters. As do the equilibrium rules, the joint probability distribution characterizes a system.

The invariant probability distributions for the endogenous variables reflect the properties of storage over an infinite number of periods. They can also be understood as cross-sectional features of the system. From the perspective of the current period, the price in, say, period $t + 250$ is a random variable: The realized value will depend on the weather and the reaction by storage and planned production over all those 250 periods. Because the system is not explosive, the probability distribution for P_{t+250} is well defined; and because the influence of the particular circumstances as of period t will have long since been dissipated, the probability distribution for P_{t+250}, as of period t, is the distribution emerging from an infinitely long time series.

Of course, it is impossible to generate an infinitely long time series. For the probability distributions in this and the following sections, 250,000 periods were simulated. The value, period by period, for, say, price was recorded in a finely graded histogram; the histogram entries were then smoothed. (The results for 25,000 periods would have been indistinguishable.) Figure 4.3 contains two of these invariant long-run distributions, along with the market demand curve seen previously in Figure 2.5. In the fourth quadrant is the probability distribution of the amount available, namely, the sum of the carry-in and the new production. Refracted through the market demand curve in the first quadrant, this probability distribution for availability causes the probability distribution for price, shown in the second quadrant.[2] From either of these distributions can be deduced the chance of the equilibrium in any one period falling at a particular spot on the market demand curve. When inspecting the system's behavioral rules, one does not know how relevant is a particular range. These probability distributions provide that information.

Lessons from steady-state price distributions

Also shown in Figure 4.3, as dotted curves, are the probability distributions of availability and price when storage is technically impossible. Their shapes parallel the normal distribution of the underlying variability in the weather. A comparison of the distributions with and without storage divulges three lessons about storage, one lesson for each of the first three moments of the price distribution.

---

[2]   Because the consumption demand curve is linear, the probability distribution for consumption is a direct transformation of the one for price.

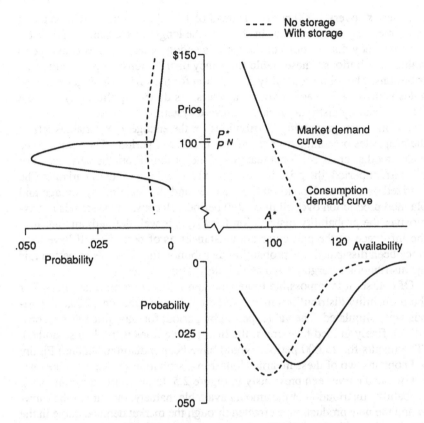

Figure 4.3. Probability distributions of availability and price.

First, as regards the means, the important message is that they are different. For this parameter set of linear demand, $\eta^d = -0.2$, and $\eta^s = 0.5$, mean price with storage is $101.27; without storage, it is $103.55.[3] The long-run means are endogenous. By contrast, most of the literature on "price stabilization" assumes that the stabilization mechanism – usually vaguely attributed to storage – does not change the mean price. But, as long as the mean price is endogenous, this cannot be true because it ignores the collective responses or

---

[3]   The calculation of mean price without storage involves a technical detail. A harvest larger than two standard deviations above mean weather (assuming planned production of 100 units), which has more than an infinitesimal chance of occurring, corresponds to a price of $0 for this linear consumption demand when there is no storage. This peculiarity is irrelevant to the calculation of the storage rule or the operation of storage, which keeps consumption at a much lower level. To keep the linear demand curve while comparing probability distributions, it was assumed, for calculating the producers' incentive price, that market price could be negative.

feedbacks of firms and individuals, as Samuelson (1972) has emphasized.[4] For the market as whole, the long-run mean of price is exogenous only if the consumption demand curve is linear and the elasticity of supply is zero.[5]

The second notable difference between the probability distributions for price is that the variance in the system with storage is appreciably lower. Storage stabilizes price (and consumption). What is perhaps surprising is that probability is shifted from both tails of the distribution toward the center. Although one commonly thinks of storage as intended to reduce the frequency of very high prices, it also reduces the frequency of very low prices.

On the other hand, the notion of a mean-preserving contraction in the dispersion of price, to use the terminology introduced by Rothschild and Stiglitz (1970), does not come close to capturing a third and important effect of storage on the long-run probability distribution. As can be seen in Figure 4.3, storage makes the distribution highly skewed, with the long tail toward high prices.[6] The effects of storage on the price distribution are asymmetric in a fashion that contradicts popular notions about storage: The tendency is to think of storage primarily as protection against shortages and their high prices. Nevertheless, storage is much more effective at precluding gluts and their low prices. Collectively, storage can always be increased to support prices (i.e., the market can always save for the future). Collectively, stockpiles cannot always be run down as much as desired in the event of a poor harvest, for aggregate storage cannot be below zero. Since equilibrium consumption may, in any given period with some stocks carried in, exceed production with positive probability, the amount stored will fall to zero with probability one in finite time, as proved by Townsend (1977). Only an infinitely large stockpile can preclude a stockout. With no comparable constraint on storage capacity, the probability distribution of price in a system with storage will be asymmetric.

Other steady-state distributions

The other endogenous variables also have steady-state (i.e., invariant) probability distributions. Figure 4.4 illustrates one of them, the distribu-

---

4   Gilbert (1986) has divided the welfare effects from stabilizing mechanisms like storage into a pure "stabilization effect" (change in dispersion with mean price constant) and a "transfer effect" (change in mean price). This nomenclature is not helpful because both effects are caused by changes in consumption stability and because both, in general, cause transfers between consumers and producers.

5   A creative search might identify special combinations of demand specification and error structure that would leave mean price unaffected by storage. From now on, we do not make explicit qualifications regarding such "probability zero" exceptions.

6   If nothing else, this result should cast doubt on the common assumption of prices or price changes (year-to-year) being distributed normally. Here the one exogenous random variable is, in fact, normally distributed and consumption demand and production response are both linear. Not one of the endogenous economic variables is close to being normally distributed.

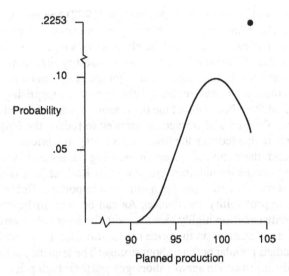

Figure 4.4. Probability distribution of planned production.

tion for planned production. This distribution is also skewed, with a large mass point at a planned production of 103.34 units. This level of planned production matches with equilibrium storage of 0.00; 0.225 is also the probability of nothing in store in any given period. Indeed, the whole probability distribution for the amount stored looks much like the mirror image of Figure 4.4. This interaction is investigated in the next section.

4.3   Sensitivity to supply and demand parameters

The system in the previous two sections is defined by a particular set of parameters. To what extent do the system's properties depend on these parameters? This section investigates that question for the parameters related to the specification of demand and supply, the next section for those related to storage costs, and Section 4.5 for the parameters determining the probability distribution of the weather.

Definition of demand curvature

Among the demand and supply parameters, the most obvious are the price elasticities of demand and supply, measured at the certainty point (q^N, P^N). Nonetheless, a third parameter, one measuring the curvature of the consumption demand curve, is also relevant.[7] Two consumption demand curves

---

[7] Because planned production varies much less than realized production, the curvature of the supply function is not especially relevant to the storage rule, which is why it is specified as linear throughout.

can have identical elasticities at the certainty point but very different elasticities elsewhere. A linear consumption demand curve, where the elasticity falls with lower price, contrasts with a constant-elasticity curve, which is convex. As will be shown in Chapter 12, the degree of curvature principally determines whether producers or consumers benefit from storage.

The relative curvature of an (inverse) consumption demand curve can be measured by a parameter C introduced by Wright (1979):

$$C \equiv \frac{-q(\partial^2 P[q] / \partial q^2)}{\partial P[q] / \partial q} \tag{4.1}$$

Because its second derivative is zero, a linear consumption demand curve has a C of 0, whereas a convex demand function has a positive C. This definition of relative curvature is analogous to the Pratt–Arrow measure of relative risk aversion with respect to income (Pratt 1964).[8] Thus, the parameter C can be thought of as an approximate measure of risk aversion with respect to the consumption of the particular commodity, in the sense of the expected Marshallian consumer surplus from consumption of the commodity compared to the welfare from the average quantity. The higher is C, the more commodity risk averse is the consumer. $C = 0$ corresponds to risk-loving preferences for the consumption of that one commodity. As Waugh (1944) showed, expected consumer surplus in the linear case exceeds consumer surplus at mean price. With $C = 1$, expected surplus is the same for uncertain consumption of the commodity around a mean of $\bar{q}$ and certain consumption at $\bar{q}$. Although over all commodities the properties of demand curves are related to the degree of income risk aversion, income risk aversion is distinct from the commodity risk aversion of a single commodity. Moreover, assuming the budget share of the commodity of interest is as small, as is typical, income risk aversion has little significance for storage and C is an excellent indicator of welfare effects.[9] (The relative importance to welfare analysis of the curvature param-

---

[8] Pope (1987) uses the analogy with measures of risk aversion with respect to income to characterize the curvature of supply functions. Kimball (1990) presents an analogous measure of the curvature of the marginal utility of income schedule, which he calls the coefficient of prudence.

[9] On the other hand, if the commodity of interest constitutes the entire economy and if supply is perfectly inelastic, the curvature parameter C can measure risk aversion with respect to income. Price in equation (4.1) would correspond to marginal utility of income and high values of C to high levels of risk aversion with respect to income (given that the utility function is additively separable across periods). The equilibrium determining the amount stored would follow the same logic as before: The decline in current utility from another unit stored is weighed against the expected utility in the next period arising from that unit. The storage rule, steady-state storage, and other allocative effects would be the same as the cases for various C's under zero supply elasticity in this section. The competitive equilibrium would not have too little storage, contrary to the presumption of Newbery (1989).

eter, degree of income risk aversion, and the budget share will be discussed further in Chapter 12.)

Although the curvature, like the elasticity, can differ at every point, it suffices to study the family of inverse demand functions with constant curvature. This family, which includes many of the functional forms used empirically, has the general form:

$$P_t = \alpha + \beta q_t^{1-C} \tag{4.2}$$

$\alpha > 0$, $\beta < 0$, and $C = 0$ is a linear curve; $\alpha = 0$, $\beta > 0$, and $C > 1$, a constant-elasticity < 1.0 (in absolute value) curve; and the curve with $\alpha > 0$, $\beta < 0$ approaches a semilog specification as C approaches 1.0.

For systems with different values of η^d, C, and η^s (all of which are measured at the nonstochastic equilibrium (P^N, q^N)), Table 4.1 displays their properties. These properties are of three main kinds: properties of the storage rules, properties of the long-run distributions,[10] and, for comparison, properties of a system with storage technically impossible. Table 4.1 has its 15 rows grouped to show, in turn, the effects of variations in the three parameters, in the same manner that numerical partial derivatives are used in single-period models. To give storage center stage, η^s is set at 0.0 in the investigations of η^d and C. To make the progressions clearer, row 6 duplicates row 2. Row 9 can be read as part of the sequence for supply elasticities beginning with row 11. The other parameters are the same as previously; namely, $r = 5$ percent, $k = \$2.00$, and $v_t \sim N(0.0, 0.1^2)$, which translates into $\sigma_h = 10$ units when $\eta^s = 0.0$.

Demand elasticity

The higher the elasticity of consumption demand (holding the curvature of the demand curve constant), the less important is storage, by any measure. With $\eta^d = -0.1$ (row 1), 11.18 percent of periods have no storage, whereas with $\eta^d = -1.0$ (row 5), 66.95 percent have no storage. Similarly, mean storage is, respectively, 14.62 units and merely 1.31 units. These steady-state properties are the direct result of the position and slope of the storage rules for systems with those demand elasticities. The point of positive storage, the kink point A^*, moves considerably to the right with a higher $|\eta^d|$. Whether measured at A^* or at the 90th percentile in the steady-state distribution of availability, the marginal propensity to store is lower the higher is η^d.

The sensitivity with respect to η^d can be stated another way. The greater the inconvenience to consumers in adjusting their consumption, as reflected

---

[10]   The steady-state properties are based on simulations of 20,000 periods. The final digits of the means and standard deviations might change if the samples were 200,000 or 2,000,000 periods long. On the other hand, the same string of random numbers was used for each row, so comparisons, which are the purpose of the table, should be even more accurate.

in the slope of the demand curve, the higher will be next period's expected price without carryin and the larger the incentive to store. On the other hand, when the consumption demand curve is relatively flat, it will absorb most of the shocks due to the weather. The smoothing provided by storage is less necessary. Out of the total variability in production equal to 10.00 units, the steady-state standard deviation of consumption is 4.29 with $\eta^d = -0.1$ and 8.49 with $\eta^d = -1.0$, whereas the standard deviation of price, of course, is the reverse, $42.94 vs. $8.49.

Demand curvature

Because a higher curvature parameter C implies relatively greater inconvenience from a shortfall in consumption, the higher is C, the greater is mean storage, and the proportion of periods with storage also is higher. The standard deviations for storage and consumption both decrease slightly as C increases from 0 through 8 (rows 6–10). Even so, nonlinearity of consumption demand is not needed to produce the broad qualitative characteristics of storage and its allocative effects in this model. (By contrast, the nonlinearity of the consumption demand curve has crucial qualitative implications for distributional effects, as discussed in Chapter 12.)

The influence of higher demand curvature on the storage rule is less emphatic than that of higher demand elasticity at the nonstochastic equilibrium. Although higher commodity risk aversion shifts the kink point $A*$ to the left, it also reduces the marginal propensity to store. The storage rules for $C = 0$ and $C = 8$ cross, with more being stored at very high availabilities in the case of the linear consumption demand curve ($C = 0$). At high levels of availability (and low price), consumption is higher with $C = 8$. This crossing property is also seen in the amount in store after a string of many good harvests, each one standard deviation above normal.[11] In such (contrived) circumstances, cumulative storage is higher the lower is C.

Behavior with respect to C emphasizes that the mean price changes with the introduction of storage. Note the final column of Table 4.1 for the mean price without storage and compare it to the mean price with storage. The change in mean increases with the curvature parameter C.

Supply elasticity

The demand elasticity and curvature parameter are stable underlying parameters. So is the one-period-lagged supply elasticity. Unlike the demand

---

[11] For $\eta^d = -0.1$ and $C = 0$, the case in row 1, the amount in storage after a string of good harvests is part of an equilibrium with a price of $0. This silly result is not attributable to storage as much as the implausibility of a demand function linear over the whole range.

Table 4.1. Sensitivity to supply and demand parameters

| | Properties of storage rules | | | Steady-state means (standard deviations in parentheses) | | | | | | | Without storage | |
	Kink point of storage rule (A*)	Marginal propensity to store at A*	at 90th percentile	Storage after many good harvests	With storage Storage	% with no storage	Production	Consumption	Price		Consumption	Price
Sensitivity to demand elasticity, holding C = 0, η^s = 0.0												
1. $\eta^d = -0.1$	96.61	.70	.90	90.00	14.62 (12.01)	11.18	100.00 (10.00)	100.00 (4.29)	$100.00 (42.94)		100.00 (10.00)	$100.00 (100.00)
2. $\eta^d = -0.2$	98.12	.66	.82	51.14	8.71 (8.51)	20.77	"	" (5.41)	" (27.04)		"	" (50.00)
3. $\eta^d = -0.3$	99.35	.63	.77	34.37	6.09 (6.81)	29.17	"	" (6.14)	" (20.46)		"	" (33.33)
4. $\eta^d = -0.5$	101.41	.60	.69	18.02	3.58 (4.90)	42.97	"	" (7.11)	" (14.23)		"	" (20.00)
5. $\eta^d = -1.0$	105.83	.55	.59	5.63	1.31 (2.70)	66.95	"	" (8.49)	" (8.49)		"	" (10.00)
Sensitivity to demand curvature, holding $\eta^d = -0.2$, η^s = 0.0												
6. $C = 0$	98.12	.66	.82	51.14	8.71 (8.51)	20.77	100.00 (10.00)	100.00 (5.41)	100.00 (27.04)		100.00 (10.00)	100.00 (50.00)
7. $C = 2$	97.43	.64	.82	49.34	8.97 (8.46)	18.48	"	" (5.34)	101.52 (30.00)		"	105.16 (52.15)
8. $C = 4$	96.82	.64	.79	45.56	9.47 (8.34)	16.17	"	" (5.25)	103.25 (33.93)		"	110.83 (58.28)

9. $C = 6$	96.11	.63	.77	43.13	9.96 (8.24)	13.78	" "	" (5.17)	105.17 (39.92)	" "	117.48 (70.60)
10. $C = 8$	95.26	.59	.78	39.67	10.36 (8.26)	11.64	" "	" (5.10)	107.44 (49.89)	" "	125.79 (94.31)

Sensitivity to supply elasticity, holding $\eta^d = -0.2$, $C = 6$

11. $\eta^s = 0.1$	97.38	.68	.81	35.71	9.68 (8.08)	15.06	100.10 (10.11)	100.10 (4.66)	103.77 (36.30)	100.73 (10.07)	113.31 (68.10)
12. $\eta^s = 0.2$	98.06	.72	.83	30.55	9.52 (7.96)	15.94	100.11 (10.25)	100.11 (4.38)	103.27 (34.36)	101.08 (10.11)	111.35 (66.91)
13. $\eta^s = 0.3$	98.49	.75	.84	27.42	9.44 (7.90)	16.41	100.10 (10.38)	100.10 (4.18)	102.99 (33.01)	101.29 (10.13)	110.19 (66.22)
14. $\eta^s = 0.5$	99.01	.76	.86	23.87	9.33 (7.81)	17.06	100.09 (10.64)	100.09 (3.94)	102.69 (31.29)	101.53 (10.15)	108.89 (65.44)
15. $\eta^s = 1.0$	99.71	.85	.89	20.32	9.18 (7.74)	18.19	100.06 (11.14)	100.06 (3.67)	102.45 (29.27)	101.78 (10.18)	107.54 (64.62)

parameters, however, elastic supply permits another economic response to the inherent uncertainty. Under the unifying assumption of rational expectations, the interactions of elastic supply, storage, and market stability are very interesting. The last five rows of Table 4.1 reveal some of the effects of η^s, the one-period-lagged supply elasticity.[12] According to the columns for mean storage and the percentage of periods with no storage, storage is slightly less important the higher the supply elasticity, although the falloff is nothing like that with demand elasticity. The most notable effect of greater supply elasticity is a lower standard deviation of consumption. In systems without storage, represented by the last columns, supply elasticity alone does not stabilize consumption. Storage and production complement each other in stabilizing consumption.

In stabilizing consumption, planned and realized production are both destabilized. The standard deviation of production for any of the positive supply elasticities (rows 11–15) is higher than either the standard deviation of production with $\eta^s = 0.0$ (namely 10.00 units) or without storage.[13] The relative destabilization of production increases with η^s. Moreover, the destabilization is even more pronounced for planned production, since that adjusts to dampen the extreme realizations of previous realized production. By definition, the standard deviation for planned production with $\eta^s = 0.0$ is 0.00 units. With storage technically impossible, planned production has the same value period to period (albeit a different value for each η^s), because the prospects for the next period's weather, and in turn the next period's price, are unaffected by current conditions. With storage and $\eta^s = 0.2$, in contrast, the standard deviation of planned production is 1.99 units; with $\eta^s = 0.5$, it is 3.44; and with $\eta^s = 1.0$, 4.76 units.

Although one approach in the stabilization literature has been to imitate the effect of storage as a decrease in the dispersion of production, these results show that storage has the opposite effect. It is obvious that the derived demands for production inputs adjusted along with planned production (which are not explicitly considered here), such as labor or fertilizer, are also destabilized by storage. Rather than being regarded as a means of stabilizing production, competitive storage should be thought of as a way of efficiently dispersing a disturbance throughout an (undistorted) economy.

In effect, storage acts as a substitute for virgin production in providing the commodity to the following periods.[14] Whenever the amount currently on hand is abundant, and in consequence the price of any quantity put into store is low, it is more economical to deliver the commodity next period by expand-

---

12 Reagan and Weitzman (1982) discuss an extreme not shown in Table 4.1, namely, one in which the one-period-lagged supply is infinitely elastic.

13 In a system in which storage is impossible, consumption equals realized production each period, so no separate column is given.

14 Lowry (1989) emphasizes this point for the case of refined oil products.

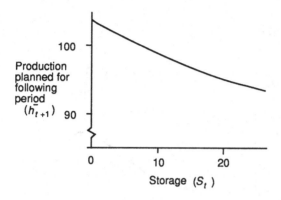

Figure 4.5. Planned production as a function of contemporaneous storage.

ing storage and contracting new production. Whenever the commodity is currently expensive, new production is relatively more attractive. The relationship between equilibrium planned production and equilibrium storage, for the base set of parameters of earlier sections (especially $\eta^s = 0.5$), is shown in Figure 4.5. Clearly, when one is relatively low the other is relatively high. Of course, high storage does not cause low planned production. Both are endogenous and simultaneous responses to the current conditions represented by A_t.

Beside increasing the dispersion of production, when supply is elastic the possibility of storage also changes the mean of production. For example, with $\eta^s = 0.3$ (row 13), mean production is 100.10 compared to 101.29 in a system without storage. The direction of the change in mean is not universal, however. It depends on the curvature in the consumption demand curve. For the cases in Table 4.1 with elastic supply, $C = 6$. If, instead, $C = 0$ (i.e., if the consumption demand curve were linear), mean production would increase slightly with storage because the equilibrium without storage would be below 100 units. Mean realized production in a system with storage is little different from 100.00 units regardless of the supply elasticity.

Elastic supply also influences the skewness in the steady-state distributions of the various endogenous variables. Figure 4.6 contrasts the probability distribution of consumption with $\eta^s = 0.0$ against the distribution with $\eta^s = 1.0$.[15] Along with a lower standard deviation, with $\eta^s = 1.0$ consumption is much more skewed. The reduction in variance comes mainly from shifting probability away from high levels of consumption; the prospect for a very low level of consumption is nearly the same whether η^s is 0.0 or 1.0. In fact, with $\eta^s = 1.0$, maximum consumption, which occurs when storage is very

---

[15] η^d continues at -0.2, and $C = 6$; the two cases are rows 9 and 15 in Table 4.1.

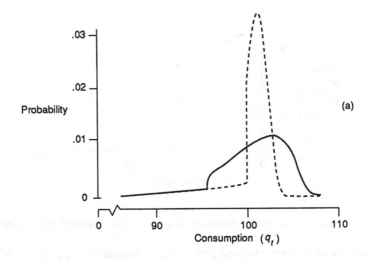

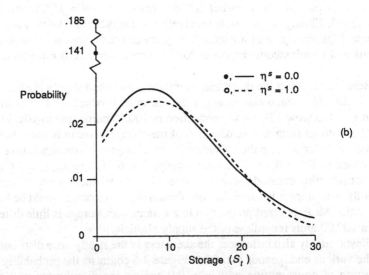

Figure 4.6. Probability distributions of consumption and storage with and without elastic supply.

high, is rarely above the maximum planned production, which occurs whenever storage is zero.

The differential effect of responsive supply on the probability distribution of consumption can be explained as follows. When supply is perfectly inelastic, very high levels of consumption ensue from consecutive years of high realized production. When supply is elastic, planned production is reduced after a good harvest, and storage is increased. Relative to the situation with fixed planned production, the net effect is a lower level of consumption that period and the next. The same kind of compensation does not occur following a poor harvest, however. Below the level of availability at which storage is zero (A^*), further shortfalls do not increase the producers' marginal incentive P_t^e; planned production is at its maximum (recall Figure 4.1(a)). The chance of a major shortfall the next period is much the same as with $\eta^s = 0.0$.

Effects on the distribution of consumption can also be compared to complete stabilization. The inherent uncertainty in the weather, when translated into realized production, has a standard deviation of 10.00 units with $\eta^s = 0.0$ and close to that value if η^s is positive. (With an additive error, it would be 10.00 regardless.) For $C = 6$ and $\eta^d = -0.2$, storage at these particular storage costs achieves 48.3 percent of complete stabilization. With $\eta^s = 1.0$, the combination achieves 63.9 percent of the conceivable stabilization. Any stabilization not achieved is, in expectation, not worth the cost.

This discussion of the sensitivity to the elasticity of supply bypassed the information in Table 4.1 on the properties of storage rules. With higher η^s, the kink point A^* is at a higher availability. On the other hand, with $\eta^s = 1.0$, the marginal propensity to store is notably higher than for $\eta^s = 0.0$, and the rule is more nearly linear. The storage rules for these two supply elasticities cross at an availability of 111.1 units. Of course, high availabilities are more common with $\eta^s = 0.0$, so that the resulting probability distributions of storage are not markedly different, as can be seen in the Figure 4.6(b).

A rough rule of thumb inferred by Newbery and Stiglitz (1982) from Gustafson's (1958a) work on storage without responsive supply is that, when storage occurs, one unit is stored for every unit consumed. That is, the marginal propensity to store is on the order of 0.5. The marginal propensities to store seen in Table 4.1, especially for the higher supply elasticities, show how inaccurate that rule of thumb can be. For $\eta^s = 1.0$, the rule of thumb is six units stored for every additional unit consumed. Table 4.1 also shows that a rule of thumb with a constant marginal propensity to store is also misguided, especially when η^d and η^s are both low. Storage rules for a system with low values of those two parameters are noticeably curved, with the marginal propensity to store increasing with the amount on hand.

Of course, when supply is not perfectly inelastic, the storage rule is not the only rule for passing the commodity onto the next period. Figure 4.7 shows the sum of the storage and planned production rules for two supply elasticities, $\eta^s = 0.0$ and $\eta^s = 1.0$. The example differs only from those in the bottom part of Table 4.1 in that the weather disturbance is additive. (Thus, the extent of weather uncertainty is not another dimension to the bequest to period $t + 1$.) The equilibrium bequest is more nearly the same whatever the cur-

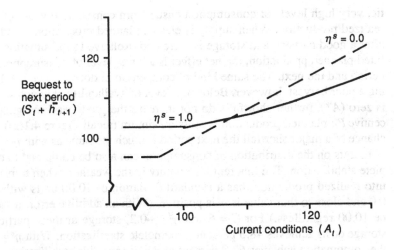

Figure 4.7. Sum of rules for storage and planned production.

rent conditions if $\eta^s = 1.0$. Of more interest, for $\eta^s = 1.0$ the marginal propensity to bequeath through either storage or planned production is lower than the marginal propensity to store when $\eta^s = 0.0$. Also, the curve for $\eta^s = 1.0$ is more nonlinear than the storage rule alone. At its kink point ($A_t = 100.17$), its slope is 0.24, whereas at $A_t = 130$ its slope is 0.52.

4.4   Sensitivity to storage costs

This section studies how the marginal physical storage cost k and the opportunity cost of invested capital r affect storage behavior. Table 4.2 gives information about storage rules and steady-state properties for five different values of k and five different values of r, with row 8 repeating row 4 in consequence.[16] Statistics for systems with storage being technically impossible were provided in Table 4.1.

The main story of Table 4.2 is not surprising. Lower storage costs, whether k or r, extend the presence of storage in the system and stabilize consumption. Differences in behavior attributable to the additive cost k or the proportional cost rP_t are not pronounced, because positive storage is consistent with a relatively narrow range of prices (recall the market demand curve pictured in Figure 4.3).

[16]   These two rows also duplicate row 9 in Table 4.1. That was the specification with a constant-elasticity consumption demand of $\eta^d = -0.2$ (namely $C = 6$) and $\eta^s = 0.0$. Supply elasticity is kept at 0.0 in the exercises in this section to evade the issue of the interest rate implicit in planting costs $H[\bar{h}_t]$.

Table 4.2. *Sensitivity to storage costs*

	Properties of storage rules				Steady-state properties (standard deviations in parentheses)			
	Kink point of storage rule (A^*)	Marginal propensity to store at A^*	at 90th percentile	Storage after many good harvests	Mean storage	% with no storage	Mean consumption	Mean price
Sensitivity to marginal physical storage costs, holding $r = 5\%$								
1. $k = \$16$	100.16	.53	.54	11.39	3.20 (3.95)	39.07	100.00 (7.35)	\$110.49 (57.10)
2. $k = \$8$	97.88	.59	.64	20.05	5.75 (5.70)	24.75	100.00 (6.31)	107.82 (49.31)
3. $k = \$4$	96.71	.62	.71	31.73	8.12 (7.15)	17.34	100.00 (5.61)	106.17 (43.57)
4. $k = \$2$	96.11	.63	.77	43.13	9.96 (8.24)	13.78	100.00 (5.17)	105.17 (39.92)
5. $k = \$0$	95.49	.66	.85	52.50	12.77 (9.85)	10.05	100.00 (4.62)	104.16 (35.45)
Sensitivity to interest rate, holding $k = \$2$								
6. $r = 10\%$	97.61	.61	.68	25.92	6.69 (6.44)	22.25	100.00 (5.99)	107.10 (47.13)
7. $r = 7\%$	96.74	.63	.79	34.79	8.36 (7.38)	17.16	100.00 (5.54)	106.03 (43.18)
8. $r = 5\%$	96.11	.63	.77	43.13	9.96 (8.24)	13.78	100.00 (5.17)	105.17 (39.92)
9. $r = 3.5\%$	95.61	.65	.81	48.81	11.63 (9.12)	11.02	100.00 (4.83)	104.54 (37.00)
10. $r = 2\%$	95.07	.66	.86	53.31	14.06 (10.34)	8.41	100.00 (4.42)	103.77 (33.53)

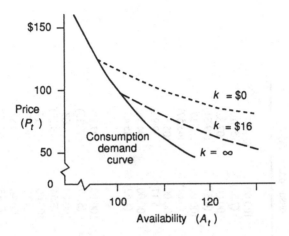

Figure 4.8. Market demand curves with different storage costs.

One subtlety in Table 4.2 is the behavior of the marginal propensity to store as a function of storage costs. Lower storage costs increase the marginal propensity to store measured at A^*. The increase is even greater at larger current availabilities; that is, the storage rules become more curved.

Storage costs and market demand curves

The implications of highly curved storage rules are better seen from the standpoint of market demand curves. Figure 4.8 shows the market demand curves for $k = \$16$ and $k = \$0$ (rows 1 and 5 in Table 4.2), along with the (inverse) consumption demand curve.[17] Consistent with the A^*'s for these two systems, the demand for storage is everywhere greater with $k = \$0$ compared to $k = \$16$. The greater curvature of the storage rule for $k = \$0$ is also manifest, however, in a more nearly horizontal market demand curve.

To put the matter slightly differently, the effect of lower storage costs on the market demand curve is more pronounced at high current availabilities than at medium availabilities (and nonexistent at low availabilities).[18] The increase in current price measured at $A_t = 100.16$, where the storage demand with $k = \$16$ causes the kink, is $17.44. Measured at $A_t = 130$ units, the price differential between the two market demand curves is $27.72. Note that both differentials are larger than the $16 difference in the storage costs. Part of the demand for current storage is to supply the desire for future storage.

[17] $k = \infty$ is equivalent to storage being technically impossible.
[18] Note also that the curve with $k = \$16$ has a differential twist compared to the curve with $k = \infty$, namely, the consumption demand curve.

The lower are storage costs, the greater the demand for future storage. The greater the current carryover, the more likely the next few periods will have substantial storage. Hence, the larger effect on the market demand curve at an A_t of 130 units. The demand for storage feeds back on itself. For the same reason, the mean amounts in store listed in Table 4.2 grow more than proportionately with a fall in storage costs.

The feedback of future storage on the demand for current storage has several lessons for the proper modeling of storage. Clearly, entire systems need to be compared or these feedbacks cannot be expressed. Feedbacks of this nature and the study of systems presume a multiperiod model. Also, the storage behavior represented must be forward looking, or these feedbacks are precluded.

Spoilage

A model of storage could include spoilage as another cost of storage. With the spoilage rate, a known constant designated as a, the arbitrage equation for positive storage would be

$$(P_t + k)(1 + r)/(1 - a) = E_t[P_{t+1}] \tag{4.3}$$

As can be seen, the spoilage rate a enters proportionately, as does the interest rate r. Consequently, the effects on storage behavior of a lower spoilage rate are much the same as the effects of a lower r.[19] The storage rule shifts to the left, and storage becomes more influential in the evolution of the system. Consequently, little new is involved conceptually with spoilage – even if it is important in practice – and so it will not be a formal feature of the models and sensitivity analysis of later chapters.

One aspect of spoilage, however, deserves brief attention: the trade-off between the collective advantage of a reserve and the dissipation of consumption through spoilage. The resulting balance is best seen through the mean steady-state consumption. Figure 4.9 traces out mean consumption as a function of the spoilage rate for two supply elasticities.[20] With $\eta^s = 0.0$, there is no storage until the spoilage rate a is below about 0.6. At the minimum of the curve, around $a = 0.18$ (i.e., the proportion of intercropyear storage left after spoilage is 0.82), nearly 0.5 units of average consumption are sacrificed for the advantages of storage. With $\eta^s = 1.0$, the minimum average consumption is at a spoilage rate of 0.0, at the right-hand side of Figure 4.9. The flexibility in supply permits adjustments in mean consumption. With consumption de-

---

[19] $a = 1.0$ is equivalent to storage being technically impossible.
[20] The consumption demand elasticity $\eta^d = -0.2$ for both; more important, the consumption demand curvature $C = 6$.

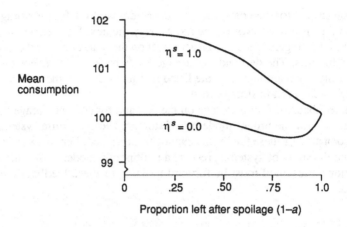

Figure 4.9. Mean consumption as a function of the spoilage rate.

mand curvature of $C = 6$, mean planned production expands in lieu of storage, and drops back as storage becomes more attractive.[21]

4.5   Sensitivity to the probability distribution of the weather

These sections on storage behavior as a function of the underlying parameters conclude with a sensitivity analysis of the parameters describing the uncertainty in the weather. The assumption so far in this chapter has been that the weather is normally distributed with a coefficient of variation of yields of 0.10. Of course, many other distributions are at least imaginable. Unfortunately, no one single parameter describes all those distributions, inasmuch as each would have a different combination of variance, skewness, kurtosis, and so forth. Here we restrict attention to, first, an investigation across different variances while continuing the assumption of normality and, second, an investigation of skewness for one particular variance.[22]

Variance of the random disturbance

For the investigation of the effect of more variable weather, the specification is otherwise familiar: linear consumption demand ($C = 0$) with $\eta^d = -0.2$, $\eta^s = 0.0$, $k = \$2.00$, and $r = 5$ percent per period. Because supply

---

[21]   If C were 0 (a linear consumption demand curve), the pattern would be the reverse; mean consumption would rise with a fall in the spoilage rate, although such computations are complicated by the implicit possibility of negative prices when the harvest is large and storage is impossible.

[22]   The means are 0.00 throughout.

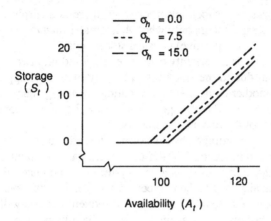

Figure 4.10. Effect of increased uncertainty in the harvest on the storage rule.

is perfectly inelastic, the underlying uncertainty in the weather can be measured directly as the standard deviation of the harvest σ_h. Figure 4.10 plots the storage rules for $\sigma_h = 0.0$ units, 7.50 units, and 15.00 units.

Not surprisingly, an increase in the uncertainty in the weather shifts the storage rule to the left. For any current availability A_t, giving rise to positive storage, the amount stored is larger the larger the standard deviation of the weather. Less obvious in Figure 4.10 is the marginal effect of uncertainty. The kink point A^* for $\sigma_h = 15.0$ is more to the left of A^* for $\sigma_h = 7.5$ than is A^* for $\sigma_h = 7.5$ to the left of the kink point with $\sigma_h = 0.0$. Also, the marginal propensity to store increases with σ_h. Measured at their respective A^*'s, the marginal propensity to store with $\sigma_h = 0.0$ is 0.61; with $\sigma_h = 7.5$, 0.65; and with $\sigma_h = 15.0$, 0.67. The marginal propensities to store are more nearly equal (at around 0.80) at higher availabilities.

The storage rule for $\sigma_h = 0.0$ provides an important insight into the function of storage, although at the risk of fostering several misconceptions. Under conditions of certainty, storage is an exercise in the optimal allocation of a surplus, in the manner of the optimal exploitation of a natural resource. The cost of new production is analogous to a "backstop technology." Solution for the storage rule involves finding simultaneously a price path increasing at the rate of interest plus physical storage costs and the number of periods for which there is storage. For example, with $A_t = 120$, the storage of 13.77 units recorded in Figure 4.10 for $\sigma_h = 0.0$, will be used up in period $t + 6$. Because there is no uncertainty, the progression back to $P = \$100$, the nonstochastic equilibrium price, will take exactly that many periods.

What a storage rule under certainty makes clear is that storage serves to spread a surplus across a number of periods. Also, it is manifest in this setting that storage works as a shock absorber when there is a surplus, not a shortage. Certainty storage occurs only when A_t is greater than q^N, whatever the (positive) interest rate or (positive) physical storage cost.

In a sense, storage under uncertainty can be decomposed into two components: one component due to the smoothing property of storage applicable under certainty and another component representing the storage necessary to cope with any uncertainty. The storage rule for $\sigma_h = 7.5$ is more or less a parallel shift to the left of the rule under certainty.

This decomposition of storage should not be pressed too far, however. Storage is important and interesting only if the system has uncertainty. Consider what is the long-run role of storage in a system with no uncertainty. If for some reason the availability in the first period is large, the next several periods will have a positive amount of storage. Subsequent periods will have no storage, however, because never again will the availability be anything but the certainty harvest h^N. Mean steady-state storage is zero. Moreover, the beginning availability presupposes some uncertainty – else how was A_0 so large? Uncertainty is intrinsic to the demand for storage.

What appear to be small differences in storage rules when they are plotted side by side as in Figure 4.10 make large differences in the behavior of the system. Because the next period's availability includes this period's carryout, an undercalculation of the proper amount of storage compounds. If the storage rule with $\sigma_h = 0.0$ is used when σ_h is actually 7.5, mean steady-state storage is 2.99, whereas the proper rule gives rise to 5.01 units of storage on average. Similarly, the rule valid under certainty when applied with $\sigma_h = 7.5$ has 43.42 percent of periods without any storage; storage should occur all but 26.89 percent of the periods. The certainty rule, if applied to $\sigma_h = 7.5$, would also understate by 22 percent the degree of stabilization of consumption achieved as measured by the reduction in its standard deviation.

Figure 4.11 looks at the effect of more dispersion in the weather on the steady-state standard deviation of price.[23] Because the consumption demand curve is linear, the standard deviation of price without storage is a linear function of the standard deviation of the harvest.[24] When storage is possible, although the standard deviation of price increases with σ_h, it does so at a decreasing rate. Storage makes a proportionately larger contribution toward stabilizing price (and consumption) as the underlying uncertainty increases.

Skewness in the random disturbance

Characterization of the sensitivity to skewness in yields is more difficult, in large part because it is not obvious which direction of skew ought

---

23   The other parameters are the same as for the storage rules in Figure 4.10.
24   If the consumption demand curvature were greater than zero, the dotted line in Figure 4.11 would bend upward as a function of σ_h.

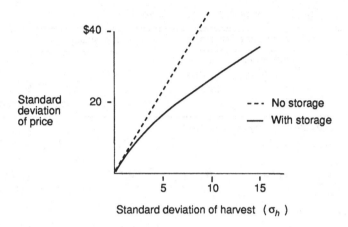

Figure 4.11. Standard deviation of price as a function of uncertainty in the harvest.

to be studied. A plausible argument can be advanced for either direction of skew. If plant biology is such that the highest yields transpire only when temperature, sunlight, and rainfall are simultaneously propitious, the probability distribution of yields should be positively skewed (assuming those three inputs are more or less symmetrically distributed and not perfectly correlated). Yields might instead have a biological maximum and plants the ability to withstand either low rainfall or hot weather but not both. Such features would cause negatively skewed yields, with the long tail toward small harvests.

We compare and contrast three cases: one with yields log-normally distributed, one with yields normally distributed, and the third with a reverse log-normal distribution; that is, one with the mirror image of the positively skewed log-normal distribution. These distributions are adjusted so that all three have a mean of 0.0 and a standard deviation of 6.0 units.[25] Also, the disturbance is additive, so that this standard deviation is the same for all cases.[26] Table 4.3 summarizes the storage behavior for these three distributions, each for two different supply elasticities.

Inspection of Table 4.3 reveals that skewness in either direction does not alter the main points about storage and storage rules. For a given η^s, the rules

[25] The other parameters are a constant-elasticity consumption demand with $\eta^d = -0.2$, $k = \$0$, and $r = 5\%$.

[26] For derivation of the respective storage rules, a finer discrete approximation – with 40 equally spaced intervals – was used for the lognormal forms. The discrete approximations to density functions are discussed in Appendix 3A above.

Table 4.3. *Effects of skewness in the weather*

	Properties of storage rules			Steady-state properties[a]		
	Kink point of storage rule $(A*)$	Marginal propensity to store at		% with no storage	Mean storage	Mean consumption
		$A*$	$A*+20$			
Lognormal distribution, negatively skewed						
1. $\eta^s = 0.0$	96.42	.68	.79	3.86	9.77 (4.21)	100.00 (3.82)
2. $\eta^s = 1.0$	99.84	.89	.92	4.59	9.99 (3.82)	100.45 (3.47)
Normal distribution						
3. $\eta^s = 0.0$	98.47	.68	.78	18.16	5.32 (4.76)	100.00 (3.24)
4. $\eta^s = 1.0$	100.34	.88	.92	23.50	4.76 (4.49)	100.12 (2.41)
Lognormal distribution, positively skewed						
5. $\eta^s = 0.0$	99.57	.73	.79	38.95	3.74 (6.98)	100.00 (2.53)
6. $\eta^s = 1.0$	100.78	.89	.92	57.32	2.35 (5.81)	99.79 (1.67)

[a]Standard deviations are given in parentheses.

for the three different skewnesses have similar marginal propensities to store; moreover, all show an increasing marginal propensity to store with increasing availabilities. It also, whatever the skewness, straightens the storage rule, shifts its kink point $A*$ to the right, and increases its marginal propensity to store. Elastic supply, whatever the skewness, complements storage in reducing the standard deviation of consumption. However, with the different skewnesses there are substantial differences in the average amount in store and the percentage of periods with nothing in store. (Such differences due to skewness may have large effects on the financial viability of any public intervention, a point emphasized by Peck and Gray [1980].) These matters fit with the general proposition that the risk of greater inconvenience induces more average storage, since the reverse log-normal distribution, which is the distribution with a small chance of an extremely small harvest, has the most storage. Last of all, storage still moves the distribution of price toward being positively skewed (and the distribution of consumption toward being negatively skewed) whatever the underlying distribution. As can be seen in Figure 4.12, storage, by the nature of the nonnegativity constraint, acts asymmetrically.

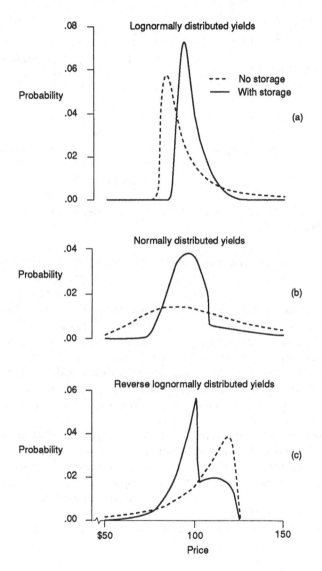

Figure 4.12. Effect of storage on the skewness in the probability distribution of price.

The endogenous change through storage in the skewness of the price distributions has another message. Observed yields, such as those studied by Timoshenko (1942, 1943), Luttrell and Gilbert (1976), Black and Thompson (1978), and Gallagher (1987), include the endogenous responses of farmers,

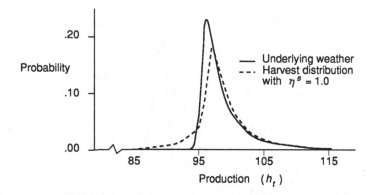

Figure 4.13. Probability distribution of the harvest with lognormally distributed yields.

both within periods and between periods, and need to be interpreted accordingly. Day's (1965) controlled results for cotton, corn, and oats indicate large changes in both the skewness and variance of yields depending on the amount of nitrogen added. (Also see Lin et al., 1963.) For farmers, individually and collectively, the amount of fertilizer to apply is a choice variable. Likewise, the endogenous planting response induced by storage may be included in observed yields. Figure 4.13 shows the distribution of realized production, with the true yield being log-normally distributed, for $\eta^s = 1.0$. If the effects of the interaction of storage and planned production are taken into account, the skewness of the underlying random disturbance may be thought to be much less than it actually is.

The view about skewness taken in this book is agnostic. With such weak evidence in favor of either positive or negative skewness, the probability distribution of yields for the many exercises is assumed to be normally distributed (with the exception of one exercise in Chapter 6 and one in Chapter 14). Of course, yields cannot be truly normally distributed, for that would admit the (faint) possibility of a negative harvest. In any case, the normal distribution is replaced by a discrete and finite version in the numerical routines solving for the storage rule.

4.6   Conclusions from the sensitivity analysis

The discussion of skewness in the probability distribution of yields completes the sensitivity analysis of storage behavior. In the following chapters, which introduce more complex models or various public interventions, it is impractical to conduct such an exhaustive sensitivity analysis. The lessons here must suffice for those other problems, except where some test of the robustness of results seems called for. Fortunately, one lesson from the sensitivity analysis in this chapter is that conclusions about storage behavior as a function of, say, the demand elasticity are not likely to be reversed if studied under other supply elasticities. The "cross partial derivatives," to speak loosely, are not such as to reverse the signs of the "partial derivatives" with respect to the principal parameters.

The approach taken in the remaining chapters is to concentrate on one or two base sets of parameters. Naturally, these are chosen to give a reasonable role for storage. The marginal physical storage cost k is kept low and the interest rate r is usually 5 percent. Because a lower consumption demand elasticity induces more storage (and accords with estimates for most actual primary commodities), η^d is usually –0.2. In keeping with estimates of agricultural supply elasticities, η^s is set at a value between 0.0 and 1.0.

The values for these particular parameters seem reasonable, and so are likely to arouse little controversy. A consensus about some parameters, such as η^d, makes all too obvious the acute ignorance about other parameters. In addition to the lack of knowledge about the skewness in the probability distribution of yields, an important gap in knowledge is the value for the curvature parameter C. People advocate government storage to aid, say, producers, without any awareness that for reasonable values of C producers are harmed. Most existing empirical work on consumption demand is of little help, because it implicitly assumes some value for C through the choice of a linear, semilog, or log-linear specification. In following exercises emphasizing allocative properties, the curvature parameter C is usually set at 0 (linear) or 6 (constant elasticity) depending on which one of them makes clearer some property under consideration. In the chapters on welfare analysis constituting the last segment of the book, many more values of C will be considered.

CHAPTER 5

Convergence to the steady state

The long-run distributions discussed in Chapter 4 can be imagined as frequency distributions from extremely long time series. Indeed, that is how they were produced. Nevertheless, there is a second way to conceive of and to deduce the stochastic steady state of a system. The stochastic steady state is the probability distribution for a single period some time in the distant future, viewed from the perspective of the current period. One can imagine from the perspective of the current period the probability distribution of, say, consumption period by period into the future. For a nonstorable commodity, the exercise is trivial. Because each future period is just like any other from the perspective of period t, the probability distribution of consumption in period $t+1$ is identical to that in period $t+2$, and so on, and also identical to the distribution that would emerge from a long time series. For a storable commodity, however, the probability distributions for the next few periods ($t+1$, $t+2$, etc.) will be sensitive to conditions in period t. Eventually, the distribution for some period ahead, perhaps eight periods ahead, will be nearly the same as that for the previous one (period $t+7$) regardless of the initial conditions. That distribution approximates the steady-state distribution.

The focus of the present chapter is understanding the process of convergence to the invariant steady-state distributions as a function of the initial conditions. The speed and pattern of convergence explain much about the system's absorption of shocks, about the patterns in futures prices, about the adjustment to a change in an underlying parameter, and about the determination of the price of land used for producing a storable commodity. Each of these subjects will be the center of attention in a section in this chapter.

5.1 Expected paths

For each initial condition, there is a set, indexed by the number of periods ahead, of probability distributions for the endogenous variables.

128

These conditional and time-varying distributions can be derived numerically by running the storage model. After solving for the storage rule, one starts with a particular initial condition, say, $A_0 = 120$ units, and simulates a number of periods, say 10, drawing from the probability distribution of the weather. In each period, including initial period 0, the amount available and the storage rule determine the amount stored, which in turn determines that period's price. For that particular path of ten periods, the values for various endogenous variables are recorded. One simulates 10,000 or 100,000 paths each for ten periods from the same initial condition but with different random draws for the weather. What emerges as the frequency distribution for, say, consumption in, say, period 4 is a conditional distribution, the conditioning variable being A_0. Its mean and variance could be denoted $E_0[q_4 | A_0 = 120]$ and $E_0[(q_4 - \bar{q}_4)^2 | A_0 = 120]$. The distribution would be different from the perspective of period 2 by which time the harvests in period 1 and period 2 would have been known. And, at least potentially, the conditional distribution for four periods ahead is different from the distribution for three or five periods ahead. For example, in a system with linear consumption demand ($\eta^d = -0.2$), $\eta^s = 0.3$, and marginal storage cost $k = \$2$,[1] and starting from $A_0 = 120$ units, the standard deviation of consumption is 0.00 units in period 0, 2.50 in period 1, 3.84 in period 2, 4.35 in period 3, 4.40 in period 4, 4.43 in period 5, and 4.46 in period 6 and farther ahead.

Conditional means

Of special interest are the means of the distributions ordered by time. This sequence of conditional means can be interpreted as the expected path of the system starting from that particular condition in period 0. Figure 5.1 displays the sequences of means for the four endogenous quantity variables for the system with the parameters just mentioned and an initial condition $A_0 = 120$ units. Recall that an availability of 120 units is substantially above average, perhaps because of the shock of unusually good weather for period 0's harvest. According to Figure 5.1(a), the expectation is for at least six periods to pass before this current surplus is dissipated and the availability is back to its long-run average. Storage principally absorbs the current shock, which is why future availabilities are expected to remain high. To a lesser extent, consumption and planned production also absorb the shock. This complementarity has already been discussed as a major theme of Chapter 4. What is new is the length of time the reactions to the shock are expected to persist – as many as five or six periods according to Figure 5.1.

Of course, the chance that the variables follow exactly these sequences of conditional means is infinitesimally small. The actual path is subject to the va-

---

[1]   Along with $r = 5$ percent and normally distributed weather with a standard deviation of the harvest of 10 percent of planned production.

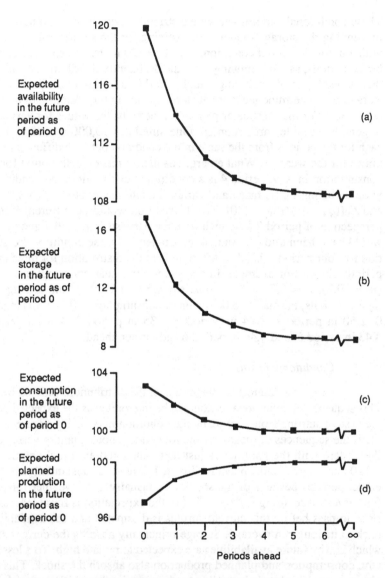

Figure 5.1. Convergence to the steady state, $A_0 = 120$.

garies of the weather. For example, the shock of good weather in the initial period might be entirely absorbed the very next period by exceptionally bad weather. Nor can it really be said that the "expected paths" in Figure 5.1 are the median or mean paths because similar paths are not grouped into some frequency distribution. These "paths" are simply the best estimates of the

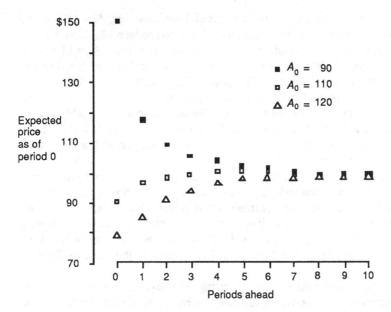

Figure 5.2. Constellations of futures prices.

quantities that will prevail in the various future periods. (That is, they are the rational forecasts as of period 0.) On the other hand, the expected paths are most definitely not the paths the various variables would track if the weather were to follow its average value (i.e., should v_t equal 0.0 for periods 1–6).[2] The means in Figure 5.1 take account of all possible sequences of the weather and, in so doing, take account of the various nonlinearities and discontinuities in the system. If by chance A_5 equaled its expected value of 108.65, the storage rule would dictate 6.49 units of storage, not the 8.60 units expected as of period 0 (given $A_0 = 120$). The discrepancy arises because an expectation taken over a nonlinear function is not equal to the function evaluated at the expected value of its argument.

Sensitivity to initial conditions

Figure 5.1 was derived with $A_0 = 120$ units. Comparable but different diagrams could be produced for other initial conditions. This point may seem obvious, but it is central nevertheless: The expected paths are highly sensitive to the initial conditions. To emphasize the importance of the initial conditions, Figure 5.2 plots the arrays of conditional means of price for three different initial availabilities. (The parameters are the same as for Figure 5.1,

[2] Such a path would be the "certainty equivalence" path, to use the terminology discussed in Chapter 3.

except that $\eta^s = 0.0$.) One of the three initial availabilities, $A_0 = 120$, is the familiar situation of current surplus, here shown to produce a low initial price. The expectation is for future weather to be less generous. $A_0 = 110$ is an availability just slightly above the long-run average, and $A_0 = 90$ is below average, with no initial storage. The sequence for $A_0 = 90$ has a high initial price and the expectation for price to be progressively lower in the future. The stockpile needs to be built up again. Because more of this buildup is expected in period 1 than in period 2 and in period 2 than in period 3, the price expected as of period 0 for period 1 is higher than for period 2, and period 2 higher than period 3.[3]

Despite the markedly different expected paths from the three initial conditions, a common characteristic is their convergence to the steady state. Far from predicting an explosion or implosion in price over the long run, the conditional means return to a steady-state value. Whether the initial price is very high or very low, the price expected for some ten periods later is about the long-run average price. $E_0[P_{10} | A_0 = 90]$ is essentially the same as $E_0[P_{10} | A_0 = 120]$.

A system with storage is mean reverting. Whatever the current condition, the expectation is for the future values of the endogenous variables to be closer to their long-run averages. Although a system for a nonstorable commodity is also mean reverting (with full convergence, in expectation, in the very next period), a system with storage is more interesting because the regression toward the mean is expected to take several periods.

A mean-reverting system is stationary; its long-run expectation does not depend on time as does an explosive system. Nevertheless, a system with storage is sensitive to the progression of time from the current period because the probability distributions differ for each of the next several periods ahead. Even more important, the extent of this time dependency depends on the current conditions. This form of time dependency is itself stationary, however. If conditions are the same in period 287 of a long time series as in period 3113, the expected progression from that state is the same.

Speed of convergence

In Figure 5.2, the price paths from both $A_0 = 90$ and $A_0 = 120$ converge to essentially the same price only six or seven periods ahead. The path of expected prices for $A_0 = 110$ converges to the steady-state mean even more quickly, by period 2 or 3 depending on one's criterion. The speed of conver-

---

3   Humps are also possible shapes, and would apply should P_0 be near the steady-state mean price and storage be positive. With positive storage along with such a P_0, as there would be with this set of parameters, $E_0[P_1]$ must be above P_0 by storage costs including interest; hence $E_0[P_1]$ is also above the steady-state mean. Such humps are yet another manifestation of the nonlinear relationships in the system.

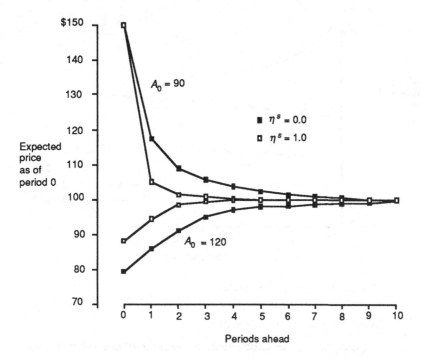

Figure 5.3. The effect of supply elasticity on the rate of convergence to the steady state.

gence for other initial availabilities would also be faster or slower depending on how far that availability is from the long-run average. Similarly, parameters influencing the extent of storage influence the speed of convergence: the greater the storage, the slower the speed of convergence.

For example, the higher is the supply elasticity the faster the convergence to the steady state. Figure 5.3 compares the speed of convergence for price for two of the availabilities from Figure 5.2. The solid squares represent the expected price path with $\eta^s = 0.0$, the open squares that of $\eta^s = 1.0$. Whereas with $\eta^s = 0.0$ the price was expected to be close to the long-run mean by period 6 or 7, with $\eta^s = 1.0$ that same degree of convergence is expected by period 3 or 4. With $\eta^s = 1.0$ any shock, whether a good harvest or a bad harvest, is expected to be almost completely dissipated within two or three periods. Because supply is elastic, it augments the cushioning effect of storage. For a given initial availability with positive storage, the distance of current price from the steady-state mean decreases with the supply elasticity, as does the time until convergence. When initial availability is such as to be too low to allow positive storage, this effect cannot work immediately, as the initial price on the upper sequence of Figure 5.3 shows.

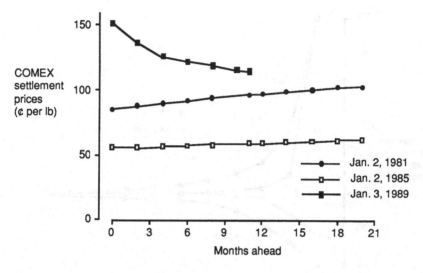

Figure 5.4. Copper futures prices.

5.2   Patterns among futures prices

The diagrams of the anticipated convergence of price to its steady-state mean from some initial condition can also be viewed as arrays of futures prices. The assumption of risk-neutral speculators who have rational expectations, encapsulated in equation (2.7), means that these expected prices are the futures prices.[4] By construction in the model, each of the futures prices is the mathematical expectation of the spot price that will prevail in a specific distant period conditional on the information available in the current period. Thus, the model of rational forward-looking storage allows one to study arrays of futures prices.[5]

The model's futures prices are each for a different cropyear, whereas the arrays of futures prices listed in newspapers are mainly for different delivery dates within the same cropyear. Possible exceptions are the metals, which have no pronounced seasonality in supply or demand. Figure 5.4 plots some actual futures prices for COMEX copper for three dates in the 1980s. Even without corrections for differences in nominal interest rates (about 20% in

---

4   More precisely, the expected prices are the perfect forward prices. Forward and futures prices differ (if indeed they do differ) because of institutional features relating to liquidity, the risk of default, or the practice of marking to market without adjusting for the timing of payments. Because these distinctions are not germane to the discussion here, the term "futures price" will be used.

5   Because the futures prices can be computed for any distance into the future, the storage model has by implication no missing markets. Similarly, rational options prices for different strike prices are implicit in the model, and could be studied if so desired.

1981 and 10% in 1989), the three arrays look very much like those of the models seen in Figures 5.2 and 5.3. When spot copper prices have been low, contracts for later delivery have had higher prices; when spot prices have been high – as in January 1989, which was near the all-time peak – distant contracts have a considerably lower price. Seemingly, the copper market's collective wisdom is for a return from whatever are the current conditions to some long-run average price in the range of 80¢ to 110¢ per pound.

Although one pictures the convergence to the steady state as taking place over time, the futures prices, whether actual prices or those in the model, are best conceived of as applying to one moment in time. The array of futures prices represents, as of period t, the price $F_{t+1,t}$ for delivery (and payment) in period $t+1$, $F_{t+2,t}$ for delivery in period $t+2$, $F_{t+3,t}$ for period $t+3$, and so on. The realized prices in those periods may be very different, but the futures prices represent the price at which someone as of period t will contract forward. The price for current delivery – the spot price – is also part of this array.

The array can and does change over time, with particular delivery dates moving to the front of the array. That is, $F_{t+1,t}$, $F_{t+2,t}$, $F_{t+3,t}$, and so on are endogenous variables contingent on the availability in period t. Figure 5.5 shows the progression of an array covering the spot price through the futures price for delivery two periods ahead for the eleven periods illustrated in Figure 2.6 to introduce the behavior of a system with storage. Each period shows the equilibrium adjustment to a new shock. A picture for copper would look much the same. Though crowded with information, Figure 5.5 covers only price; similar figures could show the progression of the conditional means for other important variables like planned production. Were the eleven arrays aligned to the same starting date, they would appear much like those in Figure 5.2 (except that the initial availabilities in Figure 5.2 were consciously chosen). Note in Figure 5.5 the forecast of a return to the steady-state mean price whatever the current price (although several of the arrays are humped).[6] Note also the corollary that $F_{t+2,t}$ is less variable than $F_{t+1,t}$, which in turn is less variable than P_t.[7]

Because of the convergence to the steady-state mean, often the differences between pairs of futures prices as of one moment in time, commonly called spreads, are below full carrying charges.[8] Indeed, the array for $A_0 = 90$ in Figure 5.2 or 5.3 has spreads in backwardation; among each and every pair

---

[6]   Contrast the reasons for differences in spot and futures prices in Figure 5.5 to Hubbard's (1986) model of spot and contract prices for oil, in which the damped behavior of the forward prices arises because they are functions of past contract prices as well as of expectations about future spot prices.

[7]   Note that this last comparison concerns the behavior of price for a particular length of time ahead, and not the movement of price for a particular delivery date over time.

[8]   "Spreads" refer to the difference between two prices for different delivery dates. Because one can take a position in a spread by simultaneously buying one futures contract and selling one for a different delivery date, on some markets the term is a "straddle."

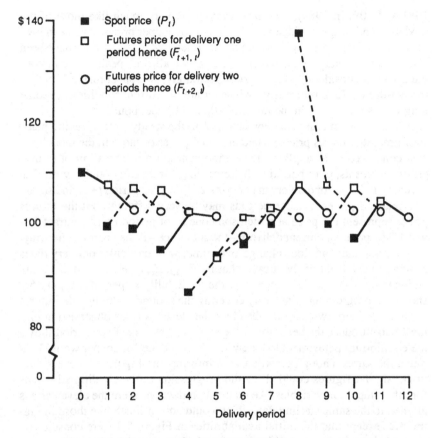

Figure 5.5. Movement of price arrays over time.

of delivery dates (representing different cropyears), the price for the later delivery is lower. Several of the periods in Figure 5.5 also have spreads in
backwardation.

These features of the model are of considerable interest because the presence of spreads below full carrying charges – in the extreme a backwardation
– is conspicuous in actual futures markets as was the case for copper in Figure 5.4. (In grains, backwardations are most frequent between the last of the
old-crop delivery months and the first of the new-crop delivery months; i.e.,
across cropyears.) Because the act of taking delivery at one time and redeliv-
ering later is the same production process as storage, Working (1948) emphasizes that spreads are the market's "price of storage." "Full carrying
charges" refer to the known expenses of storing a commodity, primarily interest and warehousing fees. In the case of Figure 5.2, those are 5 percent
and $2.00/unit, respectively.

In Figure 5.2 the spread between the prices for delivery in periods 0 and 1 for $A_0 = 120$ is at "full carrying charges" since $F_{1,0}$ is above P_0 by just that amount. The other spreads for that initial availability are below full carrying charges. This is most obvious for the pair $F_{9,0}$ and $F_{10,0}$, which are essentially equal. Apparently, should a storage firm as of period 0 buy the commodity while selling it for delivery in period 2 or later, it would not cover its expenses, whether described in terms of spreads, straddles, or price of storage. The model's futures prices, not to mention actual futures prices, seem to imply that storage must be done at an opportunity cost.

Traditionally, there have been three explanations for the prevalence of spreads below full carrying charges across cropyears. One is that the future is discounted relative to the present (Vance 1946). A second is that storers receive some benefit from having stocks on hand. They receive a "convenience yield," in the terminology first employed by Kaldor (1939). A third explanation is that observed futures prices are biased downward by risk premia. That is, if one could observe the true expected price, it would be above the spot price by full carrying charges. The futures prices in the storage model, however, do not discount the future unduly, contain no convenience yield, and are unbiased by construction; yet these arrays of futures prices show spreads below full carrying charges.

For the forward spreads, such as $F_{2,0}-F_{1,0}$, the explanation is simple. Spreads below full carry arise because of the possibility of a stockout in period 1, that is, the possibility that storage will be zero and hence the spot spread $F_{2,1}-P_1$ will be below full carry.[9] Recall in Figure 5.2 the plot of expected prices for the highest initial availability, $A_0 = 120$. Although each price expected for a particular delivery date is higher than its predecessor, the increase is progressively less. Accordingly, the spreads are progressively more below full carry. Not surprisingly, a plot of the probability of a stockout in the same sequence conditional on information as of period 0, shown in Figure 5.6(c), shows an increase with more distant periods, until that probability too reaches its steady-state value.[10] By contrast, for a low initial availability – for example the $A_0 = 90$ in Figure 5.6(a) – the probability of a stockout starts at 100 percent in the initial period and falls in smaller and smaller steps until it reaches the same steady-state value. It falls because of the probability of replenishment of stocks in future periods.

When the current stockpile is large, the probability of having a small amount available the next period is relatively low, since the current carryout can cushion a poor harvest. When the current stockpile is small or zero, the

[9]   This argument that forward spreads below full carrying charges result from the possibility of a stockout has been made by others, notably Higginbotham (1976) and Bresnahan and Spiller (1986).

[10]   Deaton and Laroque (1990) estimate the probability of a stockout for thirteen commodities, finding a range of from 0.01 for palm oil to 0.23 for sugar.

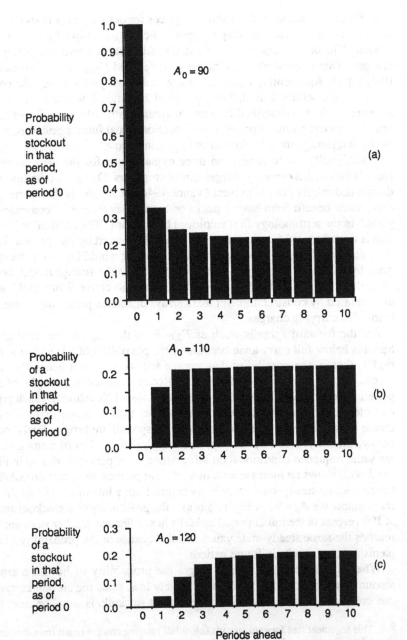

Figure 5.6. Probability of a stockout in future periods, evaluated at period 0.

probability of having a small availability the next period is obviously high. These same conditional probabilities can be expressed in terms of spreads. A current spread at full carrying charges indicates a low chance of a backwardation next period. A current backwardation, synonymous with a current stockout, forecasts a relatively high probability of a backwardation the next period.[11]

This interaction of stockouts with spreads is necessary for the existence of a (stochastic) steady state and in turn for mean-reverting behavior.[12] If sequential spreads in the array were all at full carry, this would be equivalent to the statement that a steady state did not exist, for price would be expected to rise perpetually.[13] To put it differently, because future stockouts occur with probability 1 in the model, distant spreads, if not also nearby spreads, will be below full carry. Price cannot increase at full carry indefinitely.[14]

Stockouts, and by extension forward spreads below full carrying charges, are caused by the nonnegativity constraint on storage. If the whole market could borrow from the future, there would be no reason to endure a shortage. The equilibrium relationship between the current price and the price the next period would always be one in which the marginal value of current consumption is balanced against the marginal value of future consumption, appropriately discounted. The same would hold among all the futures prices.

Also relevant is the flexible nature of an investment in the amount stored, which is adjustable each period. The observation that storage between period 0 and period 2 would seem to take place at an opportunity cost measured by the spread $F_{2,0}-P_0$ prevailing as of period 0, does not allow for the recalculation of storage at period 1. Anyone who committed to store from period 0

[11] These predictions apply to spans of a cropyear, say the July–July spread in wheat, not necessarily to the relationship between the March–May spread and the May–July spread.

[12] Whether a system with storage is ergodic or not is the central issue in an exchange between Rutledge (1976) and Samuelson (1965, 1976). Rutledge tests Samuelson's (1965) formulation of an ergodic model, in which a corollary is that futures prices become more variable as their expiration date approaches, for silver, cocoa, wheat, and soybean oil (a single futures contract in each instance), finding increasing variance for silver and cocoa but not for the other two. In both Samuelson's original model and Rutledge's alternative formulation, the stochastic process for the spot price is taken as exogenous. In the storage model here, the time-series properties of the spot price, including the speed of convergence, are endogenous.

[13] Such a perpetual rise in price might occur for a nonrenewable resource without a backstop technology. A renewable resource such as timber has a steady state of constant prices and of cuttings equaling planting. New timber growth is broadly analogous to the new production arriving every period in the storage model.

[14] Bresnahan and Suslow (1985) show that if the short-run marginal costs of mining a nonrenewable resource are rising, there can be a sequence of demand shocks such that $E_t[P_{t+1}]$ is strictly less than $(1 + r)P_t$. Consequently, spreads below full carrying charges and a tendency for transitory deviations from long-run relationships should be common features of metals markets, which they confirm for copper.

through period 2 without revision would forego the opportunity to store nothing in period 1 should total availability be small and P_1 be unusually high. Full carry should generally be observed only over the interval within which revision of plans is infeasible or undesirable.

This argument about forward spreads and stockouts addresses neither the issue of current storage in the face of the spot spread below full carrying charges, nor storage within a cropyear when intrayear spreads are below full carrying charges. Empirically it does seem that storage takes place when the spot spread is in backwardation, if for no other evidence than the disquieting fact that stockouts are never observed.[15] In Chapter 9 we shall argue that storage while current spreads are below full carrying charges is at least in part an aggregation phenomenon. One type of wheat may be in such abundance as to be stored while another type, one whose price is the standard quotation, may have zero storage. That is to say, the stockouts of particular grades or at particular locations remain important in explaining spot spreads below full carrying charges even though aggregate stockouts are not observed.

The necessary number of futures contracts

The extent and prevalence of spreads below full carry, both at one moment in time and over time, is closely connected to the speed of convergence to the steady state. The speed of convergence also says much about why so few futures markets have contracts for delivery beyond one or two years ahead. With a high speed of convergence, such as with relatively elastic supply, the price for delivery two years ahead would be essentially the same as the price for delivery three, four, or five years ahead, regardless of the initial availability.[16] Should new information emerge about the current harvest, the relationships among the very distant futures prices will change only slightly, if at all.

Nevertheless, it is commonplace for people, among them Arrow (1978), Smith (1978a), Brown (1980, p. 157), Newbery and Stiglitz (1981, p. 41), and MacBean and Nguyen (1987), to remark on the paucity of futures markets with distant delivery dates. Their message is that this gap in market prices deprives producers of an essential signal. These observers seem never to contemplate how that signal would compare to those futures contracts actually traded. The price for delivery after the next cycle of planting and harvesting is not likely to be much different from the current expected price for delivery 10, 20, or 100 years later. Given that additional contracts increase the

15   For example, wheat stocks in Chicago have never been down to zero in 120 years of warehouse statistics.
16   Added to the speed of convergence is the effect of elastic supply on the dispersion of initial availabilities. Because extremely high or low initial availabilities are less likely, the spot prices themselves are more likely to be close to the long-run mean price.

transactions costs of all the existing traded contracts by decreasing volume in each, it may be optimal for the nearest of these distant contracts to convey the prices of them all.[17]

Samuelson (1976, p. 123) has a succinct thought experiment for illustrating this logic. Consider the price of cocoa twenty years hence. Let one month pass. How different will be anyone's evaluation of that ultimate price, for delivery in 19 years, 11 months? By way of contrast, consider the price of cocoa for delivery in three months. The new information arriving over the course of one month is likely to cause substantial revision of that futures price. From this contrast in responsiveness comes the logic of the very distant futures prices being nearly redundant as allocative signals. This contrast in the variance of price changes is traceable to the ergodic nature of the system.[18]

Of course, actual futures markets do not operate in the stationary world of the storage model. As long-run production costs shift or demand changes secularly, the long-run price moves. Nevertheless, these changes in long-run relationships cause smaller period-to-period relative price changes among delivery dates than the near-term effects of transient shocks to demand or supply, because there is time to adjust to them. It is the transient shocks to current availability that are dispersed and absorbed through the familiar adjustments to storage and planned production.

5.3   Response to a change in regime

This section considers the adjustment of the system to a permanent change in regime, where the change is in some exogenous parameter such as the demand elasticity or the interest rate or in some policy such as a subsidy to storage. One can view the long-run effects of this change from the perspective of two unconnected systems, one with the original parameter set, the other with the new set; this was the "comparative-statics" approach taken in Chapter 4 by comparing properties of storage rules and steady-state distributions. On the other hand, a change in regime occurs at a specific moment in time. If the full transition to the new stochastic steady state takes time, the nature of the time path to the new steady state must be considered. From this dynamic perspective, several points become crucial.

1.   The distinction between the time of the introduction and the time of the first anticipation of the new regime. With forward-looking storers and producers, the reaction to the new regime begins as soon as it is announced.

[17]   This argument is presented in more detail in Williams (1986, chap. 6).
[18]   As Samuelson also notes, even if the system is ergodic, the variance of the return from holding the three-month futures contract until its expiration is much lower than the variance of the return from holding the other contract until its expiration in twenty years.

2. Much of the long-run effect of the new regime is transmitted to the current period.
3. This transmission is stronger the more the current period is connected to the future, that is, the more the current conditions imply a large carryover.

As an example of a change in regime, consider a decrease in marginal storage costs. Suppose that some invention lowers marginal storage costs from $2 to $0 and that this decrease in storage costs is known to be permanent, though previously the marginal storage cost of $2 was expected to prevail forever. The invention is both announced and put into effect in the current period, period 0. (One might well ask why the private agents had not foreseen at least the possibility of an invention lowering storage costs. That feature could be incorporated into the model, but a step in understanding that more complex behavior is to understand the reaction when the market is taken totally by surprise.) Once the invention is announced, the private agents recalculate completely its effects on the future, and because of their collective adjustments, a new reduced-form equation for equilibrium storage applies (whose properties were described in Table 4.2 previously).

Sensitivity to initial conditions

The effect on the current period of the change in regime depends upon the current conditions, specifically the availability, A_0. Figure 5.7 shows the expected paths from an initial condition, $A_0 = 120$. For both price and the quantity stored, Figure 5.7 gives the path that would have been expected under the old regime of $k = \$2.00$ and the path under the new regime of $k = \$0$. The mean steady-state price is the same under both regimes because, with a linear demand curve and no supply elasticity, the long-run price is $100 regardless of k. In contrast, the long-run average storage with no physical storage costs is more than 2 units higher than with $k = \$2.00$. Storage also increases in the current period in which S_0 is 16.96 units rather than 15.88 units and correspondingly price is $84.77 rather than $79.43. This increase in price is much more than the immediate reduction of $2.00 in storage costs.[19] The current demand for storage surges not only because the drop in storage costs makes current storage more attractive but because the added attractiveness of storage in future periods signals a larger current carryover to provide that future storage. Thus, much of the future effect of the change in regime is transmitted to the current period.

By contrast, when current conditions are such that S_0 equals 0.0, there is no mechanism for transmitting the change in regime to the current period (giv-

---

[19] If the decrease in storage costs were to last one and only one period, the equilibrium would have $S_0 = 6.23$ units and $P_0 = \$81.18$, which is an increase of $1.75.

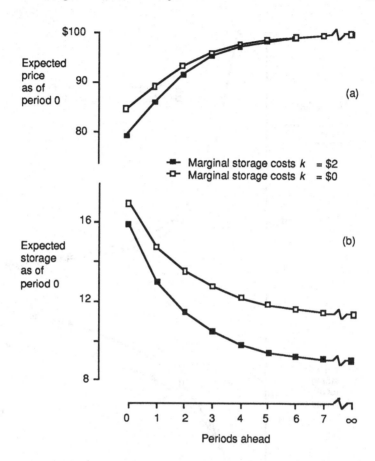

Figure 5.7. Effects of lower storage costs on expected prices and storage, $A_0 = 120$.

en perfectly inelastic supply). Figure 5.8 shows the two sequences of conditional means when $A_0 = 90$. P_0 is $150 regardless of the regime. $E_0[P_1]$, on the other hand, is higher with the new regime. As of period 0, the expectation is for a larger stockpile to be built up beginning with the next period. The expectation is for this buildup to last several periods, before the system reaches, in expectation, the new steady state. That new steady state will also be marked by lower variances for price and consumption.

Although the system is expected to follow a time-dependent path to the new steady state, the behavior is stationary. Should the announcement and introduction of the regime with lower storage costs occur twenty or forty periods from now, the path to the new steady state would be the same for the same value of availability.

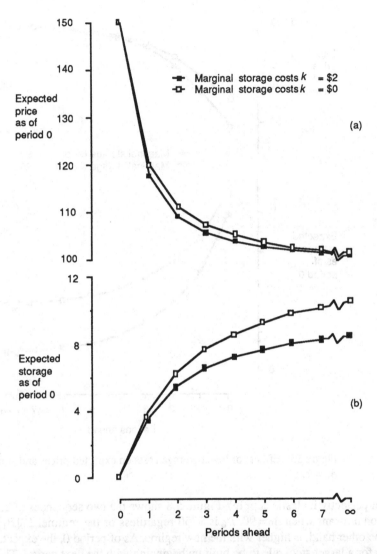

Figure 5.8. Effects of lower storage costs on expected prices and storage, $A_0 = 90$.

Anticipation of a change in regime

If the discovery and announcement of the invention of the method for storage at lower costs come some periods before it can be put into practice, the expected reaction, at the time of the introduction, from the perspective of the time of the announcement, is much more muted. This is because

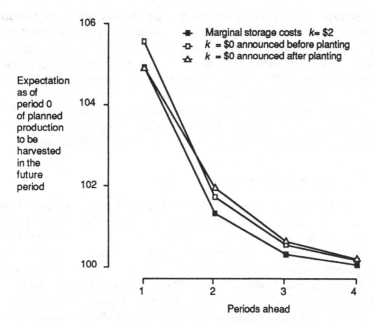

Figure 5.9. Anticipations of a change in regime, $A_0 = 90$.

part of the adjustment will have occurred before the new method is implemented. Even if a decrease in storage cost will not take effect for two periods, current storage and price both increase, precisely because the demand for current storage is, in part, derived from the demand for storage in future periods. Of course, if current conditions dictate no storage, the effects of a future reduction in storage costs cannot be transmitted through current storage. For that reason, the path for $A_0 = 90$ in Figure 5.8, which assumed the change in regime in period 0, also portrays the path if the regime were to change to lower storage costs in period 1 with that fact being known in period 0. In general, the later the implementation relative to the announcement, the smoother the path to the new steady state.

If supply is elastic (with one-period lag), the responses to anticipated changes in storage costs are more flexible. Consider a situation with elastic supply and yet no current carryover because A_0 is too low. Figure 5.9 shows that under the old regime, with k expected to be constant at $2.00, producers respond to a current stockout by setting planned production for period 1 at its highest level. The expectation, as of period 0, is for successively lower planned productions. Suppose into this environment comes word that k will be $0 starting with period 1. The timing of that announcement within period 0 is crucial. If the crop is not yet in the ground, the planned production for period 1 is increased further to satisfy the derived demand for additional future storage. But if the crop is already in the ground, nothing can be done in terms of adjusting planned production until the next planting in period 1. To catch up, the expected path in Figure 5.9 with that timing shows higher average planned production for periods after period 1 than if an adjustment was possible in period 0's planting for the harvest in period 1. Producers, however, are not necessarily worse off because the announcement came after they had committed themselves to a level of production supposing $k = \$2.00$. Had they been able to respond to the increase in derived demand, by adding to planned production, their expected revenue would have been lower.

5.4   The price of land

The themes of expected paths back to the steady state and of the changes in the paths with the introduction of a new regime make it possible to understand the calculation and behavior of the price of land in the storage model. Producers' revenue has an expected path, just as do price, storage, and planned production. That is to say, the means of the probability distributions of producers' revenue in some future period conditional on information and circumstances in the current period have the typical pattern of converging to the steady state. The price of land should be the present value of the (appropriately discounted) expected stream of net revenue. Because the path of expected revenue depends on the current conditions, the price of land is a function of the current state variable A_0. Thus, land price is another endogenous variable in the system. Its evolution is closely tied to that of storage. Because the stream of expected revenue, including the steady-state mean, immediately reflects a new regime, the current price of land will reflect the full anticipated effects of the new regime.

Before these points can be elaborated, more precise definitions of revenue and the price of land are needed. Under the accounting assumptions laid out in Chapter 2, producers are distinct from the storage industry. They sell their new production at the time it is harvested; that is to say, their gross revenue equals $P_t h_t$. Net revenue R_t is this gross revenue minus costs. These costs $H[\bar{h}_t]$ are determined by the amount of production planned, not the size of the realized harvest.[20] (They can be thought of as costs incurred in planting.) In practice, the costs are the area under the linear supply curve, so that when $\eta^s = 0.0$, net revenue equals gross revenue.[21] Net revenue is the economic rent.

20   The accounting is such that H is in dollars as of the time of the harvest.
21   The supply curve is assumed to be linear over its entire range, not just over the observed range of planned production. If a larger stable cost were subtracted from gross revenue, the equilibrium price of land would be appreciably lower. Yet, the response of the price of land with respect to changes in storage is not affected by this question of scaling.

Under the assumption of marketwide risk neutrality, the price of land is the present value of the stream of expected net revenue discounted by expected future interest rates.[22] Here, our intertemporal valuations are simplified by the assumption of an exogenous (and time invariant) interest rate. This assumption of exogeneity is realistic if the commodity has a sufficiently small share of total output and if the land for it is a small enough fraction of the whole portfolio.[23] The price of land does not include the current revenue, simply the stream of revenue from production not yet harvested (or even planted). That leaves vague whether the price of land is measured just after the current harvest or just before the next harvest, the farther limits of what is classified as period 0. Because nothing is learned about the next harvest over the interval, and hence nothing of substance changes, the issue is only whether another discount term, $1/(1 + r)$, applies. Here it will be assumed it does; the price of land is recorded just after the current harvest.[24]

Although from the perspective of period 0 net revenue in any future period is a random variable, all that matters to the price of land is the mean revenue in that future period. Likewise, under risk neutrality of potential buyers, any connection between revenue in one future period and the next – and there will be some connection through storage – is immaterial. In short, an "expected path" for revenue contains all the information about the uncertain future needed for a calculation of the price of land. The current price of land is the present value of the expected path of revenue excluding R_0.

The land price rule

Because the expected path of revenue depends on current conditions, namely the state variable A_0, the price of land does too. One can conceive of computing the path of the conditional means of revenue in future periods and its present value for each possible current availability, that is, deducing a land price rule comparable to the storage and planned production rules. The rule shown in Figure 5.10 is for the system with linear demand,

---

[22] By assumption land is homogeneous and in fixed supply. Hence all parcels sell for the same price. (It is for the convenience of calculating that price of land that planned production is adjusted through planting intensity rather than the number of acres.) "Land" is meant to represent all fixed assets associated with production.

[23] If land's share is larger, factors affecting revenues can feed back on savings via the adjustments in interest rates from portfolio reallocations. Examples of such responses can be seen in the overlapping generations models of Feldstein (1977) and Chamley and Wright (1987).

[24] As an example of this accounting for the price of an acre of land (employing the formula for a perpetuity), under certainty and zero supply elasticity and the parameters typically used, follows:

$$Land\ price^N = \left(\frac{1}{1+r}\right)\left(\frac{P^N h^N}{r}\right) = \left(\frac{1}{1.05}\right)\left(\frac{100 \cdot 100}{.05}\right) = \$190,476$$

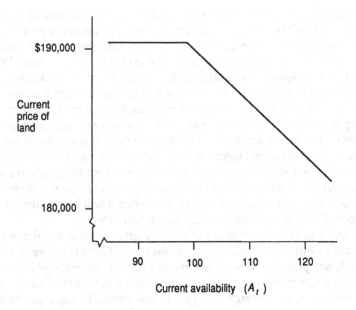

Figure 5.10. Rule for the equilibrium price of land.

$\eta^d = -0.2$, $\eta^s = 0.0$, $k = \$2.00$, and $r = 5$ percent. The horizontal axis in Figure 5.10 is labeled with A_t rather than A_0 to emphasize the stationarity of the relationship. It is another example of an endogenous variable being a function of the state variable availability.

The reduced-form relation for the price of land illustrated in Figure 5.10 has two distinct sections. The horizontal segment corresponds to those availabilities for which current storage is zero. (The effects of future storage do, however, influence the level of the horizontal segment.) Over that range future revenues are the same regardless of current conditions. Hence the price of land is the same regardless of current availability. With a higher availability, in contrast, storage plays a role, and, with a carryout from the current period, future revenue of producers will be lower than otherwise. Hence, over that range the price of land is a decreasing function of current availability.

Because both current storage and land price are direct functions of current availability, the relationship between the price of land and availability can be recast as a relationship between the price of land and the carryout, as is done in Figure 5.11. This perspective makes it clearer that the current price of land is lower whenever current storage is large because of the depressing effects that the storage has on future revenue. (That same storage, meanwhile, is boosting current revenue.) It is not proper to deduce from this effect that storage causes a depression in the price of land. Both are the rational equilibrium

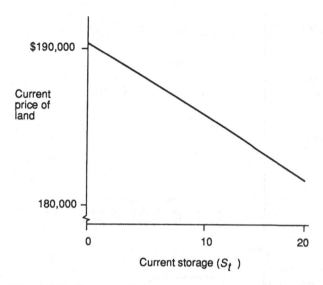

Figure 5.11. The price of land as a function of current storage.

responses to the true causal variable, current availability.[25] When first glancing at Figure 5.11, it may seem surprising that the price of land is lower by some $400 for each additional unit of storage. The typical price of that unit of storage when sold will be much less, around $100. Because the consumption demand curve is so inelastic, that additional unit sold, whenever it is sold, lowers the total revenue across all sales. From that harsh fact of life comes much of the sharp contrast between the incidence of storage interventions on producers and on consumers, to be discussed Chapter 12.

Like the other endogenous variables, the price of land has a steady-state probability distribution and, from any initial condition, an expected path back to the steady-state mean. The information about the sequence of conditional means for land is, however, already contained in the sequence of conditional means for revenue. From the perspective of period 0, the expected price of land in period 1 is the expected value of the expected net revenue from period 2 on. These expectations of expected values from the vantage point of period 0 are the same as the expected revenue used to calculate the price of land in period 0. All that is missing from the calculation of the price of land in period 1 is the revenue in period 1. If the expected revenue for period 1, as of period 0, is above the long-run mean, the price of land in period 1 is expected, as of period 0, to be lower than the current price of land.

[25] Indeed, both the price of land and the amount stored reflect the equilibrium response of planned production when supply is elastic. One could also plot the relationship between the price of land and the current planting.

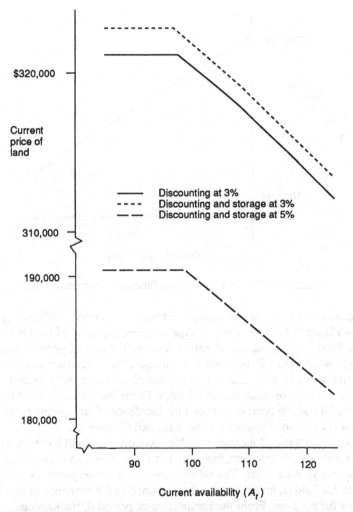

Figure 5.12. The sensitivity of land price rule to changes in the interest rate.

Regime changes and land prices

To clarify the calculations and relationships involving the price of land, an exercise with a permanent change in the interest rate is instructive. Suppose the change is from $r = 5$ percent to $r = 3$ percent and is both recognized and in effect in the current period. At first glance the sole effect on the price of land would seem to be the discounting of the previously calculated stream of expected revenues. That computation with the lower discount rate leads to the solid line in Figure 5.12, which corresponds to Figure 5.10.

With the lower interest rate, the present value of the revenue stream surges to around $320,000 from $190,000. But the effect of the new interest rate on the price of land is more than just the discounting of the stream of revenue. The stream of expected revenue also changes because the interest rate enters into the arbitrage equation for storage. The total and instantaneous effect of the change in the interest rate is represented by the dashed line in Figure 5.12. Note that there is a difference between the solid and dashed lines even over the range of availabilities where current storage is zero under both systems.

Similar analysis can be done for other changes in regimes, such as a reduction in physical storage costs. Indeed, calculation of the effect on land price is rather less complicated when the change does not involve the interest rate. For the same discount rate, the effect of a change in regime is the present value of the difference between the two paths of expected revenues for any given initial condition. Because the means of future revenues alone matter to current land values, those streams suffice. The present value of a stream of differences is the same as the difference between the present value of two streams.

From the perspective of landowners (i.e., producers), the full effect of a change in regime is encompassed in the movement in the current price of land. The full effect of the decrease in the interest rate is represented by the difference between the relationship between land price and current availability in Figure 5.10 with $r = 5$ percent, reproduced in the lower part of Figure 5.12, and the dashed line in Figure 5.12 with $r = 3$ percent. Land price is the capitalized value of future revenue. Although a change in regime may not have an effect on revenue for several periods, its effect on land price is instantaneous. Land price may change (or, more precisely from the perspective of the current period, be expected to change) with the foreseeable effects on future revenue. Nevertheless, those changes in land price are foreseeable by all parties transacting in a competitive land market. Anyone who buys land in a later period must pay for any future benefits of the regime change or receive a discount for any future harm. Those who hold land at the time of the announcement of the regime change alone experience the gain or loss.

The absorption of the effects of a regime change over all periods by the asset holders at the time of the regime change is an instance of the general principle of capitalization into inflexible assets. Here the principle of capitalization goes hand in hand with the assumption of rational forward-looking producers and storers. Because expectations about the entire future can be adjusted, the price of land changes with a new regime even when the current period has no direct connection to the future through storage or planned production. As can be seen in Figure 5.12, the current price of land reacts to the change in the interest rate even for low A_0's, which have no storage under either regime.

The principle of capitalization also applies to the effects on storers and consumers.[26] Storers, however, own no fixed assets; there are no effects on them of a change in regime unless they happen to own some of the commodity at the time of the announcement. To put the matter slightly differently, the path of expected net revenues from storage is 0.0 under all circumstances. There is nothing as obvious as "land price" for consumers because consumption rights are universal and not tradeable. But the effect on current and future consumers of a regime change can also be made as a present value calculation. These present value calculations and the principle of capitalization are at the heart of any analysis of incidence involving storage.

5.5   Tools learned

This discussion of the capitalization of regime changes into land prices concludes the material on the basic storage model. In Part II, comprising Chapters 6 and 7, are explored the time-series properties resulting from the ergodic nature of the storage model. In Part III, several extensions are made to the basic model, and in Part IV, welfare analysis takes center stage.

In these various applications and extensions, particular "tools" – "analytical techniques" is too strong an expression – used in the discussion of the basic model will be used again and again:

1. foremost, the notion of the reduced-form equation for an endogenous variable as a function of current conditions, especially the notion of a "storage rule" in the lexicon of a planner's problem;
2. studying storage behavior during a concocted sequence of good harvests;
3. the notion of steady-state (long-run) distributions;

[26] In addition, the principle of capitalization provides a simpler method for calculating land prices. The implicit method in this section's discussion is the present value of sequences of conditional means. Those expected paths – which would have to be sufficiently long that the final period when discounted was insignificant (say, 100 periods) – would have to be based on a sample of 10,000 to 100,000 paths for sufficient accuracy. The computer time required for even one initial condition is forbidding. Fortunately, that approach provides more information than is necessary for the calculation of the price of land. That calculation needs just the present value of the effect on future revenue of a carryout, precisely what is given by Figure 5.11. From the discussion of storage rules in Chapters 2 and 3, it is known that in the setting of an infinite horizon, relationships such as in Figure 5.11 are time invariant. In other words, one searches for a stable, self-reproducing function, which, as Figure 5.11 shows, is also smooth. This function can be found through the use of polynomials in the manner described for storage rules in the Appendix to Chapter 3. This approach comes up with the price of land for all imaginable availabilities with a minute or two of computer time on a fast PC. (A more detailed description of the application of these techniques to determining the price of land can be found in Wright and Williams [1984b, app. 2].)

4. comparative dynamics (introduced in this chapter), which studies the behavior of a system on its way to the steady state from various initial conditions; and finally

5. the thought experiment of comparing the behavior of systems with different parameters or different permanent policy regimes.

PART II

Implications of storage for research on time series

CHAPTER 6

Time-series properties due to storage

Measured quarterly or annually, actual time series of spot prices for major commodities have two common features. First, they display considerable positive autocorrelation: Years with high prices tend to follow years with high prices and low prices to follow low prices. Second, time series of spot prices have spikes, that is, years when the price jumps abruptly to a very high level relative to its long-run average. (See Deaton and Laroque 1990.)

Perusal of the World Bank's (1989) report on commodity prices reveals numerous commodities with these two features. Spot sugar prices, shown in Figure 6.1 annually for thirty-eight years, provide a good example. The spikes dominate visually, but the tendency for the (deflated) price to remain in the doldrums for years on end, such as the stretch over the mid-1980s, is unmistakable. The first-order serial correlation of the series is 0.53. A plot for copper looks much the same as sugar. Spikes in copper prices transpired over 1973–4, 1979–80, and 1987–9, while the mid-1970s and early and mid-1980s had prolonged low prices. The two spikes in the 1970s also occurred in other base metals,[1] in the principal grains, and in energy products,[2] each time heightening concern about general inflation (Cooper and Lawrence 1975; Bosworth and Lawrence 1982).

These two stylized facts about spot commodity prices are the natural result of storage. Whereas a series of spot prices for a nonstorable commodity subject to independent disturbances in harvests (and no systematic change in long-run demand or supply) would behave as pure white noise, a time series of prices for a storable commodity has an autoregressive structure, because storage spreads unusually high or low excess demand over several periods. Moreover, the skewness of the distribution of price under storage produces a

[1] These common booms and backwardations in metals coincide with the late stages of business cycles, as noted by Fama and French (1988).

[2] Uranium had a single spike in the mid-1970s. According to Owen (1985), the first-order serial correlation in annual spot prices over 1971–82 was at least 0.75.

157

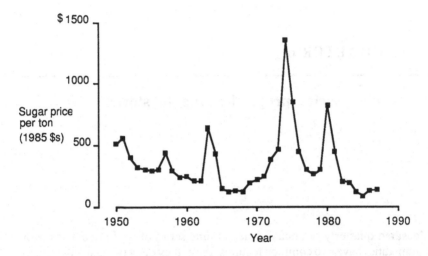

Figure 6.1. Spot price of sugar, annually 1950–87. "World" price, FOBS Caribbean ports, deflated by U.S. GNP deflator. *Source:* World Bank (1989, vol. 2, p. 74).

time series in which increases in price, while rarer, are larger than typical price decreases. This asymmetry gives a price series for a storable commodity something of a sequence of cusps. Finally, because of storage, the variance of price changes depends on the particular current spot price. The contrast in variance is most obvious between a very low current spot price, which is accompanied by an overflowing stockpile able to buffer price changes, and a very high current spot price, which finds the stockpile empty and unable to buffer price changes. Storability causes heteroskedasticity in the time series.

The purpose of this chapter and the next is to explore the implications of the smoothing properties of storage for the time-series behavior of a system. The emphasis in this chapter is on univariate properties, specifically those that would be studied under the heading of ARMA (autoregressive moving-average) processes. Chapter 7 considers how the time-series properties due to storage affect common empirical procedures performed on commodity prices. The topics include tests of the forecast power of futures prices, of the bias in futures prices, of the variability of asset prices, and of appropriate models of supply. The dividing lines between the two chapters cannot be sharp, but the material in the Chapter 7 has in common tests, implicit or explicit, of rationality.

The principal conclusions in the two chapters are that rational storage produces time series that look like ARMA processes at first inspection but, in fact, are not, and that rational storage itself biases standard statistical tests toward the finding of irrationality. These conclusions necessarily follow from the properties of paths converging to the stochastic steady state (the subject of Chapter 5). Because the expectation is for spot prices to return to the steady state over more than one period, the probability distribution of next period's spot price is conditional on the current price. This conditionality of the probability distribution of a variable for one period on the previous period's value is the essence of autoregression. Once it is admitted that the variables in the system are autoregressive, standard tests on samples of the usual size must be acknowledged to be biased.

By the same lines of reasoning, because storage is asymmetric – able to support a glut but not alleviate every shortage – changes in spot prices are asymmetric. Once that nonlinearity and that nonnormality are admitted, it follows that standard ARMA procedures and standard t-tests and F-tests are inappropriate, at least to some extent. Thus, there is a tension from the outset when discussing commodity prices as linear, Gaussian stochastic processes. Conventional ARMA techniques are not unreasonable as descriptive devices, because they capture some of the serial dependencies. A number of endogenous variables will be described here by such methods. However, conventional ARMA techniques are subtly misleading when used to infer the economic relationships in a system involving storage.

6.1 Extent of serial correlation

Positive autocorrelation, sometimes of more than first-order, is true of all the important endogenous variables in the basic storage model except the realized harvest. Storage itself is positively serially correlated, because a large carryout makes it less likely the stockpile will be exhausted.[3] Another example is expected price, which here is analogous to a one-year-ahead futures price for a commodity like corn. The sequence of such futures prices (measured annually) should be more highly autocorrelated the lower are storage costs (k and r).[4] The same relationship applies to the autoregressive behavior of the spot price, revenue, and the price of land, which are considered in more detail in this section.

Serial correlation in price

Figure 6.2 shows a series of 120 spot prices drawn from the storage model with $\eta^d = -0.2$, $C = 0$, $\eta^s = 0.0$, $\sigma_h = 10$ units, $k = \$0$, and $r = 5$ per-

---

[3] This positive serial correlation may explain why the so-called accelerator models of inventories, such as Lovell's (1961), seem to fit the empirical evidence so well.

[4] This is not to say that the corn futures price for delivery in, say, December 1995 would vary systematically from December 1991 to December 1992 to December 1993. Rather the price for delivery in December 1992 as of December 1991 should be related to the price for delivery in December 1993 as of December 1992, and that one in turn related to the price for delivery in December 1994 as of December 1993.

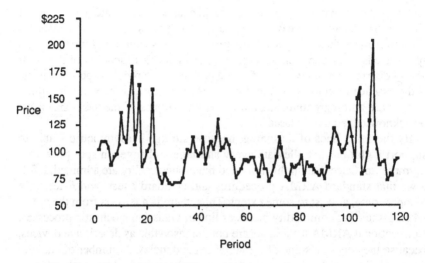

Figure 6.2. A long time series of price.

Table 6.1. *Autocorrelations in the spot price[a]*

| | Lag of | | | |
	1	2	3	4
Price	0.467	0.278	0.187	0.132
Price changes	−0.323	−0.092	−0.034	−0.008

[a]$\eta^s = 0.0$; $k = \$0$.

cent. Because the eye wants to impose order where there is chaos, it often sees patterns when the stochastic process is pure white noise. In Figure 6.2 the patterns are real, however. What is more, the model's spot prices have the two stylized facts: occasional peaks and positive serial correlation. Table 6.1 shows the autocorrelations for the price series and for the corresponding series of price changes.[5] Based on a yet longer series than Figure 6.2 – 10,000 periods to be exact – these numbers are effectively the population parameters. The first-order autocorrelation in price is 0.467, not much different from that seen for sugar. Part and parcel, the spot price in period t is also correlated via storage with price in period $t-2$, $t-3$, and $t-4$, albeit the connection gets ever fainter. These autocorrelations more than one period apart may

5   Often in time-series work, the logs of the series are used, with little justification except the belief the transformation will reduce the importance of inflation or deterministic trends. Because the price series here have no long-run trends by construction, and because the most extreme prices are in the same order of magnitude, the pure price, logs, and percentages behave much the same in any time-series analysis.

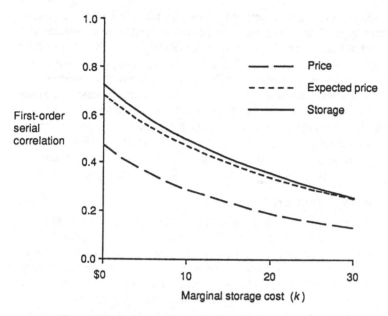

Figure 6.3. Serial correlation induced by lower storage costs.

be consistent with partial autocorrelations of around 0.0, however. It depends on how much nonlinearity in the relationship between the current spot price and the expected price for the next period is induced by storage.

The degree of first-order serial correlation in the spot price is endogenous, ultimately dependent on the potential for storage. The higher are storage costs, the weaker the connection between periods and the lower the proportion of the variance in the spot price that can be explained by the previous spot prices, as can be seen in Figure 6.3.

Serial correlation in revenue and land prices

Both producers' revenue and the price of land are autoregressive time series, like storage, the expected price for the next period, and the spot price. For the same set of parameters as in Figure 6.2, standard univariate techniques applied to the time series for revenue uncover a first-order autoregressive process because the other partial autocorrelations are essentially zero.

$$Revenue_t = \$3,770 + 0.614 Revenue_{t-1} + e_t \qquad (6.1)$$

where e_t is supposedly white noise with a standard deviation of \$1,232.[6] This

---

6   Recall that the parameters are calibrated so that certainty revenue R^N is \$10,000, and that certainty land price with perfectly inelastic supply is \$200,000 when measured just before the next harvest, or \$190,476 just after its precursor, as per Chapter 5.

positive autocorrelation parameter of 0.614 says that close to 40 percent of the variance in producers' current revenue is explained by past revenue. For the same set of parameters, the degree of autocorrelation in the price of land is yet higher, specifically, 0.704.[7] The price of land, being the present value of the stream of expected revenue, reflects directly a storable commodity's expectation of a slow return to the relevant stochastic steady state. In a study of Illinois farmland, Burt (1986) found the price of land to be well described by annual rents from the two previous years. Here rent corresponds to "revenue," and indeed the current price of land, representing revenue from the next period and beyond, has such a relationship to current and previous revenue:

$$Land\ price_t = \$183726 + 1.086 Revenue_t + 0.224 Revenue_{t-1} + u_t \ ,$$

$$u_t = 0.457 u_{t-1} + e_t \tag{6.2}$$

where e_t is (supposedly) white noise with a standard deviation of \$2,808.

The connection between the future revenue embodied in the price of land and previous revenue results from the smoothing of storage. The serial correlation in revenue and, by extension, land price is less the higher are storage costs. The serial correlation is similarly lower for any reason that speeds the expected return to the steady state. One such flexibility comes with supply elasticity. Figure 6.4 plots the degree of first-order serial correlation for several of the endogenous variables as a function of η^s. All are declining functions. Figure 6.4 also serves to emphasize that, although a system with storage is characterized by serial correlation, the degree and order of the serial correlation is a complex function of the underlying parameters.

6.2   Similarity to random walks

A degree of first-order autocorrelation on the order of 0.7 puts an asset like land in a gray zone where the properties of its price are very likely to be misidentified in samples of typical lengths such as 20 or 30 periods. Often the degree of autocorrelation seen in samples of such length may suggest a pure random walk, which has no steady state, even though the series is truly ergodic.

In a "random walk" the (population) autocorrelation coefficient is 1.0. The time series has a unit root. In terms of land prices a random walk would be

$$Land\ price_t = 1.0 Land\ price_{t-1} + e_t \tag{6.3}$$

where e_t is once again white noise, the "shock" to the series. Without "drift," the intercept is necessarily zero. An autoregressive coefficient above 1.0 implies explosive behavior; one below 1.0 mean-reverting behavior, the mean being a nonzero intercept in (6.3).

---

[7]   For the price of land, a first-order autoregressive process also seems the parsimonious description.

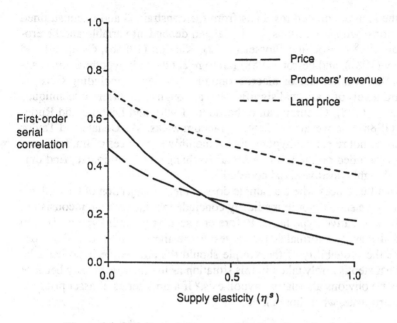

Figure 6.4. Serial correlations as a function of supply elasticity.

The evidence is fairly strong that actual prices of assets such as stocks, bonds, and futures contracts behave much like random walks (martingales, to be more precise), especially when measured daily or weekly. Even at quarterly or annual intervals, commodity prices, exchange rates, GNP, and other macroeconomic variables are highly serially correlated. Whether or not these various series are truly random walks makes a large difference to the fundamental nature of the economy, specifically how it responds to shocks. Should they be random walks, a shock to the system is not damped out eventually; nothing, including the weather, is transitory. A mistaken policy leaves its legacy forever. Normal methods of "smoothing" like storage and saving are not effective, except to the extent that they dampen movements in endogenous variables.

Statistical tests for random walks

In a regression of current land prices on past land prices, a random walk amounts to a specific null hypothesis about the coefficients for the intercept and slope – namely, the intercept is 0.0 and the slope is 1.0. Of course these values are unlikely to hold in a particular finite sample. Nevertheless, one can calculate the probability of getting the coefficients in the sample under that joint hypothesis. The natural test statistic is an F-statistic calculated from the sum of squared residuals from the constrained and unconstrained regressions, with corrections for the lagged dependent variable and hetero-skedasticity.[8] Nelson and Plosser (1982), Kleidon (1986b), Campbell and Mankiw (1987), and Perron (1988) fail to reject the null hypothesis of a random walk for a number of macroeconomic time series, including GNP, at standard levels of statistical significance, although with different techniques Cochrane (1988), Cochrane and Sbordone (1988), and Diebold and Rude-busch (1988) find weaker evidence of random walks. MacDonald and Taylor (1988a) do not reject the hypothesis for monthly spot prices of tin, lead, and zinc, as recorded on the London Metal Exchange. (All, of course, find evidence of highly positive serial correlation.)

As in all instances where a sample does not lead to rejection of the null hypothesis, one should not immediately conclude that the data are inconsistent with the alternative hypothesis. Before one accepts the null hypothesis, one should also apply a formal statistical test to the alternative hypothesis, to determine the probability of the sample should the alternative hypothesis be true. That step is rarely taken in this situation as in others, primarily because there is no obvious alternative hypothesis.[9] If a time series of asset prices is not a martingale, what should it be?

Performance of the tests with land prices

The storage model provides a well grounded alternative hypothesis. Supposing that storage is the force behind the time series, what should be the behavior in a sample of the usual length? More to the point, what is the chance of mistaking the mean-reverting prices of land for a random walk with white noise (i.e., of making a "Type 2 error" in hypothesis testing)? According to panel 1 of Table 6.2, that chance is uncomfortably high, at least for that set of parameters (those used for Figure 6.2). Behind Table 6.2 for each of the sample sizes under the heading "base case" are 1,000 samples of the series produced by the storage model. By construction, therefore, the price of land is not a martingale. Ideally, the procedure with the (adjusted) F-test should have the power to reject the false null hypothesis in all but the most unusual samples. On the contrary, for sample sizes of twenty-five land prices

8   Autoregressive coefficients tend to be biased downward in small samples. As a result the critical values are higher than for conventional F-tests. One must consult the critical values given by Dickey and Fuller (1981). Otherwise, the same principles of statistical inference apply. Phillips (1987) has derived a test statistic for the autoregression coefficient when the error term may be heteroskedastic, as it is in a series involving storage. Related to a conventional t-statistic, it is compared to Table 8.5.2 in Fuller (1976). Also see Campbell and Shiller (1989).

9   In studies of the power of these tests for a unit root, Evans and Savin (1984) and Nankervis and Savin (1985) each have proposed an alternative autoregressive parameter of 0.9, but have not given any justification for such a value.

Table 6.2. *Statistical power against (false) null hypothesis of random walk*[a]

	Number of periods in sample	Revenue			Land price		
		Probability of not rejecting null hypothesis if using as significance level			Probability of not rejecting null hypothesis if using as significance level		
		.10	.05	.01	.10	.05	.01
1. *Base case*		Using adjusted F-stat for both coefficients					
$k = \$0$	25	.692	.835	.946	.711	.817	.929
	50	.198	.345	.688	.313	.496	.766
		Using adjusted t-stat for autoregressive coefficient					
	25	.085	.195	.460	.112	.227	.490
	50	.009	.021	.119	.009	.031	.216
2. *High storage costs*		Using adjusted F-stat for both coefficients					
$k = \$10$	25	.308	.467	.752	.340	.465	.741
	50	.006	.019	.139	.038	.083	.253
		Using adjusted t-stat for autoregressive coefficient					
	25	.008	.032	.141	.030	.057	.178
	50	.000	.000	.003	.001	.005	.024

[a]Based on 1,000 simulations; with $A_0 = 110$, of which 100 units is registered for producers' revenue in that first period.

the chance of not rejecting the null hypothesis at 10 percent "significance" is 71.1 percent. The time series for revenue is also unlikely to behave markedly differently from a random walk. If the more stringent cutoff of 1 percent statistical significance is applied, it is virtually certain that the false null hypothesis of an autoregressive parameter of 1.0 will not be rejected, neither for the land price nor for revenue.[10]

In effect, in samples on the order of twenty-five periods, a time series of prices for land used to produce a storable commodity will rarely be distinguishable from a random walk.[11] With larger samples, say, those fifty periods in length, there probably would be sufficient information to make evident the stationarity of the land prices. Unfortunately, in actual samples spanning

[10] The situation seems somewhat better using Phillips's test solely on the slope coefficient. The estimated residuals were used for his test, and the intercept was let be a free parameter. For the sample size of twenty-five, some 3 percent of the time the test could not be computed because the sample autocorrelations were negative. These instances were classified as failures to reject the null hypothesis.

[11] As Hakkio (1986) has emphasized for foreign exchange, the failure to reject the false null can also be blamed on the low statistical power of the tests. Also see Clark (1988).

fifty years, other issues such as inflation or structural change so muddy the waters that a highly autoregressive yet stationary system cannot be distinguished with confidence from a pure random walk.

Thus, actual time series, such as stock prices and GNP, from systems where storage or similar behavior is important may not be true random walks. That storage is at least one possible source of stationary time series that masquerade as random walks is demonstrated with panel 2 of Table 6.2. With higher storage costs, which reduce the role of storage, a particular sample size will be more likely to support rejection of the hypothesis of a random walk.

Random walks and predictable profits

Lest there be some confusion, a finding that actual land prices, commodity prices, or the S&P 500 stock index for that matter, do not behave as nonstationary random walks does not imply that opportunities exist to profit from predictable price movements. As Danthine (1977) has demonstrated, a random walk for the spot price of a commodity is not a necessary condition for there to be no profit opportunities, contrary to the assertion of Alchian (1974).[12] The land prices in the storage model are rational and offer no opportunity for assured speculation. The predictable movements in land prices touched on in Chapter 5 reflect the predictable movements in revenue, traceable to the smoothing effects of storage. In the context of stock prices, the issue is similar to predictable movements in dividends. No one gets rich (as far as we know) from recognizing that on the day when a stock goes ex dividend its price falls.

6.3   Persistence of booms and busts

A positively autocorrelated series by its nature has high prices tending to follow high prices, a "boom," and low prices following low prices, a "bust." Thus, several years running of good times or of bad times should be commonplace for a storable commodity.

Yet the positive serial correlation has another, perhaps pernicious, effect. It makes it much more difficult to determine whether an apparent boom or bust results from a temporary shock or from a change in the long-run average price. Inferences about the long-run price from small samples are inescapable in many investment and policy settings. "Wait till the sample is big enough"

---

[12] Cox (1976) examined the autoregressive properties of spot prices for several commodities before and after the introduction of futures trading, finding less autoregressive behavior afterward. His subject is substantially different from the issues discussed in this section, which implicitly assumes a fully functioning futures market. It should be stressed in any case that there is no proper degree of autocorrelation in spot prices.

is not helpful advice. For example, MacAvoy (1988, p. xi) relates that, for him and other members of the board of Amax Corporation, "while those of other materials recovered over the 1983–1986 period, the question became that of why metals prices had remained at startlingly low levels for over five years." Their question could be rephrased to ask whether Amax should invest in new mines, which would not come into production for several years. Another example is the U.S. farm bill, which is revised about every four or five years, the U.S. Congress finding itself having to judge whether prices in the intervening years have indicated a shift in the long-run average price. Recently, the Australian Wool Corporation inferred from a few years of very high wool prices that a permanent shift in demand had occurred, and raised its support prices accordingly. As of mid-1990, it appears to be spending its multibillion dollar reserves, not to mention additional lines of credit, on this bet, although the support price has just been lowered somewhat.[13]

These problems with inferences about the long-run price from short samples are obviously closely connected to mistaken inferences about series being random walks. In this section, however, the problems arise from the incorrect assumption of an autoregressive parameter of 0.0, not from an incorrect assumption of a value of 1.0. Also, the issues are not those of statistical inference directly about the autoregressive parameter, but about the biases in other inferences from the hidden presence of positive serial correlation.

Confidence intervals for structural change

A reasonable approach to whether the long-run price has changed over the past five years is from the perspective of confidence intervals. One might imagine statements of the form: "With 99 percent confidence we can say the long-run mean price has shifted down from the previous average; indeed, with 90 percent confidence we can say the long-run price is $10 below the previous long-run mean." These statements would presumably be made after calculating the average price and standard deviation over the five-year period, and constructing the confidence interval from the *t*-statistics in the universal tables. Every elementary statistics book recommends these techniques.

Behind Figure 6.5 are confidence intervals constructed in such a fashion with 50,000 samples of each length drawn from the same long series behind Figure 6.2. The standard of $88 or $112 is one standard deviation from the long-run mean price of $100. Thus, Figure 6.5 tells the chance of concluding

---

[13] These examples are other manifestations of the perennial dispute about the terms of trade between a price index of primary commodities and an index of manufactured goods. (See Cuddington and Urzúa [1989] for a recent paper on this subject.) Because each series itself is highly serially correlated, discerning any relative trends is difficult.

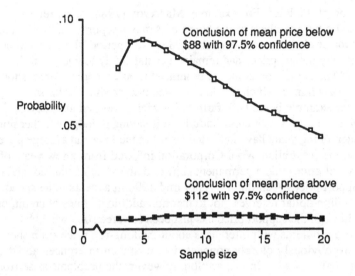

Figure 6.5. Effect of serial correlation on estimates of long-run mean price. (True mean is $100.)

with 95 percent confidence that the mean price is above $112 or below $88. Because the long-run mean price is in fact $100 throughout, this probability should be very, very small if the procedure is performing as expected. The probability, however, is not so very small: There is above a 5 percent chance of falsely concluding that the long-run price is at least $12 from $100, especially that the average price has shifted downward.

The problem with the procedure is not in the notion of confidence intervals, but in the implicit assumption of the conventional t-test that each observation is independent of the others. With a sample of spot prices from a storable commodity, that assumption is not tenable. The positive serial correlation causes the sample standard deviation to be a considerable underestimate of the population variance of the sample mean (see Flavin 1984). As a result the confidence intervals as conventionally constructed are much too small. With positive serial correlation a sample of size 5 has the information of a sample with independent observations of perhaps size 3.

Expected frequency of busts

The effect of the positive serial correlation can be seen in Figure 6.6 in a form more directly relevant to Amax's board. The implicit belief behind the question of how metals prices could be depressed for five years in a row is that in a normal market runs of such length should be very rare, as indeed they are for a nonstorable commodity. Figure 6.6 tests that belief. It asks,

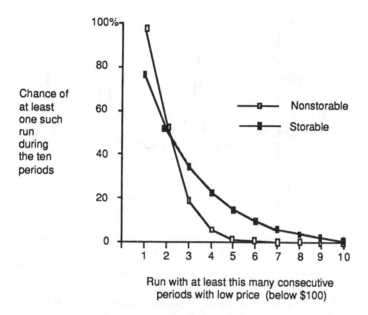

Figure 6.6. Tendency for sustained low prices.

from a starting point in period 0 with a price of $100, the long-run average, what is the chance of a run of prices below $100 of various lengths over the next ten periods? Not surprisingly, the chance of one poor period in the next ten is high; yet the chance for a storable commodity having a depression of five periods' duration is surprisingly high – above 15 percent. Thus, one explanation of the sustained depression in metals prices in the mid-1980s is that such depressions are not very unusual for easily stored commodities.

6.4   Higher-order moments

Besides the feature of autoregression, a time series of spot prices, such as in Figure 6.1 for sugar or Figure 6.2 from the storage model, is notable for the asymmetry of its price changes. Large increases in price from a previous price near the long-run mean, while rare, are more common than large decreases. This pattern arises because storage can cushion a price fall if the harvest is good but can do little if the harvest is bad. Moreover, the cushion on the bottom is more pronounced the lower the price has already gone (because the market demand curve is increasingly elastic). A stretch of the same good harvest causes progressively smaller price declines. The result of all these tendencies is a time series with cusps.

The cusplike pattern in the spot price is more pronounced when the under-

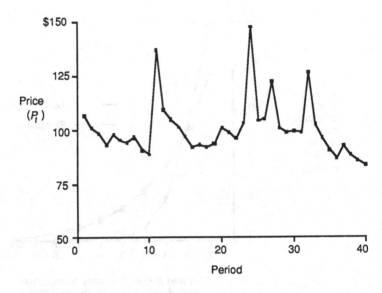

Figure 6.7. Sawtooth pattern in prices (v_t lognormally distributed).

lying uncertainty in the weather is itself asymmetric. Figure 6.7 shows a typical segment of spot prices when the distribution of yields is distributed lognormally (with the long tail toward poor harvests).[14] This asymmetry in yields reinforced by the properties of storage makes for especially long, steadily decreasing decays from high prices and occasional sharp peaks.[15] Nevertheless, these are not true cycles, since they are of random length.[16]

[14]   The variance of the weather is the same as in previous examples in this chapter; the skewness alone is substantially different.

[15]   Such cusplike patterns are of more than idle interest. In the early 1970s the State of California charged the major oil companies with a tacit price-fixing scheme (Coordinated Pretrial Proceedings in Petroleum Products Anti-Trust Litigation, MDL-Docket 150 WP6, U.S. District Court, Central District of California, dismissed on summary judgment in 1986). The State's principal evidence was a series of weekly gasoline prices, which showed a cusplike pattern. The State of California maintained that a cusplike pattern could only have arisen as a cartel first fixed the price and then broke down as its members cheated, the cycle repeating itself as discipline was reimposed. Quite apart from whether the major oil companies had market power in California, such a pattern can occur in a perfectly competitive market where inventories are important.

[16]   If a rule such as "Buy in the fifth period after a surge" is followed, many opportunities profitable in retrospect are lost, and many times there will be a long wait, possibly twenty or thirty periods, until the next surge while paying interest and warehousing fees. The difficulty in "market timing" should come as no surprise, however. Figure 6.7 has by construction no abnormal opportunities for profiting from storage.

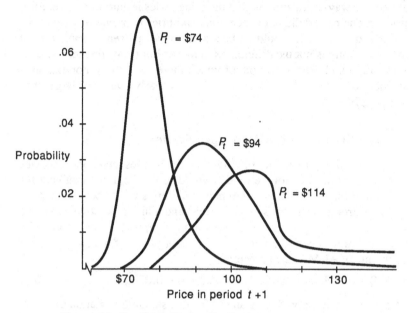

Figure 6.8. Conditional price distributions.

Conditional price distributions

The cusplike (or peaklike) behavior in spot prices is a manifestation of the higher moments of the distribution of price being conditional on the current circumstances.[17] Figure 6.8 plots, for a time series with normally distributed weather such as Figure 6.2, the distributions in price for period $t+1$ that will occur when price in period t is one of three levels. The first level, $P_t = \$74$, is one of the lower prices seen in the time series in Figure 6.2. Along with that P_t the carryover is substantial and the chance of a very high price the next period is low. When $P_t = \$94$ the carryover is much closer to average; the chance of a very high price the next period is larger. At the third level, $P_t = \$114$, the carryover is zero. There is little cushion in either direction, especially against an extremely high price. (Because from $P_t = \$113$ and higher the carryover would be zero, the distribution for P_{t+1} would be the same regardless of P_t over that range.)

The most obvious difference among these three distributions for P_{t+1} is their means, which for $P_t = \$74$ or $\$94$ is $(1+r)P_t$. The difference in means

[17] Studies of the conditional variances of commodity prices, such as by Anderson (1985) and Kenyon et al. (1987), concentrate on price movements over a horizon of at most a month. Thus, it is difficult to know whether the model replicates the conditional variances of actual series measured annually.

is yet another way of illustrating that the price series is autoregressive, for if the price in one period did not depend on conditions in previous periods, the conditional distributions would all be the same. For present purposes, what is most interesting is not the differences in means but the differences in standard deviation and skewness, both of which increase with P_t. For example, the standard deviation of P_{t+1} when $P_t = \$114$ is nearly five times larger than when $P_t = \$74$.[18]

6.5   Applicability of ARMA specifications

To a naive practitioner of univariate time-series techniques, a series of spot prices from the storage model would look like a good subject for those techniques. Without any differencing the series would be stationary. It would have strong autoregressive properties, and a hint of a moving average component. For example, with as parsimonious a representation as possible, standard techniques would uncover, for the spot prices of which Figure 6.2 is a segment, an ARMA (2,1) process:

$$P_t - 0.503P_{t-1} - 0.042P_{t-2} = 45.5 + e_t - 0.073e_{t-1} \qquad (6.4)$$

where e_t is white noise, with a mean of $\$0$ and a standard deviation of $\$20.5$. By the general properties of storage, actual series of spot prices could be described well by ARMA techniques.

Nevertheless, such a description of spot prices as an ARMA stochastic process is misleading or outright wrong, for several reasons. For one, e_t is neither homoskedastic nor normally distributed.[19] Although recent advances in time-series techniques have recognized the inherent heteroskedasticity in price series (e.g., Baillie et al. 1983; Bollerslev 1986; Engle et al. 1987), these so-called autoregressive conditional heteroskedasticity (ARCH) models do not capture the theoretical relationship between variance and price level. Generally speaking, ARCH models portray either the variance or standard deviation as a linear function of price. Figure 6.9, which implicitly includes the information about conditional variance from Figure 6.8, shows that the standard deviation of P_{t+1} is in fact a highly nonlinear function of P_t. The big break in the relationship occurs at the P_t corresponding to $S_t = 0$, for the uncertainty in next period's price is ultimately conditional on the carryover.

Were the ARMA representation kept solely as a descriptive device, there would be fewer problems. Not surprisingly, however, it is used to forecast the next spot prices. Although it performs reasonably well while forecasting, it is inferior to the true rational forecast, which is the futures price in the mod-

---

[18] This ratio would be reduced somewhat if natural logs or percentage changes were used.

[19] ARMA techniques, involving maximum likelihood estimation, require specific assumptions about the shape of the probability distribution of the white noise (see Brockwell and Davis 1987).

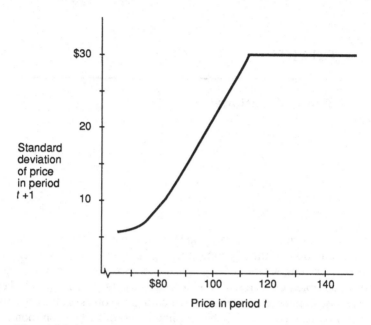

Figure 6.9. Standard deviation in next period's price as a function of current price.

el. The relative success of an ARMA representation also suggests that the spot price evolves on its own, when in fact the time series of the spot price is a creation of the storage rule. That storage rule is the fundamental economic relationship in the system, while the true stochastic process is the white noise of the weather. Description of the system as an ARMA process also misleads by suggesting the current endogenous variables are functions of several past periods. Actually a single variable, current availability, summarizes the past. Finally, the ARMA perspective suggests that the spot price can be controlled by public intervention, whereas a public intervention would change the ARMA properties of the spot price, not to mention that the observed ARMA process in (6.4) is the result of socially optimal storage.

CHAPTER 7

Tests of rationality

A great advantage of the storage model is its capacity to generate under controlled conditions infinitely long time series or infinitely many short time series. In a setting where underlying parameters and behavioral relations are known, accepted empirical techniques can be judged by how well they uncover those parameters and distinguish among hypotheses about agents' behavior. For example, it would be disquieting if ordinarily a common empirical technique for supply estimation assesses incorrectly the supply elasticity from data created by the storage model. By this standard, four basic empirical procedures are shown to be highly suspect:

1. tests of the forecasting ability of futures prices;
2. tests of bias in futures prices;
3. tests of excessive variability in the prices of assets like land; and
4. cobweb and adaptive expectations models of supply estimation.

Each of these procedures is inspected in a separate section in this chapter.

A common theme of these four empirical procedures is their implicit or explicit test of rationality. For example, if futures prices are biased, they are irrational forecasts; if supply follows cobweb behavior, it is irrational. Here we are testing the conventional tests themselves, not the rationality of futures prices or supply responsiveness in our data. Because the data are generated by stochastic simulation of our storage model, they are rational by construction. Because empirical results of these four tests have been used to question the hypothesis of rational expectations, this chapter, by calling the tests themselves into question, lends support to the assumption of rationality in the storage model.

7.1 Tests of forecasting ability

The eventual return to the steady state and, indeed, the concept of the steady state concern expectations. The spot price actually realized in particular

174

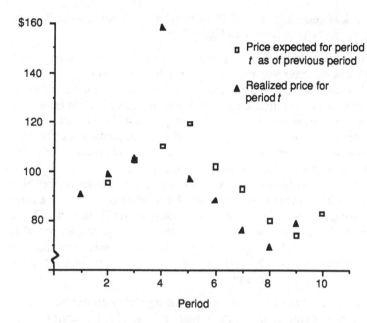

Figure 7.1. Realized spot price compared to expected price.

periods will almost surely be different from the expected price due to the random component to the harvest. Figure 7.1 gives some idea of the discrepancy between expectations and realizations.[1] It plots for nine periods the spot price in period t and the price that was expected for period t as of period $t-1$. This expected price can be compared to the realized spot price in period t. It often misses its target. Although the prediction for period 3 is close, the prediction for period 4 is considerably low, and those for periods 5–8 are all above the realized price. One could put a better light on this performance by noting that the spot series in Figure 7.1 is more variable than the series for expected price. Even though the series for the price expected in period t moves in response to past shocks to the harvest, its response is more muted than the spot price because it is anticipating a return to the steady state and it does not take the shock to the current harvest into account.[2]

In Figure 7.1 the expected prices are futures prices for delivery the next harvest. Thus, it also suggests that actual futures prices should not predict subsequent spot prices especially accurately.

Forecasting ability is a general concern raised about futures markets, at least from the time of Dow (1941). What various authors mean by forecast-

[1] Figure 7.1 has behind it the same parameters as behind Figure 6.2, namely $\eta^d = -0.2$, $C = 0$, $\eta^s = 0.0$, $\sigma_h = 10$ units, $r = 5$ percent, and $k = \$0$.
[2] The usual positive autocorrelation is clearly visible in both series, too.

ing ability is less general, however. Three broad areas of concern can be identified, and all can be illustrated with Figure 7.1:

1. How close do the futures prices come to the realized spot prices? This perspective was used in the preceding discussion.
2. How well do futures prices, in conjunction with the contemporaneous spot price, anticipate the change in the spot price? In Figure 7.1 the price expected for period 5 as of period 4, for example, is considerably below the spot price in period 4; the prediction is for a decline in price, which is what happens. Thus, this second definition compares the basis to the change in the spot price.[3]
3. How well do futures prices perform relative to other conceivable forecasting techniques? In Figure 7.1 another contender as a forecasting technique is the previous spot price itself. In period 7, for example, the spot price is lower than the price expected for period 8; because the realized spot price in period 8 is lower even than the spot price in period 7, at least in that instance the previous spot price outperforms the futures price.

These three approaches to measuring forecasting ability do not necessarily admit the same conclusion about the futures prices. That is, futures prices judged to have forecasting power in terms of the first definition may appear to perform poorly for the second or third.

Absolute ability to forecast spot prices

The first commonly employed test of forecasting ability relies on the R^2 in a regression of the realized spot price on the futures price:

$$P_t = \alpha + \beta F_{t,t-1} + e_t, \qquad t = 1,...,N \qquad (7.1)$$

where N is the number of observations and e_t is an error term. The estimated coefficients from this regression are also used to infer bias, as will be discussed in Section 7.2; but as far as forecasting ability is concerned, the R^2 is what matters. The higher the R^2, the more the futures prices "explain" the spot prices, and the lower are the proportional forecast errors.

Having inspected a number of regressions of this type, Stein (1981, p. 227) concludes (perhaps too strongly) that for futures prices "more than four months to delivery, the R^2 of the regression is negligible. Consequently, the

---

3   The "basis" is a synonym for the carrying charge observed between the spot price and some (usually the nearest) futures price. In many commodity markets, merchants do not haggle directly over the price of a particular lot of the commodity available for immediate delivery. Rather, they bargain over the price difference from some reference price, usually the nearest actively traded futures contract, and so their quotations are "based" on that futures price, and the "basis" is the price difference.

forward price at 'planting' time is a biased and worthless predictor of the price at the 'harvest'." Stein, however, does not consider how high the R^2 could be under the best of circumstances. It should not ordinarily be expected to be anywhere near 1.0, the maximum statistical value.

By construction in the storage model, the futures price for delivery the next period is the best possible estimate of the price at the next harvest. Nevertheless, for reasonable combinations of parameters in our model, the highest R^2 in regression (7.1) is merely .30, and it can be as low as .10. Were the test applied to the model's futures prices for two periods ahead, the highest attainable R^2 would be even lower.[4] Compared to these R^2's attainable by the best possible futures prices, the forecasting performance of actual futures prices does not look so bad. Prediction of subsequent spot prices is inherently difficult.

Indirectly, this evidence acknowledges that the degree of predictability depends on the system involved – the specific demand and supply parameters, storage costs, and so on. Figures 7.2(a) and 7.3(a) drive home that message, by relating the R^2 in regression (7.1) (with 10,000 observations) to the marginal physical storage cost and the supply elasticity. According to Figure 7.2(a), the lower are the marginal physical storage costs, the higher is the forecasting ability of the futures price. If the commodity could not be stored, the R^2 would be zero in this situation. Storage disperses excess availability in period t into period $t+1$, reducing the deviation from the long-run average of price in period t but increasing it in period $t+1$. It is this storage-induced component of P_{t+1} that is "explained" by the futures price, and consequently the lower the cost of storage, the higher the proportion of the variance explained.[5]

Also in Figure 7.2(a), the lower are physical storage costs, the better is the current spot price at predicting the subsequent spot price. Of course, with low storage costs, spreads between the spot price and nearby futures price are most often at full carrying charges. Consequently, as Tomek and Gray (1970, p. 373) emphasize, "[t]he element of expectations is imparted to the whole temporal constellation of price quotations, and futures prices reflect essentially no prophecy that is not reflected in the cash [i.e., current spot] price and is in that sense already fulfilled."

According to Figure 7.3(a), the higher is the supply elasticity, the lower is the attainable R^2. This relationship may be surprising. More elastic supply, by helping to absorb the shocks from good or bad weather up to planting times,

---

4 The model also abstracts from complications like unexpected inflation or unexpected changes in the real interest rate, complications that would also reduce the attainable R^2.

5 It is also worth emphasizing that the lower are the physical storage costs, the lower is the variance of the spot price to be explained. The variance of the spot price is endogenous.

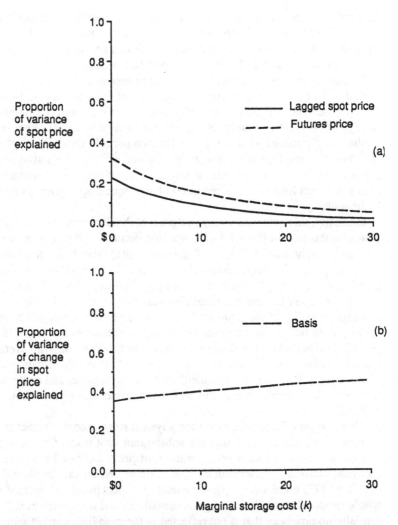

Figure 7.2. Forecasting capabilities as a function of storability.

reduces the predictable moves back to the stochastic steady state. Thus elastic supply, by facilitating adjustment to previous shocks, reduces that component of the variance of the spot price that could be explained by information in period $t-1$. While this effect diminishes the variance (of the spot price) to be explained, it also diminishes the proportion explained by the futures price.

The lessons from Figures 7.2(a) and 7.3(a) can be put together to call into question whether a higher R^2 in regression (7.1) even indicates greater rationality, the presumption behind the whole formulation of the test. Consider

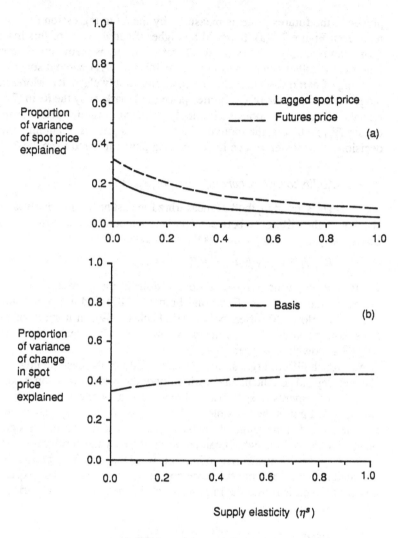

Figure 7.3. Forecasting capabilities as a function of supply elasticity.

a case where producers are irrational. Although they could adjust their planting intensity period to period (the true one-period-lagged η^s is, say, 1.0), they persist in forecasting the next price as equal to the long-run average (the effective one-period-lagged η^s is 0.0). Private storers, meanwhile, are rational, including an understanding of the effective supply elasticity.[6] The forecasting

---

[6] Peck (1976) presents (along with a fully rational model) such a hybrid model, with rational expectations for speculators and adaptive expectations for producers.

power of the futures price as measured by the R^2 in regression (7.1) can be read from Figure 7.3(a). It would be higher if supply were of this irrational form than if supply were rational. Therefore, it seems premature to interpret empirical results from regressions of the form of (7.1) without some understanding of parameters like storage costs and supply elasticity. Moreover, to judge the social value of the futures price (and market) by the R^2 in (7.1) is a mistake. The more responsive is supply to that very futures price (or its first cousin P_{t+1}^r) – that is, the more useful the futures price is in guiding planting decisions – the lower will be its forecasting power inferred from the R^2.

Ability to forecast changes in spot prices

The second method of measuring forecasting ability involves the basis, that is, the difference between contemporaneous spot and futures prices. Specifically, forecasting ability is the R^2 in the regression:

$$P_t - P_{t-1} = \alpha + \beta(F_{t,t-1} - P_{t-1}) + e_t, \qquad t = 1, ..., N \qquad (7.2)$$

where N is again the number of observations in the regression. For futures prices ten months ahead, Fama and French (1987) find in twenty-one markets R^2's below .20, often below .05. Peck (1989), in a study of grains, livestock, and silver finds comparably low R^2's.[7] The interpretation of these low R^2's, however, is open.

As French (1986) argues, the inherent ability of the basis to predict price changes depends on the natural variability of the basis of that commodity relative to movements in spot prices. French's argument can be understood in two stages. First is the possible explanatory power for any particular basis and the second is the range of the basis observed. The current basis depends on current conditions, which can be represented by the current price P_t. The basis would be the mean change in price, were the shift from period t to $t + 1$ repeated many times from the same conditions in period t. The explanatory power of the basis is thus the importance of the mean in the total variability of P_{t+1} relative to P_t. Precisely, it is

$$R^2 | P_t = \frac{(Basis | P_t)^2}{(Basis | P_t)^2 + Variance\ of\ P_{t+1} | P_t} \qquad (7.3)$$

Figure 7.4 plots this measure of forecast potential for a range of P_t, using the relationship between P_t and the variance of P_{t+1} presented previously in Figure 6.9. If by chance P_t is very high, the explanatory power of the basis is very high, despite the large variance of P_{t+1}, because the basis is so negative. At the other side of Figure 7.4, the basis is small (5% of P_t with $k = \$0$ and

---

[7]   A related study is that of copper prices by Bresnahan and Suslow (1985). While making allowance for instances of backwardation (a negative basis), they estimate what is effectively the basis regression (7.2). They too find a low R^2.

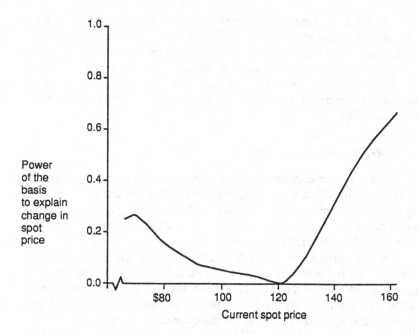

Figure 7.4. Forecasting power of the basis as a function of current conditions.

$r = 5\%$), but the large carryout keeps the variance of P_{t+1} small too. When the basis is $0, that is, when P_t equals $119.72, it cannot possibly explain any of the change from P_t to P_{t+1}.

The R^2 in regression (7.2) is the weighted average of the R^2's from equation (7.3), weighted by the frequency of particular spot prices. If very high or low spot prices are rare, regression (7.2) perforce has a low R^2. Thus, if the spot price and the basis are not especially variable, the forecast power of the basis cannot be very high. Of course, the more easily stored is the commodity, the more stable are its prices and its basis.

Storage removes most predictable price changes by transferring them to existing conditions, as argued by Working (1942) and Peck (1989). Hence, the R^2 in a regression like (7.2) should be higher the higher is the marginal storage cost, the relationship seen in Figure 7.2(b), for the same reason the R^2 in a regression like (7.1) should be lower. Yet the relatively high R^2 in (7.2) that comes with high storage costs, higher than any R^2 seen for actual futures markets, should not be taken as evidence of better or more rational futures prices. In the storage model that generated Figures 7.2(b) and 7.3(b), all the futures prices were the best rational forecasts regardless of k or η^s. Yet the forecasting power of the basis differs.

In short, the R^2 in a regression like (7.2) cannot indicate whether a futures market is performing well. That the basis in the array of silver prices poorly predicts price changes does not convict the futures market for having no allocative significance for silver. Rather the reverse is true. Responses to futures prices by producers and storers eliminate most of the predictable potential variation in silver prices, leaving a residual of variation largely unrelated to previous conditions.

Relative forecasting ability

This section concludes with skepticism about tests of the relative forecasting ability of futures prices in the genre of Rausser and Carter (1983). They compare the ability of the futures markets in the soybean complex to forecast the four harvest prices over 1977–80 with the forecasting ability of simple ARMA models fitted to monthly data over 1966–76. On the basis of the root-mean-squared error of the forecasts, these "models 'outperform' the futures markets for soybeans and soybean meal but not soybean oil for both long- and short-run horizons" (p. 477). From this conclusion comes the corollary that the futures markets are inefficient in processing information. Similarly, Epps and Kukanza (1985) study the informational efficiency of grain markets, and Bopp and Sitzer (1988) the informational efficiency of the fuel oil futures market. Bopp and Sitzer (1987) also compare futures prices for heating oil to the forecasts from the Energy Information Administration's model, Ma (1989) compares futures prices for crude oil, fuel oil, and gasoline to forecasts from various ARMA models, and Just and Rausser (1981) compare the forecasting ability of futures prices and the large-scale econometric models such as those of Data Resources, Inc. and Wharton Econometric Forecasting Associates.

One point to note about these comparisons of forecasting ability is that, for storable commodities, futures prices are by their very nature related to the spot price quoted concurrently. This is a point made nearly fifty years ago by Working (1942), who argued that spot and nearby futures prices react to news about distant harvests because all prices are connected by the amount and cost of storage. Because the current spot price contains much of the information about the next spot price incorporated in the futures price, models using ARMA techniques with spot prices should acquit themselves nearly as well as futures prices. To put the matter slightly differently, in comparisons like Rausser's and Carter's, the futures price is being compared to something closely related to itself. It should not be expected to outperform itself by a very great margin, and certainly not every time.

The potential of any forecasting method is bounded by the knowledge about the future contained in the current information set. If such information is sparse, blind guesses will have a good chance of performing better than the

Table 7.1. *Relative performance forecasting spot prices*[a]

	Chance of root-mean-square error lower than that using futures prices, for this forecasting technique:		
	AR model	"Structural" model	Long-run average price
Model fitted to sample of 20			
Forecasts:1	42.3%	39.2%	37.7%
4	39.2	31.5	33.8
8	31.6	25.7	24.0
Model fitted to sample of 40			
Forecasts:1	44.2	42.2	37.7
4	42.7	37.5	33.8
8	35.8	33.2	24.0

[a]Based on 10,000 trials for each sample size.

best-constructed forecast, whatever it is. In such circumstances it would be hardly surprising that relatively sophisticated methods such as ARMA models outperform the best possible forecasting method. For this reason the comparisons made by Rausser and Carter and the others require an outside standard, such as the storage model provides. By construction its futures prices are the best possible forecasts, and it can provide sufficient repetitions to quantify forecasting ability. In Table 7.1 the forecasting ability of the model's futures prices is compared to those of three other forecasting techniques, all aimed at forecasting future spot prices. Forecasting ability is measured by the root-mean-squared error:

$$RMSE = \sqrt{\frac{\sum_{i=T+1}^{T+N}\left(P_i - Forecast_i\right)^2}{N}} \qquad (7.4)$$

where N is the number of forecasts and T the last observation used to fit the forecasting equation.

One of the three techniques is simply to guess the long-run average price, which with the set of parameters behind Table 7.1 is $100. That is, the forecast is always $100, whereas the futures price, for delivery the next period, changes period to period. The second is an AR model fitted to two lags of spot prices.[8] The third is a so-called structural model, the idea being to take

---

[8] For each sample among the 10,000 trials, the apparently "best" ARMA structure was not selected. Rather an ARMA (2,0) structure was always fit.

account of the other variables in the system. (It is not a true structural model, but follows Rausser and Carter.) As one example of this approach, the econometric equation fitted has, in addition to the two lags of the spot price, two lags of the amount in store. Lags of the amount in store are not true exogenous variables; rather they are simply predetermined variables. Nevertheless, they may contain some information about future spot prices not found in linear functions of current and past spot prices. The AR and "structural" econometric models are fitted to time series of twenty or forty observations. That is, for each of the 10,000 trials, say, twenty periods of the storage model are simulated with draws from the probability distribution of the weather, and the econometric model fit to those data. The resulting estimated coefficients, and the relevant values for the right-hand-side variables, are used to forecast the spot prices over as many as the next eight periods.[9] With coefficients estimated over a longer sample, the forecasts should improve. That pattern is present in Table 7.1. Also, making eight forecasts should be more challenging than one forecast. That pattern is also present in Table 7.1, as each of the three contestants has a better chance of beating the futures prices if only one forecast is involved than when eight are required. None of the three contestants would have more than a miniscule chance of outperforming the futures prices if 1,000 forecasts were the standard.

The main point of Table 7.1 is found in the entry for eight forecasts by the long-run average price. There is a 24 percent chance that the simplistic forecasting technique of the long-run average price will outperform the superior futures prices. Predicting the next spot price is intrinsically difficult.[10] For four forecasts, the chance of the futures prices appearing to be less efficient forecasts than a steady price of $100 is 33.8 percent. These percentages, 24 and 33.8 percent, are the standards against which the forecasting ability of ARMA and structural models should be judged. The AR model, fitted to twenty observations, has a 39.2 percent chance of topping the futures prices over four forecasts. That performance would look impressive if the uninformed guess of $100 were beaten all but, say, 1 percent of the time. When that guess beats the futures price 33.8 percent of the time, the AR model looks much less impressive.

This observation can be recast in the terminology of hypothesis testing.

9   The forecasts go only one period ahead. That is, the realized spot price in period 21 is used in making the forecast of price in period 22, and so forth. The estimated coefficients, however, continue to be those based on the first 20 observations. Rausser and Carter use the forecast of price in period 21 to make the forecast of price in period 22. Their technique would indicate forecasting ability some place between those in the "AR" and "Long-run average price" columns of Table 7.1. Their approach makes some sense with an exogenous variable evolving with its own time-series structure. Here the nominal right-hand-side variables are not exogenous.

10   This is another manifestation of the low R^2's in the regression (7.1) of spot prices on futures prices.

Rausser and Carter find that an ARMA model has a lower root-mean-squared error than futures prices for four soybean harvests. They accept that as strong evidence of the inefficiency of futures prices, which is to say they reject the null hypothesis of informational efficiency in futures prices. This might be consistent with common standards of statistical inference if the probability of obtaining their result under the null hypothesis were small, say, 5 percent or 1 percent. Table 7.1 suggests that the probability of a "Type I" error is much higher, on the order of 30 or 40 percent. To reduce the chance of a Type I error to 5 percent, they would need to compare forecast performance over, say, sixteen or twenty harvests. Of course, the percentages in Table 7.1 depend on the particular parameters used in the storage model. But that admission only emphasizes the need for an explicit model under the null hypothesis of rational futures prices. The obvious candidate is the basic storage model.

7.2   Tests of bias in futures prices

A large literature revolves around testing whether futures prices are biased predictors of the subsequent spot prices. Apart from all the articles concerned with foreign exchange or financial instruments, the list includes Tomek and Gray (1970), Kofi (1973), Leuthold (1974), Goss (1981, 1983), Bigman et al. (1983), Rajaraman (1986), and Canarella and Pollard (1986), and covers nearly all of the important storable commodities.

The idea behind all this empirical work is simple. The realized spot price is just the futures price for that delivery observed at some earlier date plus an error term:

$$P_t = \alpha + \beta F_{t,t-1} + e_t \tag{7.5}$$

If futures prices are unbiased predictors of subsequent spot prices, α should equal 0.0 and β should equal 1.0. This null hypothesis can be tested against the estimated coefficients in the sample at hand using an F-statistic.[11] Typically, applications of these regressions involve ten or fifteen observations if taken once per cropyear or fifty or sixty observations if each of the five or six contracts per cropyear is involved.[12] The usual finding has been for $\hat{\alpha} > 0$ and $\hat{\beta} < 1.0$, although both are not far from their values under the null hypothesis of unbiased futures prices. That is, a $\hat{\beta}$ of 0.90 is not uncommon and, depending principally on the sample size, $\hat{\beta}$ is often judged to be "statistically" significantly less than 1.0.

[11]   As emphasized by Martin and Garcia (1981), the null hypothesis requires a joint test of the two coefficients, although a number of articles in this literature test them sequentially with separate t-tests.

[12]   Kahl and Tomek (1986) rightly criticize those regressions with overlapping contracts and observations. If the time span for each observation overlaps to any extent, the error terms are not independent. Canarella and Pollard (1986) have made a correction for this problem in their study of metals on the London Metal Exchange.

Statistical problems

The time-series properties of prices influenced by storage should give several reasons for pause before application of conventional statistical tests to equation (7.5), however. Most obvious is the problem of heteroskedasticity, which reflects the different variances of the price distribution at different levels of price.[13] Heteroskedasticity usually biases downward the standard errors of coefficients estimated by ordinary least squares. This bias in turn biases the conventional test statistics upward toward rejection of the null hypothesis. From the storage model, the distribution of price and by extension the distribution of e_t are also known to be skewed. Hence e_t is not normally distributed even when the underlying randomness in the weather is normally distributed and when a correction is made for heteroskedasticity. Conventional F- and t-tests are strictly accurate only under normality.

Most important is the problem arising from a connection between the error term e_t and subsequent values for the futures price, the right-hand-side variable. For $\hat{\beta}$ under ordinary least squares to be an unbiased estimate of β, $E[Right\text{-}hand\text{-}side\ variable_t,\ e_{t+j}]$ must equal zero for all j. The correlation, in expectation, for $j = 0$ is zero as required, but for $j = -1$ the correlation is positive. $\hat{\beta}$ should be biased downward. (OLS is consistent in such circumstances, however; the bias disappears in sufficiently large samples.)[14] Consider what happens when a harvest is unexpectedly large. The spot price is low and, more to the point, is lower than the futures price, as of the previous period, for delivery at that date: e_t is negative. The equilibrium with that large harvest also features a low futures price as of period t, for delivery in period $t + 1$. That futures price is the value for the right-hand-side variable for the next observation in regression (7.5). Thus, the right-hand-side variable is related to previous error, contrary to the conditions appropriate for ordinary least squares. The statistical problem is much like that of a lagged dependent variable, where even if the error term is not serially correlated, slope coefficients estimated from small samples will be biased toward zero.[15] On statis-

---

13 Emphasizing the possibility of changing structure, Gregory and McCurdy (1984) have demonstrated the presence of heteroskedasticity in tests of the bias in the 30-day Canadian $ / U.S. $ forward premium.

14 Maberly (1985) was the first to suspect a bias in the conventional procedures, based on some simulations, but he misdiagnosed the source of the bias as being due to censoring. James and Perelman (1986) and Elam and Dixon (1988) have recognized this problem with the literature on bias and efficiency of futures prices as one of serial correlation in the right-hand-side variable. They discuss the problem in the context of spot prices that follow a random walk, however. Here, although spot prices do not follow a random walk, the error term in the regression is related to futures prices for subsequent delivery dates, because of the nature of storage.

15 Goss (1981, 1983), in his study of prices on the London Metal Exchange, uses an instrumental variables estimator instead of ordinary least squares. But this is to allow for

tical grounds, therefore, for a storable commodity some bias should be expected in the conventional procedure.[16] The interaction of this possible bias with the problems of heteroskedasticity and skewness makes the whole econometric exercise even more problematic. It is far from obvious whether the nominal F-statistic is distributed at all like the one in the standard table.

With the help of the storage model, the true F-distribution can be found through "Monte Carlo" techniques. The issue is not whether the F-statistic, as a function of differences in sum of squared residuals, is calculated correctly, since the calculations are straightforward. Rather the issue is the probability distribution of that test statistic. For a specific set of parameters,[17] simulation of the model can produce any number of time series of a desired length. (Figure 7.1, seen previously, is one such series.) To each time series the regression equation (7.5) is applied, and the F-statistic calculated. With many repetitions the "empirical" probability distribution of that F-statistic emerges. If the error e_t were in fact homoskedastic, normally distributed, and unrelated to the right-hand-side variable, the distribution tabulated in every statistics book would unfold. That is not what happens.

Rather than displaying the entire empirical distribution, the top of Table 7.2 shows the probability of seeing an F-statistic greater than some critical value. These critical values correspond, for the three sample sizes of 22, 42, and 62, with the values representing .10, .05, and .01 probability in the tail of the standard F-distribution. For example, with a sample of 22 and desired significance of 10 percent, the F-tables give a critical value of 2.59. If the F-statistic resulting from a regression were greater than 2.59, the analyst would reject the null hypothesis of no bias. If the degree of statistical significance is as supposed, the entries in the first three columns of Table 7.2 should, regardless of the row, be close to .10, .05, and .01. Likewise, the average F-statistic should equal the number of observations divided by the number of observations minus 2, or essentially 1.0. On the contrary, all the entries are far larger than their supposed probabilities and the averages are far above 1.0.

In short, large F-statistics are more common than assumed in the literature and in conventional hypothesis tests. Note especially the third entry for a sample size of 22. An F-statistic thought to occur by chance under the null hypothesis only 1 percent of the time in fact occurs 11.4 percent of the time.

possible serial correlation in e_t, not for the relationship between the error term and subsequent values for the right-hand-side variable.

[16] As Gray and Tomek (1971) have argued, the test based on (5.5) for a nonstorable commodity should not in any case be expected to have $\alpha = 0$ and $\beta = 1$.

[17] Specifically, $\eta^d = -0.2$, $C = 0$, $\eta^s = 0.0$, $k = \$0$, $r = 5$ percent, and $v \sim N(0.0, 10.0^2)$. This is the same set used in Section 7.1. To avoid any effects from an initial condition, the model is simulated seven periods before the sample used in the regression is recorded.

Table 7.2. *Tendency for false conclusion of bias in futures price*[a]

	Sample size		
	22	42	62
Probability of F-statistic greater than standard table's critical value with significance of:			
10%	.254	.184	.168
5%	.201	.139	.121
1%	.114	.081	.064
Mean F-statistic	2.14	1.68	1.50
Mean $\hat{\alpha}$	17.3	8.7	6.0
Mean $\hat{\beta}$	0.825	0.914	0.941
Mean R^2	.27	.30	.31

[a]Based on 10,000 trials for each sample size.

Although this tendency for large F-statistics is less pronounced with a larger sample size, it is still substantial. With a sample of 62, an F-statistic that would be represented as having a "significance level" of 1 percent has in fact a significance level of 6.4 percent.

Table 7.2 also gives the average $\hat{\alpha}$ and $\hat{\beta}$. In a sample infinitely long, these values would be 0.0 and 1.0. As is evident from Table 7.2, even for sample sizes large by conventional standards, the estimated coefficients are biased, with the direction of bias, $\hat{\alpha} > 0.0$ while $\hat{\beta} < 1.0$, conforming to the results found in the empirical literature. As a result, evidence for rejection of the null hypothesis of no bias in futures prices may be much weaker than represented in the literature.

Related tests of bias

A variant of this test for bias in futures prices has recently emerged, mainly in tests of the prices on the London Metal Exchange (Hsieh and Kulatilaka 1982; Canarella and Pollard 1986; MacDonald and Taylor 1988b).[18] This approach focuses on the forecast error, namely the difference between the futures price and the realized spot price, and posits that it should be unrelated to information known at the time of the forecast. Otherwise, the forecast could have been improved upon. One piece of information known at the time of the forecast is the previous forecast error, or

$$(P_t - F_{t,t-1}) = \alpha + \beta(P_{t-1} - F_{t-1,t-2}) + e_t \qquad (7.6)$$

[18]   A related article in the foreign exchange literature is by Wolff (1987).

Table 7.3. *Tendency for false conclusion of systematic forecast errors[a]*

	Sample size		
	22	42	62
Probability of F-statistic greater than standard table's critical value with significance of:			
10%	.171	.188	.190
5%	.102	.122	.123
1%	.024	.044	.047
Mean F-statistic	1.44	1.46	1.49
Mean $\hat{\alpha}$	0.308	0.198	0.149
Mean $\hat{\beta}$	−0.073	−0.042	−0.031
Mean R^2	.055	.034	.026

[a]Based on 10,000 trials for each sample size.

Under the hypothesis of rationality, α and β are both zero. In actual tests, the tendency has been to find current forecast errors to be weakly related to previous forecast errors.

Again, however, the statistical setting matters. Equation (7.6) is clearly an instance of a lagged dependent variable, and in small samples the test can be presumed to be biased. James (1988) has also shown that the test's bias should increase with the skewness of the error distribution. Again the storage model, where $\alpha = 0$ and $\beta = 0$ by construction, can generate many samples of the requisite length. The salient results of that Monte Carlo experiment are shown in Table 7.3. Once again the test procedure itself is exposed as suspect. The estimated $\hat{\beta}$ tends to be different from zero, with the bias being more pronounced the smaller the sample size. Thus, in small samples, forecast errors appear to be negatively related to the previous forecast error. As with the test of the spot price level on the futures price, large F-statistics are more common than supposed. Here, too, any evidence against the hypothesis of rational expectations is overstated.[19]

---

[19] Raynauld and Tessier (1984) extend the basic test in regression (7.6) to investigate whether any variables known at the time of the forecast are systematically related to the forecast error. Among possible contributors to time-varying bias for wheat and corn, they find stocks to be related to the prediction error in the futures price. But stocks are another series known to be autoregressive and related to previous forecast errors. This evidence of time-varying risk premia must also be acknowledged as weaker than represented.

7.3   Tests of excessive variability in asset prices

Another test of rationality concerns the variance of prices and not just their possible bias. These tests could be applied to futures prices, but more naturally they involve the price of land, which often seems too variable for the realized sequence of revenue over several periods.[20] That is, the price of land can appear irrationally variable. Indeed, the boom in agricultural exports in the late 1970s induced a heady appreciation in land prices. By the mid-1980s distress sales abounded because of the decline in the prices of the major crops. More recently, land prices have revived along with prices for farm products. The impression of an excessive speculation followed by an excessive contraction is at least plausible. After the fact, those farmers who had bought at the peak certainly regretted their decision, just as did those who sold at what became the trough. Yet it does not follow automatically that land prices at either the peak or the trough were irrational.

The speed with which a system with storage is expected to return to the steady state from a particular initial condition has much to do with the variability in the price of land. The slower is the expected return – that is, the more important is storage – the more the price of land may appear excessively variable without actually being irrational.

The rational price of land is the present value of the expected stream of revenue. Of course, the possible streams of revenue are legion, and so the price of land must account for all those possibilities. If one could divine the future, to know what will be the actual path of revenue, the calculation of the price of land would be a simple matter. One way to know the future is to wait until it is the past. All this is a way of saying that one can construct a series of "perfect-foresight" prices for land based on a realized series for revenue, treating the realized series as something that can be entirely foreseen. Figure 7.5 plots for twenty-five periods in different panels three representative pairs of constructed "perfect-foresight" prices and the series for land price determined by the storage model.[21] Each panel differs from the other panels because of the difference in the random draws from the distribution of the weather. Within each panel the two series follow separate paths because of the difference between expected revenue and realized revenue.

---

[20]   This issue is behind one of the hot research topics of the last decade involving stock prices. Shiller (1981) and LeRoy and Porter (1981) offered what they claimed to be evidence of excessive variability. Then Flavin (1983) and Kleidon (1986a,b) countered that this evidence was an artifact of the time-series properties of companies' earnings. Earnings and stock prices are analogous to revenue and land price in the storage model.

[21]   The sequence of revenue used to construct the "perfect-foresight" price is much longer, 120 periods to be exact. The "perfect-foresight" price as of period 10, say, is the present value of the sequence of revenue from the period 11 through period 120. With an interest rate of 5 percent per period, the effect of periods even twenty or thirty periods ahead is negligible.

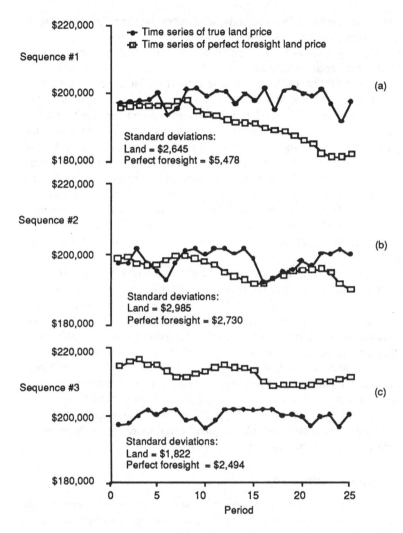

Figure 7.5. Land price compared to "perfect-foresight" price constructed from realized revenue.

Such "perfect-foresight" prices should be more variable than actual time series of the price of land. The intuition is that the "perfect-foresight" price, being based on certainty, should react to a particular change in revenue rather than the expected change, which is "smoother." Contrary to anticipations, the series in Figure 7.5 for constructed "perfect-foresight" prices are by no means distinctly more variable than the true series for land prices. Over shorter segments, say, ten or fifteen periods, whichever the panel, the constructed "perfect foresight" series looks to be less variable.

The intuitive argument for the "perfect-foresight" land price constructed from realized revenue to be more variable is not wrong. If these or similar panels spanned 500 or 1,000 periods, the "perfect-foresight" price series would be unmistakably more variable. Rather the problem arises in small samples because the serial correlation in the realized revenue is ignored. Because revenue is highly positively serially correlated, on the order of 0.6, the constructed "perfect-foresight" series changes relatively slowly. A number of periods must pass before the full extent of its variability is apparent. Kleidon (1986a) deduces that, given the serial correlation in corporate earnings on the order of 0.9, the necessary number of periods for stock prices is on the order of fifty or sixty. With the storage model it seems more like fifteen or twenty. Yet fifteen or twenty years is probably more periods than pass before observers are inclined to judge purchases of agricultural land as having been good or bad.

The insight here can be seen more clearly by considering whether too much was paid for a parcel of land for a nonstorable commodity.[22] Because the revenue from one crop is independent from the revenue from other crops, the evidence from just a few cropyears should suffice to expose a gross overpayment. For a storable commodity, what happens to one period's revenue influences subsequent periods' revenue. Without completely independent readings, it is harder to judge whether the purchase price was correct. Moreover, because the current circumstances carry over through storage, the prospects for future revenue do alter, and the price of land should change. The more storage is important to the commodity, the more variable should be the price of fixed factors like land. Consequently, the more likely those prices will be viewed, incorrectly, as excessively variable.

7.4   Supply estimation

Empirical estimation of producers' supply response is another area where the time-series properties resulting from storage may have unrecognized effect, biasing downward reported supply elasticities and supporting the view of farmers' holding unrealistic views of future prices. It is hardly in the scope of this book to discuss such a huge literature as supply estimation. Nor is it the purpose here to estimate a large simultaneous equations model of storage and production. Rather the purpose is to use the storage model to generate time series of prices and production for known parameters. Then three widely used techniques for supply estimation can be applied and judged by how well they uncover the truth. Of course, this contest uses artificial da-

22   Without complications like inflation and technological change, the price of land for a nonstorable commodity should not change period to period.

ta, although data constructed to share many of the properties of real-world time series. But it would seem to be a modest requirement of the accepted techniques, such as the cobweb model, the adaptive expectations model, and a so-called rational expectations model, that they perform well in these conditions of no measurement error, no structural change, and no ambiguity about planting and harvest times.

Consider the problem of estimating the slope coefficient when production planned for the next period is a linear function of some price-related incentive. In practice production realized in the next period is often all that is compiled, but here suppose planned production is also measured, so that the issue separating the various models is simply the representation of the price incentive. In the storage model with additive disturbances, that price incentive is the true expected price, which is also the futures price. If planned production were estimated as a function of the futures price (i.e., if the correct specification were used), it would be a perfect linear relationship with an R^2 of 1.0.[23] As an example to work with, suppose that slope coefficient is 0.3 (i.e., $\eta^s = 0.3$ at the certainty price). Let the additive production disturbance have a standard deviation $\sigma_h = 10.0$ units. To have a reasonable role for storage, let $k = \$0$ and $r = 5$ percent per period. (Except for η^s, these are the parameters used in previous sections of this chapter.) With these parameters, price and planned production have first-order autocorrelation coefficients of about 0.45.[24]

Common econometric specifications of supply

Instead of the futures price, the three standard econometric approaches to supply estimation have used some other characterization for the price incentive. According to the cobweb model, formalized by Ezekiel (1938) and a standby ever since, producers forecast that current prices will persist.[25] Thus, the model estimated is

$$\bar{h}_t = \alpha + \beta P_{t-1} + u_t \tag{7.7}$$

with u_t assumed to be an independently and identically distributed error.[26]

---

[23] In more complicated models such as those discussed in Chapters 8 and 9, planned production would depend on more than just expected price. If these variables, such as levels of groundwater or nitrogen, were not included in the estimated equation, the R^2 would be below 1.0. But in such circumstances econometric estimation would be problematic, for planned production and the corresponding futures price are both endogenous variables.

[24] Realized production – namely, planned production plus the effects of the weather – is negatively serially correlated. An unusually good harvest is compensated for by lower planned production for the next period, along with the large carryout.

[25] Most often this econometric model has been applied to agricultural supply. See Lichtenberg and Ujihara (1989) for an application to crude oil.

[26] Recall that $\bar{h}_t$ is the notation for planned production, planted in period $t-1$ for harvesting in period t.

The adaptive expectations model, used in literally hundreds of studies, supposes that expectations are updated with a new realization of price but not completely. The model actually estimated includes a lag of planned production (see Nerlove [1958] for the derivation):

$$\bar{h}_t = a + bP_{t-1} + c\bar{h}_{t-1} + u_t \tag{7.8}$$

The slope coefficient for the one-period-lagged supply curve is estimated as $\hat{b} / (1 - \hat{c})$.

Finally, the "rational expectations" model employs a single equation and the "errors-in-variables" approach of McCallum (1976). Because the true model is known to be nonlinear, the "substitution" approach cannot work; nor can the cross-equation restrictions of a multiple equation model help. The model is closest to that used by Ravallion (1985) for rice in Bangladesh. Despite its name, the so-called rational expectations model is not truly rational, for if it were, the price incentive would be identical with the storage model's futures price. It shares two features with the true model, however. One is the notion that a rational expected price for period $t + 1$ should be a function of variables known at period t. Second is the notion that the inevitable mistake in forecasting should not be systematically related to variables known at period t, for then the forecast would have been improved upon. These arguments lead to supply estimation in two steps. The first is an estimate of the rational expected price, using the fitted values in a regression such as

$$P_{t+1} = c_1 + c_2 P_t + c_3 (P_t)^2 + c_4 P_{t-1} + c_5 \bar{h}_t + c_6 \bar{h}_{t-1} + c_7 S_t + e_{t+1} \tag{7.9}$$

where c_1, c_2, and so on are coefficients. Those six variables in price, planned production, and storage surely capture most of information known about period $t + 1$ as of period t. By the properties of ordinary least squares, the fitted error $\hat{e}_{t-1}$ will be uncorrelated by construction with the variables in the information set. The series for the fitted dependent variable in (7.9), namely $\hat{P}_{t+1}$, is used in

$$\bar{h}_{t+1} = \alpha + \beta \hat{P}_{t+1} + u_{t+1} \tag{7.10}$$

Although this "rational expectations" technique includes lagged price and lagged production, as do the cobweb and adaptive expectations models, it is more than an extension to several other explanatory variables. The first-stage regression changes the effective units of those two variables by their coefficients in (7.9). Nevertheless, it too is not truly forward looking: It projects the expected price from the past.

Average performance

Although these three econometric techniques may give results close to or wide of the true slope coefficient in any particular sample, their average

Table 7.4. *Supply estimation* [a]

	Sample size	
	20	40
Cobweb model		
Mean estimated supply coefficient	.14	.11
Mean R^2 of regression	.67	.60
Proportion with "good" Durbin–Watson statistic	.71	.50
Adaptive expectations model		
Mean estimated supply coefficient	.15	.12
Mean R^2 of regression	.71	.65
Mean coefficient on expectations	.85	.78
Proportion with expectations coefficient under 1.0	.83	.97
Proportion with "good" Durbin h-statistic	.91	.90
"Rational expectations" model		
Mean estimated supply coefficient	.14	.20
Mean R^2 of regression	.36	.53
Proportion with "good" Durbin–Watson statistic	.67	.54
Mean serial correlation in planned production	.40	.47

[a]Actual supply coefficient = 0.30. Based on 1,000 trials for each sample size.

tendency – their bias, in other words – is of particular interest. These properties are shown in Table 7.4 for sample sizes of twenty and forty periods (not counting the observations lost to lags). All three are considerably biased. Generally speaking they underestimate the supply response, on average, by 50 percent. The "rational expectations" estimator improves with the larger sample size, which suggests it is a consistent estimator. Even so, its bias is substantial in the size of samples one commonly sees in real-world applications.

All three approaches to supply estimation miss the mark. Nevertheless, the answers they give, not being unreasonable, are not likely to be recognized as wrong. In some cases, the Durbin–Watson statistic would look suspicious, although with the cobweb model, reestimation taking into account the serial correlation in the residuals would lead to much the same parameter estimates. On the other hand, conventional diagnostic tests – the Durbin h-statistic, for example – are not likely to indict the adaptive expectations model. Thus, there is not the suspicion of misspecification that would arise if the models gave nonsensical results.

Two connected reasons account for the plausibility of the results of all three models. First, because of the connection through storage, past prices do give some indication of the price expected in the future. Second, storage causes the time-series behavior in prices and planned production that provide the serial correlation exploited by the various econometric models.[27]

Because in the storage model the true price incentive for producers is the futures price, for delivery in the next period, all three econometric approaches are attempting to approximate the time series for that futures price. When storage is abundant and the spot price low, the futures price is above the spot price in the regular relationship of full carrying charges. Thus, the lagged spot price will appear highly correlated with planned production, even if the causal connection is actually somewhat different. The three standard econometric models get into trouble when the spot price is high and the carryover zero.[28] The correct futures price is below the spot price: The cobweb model, for example, continues to project it above the spot price. In a scatter diagram of forty observations, only 10–20 percent of the pairs of spot price and futures price would fall in that zone. As a result, there will be at least some hint of a linear relationship between them. Nevertheless, the linear relationship implied in the cobweb model or the nearly linear relationships implicit in the other two approaches hardly do justice to the true relationship between P_t and $E_t [P_{t+1}]$, which is sharply nonlinear.

Of course, this simulation exercise with the storage model cannot establish beyond a doubt that similar econometric problems plague actual exercises in supply estimation. It should, however, give practitioners pause.

7.5   Presumption against rational storage

The apparent good performance of adaptive expectations and cobweb supply models suggests subtly that farmers, though responsive to price expectations, form their expectations in such irrational manners.[29] The apparently excessive variability in land prices reinforces that impression. The literature on bias in and poor forecasting performance of futures prices augments the case against rational expectations. Yet the exercises in the chapter suggest instead that rational forward-looking storage engenders the price behavior ac-

27   Eckstein (1985) makes a similar point by showing that Nerlovian supply estimates emerge when the system actually has rational expectations and an exogenous second-order autoregressive process in demand (and no storage).

28   In this context, it is worth commenting on MacDonald and Taylor's (1988a, p. 236) statement on spot metals prices: "Thus, given past prices, no other information should be of use in predicting future prices. . ." This claim is only true for the appropriate functional form; with linear functions of past prices, as in ARMA representations, other contemporaneous variables are needed to capture the nonlinear relationship between current conditions and the futures price, without any violation of market efficiency.

29   In the case of the adaptive expectations model, it is worth emphasizing that Nerlove and others using his framework, such as Behrman (1968) for Thailand, were refuting the belief that farmers failed to respond to incentives at all. For that argument, it was less important that the price incentive itself is completely rational.

tually observed. Rational expectations may be creating the evidence used to cast doubt on itself.

There is a remarkable dissonance, in attitudes toward public interventions, between areas where decisions are made under relative certainty and those where expectations are paramount. No one seriously proposes that most farmers in developed countries are irrational in their choice of feed for livestock and that the government would make those decisions notably more intelligently. Where there is doubt, as there might be for illiterate subsistence farmers, the public role is usually restricted to education and provision of information via extension or similar channels. In contrast, in the sphere where expectations about the uncertain future are central, especially true in the domain of storage, the presumption often appears to be that direct public intervention is needed to correct the allocation of resources.

For example, from plots of the prices over the past ten years for, say, soybeans or copper, it is tempting to view the large swings as evidence of grossly inadequate decisions about storage. Why were more soybeans and copper not released from storage in the late 1970s and early 1980s in anticipation of the surpluses of 1984 and 1985? And why immediately after 1985 were not more beans and copper saved for the tight conditions of the late 1980s? From the storers' perspective, more profits would have been made or losses avoided. From society's perspective, improved allocations would have gone far to alleviate the price swings. This conclusion is indisputable.

Nevertheless, the first "law" of decision evaluation is to judge decisions in the light of the information available *ex ante*. To have anticipated these deficits and surpluses in soybeans and copper one would have had to be clairvoyant. Such reallocation with hindsight avoids the whole problem of what to do now, when the uncertainties about the future are all too dominant. Clearly, one should not judge storage decisions *ex post*.

Even if judging with hindsight is accepted as invalid, the mere existence of *ex post* information distorts in several ways evaluation of decisions made complex by the presence of uncertainty:

1. There is at least the suggestion that *ex ante* decisions could have been improved, because with hindsight the decision could have been made substantially better.
2. Given that uncertainty about the future is difficult to quantify, the tendency will be to judge decisions once the uncertainty is resolved, and not to work toward uncovering the superior *ex ante* approach.
3. Even if the optimal *ex ante* decision is identified, it may seem insignificantly different from other plausible *ex ante* approaches, relative to the *ex post* errors. That is to say, the existence of an unattainable standard, the one available with hindsight, clouds the comparison of *ex ante* decisions.

Also, it is difficult to demonstrate that private storage is rational or that an irrational storage rule is ill advised, because of the inevitable variability in outcomes from period to period. The effects of this inevitable randomness can be seen from the perspective of conventional statistical terminology. One hopes with a sample to distinguish a null hypothesis from an alternative hypothesis. The null hypothesis is that storage is rational and competitive, the alternative that it is some version of irrational or monopolistic behavior. For the size of samples one typically has, twenty cropyears or forty quarters of metals inventories, the probability of rejecting the null hypothesis when it is in fact true is high. Likewise, the probability of not rejecting the alternative hypothesis when it is in fact false is discomfortingly high.

The inevitable variability is also the root of the doubts about the forecasting ability of futures prices and rational expectations more generally.[30] If the futures prices were always right on target, there would be little reason for them, because there would also be few temporary shortages or surpluses. Land prices can be judged *ex post* to have been irrational, but their very movement may be the rational *ex ante* reaction to the unpredictable randomness in the weather. Similarly, persistent suspicion that private storage behavior is inadequate, not to mention claims that public interventions into storage are socially beneficial, will often find *ex post* support in the empirical record.

[30]   A large literature on rational expectations and learning from experience has developed, including papers by DeCanio (1979), Blume and Easley (1982), Bray (1982), Townsend (1983), and Feldman (1987). Quite apart from whether a rational expectations equilibrium emerges from economic agents consciously improving their crude forecasting techniques (the main questions behind these papers), the considerable variability in time series with even rational storage suggests that the learning and convergence would be very slow.

PART III

Extensions of the model

CHAPTER 8

The market's reaction to news

During the oppressive heat and dryness in grain-producing regions of the United States in the summer of 1988, many believed in the arrival of the "greenhouse effect." The grain markets, more dispassionate than journalists, seem not to have given much credence to the cries of alarm over the possibility of long-run global warming and environmental degradation. If the typical weather were known to be ever worsening, the prices of corn and soybeans for delivery in later cropyears would be above the price for delivery in 1988. The actual price pattern was one in which the quoted price for delivery after the harvest of 1989 was not far above the average over the previous decade. Specifically, on May 1, 1988, during planting and before any indications of severe drought, the price of soybeans on the Chicago Board of Trade for delivery in July 1988 was $6.985 per bushel; the November 1988 contract, the first delivery month for the crop that would suffer from the weather, was $7.135. The November 1989 contract was not yet traded, but based on other contracts one can infer that it would have had a price in the range of $7.30 to $7.40. On June 22, 1988, soybean prices were near their peak, as a result of the poor weather (and prospects for more of the same). On that day, the price for July 1988 delivery was $10.545, an increase of 50 percent from May 1. Although the price for November 1988 delivery was up by a similar percentage, the November 1989 contract was trading for $7.55, an increase of 3 percent at most. This inversion in futures prices is the market's way of reflecting that, in its view, the weather conditions in 1988 were an unfortunate draw from the probability distribution of temperature and rainfall.

In the spring of 1989, the oil spill in Prince William Sound and the shutdown of several pumping platforms in the North Sea caused a temporary shortage of crude oil, exacerbated by OPEC's announcement of production restrictions. Before the disruptions, on March 1, 1989, unleaded gasoline for delivery in any month remaining in the year was selling for about $0.50 per gallon on the New York Mercantile Exchange, with a penny or two premium for delivery at the start of the summer, which is the beginning of its peak seasonal demand. Meanwhile, fuel oil, the other principal product from crude, was $0.47 per gallon for the June 1989 contract and $0.49 for the December 1989 contract. After the disruptions, gasoline, beginning its period of peak seasonal demand, had a constellation of futures prices such that the price on May 1 for June 1989 delivery was $0.72 per gallon, some 40 percent above the $0.50 quoted for delivery in December 1989.[1] Fuel oil's constellation of futures prices remained much closer to full carrying charges. Specifically, the June 1989 contract was $0.49 and the December 1989 contract $0.51 per gallon. The demand for fuel oil is at its seasonal low in the late spring and summer.

These changes in the patterns in the futures prices for soybeans, gasoline, and fuel oil with the arrival of "news" can be understood with the help of the storage model extended to allow for more complicated patterns in excess demand and production timing. This chapter considers four extensions of the basic storage model:

1. seasonality in demand, as when demand for gasoline increases during summer months of heavy driving;
2. autocorrelation in the weather, as when drought years tend to follow one another;
3. two-period-lagged supply, as when the northern and southern hemisphere alternate wheat harvests and each one plants knowing the size of the prospective harvest in the other; and
4. a quarterly model with annual production in which there is a shock (to demand) each quarter, whereas earlier the impact of the shock was only at the harvest time itself.

These four extensions are investigated primarily for the insights they provide into the equilibrium reaction to news, given situations in which variations in supply or demand are partly predictable or are revealed gradually. By news is meant the observation of any previously unanticipated exogenous shock. In the basic storage model of Parts I and II, we modeled the shock as simple, serially independent weather fluctuations in an otherwise stationary setting with a new harvest, planted the previous period, maturing each period (an "annual" model). We emphasized how storage compensates for such disturbances and the prospect of further fluctuations in the future. Here the focus is on situations where storage has a second role. In addition to damping the effects of uncertainty, it also smooths the predictable components of fluctuations in supply or demand. Clearly, storage (or the market, more generally) can absorb more easily a shock that would otherwise raise price substantially if the quantity in store is near its seasonal peak. Similarly, the quarter in the

---

[1]   Prices for delivery in the first week of May (a delivery period used in the informal forward market) were higher still, according to Verleger (1989).

crop cycle influences the equilibrium reaction to news, just as the reaction to the current harvest in the northern hemisphere should be different depending on the plantings in the southern hemisphere. When the weather is serially correlated, current storage must reflect not only the current weather but the resulting predictable component of the future weather.

By studying the time-series properties of these four models, we continue a theme pursued in the previous two chapters. In particular it is interesting to learn which of these four systems has the most pronounced appearance of an autoregressive moving-average process in price or production and which has a dominant role for storage.

A common technical feature of all four systems is that they have two state variables, one more than the single state variable of the basic storage model. In the basic model the state variable was current availability, and the control variables were the carryout and planned production. In the four problems addressed in this chapter, this state variable and two control variables remain. The second state variable is, in the first model, the stage in the cycle of seasonal demand. In the second model it is the most recent weather (which is distinct from the current availability), because it contains information about the weather the next period. In the third, it is the size of the crop in the ground in the other hemisphere, and in the fourth, it is the stage of the approaching harvest. In all but the third problem, the second state variables are truly exogenous. And in that third problem the size of the crop in the ground, previously a control variable, is no longer adjustable (being predetermined instead). These four systems, and systems involving storage more generally, are interesting largely because the legacy from current conditions and decisions must be factored into the selection of the optimal current policy.

8.1 Seasonality

The first application of the extension of the model to two state variables is to seasonality in excess demand. This particular application should provide some insight into the different reactions of gasoline and fuel oil to the disruptions during spring 1989, when gasoline was nearing its seasonal peak in excess demand and fuel oil was nearing its seasonal trough in excess demand. (That both are made from crude oil we do not emphasize here, treating processing margins in Chapter 10.)

Excess demand refers to an imbalance between demand and supply at, say, the long-run average price. "Seasonality" refers to some foreseeable and periodic addition or subtraction from the whole demand curve, as with turkeys or heating oil. This seasonal component may be only an expectation, a general tendency. In any one period the price and amount consumed may not be as anticipated, because of the unpredictable component to demand (or supply). Although with turkeys the source of the seasonality in excess demand is clearly from the demand side itself (Thanksgiving and Christmas in the United States), seasonality can arise from periodicity in supply. The most obvious example is an annual harvest of a few weeks' duration. In those few weeks excess demand is negative; in the other weeks of the year, positive. The fluctuations need not be annual: Consider, for example, the double cropping of raspberries in temperate zones and of rice in tropical climates.

For a nonstorable commodity such as fresh raspberries, seasonality in excess demand is strongly reflected in the time-series behavior of price and of planned production, and the more complex the seasonality or the greater its amplitude, the more pronounced the patterns in price and planned production. For a storable commodity like fuel oil, in contrast, seasonality in excess demand appears only weakly in price and planned production. Moreover, the time-series behavior of price and production is much the same whatever the amplitude of the seasonality. Storage absorbs the seasonality. Storage fundamentally controls the time-series behavior of all the endogenous variables.

Seasonality under certainty

The main effect of storage on seasonality can be seen under certainty. In situations with no seasonality and a positive discount rate, storage under certainty is the straightforward exercise of allocating a large initial availability in regularly declining proportions over the subsequent periods (Samuelson 1958; Houthakker 1959). With seasonality the role of storage is substantial even when there is no uncertainty.

To demonstrate this, consider an example where the random disturbance v_t for all t is 0.0.[2] Let the predictable seasonal component in demand be unmistakable. Suppose it follows a sinusoidal wave that repeats every twelve periods and has an amplitude (distance from trough to peak) of 40 units. This cycle of twelve periods is chosen, of course, to represent twelve months. In the basic storage model, the period – given one planting decision, an interest rate typically of 5 percent, and a storage cost of $2.00 over that stretch of time – corresponds to a full year. Here the storage costs accrued over one month (one period) are reduced proportionately: the marginal physical storage cost $k = \$0.17$ per period and the interest rate $r = 0.40$ percent per period. New production continues to arrive with a one-period lag and, if it were not for compensations to the seasonality in demand, would come at a rate of 100 units per month. (That is, there is no inherent seasonality in supply.) The example thus fits a commodity like fuel oil, where production decisions about crude oil translate into heating oil burned in a customer's furnace some weeks later and where the seasonal demand rises through the fall, peaks in the win-

2   Without seasonality, the equilibrium would be ($q^N = 100$, $P^N = \$100$), period after period after period.

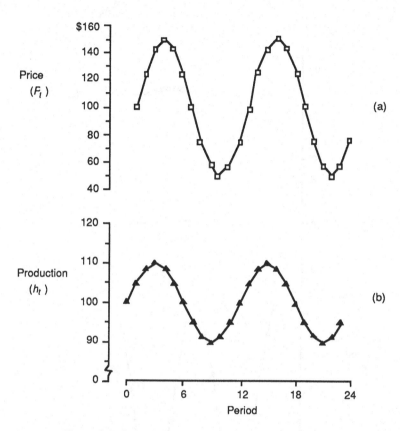

Figure 8.1. Seasonality in price and production without storage under certainty and sinusoidal demand.

ter, declines in the spring, and reaches an annual low in the summer.[3] Ignoring complications such as the source of crude oil, suppose the (one-month-) lagged supply elasticity is, like demand, 0.2, so that consumption and production compensate equally for the seasonality.

With both supply and demand curves linear, without storage the sinusoidal pattern is unaltered except for a reduction of amplitude in the time series of price and production, which equals consumption. In Figure 8.1, two full cycles of these variables are shown, starting from the point in the cycle, the autumn, when excess demand for fuel oil is rising.

[3] Of course, fuel oil is continuously produced, not as this formulation supposes, in a series of batches. The continuous-time version of dynamic programming, or equivalently, of optimal control theory, would be the technique for solving for the paths of the endogenous variables. For the purpose of describing the effect of seasonality, the discrete-time version is more intuitive.

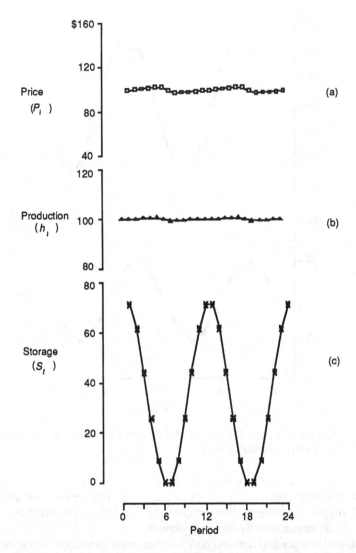

Figure 8.2. Seasonality with storage under certainty and sinusoidal demand.

As a problem in optimal storage, this situation requires two state variables. One is the current availability, which as before is the sum of the current period's new production and the carryin from the previous period, and which must be allocated between current consumption and the carryout. The second state variable is the current stage of the cycle. For a given availability, equilibrium storage is very different depending on whether the cycle is near its

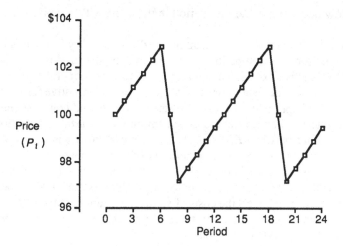

Figure 8.3. Seasonality in price with storage under certainty and sinusoidal demand.

peak or its trough. A distinct relation between S_t and A_t applies for each of the twelve months.

Cycles with and without storage

Under certainty the full storage rules for each phase of the cycle are not especially interesting, since only one combination of current availability and storage on them ever comes into play (once any extreme initial condition is dispelled). Hence the system can be discerned just with the time paths of price, production, and storage. These are shown in Figure 8.2, also for two cycles. The scales for price and production are the same as for Figure 8.1, to make the effect of storability more apparent.

The differences between Figure 8.1 (no storage) and Figure 8.2 (storage) are striking. With storage, the seasonality in price and the seasonality in production are relatively minor. Without storage, production ranges from 90 to 110 units; with storage the range is merely 99.66–100.34. The range of price is reduced proportionately. Storage instead displays the pronounced cyclical pattern, although not a perfect sine wave.

More interesting even than the reduced range is the alteration in the shape of the seasonality of price or production compared to that of a nonstorable commodity. With storage, price and production follow a sawtooth rather than a sinusoidal pattern. (Figure 8.3 shows the price panel of Figure 8.2 on a larger scale, so that it is more visible.) Price starts out low and rises steadily before a quick return to that same low. Also the cyclical low in price or production does not coincide with the cyclical low in excess demand: It precedes it, the low occurring in the first period in the cycle with negative excess demand.

Behind the piecewise "linearization" of the seasonality in price is the arbitrage condition for competitive storage. Crudely, the surplus from the five periods of negative excess demand is stored for the benefit of the five periods of positive excess demand. For there to be the proper incentive for such storage, the price in period $t + 1$ must equal the price in period t plus warehousing fees and interest. For the storage to be continuous, the arbitrage relationship must also hold between P_{t+1} and P_{t+2}, and between P_{t+2} and P_{t+3}, and so on.[4] Inasmuch as the sinusoidal pattern in excess demand causes continuous storage except for one period each cycle, the seasonal pattern in price for months with storage must be essentially linear (for moderate interest rates) to cover (but only just cover) the costs of storage. The underlying seasonality in excess demand reasserts itself in price or production only in those periods untouched by a carryin or carryout.

Because the spot price must be rising from period to period to elicit storage, in some periods the spot price is higher than the previous period's even though demand is falling. In Figure 8.2 demand reaches its seasonal peak in period 3 (and 15). Price is higher in periods 4 and 5 (and 16 and 17) because storage is still positive. Those periods have lower demand than the cycle's peak but more than the average demand over the cycle.

Another implication of this sequence of equilibria, an implication emphasized by Pyatt (1978), is that marginal production costs must be rising over the periods during which stocks are held. This rate of increase in marginal production costs is controlled by the marginal cost of storage. The role of storage is essentially to allow production in several periods to be substitutes in providing the commodity for consumption in a single period.

The same sawtooth seasonality and the same range would emerge in price or production even if the amplitude of seasonality in excess demand were much greater. For that matter the same sawtooth pattern in price would emerge even if the cycle in the excess demand were something other than sinusoidal, as long as there was a stretch of five periods with cumulative excess demand and a stretch of five periods with cumulative surplus. If the equilibrium calls for continuously positive storage, the price pattern simply conforms to the storage costs. The amount in store absorbs the seasonality in excess demand whatever its precise form and whatever its magnitude. (See Pyatt [1978] for illustrations of this principle.) It follows that one should inspect the time series of inventories, not price or production, to uncover the

---

4   If the firm were a monopolist (including over storage), the relationships between periods would involve marginal revenues. The point remains, nevertheless, that storage costs, not the seasonality in demand, dictate the rise in the price. Phlips and Phlips (1981) and Ashley and Orr (1985) have studied the monopoly version of seasonal storage under certainty, building on an early paper by Smithies (1939).

underlying seasonal component to excess demand. This is the emphasis in Brennan's (1959) study of creamery butter, cheese, and shell eggs.[5]

Seasonality under uncertainty

With uncertainty the same two features – linearity in the seasonal component of price and production and extreme seasonality in storage – dominate the time series. A span of five cycles is plotted in Figure 8.4. The situation is the same as the example just studied under certainty, except that each month there is a random disturbance. This stochastic term is additive and with equal variance each period; it can be thought of as a random shift to the demand curve (as with unusual temperatures in the case of fuel oil). The disturbance is independent each period. Its standard deviation of 2.87 units is such that over a whole cycle the cumulative randomness has a standard deviation of 10 units. Although this random component introduces roughness into the series, a seasonal pattern is evident. This seasonal pattern, however, is far removed from the underlying sine wave in excess demand. Once again, storage most strongly reflects the seasonality in demand.

Like other systems with storage, this one with seasonality and uncertainty has a stochastic steady state. Although the system does have a long-run average price or amount stored, it is more instructive to envision long-run averages for each of the twelve stages of the cycle. There is a steady-state seasonality, so to speak. Whenever the system is away from this average seasonal path, the system seeks to return to it.

In Figure 8.4 another, more subtle, aspect of the seasonality is present. There are marked differences in the variability of price depending on the stage of the cycle. The variance of price is highest just as price reaches its peak (on average) and during its cyclical decline. For example, the most pronounced move in Figure 8.4(a) occurs in one of those periods, period 42 to be precise, when storage is falling to its cyclical low.

The pattern in the variability of price is illustrated in Figure 8.5, which shows the steady-state standard deviation of price conditional on each of the twelve stages in the cycle. While the standard deviations show a marked seasonal pattern, the relationship is highly nonlinear. In this case months 6 and 7 in the year-long cycle are much more likely to show very different prices from one year to the next than even month 5, which has the highest level of seasonal demand. A plot for the standard deviation of price changes from one stage to the next would show a similar seasonal pattern: Months 6–8 are more likely to show substantial changes from the previous months than are the other months in the cycle.

---

[5] Also see Duddy and Revzan (1933) for evidence of a linear pattern to price during the season of butter storage and Vaile (1944) for the seasonal pattern of the cash price of corn.

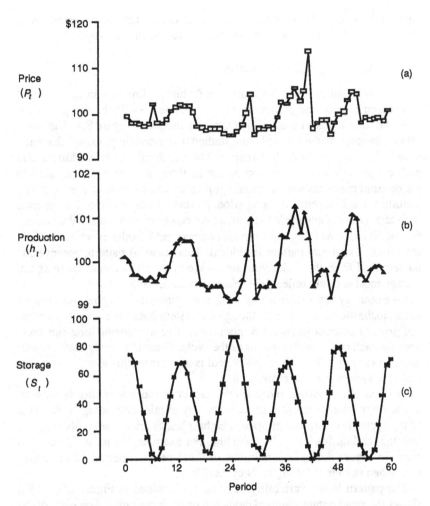

Figure 8.4. Seasonality with storage under uncertainty and sinusoidal demand.

These different price variances along the cycle are signs of the differences in the storage rules operating in each stage in the cycle. In that setting, the differences are best expressed in terms of the marginal propensity to store. Contrast the marginal propensity to store in month 5 with that of month 8. The average amount in store at either of these stages is about 10 units, but storage is cyclically declining through month 5 and beginning its cyclical rise at month 8. The marginal propensity to store, measured at 10 units in store, is about 0.76 for month 5 and 0.96 for month 8. Moreover, the storage rule for month 8 is virtually linear (over the range of positive storage), whereas the

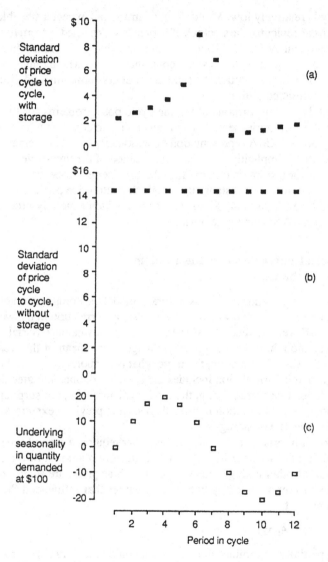

Figure 8.5. Seasonal cycle in standard deviation of price with storage.

rule for month 5 is highly nonlinear as storage rules go, the marginal propensity to store ranging from 0.60 at low availabilities to 0.95 at high availabilities. These differences make perfect sense. At month 5, if the carryover is left very small, there is a good chance for a shortage in month 6, the last month with seasonal excess demand. Consumption, and by extension price, in month 5 must shoulder a large share of the adjustments if by chance the availability is relatively low. Month 9, in contrast, can expect a sizeable surplus, which can replenish the stockpile if very little was carried in from month 8 should the amount available then have been atypically small. Hence, in month 8, a high marginal propensity to store, constant over the whole range of positive storage, translates to much the same level of consumption, and price, regardless of current conditions.

Standard deviations variable along the cycle pose problems for the standard univariate time-series techniques when applied to commodity prices. The plausibility of an ARMA representation of seasonality in excess demand suggests, explicitly or implicitly, a similar specification of the time-series process for price. But for a storable commodity, the time-series properties of an underlying seasonality are substantially transferred into price processes poorly represented by a standard ARMA specification, which generally proceed by supposing homoskedastic white noise.

8.2   Serial correlation in the random disturbance

This section adds to the basic storage model the complication of positive serial correlation in the weather. Positive serial correlation in the weather means that bad weather tends to persist (as does good weather). Serial correlation can be thought of as a temporary change in the mean of the weather. The higher the serial correlation, the more what is temporary looks to be permanent. Thus, this formulation includes the situation dubbed the greenhouse effect. Such positive correlation in the random disturbance, not surprisingly, induces more serial correlation in price than seen in previous exercises. Also it diminishes the role of storage.

A system with serial correlation in the weather requires a second state variable describing the weather just past. The equilibrium amount of the carryover, as well as other endogenous variables such as price, are functions not only of the current availability but of the weather that influenced the just-completed harvest,

$$S_t = f^S[A_t, v_t] \tag{8.1}$$

because v_t partially determines the prices that could prevail in period $t+1$. In this formulation, the serial correlation in the weather is first order, namely

$$v_t = \rho v_{t-1} + u_t \tag{8.2}$$

where u_t is independent of the realization in other periods. (With a positive ρ, good weather will tend to follow good weather.) Although, say, u_{t-10} and through it v_{t-10} has a lingering influence on the weather in period $t+1$, a distinct state variable for the weather in every one of the past periods is not nec-

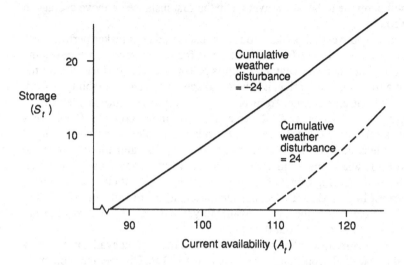

Figure 8.6. Optimal storage rules when weather is serially correlated.

essary. The possible effect of the past weather in period $t+1$ is summarized in the current weather v_t .[6]

Storage rules

As with seasonality in excess demand, a distinct storage rule (i.e., a distinct relationship between S_t and A_t) exists for each value of the state variable v_t. Unlike with seasonality, which had a finite number of stages to its cycle, the possible values for v_t are infinite.[7] To portray these relationships graphically, the best one can do is to show the relationship between S_t and A_t for some representative values of the second state variable. This amounts to cross sections of a three-dimensional diagram. Two such slices are illustrated in Figure 8.6: one where the weather in the just-completed harvest was very bad (labeled "Cumulative weather disturbance = –24") and the other for very good current weather (labeled "Cumulative weather disturbance = 24"). (The mean weather disturbance is 0, recall.) In this example, ρ is set at (the unrealistically high) value of 0.7, so more than likely the wea-

---

[6]   If the random disturbance followed a second-order process, a third state variable representing v_{t-1} would be needed.

[7]   Instead of a separate polynomial in storage (see the Appendix to Chapter 3) for each stage of a seasonal cycle, as in the previous section, $E_t[P_{t+1}]$ is approximated as a more complicated polynomial, including interaction terms, of the two state variables.

ther will continue to be below average in the first instance or above average in the second.[8]

Because bad weather is likely to follow bad weather, it makes perfect sense for the storage rules in Figure 8.6 to call for more storage, whatever the availability, for current weather 24 units below average productivity. At the cost of a higher current price, it is better to spread current availability around. Since without any storage from period t to period $t + 1$ the availability in period $t + 1$ would average 83.2,[9] an availability in period t of 100 units represents a relative surplus. Moreover, the relative surplus in period t is shared more or less equally between current consumption and the carryover to period $t + 1$, with some adjustment to cover warehousing fees and interest, because the lingering effect of the bad weather can be anticipated to depress the harvest in period $t + 2$. Because the anticipations of future shortfalls has more force the greater the current availability, the marginal propensity to store increases with A_t from about 0.65 to about 0.85.

When the current weather has been good and the current availability is very high, the marginal propensity to store is virtually 1.0. The average propensity to store from availability above long-run average production of 100 is much lower, however. The intercept for the storage rule when $v_t = 24$ is 109 (on the horizontal axis in Figure 8.6). Current price P_t must be very low, some $65, before storage begins, because the large harvest that can be expected for period $t + 1$ will keep P_{t+1} otherwise depressed.

In one sense Figure 8.6 misrepresents the interaction of storage and the state variable encompassing the weather. Figure 8.6 seems to imply that the availabilities shown are equally likely whether the current weather is –24 or +24. They are not. Indeed, if $v_t = 24$, an availability below 124 is impossible, since the minimum carryin is zero. For that reason the storage rule for $v_t = 24$ is shown as a dotted line to the left of $A_t = 124$ units. Although the storage rule below $A_t = 124$ is irrelevant for the rule with $v_t = 24$, the high range of the other storage rule could come into play. When $v_t = -24$, an availability of 110 or 120 is possible, should the carryin be large. More likely, A_t is below 90 and storage zero whenever $v_t = -24$.

Some sense of the joint probability of A_t and v_t can be obtained from time series of this system. Figure 8.7 shows the sequential equilibria for forty periods. Note that stretches of similar prices are of random length. There are no systematic opportunities to earn supernormal profits. Long stretches of low prices and long stretches of high prices are both visi-

---

8   The other parameters are linear demand with elasticity of –0.2 at (q^N, P^N); $\eta^s = 0.0$; $k = 2.0; and $r = 5\%$, in line with one period equaling one year. u_t is distributed as N $(0, 6 \text{ units}^2)$, implicitly an additive disturbance. With $\rho = 0.7$, nearly half of the variance in the current weather is attributable to the past.

9    $83.2 = \bar{h}_{t+1} + E_t[v_t + u_{t+1}] = 100 + .7 (-24) + 0.$

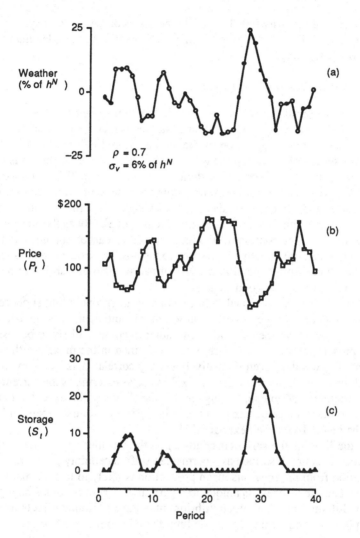

Figure 8.7. Time series when weather is serially correlated.

ble.[10] Storage is zero for many periods on end. Both series are highly auto-correlated, the serial correlation in price being 0.75. That number is just slightly higher than the value without storage, namely, the 0.70 autocorrelation assumed for the weather.[11] The price series has a second-order partial

---

10 Although the long stretches of prices either above average or below average are the dominant feature of Figure 8.7, the system does, in expectation, converge to a steady state. The expectation is simply for a very gradual return.
11 The demand curve for the example is linear, recall.

correlation of virtually 0.0. Thus, the time-series properties of a system with storage and autocorrelated weather may well be no more complex than a system with just storage.

The minor role of storage

The serial correlation in price is not much higher than the serial correlation from the weather itself because storage is relatively unimportant. Although the standard deviation of the amount stored is higher than without positive serial correlation in the weather, the average amount stored is lower and the proportion of periods with no storage is higher. When the weather has been good there is less reason to store because the next harvest is likely to be large, and when the weather has been bad there is little on hand to store. Moreover, the importance of storage decreases markedly as the supply elasticity increases, in contrast to the basic model of earlier chapters. Planned production is more effective in reacting to the positive serial correlation in the weather. It can both expand in the face of bad weather and shrink in periods with an expectation of good weather.

With bad weather inclined to follow bad weather, one might suppose that storage occurs during periods of bad weather in anticipation of the bad weather to come. Nevertheless, the bad weather to come is likely to be less bad than present; hence supplies are better consumed in the present rather than stored. The weather, even if positively serially correlated, is mean reverting – which is to say future weather is unlikely to be as extreme as the current period's weather. (Of course, the higher is ρ, the slower is the expected convergence to the stochastic steady state.) Only if ρ is 1.0 will extremely bad weather be just as likely the next period.[12]

In the limit as the serial correlation ρ in the weather approaches 1.0, the situation is better described as a permanent shift in certainty production. Any deviation from the previous mean production is likely to last for many periods.[13] The randomness u_t unique to a particular period becomes negligible. Such shifts in the certainty equilibrium may have profound effects on price and planned production. Yet in the limit there is no role for storage. Storage

---

12   Another insight into the diminished role of storage comes from rethinking the definition of a period. Even with some serial correlation in the weather, periods sufficiently spaced will have little connection in their weather. Similarly, if the period were redefined to include, say, ten of the previous periods, the serial correlation between these periods would be much reduced. The system would look much more like the basic storage model, which has no serial correlation in the weather. With the redefined, longer period, however, physical storage costs and the interest rate would be ten times greater. At these higher costs, storage would be much less practical. Also with the redefined period, the convergence would be expected to take fewer periods.

13   In the extreme of $\rho = 1.0$, that is, where $v_t = v_{t-1} + u_t$, certainty production follows a random walk. If ρ were greater than or equal to 1.0, the system would neither be stationary nor have a stochastic steady state.

is an important feature of a system when the period-by-period randomness is high. It cushions temporary surpluses or shortages, not permanent or nearly permanent ones.

8.3   Two-period-lagged supply response

A system with the harvest maturing two, not one, periods after planting has time-series properties more complex than the standard model, with or without serial correlation in the weather. This specification results in a second-order partial autocorrelation coefficient of actual production that is strongly negative, whereas those for planned production and price are slightly so. A low current harvest induces larger planned (and actual) production two periods later. Also the first-order partial autocorrelation coefficients, which are positive, are reasonably large. A large current harvest has a price-depressing effect on the current and subsequent period, incompletely damped by an endogenous production response because of the two-period lag. All together, a system with supply responding with a two-period (rather than one-period) lag has among the most complex time-series behavior of the cases studied either in this chapter or in Chapter 6 previously. Its behavior reveals more about the substitutability between storage and responsive supply in dispersing the vagaries of the weather.

Two-period-lagged supply response does not refer to the situation where only every other period has new production; rather each period's harvest is the result of planting two periods previously. Such circumstances arise, for example, with production in two hemispheres and negligible transportation costs. Each year, immediately after its harvest, the northern hemisphere decides (to personify in the idiom of the planner's problem) how much to plant based on the current worldwide availability and on what it knows to be the size of the maturing crop in the southern hemisphere. In turn the equilibrium amount planted in the southern hemisphere depends on the size of the northern hemisphere's crop in the ground.[14]

Other examples can be identified in processing or transportation activities that take longer than the interval between decisions, although in such cases the decisions are likely to be nearly continuous. The amount of oil on the high seas, along with the amount of oil already held by importers, influences the decision to send off more tankers from exporting terminals. Tree crops that take some time to mature after planting are also to be covered by the abstraction of two-period-lagged supply (ignoring that the trees might produce for many periods). To keep the model generic, all production takes place at one location.

[14]   In this formulation none of the uncertainty about the disturbance is resolved before the harvest. If the disturbance is additive, the system behaves the same whether the disturbance is in production or consumption.

A system with two-period-lagged supply requires a second state variable representing the size of the crop in the ground.[15] Each period the market, meaning producers and storers collectively, must decide how much to store and how much to plant. The storage decision need look only one period ahead; the planting decision needs to consider the expected price (or the expected marginal incentive if the random disturbance is multiplicative) two periods ahead.[16] The planting decision, once made, will affect the intervening period, however. The equilibrium storage in period $t+1$ would surely be fairly small if the prospect for a huge crop the following period, period $t+2$, was high because the crop in the ground as of period $t+1$, the amount planted now in period t, was large. Likewise, in period $t+1$, the storage decision for period $t+2$ and the planting to be harvested in period $t+3$ will be influenced by the decision to plant a small amount in period t, which is harvested in period $t+2$.

Although the crop in the ground, planted the previous period, is a distinct state variable, its influence on the price expected for the next period is not much different from the carryout. Both are sources of the commodity the next period. Indeed, if the random disturbance is additive, one more unit of crop in the ground has the same expected effect on the price for the next period as does one more unit in store. That is, while $S_t = f[A_t, \; Crop \; in \; Ground_t]$, $E_t[P_{t+1}] = E_t[P_{t+1}[S_t + Crop \; in \; Ground_t]]$.[17]

Sensitivity to current conditions

The main element of interest in this system is that new planting responds to a shock to current weather much less than if it can react with a lag of only one period. This fact can be seen from two perspectives: one showing current and expected prices as functions of the current availability (Figure 8.8) and another showing the expected path of harvests given a particular initial availability (Figure 8.9).

Figure 8.8 depicts current price P_t, the price expected for one period later $E_t[P_{t+1}]$, and the price expected for two periods later $E_t[P_{t+2}]$, each as a func-

---

15   The crop in the ground could also be thought of as the quantity of goods "in the pipeline." Once the production is set in motion it is not adjustable.

16   Because the decision to store is a commitment for one period whereas an investment in planting is a commitment for two periods, the more flexible investment, namely storage, should dominate. That is, firms should be much more willing, *ceteris paribus*, to store than to plant (Jones and Ostroy 1984). But here prices are endogenous: They adjust to make both investments equally desirable.

17   A distinction between the two variables S_t and *Crop in Ground_t* is possible with a multiplicative disturbance because the variance of the random disturbance could be a function of the size of the crop in the ground. With a high η^s, the polynomial routines have trouble quantifying this distinction. Consequently, in the examples below, the disturbance is additive.

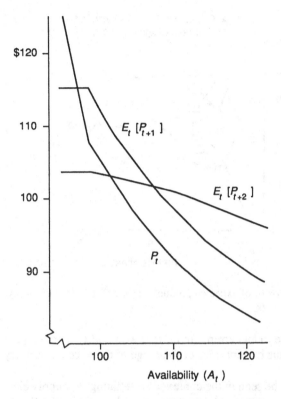

Figure 8.8. Relative sensitivity of spot and futures prices to current conditions, given *Crop in Ground$_t$* = 100.

tion of the current availability A_t, given the *Crop in Ground$_t$* has an expected harvest of 100 units. For any particular availability, the information is the same as in a plot of the expected path back to the steady-state mean. Figure 8.8 simply provides the information for many possible current availabilities (although for only one of the possible values of the second state variable).[18] The three functions in Figure 8.8 take into account the endogenous decisions to store and to plant, in period t and beyond. For example, the vertical distance between P_t and $E_t[P_{t+1}]$, for $A_t > 98.50$, represents the storage costs per period, $k = \$2$ and $r = 5$ percent.[19] As a signal for producers, $E_t[P_{t+2}]$

[18]   For precision's sake a figure like Figure 8.8 should be drawn for the full range of possible values for the second state variable, the crop in the ground (equal to 100 units in Figure 8.8). Although the precise curves would alter, they would always have the same relationship: Expected prices for the more distant delivery dates react less to current conditions, for all levels of availability, than the more nearby expected prices.

[19]   The demand curve is linear with $\eta^d = -0.2$; $\sigma_h = 10$ units.

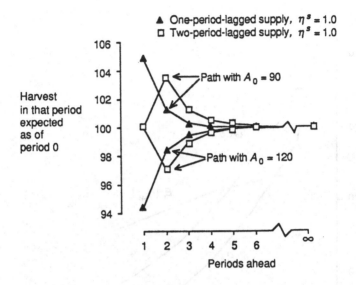

Figure 8.9. Time paths of expected production for different lags in supply, *Crop in Ground$_t$* = 100.

elicits a smaller response to an extreme in current availability than would a signal with the range of the current price or the range of the price for delivery in period $t + 1$.[20]

The point at issue can be seen in the context of estimating the supply elasticity. This example, by construction, has a two-period elasticity of 1.0 with respect to the two-period ahead futures price. As was seen in the convergence paths of Chapter 5 for the simpler model, $F_{t+2,t}$ is closer to the long-run average price than P_t, whatever are the current conditions. This relationship can be thought of as P_t measuring $F_{t+2,t}$ with some (state-dependent) error. That is, from an econometrics perspective, $F_{t+2,t} = P_t + e_t$. If the response of planting (for harvesting two periods later) to changes in the current spot price is used to infer the supply elasticity, η^s will be underestimated considerably, due to this "errors-in-variables" problem.

The muted response of planting to changes in current conditions can also be seen in the expected path of production back to the steady state. In Figure 8.9 two such paths are shown, one with $A_0 = 90$ and the other with $A_0 = 120$

---

20 Of course, if supply, with the same elasticity, could respond in one period, the curve for $E_t[P_{t+1}]$ would be different from that illustrated. The feedback effect of the superior flexibility would alter the function. Because the recomputed curve would fall between those in Figure 8.8 for $E_t[P_{t+1}]$ and $E_t[P_{t+2}]$, the adjustment in planting to the same shock in current availability would be greater. The same is true for the curve for P_t over the range of positive storage.

Table 8.1. *Steady-state properties with supply response at various lags*[a]

	2-period-lagged supply $\eta^s = 1.0$	1-period-lagged supply $\eta^s = 1.0$	1-period-lagged supply $\eta^s = 0.5$	Within-period supply response $\eta^s = 1.0$
Planned production	100.03	99.98	99.98	100.00
	(3.13)	(4.38)	(3.22)	(7.35)
Price	$99.85	100.10	100.10	100.00
	(23.21)	(19.63)	(21.12)	(7.35)
Storage	9.44	8.30	8.30	0.93
	(9.10)	(7.75)	(7.82)	(2.20)
Percentage of periods with no storage	20.92	23.03	22.64	73.75

[a]Standard deviations are given in parentheses.

(and, for both, *Crop in Ground*$_0$ = 100 and $\eta^s = 1.0$). For the same two initial conditions the paths for one-period-lagged supply with $\eta^s = 1.0$ are shown for comparison. The first possible planting for two-period-lagged supply reacts much less than the first response in the one-period-lagged case, even allowing for the delay of one more period. The system with two-period-lagged supply also takes longer to return to the steady state, which is another way of saying two-period-lagged supply is less effective at absorbing a shock.

Along with a more delayed and hence more muted response to shocks to current availability, two-period-lagged supply has more variable prices and more reliance on storage. These steady-state means and standard deviations are given in the first column of Table 8.1. The comparable figures for one-period-lagged supply are listed in the second column. Note in particular the standard deviations of planned production, 3.13 units for two-period- and 4.38 for one-period-lagged supply response. The respective values for storage are 9.10 and 7.75; extra storage substitutes for a speedier production response.

A system incorporating two-period-lagged supply with an elasticity of 1.0 behaves like a system with one-period-lagged supply with a lower elasticity. The standard deviation of planned production is 3.22, close to the 3.13 of the simpler system with $\eta^s = 0.5$. Of course, the correspondence is imperfect. In particular, with one-period $\eta^s = 0.5$, the time series of realized production does not show the negative second-order autocorrelation seen in the two-period-lag case. By the standard of price variability, a one-period η^s of 0.2 is closest to two-period $\eta^s = 1.0$, while mean storage with one-period $\eta^s = 0.0$ matches mean storage with two-period $\eta^s = 1.0$ (based on simulations not shown in Table 8.1).

In a setting of stable demand and supply curves, the main challenge to the market is transient shocks through good and bad harvests. For the purpose of absorbing period-by-period shocks, a supply function highly elastic with a ten-period lag is effectively very inelastic. In contrast note in Table 8.1 how within-period supply, also with $\eta^s = 1.0$, damps out most of the variability in price and renders storage superfluous. A within-period η^s of less than 0.1 would give the same standard deviation of price as the two-period-lagged function with elasticity of 1.0. Speed of any given response is crucial for stability. An implication of this result for empirical work on market stability is that accurate estimation of the first few coefficients in the lag structure of supply response is more important than estimation of the total response.

8.4   A quarterly model with production once a year

Actually, the basic storage model with one storage decision per production cycle implicitly contains a multiperiod problem of allocating the availability present just after a harvest. The crop cycle could be decomposed into months, weeks, or days, and the demand could display some seasonality. Such a problem is straightforward, however, as long as the uncertainty in the system is resolved only at harvest time. The two state variables are current availability and the period within the year. The allocation between harvests is then an exercise of storage under certainty. Given the optimal carryover to the next cropyear, a decision that will not be changed as the months pass, the allocation of the current harvest requires price to increase steadily at the rate of physical storage and interest costs. Even if the carryover to the next cropyear is set at zero, storage will be continuous within the cropyear.[21]

Storage within the cropyear becomes other than trivial if news about the next crop or shocks to demand become known within the cropyear. This news leads to revision of carryover plans. The prices within the cropyear change. As a relatively simple example of such a system, consider a case where there is a shock to demand each of four quarters.[22] New production, 100 units in quantity, arrives once a year (i.e., $\eta^s = 0.0$).[23] Designate that quarter as Quarter I. The random disturbance to demand is independent one quarter to

---

21   If supplies of close substitutes become available from other sources during the cropyear, storage of the commodity of interest may last less than the full year. Also note that the subject in this section is not commodities like onions and potatoes, which are not easily stored a full crop cycle.

22   The model is the same as that in Lowry et al. (1987), except for the particular values chosen for the parameters.

23   Situations with elastic supply with the crop harvested once every four quarters, or those in which news arrives about the yield of the forthcoming crop, require appreciably more complex models because they need a third state variable, in addition to current availability and the quarter. With elastic supply, the third state variable would be the size of crop in the ground. News about the prospective yield would also require a third state variable, for the storage rule in the third quarter, say, would be different if the prospects for the crop had improved since the time of planting.

the next. The standard deviation σ_u, which is the same for each quarter, is 5 units. Thus, the total variance over the cropyear is the same as in many previous exercises where the standard deviation of the weather was 10 percent of mean production. Also for the comparison's sake, let the demand curve be linear with $\eta^d = -0.2$. The demand curve needs to be put on a quarterly basis, however. It is recalibrated to pass through the point (25 units, $100).[24] But to make the seasonal pattern in prices more pronounced, the physical storage costs and interest rates are set higher than previously. The marginal physical storage cost k is $2 per quarter (thus $8 per year) and r is 2.5 percent per quarter (thus 10 percent per year). Representative time-series behavior of this system is illustrated in Figure 8.10, in which the predominance of stocks as the shock absorber is especially evident.

From the perspective of social welfare it is better to have a continuous flow of news about the random component of demand than to have all the shocks combined into the last moments of the cropyear, even if the variance of news per cropyear is the same. Adjustments are less painful if they are spread out over more of the year. Continuous arrival of news, quarter by quarter, say, is also comparable to having an early indication of a shock that arrives at the end of the year. Some piece of the total shock is known three months in advance, another six months in advance, and so on. Clearly, advance notice allows for less severe adjustments. It follows, from either of these perspectives, that carryovers from one cropyear to the next are less important if shocks arrive continuously. The average intercropyear storage with the arrival of news about demand equal across quarters is 7.36 units, with Quarter I being the quarter of harvesting and planting. If all of the total shock is in Quarter IV, the average intercropyear storage is 11.10 units. The average in the other quarters is also higher, because three-fourths (or so) of the year's projected consumption will have been gone by the time the shock is revealed. If all of the total shock is in Quarter I (the implicit formulation of the basic storage model), then the average carryover from Quarter IV to the next Quarter I is 3.65 units. Sufficiently early knowledge of the randomness during a cropyear is a substitute for storage, and vice versa.

Quarterly variability of price

Because a system with production every fourth quarter has much in common with the seasonality studied in Section 8.1, the variability of price

---

[24] As demand is measured on a shorter time scale, it becomes less plausible that the demand for the commodity in a particular period is independent of the prices for that commodity for delivery in other periods. As plausible as such nonzero cross elasticities may be, they are ignored here because they unduly complicate the storage model. That is to say, for the quarterly model, we maintain the assumption of intertemporal separability.

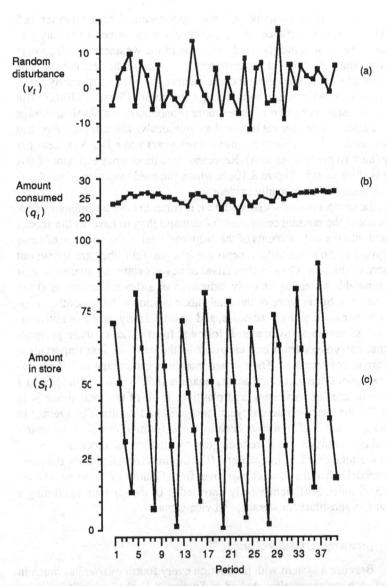

Figure 8.10. Quarterly time series when production is once a year

measured year to year is not the same for each of the quarters.[25] Even when
the total shock is distributed equally across the quarters, the standard devia-

25 This and following points about the price of the commodity also apply to the price of
    land.

Table 8.2. *Price variability by quarter*

Quarter	% of total variance in random disturbance	Price year to year		Change in price from previous quarter	
		Mean	Standard deviation	Mean	Standard deviation
1. *Randomness equally likely throughout year*					
I	25	$92.81	$22.04	–$13.74	$48.13
II	25	97.09	28.81	4.28	17.48
III	25	101.68	37.62	4.59	23.81
IV	25	106.55	55.81	4.87	41.27
2. *Randomness disproportionately likely early in year*					
I	40	$92.97	$23.96	–$13.54	$44.33
II	30	97.26	32.15	4.30	20.31
III	20	101.84	39.74	4.47	23.37
IV	10	106.50	49.43	4.67	29.82
3. *Randomness disproportionately likely late in year*					
I	10	$92.74	$20.36	–$13.71	$50.58
II	20	97.01	25.86	4.27	14.95
III	30	101.58	35.79	4.57	24.26
IV	40	106.45	60.25	4.87	48.22

tion of the distribution of prices recorded in the first quarter (the one with the harvest) is lower than the standard deviation of later quarters, with the fourth quarter having the highest. Furthermore, the variability of price changes from the previous quarter is not the same across quarters. These properties can be seen in the first panel of Table 8.2.

Thus, the relation between news and prices can be more complex than is recognized in the modern finance literature. The conventional wisdom is that asset prices move in response to news, and the bigger the move the more important the news that must have arrived. More specifically, Ross (1989, p. 16) has argued that "the volatility of prices is directly related to rate of flow of information to the market." The pattern in Table 8.2 of increasing variance by quarter suggests that his argument is not a general result wherever the potential economic response to the news, such as storage, can be greater under some conditions than under others. Even if by construction the arrival of news is constant on average, quarter by quarter, one "unit" of news (i.e., a demand shock of so many units of certainty consumption) has a larger effect during the fourth quarter, the one just before the harvest. One cannot infer the amount of news from the price move, only the combination of the amount of news and its relative impact. This incomplete correspondence between the amount of news arriving and price moves can also be seen in the two other panels of Table 8.2. In one, the randomness is disproportionately in the first half of the cropyear, and in the other disproportionately in the last half of the cropyear. In both instances, the most variable prices and price changes involve the fourth quarter.

Similarly, the responsiveness in the prices for various futures contracts to news will depend to a large extent on the cropyear in which they fall and the expectations about an intercropyear carryover. For example, suppose in the second quarter news arrives of a big, immediate, and temporary increase in current demand, that is, a reason for a major drawdown of stocks. If the expectation had already been for an insignificant carryover from the fourth quarter to the new cropyear, the futures price for delivery the first quarter of that new cropyear will react little to the news, whereas the price for delivery in the third and fourth quarters of the current cropyear – not to mention the spot price – will respond considerably. By contrast, if the expectation had been for a substantial carryover, the contract for delivery in the new cropyear will react to the news for the same reason that the prices for delivery in the remaining quarters of the current cropyear rise only slightly: The carryover bears the adjustment. In short, storage affects the diffusion of the effects of the news across periods.

Lurking behind all these results is the nonnegativity constraint on storage. The fourth quarter alone has a chance of having a zero carryout. If the second quarter experiences a sudden shortfall, the third and fourth quarters (and perhaps the next cropyear) can be made to share with it because, in the normal course of carrying stocks through the cropyear, the second quarter is storing for those quarters. If the fourth quarter finds itself high and dry, it cannot adjust downward a carryover that is already zero. Of course, the system accounts for this constraint affecting the fourth quarter by storing more on average in each of the preceding quarters. Nevertheless, that the first quarter can count on sharing a shortfall with at least three other quarters and the fourth quarter can count on none explains the greater variance of prices in the fourth quarter.

8.5   Related problems

The four models of this chapter share the basic storage model's essential feature that the market's reaction to news depends on current conditions, namely A_0. In other words, the amount of the carryout and the amount currently planted respond to the particular news arriving in the current period. Obviously, that flexibility is beneficial compared to a rigidity of a system in which the amount stored and the amount planted had been set by some plan long before and in which that plan had to be carried out regardless.

A statement that the carryout is a function of current conditions is equivalent to saying that equilibrium storage is a function of a state variable (and that stochastic dynamic programming is involved). From the perspective of a game against nature, these circumstances amount to the invisible hand, representing the collective of the market, playing a closed-loop strategy. If the strategy cannot be revised according to the current conditions, the market's strategy is open loop. The optimal open-loop strategy allows for the effects of the future random disturbances (the news), but it cannot react to the news as it unfolds. The optimal closed-loop strategy not only can react to the current news, but its current play (the chosen amount of storage) takes into account the future flexibility. In the lexicon of the planner's problem, the optimal current decision accounts for the fact that current plans can be revised. Thus, the possibility of sequential decisions (in other words, sequential equilibria) is itself a major reaction to news.

It is easy to think of many other interesting variations on the problems considered in detail in this chapter. For example, consider the problem of making storage decisions when the probability distribution of yields can only be surmised from a small sample, as when a new region opens up for production or a new disease of unrevealed virulence appears. The news contains information about the underlying parameters themselves. The current sample mean, variance, and skewness are then state variables. This system is not stationary, however. The storage rules must also be indexed by time, because the accuracy of the sample statistics increases with the length of time. Such a problem is called adaptive dynamic programming (see Rausser and Hochman 1979, chap. 8) and has been applied to such decisions as which cows to cull from a herd based on their milk production to date.

A variant to the model with two-period-lagged supply considers highly specific investments that pay back over several periods, such as especially deep plowing, which improves yields for several years running. A related example is investment in tree crops, where the vintages of the trees matter to total yield. Strictly speaking, the number of trees in each vintage should be a distinct state variable, as current storage, pruning, and planting decisions depend on the exact age distribution of the trees. Most likely, however, a narrower classification, such as into young, middle-aged, and old, would capture most of the complexity in the problem. One would not expect new plantings to respond very much to the news of temporary shocks, however large.

Roughly speaking, the difficulty of a dynamic programming problem, whether measured by computer time or by an analyst's ability to understand the answer, increases as the square of the number of state variables. The basic storage model has one state variable, current availability, and two control variables, current storage and current planting. The models probed in this chapter have the same two control variables but two state variables. One state variable is always the current availability and the other variously the stage in the cycle, the previous weather, the previous planting intensity, or the size of the crop in the ground. This basic understanding of systems with two state variables will be drawn on in the next three chapters of Part III and the last two chapters in Part IV on public interventions. Chapters 9, 10, and 15 focus on a model of two related commodities, which has two state variables and up to four control variables. Specifically, Chapter 9 considers two countries that can trade within the period and each of which can store. The systems in Chapter 14 on price-band schemes require two state variables and three control variables. The current equilibrium private storage thus reflects how the future shocks interact with the public storage agency's price-band rule. Similarly, the current equilibrium involving the two countries, encompassing current storage and current trade, reflects the future prospects of trade and storage in response to future shocks, as well as the current shocks. Thus, at the heart of these problems too is the question of the equilibrium reaction to news.

CHAPTER 9

The interaction of storage and trade

The storage studied in previous chapters is a form of intertemporal arbitrage, in a closed economy. Economists have given incomparably greater attention in research, teaching, and policy advice to another type of arbitrage, namely, intratemporal trade among open economies. What new lessons can be learned about trade and storage when both arbitrage activities are possible?

This chapter shows the fruitfulness of a combined approach. We show how storage weakens the "law of one price" and how it reduces the destabilizing effects of trade barriers in markets buffeted by random shocks. In a meaningful sense, storage has significant advantages over trade as a stabilization mechanism. Our theoretical model offers instructive rules on equilibrium international distribution of stocks. National storage responds in quite different ways to world prices and availability compared to its response to domestic availability. And FOB–CIF price bands are dubious guides to notions of national equilibrium price, given world prices.

In the basic storage model of previous chapters, the closed system could be a single country isolated by prohibitively high shipping costs or a worldwide market in which all countries are effectively combined because shipping costs are negligible. This chapter covers the intermediate case in which two countries are open to trade but the cost of shipping is not zero. This system too is closed as a whole, but within it trade is free in the sense of having no legal proscriptions, though transport costs are positive. There is a market for the commodity in each country. The amount traded and the prices in the two countries are endogenous.

Like storage, the trade emphasized in this chapter is a response to the uncertainty in the weather. In Sections 9.1 and 9.2, the economic characteristics of the two countries are identical by construction – that is, they have the same consumption demand curves, the same average production, the same storage costs, and so forth – so that trade would not occur without the weather in one location being good while bad in the other. Trade can occur in either direction

229

(or not at all) as appropriate. "Free" trade is thus a permanent policy regime (to use the terminology introduced in Chapter 1).

The prime issue here is the interaction of trade and storage in response to the inherent uncertainty, measured both in terms of steady-state properties and in terms of the dynamic equilibrium as a function of current conditions. So that we can build on the general intuition about single-period models, which has been well developed through the trade literature, we emphasize the addition of the possibility of storage to an existing regime with trade. We are thus primarily investigating a multiperiod trade model. Implicit in several figures, however, is information about the effects of adding a regime with trade to a regime with storage.[1] The symmetry of the examples is relaxed in Section 9.3, where we consider the case in which one country exports and the other imports, on average, and the case in which one country – say, the more tropical one – has a disadvantage in physical storage costs.

In a system with both storage and trade technically feasible, issues arise that would be unimportant if only one of the responses to uncertainty were possible. Examples we consider in Section 9.4 are the proportion in each location of the total uncertainty and the correlation between the weather in the two locations. Obviously, the number of countries trading freely could be expanded considerably beyond two. In Section 9.5 some flavor of that additional complexity is achieved by varying the relative size of the two countries in the model. This exercise provides some answers to questions about optimal storage rules for a small open economy. Should its carryovers decrease with a lower world price, which it takes as given? What should be its rule for releasing stocks in relation to the FOB–CIF band of export and import prices? Should such a country rely more on local stocks or on access to the world market?

As in the basic storage model, the storage is across cropyears. The trade, in contrast, is intracropyear. The cost of shipping is constant per unit shipped and is the same in either direction. These conditions hold if the shipping of the commodity of interest is insignificant in the world market for bulk freight. Most important, the cost of shipping is not zero, unlike Gemmill's (1985) and Helpman's (1988) models of trade in response to period-by-period uncertainty.

Like the storers in either location, those in the import–export business are in a competitive industry. In Chapter 11 on monopoly we discuss briefly what happens if one country recognizes the market power it could achieve by

---

[1] The thought experiment of adding trade to storage is also the one of removing such trade-restricting policies as variable levies, tariffs, and so on in favor of free trade. Grennes et al. (1978) and Tyers and Chisholm (1982) conduct such experiments with models of the world grain trade. In these thought experiments it is important that the storage be based on optimizing or profit-maximizing behavior rather than be defined as a residual.

putting its import and export business in the hands of a single agency.[2] In Chapter 15 we use the model developed in this chapter to study some public interventions to supplement private storage reduced by a regime of price ceilings, which distorts the first-best world of trade and storage examined here. Also, the model developed here has much in common with those in the next chapter designed to study the combinations of inventories of raw materials, finished goods, and goods in process. One country can correspond to the raw material industry, the other country the finished good industry, and trade the processing industry. The differences are that the "trade" as processing goes in only one direction and that processing is not likely to be achieved at constant (short-run) marginal cost.

9.1 Equilibrium with trade and storage

The model examined here is applicable to two countries, two regions, or perhaps most appropriate, two islands. Designate these two countries as a and b. (In most figures, a is the "home" country and b is the "foreign" country.) In each country, the equilibrium consumption and price without any uncertainty in the quantity available would be 100 units and $100, as before. Under certainty, each country is self-sufficient and there is no storage.

The commodity is differentiated by country. Although still wheat, wheat in one location is a slightly different commodity from wheat in a second location, just as No. 3 wheat is strictly speaking not the same commodity as No. 2 wheat. Cleaning transforms No. 3 wheat into No. 2; similarly, shipping transforms wheat in one location into wheat at another location. Shipping is in the general class of what may be called "two-way transformation technologies" because the transformation can operate equally in either direction. ("One-way" transformations are a key feature of the next chapter.)

Z_t is defined as the quantity shipped. $Z_t > 0$ if country a ships to country b in period t and $Z_t < 0$ if country b ships to country a.[3] The per-unit cost of shipping is a constant z. Thus, the spread between the spot export (FOB) price and the spot import (CIF) price at the port of country a (or at the port of country b) is a constant dollar amount $2z$. The per-unit shipping cost z is also constant from period to period. Most important for a two-way technology such as shipping is that it is costly in both directions. Far from recovering the expense of shipping from Kansas City to Galveston, the transportation of wheat from Galveston to Kansas City requires an additional outlay. The posi-

---

[2] Any effects of imports on a country's foreign exchange reserves are not considered. Bigman (1985a, chap. 3) considers such effects, but not in a model with storage of the commodity.

[3] In their formulation, Miranda and Glauber (1989) restrict $Z_t \geq 0$, which permits trade in only one direction. Thus, they are studying a regime of export restrictions rather than one of free trade.

tive per-unit cost to shipping, whichever the direction, means there is a pronounced nonlinearity in the total cost function. It is V-shaped, with the low point at $Z = 0$. The marginal cost curve is also highly nonlinear, because of the sharp discontinuity at zero. Because the per-unit cost of shipping is constant, no economic rents accrue on average to the competitive transport industry.

Trade without storage

Figure 9.1 shows a short sequence of equilibria, comprising prices in country a, prices in country b, and the amount traded each period, for a system with $z = \$5$ and storage impossible. The other parameters are familiar: In both countries the consumption demand curve is linear with $\eta^d = -0.2$ at the nonstochastic equilibrium. Throughout this chapter, η^s is 0.0 for both with mean production in both countries 100 units; the weather disturbances v^a and v^b have standard deviations of 10 units and are independent of each other.

In Figure 9.1(a), sometimes P^a is above P^b by \$5 and sometimes P^b is above P^a by \$5, depending on where the weather was worse. This can be seen more clearly in Figure 9.1(b), which plots the difference between P^a and P^b. The one exception to the two prices being separated by the value of z is period 2, in which P^b is above P^a by merely \$0.35. Coincidentally, in period 2 the amount traded is 0.00 units. Because of the symmetry of the system, country a should ship to country b as often as country b ships to country a, as by chance happened in this sample of eleven periods. There is no serial correlation in the amount traded, nor in prices for that matter.

The prices between the two countries are kept within \$5 by the power of spatial arbitrage. The analyst, though, can solve for the equilibrium prices and quantity traded from the perspective of a planner's problem. A useful tool for such problems of spatial equilibria is a "cross" diagram, such as Figure 9.2, which determines the equilibrium for the pair of availabilities in period 0 in Figure 9.1. A cross diagram has behind it a separate diagram for each country, in which the supply and demand curves are plotted. (Here both supply curves are vertical, for instance.) On the horizontal axis in Figure 9.2, exports or imports are shown as differences between the supply and demand in each country. On the vertical axis in Figure 9.2 is the price in country a.

With prices measured from the perspective of country a, the upward sloping line in Figure 9.2 plots the excess supply in country a, the amount available for export (or necessary from imports), given that the local harvest is 102.51 units. If P^a were \$87.45, all those 102.51 units would be consumed in country a, given the local consumption demand curve. If instead P^a were \$100, consumption demand would be only 100 units; 2.51 units would have to be disposed of through exports. If P^a were \$70, 3.49 units would have to be imported to satisfy the demand of 106 units at that price.

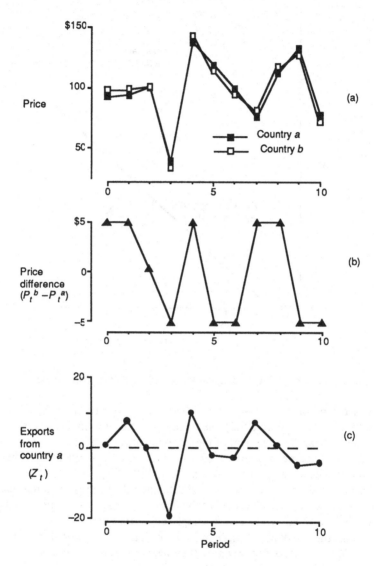

Figure 9.1. Time series of prices and trade with storage impossible.

The downward sloping curve in Figure 9.2 is the excess demand of country b for commodity a in terms of the price in a, given that the quantity harvested in b is 98.58 units. In terms of its own price P^b, it would be a straight line; but in terms of P^a it must be adjusted up or down depending on the direction of trade. If country b is importing from country a (to the right of the vertical dashed line in Figure 9.2), the price in a is \$5 below the price in b to

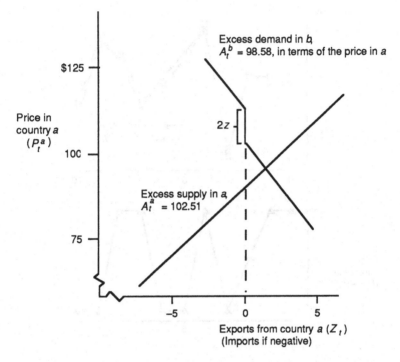

Figure 9.2. "Cross" diagram for determining equilibrium trade.

allow for the shipping costs. If country b is exporting (to the left of the vertical dashed line in Figure 9.2), the price in country a is $5 above the price in b. The vertical displacement of the excess demand curve in b corresponding to $Z_t = 0$ is ±$5 centered on $107.10, which equals the price in b when the quantity consumed is 98.58 units, namely, $P^b[98.58]$.

Each of the two curves in Figure 9.2 can be calculated without reference to the conditions in the other country, which is why the cross diagram is a convenient tool. That is, the excess supply curve for country a is a function of the consumption demand curve in a and the harvest in a, not also the harvest in b. Equilibrium is found where they happen to cross, namely, at exports from $a = 1.47$ units, $P^a = \$94.80$, and $P^b = \$99.80$.

Trade with storage

If storage is permitted, the sequence of equilibria shown in Figure 9.1 is changed markedly, as shown by the panels in Figure 9.3 where the same eleven pairs of weather are used. (The marginal storage cost k is $2 and the interest rate r is 5% for both countries.) For example, with storage possible, price in either country is much less variable.

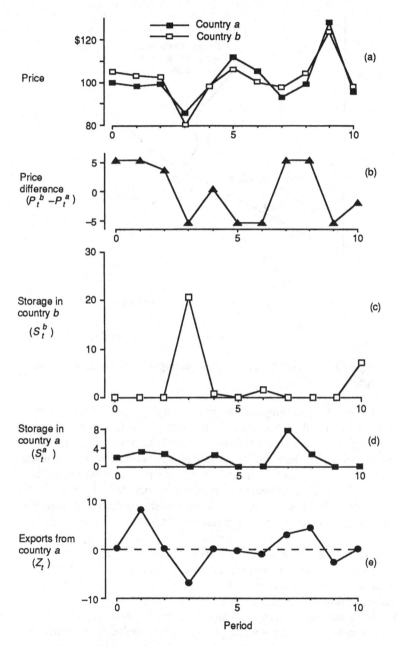

Figure 9.3. Time series of prices and trade with storage possible.

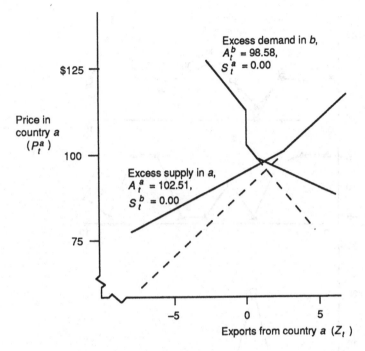

Figure 9.4. "Cross" diagram for determining equilibrium trade with storage.

As Josling (1977b) has emphasized, the underlying randomness cannot be dispensed with. If it does not manifest itself in prices, it does so in stocks or trade. With storage permitted, swings in availability are largely absorbed through storage rather than trade. For these eleven periods, the peak amount traded falls from 18.56 to 8.05 units, whereas the peak amount stored rises from zero to 20.61 units, observed in period 3 in country b. Sometimes the storage is in country a, sometimes in b, and sometimes both. For example, the second highest quantity in store is recorded in period 7 in country a, specifically 7.90 units. In all but two periods there is some storage, whereas three periods have no trade (compared to one period in Figure 9.1), the equilibrium prices being within the marginal cost of shipping in those periods. In two of these three periods, there is storage in one of the countries. And storage confers its positive serial correlation on the amount traded.

With the possibility of storage, an analyst's determination of the equilibrium amount traded is no longer a straightforward manipulation of a cross diagram taking the excess supply or demand from the situation in either country. More bluntly, the analytical techniques common to single-period static models of trade do not work.

Figure 9.4 illustrates the difficulties. (Indeed, the creation of a diagram to show the problems with the cross diagram technique itself requires some suspension of belief. What follows is *not* the way to solve for the equilibrium.) The single-period static approach, as in Figure 9.2, employs the thought experiment of varying just the spot price P^a. But with storage that may be nonsensical: The simultaneously quoted price for delivery in country a the next period must also be altered; otherwise the spread between the spot and futures price may be greater than storage costs, a situation that cannot be an equilibrium.[4] The excess supply curve for country a plotted in Figure 9.4 supposes such a simultaneous adjustment of the spot price and the futures price in country a. (The greater elasticity of imports into a with respect to P^a than found in Figure 9.2 is a result of the demand for storage augmenting the consumption demand curve in a.) For its construction, the excess supply of exports thus presumes knowledge of the equilibrium relation between S_t^a and $E_t[P_{t+1}^a]$. More important, it also presumes a particular value for S_t^b. At prices at which there would be storage in country a if $S_t^b = 0$, the demand for storage in country a would be less than if S_t^b were large, since one use of any storage in country a would be to ship it next period to country b should a shortage emerge there.[5] These properties can be summarized by observing that the expected price in a is a function $E_t[P_{t+1}^a[S_t^a, S_t^b]]$.

Figure 9.4 shows the excess supply curve assuming $S_t^b = 0$, the difference from the dashed excess supply curve being the demand for storage in a. For its part, the excess demand curve from country b in terms of the price in a is the same for most of the range as the curve in Figure 9.2, including the vertical portion corresponding to the FOB–CIF band. But over the range of positive S^b to the right of the last kink in the excess demand curve in Figure 9.4, the correspondence breaks down. The component of storage demand in the excess demand curve in b depends on the amount of storage in country a. The segment drawn in Figure 9.4 assumes that S_t^a equals 0.0. The difference between the solid line and the dashed line is the demand for storage in b, given that amount of storage in a.

As it happens, the excess demand and supply curves intersect in Figure 9.4 where they would imply positive S^a, positive S^b, and positive Z. When the crossing point implies storage in equilibrium, the shapes of the curves as drawn in Figure 9.4 are no longer valid, because they were constructed under

---

[4] If, for example, the expected price for the following period (i.e., the futures price for delivery the following period) is $97.50, no spot price P^a below $97.50/(1 + r) - k$ = $90.86 is possible, because the demand for the commodity to be put into store to deliver at $97.50 is infinitely elastic at $90.86. Of course, if a huge quantity were stored, the futures price for delivery the next period would not remain at $97.50.

[5] Contrast this treatment with that by Rayner and Reed (1978, p. 103) where "[i]t is assumed that the [stationary] excess demand and supply curves incorporate the activities of private stockholders."

the assumption that $S_t^b = 0.0$ and $S_t^a = 0.0$, respectively. That is to say, a different availability in country b requires not just a shift in the excess demand curve for b but a reformulation of the excess supply curve representing country a. Similarly, the excess supply in a over the range of positive storage depends on the availability in b.

In short, intertemporal arbitrage constrains the possible configurations of storage and trade flows so that the excess demand and supply curves, whichever the country, cannot be deduced by the analyst independently of conditions in the other country. Such independence, applicable in a regime with just trade, was exploited in finding the equilibrium in Figure 9.2. This is an important result: The standard analytical techniques of single-period trade models are inappropriate when storage is involved. Rather the equilibrium amount traded must be deduced simultaneously with the equilibrium amount stored in country a and the equilibrium amount stored in country b.

Equilibrium conditions with storage and trade

Any equilibrium, such as those in the time series in Figure 9.3, satisfies the following set of constraints:

1. the intertemporal arbitrage conditions in the two countries, including the condition that stocks cannot be negative:[6]

$$P_t^a + k^a = (1+r)^{-1}F_{t+1,t}^a, \qquad S_t^a > 0$$
$$P_t^a + k^a \geq (1+r)^{-1}F_{t+1,t}^a, \qquad S_t^a = 0 \tag{9.1}$$

$$P_t^b + k^b = (1+r)^{-1}F_{t+1,t}^b, \qquad S_t^b > 0$$
$$P_t^b + k^b \geq (1+r)^{-1}F_{t+1,t}^b, \qquad S_t^b = 0 \tag{9.2}$$

2. the zero-profit condition for arbitrage of futures prices by risk-neutral speculators:

$$F_{t+1,t}^a = E_t[P_{t+1}^a], \qquad F_{t+1,t}^b = E_t[P_{t+1}^b] \tag{9.3}$$

3. the conditions for equilibrium current trade:

$$P_t^a + z = P_t^b, \qquad Z_t > 0$$
$$P_t^a - z = P_t^b, \qquad Z_t < 0 \tag{9.4}$$
$$|P_t^a - P_t^b| \leq z, \qquad Z_t = 0$$

---

6   In contrast, Gemmill's (1985) analysis of trade and storage ignores the essential nonnegativity constraint on storage.

4. a constraint on futures prices due to anticipation of future trade opportunities:

$$\left|F_{t+1,t}^a - F_{t+1,t}^b\right| \leq z \qquad (9.5)$$

Equation (9.5) is written as a single line, unlike (9.4), because the following period's trade Z_{t+1} is not known but only anticipated. That is to say, if $\left|F_{t+1,t}^a - F_{t+1,t}^b\right| < z$, it does not follow that the realized Z_{t+1} must be 0. Rather Z_{t+1} may be positive under some circumstances and negative under others. What does matter in (9.5) is that the futures prices cannot be farther apart than the marginal shipping cost z or there is an arbitrage possibility as of period t.

We have written these various equilibrium conditions from the perspective of futures prices rather than from the usual perspective of conditional expectations. Of course, in our model (by the assumption in (9.3), more specifically), the futures prices are the rational conditional expectations. We have chosen to emphasize the perspective of futures prices here because that makes the conditions about price relationships ones simply of arbitrage. Arguments involving arbitrage are simpler both to make and to grasp.

Because (9.1)–(9.5) must all hold for there to be no arbitrage opportunities, the set implies a tighter bound on price relationships than any one condition by itself. The joint implications of (9.1), (9.2), (9.4), and (9.5) are shown in Figure 9.5. The vertical axis in the center measures the current (period t) price of the commodity in either country. On the right, the horizontal axis measures the price as of period t of a futures contract for delivery in country a to mature in period $t+1$. The horizontal axis on the left records the trade from country a to country b, with imports to the left of 0. The point of Figure 9.5 is to show which combinations of trade, storage, and prices could be an equilibrium.

Figure 9.5's analysis of the equilibrium is conditioned on the value of P_t^a as marked on the vertical axis, in the style of the "cross" diagrams. The left side of the diagram shows that if P_t^b lies between $P_t^a + z$ and $P_t^a - z$, there is no trade. At $P_t^b = P_t^a + z$ there is an indefinite amount of trade from a to b, and for $P_t^b = P_t^a - z$ there is trade from b to a. Given P_t^a, P_t^b cannot be outside the bounds imposed by the transport cost z.

Actually, the upper bound on P_t^b, given P_t^a, is tighter because of the relationships imposed by storage in country a. If there is storage in a, the futures price in a, $F_{t+1,t}^a$, is $(1+r)(P_t^a + k)$ as shown on the right horizontal axis. Thus, the futures price in b for delivery in $t+1$, namely $F_{t+1,t}^b$, cannot be above $(1+r)(P_t^a + k) + z$. Otherwise, arbitrage is possible: Buy for delivery in a in period $t+1$, simultaneously contract to make delivery in b in period $t+1$, take delivery in a the next period, then transport to b and deliver. Given this maximum on the futures price for delivery in b (all supposing the value for P_t^a), the maximum current price in b consistent with storage in b (and storage in a) is $P_t^b = P_t^a + z/(1+r)$. The implied difference between the

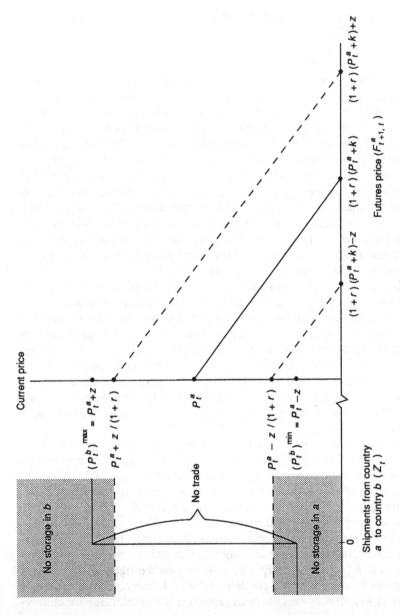

Figure 9.5. Equilibrium with trade and storage, given P_t^a.

two spot prices is less than z; current trade must be zero. P_t^b can be above $P_t^a + z/(1+r)$ (but never above $P_t^a + z$). Yet if so, the implied intertemporal spread is below the carrying charge required for storage. Thus, if there is storage in a, there can be current trade from a to b, or storage in b, or neither, but there cannot be both storage in b and shipments to b in period t. It is more profitable to store now in a and ship to b in period $t+1$, saving the interest charge on the transport cost z.

Similarly, if P_t^b is below P_t^a, there can be current storage in both countries, or storage in b and trade from b to a, but there cannot be both storage in a and trade from b to a in period t. Thus, Figure 9.5 demonstrates a very important implication of the constraints on the market (given that the marginal transport cost is constant): The importer does not store; the storer does not import.

Reduced-form relations

The requirements for equilibrium are together the first-order conditions of the planner's problem of maximizing social welfare. The planner seeks the optimal allocation of the given amounts available in country a and in country b among current consumption in each location, storage at each location, and the amount currently shipped from one country to the other. If transportation were impossible, the planner could treat each location separately. With the possibility of trade, the planner must simultaneously derive three, not one, behavioral rules: one for the storage in country a, one for the storage in country b, and one for the amount traded. These rules, including the one for current trade, take account of the uncertainty in the future.[7] Each is a function of two state variables, namely, the quantities currently available in a and b, A_t^a and A_t^b. This is the most important insight from the whole exercise of deriving storage rules: The storage in country a as a function of the availability in country a depends on the availability in country b.

For the set of parameters used for the time series in Figure 9.3, Figure 9.6 shows the reduced-form relationships for the equilibrium S_t^a, S_t^b, and Z_t. These full rules are three-dimensional; they can be seen in two dimensions by slicing through at particular values for one of the state variables. In Figure 9.6, two levels for A_t^b are given, 90 units and 110 units. Because of the symmetry within the set of underlying parameters, the illustrated rules for storage in countries a and b are interchangeable, provided A_t^a and A_t^b are also switched.

The two illustrated rules for S_t^a in Figure 9.6(b) are familiar from earlier illustrations of storage rules. The one remarkable curve is that in Figure 9.6(a)

---

[7]   Khusro (1973) considers the equilibrium of current storage and current trade, from the perspective of a planner, but without allowing for the future uncertainty.

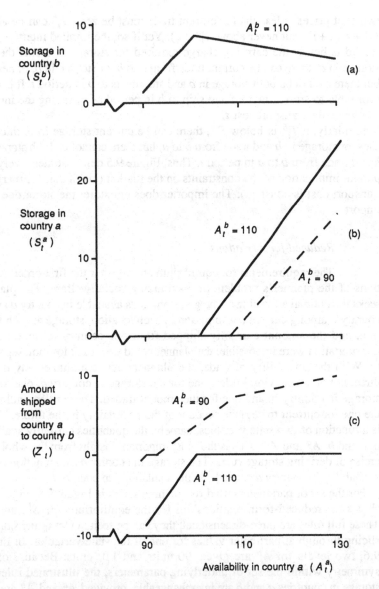

Figure 9.6. Rules for equilibrium storage and trade.

for S_t^b as a function of A_t^a when A_t^b equals 110 units.[8] At a point just beyond A_t^a equal to 100, it changes direction abruptly. Indeed, in these circumstances with availabilities in both countries relatively abundant, the marginal

[8]   When $A_t^b = 90$, $S_t^b = 0$ throughout.

propensity to store in country b out of a further increase in the availability in country a is negative. This shift to a negative marginal propensity to store at b is at the A_t^a where S_t^a first becomes positive. If commodity a is sufficiently abundant to be stored, there is less reason to store more in country b; indeed, some of the availability in b can be released for consumption.

What makes the behavior of either S_t^a or S_t^b explicable is the acknowledged connection between the two countries. As can be seen in Figure 9.6(c), the rule for the amount shipped from country a to country b is a sensible function of the amount available at country a. The higher is A_t^a, the higher is Z_t. Generally there are three discontinuities in the trade rule, the exact levels of A_t^a at which they occur depending on the amount available at country b. For $A_t^b = 90$, one kink in the trade rule occurs at the availability, $A_t^a = 107.95$ to be precise, at which S_t^a is first positive; the marginal propensity to ship out of A_t^a drops on the order of two-thirds once there is storage of a. The other two kinks demarcate the range over which Z_t is 0.0. This range is a manifestation of the discontinuity in the total shipping cost. Over it the availabilities in countries a and b are not far enough apart to induce a trade in either direction. (That is, the equilibrium prices are not z apart.) This range is far to the left on the curve for $A_t^b = 90$ in Figure 9.6(c), between $A_t^a = 89.00$ and $A_t^a = 91.00$. The range of Z_t equal to 0.0 is much larger for the curve with A_t^b equal to 110.0 because the simultaneous equilibrium storage in country a keeps P_t^a from dropping with A_t^a. This range of $Z_t = 0$ begins at $A_t^a = 100.20$ and beyond the values for A_t^a covered in Figure 9.6.[9]

It is worthwhile to visualize how these storage and transformation rules translate into market demand curves. "Market" demand curves here comprise consumption demand, storage demand, and the demand for exports or imports. They record the equilibrium price as a function of the quantity on hand. Accordingly, consider how P_t^a changes as A_t^a increases, for A_t^b equal to 90.0. At a very low A_t^a, one below 89.00 units, country a imports. This has the effect of reducing the decrease in P_t^a with increases in A_t^a compared to the responsiveness of the consumption demand curve, and as a consequence over this range the perceived market demand curve is more elastic than the underlying consumption demand curve. Over the range of A_t^a over which Z_t equals 0.0, the market demand curve is the consumption demand curve, there

---

9   This range of no transformation is an important economic phenomenon, and goes by various names within different fields of economics. In the field of monetary economics, "specie points" refers to the range of, say, the dollar/sterling exchange ratio over which deviations from the official mint values do not justify the expense of transatlantic shipment of gold. A more modern version of the same idea within the field of international finance is "parity bounds," which recognizes the transactions costs of arbitraging among foreign exchange and loans in several currencies. Within these fields of economics, the emphasis is either on the periods when prices are within the range or beyond it, depending on whether periods of no transformation are viewed as normal or abnormal.

being no storage in a. Beyond A_t^a equal 91.00 units, country a exports to country b. Once again this has the effect of making the market demand curve in country a appear more elastic than the underlying consumption demand curve in country a. When A_t^a is high enough for storage in country a to begin, at 107.95 units, the marginal propensity to trade falls. This property alone would make the market demand curve beyond that point less elastic than over the previous range, though still more elastic than the underlying consumption demand curve. But the effect of storage demand works to make the market demand curve even more elastic and that effect is much the stronger.

In short, the possibility of trade and storage both make the market demand curve in country a as a function of A_t^a more price elastic than the underlying consumption demand curve, although the effect is not continuous. Where the discontinuities occur and what the point elasticities are depend on the amount available in country b because the equilibrium demands for storage and trade are functions of both A_t^a and A_t^b. The market demand curve in country b as a function of the availability in b would display similar features: It would be sensitive to the availability in country a. Thus, the total demand for the commodity in any one country is a complex function that changes shape and slope depending on conditions in the other country.

9.2   Convergence to the steady state

Storage in either country spreads any shock in the harvest over several periods. As discussed in Chapter 5, such attenuation is seen in a plot of the values of variables expected in distant periods as of one moment in time, generated by a large number of stochastic simulations with the same initial condition. As also discussed in Chapter 5, these conditional expectations for the case of price can be interpreted as futures prices, quoted as of the initial period for delivery in the distant period.[10] Figure 9.7 provides such a plot of the path of expected prices (as distinct from the expected path of prices), along with conditional expectations of S^a, S^b, and Z for an example with A_0^a equal to 125.00 units and A_0^b equal to 85.00 units. The sum of the two availabilities is close to the long-run average total availability. Although the dispersion in availabilities is much more than seen in any of the periods in Figure 9.3, it is still well within the most extreme dispersion that would be seen in a much longer series. The 40-unit difference offers a large opportunity for trade.

With $A_0^a = 125$ and $A_0^b = 85$, the equilibrium in the current period is for country a to store some of its abundance above average production of 100, export some, and consume some – respectively, 8.17, 15.42, and 1.31 units.

---

10   These pairs of arrays derived from the storage model correspond to the actual arrays of spot and futures prices in pairs of countries studied by Protopapadakis and Stoll (1983), except that here there is only one futures contract per cropyear.

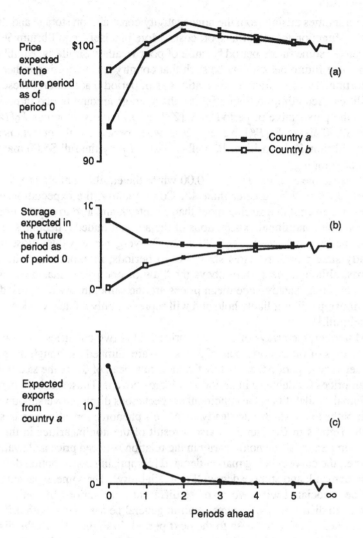

Figure 9.7. Convergence to the steady state, $A_0^a = 125$, $A_0^b = 85$.

With 101.31 units consumed in country a, the price P_0^a is \$92.92. To induce the exports, the equilibrium P_0^b must be above P_0^a by $z = \$5$. To induce the storage, $F_{1,0}^a$ must equal $(92.92 + 2) \times 1.05$. More distant periods from the perspective of period 0 are not, however, separated by full carrying charges and full shipping charges, although there is expected to be trade and storage in the future. The reasons for an expectation of positive storage but not full carrying charges, and for an expectation of positive trade but not price spreads fully covering shipping costs, are, once again, the nonlinearities and discontinuities arising from the nonnegativity constraint on storage and the V-shaped function for total transport costs. More precisely, equilibrium S^a may be zero in some future period because of poor weather. Similarly, equilibrium Z in some future period may be such that country a is importing rather than exporting. The conditional expectations as of period 0 account for these possibilities. According to Figure 9.7(c), the average amount traded in period 2 from the perspective of period 0, $E_0[Z_2]$, is 0.71 units, whereas $E_0[P_2^b]$ is only \$0.60 above $E_0[P_2^a]$. Nevertheless, when period 2 is the current period, if equilibrium Z_2 is positive, P_2^b will be above P_2^a by the full \$5.00 marginal cost of shipping.

Because the equilibrium S_0^b is 0.00 while the equilibrium S_0^a is 8.17, the average A_1^a will be greater than A_1^b. Consequently, the expectation is for country a to continue storing more than country b and also to export. For this reason, the conditional expectations of the amount traded Z decline smoothly to the long-run average of 0.00 units. Convergence to values close to the steady-state means requires six or seven periods, in expectation. In other words, although the system obeys the "law of one price" inasmuch as the two countries' steady-state mean prices are the same, in any one period this relationship will not likely hold and will represent only a fairly weak gravitational pull.[11]

Moreover, the arrays of expected prices in the two countries – that is, the two arrays of futures prices as of period 0 – are humped. Although the prices for delivery in period 0 are below the long-run mean of \$100, the steady-state mean prices for delivery in period 2 or 3 are above it. Thus, for these particular initial availabilities, the conditional expectations display "overshooting" on their paths to the stochastic steady state. This phenomenon, also seen in some of the figures in Chapter 5, is also a result of the nonlinearities in the system – in particular the nonlinearity in the relation between price and availability (i.e., the curve relating market demand [comprising consumption demand, trade demand, and storage demand] to availability). The same expected price can be associated with two or more different distributions of availability. Two such distributions, however, will in general be associated with different mean rates of price increase to the next period. In Figure 9.7(a), the dispersion in availability is less to the left of the top of the hump, and the mean rate of price increase is higher than at similar conditional mean prices on the downward sloping side.

This "overshooting" of expected prices as they converge to the steady state is an equilibrium phenomenon. It is quite distinct from the argument for the overshooting in response to macroeconomic policy, posited by Frankel

---

11 The high degree of serial correlation that goes hand in hand with the slow convergence to the steady state makes regressions of the price in one country on the price in the other country have dubious statistical validity, as noted by Ardeni (1989).

(1986). His argument relies on an assumption that prices are always at full carrying charges – an assumption that is inconsistent with the existence of a stochastic steady state, that is, a long-run invariant distribution of price.[12]

The pattern in Figure 9.7(c) of the expectation of average exports from country a for several periods after period 0 goes far to explain why, in a time series such as Figure 9.3, the amount traded has a positive first-order autocorrelation coefficient. More precisely, the system is characterized by positive serial correlation because the convergence to the stochastic steady state is not expected to be immediate, due to the possibility of storage. If storage were technically impossible while trade cost $5 per unit, the values for period 1 as of period 0 would converge immediately to their long-run values, namely, prices of $100 and average trade of 0.00. The possibility of trade does, even with storage, speed the convergence to the mean of the stochastic steady state. Like elastic supply, trade is a method for absorbing the shocks to the system.

The arrays of conditional expectations plotted in Figure 9.7 would have very different shapes with different initial conditions. For example, if A_0^b were rather large but still smaller than A_0^a, the equilibrium in period 0 would display positive S_0^a, positive S_0^b, but Z_0 equal zero. And because of the relative abundance in country a, the likelihood is for future exports from country a. Thus, the array of conditional expectations for Z would be hump-shaped, whereas those for the prices in the two countries would rise monotonically to the steady-state mean.

The arrays of conditional expectations would also look different if the shipping cost z were larger. At some larger z, the equilibrium in period 0 would be such that P_0^b is above $100, given $A_0^a = 125$ and $A_0^b = 85$. The array of futures prices for delivery in country a would be rising, whereas futures prices for delivery in country b would have a monotonically declining pattern; that is, they would be in backwardation.[13]

Apparent negative returns to storage

The possibility of storage in one country while the spot spread in the other country is below full carrying charges is especially interesting due to a conspicuous feature of actual commodity markets: dealers' and processors' practice of holding inventories even when a commodity's price for future delivery is below the price for immediate delivery. Such storage in the face of backwardations, also known as "inverse carrying charges," has been rationalized in various ways. The most popular interpretation, following the terminology of Kaldor (1939), is that stockholders gain a "convenience yield"

---

[12] For an analysis of Frankel's argument, see Moalla-Fetini (1990).
[13] In the extreme of trade being impossible, the paths for each of the two countries would be like those in Chapter 5, each a function solely of the local initial condition.

from having inventories close at hand. Manufacturers are said to store for a return below their costs of physical storage and capital invested because inventories reduce their need for frequent alterations in the production schedule and reduce the vulnerability to interruptions in deliveries. Likewise, dealers are thought to be willing to pay the opportunity cost of spreads below full carrying charges because inventories make it more likely they will have what their customers need.

What has prompted the explanation based on convenience yield is in part the strong evidence of economic responsiveness in the amount of aggregate storage. The scatter diagram of the spread between a relevant futures price and spot price and the amount of storage of a commodity, whether in registered warehouses, in the hands of processors, or in a whole region, displays a typical relationship. Working (1934) was the first to notice this relationship, in the case of wheat. He called it the supply-of-storage curve, drawing through the observed scatter of points a single curve (1949).[14] The convenience yield, it is claimed, is measured by the extent the points fall below the level of full carrying charges. The concept of convenience yield is not derived from first principles but rather from the need to make sense out of such scatter diagrams.

Yet in this chapter and in our basic model, positive storage is always at full carry. What have we missed? What must we add to our model to reproduce the observed qualitative relationship between spreads and stocks?

"Nothing" is the answer, as it happens. The model in this chapter (and in the next) can duplicate the scatter behind the supply-of-storage curves if the storage in the two countries is lumped together and compared to the price in only one of the countries. In Figure 9.7, S_0^a is positive while the spot spread $F_{1,0}^b - P_0^b$ is below full carrying charges. Should the prices in country b be taken as the return to storage at the other location, it will appear that those storers are holding inventories at an opportunity cost. The same point can be made about the time series in Figure 9.3. In periods 0, 1, 2, 7, and 8, the spot spread in country b is below full carrying charges (i.e., conditions are such that S^b equals 0) while S^a is positive. Were the prices in country a instead taken to be representative of both countries, in periods 4, 6, and 10, storage in b would appear to earn a negative return in expectation.

Thus, the pattern ascribed to convenience yield may well be an aggregation phenomenon. When the stocks of closely related commodities are combined while the prices for one are given prominence, the seeming paradox of storage at an opportunity cost appears. Yet the set of prices for each stored commodity when appropriately disaggregated displays full carrying charges; that

14   Others, including Howell (1956), Brennan (1958), Telser (1958), Weymar (1974), Gray and Peck (1981), Thompson (1986), Williams (1986), Tilley and Campbell (1988), and Thurman (1988), have found the same strong pattern for other commodities and periods.

precise commodity whose prices are below full carrying charges will not be stored.[15]

The subaggregates, which here are the commodities in the two countries, diverge in their behavior because of nonlinearities or intertemporal shifts in the technology that transforms one into the other. The convenience of having supplies on hand matters only because transformations such as transporting, processing, or merchandising are more inflexible in the short run than in the long run, or are unusually costly in the short run. Consequently, a more appropriate, although more grandiloquent, expression than "convenience yield" is "transformation cost minimization." Indeed, from this perspective "convenience yield" is a misleading term. During backwardations, stocks are held not where they are "convenient" but in fact where they are inconvenient, and they are held only because the marginal cost of transforming them into a version that is urgently required is unusually high.

The argument here is closely related to the reason offered in Chapter 5 for why forward spreads are often below full carrying charges. Stockouts are the reason. If country b in the current period desperately wants to transform the production available in the next period into current supplies because of a severe current shortage, the nonnegativity constraint on storage is an infinitely high transformation cost. Future supplies cannot be consumed now regardless of the extent the spread between the spot price in country b and the price for delivery in b that next period is below full carrying charges. Similarly, if the shipping costs from country a are not negligible, country a may keep some stocks even though the spread in country b's prices is below full carrying charges.

9.3   Trade versus storage

Paths of convergence such as those in Figure 9.7 reveal at the extreme right the mean values of the stochastic steady state. Also worth inspecting are the whole probability distributions of the endogenous variables, in the style of Chapter 4. Figure 9.8 shows the steady-state distribution for the amount traded. Because the parameters of this particular system are symmetric, Figure 9.8 is symmetric around a quantity traded of 0.00. Surprisingly, in fully 41.42 percent of the periods there is no trade, despite shipping costs of only 5 percent of the long-run average price (and lower than the typical value in international grain markets). If storage is impossible, the distribution also is symmetric but with a much greater standard deviation. All but 5.64 percent of the periods have trade.

Of course, the probability distributions of the amount traded in Figure 9.8 are a result of a particular marginal shipping cost, $z = \$5$. As in the exercises

---

[15]   We make this argument in more detail in Wright and Williams (1989).

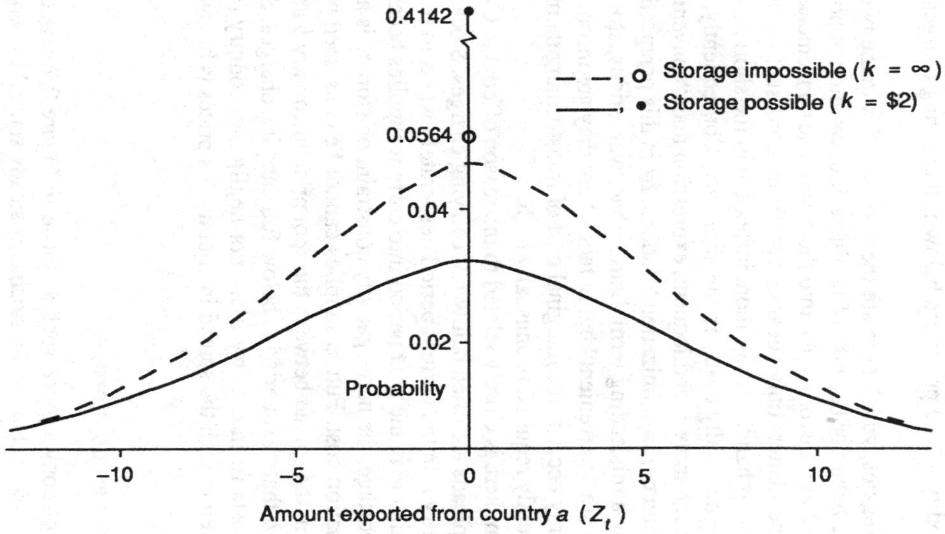
0.4142
0.0564
0.04
0.02
Probability
— —, o Storage impossible (k = ∞)
——, • Storage possible (k = $2)
−10
−5
0
5
10
Amount exported from country a (Z_t)

Figure 9.8. Probability distribution of amount traded.

in Chapter 4, one can investigate the steady-state properties of the system as a function of the underlying parameters. Figures 9.9 and 9.10 provide such an exercise for the parameter z, the marginal cost of shipping. At the left-hand side of the two figures is $z = \$0$. This amounts to the two countries being fully integrated. Storage behavior follows that of a single country whose weather has a coefficient of variation σ_h of 7.071 percent of mean production.[16] If $z = \infty$, it is as if each country is a closed economy reacting through storage to weather uncertainty with a standard deviation of 10 percent of the local mean harvest. Also in Figure 9.9 are the relationships if physical storage costs k are infinite, that is, if trade alone is possible. Figure 9.9 thus allows some conclusions to be drawn about how storage and trade substitute and complement each other in dispersing the shocks due to the weather.

Storage is relatively more effective at stabilizing consumption than is trade.[17] If neither storage nor trade is possible, the standard deviation of consumption in either country is 10 units. If trade alone is possible and costless, σ_{q^a} and σ_{q^b} are 7.071 percent of mean consumption. If storage alone is possible, the two standard deviations are 5.41 percent of mean consumption.

The relative ranking of storage is noteworthy because trade is more flexible, at least within a period, and because storage has positive physical costs of $k = \$2$ in addition to interest costs. Shipments can go from country a to b or from country b to a as need be. In contrast, collective storage can transfer supplies only one direction – to the future. The advantage of storage is that it can smooth multiple production fluctuations, whereas trade can smooth only two (contemporaneous) fluctuations at a time in the absence of storage.

More important than each one's separate contribution, the flexibility from storage and the flexibility from trade complement each other in stabilizing the system. When both are possible, either country's standard deviation of consumption is 4.18 units. This example supports the informal arguments made by Johnson (1975), Josling (1977a), Shei and Thompson (1977), Weckstein (1977), Bale and Lutz (1978, 1979), and Zwart and Meilke (1979) that removal of trade barriers helps to stabilize world prices. But our results suggest the possibility that storage substantially reduces the magnitude of the stabilizing effect of trade indicated in this literature.

Even as storage and trade combine to stabilize consumption, they substitute for each other. According to Figure 9.10, mean storage – whether measured in country a, in country b, or in total – would be, if trade were costless,

---

[16] The coefficient of variation

$$\sigma_{y^{a+b}} = \sqrt{\sigma_{y^a}^2 + \sigma_{y^b}^2} \, / \, (\bar{h}^a + \bar{h}^b) = \sqrt{10^2 + 10^2} \, / \, 200 = 7.071\%$$

because the correlation between the weather in the two countries is 0.

[17] Social welfare, of course, is the proper standard, not the coefficient of variation of consumption. For example, social welfare increases uniformly as z falls, whereas in Figure 9.9 σ_{q^a} is slightly U-shaped as a function of z. The relative importance of storage and trade are the same by either measure, however.

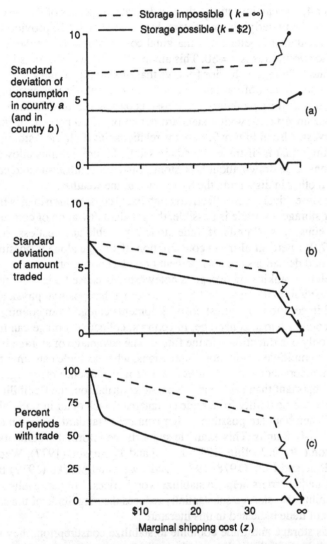

Figure 9.9. Extent of trade with and without storage as a function of shipping costs.

53 percent of average storage if trade were impossible. The percentage of periods with storage would be lower the less expensive is trade.[18] Likewise,

---

[18] In contrast, the percentage of periods in which there is storage in one country and not in the other is not especially sensitive to z, according to Figure 9.10(a). Thus, even in a system with tightly integrated markets – as measured by a low shipping cost – some storers will hold positive inventories while the spread at the other location is below

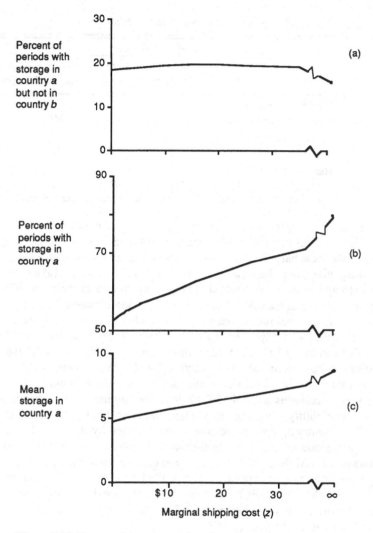

Figure 9.10. Extent of storage as a function of shipping costs.

compared to a system with trade and no storage, one with both trade and storage has a lower standard deviation of the amount traded and fewer periods in which there is trade. This result contrasts with the interaction of storage and responsive supply, discussed in Chapter 4. The possibility of storage makes rational planned supply less stable (while stabilizing consumption).

fully carrying charges. (Note that at $z = \$0$, the distribution of storage between the two countries is undefined.)

Table 9.1. *Conditional probabilities of trade*

	Country a imports		Country a exports	
	Storage impossible	Storage possible	Storage impossible	Storage possible
Harvest in a poor $(-2.1\sigma_{h^a} < h^a < -1.9\sigma_{h^a})$	.925	.440	.019	.001
Harvest in a average $(-0.1\sigma_{h^a} < h^a < 0.1\sigma_{h^a})$	.472	.327	.472	.172
Harvest in a good $(1.9\sigma_{h^a} < h^a < 2.1\sigma_{h^a})$	.019	.061	.925	.889

Storage changes the probability of importing or exporting as a result of particular local harvest. With storage impossible, common sense suggests that if the local harvest is average, country a is as likely to be importing as exporting, given that the weather in country b is independent. Likewise, without storage possible, one might anticipate symmetry in the probabilities of trade. If the local harvest is bad (defined as being between 2.1 and 1.9 standard deviations below the mean), the probability of importing is the same as the probability of exporting if the local harvest should be especially good (defined as being 1.9–2.1 standard deviations above the mean). These properties can be seen in Table 9.1, columns 1 and 3. With storage such intuition about trade, based on the size of the local harvest alone, is unreliable, as can be seen in columns 2 and 4 of Table 9.1. The amount traded depends on the local availability, which is partly a function of past harvests, in country b as well as country a, through the connection provided by storage. Also the contemporaneous availabilities in the two countries are not independent with storage. Should the local harvest be average, country a is about twice as likely to be importing as exporting, specifically 0.327 versus 0.172. (More likely yet, it would do neither.) But then, should the local harvest be good, it is much more likely to be exporting (0.889) than it would be to import should the local harvest be poor (0.440).

9.4   Storage with a general tendency for net trade

These conclusions about the relative roles of trade and storage are, strictly speaking, for systems in which all the economic characteristics of the two countries are identical. In this and the next two sections, we consider variations in which the two countries are asymmetric. In Section 9.6, one country is much larger than the other. In Section 9.5, one country has the majority, rather than half, of the total variation due to the weather. In this section, one of the countries has excess demand and the other excess supply;

that is, under certainty there would be trade. The results of this comparison suggest some inferences about the effects of differential physical storage costs, which we will discuss briefly. As an importer–exporter problem, the model offers insights into an important policy question of whether the net importer or the net exporter should be the principal storer.

Asymmetry in demand

In the two previous sections, the markets were symmetric, with the result that country a exports to b as often as b exports to a. Here the demand in country b is greater than in country a. Although the average shipment thus is from country a to b, shipments can go from b to a if there is an unusually small harvest in country a and a large harvest in country b. Country a, the "home" country, is on average an exporter of foodstuffs; the other, "foreign" country, a net importer.

The tendency for net trade is introduced into the model by changing the consumption demand curves: in the case of country b by shifting the curve out, and for country a by shifting it in. The collective consumption demand remains the same. (Also the equal distributions of production are maintained, with the means at 100 units.) The linear consumption demand curves are rotated slightly, so that the price elasticities of consumption demand remain -0.2 at \$100. An example is the case in which the consumption demand curve in country a goes through the point (95 units, \$100) while that in country b goes through the point (105 units, \$100). This situation is designated as a "gap" of 10 units, which would be closed by costless trade of 5 units. (h^{aN} and h^{bN} are 100 units because the supply elasticity is 0.) With $z = \$5$, the nonstochastic equilibrium is $P^{aN} = \$97.37$, $q^{aN} = 95.50$ units while $P^{bN} = \$102.37$, $q^{bN} = 104.50$ units, with an amount traded of 4.50125 units (continuing to define Z as exports from country a).[19]

Precisely how the tendency for net trade is introduced into the model (with random weather) is relatively unimportant, however. The gap $q^b - q^a$ at \$100 is closely related to the tendency for net trade. What is important is that the gap can be treated as a parameter and varied. Figures 9.11 and 9.12 plot various steady-state properties as functions of the gap. (A negative gap represents country a being a net importer.)

Naturally, the percentage of periods with trade increases with the imbalance in demand, as can be seen in Figure 9.11(c). Also as mean trade increases in absolute value from 0.00 for a gap of 0.00 to 12.00 with a gap of 25, the

---

[19] The need on average to ship some quantity at a positive shipping cost depletes social surplus compared to the situation where both demand curves go through the point (100 points, \$100), and one manifestation is the higher standard deviation of consumption seen in Figure 9.11(a). The social surplus is higher than if nothing is shipped, however.

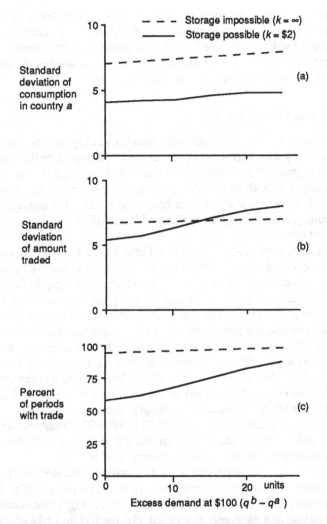

Figure 9.11. Extent of trade with fundamental trade imbalance.

standard deviation of the amount traded rises. On occasion very large amounts
are shipped. Nevertheless, storage is still the more important means of damp-
ening the uncertainty in the system. The standard deviation of consumption in
country a (the importer) is appreciably lower with storage and trade possible
than with trade alone. This conclusion, at least, is unaffected by trade that
would take place under certainty.

The main message of Figure 9.12, which is constructed to give information about both the net exporter and the net importer by letting the "gap" be

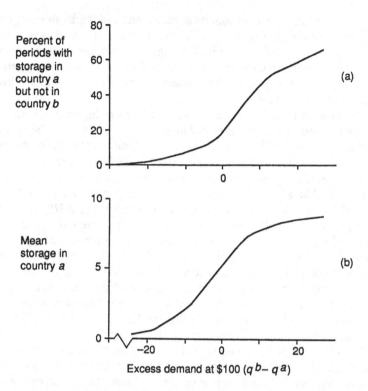

Figure 9.12. Extent of storage in "home" country with fundamental demand imbalance.

negative as well as positive, is that the net exporter should be the principal storer. The more negative is the gap (i.e., the more the home country is the net importer), the lower is the average storage in country a, the fewer periods it has positive storage, and the fewer the periods it has positive storage while country b has no storage. This pattern occurs despite the stronger demand on the part of the net importer. That stronger excess demand, however, concerns the location of the demand curve, not its shape as reflected in its elasticity and curvature. The lower the elasticity and higher the curvature the more is stored on average. Since the elasticities and curvatures at $100 are the same for the two locations, one consumption demand curve having higher consumption at any price provides no special inducement for extra storage at that location. Rather, total storage would be lower the greater is the net trade. For example, with no gap, total storage averages $5.20 + 5.20 = 10.40$, whereas with a gap of 25 it averages $8.54 + 0.22 = 8.76$.

The outward shift in the consumption demand curve in country b when the gap is positive actually works against storage in country b. Typically, the price in b is higher than in country a, on the order of the $5 shipping charge. Because one cost to storage is the interest on the value of what is stored, on average that interest expense will be higher for storage in the net importer than for storage in the net exporter. It is as if the physical storage costs were higher for the net importer, which would clearly work against higher average storage in that country.

The point at issue can also be understood by picturing the equilibrium for a particular pair of availabilities in countries a and b. Suppose they are equal and large – say, 110.00 units each – in which circumstance, for the case of no "gap," the prices and the amounts stored in the two countries would be the same. Specifically each country would store 7.50 units and the local spot price would be $87.51. The prices expected for period $t+1$ would be above $87.51 by full carrying charges. These expected prices $E_t[P_{t+1}^a[7.50,7.50]]$ $= E_t[P_{t+1}^b[7.50,7.50]] = \$93.99$ are examples from the more general functions relating expected prices to current storage in the two countries. If instead there is a gap of 10 units, which leads to trade in most periods, under this pair of availabilities there is no trade but there is storage in both locations in equilibrium. P_t^b is higher than P_t^a, because of the difference in demand curves. Were the same quantity stored at country b 7.50 units, as in a system with no gap (and assuming briefly that the function $E_t[P_{t+1}^b[S_t^a,S_t^b]]$ is unchanged), that amount of storage would lose money, because $P^b[110-7.50]$ is $111.90, not $87.51. The response would be to cut back, until P_t^b and $E_t[P_{t+1}^b[S_t^a,S_t^b]]$ differ by full carrying costs. The same reasoning would dictate an expansion of the storage at country a. These effects feed on one another and change the functions for expected prices depending on the amounts in store. Among other properties, $E_t[P_{t+1}^b[0,0]]$, which is the price expected for period $t+1$ when there is nothing in store, is higher than $E_t[P_{t+1}^a[0,0]]$. The two equilibrium expected prices are $91.18 and $95.45, respectively, a difference of $4.27. As a result for a gap of 10 units, when A_t^a equals 110 and A_t^b also equals 110, S_t^a equals 12.12 units while S_t^b equals 2.61.[20] (If the two equilibrium expected prices differed by $5, exports from a in period $t+1$ would be certain.)

Asymmetry in storage costs

Another reason for storage disproportionately at one location is a difference in storage costs, whether physical storage costs, the spoilage rate, or the interest rate. For example, a crop may be produced and consumed in both temperate and tropical zones, but expenditures on fungicides and insecticides cause relatively higher storage costs in the tropics. Relatively small differentials in storage costs shift storage markedly to the country with the cost

[20] If most of the uncertainty is in the harvest for the net importer, country b, the average storage in b may be higher than the average storage in a.

advantage, at least compared to the change in total storage if both countries had the same increase in physical storage costs.

Yet it may seem surprising that high-cost storage is ever used. It is used because even less attractive is the expense of shipping from one country to store more cheaply in the other only to have a good chance of needing a reverse shipment the next period. In the extreme, the storage cost differential cannot be greater than the round-trip freight rate. By the same token, when high-cost storage is used, it is in small amounts and usually complementary to low-cost storage in the other country.

The tendency for storage in one country to dominate with even small differentials in storage costs is even more pronounced when there is net trade because of a gap in demand in the two countries. If the country that imports on average also has higher storage costs, the importance of storage in the exporting country is reinforced. But if the net exporter suffers the higher storage costs, the issue is rather less clear and depends on the likelihood of trade going against the usual direction. If exports are certain, holding back some in country a at most saves the interest expense on the shipping costs. If storage costs in country a, say, are greater than in country b by more than the interest saved by delaying shipment (5% of $5, or $0.25 per period for the parameters we have been using here), the shipment should be made immediately, perhaps for storage in country b.

9.5   Sources of inherent randomness

In previous sections each of the two countries has had equally variable weather. That is not to say the random disturbances in the two countries were posited to be identical. The contrary was the case: The correlation between the two random disturbances was always 0.0. In this section, these conditions are relaxed. First we investigate disproportionate shares of the total variance, holding the correlation at 0.0, and then different correlations, keeping the share of the total variance equal.

Differential weather variances

How are storage and trade affected in an otherwise symmetric setting where one country has more variable weather than the other? Figures 9.13 and 9.14 give information similar to that in Figures 9.9 and 9.10, but as a function of country a's share of the total weather variance rather than as a function of the shipping cost. Previously, the total weather variance was $(\sigma_{ya})^2 + (\sigma_{yb})^2 = 10^2 + 10^2 = 200$ square units. Here we keep the total variance as before but vary the share of home country a. For example, when country a has an 80 percent share, $\sigma_{ya} = 12.65$ while $\sigma_{yb} = 6.32$. A share of 60 percent for country a is the mate to one for b of 40 percent, 70 percent to

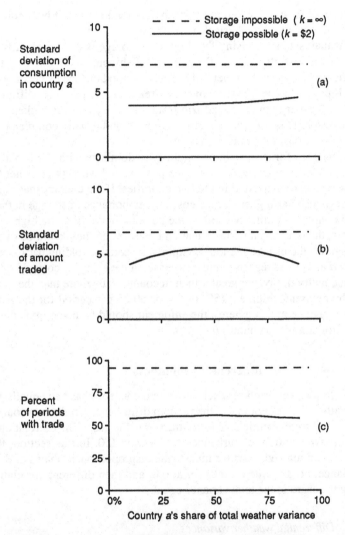

Figure 9.13. Extent of trade and location of variable weather.

30 percent, and so on, so that information about both countries can be read off Figures 9.13 and 9.14. The results for 50 percent duplicate those seen in Figures 9.9 and 9.10 for $z = \$5$. Each point along the continuum in Figures 9.13 and 9.14 represents the steady-state properties for a distinct system,[21]

---

[21] The other parameters remain: linear consumption demand with $\eta^d = -0.2$, $\eta^s = 0.0$, $k^a = k^b = \$2$, and $r = 5$ percent.

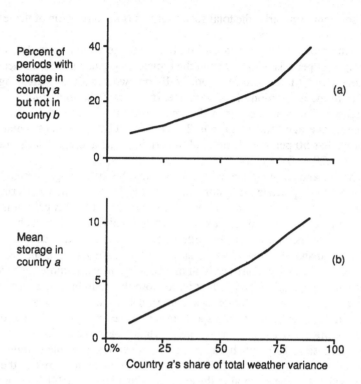

Figure 9.14. Extent of storage and location of variable weather.

each with its own set of reduced-form equations for equilibrium S_t^a, S_t^b, and Z_t as functions of the underlying parameters and current availabilities A_t^a and A_t^b.

With storage technically impossible, the relative sources of the randomness in the combined harvest are immaterial to the allocative properties of trade.[22] Trade compensates for a difference in current availabilities (i.e., harvests) in the two countries. Whether a difference of 15 units arises because h^a is 115 units due to the weather being variable in that country while h^b is its unvarying value of 100 units (i.e., a's share of the variance is 100%) or because h^a is its unvarying value of 100 units while h^b is 85 units due to local bad weather (i.e., a's share is 0%), the same amount of trade results – namely, 7 units (because the consumption demand curves are the same in the two countries). Consequently, in Figure 9.13 the relationships marked "storage impossible"

---

[22] The welfare effects will depend on the relative sources of randomness, a point made by Bigman (1985b).

are constant. Similarly, the total social surplus is not a function of the relative variance.[23]

In the more complex systems involving storage as well as trade, the percentages of periods with trade and the typical magnitude traded, as measured by the standard deviation of trade, fall somewhat with an increasing disparity in the proportion of the variance. In contrast, the role of total storage increases. For example, when the uncertainty is distributed 20 versus 80 percent, average total storage is $2.83 + 9.14 = 11.97$; whereas when each country has 50 percent of the total uncertainty, the average total storage is $5.20 + 5.20 = 10.40$ units.

The storage taking place, whether indicated by the average storage or the percentage of periods with storage, is mostly in the country suffering the more uncertain weather, as can be seen in Figure 9.14. This pattern is little changed from the broad result without trade involved at all. If each country were a closed economy, the one with the greater weather variance would store more often and more on average, as was noted in Chapter 4. If the source of the total uncertainty is primarily in one country, it makes more sense to use that harvest variation itself – that is, to store the main part of a local abundance – to offset a poor future local harvest than to rely on imports (given the magnitudes of storage and transport costs in these examples). If the prospective trading partner is used to dampen variations and the availability there is always close to 100 units because the harvest varies little, the marginal cost of imports, apart from transport fees, is likely to be on the order of the marginal value of consumption in the exporter – that is, near $100. The marginal cost of something put into store locally during a huge harvest would be much below $100.

The presence of storage can also be said to make the market demand curves more elastic. Moreover, the greater the local uncertainty, the greater the elasticity over the range of positive storage. (At low availabilities, the market demand curve's elasticity remains the consumption demand curve's.) For a given distribution of harvests and a given shipping cost z, the more elastic are the effective demand curves, the less often would the differential between P^a and P^b be large enough to justify trade. Of course, as the total uncertainty is located more in one country, the effective demand curve in the other is becoming less elastic because of the lower demand for storage. But the distribution of availabilities in the other country is also less dispersed. All these effects interact to reduce the role of trade relative to storage in a system with greater concentration in the uncertainty.

---

[23] The welfare of the individual countries, however, is a function of the (rather slight) increase or decrease in stability they experience through trade, as exhibited in Figure 9.13(a).

Correlation between the weather in the two countries

In this entire chapter so far, we have assumed that the weather in country a is uncorrelated with the weather in country b. How does the interaction of trade and storage change with the correlation ρ between the weather in the two countries?

To ask the question is practically to answer it.[24] If the correlation is -1.0, so that good weather in country b is always contemporaneous with bad weather in country a, and if the shipping cost z is $\$0.0$, trade alone fully compensates for the uncertainty. Indeed, there would be no uncertainty in the aggregate. Even if z is positive but smaller than the costs of storage, it never pays to store when ρ is close to -1.00. A poor local harvest next period can be more cheaply satisfied with imports despite the transport costs. On the other end of the spectrum, if ρ is 1.0, in which case the disturbances in the two countries are identical, there is no role for trade. Each country might as well be considered a closed economy. Storage is the only response to the uncertainty.

Although the weather correlation ρ is crucial to the analysis of trade as a response to uncertainty, it is ignored in the literature. To take but one example, Bigman (1985a, chap. 3) assumes in his analytical models a ρ of 0.0, and, while offering in his empirical sections import instability indexes and coefficients of variation of nominal protection coefficients for a number of countries, he provides no information about the correlation of weather (or similar shocks) across the countries. Where the analysis is solely about trade, the omission of ρ may be reasonable. As long as ρ is somewhat below the extreme of 1.0, there would be gains in world surplus from free trade. But unless the correlations are negative, one might well consider whether a regime with storage, not trade, should be the focus of the analysis.

9.6   Relative size of countries

This section concludes the "comparative statics" of the storage and trade model laid out in Sections 9.1 and 9.2. Here the exercise is to vary the relative sizes of the two countries. This is done in the model by keeping one country's demand curve passing through the point (100 units, $100) while the other country's demand curve passes variously through (200 units, $100), (300 units, $100), and so forth, always with an $\eta^d = -0.2$ at that point. In the extreme is the case of a small open economy, which takes the prices in the other country as given. Of particular interest is the small open

---

[24]   We have constructed figures as a function of ρ comparable to Figures 9.9 and 9.10, but on inspection their results seemed unsurprising.

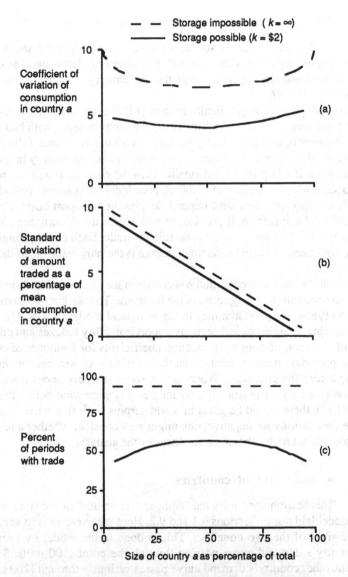

Figure 9.15. Extent of trade and relative size of country *a*.

economy's storage rule compared to the FOB–CIF band around the "world" price.[25]

As in Sections 9.4 and 9.5 the steady-state properties of systems with

---

[25] Knapp (1982) derives a storage and transformation rule for a small open economy, and Buccola and Sukume (1988) a rule for a small open controlled economy (Zimbabwe).

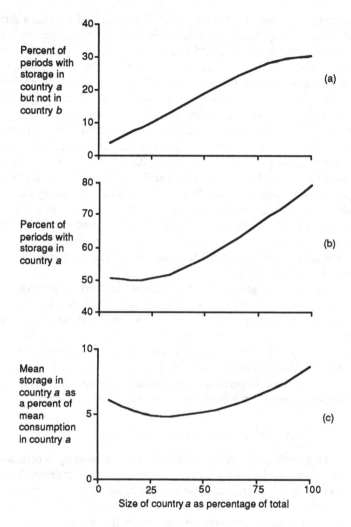

Figure 9.16. Extent of storage and relative size of country a.

countries of different relative sizes are organized into two figures: Figure
9.15 for statistics about trade and Figure 9.16 for statistics about storage.
Both figures take the perspective of country a and show the quantity stored as
a percentage of average consumption in country a. The properties for country
a's size of 25 percent are the mates for the properties for country b's size
of 75 percent, and so forth. For Figure 9.15(b)–(c), concerning trade from
either the small or large country's perspective, the relationship is symmetric
around a 50 percent share. The values at country a being 50 percent of the

world market correspond to the entries in Figures 9.9 and 9.10 for a shipping cost of $5. (Contemporaneous weather shocks v_t^a and v_t^b are uncorrelated.)

Several patterns in Figures 9.15 and 9.16 are understandable from previous discussions of trade and storage. The weather in the larger country dominates the total weather of the pair. Consequently, the whole system behaves more like a single closed economy, in which storage is the only available response to the uncertainty in the harvest. Storage in the larger country is less influenced by conditions in the smaller country; hence in Figure 9.16 the proportion of periods in which there is storage in country a is higher if country a is the bigger of the pair rather than the smaller. Similarly, the coefficient of variation of consumption for either the smaller or the larger country is higher the greater the disparity in size. Because a small open economy can buy or sell what it wants with little effect on prices, the importance of trade – measured as a percentage of average consumption in country a – is greater the more unequal in size are the two countries. And Figure 9.16(c) confirms that mean storage (as a percentage of mean consumption) actually rises as country a becomes relatively small.

Other patterns in Figures 9.15 and 9.16 may be more surprising. For example, why is the percentage of periods with trade lower in a system in which the countries are unequal in size? Why is mean storage (as a percentage of mean consumption) not symmetric around a 50 percent share? More perplexing, why does the relationship between the size of country a and the percentage of periods with storage at country a flatten out below a size of 25 percent at a value of 50 percent of the periods? The answers to these questions can best be seen in the extreme of the small open economy.

Price relationships in a small open economy

To a small open economy, the prices of the large open economy are virtually exogenous, including futures prices as well as spot prices. These futures prices – or, more precisely, the spreads in the large economy – impose strong conditions on the possible equilibrium configurations in the small economy. These conditions have not been explicitly recognized in other discussions of the storage rules for small open economies, such as those by Reutlinger et al. (1976), Feder et al. (1977), Alaouze et al. (1978, 1979), Knapp (1982), Reutlinger (1982), and Pinckney (1988, 1989).[26]

Consider a case in which the current availability is considerable in the large country and even more so, in proportional terms, in the small country. The equilibrium is for storage in both locations and for no trade. The spot price in the small country is above the FOB export price unless the availability in the

---

[26] The analysis here concerns an equilibrium. In contrast, Moore (1989) studies inventories in a disequilibrium macro model of a small open economy. (Recall the discussion in Chapter 2 of disequilibrium models of closed economies.)

small country is so high that it exports to the big country and the big country does not store. Indeed, that spot FOB export price is irrelevant when both countries store. What is relevant is the forward FOB price. Always an alternative to exporting in the current period is a contract to export the next period. At the minimum, therefore, the price for delivery in the small country the next period must be the futures price in the large country minus the stable shipping costs. This minimum small-country futures price, when divided by $(1 + r)$ and adjusted for physical storage costs (which are the same in the two countries) must be greater than the spot FOB price. The futures price in the large country itself cannot be above the spot price in the large country by more than storage costs.

Thus, it is better to store in the small country rather than export immediately when the large country is storing, because at a minimum the savings are equal to the interest on a delayed investment in shipping costs. More likely, the savings are greater, because this argument supposes the futures price in the small country is below the futures price in the large country by the full marginal cost of shipping. Such a spread would occur only if exports from the small country would be appropriate under all circumstances the next period. At the very least, some circumstances may dictate storage in both countries and hence spot prices in period $t+1$ closer together than z. If the small country's futures price for delivery in period $t+1$ is closer to the large country's futures price, the small country's spot price is correspondingly farther above the FOB export indicator. In short, the pressure of arbitrage limiting the spread between spot and futures in the large country indirectly puts a floor under the spot price in the small country that is above the FOB export price when the large country is storing.

As seen earlier, a country should never import in order to store, given that the cost of shipping is the same the next period as the current period. It would be cheaper to have a quantity the next period by contracting in the current period for delivery in the large country the next period and shipment then. Indeed, the maximum spot price in the small country consistent with positive storage should be below the threshold CIF import price, at least by the interest saved by delaying expenditures on shipping for one period. More likely, the future price for delivery in period $t+1$ in the small country is not above the large country's futures price by the full shipping cost. The spot price in the small country consistent with the futures price being at full carrying charges, and hence supporting storage, would be further below the CIF import price.

If the small country is importing in order to store, it is actually speculating that the futures price in the large country is below the expected spot price or that shipping costs will be substantially greater the next period. But that speculation is more directly achieved by long positions in the appropriate futures contracts (e.g., the freight index contract on the Baltic Exchange in London).

The bounds on the small country's spot price imposed by storage arbitrage as well as spatial arbitrage can be seen in the market demand curves. Figure 9.17 shows the equilibrium price in the small country, country b, as a function of its own availability, for two different levels of availabilities in the large country. In Figure 9.17(a), the large country has an availability equal to 100 percent of its average harvest, whereas in Figure 9.17(b) A_t^a is 110 percent, which is close to the long-run average availability with storage possible. Country a is the large country and is nineteen times bigger than country b. The equilibrium price in the larger country can be inferred from the direction of trade, which can be inferred from the kinks in Figure 9.17. To the left of the double kink, country b imports: P_t^a is below P_t^b. To the right of the double kinks, P_t^a is above P_t^b. The price in the larger country is lower in the lower panel than in the upper panel for any availability in the small country. In each panel, the dotted lines represent the market demand curve in the smaller country with trade alone possible, the solid lines the situation with storage and trade both possible. In each of the two relationships for trade alone possible, the FOB–CIF band is prominent. (The example has $z = \$10$ to make it more visible.) For the small country's market demand curves involving storage, however, imports cease at a higher price (the price at the left-hand kink) when there is storage, because the smaller country's demand must compete for the availability in the larger country with storage demand in the larger country. The steeply sloped segment after the left-hand kink is a portion of the smaller country's consumption demand curve, because there is no storage in the smaller country at prices near the import price, namely, the CIF threshold. (Recall Figure 9.5.) The vertical height of this steep drop is at least zr (i.e., $\$10 \times .05$), the interest on the transport cost.

Knapp (1982, p. 204) has concluded: "Generally speaking, optimal carryovers [of a small open economy] increase with domestic supply and decrease with the world price." The first of these features is present in Figure 9.17 but not the second. The small country's marginal propensity to store out of its local availability (when local storage is positive) is between 0.0 and 1.0. That is, the market demand curve, comprising consumption demand, storage demand, and trade demand, slopes down. Thus, if domestic availability is larger, the smaller country stores more (over the range of positive storage). The greater is the availability in the larger country, the lower will be the equilibrium spot prices in the two countries. For any given availability in the small country, a lower spot price in the world market is consistent with higher consumption and lower storage. For example, for a local availability of 110 units, the equilibrium in Figure 9.17(a) is a "world" price of $\$104.83$ with storage in the small country of 5.24 units, compared to the equilibrium in Figure 9.17(b) of $\$90.36$ and 4.21 units. (Total storage, however, is greater in the latter case, because much more storage occurs in the larger country.) Knapp is wrong about the relation between the small country's storage and

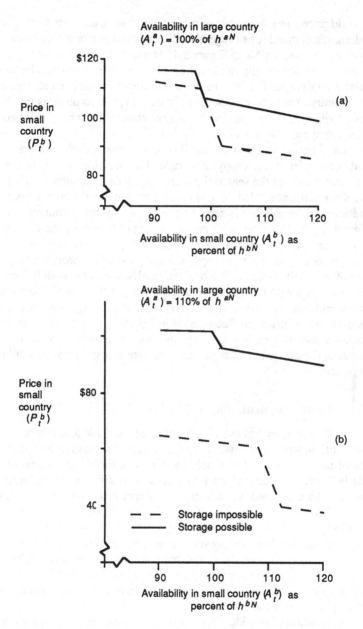

Figure 9.17. Market demand curves in the small country, country *b*.

the world price (over this range of prices), because he does not recognize that the domestic demand for storage is itself a function of worldwide stocks.

Another feature visible in Figure 9.17 is that over the range of imports on the left of the panels, the market demand curve is more price elastic (i.e., flatter) with storage. The imports are being drawn in part from storage in the large country. Yet another aspect of Figure 9.17, one so obvious that it may be overlooked, is the possibility that storage affects the "world" price considerably, much more than trade.

It should be stressed that the small country's storage rule and market demand curve refer to intercropyear storage. Seasonal storage may be a different matter, although the seasonal patterns in the large country would have a controlling influence. Also there is the assumption that the contemporaneous correlation in the weather is zero. For an individual small country in a very different region from the main producer (or producers) of the commodity, that may be a reasonable characterization. But it is implausible on its face if the large country is meant to represent the "rest of the world" comprising many other small countries. Each of the small countries cannot in turn have zero correlation with the aggregate of the others, or there would be no uncertainty worldwide. If there were no worldwide uncertainty, there would be no reason for world prices to fluctuate (although there would still be scope for trade). An analysis presuming many small countries whose weather is independent of the others but who face unstable world prices leads to a fallacy of composition.

9.7   Final comments on trade

This chapter has examined within-period trade as a response to the uncertainty in harvests of two countries. Except for those in Section 9.4, in none of the systems studied would there be any trade under certainty. The trade is "free," constrained only by a fixed per-unit cost of shipping. It is conducted by a competitive industry. As in previous chapters, the emphasis here has been on the allocative effects of trade. A contrast has been drawn with storage, which is a response across periods to the uncertainty. If storage or trade alone is technically possible, then it is the socially optimal response to the uncertainty. Obviously, if both trade and storage are technically possible, social surplus is higher still. Thus, the discussion of trade underscores the insight that analysis of the effects of uncertainty must be cast against the backdrop of the feasible technology.

In the situation of two identical countries with weather uncorrelated across time or space, ideal, costless trade alone would reduce the coefficient of variation of consumption to a factor of $1/\sqrt{2}$. Costless storage would achieve a reduction of close to 1/2. (Gains in social surplus would be more or less proportional.) Thus, it is fair to say storage appears more effective as a response to the aggregate risk, even if in practice both storage and trade are costly. That ranking is even sharper should the countries be of unequal size or the contemporaneous weather positively correlated. Trade would be of greater use if the contemporaneous correlation were negative, so that one country's poor harvest was offset by the other country's good harvest.

The analysis here has been simplified by restricting the one-period-lagged supply elasticity in both countries to be 0.0. If planned production could be adjusted, the response to the social uncertainty would be yet more effective. For example, if country a had a harvest failure and country b had a large quantity on hand, elastic supply would permit more to be shipped from b to a at the expense of depleting reserves in country b because plantings in both locations could be increased to restore, in expectation, the normal level of stocks. This added flexibility, however, is due to storage. In a system with elastic one-period-lagged supply and trade but no possibility of storage, planned supply would be the same period after period (although that stable value might be influenced by the prospects for trade). Planned production for next period's harvests cannot help disperse the vagaries of this period's harvests unless storage connects the periods.

Were there more countries in the model, the analysis would be correspondingly more complex. The increased complexity of the spatial equilibrium – the price in each country could not be above or below any other country's price by more than the price of transport adjusted for distance – is obvious, but the increased complexity of the intertemporal equilibrium is even more demanding. Those countries that would be storing must have futures prices (i.e., expected prices for the next period) above their local spot prices by full carrying charges and no more. The set of futures prices also cannot be outside any FOB–CIF band; otherwise there is the opportunity for arbitrage. These additional equilibrium conditions impose much more stringent conditions on the spatial equilibrium of spot prices than would intraperiod trade alone, as was pointed out in Section 9.1. A model with many more countries than two also puts a spotlight on the correlation matrix of the weather. Which countries store and which trade will primarily be a function of such cross-sectional correlations. On that score it should never be forgotten that a model of a single small open economy is imbedded in a broader model. In that larger model it is essential to ask how does the aggregate uncertainty arise and what are the endogenous responses to it, such as storage.

In the model studied here, the shipping cost was constant per unit and constant over time. If the commodity of interest were significant in total world trade, the cost of shipping the commodity might increase with the quantity shipped. (The total cost function could still be fixed over time, however.) Under such circumstances, it would be much less likely to get corner solutions such that it would not be sensible to export some amount only to have it put into store. Nevertheless, the general point of trade decisions being in equilibrium with storage decisions would still hold. If shipping costs were always constant within a period but changed over time (and independently of the circumstances specific to the commodity of interest), they would have to be represented by a third state variable in the dynamic programming algorithm. Such a modeling complication, of course, would matter only if the commodity were storable, for only if storage connected the future with the present would the current spatial equilibrium be influenced by the prospects for future shipping costs.

Similarly, storage complicates the conventional single-period analysis of trade because the positive autocorrelation induced by storage appears in the quantity traded. Among other things, that feature complicates not only the interpretation of the law of one price but the empirical determination of whether a particular country is truly self-sufficient. (Recall the problems with testing for booms or busts, discussed in Chapter 6.) Also, through the transmission mechanism of storage, current conditions result from past trade decisions: Current availabilities are predetermined variables, instead of strictly exogenous variables. And in terms of analytical techniques, the usual "cross" diagrams of excess demand and supply are inadequate for determining the equilibrium amount traded.

The main reason for neglect of the rich potential of models with both trade and storage is no doubt the added complexity of the models. This chapter shows how much can be learned using an extension of our modeling approach.

CHAPTER 10

Inventories of raw materials, finished goods, and goods in process

In the recent macroeconomics literature, discussion of inventories has revolved around a "production-smoothing" function for holding stocks. As Blinder (1986, p. 12) puts it: "A firm is said to smooth production if its production responds less to a sales [that is, a demand] shock than it would if it could not carry inventories." At first glance this role for stockholding appears to be different from the consumption-smoothing buffering effect emphasized so far in this book. It also seems intuitively plausible. Because of unforeseeable fluctuations in the demand for final goods, a firm would have to alter its contemporaneous production schedule a great deal and at considerable expense, unless it held inventories of finished goods.[1] By extension (so the argument goes), aggregate production should be less variable than aggregate final consumption, both for particular industries and for the economy as a whole. Nevertheless, this production-smoothing role of inventories, at least as formally modeled, appears to be contrary to the facts in the U.S. economy. As Blinder (1986) observes, a broad stylized fact is that aggregate current production is more variable than aggregate current final consumption. West (1986) also tests the model for particular industries, specifically food, tobacco, apparel, chemicals, petroleum, and rubber, and decisively finds final consumption to be less variable than production.[2]

[1] In the context of agricultural commodities, "production" as used in this literature refers to processing rather than new plantings.

[2] Ghali (1987) offers evidence for several more disaggregated industries suggestive of seasonal movements confounding these simple comparisons. He concludes that there is some support for the production-smoothing model, although Miron and Zeldes (1989b) offer evidence for other seasonal industries that do not seem to have less variable production than final consumption. Fair (1989), in contrast, finds support for the production-smoothing model in seven industries, and argues that the other results are due to the poor quality of the inventory data used. Miron and Zeldes (1989a) also cast doubt on the quality of the data representing new production.

273

In the model and its variations here – by construction a model of inventories and production rationally atuned to the costs of irregular production – inventories smooth production, by Blinder's standard, even though they conform to the stylized fact of production (i.e., processing) being more variable than consumption. For the amount processed is less variable than it would be without the possibility of inventories of finished goods, provided there are inventories of raw materials. Thus, across many combinations of underlying parameters, the model developed here accords with intuition and observation. The probability is large, therefore, that the problem with the recent macroeconomics literature is a failure to comprehend inventory behavior within a full system at the level of aggregate behavior. The conventional production-smoothing model misses the feedback effects present in a model of the whole industry, including raw material as well as processing. It does not portray price, storage, production of raw material, and processing as interacting in sequential equilibria (i.e., period by period) for the optimal assignment of the responses to shocks.

The models of this chapter are adaptations of the trade model of two locations, introduced in Chapter 9, to the situation where one commodity is solely an input without independent consumption demand and the other is solely an output. We develop the model from this perspective in Section 10.1. Having formulated and elucidated the reduced-form relationships for equilibrium behavior for this case, we conduct a sensitivity analysis in Section 10.2. This sensitivity analysis clarifies the roles of inventory of raw materials and inventory of finished goods in smoothing the amount processed. In Section 10.3, we present the yet more complicated case in which the processing requires one period, instead of being accomplished instantaneously, and explore its behavior. This case permits the study of the interaction of storage of raw material, goods in process, and inventories of finished goods. The main conclusion is that inventories of finished goods and goods in process overshadow inventories of raw materials, in contrast to the case where processing must be within the same period.

Modeling approaches in the macroeconomics literature

Our results bring to light the consequences of seemingly small differences in modeling approaches. Some of these differences can also be seen in a brief review of the inventory models presented in the macroeconomics literature, all of which are more appropriately models of a small industry rather than models of an entire economy. Confronted with the finding of production (i.e., processing) being more variable than contemporaneous consumption, Blinder (1986) asked how can the production-smoothing model be "saved"? One modeling response has been to consider the possibility of shocks to costs of processing in addition to demand, and to convert the model to one in which inventories smooth not the level of processing but the costs of processing. Eichenbaum (1989) finds empirical support for this reformulation but Miron and Zeldes (1988, 1989b) do not. Another approach has been to model a cost of adjusting inventory levels. Eichenbaum (1984) and West (1986) present such a model, although West's tests also decisively reject that formulation. Blinder (1986) has taken a third approach, by representing the shock to demand as a combination of two components: one that the firm knows but the econometricians cannot measure and another that does surprise the firm. This second type of shock occurs after the firm commits to the amount to process. (This setup is similar to a model of agricultural production with one-period-lagged supply.) Blinder interprets the empirical evidence as suggesting the first type of shock is more important. In all these approaches, the emphasis is on inventories of finished goods; with the exception of Ramey (1989), there is no provision for inventories of raw material or goods in process. It is not clear that any of these approaches save the production-smoothing model.[3]

Unfortunately, the distinction between firm and industry is rather vague in this literature. The standard production-smoothing model of inventories and its various extensions envision single firms making decisions about inventories and current production of finished goods. This emphasis on a single firm is strongest in articles such as Blinder (1982) and Kahn (1987) in which the firm is a monopolist. More often in the models, the firm is taken as a representative of a competitive industry, although whether the demand disturbance affects the single firm or the whole industry is often unclear. The firm is portrayed as explicitly maximizing the discounted present value of profits while recognizing that its current decisions influence its position in the future. Its problem is then a hybrid of the forward-looking planner's problem. As a signal for storage, the expected price for the next period (or the futures price more concretely yet) is not explicit, because the firm as the storer trades with itself when putting goods into or taking goods out of inventory. As regards the current spot price for the finished good, the model views it as given, the disturbance being a fluctuation in demand at that set price. How the price happens to be at that level is not addressed.

As a model of aggregate inventory behavior, the standard production-smoothing model has a number of dissatisfying properties and internal inconsistencies. For one, it assumes a quadratic total cost to the firm of its inventories, including negative inventories. This assumption is advantageous for permitting analytical solution of the model; but it implies that if the demand shocks are idiosyncratic, some firms hold much inventory at a high marginal

---

3   Christiano and Eichenbaum (1989) argue that some of the problem with the empirical performance of the production-smoothing model may be in the temporal aggregation of what are in fact quantities continuously adjusted by firms into monthly or quarterly production and stock figures.

cost while others hold little inventory at a low marginal cost. Obviously, the firms with the large holdings could try to rent warehousing space from the others or some similar arrangement. Because they are assumed not to, the model countenances discrepancies in storage costs that amount to a disequilibrium. More important, the model permits negative inventories, under the presumption that these are equivalent to backorders, although physically it is impossible to have negative inventories.[4]

Kahn (1987) has reformulated the production-smoothing model to include a nonnegativity constraint on inventories (in the context of a monopolistic firm). Nevertheless, Kahn's model retains another of the dissatisfying features of the production-smoothing model: Price does not change from period to period. As a result, in his model and more generally, the production-smoothing model presupposes a disequilibrium. As Summers (1981) has argued forcefully, it is difficult to imagine that price does not fall to some extent, when many firms experience a decline in demand (a negative industrywide shock). Also, as Summers points out, the model is tested on aggregate inventories. Because of the collective feedback of individual decisions, there is no reason to suppose that a model of an individual firm taking prices as given should explain aggregate behavior (the fallacy of composition). Price should be endogenous at the industry level.

The same fallacy of composition results from the assumption that each firm can buy all the raw material it needs at the given price. Surely, to the industry as a whole, the within-period supply elasticity of the raw material is not infinitely elastic. Indeed, if the production of the raw material takes time, the industry-level within-period supply may be infinitely inelastic if the raw material is used exclusively in that industry. If the supply of raw material is not infinitely elastic, one would imagine that firms would hold inventories of raw materials (as, of course, they do). The production-smoothing model does not, however, address the interaction of inventories of raw material and finished goods.

This chapter does address that issue. It builds in Section 10.1 a model of a system with a raw material, within-period processing, and a finished good. Inventories of both the raw material and the finished good are possible, and there is a disturbance both to the supply of the raw material and to the final consumption demand. Specialist firms are presumed to produce the raw material with a one-period lag, others to store it, others to process it within the period, others to store the finished good, and others to distribute it to the final consumers. By unbundling the functions of the firm in the standard production-smoothing model, this approach forces the analysis to make the spot and futures prices explicit and endogenous. The relationships among the

---

4   Schutte (1983) observes, with an argument more generally applicable, that in Blinder's (1982) model the mean steady-state quantity of inventories is negative.

various spot and futures prices are constrained to obey the conditions for the sequential equilibria of aggregate behavior. The analysis considers the market as a whole and allows no hidden, unexplained disequilibria.

10.1 Inventories of raw material and finished goods

The basic storage model of Chapters 2–7 considered a single commodity. The raw material and finished good were one and the same. In this and the next section, the raw material and finished good are distinguished and the cost of processing is made explicit, so that we can investigate at which stage of processing there is storage. To do this, a model of two related commodities is needed.

A helpful insight is that a model encompassing raw materials and finished goods shares essential features of the two-country model of trade and storage developed in Chapter 9. What was the commodity in country a is here the input, and any storage in a is the inventory of raw material. Country b represents the output after processing, and any storage in b is the inventory of finished goods. If processed, one unit of commodity a is transformed into one unit of commodity b within the same period. Z_t now represents this amount processed within a period and z the marginal cost of processing instead of the marginal cost of shipping.

This easy adaptation of the model for trade should come as no surprise. Trade is a transformation of a commodity through space and processing a transformation in physical quality (just as storage is a transformation through time). Interpreted as the amount processed, Z_t no longer is sensible as a negative value, however. Wheat cannot be reconstituted from flour. For this reason, in an all-encompassing model, trade can be classified as a "two-way transformation technology" whereas processing is a "one-way transformation technology."[5]

Another alteration necessary to recast the trade model into a processing model is to disallow independent consumption demand for commodity a. The consumption demand for a is set at zero everywhere, so that commodity a has a positive price only through the demand derived from the final consumption of commodity b. Nor does it make sense to allow any supply of the finished good b except through processing of the raw material a. (There can still be a random component to the excess demand for the finished good.) That is, $\bar{h}^b$ is set equal to zero. In all periods, therefore, some raw material is transformed into finished goods. For the same reasons, in any period the price of the input a is below the price of the output b. Thus, this model for raw material, within-period processing, and finished goods is like the variant of the

---

5   If one country prohibited imports but allowed exports of a commodity, the trade model too would have a one-way transformation technology.

trade model of Section 9.4 in which country a almost always exports to country b.

One of the lessons from that trade model is that if country a is almost certainly exporting and if the marginal shipping costs z are constant, any storage will be in country a. If it costs no more to ship an additional unit next period than this period, it makes no sense to (i.e., equilibrium prices cannot be such as to) incur the shipping expense this period only to put the commodity into store in the importing country, provided physical storage costs and interest rates are the same for the two commodities. The same calculations apply if the transformation is processing rather than trade. There will be no inventories of finished goods if the marginal cost of processing is constant.

For the situation with processing to be at all realistic, therefore, the technology of transforming one commodity into the other cannot be at constant marginal cost. Rather the marginal processing cost $z[Z_t]$ must rise at some point (and perhaps continuously) over the relevant range of Z_t.[6] Considering the inflexibility in the capacity of copper smelters, soybean crushers, sugar refineries, and flour mills even over several years, the short-run variable cost curves relevant to a single period will very likely be highly nonlinear.[7]

Figure 10.1 illustrates the curve for the marginal processing cost of the "base case" for this and the next section. The relationship, for the representative firm or for the market as a whole, is

$$z[Z_t] = 10 + .025 (Z_t - 80)^2 , \quad Z_t > 80$$
$$z[Z_t] = 10, \qquad\qquad\qquad 0 \le Z_t \le 80$$

(10.1)

This function $z[Z_t]$ is far from the constant marginal cost curves of the trade examples, but as in those models, the marginal processing cost function is exogenous. The properties of systems with different marginal processing cost curves can be studied, as they are in Section 10.2.[8]

The other parameters of the base case are chosen to make it comparable to systems in other chapters. Specifically, the consumption demand for the finished good, commodity b, is linear with $\eta^d = -0.2$. The one-period-lagged

---

6   Specifications with the function $z[\cdot]$ itself varying with time (it would be written $z_t[\cdot]$) are interesting and relevant; but they are too complicated to be dealt with here.

7   The long-run marginal cost curve is plausibly horizontal. This would be consistent with a processing industry of many price-taking firms with no inputs that are specific to the industry, given sufficient time to adjust. The issue in this chapter, as in the others, is the response to temporary disruptions, not the long-run number of firms in a market.

8   This specification does not include a random component to the marginal processing cost. The reason is a technical one: A third state variable would be required, making the computations much more time consuming. On the other hand, the stochastic component to the availability of the raw material will appear as a "cost shock" if those two levels are combined, as they are in effect in Eichenbaum (1989) and similar adaptations of the production-smoothing model.

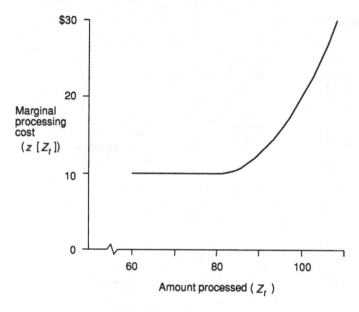

Figure 10.1. Marginal processing cost assumed.

and within-period supply of the raw material are both perfectly inelastic; $\bar{h}^a$ = 100 units. The nonstochastic equilibrium would be that pictured in Figure 10.2. Every period 100 units would be processed. The finished good would sell for $100 and the raw material for $80, the marginal cost of processing at 100 units being $20.

But there is uncertainty in the supply of the raw material and in the consumption demand for the finished good. The additive random disturbance to the virgin supply of the raw material v^a has a mean of 0.00 and standard deviation of $10/\sqrt{2}$ units. The same is the case for v^b, which acts as a horizontal shifter of the consumption demand curve. A negative v^b shifts the consumption demand curve out (causing high prices just like bad weather), whereas a positive v^b shifts it in. The disturbances v_t^a and v_t^b are uncorrelated contemporaneously and serially. (If there were no processing involved, the standard deviation of the random disturbance of the single commodity would be the familiar 10 units.)

These two sources of uncertainty induce storage of both the raw material and the finished good. The relevant storage costs are the same for both commodities: $k^a = k^b = \$2$ per unit stored while the interest rate r is 5 percent per period.[9] Because the price of the raw material is always below the price of the finished good, storage of the raw material has an interest cost advantage.

9   Also, there are no costs to changing the level of inventories.

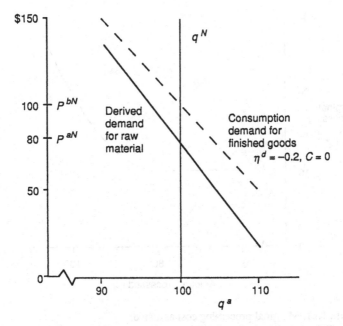

Figure 10.2. Nonstochastic equilibrium in the raw material's market.

Sequential equilibria

As in other systems, the competitive equilibrium is the same whether there are storage industries separate from processing or integrated firms handling all three activities. What is interesting within the model is the movement in the amounts stored and processed in the sequence of equilibria. Figure 10.3 plots a short sequence of equilibria for the base case.

In Figure 10.3(a) are the random shocks to the supply of the raw material and to the demand for finished goods. As it happens, over these eleven periods the random component in supply was somewhat more variable than the one in demand. Also, the sequence was selected to start with a clean slate. The carryin into period 0, whether of raw material or finished goods, was 0.00 units.

The shock in period 0 for the raw material was relatively bad. Consequently, although all of the raw material was processed, the price of the finished good was high: $P_0^b = \$147.05$. The competition among the many processors for the raw material ensures that P_0^a was below P_0^b by the marginal cost of processing. That marginal cost was $11.96 given the 88.87 units being processed, so P_0^a was $135.09. These high prices were not expected to persist, however. $F_{1,0}^b$ was $120.43 while $F_{1,0}^a$ was $102.56. (That the expected spread in period 1 as of period 0 between the price of the raw material

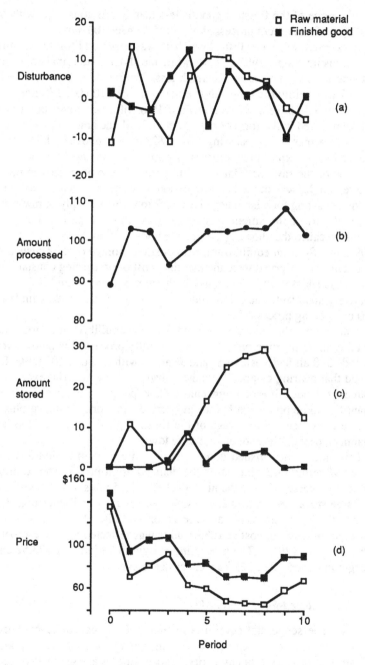

Figure 10.3. Time series for raw material and finished good.

and the price of the finished good is less than $20 is consistent with an expectation of an amount processed in period 1 under 100 units.)

In the event in period 1, the "weather" was very good for the raw material, increasing supply substantially, while the shock to the final consumption demand shifted that curve out much less. The resulting equilibrium P_1^b at $93.75 was below the long-run average price of $100.00. P_1^b, not to mention P_1^a, would have been even lower if 10.63 of the relative abundance had not been stored in the form of raw material. With the amount processed Z_1 at 103.06, the marginal processing cost of $23.40 was above its long-run average, and so, in expectation, processing costs could be saved by waiting.

Some of the raw material stored in period 1 was processed in period 2. The remainder was carried over to period 3, where it turned out to be useful in compensating for a large negative shock to the new supply of raw material. A small part of the amount processed was stored in period 3 as finished goods, because the shock v_3^b shifted the consumption demand curve inward 6.09 units. Such an equilibrium, with positive storage of the finished good, would not be observed were the marginal cost of processing constant. In period 4 the shocks worked to make both the raw material and finished good relatively abundant. The equilibrium called for storage of both, with less than 100 units being processed.

It should not, however, be inferred from the equilibria in periods 3 and 4 that S^b can be positive only when the quantity processed is below average. Periods 5–8 all had positive S^a and S^b along with Z above 100 units. It happened that a string of good "weather" made the raw material exceptionally abundant. Under those circumstances the expectation is for above-average quantities to be processed for several periods, to work off the surplus. This can be consistent with storage of the finished good (albeit not too large a quantity), because its spot price is very low.

This storage of finished goods served its purpose in period 9 when the shock v_9^b temporarily increased the demand at all prices. The equilibrium amount processed Z_9 was the high level of 108.05 units; a substantial part of the large stockpile of raw material was used up. P_9^a was higher than P_8^a, although the increase was not as large as for the finished good. The increased marginal processing cost at 108.85 units was reflected in a spread between P_9^a and P_9^b of $29.67. The processing margin in period 8 of $23.52 and the margin in period 10 of $21.73 were closer to average.

Reduced-form relationships

The sequential equilibria in Figure 10.3 suggest several patterns among the storage of the raw material, the storage of the finished good, and the amount processed in any period. Those patterns are seen more precisely in the reduced-form equations specifying the equilibrium values of the endogenous variables as functions of the underlying parameters and predetermined variables. In the planner's lexicon, the fundamental information about the interaction among S_t^a, S_t^b, and Z_t is contained in the storage and processing "rules" as functions of the state variables:

$$S_t^a = f^{S^a}[A_t^a, A_t^b]$$

$$S_t^b = f^{S^b}[A_t^a, A_t^b] \tag{10.2}$$

$$Z_t = f^Z[A_t^a, A_t^b]$$

A_t^a is the sum of the carryin S_{t-1}^a plus new production $\bar{h}^a + v_t^a$. The other state variable A_t^b does not include the amount processed in period t. Rather it represents the carryin S_{t-1}^b minus the shock to final consumption demand v_t^b. (Because A_t^b by this definition can be negative, it may be better to think of A_t^b as a percentage deviation of excess demand from the nonstochastic equilibrium, in which case the axes of the figures will have a familiar scale.)

As with other reduced-form relationships in three dimensions, these three are difficult to illustrate in two dimensions. Figures 10.4 and 10.5 instead show two perpendicular slices through the three rules. Figure 10.4 shows S_t^a, S_t^b, and Z_t as functions of A_t^a holding A_t^b at 100 percent of q^{bN}, where q^{bN} is the nonstochastic equilibrium value of q^b. Figure 10.5 shows the slice along A_t^b holding A_t^a at 100 units. Similar diagrams were seen in Chapter 9.

The continuity of the rule for Z_t, in either Figure 10.4(c) or 10.5(c), is the major difference from earlier examples involving trade where discontinuities at $Z = 0.0$ coincided with a range of autarky. Here in Figure 10.4(c), for low A_t^a, the marginal propensity to process a into b is a steady 1.0. If it were impossible to store the raw material a, the transformation rule would be linear over the whole range of A_t^a, since there is no use for raw material except to convert it into finished goods.[10]

Together the rules for storage of raw material and for the amount processed must add to a line with a slope of 1.0, because there are no other uses for the raw material.[11] Storage of the input serves as a substitute for the immediate processing of a large quantity at a correspondingly high marginal cost. Postponement of the processing when a large supply of the input is currently available until a period when the harvest is small lowers the combined processing costs. This pattern is visible at the right of Figure 10.4. Even with A_t^b equal to 100 units, and A_t^a equal to 110 units, just slightly more than half of the surplus above the long-run average new supply of 100.00 units of the raw material is processed; the rest is stored. This pattern is also present in

[10] On the other hand, the relationship between the spot price for a and the spot price for b is not linear, despite the linearity of the consumption demand for b. The difference between the input and output prices is the marginal cost of processing, and that marginal cost increases with a greater amount transformed.

[11] Note that we are assuming no wastage.

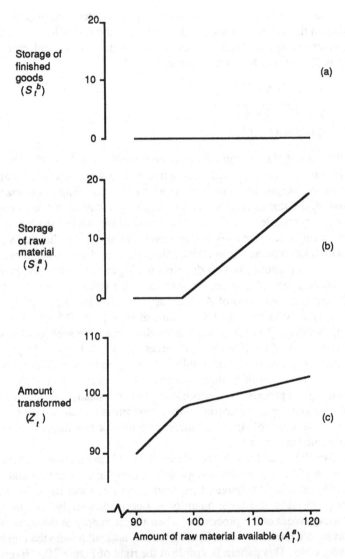

Figure 10.4. Storage and transformation rules, $A_t^b = 100$.

Figure 10.5. With $A_t^a = 100$, over the range 97.60–100.56 units for A_t^b, some of the raw material is stored rather than processed. Storage of the input helps reduce processing costs.

In contrast, storage of the finished good is aimed at avoiding those periods when final goods are in relative shortage (i.e., A_t^b is low). In Figure 10.5(a) over the range of positive S_t^b the marginal propensity to store is similar to

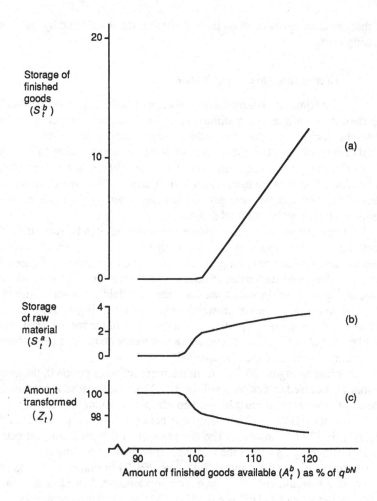

Figure 10.5. Storage and transformation rules, $A_t^a = 100$.

those of the basic storage model for a single commodity. Indeed, over the range of A_t^a where all of it is transformed into finished goods, storage of the finished good reverts to a function of the sum of A_t^a and A_t^b, rather than a function of the two arguments separately. The initial dispersion between a and b is immaterial to the decision to store b.

At first glance, it might seem odd under some combinations of A_t^a and A_t^b to transform all of the raw material into finished goods only to store some. Given that the price of the input a is lower, why incur higher interest expenses? The answer is that the amount transformed, and hence marginal processing costs, are below their long-run averages. It is best to take advantage of that opportunity. Savings on interest cost would be nullified by higher processing cost.

Convergence to the steady state

An equilibrium with positive storage of both the raw material and the finished good reflects the nonlinearity in the total cost of processing. Likewise, the decision to store at all reflects the extreme nonlinearity in the marginal cost of storage, the infeasibility of negative storage being equivalent to an infinite marginal storage cost over that range. The storage and transformation rules reflect these nonlinearities in the current period as well as the prospect of their effects in future periods as determined by the random components in virgin supply and final demand.

The interactions among the various nonlinearities can be seen in the "expected paths" back to the stochastic steady state, that is, in the means of future variables conditional on particular current circumstances. Figures 10.6 and 10.7 show two such paths of conditional means. Both are for initial conditions, A_0^a and A_0^b, in which the combined availability is very close to the long-run average. In the circumstances represented by Figure 10.6, however, initial quantities are disproportionately in the form of the raw material, whereas Figure 10.7 represents the reverse – a temporary abundance of the finished good and a shortage of the raw material.

According to Figure 10.6(c), from the perspective of period 0, the average amount processed in period 1 will be 102.37 units, because the large abundance of raw material must be worked off. The marginal processing cost at 102.37 units is $22.51. The difference between the two prices, $E_0[P_1^b] - E_0[P_1^a]$, is $22.65, however. The discrepancy, although slight, reflects the effects of averaging across the nonlinear marginal processing cost function, illustrated in Figure 10.1 above. Likewise, $E_0[Z_1]$ in Figure 10.7(c) is 96.40 units, which would cost, if it were a certain amount, $16.72 at the margin, whereas the spread $E_0[P_1^b] - E_0[P_1^a]$ is $17.44. The long-run average price of the finished good is $100.00 (because the consumption demand curve is linear). The mean steady-state price for the raw material is $79.45, not $80.00 as under certainty.

Another interaction between the nonlinearities and the inherent uncertainty can be seen in the spreads between prices for delivery in various periods. According to Figure 10.6(b), in period 1 it is expected, as of period 0, for 1.60 units of the finished good to be in store. Yet the expected price difference between periods 1 and 2 is not at full carrying charges. $E_0[P_1^b]$ ($\equiv F_{1,0}^b$) is $97.32. Full carrying charges would require $(97.32 + 2) \times 1.05 = \$104.29$, not the $98.92 that is $E_0[P_2^b]$ ($\equiv F_{2,0}^b$). Of course, any storage of b that does occur between periods 1 and 2 is at full carrying charges. The appearance to the contrary in Figure 10.6 or 10.7 is due to the possibility of a stockout in

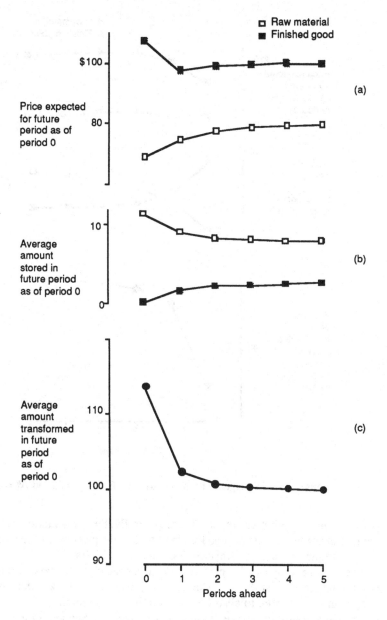

Figure 10.6. Convergence to the steady state from $A_0^g = 125$ and $A_0^b = 85$.

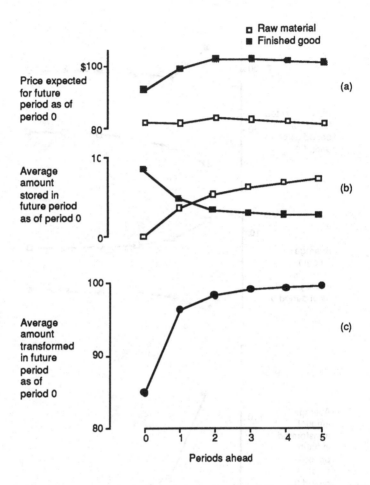

Figure 10.7. Convergence to the steady state from $A_0^g = 85$ and $A_0^b = 125$.

period 1 and P_1^b being above $F_{2,1}^b$. More generally, these interactions among the nonlinearities are responsible for the humps in the plots of expected prices – for example, those of the finished good in Figure 10.7(a).

These two examples of expected paths to the steady state have two other notable features. First, from the same initial dispersion, it takes the system longer, in expectation, to absorb an unusually large amount of the finished good than an unusually large amount of raw material. Second, in the initial period, storage of one of the commodities takes place while there is no storage of the other. In Figure 10.6(b) S_0^g is positive whereas in Figure 10.7(b) S_0^b is positive. The carrying charges as measured by the other commodity's prices are below full carry. (In Figure 10.6(a), $F_{1,0}^b - P_0^b$ is a backwardation.)

Table 10.1. *Correlation among amount processed and inventories*

Correlation with	Final consumption	Amount processed	Inventory of raw material	Inventory of finished goods
Series itself lagged	.456	.317	.752	.493
Amount processed	.415			
Inventory of raw material	.689	.474		
Inventory of finished goods	.544	−.148	.342	

Correlation with	Value added in processing $((P_t^b - P_t^a)Z_t)$	Value of inventories $(P_t^a S_t^a + P_t^b S_t^b)$
Series itself lagged	.312	.665
Value of inventory	.254	

These are instances like those discussed in Section 9.3 in which the stock in one country appears to be held at an opportunity cost if measured against the prices in the other country. These examples strengthen the suggestion we made in Section 9.3 that "supply-of-storage" relationships are better explained as an aggregation phenomenon than as "convenience yield."

Degree of serial correlation

Another manifestation of the speed of convergence to the stochastic steady state is the degree of serial correlation in the system. In Figures 10.6 and 10.7, we have selected the combinations of values for the state variables. In the system itself, the state variables evolve according to their own degree of serial correlation, with the result that the degree of serial correlation in the endogenous variables cannot be inferred directly from figures such as these. Table 10.1 shows those autocorrelations. This is a system characterized by a reasonably high degree of auto- and contemporaneous correlations, although not as high as some of the systems studied in Chapter 6.[12] All these correlations would be 0.00 if the raw material and the finished good were not storable. The correlation between the amount processed and final consumption is within the range Pindyck (1990) observes for several primary commodities, but at the low end of the range. The positive correlation between inventory of raw material and inventory of finished goods is typical of actual inventories (e.g., those of crude oil and refined products [Krol and Svorny 1981]).

Of particular interest in Table 10.1 is the degree of serial correlation in in-

[12] Because price P_t^b is a linear function of q_t^b in this system, the serial correlation for price is identical to that for final consumption in Table 10.1. The contemporaneous correlations, those between consumption and the amount processed, etc., are the negative of the values shown.

ventories. The highest degree of serial correlation, 0.752, is for the physical units of inventory of raw material, but the positive correlations for inventory of finished goods, 0.493, or of the value of total inventory, 0.665, are substantial.[13] Because of this positive serial correlation, it would appear that inventories slowly adjust back to some "desired," long-run level. That is to say, econometric models of inventories emphasizing costs of adjustments, such as Lovell's (1961), will appear to fit reasonably well. But in the system behind Table 10.1 there are by construction no costs to adjusting the level of inventories (such as in-and-out charges).

10.2   Sensitivity analysis

The discussion in Section 10.1 of inventories of raw material and finished goods revolved around a single system, with a single set of underlying parameters. The purpose of this section is a sensitivity analysis in the style of Chapter 4. Specifically, the shape of the marginal processing cost curve, the location of the random disturbance, the relative storage costs of the raw material and the finished good, and the one-period-lagged supply elasticity of the raw material are varied. These "experiments" are designed to reveal whether inventories are better described as smoothing the amount processed, buffering costs, or buffering demand.

Table 10.2 contains the results of these experiments, with the exception of the one involving physical storage costs, which is shown in Figure 10.8. Table 10.2 contains information only on the steady-state behavior of the various systems, and no material on storage rules, kink points, and so on. The base case of Section 10.1 is row 7 of the table. The parameters held constant are as follows: an interest rate of 5 percent, a standard deviation of the sum of the disturbances equal to 10 units, and a linear consumption demand for the finished good with an elasticity of −0.2 at the nonstochastic equilibrium. Because the demand curve is linear with a slope of −5.0, the standard deviation of final consumption can be deduced easily as one-fifth of the standard deviation of the price of the output, listed in the final column.

Sensitivity to the shape of the marginal processing cost curve

As for the consumption demand curve, one can distinguish among the family of marginal processing cost curves by their elasticity and curvature, both measured at the nonstochastic equilibrium (and holding constant the $20

---

13   The value of inventory would be an index typically constructed to aggregate across different physical units. Such series would be used in many macroeconomic studies. As Reagan and Sheehan (1985) observe about monthly U.S. data, raw material inventories and finished goods inventories, while positively correlated, do not move together perfectly. (Here the correlation is 0.342.) Some information is lost should they be aggregated into one series.

processing margin at the nonstochastic equilibrium). Elasticity η^{proc} and curvature C^{proc} can be varied independently, as in rows 1–7 of Table 10.2.[14]

Between the two parameters η^{proc} and C^{proc}, a difference in η^{proc} has a larger effect on the steady-state values of the system. The larger is η^{proc} (i.e., the more nearly horizontal at \$20 is the marginal processing cost curve), the more important is storage of the raw material relative to storage of the finished good. In the extreme when $z[Z_t]$ is constant (row 4), all storage, should there be any, is in the form of the raw material.[15]

In row 4, σ_Z is 5.18, significantly below the value of 7.07 units that would occur if storage were technically impossible. Thus, according to Blinder's standard, storage is production-smoothing, because the amount processed responds less to a shock to demand than if inventories could not be held. This smoothing of the amount processed, all of which is achieved by inventories of raw material, cannot be attributed to a desire to average out low processing costs with high processing costs because the marginal cost of processing is constant in this case. Comparison with row 4 should reveal any effect due to a rising marginal cost of processing. By this standard, over some range of elasticities η^{proc} (namely, row 3 with $\eta^{proc} = 1.0$), σ_Z is above 5.18; thus, it is not possible to say that inventories are specifically intended to smooth the amount processed. Similarly, because σ_{q^b} as well as total storage are little different across rows 1–4, the conclusion is that the main response to an inelastic supply of processing services is in the distribution of storage, the finished good more likely to be stored the lower the elasticity η^{proc}. In other words, the less flexible is processing, the more the inventory of finished goods is used as a buffer against shocks. Conversely, when processing is flexible, total costs are minimized by storing inventories in their raw form. In comparison to this effect of elasticity, the sensitivity of the steady-state values to the curvature of the marginal processing cost curve is less pronounced, at least over the range of C^{proc} examined.[16]

As can be seen in rows 8 and 9 of Table 10.2, storage goes with the source

---

[14] $C^{proc} \equiv (\partial^2 z / \partial Z^2) / (\partial z / \partial Z)$. Unlike the curvatures of the consumption demand curve considered in Chapter 4, which were constant along the whole demand curve, those for processing cost are the curvature just at the nonstochastic equilibrium. (Similarly, the elasticities of marginal processing cost curves are not constant.) The curve for $C^{proc} = 5.0$ is that in equation (10.1); for $C^{proc} = 0.0$, $z[Z_t] = 1.0(Z_t - 80)$, beyond 80 units; for $C^{proc} = 2.5$, $z[Z_t] = 5.0 + 0.5(Z_t - 80) + 0.0125(Z_t - 80)^2$. The extreme for C^{proc} is a right-angled marginal processing cost curve, such as the one Bresnahan and Suslow (1989) say is the case for the aluminum smelting industry.

[15]   The system behaves like the basic storage model of a single commodity, with the nonstochastic equilibrium at (100 units, \$80) and $\eta^d = -0.16$, the result of the vertical shift by \$20 along the consumption demand curve.

[16]   At an amount processed of $100 + 2\sigma_{y^s}$, namely, 114.14 units, the difference between z with $C^{proc} = 5$ and $C^{proc} = 0.0$ (both with $\eta^{proc} = 0.2$) is about the same as between a linear z with $\eta^{proc} = 0.2$ and 0.4.

Table 10.2. Steady-state statistics on raw materials, processing, and finished goods (standard deviations in parentheses)

	Mean storage of a (raw material)	Mean storage of b (finished goods)	% with no storage	% with storage of a but not b	% with storage of b but not a	Mean amount transformed	Mean price of a	Mean price of b
Sensitivity to processing elasticity, holding $C^{proc} = 0.0$, $\eta^s = 0.0$								
1. $\eta^{proc} = 0.2$	8.16 (7.84)	2.43 (3.48)	16.38	29.04	3.39	100.00 (4.35)	80.00 (27.31)	100.00 (25.26)
2. $\eta^{proc} = 0.4$	8.63 (8.18)	1.68 (2.77)	17.79	36.88	1.90	" (4.69)	" (26.46)	" (25.51)
3. $\eta^{proc} = 1.0$	9.64 (8.95)	0.57 (1.45)	18.03	58.16	0.38	" (5.44)	" (25.92)	" (25.59)
4. $\eta^{proc} = \infty$	9.98 (9.36)	0.00 (0.00)	18.28	81.72	0.00	" (5.18)	" (25.92)	100.00 (25.92)
Sensitivity to processing cost curvature, holding $\eta^{proc} = 0.2$, $\eta^s = 0.0$								
5. $C^{proc} = 0.0$	8.16 (7.84)	2.43 (3.48)	16.38	29.04	3.39	" (4.35)	80.00 (27.31)	" (25.26)
6. $C^{proc} = 2.5$	8.13 (7.87)	2.51 (3.52)	16.42	27.67	3.66	" (4.32)	79.77 (27.11)	" (25.30)
7. $C^{proc} = 5.0$	8.10 (7.94)	2.59 (3.55)	16.81	26.48	3.84	" (4.28)	79.45 (27.06)	" (25.45)
Sensitivity to location of disturbance, holding $\eta^{proc} = 0.2$, $C^{proc} = 5.0$, $\eta^s = 0.0$								
8. $\sigma_{\mu a} = 2\sigma_{\mu b}$	10.14 (9.52)	0.96 (1.63)	16.38	40.06	2.01	" (4.87)	79.25 (27.81)	" (24.91)
9. $\sigma_{\mu b} = 2\sigma_{\mu a}$	5.74 (5.63)	4.27 (5.26)	17.21	18.82	4.28	" (3.21)	79.75 (33.08)	" (25.79)

						"		"
10. $\rho_{ya,yb} = 0.7$	12.93 (11.04)	2.71 (3.57)	13.86	26.35	0.33	(3.51)	79.63 (33.08)	(31.26)

Sensitivity to elasticity of supply of raw material, holding $\eta^{proc} = 0.2$, $C^{proc} = 5.0$

11. $\eta^s = 0.0$	8.10 (7.94)	2.59 (3.55)	16.81	26.48	3.84	100.00 (4.28)	79.45 (27.06)	100.00 (25.45)
12. $\eta^s = 0.5$	6.68 (6.09)	3.43 (4.18)	14.64	21.77	6.71	99.81 (3.25)	80.01 (20.59)	100.95 (19.49)
13. $\eta^s = 1.0$	6.57 (5.94)	3.31 (4.06)	14.69	22.24	6.92	99.79 (3.24)	80.15 (19.25)	101.05 (18.59)

of the uncertainty. If the uncertainty is disproportionately in the virgin supply of the raw material, storage of the raw material dominates. If the uncertainty is disproportionately in final demand, more finished goods are stored than otherwise. Thus, the relative importance of inventories of raw material versus finished goods depends as much on the balance of the random disturbances as on the shape of the short-run marginal processing cost curve, if not more so.

The correlation between the two disturbances is also important. Row 10 of Table 10.2 suggests that if the two random disturbances are positively correlated,[17] storage of the raw material is more important relative to inventories of the finished good. Because periods with a deficit of finished goods and a surplus of raw material or with a surplus of finished goods and a deficit of raw material are less likely, the amount processed is relatively less variable. But because there are fewer compensating disturbances, the system as a whole – as measured by the standard deviation of prices – is more variable.

Sensitivity to relative storage costs

Perhaps the most revealing of the sensitivity experiments concerns the physical storage costs. Figure 10.8 plots the result of having one of the two commodities with higher physical storage costs than the other. A differential of $0, in the middle of the diagram, corresponds to the base case of Section 10.1 (and row 7 of Table 10.2) in which both k^a and k^b equal $2 per unit. A differential of –2 in Figure 10.8 means, therefore, that $k^b = \$4$ while $k^a = \$2$. A differential of $-\infty$ means that storage of the finished good is physically impossible, whereas one of $+\infty$ corresponds to storage of the raw material being physically impossible.

A clear pattern in Figure 10.8 is that storage, not unexpectedly, gravitates toward the cheaper-to-store commodity. Obviously, the system as a whole is better off (i.e., social welfare is higher) if k^a and k^b are both $2. That is where the standard deviation of the amount processed and of final consumption are both lowest. (A differential of $0 does not, however, mark the low point of the curve for the standard deviation of the price of the raw material.) More surprisingly, the standard deviation of the price of the finished good does not differ that much depending on whether storage of the input or output is cheaper. The stabilization (from $\sigma_{p^b} = \$50$ and storage impossible) and the gain in social welfare comes primarily from having one of the two commodities be storable.

The two extremes of Figure 10.8, where one of the commodities is technically impossible to store, actually reduce to systems with only one commodity. This is an important insight, for two reasons. First, it places the steady-state statistics for this extension of the basic model into a larger context. Second, it identifies which inventory type is necessary for a production-smoothing role.

[17] The total variance is the same.

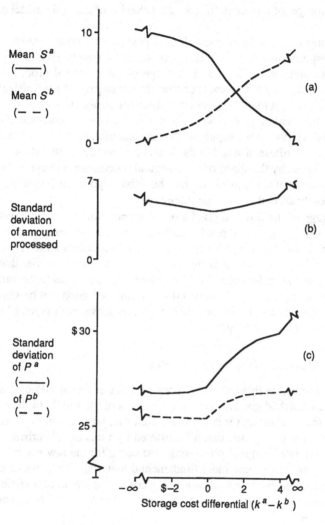

Figure 10.8. Effect of physical storage cost advantage between material and finished good.

If the finished good cannot be stored, then in any period the derived demand for the input, such as was pictured in Figure 10.2 above, is effectively the final consumption demand. That is to say, the demand curve for the input is exogenously given and its shape is the same every period. (Its placement, however, may move with the exogenous shock.) An exogenously given demand curve results in storage of the commodity – in this case the raw material – according to the demand curve's elasticity and curvature.[18] Storage, of the input, follows the behavior of the basic model of earlier chapters.

If storage of the finished good alone is possible, the system reverts to storage in response to a linear consumption demand, supply elasticity $\eta^s = 0.0$, and uncertainty $\sigma_h = 10$ units. The shape of the marginal processing cost curve is immaterial to the levels of equilibrium storage of the finished good. If the raw material must be processed within the period, it must be processed. That is, the standard deviation of the amount processed corresponds to the standard deviation in the supply of the raw material, namely, 7.07 units. It is this value regardless of whether the finished good can be stored. Social welfare is affected by the shape of the marginal processing cost curve, but from the perspective of allocative behavior, the finished good can be taken as arriving randomly around an average supply of $\bar{h}^b$.

If storage of the finished good alone does not dampen fluctuations in the amount processed, nor respond to different processing costs, it follows that inventories of finished goods are not in and of themselves aimed at "production smoothing." Rather, it is the storability of the raw material that is the necessary and sufficient condition for cost-saving reductions in the variability of the amount processed. If in addition the finished good can be stored, the amount processed is further stabilized. In this sense, both types of storage are "production-smoothing."

Elastic supply of the raw material

Implicit in this argument about the roles of inventories of raw material versus finished goods is an assumption about the supply of the raw material to the market: that it is perfectly inelastic, both within the period and with a one-period lag, and that it is buffeted by a random disturbance v_t^a. In effect, there is a marginal processing cost curve for the raw material as the finished good from some more fundamental material. The shape of such an (exogenously given) marginal processing cost curve would be a vertical line. It dominates the economic responses at the other levels of processing and consumption.

If the supply of the unstorable raw material can be adjusted within the period, with the result that processing does not have to occur regardless, it no longer follows that the storage behavior of the finished good is insensitive to the shape of the marginal processing cost curves. Both types of inventories

[18] Here the demand curve for the finished good b with an elasticity of -0.2 and $C = 0$ at the nonstochastic equilibrium appears to commodity a as a demand curve with $\eta^d = -0.1333$ and $C = -0.138$ at the nonstochastic equilibrium of (100 units, \$80). Were one to extrapolate using Table 4.1 from Chapter 4, the average storage in such a system would be the same as that here for storage of the raw material with storage of the finished good impossible.

will serve to dampen the fluctuations in the amount processed induced elsewhere in the system, while inventories of raw material also serve to smooth the cost of supplying the raw material.

It is more in keeping with the emphasis on agricultural commodities in this book to assume elastic supply of the raw material only with a one-period lag.[19] That is, while the supply of the raw material is unalterable in any one period, planned production responds to the anticipated price of the raw material the following period if the production disturbance is additive, or to the comparable producers' incentive price if v_t^a is multiplicative. Two such systems (with additive errors), one with $\eta^s = 0.5$ and the other with $\eta^s = 1.0$, are included as rows 12 and 13 in Table 10.2.[20] When these are compared to row 11 representing a system with $\eta^s = 0.0$, several differences stand out. With one-period-lagged elastic supply of the raw material, the role of storage of the raw material is reduced, while the role of storage of the finished good is increased. The system is more stable, as measured by the standard deviations of the amount processed and of final consumption. (The standard deviation of the amount of the raw material is higher, however.) The average price of the finished good is higher (and average consumption lower). Finally, the mean differential in prices is also larger.

Actually, all these patterns are consistent with the interaction of storage and planned production for a single commodity. As discovered in Chapter 4, while elastic supply reduces the role of storage and is destabilized by storage, together they stabilize consumption. Also, the direction of the response in average production depends on the curvature of the final consumption demand curve, with average supply below q^N with a low C and above q^N with a high C. Here, due to the intervening marginal processing cost curve, the effective demand curve from the perspective of the producers has a very low curvature, indeed one below 0. Consequently, the uncertainty reduces the average supply and increases average prices.

Although one-period-lagged elastic supply changes the mean and variance of the amount processed, it does not change its skewness appreciably, as is the case for final consumption. (Recall Figure 4.6(a).) Indeed, the effect of storage itself on the skewness of the amount processed is nothing as pronounced as its effect on price. Figure 10.9 illustrates the distributions of the amount processed for these three cases: one with $\eta^s = 0.0$, $k^a = \infty$, and $k^b = \infty$; another with $k^a = k^b = \$2$ and $\eta^s = 0.0$; and a third with $k^a = k^b = \$2$ and $\eta^s = 1.0$. Note that if the two commodities were not storable, the one-period-lagged supply elasticity would be immaterial.

[19] Christiano (1988) has a similar formulation in a macroeconomic setting. Firms must commit to their quarterly production schedules before they know the quarter's shock to demand or production. His "production" encompasses both raw material and processing.
[20] The elasticity is measured at the point of nonstochastic equilibrium, namely, (100 units, \$80).

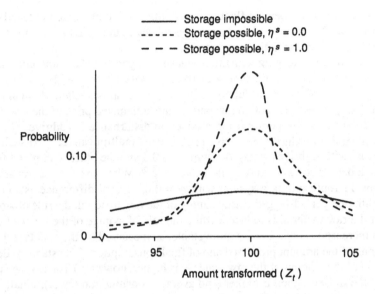

Figure 10.9. Probability distributions of amount processed.

Because the degree and nature of the supply elasticity of the raw material has such a large effect on the probability distribution of the amount processed, it seems bold, to say the least, to make any generic claims about the role of inventory. Yet this is precisely the purpose of the macroeconomic literature on the production-smoothing role of inventories of finished goods, models in which treatment of the supply of raw material is noticeably lacking. Moreover, the sensitivity analysis of this entire section suggests that any econometric test of a theory of inventories must be done with caution. The models in the macroeconomics literature are not at all robust to small changes in specification, the most important being the relative costs of storage in various forms and the nature of the supply of the raw material. At the very least, these models need to be reformulated to allow the simultaneous determination of inventory of raw material and inventory of finished goods, because a model with only one type of inventory cannot capture all the uses of inventories. As Reagan and Sheehan (1985) counsel, actual U.S. inventories at different levels of processing behave very differently.

10.3   Goods in process

Unfortunately for the purpose of disaggregating the level of inventories, the case including goods in process is one degree more complex. In each period not only is there a decision about how much to store of the raw material S_t^a and the finished good S_t^b, and how much to transform from raw material into finished goods in the current period Z_t, but how much to transform more slowly for delivery as finished goods the next period.[21] The amount of this slower transformation – call it Y_t – is the quantity of goods in process from the perspective of period t. Y is meant to represent goods flowing at the normal pace of business, whereas Z is meant to represent goods expedited at higher costs, such as those produced on an overtime shift and rushed to customers by air freight. Both Y and Z represent processing of commodity a into commodity b; to make clear that Y alone represents goods in process by the normal meaning of the expression, we shall refer to the two types of processing as "transformations."[22]

Consumption of the final good can be satisfied in any of three ways: a carryin of finished goods, transformation done at the regular speed and set in motion in the previous period, or express transformation. The first two of these three, as well as storage of the raw material, involve time and are storage in that sense. Yet only inventories of raw material and the finished good are storage in the direct sense; goods in process are an indirect version of storage. Direct storage, although fundamentally a response to the underlying uncertainty, needs to be evaluated against other indirect methods of influencing the quantity of finished goods available the next period. Thus, the role of direct storage, whether of the raw material or of the finished good, is determined in large part by the shape of the marginal processing cost functions, both that for express transformation and for the more normal, slower transformation. The important issue about this system, from the perspective of the macroeconomics literature, is whether storage of the raw material or of the finished good can be said to "smooth" the amount processed.

An arbitrage equation for the amount of the slower transformation – call its marginal cost $y[Y]$ – connects the current price of the input with the price expected for the output the next period.[23]

$$P_t^a + y[Y_t] = E_t[P_{t+1}^b], \qquad Y_t > 0 \tag{10.3}$$

The input price P^a is now a function of Y as well:

$$P_t^a = P^a[A_t^a - S_t^a - Y_t - Z_t] \tag{10.4}$$

---

[21] That the slower transformation takes the time between period t and $t+1$ is technologically given and is inflexible. More generally, the "lead time" could be endogenous.

[22] This model is related to that proposed by Schutte (1984), in which final demand is satisfied at lowest cost through holdings of finished goods inventories at a distribution center but can be satisfied by direct, within-period shipments from the factory. Differences in his model include monopoly rather than competition, no nonnegativity constraint on storage, and an infinite within-period supply elasticity of the raw material.

[23] Note that in this formulation Y is the only argument of the function $y[\cdot]$, just as z is the only argument of the function $z[\cdot]$. Christiano (1988), Lowry (1988), and Ramey (1989) include stocks of raw material as factors of production in which case the marginal processing cost function is $y[Y_t, S_t^a]$.

Because the goods in process appear on the scene in period $t+1$ indistinguishable from any amount of finished goods b that had been stored, the expected price for period $t+1$, whether for the raw material or the finished good, is a function of the arguments S_t^a and $S_t^b + Y_t$.[24] With the spot price for the raw material connected to the expected price of the finished good for the next period through (10.3) and connected to the spot price for the finished good through the arbitrage relationship involving Z – not to mention the connection, through storage, to the expected price of the raw material for the next period – the equilibrium is much more intertwined. It is possible for four industries to be active at the same time, related respectively to S^a, S^b, Y, Z.

Although one could imagine express transformation of the raw material into the finished good and storage of the finished good even as use is made of the slower transformation – as when the slower transformation has steeply rising marginal costs – it seems more reasonable to imagine that the express transformation is so much more costly than the more leisurely transformation that the express transformation is only undertaken when there is a current shortage of the finished good. Consequently, we have chosen parameters for $z[\cdot]$ and $y[\cdot]$ such that Z and S^b are never both positive in the same period. (In contrast, it is perfectly reasonable that Z and S^a are positive simultaneously.) Because the only source of finished goods b is transformation from the raw material a, no emergencies could be so great that all of the current availability of the raw material is transformed immediately into finished goods, for that would make certain a low availability of the finished good the next period. That is to say, the amount of goods in process Y is always positive. It does adjust, however, depending on the current availabilities A_t^a and A_t^b.

Accordingly, we set the parameters for an example so that the express transformation is used in some 10 percent of the periods and so that the regular transformation ranges from about 90 percent to 110 percent of its mean. Specifically, $z[Z] = 30.0 + 0.02Z^2 + 0.002Z^3$ and $y[Y] = 0.001(Y-75.0)^2 + 0.0002(Y-75.0)^3$. The nonstochastic equilibrium would have 100 units of goods in process every period and a price of the output $P^{bN} = \$100$. The input price P^{aN} would be $P^{bN}/(1+r) - y[100] = \$91.49$. Since the minimum cost of an express transformation is \$30, Z^N would be zero. As in Section 10.1, the additive error term for each of the commodities has a standard deviation of $10/\sqrt{2}$; the two disturbances are uncorrelated. The one-period-lagged supply of the input a is perfectly inelastic.[25] The consumption demand curve for

---

24 The two-hemisphere problem of Chapter 8 had a similar feature, namely that $E_t[P_{t+1}]$ is a function of $S_t + Crop\ in\ Ground_t$.

25 The regular transformation Y_t creates virgin finished goods in period $t+1$, just as in the basic single-commodity model, $\bar{h}_{t+1}$ represents new production planned as of period t for harvesting in period $t+1$. The marginal cost function y is comparable to the exogenous supply curve, defined by the parameter η^s. An equilibrium Y_t is the more

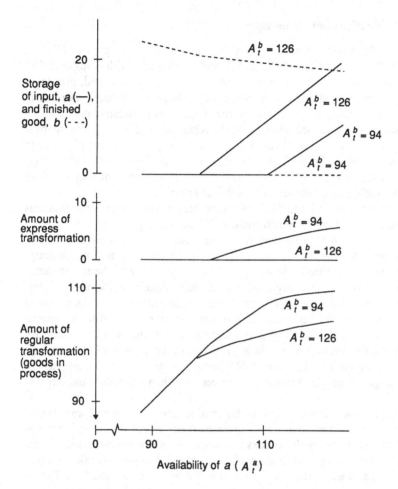

Figure 10.10. Storage and transformation rules including goods in process.

the finished good b is linear, with η^d equal to -0.2. Marginal storage units k^a and k^b both equal \$2.00 (a lower physical cost to storage encourages simultaneous express transformation and storage of the finished good), and as usual r is 5 percent. Representative rules for the two types of transformation and the two types of storage are shown in Figure 10.10.

complex formulation, however. It depends on current conditions (i.e., the current availabilities) through current price P_t^a as well as through the effect on the price expected for b the following period.

Equilibrium relationships

The reduced-form relationships such as those in Figure 10.10 must be such that the ones for S_t^a, Y_t, and Z_t add up to a line with a slope of 1.0. Commodity a is only used as an input, so that it must be stored, processed slowly, or processed quickly. As intended by the choice of cost curves, there is express transformation only when the availability of finished goods is low and that for raw material relatively high. When A_t^b is relatively low, there is also less storage of raw material. More surprising, the amount of goods in process Y_t is also higher.[26] The shortage of finished goods precluding their being stored, goods in process will be the only economical way to avoid another costly emergency transformation the next period.

As in Sections 10.1 and 10.2 where the only possible transformation was immediate (the express transformation Z here), storage of the raw material serves mainly to reduce the transformation costs of goods in process, whereas storage of the output is aimed at the possibility of a shortfall in consumption. Here, the (dashed) rule for S_t^b decreases with more of the raw material available, however. The high costs for an immediate transformation Z_t impede the natural sharing of a large amount of raw material between current consumption of finished goods and future consumption of finished goods. Adjustment of the amount of goods in process Y_t is the next best thing. By increasing the amount of goods in process and the storage of raw material while cutting back on the storage of finished goods, current consumption of finished goods can be increased at lower cost than via additional express transformation.

Perhaps these various trade-offs designed to minimize average transformation costs can be seen more easily in the behavior of the system as it evolves over time, buffeted by the shocks to the supply of raw material and the demand for finished goods. Figure 10.11 plots thirteen periods taken from a much longer time series. As always, the dominant impression from Figure 10.11 is the strong serial correlation in all the variables. (The series for the price of the input has $10 subtracted from it, to make it visually distinct from the other series in Figure 10.11(a).)

The segment begins with $A_0^a = 100.05$ and $A_0^b = 100.79$, which are close to the values they would have if there were no uncertainty, namely, 100.00 units each. Consequently, all of the raw material available is earmarked for

---

26   That the equilibrium amount of goods in process as a function of availability of the raw material changes depending on the current availability of the finished good makes it difficult to distinguish econometrically a "demand curve for processing" from a "supply curve for processing." This result is an extension of Gardner's (1975) result for a single-period, long-run equilibrium model. As he points out, shifts in the supply curve for processing services (say, because of technical change) themselves cause a shift in the demand curve for processing services, because that demand is a derived one.

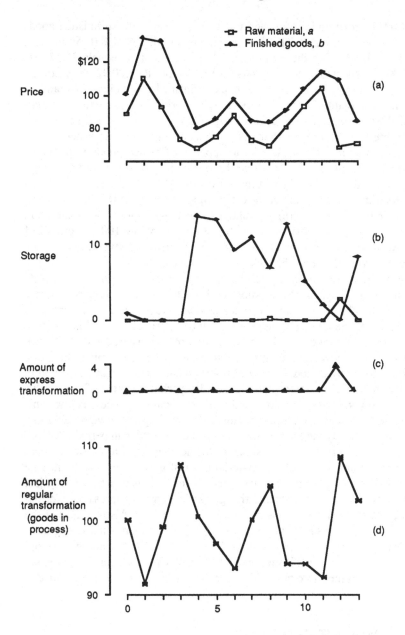

Figure 10.11. Time series of prices, storage, and goods in process.

slow transformation into finished goods while nearly all the finished goods available are consumed. That is, the stage is set with $S_0^a = 0.0$, $S_0^b = 0.87$, and $Y_0 = 100.05$. The shocks in period 1 are such that A_1^a equals 91.57, not the 100.00 expected, and A_1^b equals 93.12, also not the 100.92 units expected. (One can think of the negative shock to finished goods either as a random loss in the amount of goods in process from period 0 or as a temporary outward shift in demand for the finished goods.) Although P_1^b is high as a result, there is no emergency transformation, since that would further deplete the small amount of raw material to appear as finished goods in period 2. Period 2, in contrast, is one where the availability of raw material is high enough and the availability of finished goods low enough for there to be an express transformation, albeit for the small amount $Z_2 = 0.18$ units just barely visible in Figure 10.11(c). The shock to the new supply of raw material in period 3 is large and positive. Nevertheless, A_3^b is below 100.00, and all of the raw material is devoted to goods in process; neither commodity is stored. Only in period 4, when there is a large positive shock to A^b, does S^b become positive. Storage of finished goods continues for another seven periods, through period 11. During those periods the amount in process Y varies considerably. Y_6, for example, is much below average. Precisely for that reason, some of the abundant current supply of the finished good is reserved for period 7. In period 8, both the availability of raw material and of finished goods are high. With no pressing need to have raw material transformed into finished goods by period 9, some of it – 0.16 units to be exact – is stored in order to reduce the transformation costs. By period 11, most of the surplus of finished goods has been absorbed and the amount in process is low. This calculated risk leaves the price of finished goods especially vulnerable to a negative shock. By the luck of the draw, that does happen in period 12; but it coincides with a large positive shock to the new production of raw material. Some of this abundance of raw material is transformed immediately into the finished good. Consumption of the finished good q_{12}^b is constrained not just by the low A_{12}^b but by the steeply rising marginal cost of express transformation. Consequently, Z_{12} is positive while S_{12}^a is positive. Also because of the relative abundance of the raw material, much more than usual is begun as goods in process, although not all of the remainder. That is stored, to avoid the rising marginal transformation costs. Period 13, which concludes the series, returns to the more normal condition of S^b positive while S_{13}^a and Z_{13} equal 0.0.

Steady-state properties

In the short segment just examined, the proportion of periods with the various activities is fairly representative. More precise statistics on the long-run averages of this base case are given in Table 10.3. The table also

Table 10.3. *Statistics on amounts stored and in process (standard deviations in parentheses)*

	Mean storage of a (raw material)	Mean storage of b (finished goods)	% with no storage	Mean amount transformed promptly	% with none transformed promptly	Mean amount transformed regularly	Mean consumption of b	Mean price of a	Mean price of b
Base case	0.63 (1.75)	4.33 (4.19)	23.44	0.25 (1.04)	89.96	99.75 (5.51)	100.00 (3.36)	$92.97 (13.29)	$100.00 (16.81)
Storage of a impossible	0.00 (0.00)	4.66 (4.71)	26.62	0.25 (1.02)	89.78	99.75 (6.21)	100.0 (3.46)	92.93 (14.59)	100.00 (17.28)
Storage of b impossible	2.94 (3.94)	0.00 (0.00)	42.09	0.86 (1.87)	69.99	99.14 (4.14)	100.00 (4.43)	88.74 (15.10)	100.00 (22.14)
Express transformation impossible	1.17 (2.44)	5.65 (4.00)	9.68	0.00 (0.00)	100.00	100.00 (5.29)	100.00 (3.43)	95.13 (15.46)	100.00 (17.17)
Four-fifths of uncertainty in a	1.50 (3.22)	4.21 (3.79)	20.68	0.31 (1.22)	89.42	99.69 (6.44)	100.00 (3.61)	92.71 (15.36)	100.00 (18.07)
Four-fifths of uncertainty in b	0.19 (0.80)	4.36 (4.21)	24.13	0.16 (0.76)	92.38	99.84 (3.76)	100.00 (3.04)	98.81 (10.44)	100.00 (15.18)

compares the cases where one of the commodities cannot be stored, where the express transformation is prohibitively expensive, and where the bulk of the total uncertainty is located in the error term of one of the commodities. Three surprising patterns stand out in Table 10.3.

1. *Relative standard deviations of price:* The conventional single-period model schools one to expect that an input's price has the higher standard deviation, because derived demands are more price inelastic. Yet, in this system, the price of the output is more variable. The explanation is that the derived demand for the raw material comes not only from within-period transformation but also from storage and, more important, from slow transformation. The effective demand curve for the raw material is made more elastic by these substitute uses.

2. *Standard deviation of consumption of finished goods vs. that of production:* The standard deviation of production as measured by the standard deviation of the slow transformation is always higher than that of consumption (or "sales") whenever the finished goods can be stored. This is most obvious for the row with the express transformation impossible. The standard deviation of the amount transformed slowly is 5.29 while that of consumption of the finished good is 3.43. Perhaps it should not be said that this pattern is surprising, since it is one of the main stylized facts of many actual industries. What is surprising is that economists have not recognized that it is a natural result of rational competitive storage.

3. *Storage for the finished good vs. that for raw material:* The average storage for the finished good is higher than that for raw material, despite the lower average price for the raw material. The explanation is that the goods in process are a close substitute for storage of the raw material; storage of raw material mainly reflects the increasing marginal cost of that regular slow transformation, since it only occurs when the slow transformation is running close to or above average.[27]

---

[27] The balance of direct storage versus indirect (in process) storage may help settle a controversy concerning the medieval economy. McCloskey and Nash (1984, p. 177) argue "that the medieval economy was haunted by starvation, in short, implies that it had little in stores of grain." They attribute the low amount of carryover to extremely high storage costs, in particular to an interest rate on the order of 30–40% per annum. (Also see Taub 1987.) McCloskey and Nash fail to recognize that sowing is an investment akin to storage. The amount stored is related to the possible return to planting the marginal seed. The rate of interest may well be high, but the lack of storage cannot confirm that fact without providing the additional evidence regarding average and marginal yields, which McCloskey and Nash do not present. (They do also analyze price data, with which we are not concerned in this instance.)

Of course, if the marginal costs of the two types of transformations were even more steeply rising, or if the level of the two marginal costs were higher (with the result, say, that the mean price of the raw material were on the order of $50.0 instead of $90.0), there would be appreciably more storage of raw material. Such a sensitivity analysis, however interesting, is beyond the objective of this section. The few examples here can leave little doubt that the understanding of these systems – which are far from intricate by any comparison with the actual world's welter of grades and locations and transformations of various speeds and directions – is sadly underdeveloped. In particular the role of inventories is not adequately understood.

10.4 Firm-level versus industry-level behavior

The discrepancy between results of models for individual firms and of those for the whole industry (albeit with individual firms) has been an underlying theme in this chapter. The venerable production-smoothing model of inventories considers a single firm with a price for its output and a price for its input set by the market. But if all firms in the industry react to the collective demand or cost shock in the same way as the representative firm, those prices are unlikely to be the equilibrium prices. If the price responses are different than assumed in the production-smoothing model, it follows that the representative firm's inventory and production decisions are different too. The models of Sections 10.1 and 10.3 should be understood as attempts at presenting the industrywide behavior when the underlying technology of processing gives an incentive to smooth the amount processed. These two models should be viewed as being firmly in the macroeconomics tradition, for all important variables are endogenous.

The recent macroeconomics literature on the theory of inventories of finished goods can be found lacking for succumbing to the fallacy of composition. In particular, only if the implicit assumption that the within-period elasticity of supply of the input is infinitely elastic is true are the models in the macroeconomic literature valid. Of course, the supply of raw material may be

In the subsistence economy of the middle ages, the principal output, wheat, was also a major input, seed. Although sowing is a competitor of current consumption, it is also a substitute for storage in producing the commodity for the next period. Storage can turn one current unit of the commodity into at most one unit of the commodity next period. If, for purposes of illustration, seed were the only production cost, storage would be comparable to sowing with a marginal yield of $(1.0 - a)$, where a is the spoilage rate. The average return to seed was by some accounts as low as 4 or 5 to 1 in the medieval economy, much lower than at present. Nevertheless, if the elasticity of the marginal yield was high in the relevant range, it is conceivable that adjustment to variations in availability would principally take the form of adjustments in sowing intensity or area sown, rather than in storage, except when availability was extremely high, even if interest rates were lower than inferred by McCloskey and Nash.

relatively elastic because of inventories of raw material. But if that is the case, the model obviously needs to consider the simultaneous determination of both types of inventories. Similarly, the speed of processing needs to be considered in an industrywide model.

In Section 9.3 of the previous chapter, we argued that the phenomenon of firms holding inventories at an apparent loss, reconciled through the concept of convenience yield, may well be the result of aggregating very similar commodities in terms of grade or location into a composite. Our questioning of the concept of convenience yield concerns the difference between arguments plausible at the level of the firm and those that may hold at the level of the industry. Although the supply-of-storage scatters for wheat, cocoa, and so on use data on inventories at the industry level, the verbal arguments for the plausibility of convenience yield – as in Brennan (1958), Telser (1958), Cootner (1967), and Weymar (1974) – refer to single firms. It does not follow that those arguments necessarily hold at the level of the industry. For example, Williams (1986, chap. 4) presents a formal two-period model of an individual firm facing a backwardation in prices and shows that given its cost structure it will store despite the backwardation. But when many such firms are aggregated – when the model's prices are made endogenous – such an equilibrium does not emerge; the industry stores only at full carrying charges. The other arguments for convenience yield applicable to the individual firm do not readily extend themselves to a model of the industry, or at least we have not been able to so capture them.

The large consequences of the assumption of exogenous prices or quantities can be seen in two areas of the agricultural economics literature. The standard models of farmers' optimal applications of fertilizer – including those of Kennedy et al. (1973), Stauber et al. (1975), Godden and Helyar (1980), Kennedy (1981), and Taylor (1983) – are sophisticated applications of dynamic programming. However, all assume that the price of the fertilizer and the crop are given, although presumably if many farmers were to add more fertilizer, the price of fertilizer would be higher and the price of the crop lower than otherwise.

Should there be carryovers in land quality from previous cropping decisions, a model of an individual farmer suggests an oscillation in amounts planted, given an exogenous price process. Seemingly, one would anticipate negative first-order serial correlation in the planting intensity. Such is the argument Eckstein (1984) made for his study of dynamic supply functions for Egyptian cotton. But the price process is endogenous at the level of the whole market. If many farmers have such land, one can show that the individual responses collectively would alter the price process such that there would be little oscillation in their planting intensities.

The endogeneity of the time-series properties is an important point in its own right. Consider some of the recent extensions to the standard production-smoothing model. They often propose a supposedly exogenous second-order process for either the shock to demand or the cost shock to supply, each with a new random component each period. At first glance, this formulation looks like a reasonable simplification of the obvious serial correlation in U.S. macroeconomic aggregates. Nevertheless, it is questionable, because the degree of serial correlation is almost surely endogenous.

As we stressed in Chapter 6, the possibility of storage induces positive serial correlation in market-level variables. Thus, the observed correlation in macroeconomic aggregates could very well be due to storage (or to savings more generally), as is the case for the systems studied in this chapter. If the observed serial correlation is at least partly due to storage, those supposedly exogenous stochastic processes are partly endogenous; for one, the degree of serial correlation would change were it possible to store finished goods. More troubling is that the supposedly new exogenous shocks may be partly endogenous. If, say, the unanticipated current shock to demand is truly exogenous, what is represented as the shock to processing costs may be an endogenous response, perhaps through adjustments in inventories of raw materials, to that very shock in demand. The only hope of sorting out these endogenous reactions to uncertainty is an industrywide model encompassing all levels of inventories and savings.

CHAPTER 11

Market power and storage

Most people feel sure that storage monopolization reduces their welfare, but they generally have no clear perception of why or of how a storage monopolist behaves. For example, in times of shortage, observers often jump to the conclusion that a storage monopoly involves excessive withholding of supplies from the market, that is, storing too much. But Adam Smith (1784) found the answer.[1] If the monopoly is truly over storage, as when someone holds a patent for warehousing technology, too little is stored. Abnormal profits cannot be earned by buying up the current availability and holding it off the market.

Confusion comes from imprecision in the scope of the monopolist. Is the monopoly power over storage specifically or over all current and prospective supplies? Monopoly over all distribution such that consumers could buy solely from one party (as in Kennedy 1979) is a different matter entirely from a monopolist over the storage technology alone. Here in Section 11.1 we examine a monopolist over distribution. In Section 11.2 we examine the distinctly different subject of a monopoly over storage technology alone.

Control of storage is likely to be a side issue if one party controls the whole distribution of the crop and is free to charge each period what the traffic will bear. A firm with a monopoly over distribution would want to restrict its sales each period to an amount where demand becomes elastic. If supplies received are excessive, destruction may be much the most effective method. Storage is, however, more important for a monopolist over distribution if the firm for some reason sets its price in advance, absorbing shocks in demand and supply through inventories. Here we show how a monetary value can be put on this flexibility, or conversely on the cost of a policy of list prices compared to a policy of adjusting price within the period, for various assumptions about the flexibility of storage and production. We also expose the rather special as-

---

[1]   Rashid (1980) disputes Smith's premise that the grain trade was competitive.

sumptions about market power and flexibility implicit in a popular operations research approach to inventory decisions, namely the (S,s) model.

Even monopoly over storage alone leaves some imprecision. Does the monopolistic firm do its own storing or does it rent (or license) its storage technology to others? If it is capturing its monopoly profits from or through these other forward-looking agents whose current actions depend on their anticipation of the monopolist's later actions, it is entangled in a strategic "game." Because the monopolist may be free to revise its fees or revoke its commitments, its optimal strategy may be "time inconsistent." Thus, an added benefit of this inquiry into a storage monopoly is an introduction to the subject of the time inconsistency of optimal plans. Other examples of time inconsistency arising from market power we discuss in the conclusion here, Section 11.3. Also time inconsistency is a surprising feature of the designs of a public agency to supplement private storage that is inadequate due to some distortion such as a regime of price ceilings. Those particular policy interactions are to be the focus of Chapter 15.

11.1   Market power over distribution and storage

A monopoly over supply, distribution, and storage is treated first because it does not involve features of a strategic game.[2] Final consumption in any one period is not dependent on the consumers' anticipations of the monopolist's future actions, because by assumption consumers do not store and have intertemporally separable utility. (The situation could be different, e.g., in the case of monopoly over a finite resource [Karp and Newbery, in press] or in the case of a durable good [Stokey 1981].) If new supply cannot be adjusted within the period or with a lag (i.e., if $\eta^s = 0.0$), there is no strategic interaction with producers. If the monopolist itself controls the new supply, obviously there is no strategic game, whatever the supply elasticity. That is the perspective taken here, so that one-period-lagged supply can be elastic. In sum, the monopolistic firm can take the technical features of supply and the consumption demand curve as stationary and exogenously given.

Rather than strategic interactions, the main issue in this section is the value of flexibility in the face of uncertainty. At the inflexible end of the spectrum is a price set for all periods. A common practice, at least in retail stores, is to specify a "list" price. If demand proves unusually strong that period or, equivalently, if some bottleneck limits supply, the quantity on hand is sold out and potential sales are lost. Additional supplies arrive only with a lag. If demand proves unusually weak at the list price, the excess incurs warehous-

---

[2]   Rotemberg and Saloner (1989) consider inventories in an oligopolistic industry where inventories may be used as a strategic weapon to enforce collusive agreements. Sengupta (1988) considers the game theoretic interactions of oligopolistic producers (and storers) in the world coffee market.

ing and financing charges. A firm with such fixed prices is much less flexible than one that can reset price each period depending on market conditions that period.[3]

With a fixed price period after period, the role of storage is that of a residual. It is neither a control variable nor the result of any explicit maximizing behavior. This is the role given to inventories in much of the operations research literature, especially in the so-called (S,s) model, which emphasizes instead the decision about a new order of the commodity, to be delivered in the subsequent period. In the agricultural setting emphasized here, that flexibility in ordering amounts to letting planned production for harvesting the next period adjust period to period, with perfectly elastic one-period-lagged supply. The rule for placing orders (or for planning the next harvest) must anticipate the current order's effect on the future course of lost sales or inventory expenses. Derivation of the rule requires stochastic dynamic programming. In that way, inventories are the indirect result of maximizing behavior over orders or planned production. Nevertheless, the analysis starts with the assumption that price cannot be adjusted optimally within the period or, equivalently, that current inventories are not under the direct control of the firm.

Within the economics literature, the model closest to this specification of unadjustable price and adjustable one-period-lagged supply is Blinder's (1986). (Bivin [1986] and Kahn [1987] present models of a monopolistic firm that has a fixed price and that can obtain new supplies within the period.) Abel (1985), Seidmann (1985), and Haltiwanger and Maccini (1988) model a monopolistic firm that sets each period both a list price and planned production for the following period. That is, although price is not fixed for all periods, neither is it adjusted to clear the market within the period. Irvine (1981) has a similar model in which a stockout affects future demand detrimentally through "reputation." (In a model designed to investigate Keynes's notion of sticky prices, Ball and Romer [1989] consider prices adjusted every period. Production, however, can be adjusted within the period, and so their model does not fall within the class studied in this section.) Carlton (1979) has a model in which a firm fixes price and planned production for all periods but it cannot store. This combination offers the least flexibility in the face of the uncertainty.

At the other end of the flexibility spectrum is a monopolistic firm that can set price within each period (simultaneously selecting its carryover) and select its planned production for the next period.[4] Amihud and Mendelson (1983)

---

3   Of course, actual retailing establishments conduct clearance sales or sell their excess holdings to discounters through a secondary market. The discussion here centers on models of retailing firms, in which price is frequently assumed to be fixed.

4   Hay (1970) includes a cost to adjusting price within the period, along with costs to adjusting within-period production and inventories.

model a monopolistic firm with these opportunities (although their general model permits negative inventories). Reagan (1982) has exactly this model with the extreme of infinitely elastic one-period-lagged supply (although there are no physical storage costs for the inventory).[5] Some place in the middle of the flexibility spectrum is a monopolistic firm that can reset the current period's price and the production planned for the following period but that cannot store.

In all these formulations, the technology constrains the order (i.e., the planned production) from arriving until the following period. In this dimension these various models differ from those models of finished goods inventories and within-period adjustable supply studied in the previous chapter. They differ among themselves in the pricing and storage flexibility they assume. The main question here is the implicit cost of such constraints, given that production cannot be adjusted within the period.

The monetary value of flexibility

The value of the various degrees of flexibility in response to supply or demand shocks can be approached by asking what some firm would pay to be a monopolist constrained by the various policies. Specifically, in the setting of an agricultural crop common to earlier chapters that is harvested one period after planting, what would a firm pay for all the land devoted to the crop?

If the consumption demand curve has a elasticity less than 1.0 (in absolute value) for any positive level of consumption, as in our previous examples, the answer is an infinite amount. Consequently, for the exercise to be sensible, the consumption demand curve must be elastic. And obviously the exact present value of the monopoly rents depends on the specific parameters selected. Consider the case in which consumption demand is linear, having $\eta^d = -1.0$ at the point (150 units, $150). (The inverse consumption demand curve is thus $P_t = 300 - 1.0q_t$.) The linear marginal revenue curve thus goes through the point (100 units, $100) with twice the slope. Let the one-period-lagged (linear) supply curve also go through the point (100 units, $100) with elasticity $\eta^s = 1.0$. Under these circumstances, the nonstochastic competitive equilibrium would be 150 units planted for each period, at a price of $150, with net revenue for landowners of $11,250 per period.[6] If one firm alone owned the land, the nonstochastic monopolistic equilibrium would be (100 units, $200), with a revenue after production costs of $15,000 per period.

Under either competition or monopoly, the nonstochastic equilibrium has

---

5   Newbery (1984) models a cartel of agricultural producers in which the random harvest has a one-period-lagged supply elasticity of 0.0.

6   Because the supply curve is a 45° line from the origin, the land rent is half the gross revenue of $150 × 150 units.

the same price period to period. A distinction between a list price and a market-clearing price is irrelevant. If there were shocks to demand or supply each period (independent of the shocks in other periods), any inflexibility, especially that of the same list price period after period, reduces the present value of the stream of net revenue. (Even in a competitive setting, the prospect of random disturbances to supply in future periods lowers the value of land with this linear specification of the consumption demand curve.) Specifically, consider the case in which the disturbance is an additive shock to supply, normally distributed with $\sigma_h = 15$ units.[7] Finally, under such uncertainty, storage costs matter. Let $r = 5$ percent per period and $k = \$10$.

With these underlying parameters, six degrees of flexibility can be distinguished. Each is included in Table 11.1. The least flexibility is that imposed by fixing price and planned production at the same levels period after period and storing none of the occasional surpluses. The most flexibility is allowed by adjusting price and planned production every period and storing when appropriate. The present value of monopoly rents (with nothing initially in store) is in direct relation to the degree of flexibility allowed. The regime of fixed price, fixed planned production, and storage impossible has the greatest drop from the potential rent under certainty, from $15,000 per period to $13,809. In Table 11.1 it is given a score of 0 percent in the final column.

In the regime of fixed price, fixed planned production, and no storage, flexibility is allowed to the extent that the fixed price and fixed planned production can be selected once and for all by the monopolist *ex ante*. The optimal combination of fixed price and fixed production weighs the possibility of losing revenue if the price selected or the planned production is too low against the possibility of wasting production, which is costly *ex ante*. If, for example, the list price is set at $210 (corresponding to 90 units consumed), any quantity harvested in a particular period above 90 units simply spoils; any quantity below 90 units represents lost sales at $210.[8] For this particular set of parameters, the balance between lost sales and wasted production is struck at a list price of $198 along with 102 units planted.[9] (That is, $\overline{h}_{t+1} = 102.00$ for all t.)

With storage possible, although at $k = \$10$, the optimal *ex ante* fixed price and fixed planned production are different. Because of the cost of storage, the optimal fixed planned production will be less than the production consistent with the fixed price. If, for example, price is fixed at $210 and $\overline{h}$ is fixed at the corresponding value on the consumption demand curve, namely, 90

---

[7]   To have the results comparable to those in earlier chapters, the shock is kept as one to realized production.

[8]   The fixed planned production need not equal the number of units corresponding to the list price, but it will in this instance because the marginal revenue curve is linear.

[9]   Because there is no storage (or backorders) to connect the periods, the optimal planned production would be constant regardless of whether price were fixed.

Table 11.1. *Monopoly rents and responsiveness to uncertainty (means and standard deviations)*

Regime	Price	Planned production	Storage	Monopoly rents (scaled)[a]
Certainty	$200.00	100.00	0.00	100.00%
	(0.00)	(0.00)	(0.00)	
Fixed price:				
FPP, storage impossible	198.00	102.00	0.00	0.00
	(0.00)	(0.00)	(0.00)	
FPP, storage ($k = \$10$)	197.57	99.84	36.72	44.05
	(0.00)	(0.00)	(45.50)	
APP, storage ($k = \$10$)	199.50	99.33	18.08	64.58
	(0.00)	(9.02)	(13.95)	
One-period-lagged adjustable price:				
APP, storage ($k = \$10$)	199.03	99.83	17.50	65.68
	(3.84)	(6.74)	(13.45)	
Within-period adjustable price:				
APP, storage impossible	200.03	99.97	0.00	81.08
	(15.00)	(0.00)	(0.00)	
APP, storage ($k = \$10$)	200.00	100.00	3.95	85.18
	(10.59)	(3.51)	(6.47)	

Abbreviations: FPP, fixed planned production; APP, adjustable planned production.
[a]Present value from initial condition of $A_0 = 100$ units.

units, on average none of the existing stocks are used up. Because the probability distribution of harvests is symmetric around $\bar{h}$, those low harvests that would draw down stocks have a matching large harvest that would add to them. Therefore, if $\bar{h}$ corresponds to the list price, in expectation any surplus will not be depleted but will continue to accrue warehousing charges. (Of course, no monopolistic firm would countenance the expenses of a huge stockpile. If its stockpile were already so huge that the discounted present value of net revenue from an additional unit was negative, that unit would be left to spoil.) For these reasons, the monopolistic firm sets the fixed planned production lower than the units on the consumption demand curve corresponding to the list price selected simultaneously, so that on average a stockpile is consumed. With marginal physical storage costs $k = \$10$, the optimal fixed planned production of 99.84 units is 2.59 units below the consumption corresponding to the optimal fixed price of $197.57.

Because in this regime planned production cannot be cut back from 99.84 units even if there has been a string of good harvests, average storage is large, as can be seen in Table 11.1. Put another way, the present value of another unit in store is much below the list price. Nevertheless, "storability" adds considerably to the monopoly rents, as also can be seen in Table 11.1.

From the perspective of the present value of expected monopoly rents generated, a much better response than adjusting planned production once and for all is to adjust the planned production for each and every period depending on current conditions (given price is the same every period). The level of inventories is dictated by the surplus or deficit at the specified fixed price; inventories cannot be controlled directly. Yet if inventories happen to be large, because of a string of good harvests, it makes sense that the amount planted for the next period should be adjusted down. Or if inventories are exhausted temporarily, a temporarily higher level of planting might be advisable. More precisely, the amount of planned production for next period, period $t + 1$, should be such that the marginal cost, as represented by the one-period-lagged supply curve, equals the present value of the expected net marginal revenue from new production.[10] With this flexibility in responding to the uncertainty, monopoly rents are not reduced so much compared to a nonstochastic regime.

Higher (but only slightly higher) monopoly rents occur under a regime with adjustable planned production, storage possible, and list prices adjustable with a one-period lag. That is, depending on current conditions, the firm selects its planned production and list price for the following period. For example, if the current list price, set in period $t - 1$, is such that 40 units remain unsold, the optimal $\bar{h}_{t+1}$ is 88.71 units and the optimal list price for period $t + 1$ is \$194.62 compared to values of 108.90 units and \$204.00 if $S_t = 0$. (Of course, if the firm could only adjust price with a one-period lag, that option would be useless without storage.)[11]

Nevertheless, the present value of monopoly rents under a fixed-price regime, even with the flexibility of storage and adjustable planned production, is much lower than under a regime of prices adjustable within the period, even without storage. That is, if the monopolistic firm had the choice between being able to store while keeping price fixed and not being able to store while

[10] The amount planted will be a declining function of current storage. The marginal revenue does not necessarily accrue in period $t + 1$. If it causes additional storage, the marginal cost of storage must be subtracted off. In brief, this marginal revenue curve is found as a self-replicating polynomial in storage.

[11] A regime with the same fixed price and fixed planned production every period is an "open-loop" system, since no use is made of the information about the realized harvest in any particular period. A regime with price adjustable within each period is a "closed-loop" system, in the terminology discussed in Chapter 3. Also in this class of closed-loop systems is the regime with fixed price, adjustable planned production, and storage possible, because there is feedback from current conditions to the production planned for the next period.

adjusting price within the period, it would much prefer not to store.[12] Best of all, it would prefer to have the option to store and adjust price within each period (while adjusting production planned for the following period).[13]

The implicit cost of the constraint of the same price every period or even the constraint of price set one period in advance is substantial, relative to variations in other parameters.[14] For instance, the present value of the monopoly rents for the most flexible regime (i.e., adjustable price, adjustable planned production, and storage) would compare to that for fixed price, adjustable planned production, and storage at about half the standard deviation of the weather. Also, the fixed-price restriction makes it appear that the benefit of attention to "optimal" inventory and order management is much more valuable than if price were adjustable within the period. At a practical level, therefore, specialists in operations research should be advising clients to improve their price flexibility rather than their ordering and inventory systems. At the level of modeling, the assumption of a fixed-price regime seems to be very important to the results.

Implicit monopolistic competition

The conclusion is therefore strong: Flexibility in price is very helpful in alleviating the inherent uncertainty. Perhaps the reverse also holds. If firms are observed to rely on list prices (with no closet renegotiations), it is difficult to believe that the degree of randomness in excess demand is very high.

Nevertheless, the practice in many industries is to set list prices in advance, although this practice is rare for bulk commodities. A list price in the presence of uncertainty implies a sequence of disequilibria. Such disequilibria in turn suggest the absence or difficulty of some form of arbitrage.[15] If price at one shop is fixed noticeably lower than at a nearby shop, consumers should patronize only one. For that matter, the owners of the shops could trade among themselves. In short, the same commodity should sell at the same price. If

12 Because the consumption demand curve is linear, the monopolistic firm stores more than the competitive consumers would at the prevailing prices. If the consumption demand curve is highly nonlinear (while still relatively elastic), consumers may dominate the monopolistic producer as the storer. The difference in the cases derives from the shape of the marginal revenue curve, as is shown by Newbery (1984).

13 Young and Schmitz (1984) make a "revealed preference" argument (for a monopolist in a two-period setting): The added flexibility permitted by the monopolistic firm's own storage cannot make it worse off.

14 The present value of monopoly rents is much more sensitive to the regime than to the precise fixed price or precise fixed planned production.

15 Gould (1978) studies the competitive equilibrium of retail shops with a list price, a total quantity on hand, and customers that randomly select a particular shop. (There are no carryovers across periods.) Customers cannot go to another shop, and shops with too many customers for their quantity on hand cannot get goods from other stores.

it does not, the implication is that the different versions of the commodity, properly defined, are not identical. Thus, the list price model of inventories has behind it a formulation encompassing a commodity in many forms or locations, in the style of the two-location model of Chapter 9 or the processing models of Chapter 10. That is, each shop or firm is part of a much larger system yet separated by transport or transactions costs. These wedges caused by transport or transactions costs imply that each firm faces a downward sloping demand curve. Here then is the principal discovery of this section: The "list-price" models of inventories are implicitly supposing a degree of market power. They belong in the class of oligopoly or monopolistic competition models. The choices of the firm, which indirectly determine the inventories, are used to price discriminate between periods, a point emphasized by Shaw (1940) (also see Phlips 1983).

Once these "list-price" models of inventory accumulation are recognized as being related to the trade and processing models, lessons from those models raise several issues. In discussing the trade model of Chapter 9, we stressed that the analysis of a small open economy suffers from a fallacy of composition. At the level of many small open economies combined, price is endogenous. For the list-price ordering models similar logic implies that each firm should allow for the possibility that many others will try to order when it does, if all are experiencing similar random shocks. This amounts to the firm recognizing the correlation between its shock and the shock in the system as a whole. This subject in turn focuses attention on the disturbance term as formulated in the literature.[16]

Similarities to (S,s) inventory models

These comments about the implicit assumption of market power apply with particular force to the (S,s) inventory model. This standard model of the operations research literature takes the perspective of a single expected-profit-maximizing firm, most often a retailing store. Its output is sold at only one retail price, into the face of random demand. Backorders are possible, although stockouts incur a cost in terms of customers' goodwill. There is a fixed and a per-unit cost to an order, which will arrive from the supplier the next period. These features are emphasized to make the ordering (i.e., the replenishment) decision interesting. The optimal ordering strategy is to let the stock in the store fall to the level s and then to place an order to bring them up to the level S. Scarf (1959) provided a general proof of the optimality of these (S,s) policies. The solution requires an application of stochastic dynamic programming with a multiperiod or infinite horizon.

---

16 Caplin (1985), in contrast to most of the literature on the (S,s) model, both takes an industrywide perspective and acknowledges the correlations in the disturbance terms across the firms. Also see Blinder (1981).

One question is, why does the firm look ahead more than one period, considering that it takes only one period for the order to arrive? The conventional answer is that the order may not be completely sold off the next period, should the random component cause demand to be less than anticipated. The excess will be carried over as inventory, incurring a storage cost, and so subsequent periods enter into the calculations. But that answer presupposes no possibility of selling the excess in the open market immediately. If the firm could sell all it wanted at its list price, whether to customers or other firms, it would need plan no farther than one period ahead. That such flexibility is not possible suggests either that the list price is not an equilibrium value, or that it is set to take advantage of market power, or both. This contrast between the concept of an equilibrium (marketwide) spot price and the individual firm's list price would be all the sharper if many firms following (S,s) policies were aggregated.[17]

If the list price (for the next period) is not the firm's signal for ordering, it follows that some other price or marginal valuation is the proper signal. As Blinder (1980) has pointed out, there is a shadow price for inventories within the (S,s) model. This is a key insight, although what is happening within an (S,s) model can be made even clearer by introducing a second explicit price in addition to the conventional list price. Call the list price the customer pays the checkout price and the other price the shelf price. Suppose this second spot price, the marginal value of inventories, is not only an explicit spot price but part of a constellation of futures prices for various delivery dates.

Even if the spot checkout price (and, by implication, the futures checkout prices) stays the same from period to period, the spot shelf price varies in response to the demand shocks. Also the spot shelf price is not in a steady relationship to the futures shelf price for delivery the following period. If too little is on hand to satisfy all customers currently, the spot shelf price would be above the expected value for the next period. (It would also be above the spot checkout price, given the shortage penalty.) If not enough customers buy at the checkout price in the current period, the spot shelf price is below the futures shelf price by full carrying charges. That is to say, the shelf prices, spot and futures, display a sequence of equilibria. The price for delivery on the shelf next period (i.e., the futures shelf price) dictates decisions about orders. So perhaps it is better to say: If a particular quantity must be stored because not enough customers will pay the list price, the equilibrium shelf price is the one that accords with the price for future delivery on the shelf given that orders also follow that signal.

The point of this formulation is that it makes clear that those placing the orders need look only at the futures shelf price for delivery the next period;

---

[17] Note in Caplin's (1985) model of aggregate demand under individual (S,s) policies that firms cannot trade the retail good among themselves, so there is not an equilibrium.

that is, the ordering decision itself is not especially complicated. What is complicated is deducing the futures price (i.e., the expected shadow price); it requires the technique of stochastic dynamic programming. But not if that price can be read off in the market, nor if it equals the futures price of the retail good. As Blinder (1980) has noted, that the shadow price does not equal the list price must indicate some degree of monopoly power, transactions costs, or similar market imperfection. In the (S,s) model, the market power and inflexibilities are all on the demand side, whereas on the supply side the firm is assumed to be in a perfectly competitive industry, which is a small part of a larger sector.

11.2   Monopoly over storage alone

In this section we study monopoly over storage alone, unlike in the previous section where the firm was a monopolist over all distribution. Here consumers can deal directly with producers through the market but neither group can store on its own. Only one firm has the right or the technology to store (a technology that it may license, however). The one-period-lagged (and within-period) supply elasticity η^s is 0.0. Current consumption is a function only of current price, not current and all future prices.

A monopolistic storage firm does not extract its extra profits by keeping the commodity off the market to keep the price high, because it is not the only source for consumers, the producers bringing their new harvest to market every period. Likewise, the firm competes with consumers for any quantity on the market. The monopolistic storer, ignoring shrinkage, must expect to sell at some point any amount it buys. A policy of "buy low, hold high, sell low" is no more conducive to success for a storage monopolist than for a price taker. Hence, the true offense of a monopolistic storer is the reverse of the standard charge of overwithholding the commodity from the market. A monopolistic storage firm profits by restricting its output, its output being not supplies of the commodity but the provision of the service called storage.

Versions of monopolistic storage

Even within the class of storage monopoly, care must be taken in specifying the nature of the monopoly. Three variants are distinguished here. Each can be expressed in a form where the firm with sole rights to the storage technology does the storing itself or in a form where it rents its warehousing service to others. These others could be the producers, or the consumers, or separate entities. All that matters is that they are competitors who follow the usual competitive arbitrage equation for storage, except that the marginal physical storage price is in the control of the monopolist and can be different each period. (Call it W_t for "warehousing fee.") These competitors' rational expectations include the possible future actions of the monopolist in adjusting its fees.

Expressed from the perspective of renting warehousing space to others, the three forms are as follows:

1. a fee structure tailored to the circumstances in each period but with that structure set once for all time and the monopolist bound to stick to it by some means such as deposit of a performance bond;
2. a fee structure negotiated anew each period; and
3. a single fee applicable across all periods, again backed by a performance bond.

In all three approaches the monopolistic firm maximizes the expected present value of the fees it would collect, subject to the flexibility and degree of commitment in the fees. Its profits are highest given a flexible fee with the schedule committed in advance, next highest with the fee renegotiated each period, and lowest with a single fee across all periods.

Expressed as a monopolistic firm doing its own storing, the three variants are as follows:

1. A flexible fee with the schedule committed in advance and enforceable by a performance bond corresponds to a monopolist selecting its own storage in a particular period with reference to the effect on the firm's own past (back as far as the date of the commitment), current, and future profits.
2. A fee renegotiated each period corresponds to a monopolist who owns stocks ignoring the effects of its marketing decisions on the value of those current stocks. In effect the firm is constrained to act as if it does not currently own any of the commodity.
3. The single fee across all periods corresponds to the monopolist, when storing itself, not taking account each period of the effect of its releases or additions to its stockpile on the market price.

When formulated from the perspective of a monopolist doing its own storing, one sees that the second and third approaches, by imposing a constraint on which of its own actions the monopolist can account for, cannot increase profits beyond that of the version equivalent to a precommitted fee schedule. The formulation of the problem from the perspective of the monopolist doing its own storing gives the correct ranking. Thus, an immediate result is that the opportunity to renege on a fee structure may actually be harmful to a monopolist.

The conceptual differences in these three versions of storage behavior can be seen in the first-order conditions of a simple three-period example with certainty under the formulation of the monopolist storing itself. (Behavior under uncertainty and an infinite horizon follows.) These first-order conditions make unambiguous what the monopolist accounts for when selecting its level of storage in the first period, period 1. Suppose A_1, none of which is owned by the monopolist, is sufficiently large to induce carryovers to both periods 2 and 3. The harvests h_2 and h_3 are fixed. Suppose true physical storage costs and interest are zero.

If the monopolistic firm controls all storage, its profits are

$$\Pi = -P_1[A_1 - S_1]S_1 + P_2[h_2 + S_1 - S_2]S_1 - P_2[h_2 + S_1 - S_2]S_2 + P_3[h_3 + S_2]S_2$$
(11.1)

The first two terms can be thought of as profits attributable to storage in period 1, Π_1, and the last two terms thought of as Π_2. Profits are maximized where:

$$\partial \Pi / \partial S_1 = 0 = -P_1 + (\partial P_1 / \partial q)S_1 + P_2 + (\partial P_2 / \partial q)S_1 - (\partial P_2 / \partial q)S_2$$
(11.2)

$$\partial \Pi / \partial S_2 = 0 = -(\partial P_2 / \partial q)S_1 - P_2 + (\partial P_2 / \partial q)S_2 + P_3 + (\partial P_3 / \partial q)S_2$$
(11.3)

where derivatives with respect to q refer to the consumption demand curve, specifically its slope evaluated at q_1, q_2, and q_3. The monopolist's profits are maximized where S_1 and S_2 are the solutions to the pair of equations (11.2) and (11.3).

Note that the last term in (11.2) is $\partial \Pi_2/\partial S_1$, while the first term in (11.3) is $\partial \Pi_1/\partial S_2$. This term $\partial \Pi_1/\partial S_2$ is crucial. Consider the monopolistic firm's profit if there were only two periods to the problem, specifically periods 2 and 3, and of the given A_2 the firm owned nothing:

$$\Pi_2 = -P_2[A_2 - S_2]S_2 + P_3[h_3 + S_2]S_2$$
(11.4)

These profits are maximized where

$$\partial \Pi_2 / \partial S_2 = 0 = -P_2 + (\partial P_2 / \partial q)S_2 + P_3 + (\partial P_3 / \partial q)S_2$$
(11.5)

Equation (11.5) is the same as the first-order condition (11.3) except for the term $\partial \Pi_1/\partial S_2$ (i.e., $(\partial P_2/\partial q)S_1$). Obviously, if (11.5) is used with (11.2), the solutions for S_1 and S_2 will be different and, more important, will not be optimal. The solution for S_1 and S_2 using (11.2) and (11.5) misses the connection between the amount stored in period 2 and profits attributable to storage in period 1. Or to put the matter slightly differently, if S_1 is positive, then A_2 is partially owned by the storage monopolist, and that partial ownership should influence its choice of S_2. By withholding some of its share of A_2 from the market, perhaps even to the extent of taking a loss on it, the monopolistic storer supports the price in period 2 and makes higher profits on what it does release, a profit accruing to its carryout from period 1. Under (11.4) its share of A_2, if any, does not influence its choice of S_2, and by extension the monopolist's selection of S_1 leads to lower total profits.

From the perspective of a warehousing fee structure for storage space, the underlying mathematics are the same; but the interaction between the monopolist and the market is different. The monopolist's profits (11.1) can be rewritten as

$$\Pi = W_1 S_1 + W_2 S_2 \tag{11.6}$$

where the fees W_1 and W_2 are now in the monopolist's control while S_1 and S_2 are implicit in the competitive arbitrage equations:

$$P_1[A_1 - S_1] + W_1 = P_2[h_2 + S_1 - S_2] = -W_2 + P_3[h_3 + S_2] \tag{11.7}$$

in which W_1 and W_2 are taken as given by those renting the storage space. The monopolist's profits are maximized by solving jointly for W_1 and W_2 in

$$\partial\Pi / \partial W_1 = 0 = S_1 + W_1(\partial S_1 / \partial W_1) + W_2(\partial S_2 / \partial W_1) \tag{11.8}$$

$$\partial\Pi / \partial W_2 = 0 = W_1(\partial S_1 / \partial W_2) + S_2 + W_2(\partial S_2 / \partial W_2) \tag{11.9}$$

where $\partial S_1/\partial W_1$, $\partial S_2/\partial W_2$, and so forth are found by implicit differentiation of the competitive storers' arbitrage equations in (11.7). The profits achieved with the joint selection of W_1 and W_2 are the same as achieved through the profit-maximizing S_1 and S_2 based on (11.2) and (11.3).

Monopolistic storage and time inconsistency

From this perspective of fees collected from a competitive industry, it is much less intuitively reasonable that the monopolist jointly maximizes the two fees. If nothing binds the monopolistic firm to stick to the W_2 it proposed as of period 1, it can increase its profits in period 2 by adjusting its fee. (From the standpoint of period 2 alone, given all decisions made by the firm and others in period 1, the chance to renege on its promised fee W_2 cannot make the firm worse off – it could always keep its promise.) Yet the people contemplating storing by renting warehousing space in period 1 will see that the firm has an incentive to depart from its announced value for W_2 given circumstances as of period 2, and that P_2 will be lower as a result. Consequently, they will store less in period 1, which reduces the monopolist's revenue directly in period 1 and indirectly in period 2 through the effect on A_2. Those renting warehousing space from the monopolistic firm see the time inconsistency in its announced plans.

When the problem is formulated with the monopolist as storer itself and with the harvest producers bring to market exogenous, the monopolistic storage firm is playing a game against nature. If the firm does not follow its intended actions for later periods, designed for all possible conditions, it only harms itself. When the problem is formulated as fees paid by competitive storers, the monopolist is playing a game against those agents, who are forward looking. The resulting difference in the monopolist's storage behavior makes clear the role of the "competitive fringe's" expectations.[18] Their presence tempts the storage monopolist to remaximize in the last period, since it appears the private agents can be exploited. The private agents anticipate this exploitation and so change by their earlier actions the conditions that the dominant player will be taking as given. This means the monopolist has no incentive not to remaximize in all earlier periods as well.[19]

Whether the objective is social welfare in the case of a public agency supplementing private storage distorted by a price ceiling (discussed in Chapter 15) or profits in the case of a storage monopolist charging a fee, the results can be improved if the dominant player can bind itself from reoptimizing each period. In the case of the government, that commitment is not credible, because governments by their sovereign nature cannot bind their future actions. More credible is a storage monopolist's effort to convince private agents of its commitments. Perhaps it can make binding contracts or post a bond (or store everything itself). The avoidance of time inconsistency is at least feasible. Nevertheless, it is by no means obvious which formulation of monopoly storage is more appropriate. Wright and Williams (1984a) examined the system with renegotiated flexible fees, that is, without a credible commitment. Here we emphasize the case where the monopolist can commit to its flexible fees through a performance bond or do its own storing.

The issue here is not the rationality of the monopolist but whether the firm can convince other agents that it will stick to its commitments. Either way the firm takes account of the effect of its current actions on its future profits and the effect of its current purchases and sales on current market price. It balances marginal expenditures with marginal revenue. The first-order condition for storage in period 1 (i.e., equation (11.2)) can be rewritten as

$$\partial \Pi / \partial S_1 = 0 = -MX_1 + MR_2 + (\partial \Pi_2 / \partial S_1)S_1 , \quad S_1 > 0 \qquad (11.10)$$

where MX_1 denotes marginal expenditure $\partial(P_1 S_1)/\partial S_1$, and MR_2 is marginal revenue.

In the three-period model, the difference between monopoly storage with precommittted flexible fees and monopoly storage with renegotiated fees is the single term $\partial \Pi_1/\partial S_2$. This difference feeds on itself as time moves backward from the last period. The difference in storage behavior in period $t+8$ because of reoptimization in period $t+9$ affects the demand for storage in period $t+7$, as does the prospective reoptimization in period $t+8$. Similar considerations feed back to the current period, period t.

[18] As Newbery (1981) has emphasized in the setting of an oil cartel and a competitive fringe, the competitive fringe's expectations give substance to the issue of dynamic inconsistency.

[19] If the monopolist does not anticipate that there will be a final period, there could be a multiplicity of equilibrium storage behaviors in the current period.

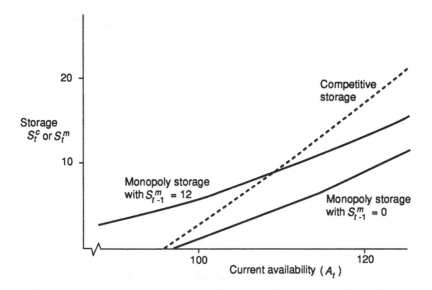

Figure 11.1. Storage rules for monopolist with committed flexible warehousing fees.

Storage rules under monopoly

As the final period recedes over the horizon toward infinity, current monopolistic storage behavior becomes independent of time. It is a stable function, as were the reduced-form relationships for competitive storage studied in earlier chapters. In the case of the flexible but committed fee structure the amount of storage is a function of two state variables:

$$S_t^m = f^m[A_t, S_{t-1}^m] \tag{11.11}$$

A_t, of course, equals $h_t + S_{t-1}^m$. The system with period-by-period reoptimization has the control variable a function of one state variable:

$$S_t^m = f^m[A_t] \tag{11.12}$$

Either of these storage rules for an infinite horizon can be found through numerical methods. Figure 11.1 plots the relationship between S_t^m and A_t for the system with precommitted flexible fees for two levels of S_{t-1}^m, the second state variable. The example is one familiar from earlier chapters: constant elasticity of demand of -0.2, perfectly inelastic supply, $\sigma_h = 10$ units, and $k = \$0$. When the monopolist owns some of the current availability the whole storage rule shifts more or less in parallel to the left; the firm stores more.

The storage rule for the system with renegotiated flexible fees is essentially that of the other system shown in Figure 11.1 with $S_{t-1}^m = 0$. The rule is slight-

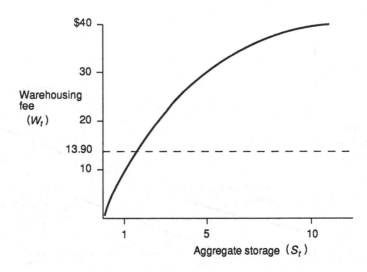

Figure 11.2. Implicit monopolistic warehousing fees.

ly shifted to the right, reflecting dampened future storage demand. It has essentially the same marginal propensity to store of about 0.35.

Now consider the relationship between the total storage and the fee W_t the monopolist would charge when credibly committed to that fee structure. That relationship is shown in Figure 11.2. The adjustment in the profit-maximizing fee is considerable. Not surprisingly, the monopolist sets the fee noticeably higher when the storage is high (or, more precisely, when the current availability is high).

For its part, the optimal single fee across all periods, given that the monopolist is constrained to charge only one fee under all conditions, is $13.90, shown in Figure 11.2 with a dashed line. The storage rule for this version of monopoly corresponds to that under competition when k equals that value of $13.90. Namely, it would be a nearly parallel shift to the right of the competitive rule with $k = \$0$ that is shown in Figure 11.1, with a kink point at an A_t of about 100 units and, more important, a marginal propensity to store of about 0.70, double that of the other two monopoly rules.

The salient feature of monopoly storage rules derived under either version of flexible fees is the low marginal propensity to store. Basically, a monopolist over storage technology gains its profits by restricting how much is stored out of each additional unit available.[20]

---

[20] Wright and Williams (1984a) give some additional intuition for why a monopolist's marginal propensity to store is less, using a two-period model with an anticipated disturbance to production. Also see the two-period model of a monopolistic storer in Sarris (1982).

Because the marginal propensity to store is lower under monopoly than under competition, monopolistic storage of whatever form will generally be less than competitive storage. The exception is the precommitted flexible monopolistic storage when the monopolist has a large carryin. This is seen in Figure 11.1 where the storage rule given $S_{t-1}^m = 12$ units shows positive storage even at very low availabilities. Thus, under this type of monopolistic storage, the monopolist may sometimes store something even when the price is very high, which is seemingly perverse behavior. The reason is that the monopolist recognizes that holding some amount off the market increases the revenue from what it does sell from its carryin.

Time-series behavior

The operation of this type of monopoly storage, one with precommitted flexible fees, is best explained with a short time series, such as that in Figure 11.3. Periods 14–17 are of particular interest. The carryout from period 14 with this type of monopoly behavior is 14.31 units, a relatively large amount. The harvest in period 15 is unusually bad, such that A_{15} under monopoly is merely 94.69 units. At this availability competitive storage would be zero.[21] The monopolist storage firm, in contrast, retains 5.77 units in store, which keeps the price very high, $179.95 to be exact. More surprisingly, over the next two periods it reduces its stocks further despite the falling price. The competitive equilibrium always involves more storage at lower prices. Note, however, that the monopolist did release the majority of its stocks when the harvest was poor, and that it accumulated its large stockpile as of period 13 by the conventional practice of buying when the price has fallen.

The monopolistic firm acts as it does during the shortage in period 15 because it owns some of the availability. By withholding some of its share from the market, even taking an expected loss on it, the firm supports the current price and makes a substantial profit on what it does release. True, its share of current availability is relatively small, less than 20 percent, which implies that the demand curve it faces is elastic. Although in models with a single period such an elastic demand curve would dictate complete release, this monopolistic firm is working not just with the market in period 15 but with later periods too. The firm obtains greater monopoly profits because it can discriminate among the periods. A price discriminator makes money when other parties cannot arbitrage between the submarkets. By the nature of a storage monopoly with no production response, no other parties can arbitrage between the periods. In any case, it would be physically impossible for them to convert

---

[21] Note, however, that under competition, availability and storage are higher in this period, because of the cumulative effects of higher carryouts from periods 1–13.

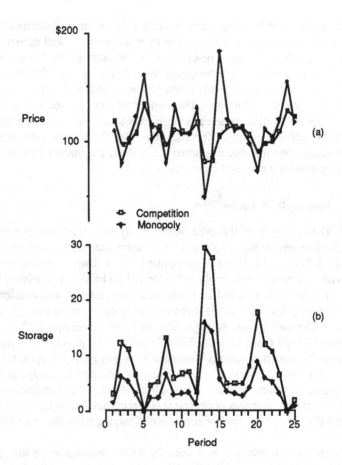

Figure 11.3. Time series comparing competitive and monopoly storage.

supplies available in period 16 to those available in period 15, in order to sell at the high price in period 15.

Thus, any firm that owns a share of the current availability and that is not a pure price taker may want to release its holding too slowly from society's viewpoint. It may be willing to hold stocks despite spreads below full carrying charges.[22] Yet this possibility begs the questions of how the monopolistic firm acquired its share of availability in the first place and how total availability happened to be that number. Although for a given availability monopoly

---

[22] Expressed in the context of a monopolistic fee, storage at spreads below full carrying charges correspond to a negative W_t. Precisely because those renting warehouse space in earlier periods doubt the monopolist would keep to a promise of a subsidy, the system without credible commitment degenerates into a system where all renegotiated W_t's are positive and where the monopolist's total profits are lower.

Table 11.2. *Long-run means under competitive and monopolistic storage* *(standard deviations in parentheses)*

	Competitive storage	Flexible-fee monopoly	Flexible-fee monopoly	Fixed-fee monopoly
Price	$104.12	108.42	111.87	109.84
	(35.54)	(47.89)	(58.94)	(55.44)
Storage	12.74	6.26	2.34	3.68
	(9.86)	(4.88)	(2.40)	(4.29)
% with no storage	10.09	10.31	27.87	35.15
% with storage at less than full carry	0.00	32.84	0.00	0.00
Maximum observed storage	57.58	29.17	15.20	30.01

storage derived as with a precommitted, flexible fee structure may be higher than competitive storage, the actual availability is generally much higher under competition. Period 15 is a case in point. Competitive carryin from period 14 is 27.54 units, not 14.31. With a higher A_{15} and higher marginal propensity to store, competitive storage in period 15 is 8.34 units, higher than the monopoly level. With the same long sequence of random weather from which this example was excerpted, comparing competitive and this form of monopolistic storage side by side, less than 0.5 percent of the periods have higher monopoly storage. For monopoly storage with renegotiated flexible fees, that probability is 0.0 percent. Average storage and average availabilities under monopolistic storage of any form are lower than under competition, as can be seen in Table 11.2.

Monopolistic storage profits and social welfare

Even if monopoly storage derived as with a precommitted, flexible fee structure has occasions with positive storage and high prices, it is by no means obvious that it is inferior socially to the other types of monopoly. As can be seen in Table 11.2, among the three types of monopolistic storage it has the lowest standard deviation of price. Some occasions of high prices are traded against fewer periods of extremely high prices. More to the point, the deadweight loss, for these particular parameters, is lowest. Among the three, the system with renegotiated flexible fees has the highest deadweight loss. Compared to the fixed-fee monopoly, a monopoly with precommitted, flexible fees can price discriminate more across periods. Just as in the static, single-period setting, a discriminatory monopoly leads to a lower deadweight loss even as it achieves higher profits.

A discriminatory monopolist's market power comes from its share of current availability. The firm had to acquire that stake somehow. In a world with free entry, that is, one in which the monopoly is not legally sanctioned, it would be irrational for anyone to bid for supplies in order to control the market later. Note that with $S_{t-1}^{m} = 0$, the competitive storage rule in Figure 11.1 lies everywhere to the left of the monopoly rule. A prospective monopolistic firm would have to outbid competitive storers for its stock. Its prospects for profits would disappear. By construction, competitive storers are willing to store with no prospect of abnormal long-run profits. Outbidding them would only lead to expected losses, the opposite of monopoly profits.

11.3   Implications for modeling market power

The implications of market power over storage depend very much on how much further that market power extends, and upon the broader economic environment. If there is monopoly over all supply and distribution, storage manipulation might well be a relatively minor aspect of overall exploitation, unless other decision variables regarding pricing and production are highly constrained.

Our analysis of market power and storage has furnished insights into the (S,s) model, popular in the operations research literature. The behavioral rules derived in that model and its relatives have a natural interpretation in terms of shadow prices. But the rules themselves depend upon a peculiar blend of assumptions, including competition in the input market, market power in the output market, and inflexibility in pricing decisions.

If the monopoly is over storage alone, the distortion it causes takes the form of too little storage, not excessive withholding of stocks. This insight, enunciated by Adam Smith, is not yet recognized sufficiently widely in either developed or less developed economies. The effects of this type of storage monopoly depend on the feasibility of commitment by the monopolistic firm to an announced policy, in the presence of private sector responses by producers and speculators.

In the discussion in Section 11.2 of a monopolist over storage technology, a crucial simplifying assumption was that the supply elasticity $\eta^s = 0.0$. If new production were elastic with a one-period lag, all three versions of the monopoly problem would involve the issues of time consistency and believable commitments. Producers, making a commitment to plant an extra large quantity, would anticipate that a monopolistic storage firm promising to buy up a large quantity to store itself or promising to license the warehousing technology to others at a low fee, would have an incentive to renege, to extract some extra revenue when the harvest matures. Whether or not the monopolist would renege (or would find it advantageous to deposit a performance bond) depends on the particular underlying parameters. Thus, general results are not likely.

This issue of dynamic inconsistency arises in many other settings, whenever a dominant "player" is repeatedly interacting with competitive forward-looking agents who can respond. One example, to be the focus of Chapter 15, is when the government attempts to run its own stockpile to supplement private storage while taking into account the reactions of the private sector. Another example is that of a state-authorized monopoly of international trade in a primary commodity (e.g., rice in Indonesia). Such an agency is entangled in the web of other parties' expectations of its actions. Domestic producers must produce and domestic storers must store with the worry that the agency could renounce its planned export/import program if it could profit after the fact. Likewise, the foreign producers and storers are calculating whether the agency will renege on plans to import if the domestic country has a relative (and temporary) abundance or plans to limit exports if the domestic harvest is huge.

The existing literature on stabilization in the context of market power in international trade in commodities, including Bieri and Schmitz (1973, 1974), Schmitz et al. (1981), Eckstein and Eichenbaum (1985), Danielson and Cartwright (1987), and Wong (1989), take the demand and supply curves as given (apart from weather shocks). But the market demand curve in the foreign country, to take one example, includes the demand for storage at that location. That demand for storage incorporates the private storers' anticipations of the monopoly trade agency's operating procedures. As a result, that foreign country's demand in the current period is not exogenous. Rather, it is partly a function of the monopolist's own behavior, a point made by Aiyagari and Riezman (1985). Treatment of such curves as exogenous is likely to overstate the advantage gained from the market power. Maskin and Newbery (1990), for example, show how the ability to levy tariffs in the future may make a large importer worse off because of the anticipation of those tariffs by exporters.

Thus, one lesson from this chapter on monopoly and storage is that any multiperiod analysis must represent carefully whether the other behavior within the system is exogenous or endogenous. A second lesson concerns the nature of the market power and the industrial organization of the industry. In Section 11.2 we carefully distinguished between a formulation with the storage monopolist doing its own storage and a formulation in which the monopolist rents its warehouse to others. The second formulation seems very strained, of course. But the parallel formulations did have the advantage of demonstrating that the ability to renege can be detrimental to the monopolist, by showing what component is omitted from the first-order conditions of profit maximization when the monopolistic firm does its own storing. The parallel formulations have a more general advantage in uncovering hidden instances of dynamic inconsistency. Any problem involving market power should thus be recast as many ways as possible in terms of the industrial structure, to expose hidden assumptions about the exogeneity of behavior.

Maskin and Newbery's article (1990) is a case in point where this multiple formulation could have been used to advantage. They argue that one way to overcome the dynamic inconsistency of promises not to impose tariffs (on oil) is for the importer to store. They work through some examples, suggesting that the storage could be done either by the government or by private speculators in the importing country. But those two formulations are not the same except in a first-best world with no market power. If domestic speculators do the storing, they will be attempting to understand under which circumstances in the future the government will impose a tariff or will confiscate their speculative profits. They will not store the same amount as a government agency, for they will see the dynamic inconsistency in the government's plans.

PART IV

Public interventions

CHAPTER 12

Welfare analysis of market stabilization

The existence of competitive storage stabilizes price, as was evident in the comparative-statics exercises of Chapter 4. Is this a desirable result? An affirmative answer may seem obvious, not just to "practical" men but to academics as well (e.g., Cochrane 1980). Indeed, many studies adopt price stability or income stability *per se* as the principal targets of policy (e.g., Arzac and Wilkinson 1979; Dixon and Chen 1982; Ghosh et al. 1987).

It seems that the main attraction of stability as a criterion is its simplicity; nevertheless, that simplicity is more apparent than real. Even those concerned solely with stability confront unavoidable trade-offs when the underlying source of disturbances, such as weather-related randomness in production, is not neutralized. As Josling (1977b) stresses, the underlying variability must express itself somewhere. In storage-induced stabilization, for example, more stable prices may mean less stable production or less stable net revenue, as noted in Chapter 4. In making these trade-offs involving stability, some other standard must be invoked. For economists in the neoclassical tradition, the natural choice of policy objective is some function of the welfare of individuals. Here we concentrate on the effects of stabilization on individual welfare, using where necessary the simplest possible method of aggregation: assuming equal weight for each individual's monetary measures of gains and losses.

This chapter offers a primer on welfare analysis of policies affecting market stability, such as a public buffer-stock scheme or public R&D that increases production stability or lowers storage costs. Its focus is on the methodology; it does not claim to be the definitive statement of the welfare effects of each and every storage program.

The following are five mistakes commonly made in the welfare analysis of public programs intended to stabilize the market.

1. *Inappropriately narrow focus:* An example is justifying market-level intervention with analysis of a single consumer or producer, holding the responses of others constant. Collective reactions to the stabiliza-

335

tion may invalidate the conclusions. A model of the whole market is required, even though the effects are measured in terms of the welfare of individual participants.

2. *Inappropriate generalization of specific results:* Analysts often do not recognize the extreme sensitivity to seemingly small differences in specification of conclusions drawn from analysis of a particular model with a particular set of parameters. Examples of crucial details are the distinction between additive and multiplicative weather disturbances or between linear and constant-elasticity consumption demand curves. Indeed, in theoretical or empirical studies on stabilization policy, one can often read the equation for consumption demand, which is usually linear or log-linear for analytical tractability, and know whether the producers will gain or lose in the long run, regardless of the other details of the model or any empirical results.

3. *Ignoring the implications of capitalization:* At the time of the announcement of some public program, the prices of capital assets, such as land or the current stocks of the commodity, will change by the present discounted value of the program's anticipated effects in future periods, if the capital market is competitive. Later entrants into farming are not helped by the program.

4. *Neglect of dynamic (i.e., time-related) responses:* This is closely related to this principle of capitalization. The conditions prevailing – the size of the initial availability and its ownership – at the time of the announcement of some program and the lag, if any, between announcement and implementation, are important determinants of the welfare effects of interventions in markets with storage; conventional long-run comparative statics give the wrong answer.

5. *Assumption, without explicit justification, of suboptimal performance by the private sector:* Until recently, private price forecasts were routinely specified as irrational in welfare analyses of public interventions. Furthermore, analyses of market fluctuations and the design of public storage programs have often ignored the role of private storage (not to mention its response to the program).[1] Such misspecification can easily make a wasteful and undesirable public program appear to be just the opposite.

Each of these pitfalls in the welfare analysis of storage will be discussed further in this chapter, although more emphasis is given to the fifth one in Chapters 13–15. The first two pitfalls apply not just to storage-based schemes

---

[1] One of the many examples is Adams (1983). In a paper on the role of research in the creation of the IMF's Cereal Import Facility, variability in staple food consumption is presented (Table 1, p. 550) as production plus net imports and changes in public stocks. The only recognition of private storage is in a footnote: "Actual consumption might be slightly higher or lower because of fluctuations in private cereal stocks."

but also to other types of stabilization, in particular to "ideal stabilization," which represents the complete removal of uncertainty from the system. As was discussed in Chapter 4, this complete stability is an extreme case and cannot be attained by storage. In an agricultural context, one could think of it as stabilization achieved through a new plant variety with unchanged mean yield but insensitive to the weather. Ideal stabilization in a world without storage is both a useful standard against which to measure the welfare effects of public storage, and an analytically simpler case for illustrating some of the modeling pitfalls that we discuss.

12.1   The effects of stabilization on individual welfare

The effects of price stability on welfare have interested economists for a long time.[2] The seminal paper by Waugh (1944) in which a representative consumer faces exogenous and variable prices produced a remarkable result: Consumers may be better off with price instability.

Like many of the authors who followed in his footsteps, Waugh studied the implications of stabilization without explicitly modeling how it is achieved. Using a linear demand curve, he showed that variable prices lead to higher average welfare (measured by the consumer surplus under the consumption demand curve) than if price is fixed at its arithmetic mean. His result is illustrated in Figure 12.1. If price is fixed at $\overline{P}$, then consumer surplus is the area under the demand curve above that price. If price is high at P_{high}, then consumer surplus is lower by the horizontally striped area. If price is low at P_{low}, consumer surplus is higher than at $\overline{P}$ by the vertically striped area. (For now, ignore the shading in Figure 12.1.) If the price deviations are symmetric and have equal probabilities of 0.5, then the average of the striped areas exceeds the smaller of the two, the horizontally striped area: Average consumer surplus is higher in the regime with variable price than in a regime with price fixed at $\overline{P}$. If the demand curve were vertical (had zero price elasticity), this obviously would not be true; the more gentle slope seen in Figure 12.1 gives consumers flexibility to take advantage of lower prices by consuming more.

This result does not depend on the linearity of demand, the accuracy of consumer surplus as a welfare indicator, or even the presence of risk (as distinct from anticipated price variation). To verify these assertions, consider the case where the variable prices consist of a series that consumers know alternates between high and low values, so there is no uncertainty at all. Assume further that there are no enduring effects of price in one period on utility in others. Thus, storage is ruled out, and utility in any period is assumed to be

---

[2]   The literature on this subject is voluminous. Excellent surveys include Turnovsky (1978), Labys (1980), and Schmitz (1984). Gardner (1979) also contains many useful references.

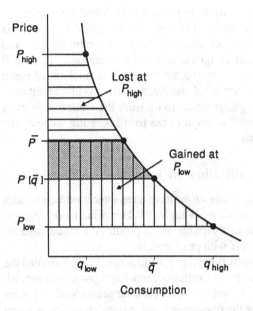

Figure 12.1. Consumer surplus with variable prices.

independent of (i.e., additively separable from) utility in other periods. The discount rate is assumed to be zero.

Given these assumptions, consider Figure 12.2 in which the curve marked V^* shows the consumption expenditure needed to maintain a given level of utility $U = V^*$ as a function of the commodity price P, holding all other prices constant. The curve has positive slope, because to maintain utility at V^* with a higher price, higher expenditure is necessary. V^* is an indifference curve in price–expenditure space.[3] (The curve marked V^{**} shows price–expenditure combinations giving a lower level of utility.) This expenditure function $EXP[P,U]$ is concave in price regardless of demand specification.[4] Consequently, the average expenditure needed to maintain the level of utility V^* under alternating prices P_{low} and P_{high}, namely, $EXP_A = (EXP[P_{low}, V^*] + EXP[P_{high}, V^*])/2$, will support a level of utility no higher than V^{**} if price is fixed at $\bar{P}$. Because V^* is strictly preferred to V^{**}, pure price stabilization causes a fall in consumer welfare equivalent to the fall caused by a program that changes income by $EXP_A - EXP_S$; this is the average *equivalent variation* of eliminating anticipated price variation.

---

3   The custom is to use V to represent the indirect utility function, just as it is the custom in the literature on dynamic programming to use V for the value function.

4   See, for example, Varian (1984). The slope of the curve V^* is the quantity consumed at (P,U).

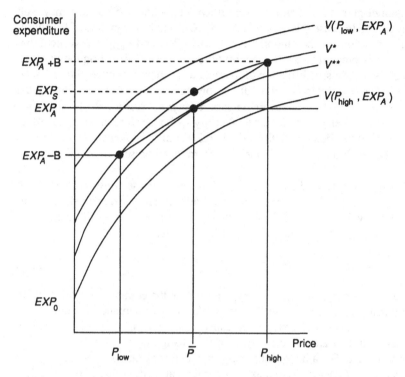

Figure 12.2. Consumer expenditure with unstable prices.

What if the price is uncertain in these circumstances rather than known to alternate between low and high? Then the value of fixing price at $\bar{P}$ is illustrated for a one-period case in Figure 12.2. If the consumer spends EXP_A, he attains utility $V[P_{low}, EXP_A]$ if price is P_{low}, and $V[P_{high}, EXP_A]$ if price is P_{high}. Assume each price has probability of one-half. Now because we have assumed no income effect, the price-expenditure indifference curves $V[P_{low}, EXP_A]$ and $V[P_{high}, EXP_A]$ are a vertical distance B above and below curve V^*. If the consumer is risk neutral, and $V[\cdot]$ is reinterpreted as a cardinal (and not just ordinal) indirect utility function, then V^* is $1/2(V[P_{low}, EXP_A] + V[P_{high}, EXP_A])$, the expected utility of consumption of uncertain price. This is also the average utility of consuming at alternating prices, as was just discussed. So the equivalent variation of stabilization is, once again, $EXP_A - EXP_S < 0$.

If the consumer is risk averse, the marginal utility of expenditure (equal to income here) declines as expenditure rises. An increase of B adds less utility than a decrease of B. Thus, $\hat{V} = 1/2(V[P_{low}, EXP_A] + V[P_{high}, EXP_A])$ lies below the curve for V^* in Figure 12.2. Only if $\hat{V}$ falls below V^{**} will the consumer gain from stabilization of price. The income effect here may well be too small to cause this reversal. At $(\overline{P}, EXP_A)$, the magnitude of the equivalent variation for the random combination P_{low} and P_{high}, the vertical distance B, is typically a small fraction of average expenditure on the product, which is itself a small fraction of average total consumer expenditure EXP_A, except for some staple commodities for very poor consumers. For typical values of the relative risk aversion parameter $\rho \equiv -y(\partial^2 V / \partial y^2) / (\partial V / \partial y)$, measuring the elasticity of marginal utility with respect to income, the effect of commodity price fluctuations on marginal utility is likely to be negligible, with the result that the consumer loses from mean-preserving stabilization of price.

To pursue further the effects of risk aversion on the consumer gain from price stabilization, it is convenient to move from graphical analysis to calculus. Turnovsky et al. (1980) show that stabilizing price at its arithmetic mean gives the consumer a gain approximately equivalent to

$$\frac{1}{2} \, \overline{P} q[\overline{P}, y] (\gamma(\eta^y - \rho) - \eta^d)) \Delta \sigma_P^2 \tag{12.1}$$

Here γ is the share of consumer expenditure on the commodity, $\overline{P} q[\overline{P}, y]$, in the consumer budget, η^y is the income elasticity of demand, ρ is the coefficient of relative risk aversion with respect to income, η^d is the price elasticity of demand, and $\Delta \sigma_P^2$ is the square of the change in the coefficient of variation of price. For a budget share of 1 percent, for example, ρ would have to be very high (at least 20) to make price stabilization desirable if η^d is less than $|-0.2|$, even if the consumer had no means at all of rearranging his assets (e.g., buying a share in a farm, working as a sharecropper, or saving in low-price years) to reduce exposure to this risk.

A parallel result to Waugh's holds on the supply side, if supply responds to the contemporaneous price. In Figure 12.3, the average of the horizontally and vertically hatched areas for producer surplus exceeds the latter. Risk-neutral producers are better off with variable prices than with price fixed at the mean if short-run supply curves slope upward, that is, have price elasticity between zero and infinity – a result first established by Oi (1961). The logic is similar to the case for consumers. Producers take advantage of high prices by producing more, and avoid part of the loss due to low prices by producing less. The argument can also be expressed, as by Tisdell (1963), in terms of the profit function, which is convex in terms of the prices of output, as well as of inputs. (If price is uncertain and not just variable, sufficient producer risk aversion could reverse this result.) These results for producers' profits along with those for consumers' utility might tempt one to suspect, as did Waugh, that price destabilization might be a good idea for the market as a whole.

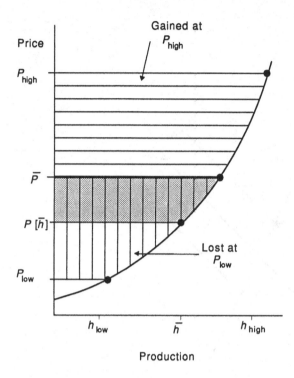

Figure 12.3. Producer surplus with variable prices.

12.2   Marketwide analysis

Can fluctuating prices – for example, prices regularly alternating as in Figures 12.1 or 12.3 – be Pareto superior to prices fixed at their arithmetic mean values, where the latter are feasible? The answer is no if producers and consumers are weighted equally. The situation illustrated in Figure 12.1 for consumers and the comparable diagram for producers in Figure 12.3 obviously cannot occur in the same market at the same time. Except at mean price, the market will not clear. In a supply–demand diagram, price disturbances cannot occur if the demand curve is fixed (as in Figure 12.1) and the supply curve is also fixed as it would be in the comparable diagram for producers. As emphasized by Samuelson (1972), price disturbances are not fundamental; they arise from shifts in demand or supply.

In Figure 12.1 the disturbance is implicitly caused by shifting supply. When high and low supply curves alternate, costless smoothing that transfers consumption from high-output periods to low-output periods is potentially Pareto-improving. That is, gainers could fully compensate losers and still be

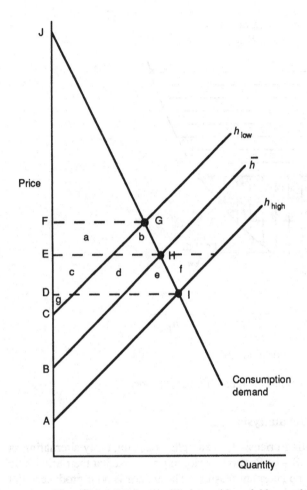

Figure 12.4. Market equilibrium with variable supply.

better off than without the smoothing. This result, foreshadowed by Meade (1950) and established by Massell (1969), is illustrated in Figure 12.4 for linear supply curves elastic within the period. The smoothing transfers the quantity beyond average supply that would be produced at price E in a high-supply period to supplement the quantity produced at price E in a low-supply period. The effect on producer surplus from such smoothing is an increase equal to areas $c + d + e + f$ in high-supply periods, but a loss of area a in low-supply periods. Consumers lose a surplus represented by areas $c + d + e$ in high-supply periods and gain areas $a + b$ in low-supply periods. The net social gain from smoothing (the loss from destabilization by prohibiting smoothing) is an area the size of area e, assuming producer and consumer surpluses can be aggregated "dollar for dollar." A similar analysis for demand shifts has a similar implication: Market stabilization via costless consumption smoothing increases net social welfare when the surpluses accruing to each party have equal weight.

This result in favor of market-level stabilization can easily be misinterpreted. It means costless smoothing of consumption given variable supply is socially desirable in the sense of a potential Pareto improvement. It does not mean that a stable supply curve is always socially preferable to a supply shifted back and forth by some disturbance, because a stable supply curve, such as the one marked $\bar{h}$ in Figure 12.4, is not the same as costless smoothing. In Figure 12.4 the net social surplus given the stable supply curve $\bar{h}$ is area BJH; this is less than the average of areas CJG and AJI, the net social surpluses with fluctuating supply.[5] Costless smoothing allows a large quantity to be produced at the low production costs represented by the supply curve h_{high}, whereas only a small quantity is produced at the high costs represented by h_{low}. The average cost is lower than the within-period production costs represented by the stable curve $\bar{h}$. Thus, even though costless smoothing would suggest itself as an analytical representation of stable supply (or vice versa), it is not. More generally, the form of the stabilization needs to be specified carefully.

Another imprecision in the analysis of the welfare effects of stabilization arises through the practice of assuming stabilization to be at the mean price. As emphasized in Chapter 4, mean price is an endogenous variable. With any shape for the consumption demand curve but one exactly linear, the price at mean quantity is not the mean price in general, except for specially constructed combinations of demand specifications and distributions of disturbances. Stabilization at mean price, whether the instability arises through shifts in demand or supply or both, implicitly supposes a change in mean quantity. This can be seen in Figure 12.1 in the difference between the price at the mean quantity $P[\bar{q}]$ and the mean price $\bar{P}$. This change in mean consumption alters net social welfare and its distribution, just as it would in an analysis conducted in a world of certainty. For consumers, for example, stabilization at $\bar{P}$ rather than $P[\bar{q}]$ causes a loss in surplus equal to the shaded area in Figure 12.1.[6] In Figure 12.3 the shaded area demonstrates the comparable point for producers.

---

5   This result in favor of instability also depends crucially on the supply specification and the nature of the supply shift. If, for example, all the linear supply curves in Figure 12.4 were price inelastic (cut the horizontal axis at positive quantities), the results are different; on average consumers gain, producers lose, and there is a net social loss from variability. Illustrations of these propositions for linear supply and demand curves are found in Massell (1969).

6   The effect of this type of stabilization on producers was noted by Bateman (1965), who also recognized the relevance of the slope of the market marginal revenue curve.

A more reasonable representation than complete price stabilization is stabilization of the underlying disturbance, which must be in the supply or demand function. Unless either supply or demand is perfectly price inelastic, both mean price and mean quantity will be different under stability than instability, at the level of the whole market. Analysis of the effects on a representative atomistic consumer or producer, assuming either price or quantity is stabilized at its mean, will fail to capture all the welfare effects of a marketwide stabilization program.

12.3   Sensitivity of distributive effects to specification

Even in a marketwide model, seemingly small differences in specification can alter conclusions about the effect on, say, producers of a stabilization program. In particular, the models of Waugh, Oi, and Massell include several assumptions that are jointly crucial to their results: (1) linear demand, (2) totally instantaneous demand and supply response, (3) additive disturbances in demand or supply, and (4) homogeneous producers. Here we consider the implications of obvious generalizations.

Demand curvature

Linearity of demand means that mean price induces mean consumption, as in Figure 12.4. We have already noted that if demand is nonlinear, this relationship in general does not hold, as illustrated in Figure 12.1, in which demand is convex. For example, assuming no supply response, storage (without spoilage losses) reduces consumption variation without changing its mean in the steady state, but in general changes mean price. The extent of this change in mean price depends on the degree of convexity in the consumption demand curve (recall Table 4.1). We have been measuring this degree of convexity with the parameter C. Thus, C proves to be central to the welfare effects of stabilization. More generally, the effects of producers' incentives and supply elasticity determine the direction of any induced supply response, which changes mean consumption. In these cases too, the curvature of consumption demand is crucial.

Strictly speaking, Figures 12.1 and 12.4 presume consumer welfare can be measured by Marshallian surplus, whereas it is not the exact measure under either certainty or uncertainty. But the distinction is unimportant for most cases of practical interest. As shown in Wright and Williams (1988b, p. 619), the proper *ex ante* equivalent variation of one-period stabilization of uncertain consumption is approximately

$$(\tfrac{1}{2}\bar{q}\,P[\bar{q},y]\,/\,\eta^d)((\gamma\,/\,\eta^d)(\eta^y-\rho)+C-1))\Delta\sigma_q^2 \qquad (12.2)$$

where $\Delta\sigma_q^2$ is the squared reduction in the coefficient of variation of consumption.[7] For any primary commodity consumed in developed countries, the budget share γ is very small, even compared to the demand elasticity η^d. Thus, the term in (12.2) involving the difference between the income elasticity and the income risk aversion parameter is essentially zero. In such circumstances, the dominant determinant of the welfare effects remains the curvature parameter C.[8]

There is also an issue of intertemporal aggregation of single-period welfare effects of stabilization. Blackorby and Donaldson (1984) have shown that aggregation of single-period compensation measures under uncertainty does not yield the same result as the correct compensation measure over a multiperiod horizon. But in this context in which *ex ante* period-by-period evaluation of uncertain prospects and saving along with other alternative smoothing methods are ruled out for consumers, this aggregation issue seems minor. In fact, intertemporal aggregation of consumer surplus, used in many of our calculations, is a good approximate indicator of the effects of stabilization in our storage model.

Production response lag and expectations

Demand parameters alone do not determine the effects of stabilization on consumer welfare. Producers' responses also have an important influence on the results. One issue in particular is the lag, imposed by technology, with which producers can respond to shocks.

To assume instantaneous response, as did Waugh, Oi, and Massell, is to imply that there is no difference between the effects of uncertainty and perfectly anticipated variability on production decisions. Expectations are irrelevant; all relevant decisions can be made with full knowledge of prices. This means, for example, that there is no production input that is fixed in the short run but variable given more time to adjust. Here, for reasons presented in Chapter 2, we specify supply response to have a one-period lag from time of input commitment to time of harvest.

Figure 12.5 shows the equilibrium with elastic one-period-lagged supply and an additive two-point disturbance. Thus, for Figure 12.5 the supply function is

$$\bar{q}_{t+1} = \bar{h}_{t+1} = \bar{h}[E_t[P_{t+1}]] + v_{t+1} \tag{12.3}$$

---

[7] This approximation is very close to the "exact" measure derived from analytical or numerical integration of demand (see Hausman 1981; Vartia 1983) except in extreme cases such as large budget share, high risk aversion, or very high initial coefficient of variation σ_q. In such cases a general equilibrium approach may well be needed. (For more on this, see Wright and Williams [1988b], especially p. 622.)

[8] C measures the curvature of the consumption demand curve and not the market demand curve, which includes the demand for storage and which perforce is more convex. Hughes Hallett (1986), for example, confuses these two.

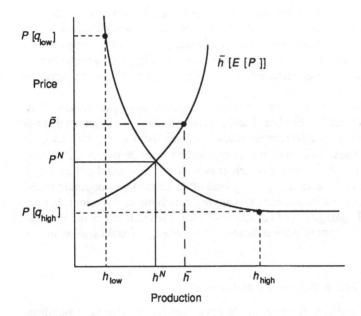

Figure 12.5. Change in planned production with ideal stabilization.

(Without storage, q and h are the same.) In Figure 12.5, $\bar{q}$ is the planned production consistent with $\bar{P} = (P[q_{\text{low}}] + P[q_{\text{high}}])/2 = E[P[\bar{q}]]$. Ideal (i.e., complete) stabilization would move the equilibrium to the nonstochastic equilibrium (q^N, P^N). With the demand curve as drawn, the mean quantity produced (and consumed) would fall.

Specification of the disturbance

With supply adjustable only with a lag of one period, the relationship between the level of planned supply and the distribution of the disturbance becomes crucial. Should the weather disturbance be additive or multiplicative, that is, in terms of quantity or yields? For most problems, the multiplicative (i.e., proportional) representation is more sensible: The effects of weather, for example, are likely to be roughly proportional to the amount of planned production. With a multiplicative disturbance such as modeled in Chapter 2, the equilibrium planned production would not be the $\bar{q}$ of Figure 12.5. From equation (2.15), for the two-point disturbance, the marginal expected revenue from planned production is, for a competitive producer,

$$P^r = \left(h_{\text{high}}P[h_{\text{high}}] + h_{\text{low}}P[h_{\text{low}}]\right)/2\bar{h}[P^r] \tag{12.4}$$

whereas

$$\bar{P} = E_t[P_{t+1}] = \left(P[h_{high}] + P[h_{low}]\right) / 2 \tag{12.5}$$

Because the higher price is weighted by the lower quantity and the lower price by the higher quantity, P_{t+1}^r is below $E_t[P_{t+1}]$ whatever the (downward sloping) demand curve (but for the curves in Figure 12.5 would be above P^N). Thus, the effect of ideal stabilization for multiplicative disturbances is different from the situation with additive disturbances, the form assumed by Waugh, Oi, and Massell. With multiplicative disturbances and the demand curve in Figure 12.5, price falls under ideal stabilization and consumers gain at the expense of producers. If demand were linear, planned output would increase by $(\bar{h}[E[\bar{P}]] - \bar{h}[P^r])$ after stabilization, whereas with additive disturbances planned output would be unaffected. The increase in output could be sufficient to enable consumers, as well as producers, to gain from ideal stabilization. Thus, distributional effects can be extremely sensitive to the nature of the disturbance.

Heterogeneous producers

In this discussion of welfare analysis, we have assumed that all the producers are identical in all relevant respects and face the same output disturbances. Once we relax these assumptions, generalizations are naturally more difficult.

One interesting stylized case, explored in Wright (1979), is the case of one consuming region but two independent production regions, each with identical producers with positive one-period-lagged supply response and independent multiplicative yield disturbances. In this setting with no storage, the yield disturbance of one region is perceived as a demand-shifting disturbance in the other. (Many important demand fluctuations faced by commodity producers are related to supply shifts elsewhere.) In this setting, ideal stabilization of output in one risky supply region causes a loss of wealth at the time of stabilization to landowners in another stable region sharing the same consumer market. This result, of course, parallels Oi's (1961) result that demand variation increases producer surplus.

In Chapter 9 we studied two production and consumption regions connected by trade and storage. The general insight that market-stabilizing interventions may favor only a subset of all producers is useful in evaluating such cases. The point will be especially true when the two countries are not perfectly symmetric.

Summary of welfare effects of ideal stabilization

Using second-order Taylor series approximations to the demand and supply curves, Wright (1979) has distinguished three general cases for the

Table 12.1. *The effects of ideal stabilization on the flows of producer and consumer surplus*

	Sign of:		
	Expected producer gain	Expected consumer gain	Change in expected output
Linear demand ($C = 0$)			
$\eta^s/\eta^d < -1$	+	+	+
$-1 < \eta^s/\eta^d$	+	−	+
Constant elasticity demand ($C = 1 - 1/\eta^d$)			
$0 > \eta^d > -1$	−	+	−
$-1 > \eta^d$	+	+	+
General case:			
$C < (1 + \eta^s/\eta^d)$	+	−	+
$C > (1 + \eta^s/\eta^d)$			
$\quad C < 2$	+	+	+
$\quad C > 2$	−	+	−

welfare effects of ideal stabilization of multiplicative production disturbances. If the index of relative demand curvature $C < 1 + \eta^s/\eta^d$, producers gain (in terms of expected current surplus flows) and consumers lose from ideal stabilization. If $1 + \eta^s/\eta^d < C < 2$, expected consumer and producer surplus both rise. If $2 < C$, as it would be for a constant elasticity demand curve with $|\eta^d| < 1.0$, expected consumer surplus rises and producer surplus falls. These results are summarized in Table 12.1. The importance of the curvature parameter C to the welfare effects of stabilization, including storage, is the main reason why we give it prominence. The importance of rational supply response is also obvious.

12.4 Dynamic welfare analysis

Most of the literature on market stabilization has used comparative statics, that is, has compared the stabilized and unstabilized long-run equilibria. If the change is an immediate and permanent transition between the initial stochastic steady state and the deterministic stabilized steady state, as through ideal stabilization, comparative statics suffices to indicate the effects on prices and quantities. But even in these circumstances, the effects on market participants are dynamic, so that welfare effects in Table 12.1 must be interpreted with care. One should not infer from Table 12.1, for example, that if $2 < C$, any producer in periods after the initiation of ideal stabilization is worse off.

Expected producer surplus flows are reflected in the demand for the fixed assets needed to obtain those flows, such as land and, in the short run, machinery, education, or other productive investments. In any period the price of the necessary assets should equal the expected present value of the stream of producer surplus, adjusted, if necessary, for any risk premium. That is, the expected surplus stream is capitalized.[9] If the land market is competitive, the buyers of land in subsequent periods, who receive the flow of producer surpluses that the market expected at the time of their purchase, experience no gain or loss in wealth from that flow; its expected value will just cover the opportunity cost of the investment. Thus, a producer who held land at the time when ideal stabilization was initially pronounced would gain, but subsequent land purchasers expect no gain or loss from stabilization; anticipated movements in producer surplus are fully offset by changes in land cost. Therefore, in our terminology, "producer gains" refer to those owning land at the time of the announcement of the intervention causing the change in the value of land.

Figure 12.6 shows one example ($\eta^d = -0.2$, $\eta^s = 0$, $C = 6$, $r = 5\%$) of the expected effects of ideal production stabilization announced in period 0, effective for the period 1 harvest. The expectations as of period 0 of the effects on consumer and producer surplus in later periods, $E_0[Consumer\ Surplus_t]$ and $E_0[Producer\ Surplus_t]$, $t = 1, 2, \ldots$, are constant at their new steady-state values. The price of land immediately jumps down, one period before producer surplus changes, by the change in the expected net present value of steady-state producer surplus. The arrows in Figure 12.6 are included to emphasize that this change in the price of land occurs in period 0. After this downward jump, the price of land is expected to remain constant. Purchasers at this new price of land neither gain nor lose from the expected change in later producer surplus flows. Only unanticipated variations in realized producer surplus due, for example, to subsequent policy surprises, affect the wealth of those who purchase land after period 0.[10]

Figure 12.6 emphasizes that even in this example, in which comparative-statics analysis provides the necessary information for incidence, an analysis of the incidence itself is dynamic. Whether a landowner is affected depends

[9] Here we simplify the exposition by assuming risk neutrality and denoting land as the only fixed asset, all others being fully variable at constant cost after a lag of just one period. To simplify the accounting, we also assume that producers own their land.

[10] Changes in consumer surplus are not so easily capitalized. Although expected changes in consumer surplus flows may be reflected in the prices of complementary durables – for example, high gasoline prices may reduce automobile prices – in general access to consumption comes with citizenship, and is not bought and sold like investment goods. Nevertheless, future consumer benefits, if foreseen, may change the bequests left by the current generation, or even national debt policy. Here we ignore these intertemporal links on the consumer side and assume that expected consumer surplus changes in the future measure welfare changes to the recipients.

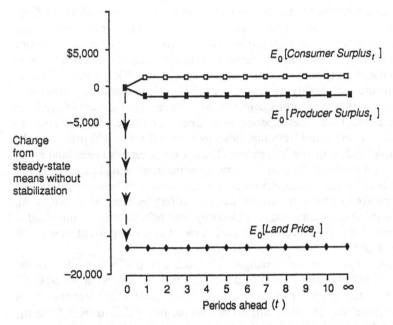

Figure 12.6. The welfare effects of ideal stabilization as of the period before the stabilization operates.

not just on the comparative-statics results but also on the calendar time during which the land is owned.

Dynamic welfare implications of storage

Because storage forges intertemporal links, it makes the incidence of policies inducing stabilization more complex than implied by Figure 12.6 for ideal stabilization. Figure 12.7 shows the equilibrium in a particular period t for a specific availability A_t, which is split between q_t and S_t. If the carryin is positive, the revenue from sales of that A_t accrues solely to producers only if they own all the stocks as well as current output. Figure 12.7 is drawn under the assumption that all of A_t has come from the current harvest.

Surplus measures in this static diagram fail to capture the full effects of the current period's storage on market participants. Current producer surplus (horizontally hatched) overstates the expected net gains to producers current and future from having grown that amount A_t. The carryout S_t will depress some future price, and hence some future producer revenue, in period $t + 1$ or later. Similarly, the current consumer surplus, represented in Figure 12.7 by the vertically striped area, understates the total present value of expected consumer surplus flows associated with A_t. What is stored will be consumed eventu-

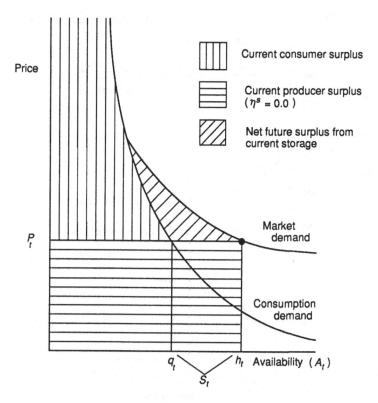

Figure 12.7. Current surplus with storage.

ally, and the future consumer surplus generated should properly be credited to the current harvest.

Thus, the diagonally hatched area between the consumption demand curve and the market demand curve, above the current price, is the present value of the net social surplus from the current storage. The present value of consumer surplus is much larger than indicated by this area; future producer surplus due to current storage is negative, as was seen in Chapter 5. In expectation, the constant-cost storers in our model gain no surplus from their storage, because they store up to the point where they expect to cover their marginal and total costs.

The incidence of the introduction of storage

To understand the dynamic welfare effects more fully, it is helpful to consider their evolution period by period. An instructive example is the simple case in which storage is initially impossible, then suddenly made possible

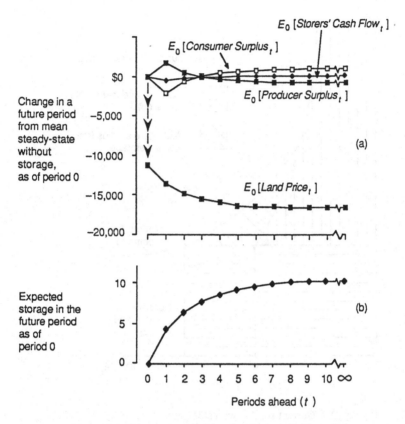

Figure 12.8. Expected evolution after the introduction of storage.

by a technological innovation. If the possibility of storage is announced in period 0, effective period 1, the expected paths, generated by multiple simulations of sample paths as in Chapter 5, evolve as in Figure 12.8. The parameters are specifically those for Figures 5.1 and 5.2, which showed representative paths of conditional means.

In period 1, if output is high, some is purchased by storers, lowering consumption and consumer surplus while raising producer surplus. If output is low, there is no change from circumstances without the possibility of storage. In period 2, if output is high, more is stored (or some is stored for the first time), lowering consumer surplus. If output is very low in period 2, the carryover from period 1, should there be one, is entirely consumed, raising consumer surplus and storer revenue but lowering producer surplus. In immediately subsequent periods the probability of purchases for storage declines while the probability of sales from stocks rises, so the expected marginal additions to stock decline over time as in the bottom of Figure 12.8, until an expected steady state is reached. Price evolves as in Figure 5.2 for the case with $A_0 = 90$. The path, as of period 0, of expected producer surplus initially rises then falls as the early storage-boosted periods give way to the influence of the steady state, which is negative for these parameters, principally because C exceeds the break-even level of 2. Because stocks must be bought before they can be sold, the initial effects are always favorable to producers and unfavorable for consumers, and discounting at a positive interest rate makes the initial effects have extra weight. Thus, land price, which in any period is the present value of the producer surplus over the remaining periods, is expected after its initial drop in period 0 to decline further as the initial, partially offsetting demand boost from stock buildup dissipates. (That a drop in the price of land occurs in period 0 even though storage is not possible until period 1 is again emphasized by the arrows in Figure 12.8.)

These effects on producer surplus and land value are shown in percentage terms in Figure 12.9, which also shows how elastic supply affects the dynamic response. If supply is elastic, the size of the initial demand-boosting effect is moderated by the planned production response $E_0[\bar{h}_t]$. If the introduction of storage is anticipated one period ahead, production decisions respond in advance of the initial anticipated demand boost due to storage. But the consumption demand is inelastic, and so revenue in period 1, calculated in period 0, which is one component of the effect on land value, is lower than if supply were unresponsive or storage unanticipated. More generally, a small carryout induces an increase in planned production and a large carryout a decrease, moderating the immediate welfare effects of the storage activity. In the long run given these parameters, the greater stability induced by storage dampens the average producers' incentive price, so long-run average production is slightly lower. Furthermore, the weight of initial effects, relative to steady-state differentials (the far right of Figure 12.9), is reduced by a faster convergence to the steady state, so that the discounted influence of the latter is increased. As is the case for ideal stabilization, the comparative statics effects of introduction of storage on consumer and producer surplus are more even-handed with elastic supply.

The results illustrated in Figures 12.8 and 12.9 are for $C = 6$. The effects of this demand curvature parameter on incidence are crucial, as shown in Figure 12.10, where results using ideal stabilization and comparative statics are also presented as a function of C for comparison. Those owning land at the time of the regime change gain a greater share of the net social benefits than indicated using comparative statics or assuming ideal stabilization rather than storage. The relationship to C appears to be approximately linear. The producers' relative gain, less unity, is the relative loss in the present value of consumers' surplus.

Producers and consumers both gain within the shaded region in Figure 12.10. If $\eta^s = 0$, the gain is shared only over a narrow range of C – otherwise

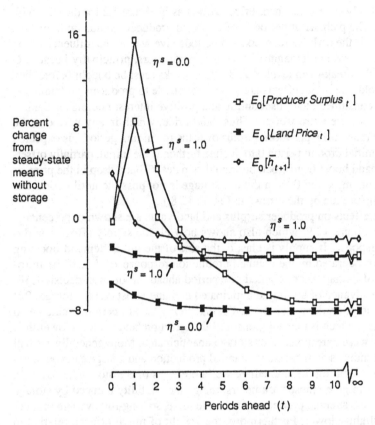

Figure 12.9. Expected evolution with different supply elasticities after the introduction of storage.

the gross redistribution due to the introduction of storage exceeds the net social gains. Consistent with Figure 12.9, responsive supply makes the incidence effects less one-sided. When the introduction of storage is anticipated, consumers and landowners gain over a much larger range of C, as shown by the lower of the dashed lines for $\eta^s = 1.0$ in Figure 12.10. And the net social gain, normalized to unity for each case illustrated, is actually somewhat higher with elastic supply.

If the first period in which storage is possible arrives unanticipated by suppliers, the distributive effects for $\eta^s = 1.0$ are much more beneficial to producers, as shown by the upper of the two dashed lines. At any C, lack of anticipation means producers gain more from the initial demand boost because their production does not initially increase while their subsequent supply re-

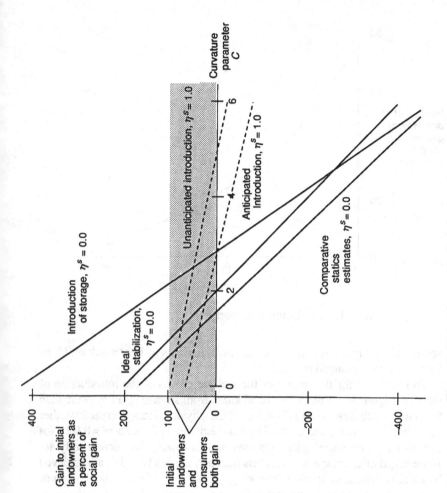

Figure 12.10. Incidence of the introduction of storage.

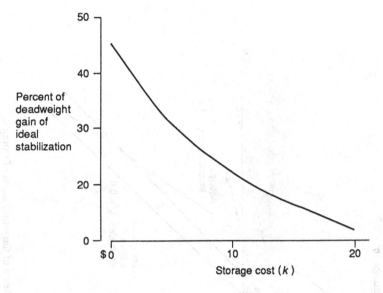

Figure 12.11. Social gains from storage.

sponse allows them to reduce the depressing effects of later stock buildups by cutting back planned output.[11]

To round out the discussion of the welfare effects of the introduction of storage, Figure 12.11 plots the social gains from storage relative to the gain from ideal stabilization as a function of the physical storage costs k. (Other parameters are the same as for Figures 12.8 and 12.9, with $\eta^s = 0.0$.) Not surprisingly, the social gain increases as k is lower, and increasingly so. More surprising, storage achieves less than half the deadweight gain achieved by ideal stabilization. Roughly speaking, ideal stabilization can be thought of as removing completely the instability in the weather, by lending the commodity to the future if the current harvest is large or borrowing from the future if the current harvest is small. Storage can work in only one of those directions, namely, lending to the future, and must pay an interest cost. Hence it makes some sense that storage can recover at most half the deadweight loss caused by the randomness in the weather.

---

11 Note that in this case producers do not share the information set on which the expectations of storers are based in period 0, in contrast to our usual assumption. Other issues of specification affect welfare calculations when supply is not perfectly inelastic. If the production disturbances are additive in the case for $\eta^s = 1.0$ illustrated in Figure 12.10, consumers lose over the entire range of C shown. This qualitative result is shown in Wright and Williams (1984b).

12.5   The necessary range of welfare analysis

In all this discussion of the welfare effects of stabilization, the possible permutations of demand curvature, disturbance structure, initial conditions, supply elasticity, and so forth seem nearly infinite. But that is the main point: Few, if any, general propositions are possible. Often seemingly small differences in specification or assumptions can reverse the sign of the presumed welfare effect.

Among the possible influences on the welfare effects of stabilization, several parameters stand out. One is the curvature of the consumption demand curve. Second in importance is the elasticity of supply. When supply elasticity is positive with a lag, the nature of the random disturbance, whether it is an additive shift in supply, a multiplicative shift in supply, or a shift in demand, becomes very important. When supply is elastic, the initial conditions – that is, those at the time of the announcement of a public intervention or of the invention of storability – become relevant. If the crop is already planted, the welfare effects are very different from the situation with current planting still adjustable. Similarly, the amount of the commodity already on hand has a major influence on whether producers are helped or hurt by stabilization programs. Likewise the nature of the stabilization program is far from trivial. Reductions in the susceptibility of yields to weather variance, public buffer-stock schemes, and reductions in spoilage rates under storage, to name a few possibilities, all have substantially different welfare effects, even though all stabilize the market. Thus, the analyst's first concern should be an accurate representation of the policy under consideration in the context of the entire market.

CHAPTER 13

Floor-price schemes

Markets for storable commodities are often subject to public interventions in the name of market stabilization, including price supports, price ceilings, prohibitions on private hoarding, marketing boards, and production controls. Often such measures are really designed to redistribute income among producers, consumers, and the public treasury by raising or lowering mean price. Others, however, are plausibly aimed at stabilization, because they do not directly interfere with sales to consumers when price is around its mean level.

Even those interventions ostensibly for stabilization can result in substantial transfers between risk-neutral consumers and producers. Indeed, they can change mean price. Hence, consumers and producers need not be risk averse with respect to fluctuations in income to be affected by market-stabilizing interventions. Also, if there is a complete and otherwise undistorted set of markets, a market-stabilizing intervention causes a social deadweight loss; the degree of instability resulting from undistorted private storage is optimal given the cost of storage. Thus, for any market-stabilizing intervention there are questions about its allocative and welfare effects.

Types of market-stabilizing price supports

Three common types of scheme aimed at keeping the price paid to producers at or above a support level are distinguished by the method of market intervention. In one, the government pays producers deficiency payments, which consist of the difference, if positive, between a "target price" P^D and the market price P_t paid by consumers in period t. Under this scheme, the producer price $= Max[P_t, P^D]$. In another type of scheme the government itself stores the commodity.[1] The simplest version of public storage has the

---

[1] The government need not own the warehousing space but could rent it. Whatever the precise logistical arrangement, the stocks are under public control and result from the official price policy.

government making an open offer to buy any available supplies for its own stockpile at a "floor price" P^F.[2] Under such a scheme, called a "floor-price" scheme here, the government, unconstrained by limits on its financing, ensures that the producer price, which is also the market price, does not fall below the floor price: $P_t \geq P^F$. A variant is a "peg" scheme, in which the government uses its buffer stock to keep the price at P^{peg}, but the market price may erupt in either direction should the stockpile or financing be exhausted. Another variant is a "price-band" scheme, wherein resale of stocks acquired at P^F may not be triggered until the price has risen substantially above P^F. In a floor-price scheme, in contrast, the government stands ready to sell them for the full prevailing price whenever the market price is P^F or higher. Hence such a scheme is less restrictive from the government's perspective than a price-band scheme. A third type of scheme uses extramarket disposal, as via destruction (allowing tart cherries to rot on the trees), marketing orders (feeding oranges to cattle), or disposal outside of normal marketing channels (foreign famine relief), to ensure that both the producer and market price do not fall below some price P^R at which supplies are removed from the market. Because we consider plausibly stabilizing interventions, we assume that the support prices P^D, P^F, and P^R are below the free-market mean price, although P^{peg} need not be. In actual applications these three types of schemes are often blended or used in conjunction with programs like acreage set asides.

With storage our focus, we discuss public interventions involving deficiency payments or extramarket disposal only on those occasions when they clarify the properties of public interventions involving storage. Many aspects of market-stabilizing storage interventions, including producers' political support for them, can be understood by considering the simplest intervention of that type: floor-price schemes. These schemes are discussed in this chapter, and price-band and peg schemes in Chapter 14. We show in Section 13.1 how the market, including private storage, behaves under a floor-price scheme. We explore the welfare effects of such a scheme in Section 13.2, and in Section 13.3 examine the merits of "speculative" private storage, which from time to time "frustrates" the public agency operating the floor-price scheme.

Floor-price schemes, as well as price-band and peg schemes, involve unalterable intervention rules. That is, P^F is a constant regardless of circumstances in any particular period. From the producers' perspective, less simplistic rules for government behavior may be superior. But the prevalence of relatively simple or arbitrary rules suggests that governments find it difficult to identify and to implement more complex alternatives even when their objective, such as helping producers, is clearly known.[3] In Chapter 15 we investigate more complex alternatives for public storage designed to supplement private storage, which may be insufficient because of the threat of price ceilings or some other market distortion.

13.1   Market behavior with a price floor

When operating the floor-price scheme considered here, the government can expect to lose money, although it sells its stocks for the full prevailing price whenever it sells. It cannot expect to make a profit above the normal rate of return on capital, because private storers, who are willing to store at the normal rate of return, compete away any supernormal profits. The introduction of a floor-price scheme is, however, unanticipated by private storers and producers, although once in place it is assumed to be in effect forever with its operating rule understood by private decision makers.

Although there is no limit on the size of the public holdings or on cumulative government losses, the government does not store every period. Sometimes there is private storage, although in some periods no storage at all, depending on the current availability. Thus, the intervention should not be judged as a success or failure depending on the size of public stocks in a particular period. The intervention is a regime, a different one for each P^F.

Under a floor-price scheme, the quantities produced, consumed, and stored satisfy the market-clearing condition:

$$q_t = h_t + S_{t-1}^c + S_{t-1}^g - S_t^c - S_t^g = A_t - S_t \tag{13.1}$$

where $S_{t-1} \geq 0$ is now total storage carried from period $t-1$ to period t, comprising private storage S_{t-1}^c and government storage S_{t-1}^g. For private storage the familiar complementary inequalities continue to apply:

$$
\begin{aligned}
0 \geq (1+r)^{-1} E_t[P_{t+1}] - P_t - k, & \quad S_t^c = 0 \\
0 = (1+r)^{-1} E_t[P_{t+1}] - P_t - k, & \quad S_t^c > 0
\end{aligned}
\tag{13.2}
$$

Implicitly these conditions and the government's commitment to buy any amount at the floor price and to sell, subject to the availability of stocks, at any price not less than the floor price, jointly determine private and public storage as functions of the amount available and the floor price,

$$S_t^c = f^F[A_t | P^F] \tag{13.3}$$

$$S_t^g = Max[A_t - S_t^c - q^F, 0] = g^F[A_t | P^F] \tag{13.4}$$

where q^F is the amount consumed at the price floor, $P^F = \alpha + \beta(q^F)^{1-C}$. Salant (1983) has proved the existence and uniqueness of rational expectations equilibrium equivalent to the rule $f^F[A_t | P^F]$. The numerical algorithm for calculating competitive storage described in the Appendix to Chapter 3 can derive this reduced-form equation (13.3) to any arbitrary degree of accuracy. The public rule (13.4) does not require stochastic dynamic programming because S_t^g is determined by the need to keep current price at least at P^F rather than by expectations about period $t+1$. Using these two reduced-form equations (13.3) and (13.4), one can calculate the expected path of net revenue, the price of land, and the stream of government expenditures.

Behind the complementary inequalities (13.2) describing private storage are fundamental issues of modeling public storage schemes. The first, quite clearly, is that the intervention is into a market with private storage technically possible. If the public agency can store physically, it seems implausible to assume that private storage is impossible. The second is that private storage is rational and forward looking; that is, the private storers attempt to anticipate the effects of the public intervention on future prices. The other extreme, such as in the model of Lee and Blandford (1980), represents private storage as backward looking. In such a formulation, private storage is entirely mechanistic and is altered in no fundamental way by the public intervention. Many other authors, including Burt et al. (1982) and Dixon and Chen (1982), make a similar assumption – more bluntly, a mistake – about the expectations of producers, representing the expectations as functions of past prices alone.[4] The inconsistency within the modeling framework between producers' political support for the intervention based on its future effects and the producers' backward-looking supply response goes unrecognized.

Storage rules with a price floor

To understand how a floor-price scheme operates in the market for the commodity, it is essential first to understand the public and private storage rules, which remain the same from period to period. Figure 13.1 shows these storage rules, that is, the relationships between current storage and current availability, for a relatively simple case: $\eta^s = 0.0$ and a public agency committed to defend a price floor of $90.[5] It bears repeating that these storage rules in Figure 13.1 and the corresponding relationships in Figure 13.2 are the precise relationships as derived from first principles; they are not conjectured, as in Rojko (1975).

Figure 13.1 as a whole does not look that much different from storage rules discussed previously, and indeed it is not. Except for the omnipresent constraint that storage cannot be negative, total storage – and by extension price and consumption – are smooth functions of availability. The marginal propensity for total storage is everywhere in the interval [0, 1]. What is interest-

---

4   The choice between modeling producers as attempting to look ahead to the effects of public programs or as projecting prices from the past also arises in empirical work. See Shonkwiler and Maddala (1985) for an empirical rational-expectations model of corn prices bounded by price supports.

5   Other parameters are $\eta^d = -0.2$, $C = 0.0$, $r = 5\%$, $k = \$2$, and $\sigma_h = 10$ units.

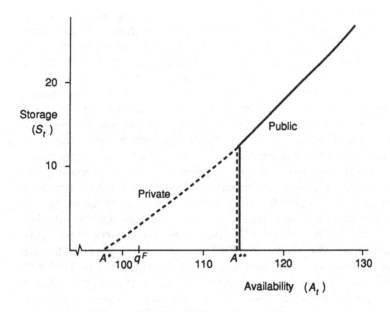

Figure 13.1. Public and private storage rules with a price floor.

ing about the storage rule in Figure 13.1 is the breakdown between private and public storage. The dashed line represents the rule for private storage and the solid line the rule for public storage. Both are discontinuous functions of current availability.[6]

When examining the storage rules in Figure 13.1, one should keep in mind two other storage rules: that for the same price floor when only public storage is allowed, and that for solely private storage undistorted by the floor-price scheme. For solely public storage the solid 45° line in Figure 13.1 extends to the horizontal axis, meeting it at q^F, the consumption corresponding to the price floor (for this linear demand curve, with $P^F = \$90$, $q^F = 102$ units). Because the public agency cannot let price fall below P^F, its marginal propensity to store is 1.0 at any availability beyond q^F. The solely private rule, with no price floor, has a marginal propensity to store increasing with A_t but everywhere less than 1.0. For this set of parameters, the solely private rule shows positive storage over a range of availabilities less than q^F but strictly greater than A^*. There is very substantial private storage above q^F, absent public storage. Part of the latter merely replaces private storage that would have occurred without the scheme.

The storage rule for a system with both private storage and a price floor de-

---

6   In this formulation, as before, the source of the current availability – whether the new harvest, private carryin, or public carryin – is immaterial.

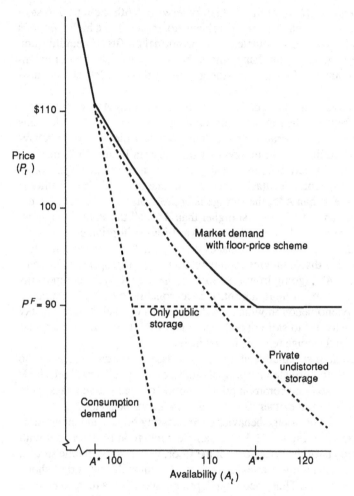

Figure 13.2. Market demand curves with a price floor.

fended by public storage is like a rule constructed by choosing, at each availability, the maximum of the storage indicated by the solely public rule or the
solely private rule. For a given current availability, greater storage is equivalent to a higher spot price (see Figure 13.2). If the public agency will bid a
higher price (namely, P^F), it supplants private storers. If private storers collectively will bid above P^F, they store and not the public agency.

The private segment of the rule in Figure 13.1 (and the private segment of
the market demand including the derived demand for the commodity to put
into store, shown in Figure 13.2) is itself affected by the floor-price scheme.
Because the public agency keeps the price in period $t+1$ from falling below

P^F, for a given S_t, $E_t[P_{t+1}]$ is higher than otherwise. With the return to storage higher, in order to store more the private storers will bid a higher price in period t (and in so doing eliminate any supernormal profits). In equilibrium, the private storage is greater than without the floor-price scheme; for example, the kink point A^* of the private storage rule shifts to the left of the undistorted rule's.

The total storage rule in Figure 13.1 and the availability A^{**} where a transition occurs between the segments for public and private storage reflect this feedback of the future operation of the floor-price scheme on current behavior.[7] This availability A^{**} in Figure 13.1 (and also in Figure 13.2) marks a critical discontinuity between private and public storage, at which a phenomenon known as "speculative attack" occurs. If in one period the availability is just a little bit less than A^{**}, the storage is entirely private. If by chance the next period has an availability just higher than A^{**}, all the storage is public. Right at A^{**} there are downward and upward jumps in private and public stocks, respectively, as the latter replaces the former. Although the total storage rule also has a discontinuous change in the marginal propensity for combined storage at A^{**} (going from 0.87 to 1.0), the change in the components of total storage is much more abrupt. It is reasonable to define speculative attack as the phenomenon in which the components of total storage display marginal propensities to store outside the interval $[0, 1]$ while the marginal propensity of total storage remains in that interval.

This definition of speculative attack encompasses both private runs on the public stockpile and private dumping of stocks on the public stockpile.[8] Although runs are the more common popular notion of speculative attack, here if there is one there is the other. Both are discontinuous behavior.

The implications of storage behavior encompassing private and public storage are illustrated in Figure 13.3 by a sample simulation of the model with $P^F = \$90$ for fifty periods. Price starts at the floor, with positive public stocks. After a few periods, a low harvest increases the probability of future shortages and higher prices. Thus encouraged, private speculators (described here in net terms) buy up ("make a run on") all the unconsumed public stocks. Then three more bad harvests (through period 6) result in a sequence of equilibria with rising prices and falling private stocks. In period 7 a good harvest causes prices to fall and encourages private speculators to increase their hold-

The availability A^{**} at which this transition occurs depends upon the price floor P^F. The higher is P^F the lower is A^{**}. More of the total storage rule is the segment of the 45° line applicable with only public storage. The remaining segment of the private storage rule is shifted farther to the left (or to the right in Figure 13.2 for price).

The runs and dumpings of so-called speculative attack are most often associated with markets for foreign exchange (Salant and Henderson 1978; Salant 1983, and references therein). This is not surprising because prices in currency markets are much more often fixed than are agricultural markets and, as Buiter (1989) has emphasized, regimes of fixed prices invite speculative attacks.

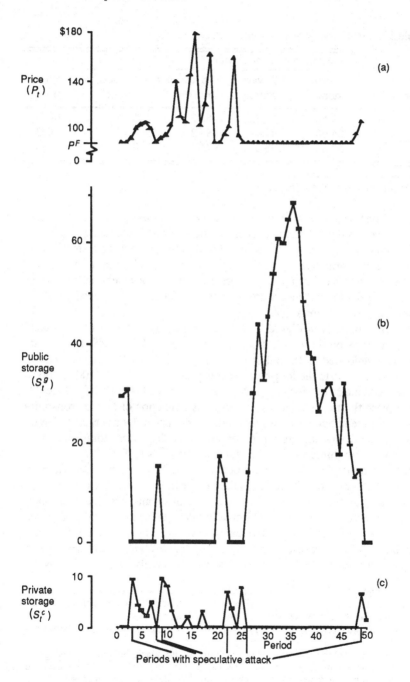

Figure 13.3. Time series under a floor-price regime.

Table 13.1. *Probability of speculative attack*

Price floor (P^F)	Percentage of periods with:				
	Public storage	Private storage	Private after public[a]	Public after private[b]	No storage
$80	19.56	61.82	6.43	6.34	18.63
$85	34.06	49.41	8.02	7.70	16.53
$90	53.35	33.67	7.78	7.34	12.98

[a]Run on the public stockpile.
[b]Dumping on the public stockpile.

ings in hope of a lower, more normal harvest the next period. Yet another good harvest occurs in period 8, causing prices to fall further and private storers to sell out to the public stockpile. But the very next period a smaller harvest improves price expectations, and private storers buy up all the public stocks not consumed that period. Note that public stocks tend to be large or zero; small public carryovers are not observed in the model, because of the actions of private storers.

The fifty periods of Figure 13.3 have six instances of speculative attack. There are runs on the public stock in periods 3, 9, 22, and 49, and private stocks are unloaded on the public stock in periods 8 and 26.[9] The percentage of attacks is close to the long-run frequency over 10,000 or 100,000 periods. Those frequencies of speculative attack are shown in Table 13.1 for three different price floors. As might be expected, as a function of P^F the probability of speculative attack first rises then falls as the price floor is raised.[10] With higher price floors, the proportion of periods with private storage declines, from about two-thirds to about one-third for the P^F's in Table 13.1.

All the private behavior in this model is rational and competitive. The runs on public stocks are neither manipulative nor hysterical.[11] By construction the private storage rule is rational for the set of parameters and price floor. The risk-neutral private storers objectively calculate the price expected for the next period, given the prospective carryout from this period, the probability distribution of the harvest, and the public agency's commitment never to let the price fall below P^F. If that expected price, when discounted, is below the

9   In Figure 13.3, the serial correlation, made greater by the floor-price scheme, is pronounced in each of the three series. Because of the positive serial correlation in the current availability, instances of speculative attack cluster.

10 This statement refers to the long-run probabilities in systems with different floor-price schemes.

11 Obstfeld (1986) presents a model in which speculative attacks on foreign exchange reserves can be self-fulfilling, because the demand for currency is a function of the price level which itself depends on the exchange rate. Here there is not this feedback because consumption demand is solely a function of quantity.

minimum cost of physical storage plus a spot price at the price floor, private storers leave storage to the public agency. If the expected price for the next period is sufficiently high – which it will be if the current availability is not so high that the carryover will be large – in equilibrium the private storers will pay more in the present period than the price floor, increasing storage and lowering expected price, so that no abnormal expected profit remains. This carryover lies entirely in private hands. In the literature, speculative attack is often associated with positive speculative profits arising from transactions with the public stockpiling authority at non–market-clearing prices, as implied by Gardner (1979, p. 91) and by Ghosh et al. (1987, pp. 186–92). But that is not true in general. Here the public agency never sells below the market price.

The starkness of the switch from all stocks in public hands to all stocks in private hands or vice versa is due to the simplicity of the model and of the floor-price scheme. Private and public stocks never coexist. In the real world, one would not expect private stocks ever to fall completely to zero when the government was heavily in the market. The government program most likely concentrates on particular grades and locations. Even as the program distorts various price relationships, it leaves some room for private storage of other grades in other locations, and in transit and undergoing processing. In such a system, however, there would still be sharp changes in storage and shipping behavior, the hallmarks of speculative attack. Furthermore, if the public agency conducts a price-band scheme rather than a floor-price scheme, substantial amounts of public and private storage may well coexist, as shown in Chapter 14.

In the more complex environment of real-world markets, movement of the public and private components of storage in directions strongly opposite to total storage is in fact observed. An example is the U.S. corn market over the decade 1965–74, during which the government was heavily involved in storing corn. Involving frequent changes in support prices and complicated regulations for releasing stocks, the public storage scheme does not correspond perfectly to the permanent intervention of a simple floor-price scheme. Nevertheless, the last column of Table 13.2 shows that in five out of the nine year-to-year changes over that decade, private end-of-cropyear stocks and total stocks moved in opposite directions. In particular, the reduction of public stocks from 925 million bushels in 1965 to 437 million bushels in 1966 was partially offset by an increase of 181 in private hands. Likewise, of the release of 193 million bushels of public stocks in 1970, 85 million were absorbed into private stockpiles. When by the end of 1974 the government had disposed of 628 million bushels, 402 emerged as private stocks. The change from 1968 to 1969 could be classified as the private stockpile being partially dumped on the government. From the Commodity Credit Corporation's perspective, on many occasions, private actions must have frustrated the manage-

Table 13.2. *U.S. corn carryover (in millions of bushels)*

Cropyear ending in	Average support rate	Private stocks	CCC stocks	Total stocks	Change in private as a % of change in total	Change in total as a % of change in CCC
1965	$1.10	222	925	1147		
					−59	63
1966	1.05	403	437	840		
					−270	27
1967	1.00	449	374	823		
					−12	89
1968	1.05	412	714	1126		
					269	−59
1969	1.05	377	736	1113		
					−78	56
1970	1.05	462	543	1005		
					37	158
1971	1.05	337	330	667		
					15	118
1972	1.03	408	718	1126		
					78	463
1973	1.05	81	628	709		
					−178	36
1974	1.05	483	0	483		

Source: USDA *Feed Grain Situation*, various issues.

ment of public stocks. An extra bushel of public stocks did not mean an extra bushel of aggregate stocks. As the last column shows, the marginal effect ranged from a low of 27 percent to a high of 463 percent.

Whatever the CCC's opinion of contrary shifts in private corn stocks, almost surely the collective private actions were a rational response to the agency's own policies, not aberrations. Changes in private behavior by their very abruptness emphasize a fundamental inflexibility in public behavior, such as the commitment to defend a particular price regime.

Replacement of private storage by public storage

In the U.S. support program for corn, some proportion of public stockpiles simply replace what would otherwise be held privately in a regime without the support program. That proportion is difficult to deduce empirically, because the other regime with no public program cannot be observed simultaneously.[12] The storage model provides that comparison.

[12] See Gardner (1981), Just (1981), Sharples and Holland (1981), and Wright (1985) for attempts at empirical estimation of the replacement of private storage by public storage.

Even within the confines of the storage model, there remains ambiguity in the concept of the replacement of private storage by public storage defending a price floor. Is the proper measure the marginal effect or the average effect? And given that a system is in a different position each period, is it the average of the marginal effects or the marginal effect on the average amount stored that is more relevant? The answers would be the same if the marginal propensity to store differed little over wide ranges in availabilities, but by its nature storage behavior has pronounced nonlinearities.

In a sense, a comparison of storage rules with and without the floor-price regime places a lower bound on the net addition of public storage to total storage whereas the steady-state properties place an upper bound on such a measure. The public storage section of a storage rule in a regime with a floor price has by definition a marginal propensity to store out of current availability of 1.0. The marginal propensity to store privately at the same high current availabilities would be on the order of 0.80. This suggests that the addition to total storage is only some 20 percent of any public storage. But there is a positive feedback effect: The higher storage under a floor-price scheme for any current availability results in higher availabilities the next period. Those higher availabilities thus induce more storage, which is more likely to be public, and so on. Such steady-state properties of floor-price schemes are illustrated in Figure 13.4 as a function of the floor price P^F. Only when the floor price is very high, nearly the mean price of $100, is a large percentage of average public storage not simply a replacement for private storage; and even at those high floor prices the percentage addition is less than 100 percent. Private storage, at least for these parameters, will persist in many of the periods, though always in small amounts. Hence the paradox: Government storage is most effective at increasing storage in states of the world where increased storage has the least value.

13.2   Welfare analysis of floor-price schemes

The more the public storage under a floor-price scheme represents additions to total storage, the more the total amount of storage is socially excessive, since undistorted private storage is the socially optimal amount of storage. Because private storage revenues just cover the cost of storage but no more, the extent that public storage adds to total storage directly determines the extent of the present value of losses of the public storage agency. Those who credit a public floor-price scheme with raising price substantially are also admitting that the expense to the public treasury is larger than otherwise. But the fiscal cost is just one component of the welfare cost of floor-price schemes. The appropriate welfare analysis follows the methodological approach presented in Chapter 12. As emphasized there, the analysis must be

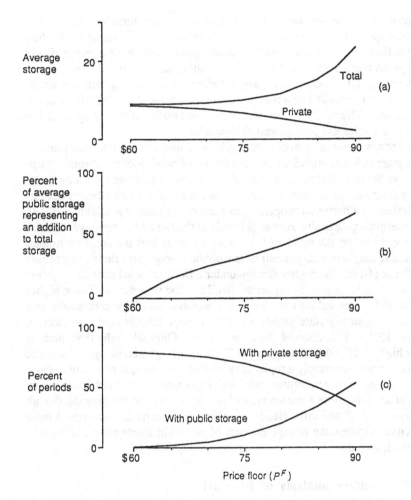

Figure 13.4. Substitution of public for private storage.

dynamic, and the results will depend on the conditions of the market at the time the scheme is announced.[13]

Consider in detail the effect of the introduction of a floor-price scheme with $P^F = \$90$ into a market where private storage is already operating.[14] In Figure 13.5, initial availability is low enough ($A_0 = 90$) to preclude carryout from period 0, and initially there is a free market. The evolution of the free-market producer surplus $E_0[Producer\ Surplus_t]$ replicates the path for the in-

[13]   The same methodology is appropriate for the opposite thought experiment, as in Campbell et al. (1980), of removing a scheme.
[14]   The other parameters are $\eta^d = -0.2$, $C = 6$, $k = \$2.00$, $r = 5\%$, $\eta^s = 0.0$, and $\sigma_h = 10$.

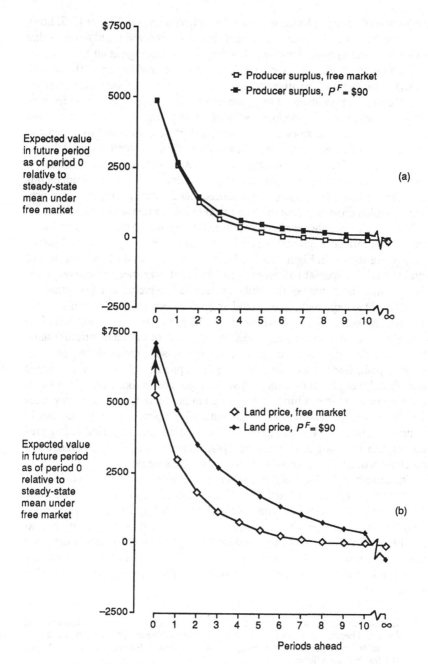

Figure 13.5. Contrasting evolutions between free market and system with floor-price scheme, $A_0 = 90$.

troduction of storage plotted in Figure 12.9 previously. (In Figure 13.5, however, the base steady state is different; it is the expected steady-state value with undistorted private storage rather than with no storage at all.)

With the floor-price scheme with $PF = \$90$ announced in period 0, and with $A_0 < A^*$, the point of positive storage, there is no immediate effect on revenue or consumption, because there are no private stocks to relay anticipations from the future. But if outcomes with especially large harvests occur in the next few periods, the floor-price scheme will raise prices, and by extension producer revenue, above the free-market value. Thus, beyond period 0 the expected path $E_0[Producer\ Surplus_t]$ for $PF = \$90$ in Figure 13.5(a) runs above the free-market curve; but later resales of acquired public stocks dampen this increase. In fact, converging to its reduced steady-state mean, expected producer surplus crosses below the free-market path for this set of parameters.

The floor-price scheme also delays the convergence to the new steady-state mean. The related expected paths (i.e., anticipations) of private and public storage are shown in Figure 13.6, where the slower speed of convergence of total storage is especially obvious.[15] Due to the slower speed of convergence, the dynamic component of the welfare effects is relatively more important.

Paths of the expected price of land under the floor-price scheme and under the free market are also shown in Figure 13.5. In the free market with low availability, land price (the expected present value of producer surplus) starts high and converges, in expectation, to its steady-state mean. Along the converging path, landholders have zero expected profits – the declining price is just offset by expected revenues above average. The introduction of the floor-price scheme induces a jump in land price in period 0, even though revenues do not change until later. This jump, which is emphasized by the arrows in Figure 13.5(b), is a windfall gain to those owning land in period 0. For producers, this windfall constitutes the dynamic incidence of the scheme. Later purchasers of land neither gain nor lose from the scheme.

The differential effects of the floor-price scheme on the expected time paths are brought together in Figure 13.7. The producer surplus curve is the vertical difference between paths for $E_0[Producer\ Surplus_t]$ in Figure 13.5; similarly for the land price. The anticipated change in the flow of government expenditure on the scheme (which is zero under the free market) and expected consumer surplus are also shown in Figure 13.7. The latter falls as stocks are accumulated at the expense of consumption, then rises to the new higher steady state.[16]

---

[15] Because a demand curve with $C = 6$ has more consumption at $PF = \$90$ than one with $C = 0$, and because it induces more average private storage in a free market, the steady-state addition of public storage to total storage is less in Figure 13.6 than in Figure 13.4 for that price floor.

[16] With a consumption demand curve with $C = 6$, consumption stabilization favors consumers in the steady state, and reduces steady-state producer surplus.

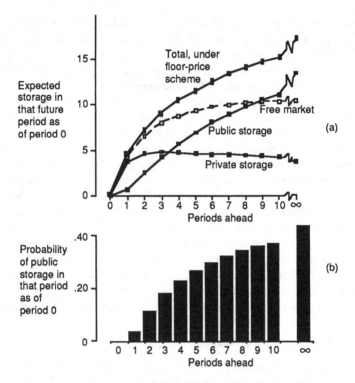

Figure 13.6. Expected evolution of storage from $A_0 = 90$ after imposition of a floor-price scheme with $P^F = \$90$.

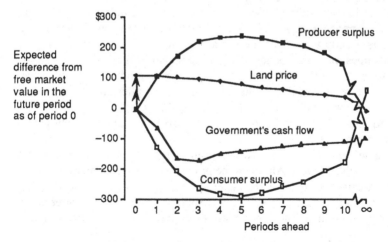

Figure 13.7. Evolution after imposition of floor-price scheme from a low initial availability, $A_0 = 90$.

The expected flow of net government expenditure on the scheme (which includes interest) initially rises with the anticipated increase in government stocks. Then it falls, as sales begin to match acquisitions, to its steady-state mean, which derives from expected carrying costs, offset by any excess of sales price over purchase price P^F. (The government's opening stocks may be insufficient in some periods to drive the market price down to P^F.)

It is absolutely crucial to note that this steady-state mean level of public expenditures, which is $99, does not imply either that government expenditure is likely to be at its mean in the long run, or that the scheme only costs, in the long-run, this mean value. The long-run cumulative expenditure has no upper bound. For example, there is a 6 percent probability that net expenditures to date after the scheme has been in operation for only ten periods will be above $5,000 (i.e., about 50 times the average net annual government expenditure in the steady state, or 50 percent of average annual producer gross revenue). Also, a full accounting of the expected current cost of the scheme should include the net accumulated cost of those intermediate acquisitions needed to build up to the (stochastic) steady-state stock levels. The appropriate measure of the government's expected financial commitment is the discounted present value of net expenditures calculated as of the announcement of the scheme.

Different initial availability

If the initial availability is high enough to support a positive carryout at a price below $90, the welfare incidence of a floor price scheme is different. Upon announcement and implementation of the scheme in period 0, the value of supplies available from private storage and the current harvest increases to $90 immediately, while the government acquires all stocks, increasing aggregate storage and lowering current consumption. Consequently, it matters greatly who owns the initial availability. For simplicity, Figure 13.8 assumes that the producers-landowners also own all of A_0; hence the increase in value of A_0 is credited as an increase in producer surplus for period 0. Another possibility is that all available supplies are already in the hands of private middlemen, including storage firms, when the scheme is announced. Under these conditions, these middlemen unambiguously gain a windfall from the scheme.

In the next period, period 1, two opposing forces affect producer revenues for any possible harvest. Although the price floor raises minimum price, the increased carryover reduces the chance of high prices. As the scheme has been in operation more periods and accumulation proceeds, the latter effect gains more weight.[17] The expectation, as of period 0, is that producer sur-

---

[17] As emphasized by Shepherd (1945, p. 81), "[w]hatever is put into store must eventually come out, and when it comes out it will depress prices about as much as it raised them when it was put in."

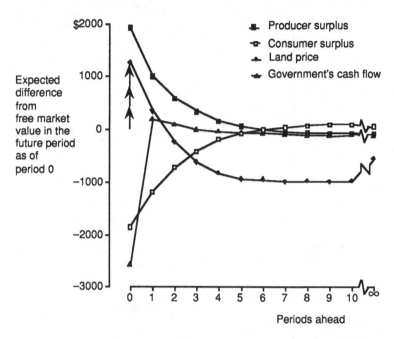

Figure 13.8. Evolution after imposition of floor-price scheme from a high initial availability, $A_0 = 130$.

plus in period 7 and beyond will be below the mean value without the floor-price scheme. Indeed for several periods, the expected differential will be below the mean steady-state effect on producer surplus.

Because the scheme's long-run effect is to depress net revenue, as of period 0 the price of land is expected eventually to be below the comparable value under the free market. But the incidence of the scheme is on those who own land in period 0.[18] Because of the boost in expected revenue for periods 1–6, the floor-price scheme increases the price of land in period 0. Thus with $A_0 = 130$, both the initial landowners and the owners of the initial availability gain (unless either must pay a tax to cover the government's expenditures). Neither group rationally expects any later net gains or losses; the subsequent net return to landowners in any period, whether in the form of rents that period or the change in the price of land, just covers interest costs on the land.

Thus, the incidence of the floor-price scheme depends on the initial availability. Figure 13.9 makes this point more obvious, by plotting the changes in asset values in period 0 over a much wider range of initial availabilities. The main feature to notice in Figure 13.9 is that the owners of the initial availabili-

[18] The argument for full capitalization is the same as for the effects of programs in a nonstochastic setting made by Floyd (1965).

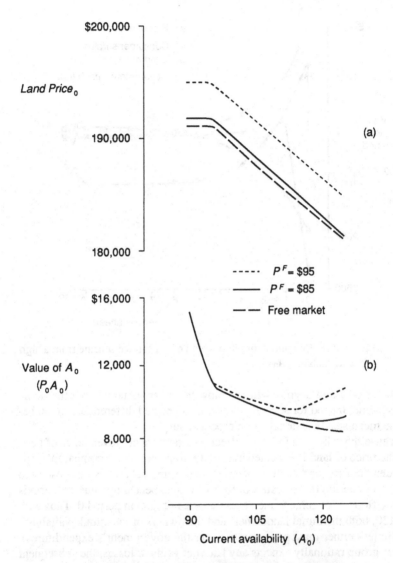

Figure 13.9. Asset values in period 0 as a function of A_0.

ty – be they producers, storers, or consumers – are the primary beneficiaries of a floor-price scheme when the initial availability is high. For a floor of $85, for an A_0 larger than about 130, the price of land in period 0 is below that under the free market. Owners of the initial availability can benefit from the scheme even if the public storage is not required immediately. The prospect of the future price support induces more private storage in the initial peri-

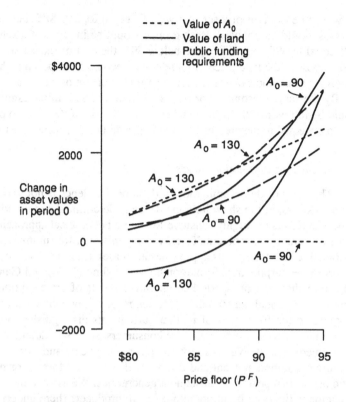

Figure 13.10. Incidence of a floor-price scheme on values of land and on the current availability.

od (as in the range $A^* < A_t < A^{**}$ shown in Figure 13.1), which raises the price and by extension the value of A_0. There is some wealth boost to owners of A_0 from a P^F of $95 even with an A_0 between about 92 and q^F.

To round out this discussion, Figure 13.10 shows the highly nonlinear relation between incidence and the floor price, for $A_0 = 90$ and $A_0 = 130$.[19] For $A_0 = 90$, the incidence is simple: Initial landholders gain, with the gain larger the larger is P^F. With $A_0 = 130$ owners of the initial availability gain over the whole range of price floors illustrated, because the free-market price would be below $80. For $A_0 = 130$ and P^F's below about $88, initial landholders lose. At higher P^F's, initial stockholders gain increasingly, then initial landholders start to gain at a "high" P^F, that is, a P^F approaching the free-market mean price.[20] Thus, conflict is possible. Owners of the initial avail-

[19] To construct this figure, the incidence on land of some twelve different price floors was computed with the dynamic programming routines, and the resulting values smoothed.
[20] P^F must be below the price at mean consumption or there is no steady state.

ability would be in favor of a scheme with P^F equal to, say, $85, but initial landowners would be opposed. Both groups would be in favor of a scheme with P^F equal to $90. But if P^F were below $95, the cost of the scheme exceeds the boost in the land price. So landowners would be opposed if the financing for the scheme came from a lump-sum tax on the obvious candidate – land. By the same reasoning, for floors above about $85, initial landowners would be in favor of the scheme when A_0 is 90, even if they had to pay a lump-sum tax equal to the present value of expected public expenditures.

Surplus transformation curves

The point of this examination of dynamic incidence is not to derive definitive answers, but to show how incidence is determined and on what it depends. The results are highly sensitive to the methodological approach and to the parameters of the problem. To emphasize this fact, we summarize the distributional results for various approaches and cases using incidence curves analogous to the surplus transformation curves Josling (1974) and Gardner (1983) use to show the one-period comparative statics of price supports in a deterministic Marshallian model. To present results in two dimensions, we must aggregate the four types of market participants distinguished above: producer-landholders, present and future consumers, storers-middlemen, and the government budget. We do so by combining producers and storers, and aggregating consumers present and future, as if they lived forever or made altruistic bequests repeated in subsequent generations. We assume the floor-price scheme is financed by lump-sum taxes on producers (here understood to include initial landowners and initial storers); equivalently, the scheme is run and financed by producers themselves.

In Figure 13.11 the origin represents the situation without the floor-price scheme: the first-best world of perfect competition. Consumer benefits from the introduction of a floor-price scheme are measured by the change in the expected present value of consumer surplus, and producer benefits by the change in the value of land plus current availability less the present value of expected program expenses as of period 0. Both are expressed as percentages of R^N, producers' one-period gross revenue at the nonstochastic equilibrium.

For the case of zero supply elasticity and constant elasticity of demand examined thus far in this section, the welfare transformation curve marked $C = 6$ in Figure 13.11 (the stubby curve that starts from the origin, loops into the fourth quadrant, and passes through the third quadrant) shows the effects of introducing various price floors in period 0 in which availability A_0 is 130. Of course, the curve would be different for a different A_0. Selected price floors P^F are marked on the curve. The information on the change in producer wealth corresponds to that in Figure 13.10 for storers and landowners less the present value of program costs. At a P^F of $80, producers lose while there

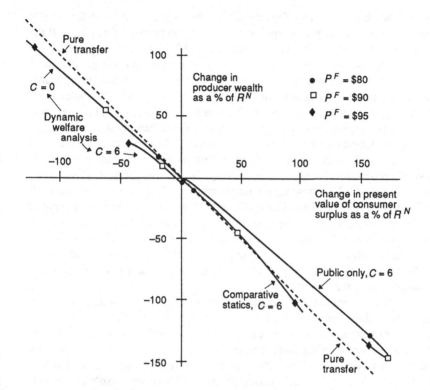

Figure 13.11. Incidence of floor-price schemes.

is a net transfer to consumers present and future, considered as a group. For higher floors the schemes are much less favorable to consumers. Over a range of floors of about $80–$85 the scheme reduces the welfare of consumers as well as the wealth of current producer and storers as a group. But if P^F is above $85, this latter group has a clear gain in wealth, even though they pay for the scheme, while consumers lose.

The vertical (or horizontal) distance from the diagonal dotted line shows the deadweight loss relative to a fully efficient redistribution between consumers and producers. The transfers through floor-price schemes are clearly rather inefficient. At a P^F above $90, the marginal deadweight loss is above 40 percent.

The importance of correct specification of the model and correct methodology for measuring incidence are dramatized in Figure 13.11. Three other curves are shown, one for a linear demand curve ($C = 0$), another for comparative-statics analysis, and the third for an analysis assuming there was no private storage. In all cases the curves represent the change from the free-market situation, using the same approach. Thus the comparative-statics curve shows the change from the free-market steady state, and the curve for "Public only," the dynamic change from a system with no storage of any kind. If the true welfare incidence of, say, a scheme with $PF = \$90$ is represented by the open square on the curve marked $C = 6$ in the northwest quadrant, the open squares on the other three curves show what the incidence would be measured according to the other approaches. All three would be drastically misleading.

As discussed above in Chapter 12 under ideal stabilization, long-run surpluses (those measured by comparative statics) are heavily dependent upon the consumption demand curvature parameter C. More precisely, as derived in Wright and Williams (1988b), the effect on mean consumer surplus is roughly proportional to $(C - 1)$. Because $C = 6$ with this constant-elasticity demand curve of -0.2, comparative statics suggest a large consumer gain from a floor-price scheme. The comparative-statics surplus transformation curve in Figure 13.11 also tempts one to conclude that producers in the distant steady state lose from a floor-price scheme, at all possible floor prices. In fact, as emphasized above, producers neither gain nor lose in the steady state; the incidence is on the owners of available supplies and land at the time of announcement of the scheme.

Part of the surplus transformation curve for comparative statics lies above the dashed line representing efficient transfers in Figure 13.11 (i.e., consumers gain more than producers lose). Should one infer that a floor-price scheme can yield a deadweight gain (the reverse of conventional deadweight loss of a market distortion)? Such an inference is erroneous: The comparative-statics partial-equilibrium approach misses the expected (dynamic) costs of accumulation of stocks along the path to the new stochastic steady state.[21]

Even if incidence is assessed using the appropriate dynamic framework, neglect of competitive private storage (a commonplace in the literature) can make the analysis totally misleading, as shown by the curve marked "Public only, $C = 6$." The curve shows a deadweight gain and large losses to initial producers and expected gains to present and future consumers, at all significant floor prices. The apparent deadweight gain comes because the exercise implicitly includes the "introduction of storage," a highly socially beneficial innovation, even if the scheme would not store optimally in the absence of private storage.[22] Second, the large transfers from initial producers to consumers reflect the fact that, with the constant-elasticity demand curve, the introduction of competitive storage reduces land value, as noted in Section 12.4

---

21   Readers familiar with neoclassical growth theory will know that one cannot evaluate the desirability of a move to a new steady state without taking account of the cost of capital accumulation needed to attain it. Also see Burt and Cummings (1977) for the similar argument in the context of natural resources.

22   A floor-price scheme with only public storage could furnish up to about 85% of the net social gain from introducing private storage in this example, the highest gain coming with PF in the range $80–$85.

above. If the analyses of a floor-price scheme is done without storage, these effects are incorrectly attributed to the scheme itself, as Weaver and Helmberger (1977) and Sarris (1984) have emphasized.[23]

Even with the correct dynamic approach, and proper accounting for private storage, great errors in deducing the incidence can arise from incorrect model specification. We have already noted the sensitivity of stabilization effects, whether in the context of ideal stabilization or the introduction of storage, to assumptions about demand curvature and supply elasticities. The curve labeled $C = 0$ in Figure 13.11 shows that the same point applies to analysis of price-floor schemes. The same price floor is much more favorable to producers if the consumption demand curve is linear rather than constant elasticity with the same point elasticity at the nonstochastic equilibrium.

Section 12.2 also showed that great differences in incidence can occur if ideal stabilization of supply elsewhere appears as stabilization of demand in the sector under study. This point is also on the mark for floor-price schemes. If the same random disturbance appears as a shifter to market demand, due to fluctuations in a foreign excess demand curve,[24] initial domestic producers lose more from the floor-price scheme. The scheme raises foreign expenditures on imports when foreign production is high and excess demand is low, and reduces foreign costs of purchases when foreign production is short and imports are high. This benefit to the foreign component of the market comes at the expense of initial domestic producers; the comparable surplus transformation curve would appear in Figure 13.11 as a downward shift of the curve marked "$C = 6$" into the southwest quadrant, as illustrated in Wright and Williams (1988a).

The increased openness of U.S. agriculture to foreign disturbances may be one reason why domestic agricultural policy has shifted from reliance on storage-based price support (such as the nonrecourse loan programs) to include deficiency payments as a major policy instrument. The incidence of deficiency payments is very different from floor-price schemes. The deficiency payment to domestic producers in period t consists of the difference, if positive, between a P^D and the market P_t paid by consumers. With $\eta^s = 0$, the deficiency payments do not affect market allocation at all.[25] The dynamics of their introduction are quite simple, as shown in Figure 13.12. (It is assumed that the scheme first pays out for the harvest in period 0; A_0 is entirely from that harvest.) Convergence of the means of the sample paths of net revenue

---

[23] The criterion is also relevant in analyses that include processors, such as Hinchy and Fisher (1988).

[24] This might be a stylized description of a rigidly centrally planned economy with stochastic domestic production and fixed producer and consumer prices.

[25] If $\eta^s > 0$, deficiency payments have direct allocative effects not present here. If producers are risk averse, Innes (1990a) has shown that for plausible parameters producers may lose from such a scheme.

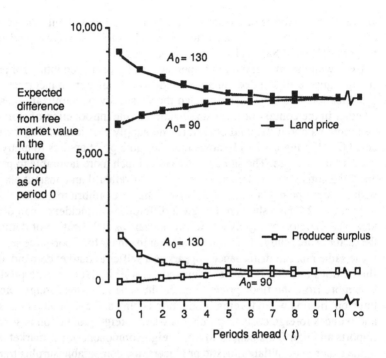

Figure 13.12. Expected evolution to new steady state with scheme of deficiency payments, $P^D = \$90$.

and land price to their new steady states is monotonic from either initial availability.[26] Flows to producers equal government expenditures. Under assumption of lump-sum financing by producers, the deficiency payments scheme, for any P^D, would appear in Figure 13.11 as a point located at the origin.[27]

Often back-of-the-envelope calculations assume a price-support scheme reduces supply to the level that drives consumption price up to the support level, ignoring later effects of the increased carryover. If the carryover disappears (many farmers and policy makers wish it would), the incidence in the basic storage model is extremely favorable to initial producers, because there is no carryover to depress future revenues. The points for the various support prices would be off Figure 13.11 far into the northwest quadrant. This type of price support, whether through a policy of destruction of surplus or foreign aid to recipients excluded from access to the commercial markets, is also much more efficient as a transfer in the case examined here, though the waste

[26] The expected paths of storage, market price, and consumption are unaffected by the program, for $\eta^s = 0$.

[27] For more discussion of the deadweight loss of deficiency payments relative to other schemes, see Glauber et al. (1989).

of destruction is much more obvious and superficially more repugnant than the waste of excessive storage.

Floor-price schemes with risk-averse producers

The welfare analysis culminating in Figure 13.11 assumes that the producers and consumers are risk neutral with respect to fluctuations in income. Of course, most analysts presume the major benefit from market-stabilizing public storage schemes is the reduction in risk faced by risk-averse producers. Indeed, some readers of Chapter 12 who are new to this field may have been surprised to find that stabilization has any welfare effects at all without risk aversion. Market-stabilizing interventions have welfare effects even if all market participants are risk neutral with respect to income changes because of the feedback of the public policies on endogenous variables such as mean price and mean revenue, and because of the dynamics of the interventions themselves. We believe that these welfare effects can explain the producers' political support for public storage interventions.

Also, it is not clear that the effects of floor-price schemes would be more favorable to producers were they risk averse, despite the common message in the literature. For agricultural commodities, the bulk of the theoretical literature has defined the utility of a farm owner-producer as a function of a single period's income, and such income is usually defined as net farm profits where the meaning of "net" is often unspecified. Leisure or labor effort is also often included as a second argument of the utility function. Typical of this approach, at least one input is committed before the realization of income is observed – the farmer sows before he reaps.[28] This specification presumes:

(a) no portfolio diversification beyond the operating unit (farm activities may be diversified, however);
(b) no distinction of income from consumption; and
(c) no income smoothing by borrowing, lending, or other means.

Assumption (a) means that the farmer is not represented as a utility-maximizing investor, as in modern finance theory of portfolio selection, but more like a risk-averse corporate manager whose performance cannot be directly observed, with human capital that cannot be diversified outside the firm. Constraints on diversification appear to be a plausible feature of modern as well as traditional farmers' investments inasmuch as most farmers have a large part of their assets invested in the farm. Nevertheless, where these constraints are not made explicit in models of farmers' behavior, conclusions re-

---

[28] For example, Newbery and Stiglitz (1981, esp. chap. 6) model the farmer as maximizing a function separable in consumption and leisure: $E[U[Y]] - wx$, where w is the return to his labor x committed in advance, Y is random income, and $E[U]$ denotes expected utility.

garding second-best interventions, such as a floor-price scheme, have a dubious analytical base.

Assumptions (b) and (c) rule out intertemporal reallocations, consistent with the essentially timeless nature of the original Von Neumann and Morgenstern theory of expected utility. The obvious time lapse between some necessary inputs and outputs in agriculture and the need for consumption in each period mean that an intertemporal trade-off is, in fact, being made by the farmer. Adjustment of this investment can help smooth the consumption stream between the two periods. Similarly, if savings and wealth accumulation are possible, interperiod adjustments are possible. According to Paxson (1989), Thai farmers responded to recent severe and unanticipated income declines by adjusting their savings about one for one. Langemeier and Patrick (1990) report that, for a sample of Illinois farmers followed for eight years, family consumption responded little to fluctuations in current income, being determined instead by life-cycle considerations. Clearly, a single-period model overstates the correspondence between current income and current utility.

A true multiperiod model also requires attention to hypotheses about asset integration and linearity of preferences in probabilities.[29] As Quizon et al. (1984) note, Binswanger's (1980, 1981) finding that experimental subjects in India do not appear to follow asset integration and linearity of preferences in probabilities is inconsistent with the expected-utility hypothesis but not with the "prospect theory" of Kahneman and Tversky (1979) or the generalized expected utility analysis of Machina (1984). Newbery and Stiglitz (1981) interpret Binswanger's experimental results as justifying the abandonment of asset integration in their own analyses. Because our analysis recognizes more explicitly the intertemporal nature of production, storage, and stabilization, we could not have taken that route without making obvious the inconsistency between the specification of utility and the stylized facts of producers' investment in planned production.

In any case, it does not follow, especially as a general proposition, that risk-averse producers are helped by public stabilization schemes more than risk-neutral producers. Farmers' borrowing ability is surely related to land value as well as current income. Public interventions that increase total storage may well destabilize land values even as they stabilize income in any one period. The simplest illustration of this possibility is the thought experiment of the introduction of storage performed in Chapter 12. With no storage, the price of land is constant, although the price of the commodity and income are highly variable. With storage technically possible, income may be stabilized but the price of land becomes variable, fluctuating inversely to movements in

---

29   Asset integration means that current income Y is viewed by the recipient as an addition to wealth W. The added assumption of linearity in the probabilities means that preferences can be represented by a function of the form $\Sigma \pi_i U[Y_i + W_i]$, where π_i is the probability of the ith outcome.

Table 13.3. *Price floors and autocorrelations in net revenue*

Price floor (P^F)	Standard deviation of revenue	Partial autocorrelations of net revenue		
		R_{t-1}	R_{t-2}	R_{t-3}
None	$2581	.370	.051	.029
$85	2364	.331	.063	.054
$90	2098	.309	.071	.072
$95	1640	.236	.086	.059

carryover.[30] Although the role of credit markets in stabilizing income is beyond the scope of this book, it is easy to imagine that the fluctuations in collateral value may reduce the amount of smoothing possible through loans. Furthermore, the duration of smoothing needed tends to increase because of the correlation induced in net revenues.

Table 13.3 shows three partial autocorrelations in net revenue under regimes with three different price floors and the regime with undistorted private storage. With storage technically impossible, all these partial autocorrelations are 0.0. The positive autocorrelations in Table 13.3 mean that with private storage, and more so with the regimes of price floors, strings of low revenue are more likely, even though the variance of revenue in any one period is lower (also see Gelb 1979). Producers may survive one very bad period, but four mediocre periods in a row may bankrupt them.[31]

Moreover, lower variance in consumption in any one period at the expense of higher variance over three or four periods may not make producers better off, if their utility functions are not additively separable but weight two lean periods more heavily should they be in succession. Expected-utility theory, as currently formulated, cannot accommodate such considerations, although that fact does not imply they are unimportant. The intertemporal version of the theory is at a much less developed stage and is struggling to cover obvious deficiencies revealed in essentially one-shot tests of the theory.[32] (See Machina [1987] for an introductory essay.)

Even this issue of the induced serial correlation in revenue concerns an in-

[30] Also, as Holly and Hughes Hallett (1989, p. 37) have emphasized, intervention in and "control" of some endogenous variables in a complex system may increase the variance of the other endogenous variables.

[31] Yet another consideration is the effect on long-term investment with a change in the profile of multiperiod risk. Timmer (1989) argues that a major benefit of stabilization is a better environment for investment.

[32] The analytically tractable specifications of multiperiod utility recently put forward by Farmer (1990) and Weil (1990) may allow a wide range of welfare analysis. Also see Hughes Hallett (1984) for an effort at specification of multiperiod risk aversion in the context of commodity storage.

dividual risk-averse producer among many risk-neutral producers. If all producers are risk-averse, the feedback of their reactions to storage programs must be accounted for. These feedbacks may negate any of the gain hypothesized for the individual producer. Just and Hallam (1978) present a model in which a price-taking farmer responds positively to the mean and negatively to the variance of price, which is assumed to be exogenous. A reduction in price variance causes an outward shift in the supply curve, which, they claim, increases the benefits to producers from stabilization. In the context of a commodity market with inelastic demand, the result can be quite different. Due to the outward shift in supply because of the aggregated response of producers, greater certainty of output is accompanied by lower expected revenue (see Innes 1990b). Consequently, there is no general result that the presence of risk aversion on the part of producers increases their welfare gains from income stabilization, even in this model, which is extremely favorable to such a finding.

Finally, it must be acknowledged that rational market participants put a price on risk aversion in the markets for capital assets, should those markets exist. In a developed economy, if the profession of a farmer is especially risky and farmers are risk averse, that risk is capitalized into the prices of assets associated with farming, principally land. If the government promulgates a program that reduces the risk to farming, the main beneficiaries of the program are, by the remorseless logic of capitalization, the owners of land and other fixed productive assets at the time of the program's announcement. Those who later enter farming are neither helped nor hurt by the program.[33] All landowners become exposed to the risk of a capital loss should the program be ended.

13.3   The merits of private speculative storage in a floor-price scheme

Earlier in this chapter we showed that private storage, including episodes of speculative attack, appears to frustrate the aims of a public floor-price scheme. A very natural inference is that private storers in general destabilize the market, and so should be restricted or banned. Here we demonstrate that such an inference is wrong.

One difficulty with this issue has been raised in Section 13.2: Policy evaluation must be dynamic, and the dynamic definition of stabilization is elusive. But if one defines stabilization as a mean-preserving contraction (the opposite of a mean-preserving spread in the terminology of Rothschild and Stiglitz

---

[33]   This statement assumes that all potential producers have the same degree of risk aversion. If their risk preferences are heterogeneous, there may be some redistribution between more and less risk-averse purchasers of land.

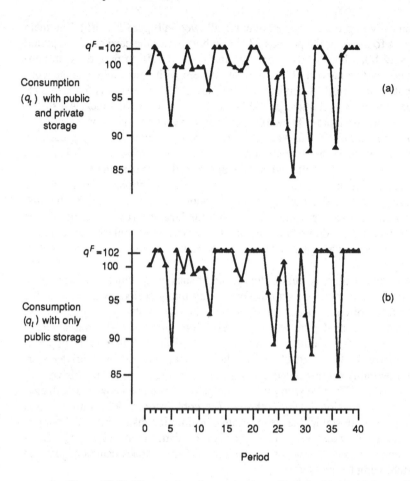

Figure 13.13. Time series of consumption with and without private storage in addition to public storage defending P^F = $90.

[1970]) of the steady-state dispersion of consumption in our model, the common intuition is wrong.[34]

Some insights into the reasons private storage, operating in the setting of a floor-price scheme, further stabilizes consumption can be grasped in Figure 13.13. Both time series of consumption in Figure 13.13 have the same availability in the first period and the same subsequent sequence for the weather. Both have the same price floor of $90, corresponding to q^F = 102 units. They

[34] Building on Salant (1983), Wright and Williams (1988c) show that a solely public price-floor program stabilizes steady-state consumption, and private storage, with speculative attack an integral feature, further stabilizes steady-state consumption (with perfectly inelastic supply) in the Rothschild–Stiglitz sense.

differ only in private storage not being allowed in Figure 13.13(b). The main story is found over the periods 33–38. In both series the carryout from period 33 is 12.80, which leads to an availability of 107.56 in period 34, in conjunction with a harvest of 94.76. In the system with only public storage, consumption in period 34 persists at 102 units, and the carryout is 5.56. In a regime with private storage, period 34 is one of speculative attack. All stocks shift to private hands. They total 6.87, and in consequence consumption is 100.69 units, not 102.00. Again in period 35 consumption in the regime with private storage is lower; but, more important, total storage, which is in private hands, is 3.41 units, whereas storage in the other system is 0.0. That storage comes in handy in period 36, which has exceptionally poor weather. Private storage is also higher than solely public storage in period 37, but that speculation proves less successful. With the large harvest in period 38, the private stocks get dumped on the public agency. Nevertheless, consumption is less variable when private storage operates in conjunction with public storage.

A system with only public storage, and hence no speculative attack, gives the appearance of more stability by having many periods with price at the price floor, often in succession. That appearance of stability comes at the expense of occasional extremely low levels of consumption and extremely large increases in price. Taking into account the possibility of these profit opportunities, private storage attacks the public stockpile. The ride with private storage, inevitably accompanied by speculative attack, is similar to a drive over cobblestones. The ride with private storage outlawed is one over smooth concrete with occasional deep potholes. The cobblestone ride, for all its small bumps, is more stable; the steady-state consumption distribution without private storage is a mean-preserving spread of the distribution with storage. Laws prohibiting private storage or restraining speculative attack cannot be justified as stabilizing the market.

Even if measures against speculative attack and private storage actually decrease market stability, it does not necessarily follow that such measures have no economic justification. A conventional second-best argument can justify some of the interventions without appealing to risk aversion. Because competitive private storage in a market with no distortions maximizes the expected value of total surplus, any other storage rule is, by this measure, inferior to pure private storage. Under a public floor-price scheme with no private storage, too much is stored at some availabilities and too little at others. Storage behavior with public and private combined has too much storage everywhere. This comparison suggests the possibility that the deadweight loss of public and private storage combined may be greater than the deadweight loss of public storage alone. In other words, a net gain in social welfare may emanate from outlawing private storage, and with it speculative attack, given that there must be public storage to support a price floor.

Table 13.4. *Welfare effects of private storage with speculative attack*

Price floor (P^F)	Change in total surplus[a]	
	Private storage allowed	Public storage only
$95	-61	-43
90	-27	-11
85	-8	-7
80	-2	-14
0	0	-100

[a]As a percentage of the effect of allowing undistorted private storage. The initial condition is 100 units available, the amount consumed and produced under certainty.

This possibility is confirmed by a numerical example, using the same parameters as for the storage rules in Figure 13.1.[35] In Table 13.4, the discounted expected dynamic welfare effects (sum of expected consumer and producer surpluses, less the public buffer stock's revenue losses) of introducing each given policy, with initial available supply equal to mean production, are given as a percentage of the value of allowing undistorted private storage with a price floor of $0. As would be anticipated, a floor-price scheme with either version of storage incurs a deadweight loss if measured against allowing undistorted private storage (column 1, floor of $0). This loss is greatest when the price floor is $0 and private storage is prohibited so that there is no storage at all (bottom row, column 2). For higher price floors, the higher (solely public) storage initially increases welfare but, beyond a floor of $85, the storage is becoming excessive on average and welfare decreases as the floor is raised.

If private storage is allowed, the social cost of a low price floor (like P^F = $80) is smaller than if public storage alone is permitted. But, as the floor is raised and average storage becomes increasingly excessive, the marginal contribution of private storage becomes less beneficial. At a floor of $85 or higher, the expected deadweight loss is lower if private storage and speculative attack are banned.

To sum up this section on speculative attack: Economists and policy makers commonly subscribe to the proposition that private storage, with speculative attacks, is a problem because it destabilizes consumption, offsetting the

[35] The exception is the curvature parameter C, which is set at 6 instead of 0, so that the demand curve does not cross the quantity axis; price remains positive for large harvests when storage is impossible.

effects of the floor-price scheme. That proposition is dubious at two levels: First, the seemingly perverse private behavior is a rational result of the original public intervention. Second, as a matter of positive economics, competitive expected profit-maximizing storage with sporadic speculative attacks unambiguously complements the consumption-stabilizing effect of a floor-price scheme. From a normative viewpoint, however, the extra consumption stability associated with speculative attacks is not necessarily socially desirable. Prohibition of speculation or some finite tax on private storage might in some cases be a defensible second-best policy, given the inevitability of the floor-price scheme, because it reduces the excess resources used in storage. Of course, a more judicious and flexible public storage policy could be even better.

CHAPTER 14

Public storage under price bands and price pegs

Many recent market-stabilizing schemes involving storage, and most of the concrete proposals for such schemes by economists, are some type of price-band scheme. For example, the analytical framework of Ghosh et al. (1987) is centered around price-band schemes, from the econometric exercises to the policy simulations. Following earlier writers like Keynes (1972 [1942]), just a few of the more recent examples of an analytical focus on price bands include Brown (1975), Behrman and Tinakorn-Ramangkura (1978), Chaipravat (1978), Ford (1978), Behrman (1979), Gardner (1979, chap. 5), Hallwood (1979), Sarris et al. (1979), Gardner (1982), Miranda and Helmberger (1988), Ahmed and Bernard (1989), and Glauber et al. (1989). In many actual international commodity agreements, the manager of the public stockpile is charged with keeping price within some band, with rules mandating accumulation of stocks at the bottom of the band and release at the top, often with some managerial discretion within intermediate price ranges (Gardner 1985; Gilbert 1987). For example, the various International Cocoa Agreements have had a ceiling price and a floor price symmetric about an "indicator" price, with the price band comprising both a trigger range, in which the buffer stock's manager can intervene at his discretion, and a nonintervention range. Many U.S. farm programs have had what amounts to a floor price and a much higher release price (Langley et al. 1985).

Price-band schemes have a superficial attractiveness and logic. Seemingly the disruptions of price changes are reduced by efforts to keep prices in a narrow band. Seemingly the symmetry of the band around the long-term mean price favors neither consumers nor producers. By the same implicit reasoning, the distribution of observed prices is close to symmetric. Most obvious, the restriction on the release of public stocks to a price at least equal to the top of the band seems a judicious and feasible storage policy.

As this chapter demonstrates in turn, none of these beliefs is valid in general. Most important, price-band schemes have an inherent tendency for an

391

enormous accumulation of stocks. Their effect on the distribution of price is not symmetric. Moreover, the requirement that public stocks be released only at the top of the band frequently leaves them in store when they would have higher social value if consumed immediately. Thus, price-band schemes have substantial deadweight losses compared to other market-stabilizing schemes, such as deficiency payments or price floors. Nor does it seem that a coalition of producers alone would prefer them.

Definition of a price-band scheme

Some of the analytical support for public storage under a price-band scheme stems from a failure to specify the alternatives to such a program. Many authors use price bands synonymously with buffer stocks, as if they suppose the only way to operate a buffer stock is with different floor and release prices. A buffer stock is more general and can be taken as synonymous with public storage whatever the rule for public intervention.

Within the broader category of public buffer stocks, a price-band scheme involves two prices: P^F, the floor price at which the government is willing to buy any amount offered to it, and P^B, the minimum price at which the government will release anything from its buffer stock. Naturally, P^B is greater than or equal to P^F. When P^B equals P^F, we call the scheme a "floor-price scheme," in which the government's behavior follows that with the price floors studied in the previous chapter. As emphasized in Chapter 13, even if P^B equals P^F, the government does not necessarily make all its sales at P^F. More generally, under a price-band scheme, the government hopes its stockpile will suffice to restrain price to P^B; but if the harvest proves to be extremely meager, the government will sell its entire stock for what the market will bear. P^B is not a statutory price ceiling: Private agents can transact freely at prices above it. Once again this formulation envisions an auction each period in which all sellers receive and all buyers pay a single price. No arbitrage is profitable within a period. Of course, in the continuous time of the real world, some parties, perhaps the government, may not recognize changing conditions and so sell for less than they should.[1]

---

[1]   Selling for too little given current conditions should not be confused with selling at a lower price in one period than could have been obtained in the next. It may happen that in a particular period the government sells some of its stockpile at P^B; that is to say, it defends the top of the band. Conditions next period may be such that the market price rises far above P^B despite the sale of the remaining public stockpile. That outcome makes it appear that the government made a bad decision by giving some of its stockpile away at too low a price. The inference is unfair, however: The government, not to mention the buyers of the stockpile were they private speculators, could not foresee the outcome of the next period's harvest. No arbitrage profits were possible in expectation.

A price-band scheme could also be defined from the perspective of a middle price and a bandwidth. The middle price is the average of P^F and P^B, and the bandwidth the difference between them. The middle of the band need not be the mean price if the scheme were in operation.

Some of the confusion about price bands comes in discussing P^B as if it were the bandwidth. One could investigate the effect of lowering P^B while holding P^F constant, or the effect of narrowing the bandwidth while holding the middle price constant (and thus the effect of lowering P^B while raising P^F the same amount). Both are interesting questions, but it is important to make clear which is being asked.[2]

The definition of a price-band scheme as a pair P^F and P^B makes clear the relationship to a regular floor-price scheme. A price-band scheme is a floor-price scheme with the additional constraint that the government cannot dispose of its stocks in the range between P^F and P^B. A floor-price scheme is the more general policy because the manager of the public stockpile does have the flexibility to release stocks in the interval between P^F and P^B. The manager could always choose to store as under a price-band scheme, only releasing if the current price is P^B or higher.

A third type of public buffer-stock policy can be distinguished as a "price-peg" scheme. In a price-band scheme, the government tries to keep the market price within a specified range. Under a price-peg scheme, it tries to keep the market price at a particular price P^{peg} near or at what is thought to be the long-run mean. In this chapter a price-peg scheme is a floor-price scheme with a capacity constraint on the public stockpile.[3] Price can fall below the intervention price P^{peg} if the limit of the public stockpile is reached, just as price can rise above P^{peg} if the public stockpile is exhausted. The floor-price schemes of Chapter 13, in which the government can buy all offered to it, exhibit the limiting behavior as capacity increases, with P^{peg} being below the nonstochastic equilibrium P^N as well as the stochastic steady-state mean. Because of the capacity constraint, P^{peg} can be as high as or indeed higher than P^N without causing the excessive accumulation that would eventually occur under a floor-price scheme.

Finally, one could combine the features of a price-band scheme and a price-

2   For example, Miranda and Helmberger (1988, p. 57) claim as a surprising result that "widening the price band by raising the release price lowers price variability in the case of nonexplosive policies." But most people would mean a wider band to be around the same center. Miranda and Helmberger's own results (Table 1) show that as the floor is lower as the release price is raised, price variability increases.

3   In some actual public programs, the binding constraint is on financing, that is, on the total funds a buffer stock manager can spend buying up a surplus. For each price, a financing constraint corresponds to a capacity constraint. Because price is endogenous, it seems simplest for analytical purposes to specify an exogenous capacity constraint rather than a funding constraint.

peg scheme. That would be a band of some specified width around a specified middle price along with a capacity constraint.[4] Thus a regular peg scheme is the limiting behavior as the bandwidth collapses to the (middle) price P^{peg}.

All these schemes are to be studied in this chapter as permanent regimes. A system with public intervention at a price peg will not always keep the market price at that level, but the public agency continues its general policy: It does not switch continuously among price floors, price bands, and price pegs. That consistency of regime is what we denote as a pricing "scheme."

14.1   The inherent explosiveness of symmetric price-band schemes

Conventional price-band schemes, with P^F and P^B symmetric around a plausible long-run price, have an intrinsic tendency to accumulate very large stocks. Indeed, a stochastic steady state may not exist; in expectation, accumulation of stocks may continue indefinitely. These properties are not the result of the interaction of private storage or production with the public policy; nor are they the result of misidentifying trends in production or consumption. Rather they result from the prescribed inflexibility of the buffer stock, which can only release its stocks at P^B or higher.

These general observations are best illustrated with a relatively simple example. Consider a situation where the consumption demand curve is linear, new production is perfectly inelastic with a mean of 100 units, the harvest is normally distributed with $\sigma_h = 10$ units, and there are no trends to average yields or to demand. The long-run average price without storage is $100. Also suppose only the government can store in this closed economy and that it uses a price-band scheme.[5] Without elastic supply and without private storage, any strange behavior must be attributed to the government's storage policy.

As the top of the price band P^B is raised, for a given P^F, the average amount stored increases explosively. This feature of price-band schemes can be seen starkly in Figure 14.1, for which each P^B was simulated for 100,000 periods. With P^F set at $80, a symmetric P^B is $120. Yet if P^B is set at even $117, average storage is enormous compared to the average under a simple floor-price scheme (i.e., where $P^B = $80). At the symmetric P^B of $120, average storage in that particular run of 100,000 periods is close to fifteen times average production.

---

[4]   McNicol (1978, pp. 62–5) argues that a price-band scheme should have a financing cap, to ensure that it does not become a method for raising the average price. What a spending cap actually achieves is a limit on the expected length of continuous operation of the scheme; it does not ensure against the raising of average prices over that period of time.

[5]   Pinckney (1988) studies optimal public storage versus only public storage with price bands in a setting with a small country facing world prices.

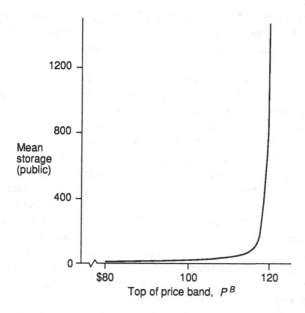

Figure 14.1. Explosion in quantity stored with higher top to price band, $P^F = \$80$.

Table 14.1. *Storage behavior under symmetric price bands[a]*

Band (P^F-P^B)	Mean storage	Maximum observed storage	Standard deviation of price
$50–150	589.69	1327.32	$35.96
60–140	853.18	1887.65	31.00
70–130	1164.67	2463.62	24.98
80–120	1472.10	3041.74	17.85
90–110	1909.72	3878.55	9.61

[a]Simulations of 100,000 periods.

Although the average storage in a simulation of 100,000 periods is lower for wider price bands, as shown in Table 14.1, it is very large compared to the average storage under a floor-price scheme with a P^F at the bottom of the band. Periods without any storage still occur but become extremely rare – merely 0.14 percent in the case of the price-band scheme of $90–$110.

It should also be emphasized that these values in Figure 14.1 and Table 14.1 for average storage are not steady-state values since a stochastic steady state does not exist. Simulations 10,000 periods long would show lower averages, and simulations 1,000,000 periods long substantially higher ones. In contrast to simulations of a price floor or of purely private storage, both of which have a stochastic steady state, under a symmetric price band the tendency is for continuous accumulation of stocks, reducing consumption below mean output.

With a symmetric price-band scheme, the amount in store on average increases over time, even though the buffer stock is also sure to run out at some point in finite time, because the changes in stocks are not fully symmetric. The additions are unbounded, but the releases are always bounded by the current stock. This expectation of indefinite accumulation under a symmetric price-band scheme stands in sharp contrast to a floor-price scheme with q^F below q^N. If the current storage in a floor-price scheme is above some specific critical value, the expectation is for release next period; if below, for accumulation.[6] Under a floor-price scheme the public stockpile can be released as long as the resulting price is above P^F. Thus, given a sequence of harvests over which no acquisitions or releases of stocks are needed to maintain a price band, there could be a fall in storage under a floor-price scheme with initially positive stocks. For large current holding under a floor-price scheme, the expected stock adjustment across all possible harvests can be negative, despite the nonnegativity constraint.

The peak funding requirement for the symmetric price-band schemes can be, to take as a sample the strings of 100,000 periods used for Table 14.1, a stockpile on the order of twenty or thirty periods' total production, equivalent to 300 times the harvest coefficient of variation σ_h. Even if the weather were bad – say, $v_t = -2\sigma_h$ – many periods running, it would take 150 periods to use up the stockpile. Of course, such a stockpile, far in excess of reasonable stabilization needs, is not financially sustainable. The public budget would long since have been reformed; the public buffer-stock agency would have been declared bankrupt. This is the certain fate of all such schemes if new supply does not contract in the face of the large overhang. According to the surveys by Gardner (1985) and Gilbert (1987), most actual schemes disintegrate in a rather few years.

The symmetric price-band schemes of Table 14.1 accumulate a budget-busting stockpile much faster than a comparable floor-price scheme. Figure 14.2 illustrates the probabilities of "bankruptcy" for the case with $P^F = \$80$. "Bankruptcy" is (arbitrarily) defined as a stockpile greater than 50 units, that is, equivalent to $5\sigma_h$ (and some seven times average storage under the floor-price scheme). Bankruptcy, so defined, can occur with a floor-price scheme if

---

6   This critical value for a floor-price scheme with only public storage, with P^F equal to $80 and the other parameters the same as in the examples in Table 14.1, is 3.99 units of storage. This value is the amount of storage solving

$$0 = S^g - 1 / \left(\left(\sqrt{2\pi} \right) \sigma_h \right) \int_{q^F - S^g}^{\infty} (h + S^g - q^F) \exp\left(-((h - \bar{h}) / \sigma_h)^2 / 2 \right) dh$$

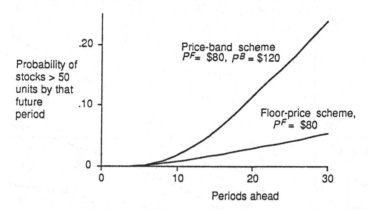

Figure 14.2. Probability of budget-breaking accumulation of public stocks under price-band and floor-price schemes, $A_0 = 100$.

several very large harvests come in a row. For example, there is close to a 1 percent chance that some time in its first ten periods of operation, starting from nothing in store, the stocks will breach the barrier of 50 units. But that chance is nearly double for the symmetric price-band scheme with $P^B = \$120$. Similarly, the chance of the floor-price scheme going bankrupt within the first twenty periods is just over 3 percent, whereas the risk for the price-band scheme is close to 12 percent. If P^F were \$90 rather than \$80, the probability of bankruptcy would be higher under a floor-price scheme, but higher yet under a symmetric \$90–\$110 price-band scheme.

The propensity for endless accumulation under the price-band scheme in Table 14.1 derives in part from the symmetry of the situation: P^B and P^F symmetric around \$100, the linear demand curve and hence symmetry in q^F and q^B around $\bar{h}$, and the symmetry of the yield distribution itself. With a constant-elasticity demand curve with the same elasticity of -0.2 at the point (\$100, 100 units) as the linear curve, q^B is closer to $\bar{h}$ than is q^F. Hence a given stockpile will be released over a greater range of harvests; other things equal, the expected increase in storage is smaller. For this reason, the accumulation of storage is less rapid for constant-elasticity demand, for the same width of the price band. This comparison can be seen in Figure 14.3, which plots the average amount stored in a particular period, for several cases with the same price band with $P^F = \$80$ and $P^B = \$120$. In Figure 14.3, 120 periods are shown (starting from $A_0 = 110$ units). In previous chapters it was necessary to illustrate only eight or ten periods, because the paths quickly approached the steady-state mean. For $C = 0$ the average storage is, of course, still rising after 120 periods because there is no steady state. The expected path of storage with constant-elasticity demand falls below that for linear demand. For similar reasons, the expected accumulation path with an asymmet-

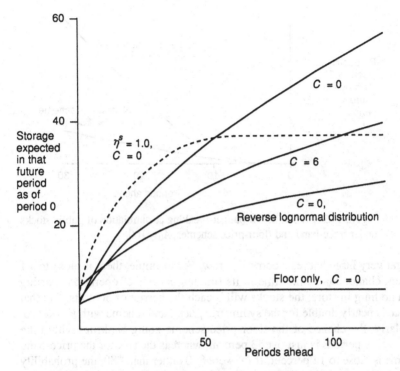

Figure 14.3. Variations in expected time paths of storage under a price-band scheme with $P^F = \$80$, $P^B = \$120$, $A_0 = 110$.

ric distribution of yields – specifically a reverse lognormal distribution skewed toward low harvests with the same mean and variance – rises less steeply. Nevertheless, even in these asymmetric cases, the expectation, as of period 0, is for a budget-breaking accumulation of stocks. The schemes with unresponsive supply do not work in the long run. And when they fail due to excessive stocks, they go out with a bang, not a whimper. Once the price crashes, the accumulated overhang tends to keep price at depressed levels for a long time – arguably the very consequence producers fear most.

14.2 Price-band schemes with private storage and elastic supply

When planned production is elastic, its response to the negative effect of current accumulation on returns to output next period can put a bound on the expected accumulation, as in the path for $\eta^s = 1.0$ illustrated in Figure 14.3. Storage is expected to approach, after many periods, its steady-state mean of 37.14 units.[7] Because a stochastic steady state exists, the long-run effects of a price-band scheme on price distributions, mean consumption, and producers' welfare can be studied. Accordingly, in the remainder of this chapter only cases with elastic supply will be examined. (Of course, the more elastic is supply, the more stable is the free-market price and the weaker is the case for public intervention.)

Because the focus of this section is the welfare significance of price-band schemes, the assumption of no private storage, convenient for demonstrating the tendency for large accumulations of stocks, must be dropped. As argued in Chapter 12, no welfare analysis without private storage can purport to be accurate, for the welfare effects of purely private storage will be misattributed to the price-band scheme. Of course, solving for the equilibrium with private storage requires stochastic dynamic programming.

In this application the problem has two state variables.[8] In a floor-price scheme, public carryin is indistinguishable from private carryin and from the new harvest; all are available to the market at any price above P^F. The single state variable is total availability. Under a price-band scheme, the public agency does not release any of its holdings unless price is P^B or higher. Instead of total availability, which is the sum of the commodity in private hands and the carryin in public hands, the first state variable is solely private availability, that is, the private carryin plus the new harvest. The amount of the public carryin is the second state variable. The public agency, waiting on the sidelines, intervenes to add or release some of its stockpile depending on its current stocks and the private availability. Because public behavior will be different next period depending on the carryover – most noticeably whether public stocks are available to defend the top of the band P^B – current private behavior is affected. That is to say, $E_t[P_{t+1}]$ is a function of private storage and public storage separately, namely, $E_t[P_{t+1}[S_t^c, S_t^g]]$, rather than just their sum as in a problem with a floor-price scheme.

Figure 14.4 illustrates storage rules for two amounts of public carryin, 0.0 units and 24.0 units, when $P^F = \$87.5$ and $P^B = \$112.5$. The range illustrated for the other state variable, private availability, is 90–130 units.[9] Private storage is represented by the dashed line, public storage by the solid line. Comparable rules exist for the continuum of levels of S_{t-1}^g.

---

7   That number too is very large compared to the long-run average with a floor-price scheme with the floor at $80.

8   Plato and Gordon (1984) and Miranda and Helmberger (1988) have also developed computer routines to solve this dynamic programming problem.

9   $\eta^s = 1.0$, $C = 0.0$, and the random disturbance, which is additive so that the amount of inherent uncertainty is not endogenous, has a standard deviation of 10 units. P^F was chosen so that a floor-price scheme at that level would have some periods with private storage.

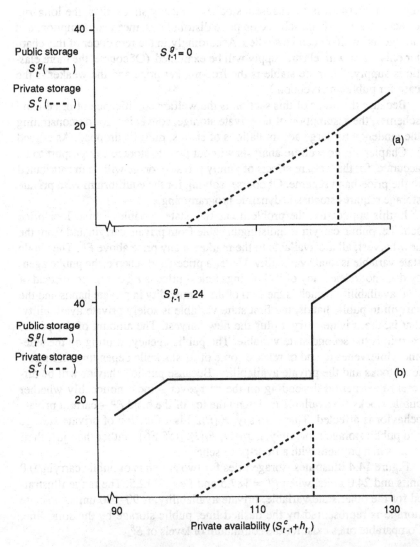

Figure 14.4. Storage rules under a price-band scheme for two different levels of public carryin.

Several points are worth noting about the reduced-form relationships for equilibrium storage plotted in Figure 14.4.

1. Private storage and public storage can coexist at prices other than P^F and over a wide range of availabilities, unlike with a price-floor scheme. With $S_{t-1}^g = 24$, over the range of private availability of

about 101.2–116.5, S_t^c is positive, because the price expected for period $t+1$ is sufficiently high to cover carrying costs. Of course, P_t is above P^F over this range; but it is not so high that P^B is broached, and the public carryin released.

2. Private storage for a given private availability is less with a higher public carryin.[10] For the same reason, with a larger public carryin the public agency must intervene at a lower private availability in order to support the price at P^F.

3. With no public carryin, private storage is the same as if the scheme were a pure price-floor scheme. With no carryin in period $t+1$, the next intervention of the public agency will be to purchase at P^F, which has the same effect on price as a floor-price scheme.

More generally, when the public carryin is positive, private storage is distorted (sometimes upward, sometimes downward) relative to the socially optimal level given the public storage behavior. This is because a price-band scheme by definition imposes inflexible management on the public stockpile. Consider public behavior in period t when the public carryin S_{t-1}^g is 10 units and the new harvest is such that price is $110. Because $110 is just below the top of the band, $112.50, none of the 10 units is released. Nevertheless, the price expected for the next period, period $t+1$, is below $110: $102.29 to be exact. Any private stocks are therefore sold (i.e., the equilibrium $S_t^c = 0$). Such conditions should also be a message to release some of the public stockpile immediately, because its current marginal value is higher than its expected marginal value the next period.[11] Because in this and similar instances the carryin of 10 units is not released, from the perspective of the preceding period, period $t-1$, price in current period t is higher than it would otherwise be. This higher expected price can induce private storage in period $t-1$, despite the existence of a public carryout.[12]

Thus, this price-band scheme constrains the public stockpile to store even when the current marginal social value of its holdings is higher than the undiscounted expected future marginal value. A floor-price scheme with the same P^F does not do this. Hence, a price-band scheme has a higher social deadweight loss. Figure 14.5 makes this clear by plotting the deadweight loss as a function of P^B for $P^F = 87.50. The social deadweight loss of a symmetric price band – $87.50 and $112.50 – is some seventeen times that of a floor-price scheme at $87.50.

---

10 Adams (1978) has emphasized that private storage behavior will differ depending on the level of public stocks in a price-band scheme. Also see Smith (1978b) and Gardner (1979, chap. 5).

11 The signal is similar with the true marginal social value rather than the expected price.

12 The private storage industry's attention to these opportunities persists until expected profits are zero. From that fact it follows that, in expectation, the price-band scheme must run a deficit.

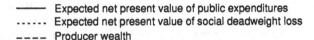

Expected net present value of public expenditures
Expected net present value of social deadweight loss
Producer wealth

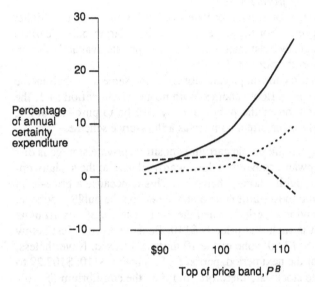

Figure 14.5. Dynamic incidence of price-band schemes, P^F = $87.50.

Moreover, the present value of public expenditures on the price-band scheme are considerably higher the higher is P^B, as can also be seen in Figure 14.5. With the competition of private storage, the expected profits from public storage are at best zero under all circumstances. The rule that the public agency can release stocks only at P^B above P^F exacerbates the cost of interest payments and warehousing.

Figure 14.5 also shows the capitalized value of the change in the stream of net revenues to producers compared to solely private storage. This capitalized value, equivalent to "producer wealth" if producers are taken to own their land and the initial private stocks, is shown net of the present value of public expenditures on storage.[13] This information can answer whether producers would be willing to tax themselves (lump sum) to run a price-band scheme. The answer is yes, but a price-band scheme is only slightly preferable to a straight floor-price scheme. More surprising, the P^B that creates the largest transfer to producers is not at all close to the level symmetric with P^F. Such a symmetric scheme is usually what people have in mind when they recommend price-band schemes. Producers in this instance of linear demand and

---

[13] The present value of the stream of loss of consumer surplus can be inferred as the curve for the social deadweight loss plus the curve for producer wealth.

supply elasticity almost surely would prefer some scheme other than a price band – destruction, deficiency payments, a price floor – given that the government is prepared to spend some set amount (in present value). Inasmuch as a linear demand curve makes stabilization especially attractive to producers, the conclusion appears inescapable that, for more curved demand curves, price-band schemes are far from producers' first choice.

Of course, price-band schemes are rarely put forward with the explicit objective of increasing producers' wealth. Generally the immediate objective is presented as a reduction in the variance of price. The way in which this benefits producers or consumers is not directly discussed.

Price-band schemes do reduce the variance of price compared to the free market. Nevertheless, that simple characterization misses the complex alteration in the probability distribution of price. Figure 14.6 plots the distribution of price for three cases. One is the distribution with no public intervention but private storage, to serve as a frame of reference. The important comparison is between the price-floor scheme with $P^F = \$87.50$ and the price-band scheme with $P^F = \$87.50$ and the symmetric $P^B = \$112.50$.[14] Although the price-band scheme reduces the percentage of prices above $112.50 from 14.9 percent to 6 percent, it primarily rearranges the distribution within the range $87.50–$112.50. By far the most common price becomes P^B, where there is a mass point as shown on Figure 14.6. The frequency of P^F, in contrast, falls from that under the price-floor scheme. Because of private storage, which coexists with a price below about $97, the distribution in the range $87.50–$112.50 is highly skewed.

Another feature of price-band schemes is obvious in the probability distribution in Figure 14.6. Prices above P^B are not unknown, whereas there are no prices below P^F, given that funding is unlimited.[15] In other words, the symmetry of the price-band scheme is not present in practice: Producers are better protected against low prices than are consumers against high prices.

14.3   Price pegs

This section examines price pegs, which are a variation of both price bands and price floors. Operating a peg scheme, the public agency attempts to

---

[14]   The parameters are those used in the previous two figures, namely, $C=0$ and $\eta^s = 1.0$. The floor of $87.50 is such that most periods, the storage, if any, is private. Note that the floor scheme mainly redistributes the probability of low prices, that is, those below $87.50. The remainder of the distribution tracks closely the distribution with undistorted storage.

[15]   In his analysis of a public buffer stock, Hallwood (1979, chap. 4) assumes that all prices are within the band, that is, that the scheme truncates the tails of the probability distribution. Figure 14.6 makes clear that this characterization is not correct. The buffer stock should be expected to be empty in some states and prices then rise above P^B. Note that the distribution of prices would also have some finite probability below P^F if financing had some finite limit.

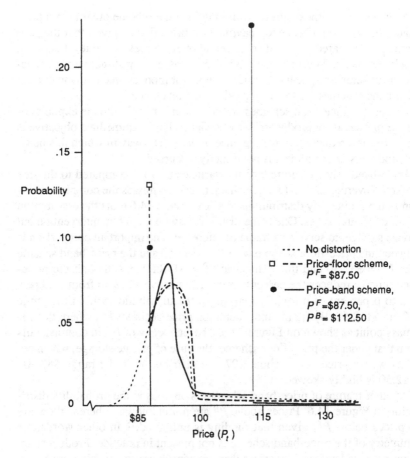

Figure 14.6. Price distributions in floor-price and price-band schemes.

keep price at a set level, perhaps one near the long-run mean. It will not always achieve its goal. In one direction it faces the possibility of exhausting
its stockpile; the market will equilibrate with a price above the peg. In the other direction, it may run out of warehousing capacity (or funding); the equilibrium price will be below the peg.

Three topics about such schemes are worth attention: the impact of a peg
scheme on the storage rule; the anticipated level of public expenditures on
such a scheme;[16] and whether producers would prefer a floor, without a capacity constraint, to a peg for a given support price. Surprisingly, producers
who must fund the scheme themselves prefer a peg scheme.

16   MacBean and Nguyen (1987) study the difficulty and expense a public agency has keeping price at a peg, but not in a model with rational forward-looking private storage.

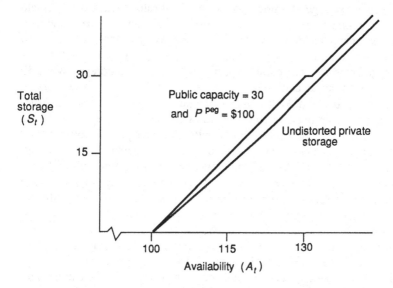

Figure 14.7. Storage rule with a price-peg scheme.

Figure 14.7 contrasts a storage rule with a peg scheme to the rule with un-distorted private storage.[17] In this particular case P^{peg} is $100.0, the nonstochastic equilibrium price. The capacity constraint is 30 units, which is large compared to mean steady-state storage but small enough to be germane. The parameters are the same as in the previous section. The two most noteworthy are η^s, which is 1.0, and C, which is 0 (linear demand).

The undistorted storage rule, with its marginal propensity to store close to 0.9, is typical of the genre with a high supply elasticity, as noted in Chapter 4. Because the private market itself supports price to a considerable extent if the harvest is large, the public agency has a much smaller effect on, say, the variance of price than would be expected from the average size of its holdings.

This peg scheme alters the marginal propensity to store to 1.0 over the range of the public agency's capacity. In addition, it shifts the point at which storage is just positive to the quantity corresponding to consumption at the peg price, if the point is lower than with only private storage. (In Figure 14.7 that shift is merely from an availability of 100.2 to 100.0.) That is, the storage rule up to the public capacity of 30 units is entirely public, although this is not a general feature. For other sets of parameters, such as those that would

[17] The storage rule with a price peg is a function of the single state variable – total availability – because the public agency releases its stockpile should the equilibrium price be above P^{peg}.

induce private storage at a price >$100, the total rule would have a private segment over one range of availabilities, then a public only segment, and then a private segment in addition to public over a range of yet higher availabilities.

The most interesting alteration in the storage rule in Figure 14.7 is the horizontal segment at the peak public capacity of 30 units. The storage beyond 30 units – for example, an additional 7.98 when $A_t = 140.00$ – is private storage. Private storage does not kick in just as the public capacity is reached, however. Current price must be lower (here in the neighborhood of $90) and availability higher (here just below 132 units) to induce private storage.[18]

If the public capacity were larger (holding the other parameters behind Figure 14.7 constant), this range of no private storage along with full public capacity would be longer. Even so, total storage is everywhere at least as large as with solely undistorted private storage. The possibility of future public demand for the commodity to put into store increases private storage in the current period. Of course, if P^{peg} is relatively low, say, $92.50, and the public capacity sufficiently small, the public agency has no substantive effect. The rule for total storage remains the same, since at that price private storage would have been larger than the public capacity anyway. Public storage simply replaces some part of private storage one unit for one unit.

At those high availabilities where public and private storage coexist at similar storage costs, the anticipated loss from holding the public stocks until the next period must be zero. Private storage, after all, requires the discounted expected price to cover the price of the commodity put into store and any physical storage costs. The present value of net public expenditures on the scheme will be positive nevertheless, because the large amount in store this period makes it likely in some future period that the government alone will be holding stocks, and so expecting a loss. In the extreme of the public stockpile merely replacing private holdings one for one, the present value of public losses is zero. More generally, losses will be a highly nonlinear function of the total amount currently in store. As the total amount rises beyond the public stockpile's capacity, the present value of losses may fall, since there is no expected loss from storage until the next period. Under a floor-price scheme, in contrast, the present value of net public expenditures is a steadily increasing function of total storage.

To put the matter slightly differently, for a given current availability, current price is a highly nonlinear function of the maximum size of the public stockpile, being insensitive to increases in public capacity from low levels but highly sensitive to marginal capacity increases at some higher capacity levels. By extension, the welfare effects of the introduction of a peg scheme are extremely sensitive to the size of the limit on the capacity.

---

[18] In the horizontal section of the upper curve between about 130 and 132 units the change in availability equals the change in consumption.

Figure 14.8 plots the change in producer wealth from the introduction of three different peg schemes, $P^{peg} = \$92.50, \$100.00,$ or $\$107.50$, for a range of capacity of 0–45 units. "Producer wealth" combines the initial change in land price with the value of the initial availability, minus the present value of net public expenditures. Most important, initial availability A_0 is 130 units. Thus, for $P^{peg} = \$100$, the capacity of 30 dominates the plot, for it is the minimum capacity able to keep price at $\$100$ for that availability. The capacities 28.5 and 31.5 are the equivalent for the other two peg prices. The steep rise in all three cases in Figure 14.8 corresponds to the horizontal segment on the relevant storage rule.

A figure for a different initial availability would have similar sharp increases in producer wealth over a small span of capacities, except that the point of the increase would be different. For example, if A_0 were 120 units, the important capacities would be 18.5, 20.0, and 21.5 for the same three values of P^{peg}. The boost to producer wealth would not be as high, however. Also, the function would rise slightly beyond a capacity of 20.0, before falling.[19]

The shape of the increase in producer wealth as a function of capacity implies that a coalition of producers will have very different opinions about a price-peg scheme depending on the capacity of the public stockpile. The steady-state distributions of, say, total storage or revenue are not that much different if the public capacity is 27 units rather than 33 units. Thus, it might not seem that producers should have a strong reason to prefer one. Yet they do, because of the dynamics of capitalization of gains; the short-term revenue boost dominates their calculations. Even more interesting is the capacity at which producer wealth is maximized.[20] It is not an infinite capacity. This is the principal discovery of this section: A coalition of producers would prefer a price-peg scheme to a floor-price scheme at the same support price (assuming it is feasible). With a price-peg scheme, producers get an initial boost without the disadvantage that comes with a floor-price scheme building up such a large stockpile that average revenues in distant periods are depressed.

In the welfare calculations the initial conditions are dominant. Producers feel much more favorably toward a scheme that improves conditions in the current period. This presumes, of course, a particular initial availability and that the introduction of the scheme was not anticipated in an earlier period. More important, this presumes that producers own the initial availability. Because whenever initial availability is large the major benefit of a peg scheme goes to owners of initial availability, those holders may have divergent opinions from the initial owners of land. Indeed, this split is much sharper than

---

[19] A comparable figure with a different demand curve, say, $C = 6$, looks much the same.

[20] The functions asymptote to a positive value. The operational difference between a peg scheme with a capacity of 80 units and one with 90 units is minute. Moreover, both are similar to a scheme with infinite capacity, that is, a floor-price scheme.

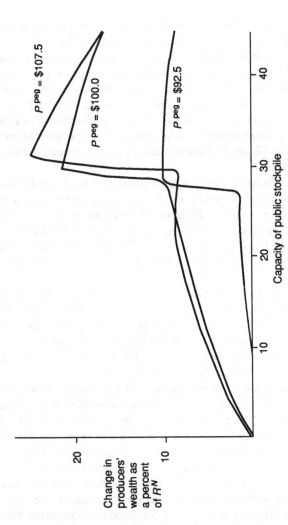

Figure 14.8. Producer wealth and capacity of public stockpile under various price-peg schemes, $A_0 = 130$.

previously observed in Chapter 13, which analyzed the incidence of floor-price schemes. If initial stocks are substantial, the primary, if not sole, beneficiaries of a price-peg scheme are the owners of the commodity at the time of the announcement of the scheme. Land values may well be reduced by the scheme, the extent depending on parameters such as the curvature of consumption demand.

All this analysis presumes that the schemes are financed with a lump-sum tax on producers equal to the present value of the expected net public expenditures. Naturally, if the producers can get some other group to pay, they would prefer, for a given P^{peg}, the maximum conceivable capacity, just as, for a given capacity, they would want the highest possible P^{peg}.

14.4 Further doubts about price-band schemes

Although producers would prefer a floor-price scheme to a symmetric price-band scheme with the same P^F, better yet is a price-peg scheme. That ranking leaves open the possibility of a price-band scheme with a capacity constraint being even better. At least for the combinations of parameters studied in this chapter, that possibility does not hold up. A peg, with P^F and P^B implicitly at the same price, is superior, from the perspective of producers who must finance the scheme, to a price-band scheme with the same capacity constraint. The same is true from society's perspective, as the deadweight loss of the price-band scheme is markedly larger. It is bad enough to store a large quantity at $P^{peg} = \$100.00$; worse is to acquire those stocks below $100, say, at $92.50, but not release them unless price reaches $107.50.

In conclusion, price-band schemes offer few if any advantages over straightforward floor-price or price-peg schemes. Their symmetry is superficial: They can ensure that prices do not fall below the bottom of the band but cannot ensure that prices do not break through the top of the band. They have substantial welfare effects even on market participants who are risk neutral. They tend to accumulate excessive stocks and to incur a considerable social cost by releasing public stocks only at a price above the marginal social value expected for later periods. The mystery is why they have been so often advocated by economists and so often used by public agencies.

CHAPTER 15

Public policies to supplement private storage

This chapter examines public policies sensibly designed to augment private storage thought to be inadequate because of some distortion. The public interventions examined in the two previous chapters are modeled as interventions in a first-best world of optimal rational storage. Judged from the perspective of total social welfare, not one of those price-support programs can be defended, because they cause a social deadweight loss. The public policies we consider in this chapter can make positive contributions to social welfare because existing private storage is suboptimal for some other reason. Moreover, these public policies can be ranked by their contribution to social welfare.

A good example of a policy aimed at supplementing private storage is the Strategic Petroleum Reserve (SPR) housed in the salt domes of Louisiana. Supporters of the SPR argue that the U.S. economy is extremely exposed to supply interruptions on the part of nefarious exporters because domestic oil companies have too little incentive to store. Reasons offered include the effects of price controls on the profits from storage, macroeconomic repercussions not considered by an individual firm, and appeals to national security.

Similar intentions to increase the size and effectiveness of shared reserves are embodied in the rules of the International Energy Agency (IEA), a consortium of twenty-one industrial countries. Although Smith (1988) worries about the mismatch between the IEA's actions and goals, the agency has devised complex oil-sharing plans, imposed policies of demand restraint, and required its members to have at least a ninety-day supply of crude oil and products in store. A concern to increase aggregate reserves underlies the calls for an international stockpile to improve world food security, discussed by the U.N. Food and Agricultural Organization (1983) and its World Food Council. It also underlies many national grain stockpiling schemes, including the Indian stockpiles of the 1960s (Chopra 1981) and the "farmer-owned reserve" in the United States under the Carter administration.

Concerns about the adequacy of private storage are hardly a modern pre-

410

occupation. In the Ch'ing Dynasty in China, for example, a nationwide granary system was administered with three aims: moderation of seasonal fluctuations, grain loans to peasants in times of need, and famine relief (Liu 1985). Tilly (1971) and Kaplan (1976) have emphasized how the eighteenth-century French view of the king as "father" of his people meant that the masses held the king and his government responsible for subsistence crises. (Also see Jongman and Dekker 1989.) Because only as a last resort was the king himself the victualer, the characteristic expression of government intervention was regulation of the grain trade. Of particular interest is the directive that all religious, hospital, and educational communities in Paris hold three times their annual grain consumption, this "community" granary to be released onto the market at the government's orders (Kaplan 1977).[1]

Public policies to supplement private storage raise two closely related issues. One is the operating rule of the public policy. How should stock management be coordinated internationally, what is the proper "drawdown" rule in a shortage, and how should the stocks be allocated to processors and refineries? The nature of the ideal public contingency plan is well worth considering as a guide to practical policy.[2] We show, in Section 15.6 specifically, that the ranking of public policies for supplementing private storage is by no means clear. No one class of contingency plans is best under all conditions. This striking result happens because seemingly optimal storage policies can suffer from what Kydland and Prescott (1977) have identified as the time-inconsistency of optimal public plans. This difficulty is similar to the problem of a profit-maximizing monopolist who rents warehousing space to others, which we discussed in Chapter 11. The problem arises when forward-looking private agents anticipate public policies, as is eminently reasonable in the case of speculative storage. Because of the private agents' anticipations, the public storage agency's current situation is a function of its own policy. Consequently, ranking of the various public policies depends crucially on mundane matters like physical storage costs and shipping costs because they also influence private actions.

One concrete feature of public stockpile management is the extent to which it can control total stocks via its own purchases and sales. In general, public storage reduces the amount of private storage that would otherwise have been

[1] The West German government today follows a similar policy by directing all local oil companies to hold inventories of at least a ninety-day supply as reckoned from the imports they used the previous year (Krapels 1980, pp. 65–8). The West German government in the 1970s also established a small Federal Reserve of crude.

[2] Plummer (1982), Hubbard and Weiner (1984), and Weyant (1988) have emphasized this topic in the case of oil; although, as recounted by Weimer (1982), much of the managerial effort expended on the SPR has simply been to prepare the salt domes and to acquire the stocks. No supply disruption has yet been classified as sufficiently severe to open the SPR, and if the U.S. government's management of inventories of metals is any guide, the oil may never be released.

present when recent harvests have been good. And as public reserves are released during a harvest failure or an oil cutoff, some may disappear into private reserves rather than adding to current consumption.[3] This second issue, concerning the substitution of public for private storage, arises, of course, for a floor-price or a price-band scheme, but it becomes central when the objective of the public intervention is explicitly to raise total stocks.

As argued forcefully by Sarris (1982), the displacement of private storage by welfare-maximizing public storage can be complete if the private storage is competitive and risk neutral, the commodity is in a single form and location, and no taxes, price controls, and regulations distort private decisions. Sarris's proposition is a corollary to the first fundamental theorem of welfare economics that (under additional technical assumptions) a competitive equilibrium is Pareto optimal. Two points follow: One is that the ostensibly private behavior studied extensively in Chapters 2–10 can guide social-welfare-maximizing public storage. The second point is less obvious and has to do with the fact that no one proposes the SPR or state granaries as a complete replacement for private storage. Why not? If the answer is to be found within a model, the model must encompass at least two locations (or two commodities), as in the model developed in Chapters 9 and 10, which allows for simultaneous public and private storage. Otherwise, the subject is not one of public supplementation of private storage. This chapter accordingly examines policies where the public agency stores at one of the locations while the private storage industry continues to store at the other location.

The distortion motivating the public role in storage could be nearly anything that reduces the private incentive to store. Here we will posit one distortion in particular, a price ceiling, imposed on the market price and hence on producers and storers whenever the amount available is especially low. (The existing quantities are rationed among consumers by some system of quotas or coupons.) Obviously, the prospect of receiving less than consumers' marginal valuation when the market is tight discourages storers. For that matter so would a per-unit tax on storage or a tax on capital, but these other distortions, however interesting, probably involve broader sectors of the economy than the market for the one commodity under study.

It should be stressed that the price ceiling is not binding in every period; rather there is a regime with a price ceiling. The exercises in this chapter are comparisons of regimes or, equivalently, of systems. For example, a system with price ceilings and solely private storage is contrasted to a system with

---

3   The substitution of the Strategic Petroleum Reserve for private storage is a concern addressed by, among others, Plummer (1982), Wright and Williams (1982b), Hubbard and Weiner (1984), and Murphy et al. (1986). In discussions of food security Hallwood (1977), Peck and Gray (1980), and Josling and Barichello (1984) have made the substitution of public for private storage a major theme.

price ceilings and private storage supplemented by public storage. The price ceilings and the public storage policies are assumed to be permanent.

Involving the private reactions to flexible public policies in a setting of price ceilings and trade between two locations, the model used in this chapter is by far the most complex in this book. It may seem that we have made the situation unnecessarily complicated. On the contrary, our main message is that such a complicated model is required: Further simplifications undermine the internal consistency of the arguments. For example, it is easy to make appeals for public programs to supplement private storage, but many of the rationales do not withstand close inspection, as we argue in the next section. Many actual programs may result in public and private storage at the same location, but this is almost surely the result of inflexibilities in the public program, such as is the case with price-band schemes. A discussion of optimal public interventions should not rely on suboptimal inflexibilities to provide simultaneous public and private storage. We ourselves (1982b) relied on lower private storage costs to permit both public and private storage in a simpler model of a single commodity; but that assumption has the look of "ad hockery." The model we present here is internally consistent, with all behavior derived from first principles. Although the best modern application of our model is to the SPR, it also speaks to the calls for international food reserves, such as those discussed in Josling (1976). For continuity, we use the same calibration, appropriate to grains, as in previous chapters.

Whether for oil, grain, or "strategic" metals, these public policies to supplement private storage are useful solely against short-term disruptions. As Weyant (1988, p. 181) observes, "[m]inimizing the short-run costs of sudden oil supply interruptions ought to be the major objective of both cooperative and unilateral stock drawdown policies." A ninety-day supply of oil at current rates of importation is a drop in the bucket if the Middle East's oil wells, pipelines, and terminals are destroyed during a war. A reserve of grain equal to 10 percent of annual world production cannot counteract a significant long-term climatic change. Our storage model, without trends or the limits of a finite resource, brings into focus the response to temporary disruptions.

15.1 Rationales for public intervention

Mind boggling is the treatment of private inventories in the U.S. Emergency Petroleum Allocation Act of 1973 (and supporting regulations issued by the Department of Energy). If inventories beyond working stocks were to have appreciated in value because of an oil cutoff, the lucky oil companies would have had to share their inventories with firms caught unprepared. With private storage repressed by the government itself, justification for public storage was not difficult to make.

This example illustrates that most public interventions into the business of storage are necessary only because of previous or existing government actions. In the literature, five broad rationales are offered for viewing private storage as inadequate. (A number of these are reviewed in Plummer [1982].) This section addresses each in turn. On close examination several turn out to be fallacious, and others are appropriate only in the setting of an open economy where the objective is the maximization of local welfare. The fifth one, the effects of a regime of price ceilings, is both most plausible and most relevant for our purposes later in this chapter.

Private speculation contrary to social needs

The argument for public stockpiles made by Khusro (1973, p. 4) for India exemplifies one view of the undesirable effects of private storage:

> For one reason or another – such as the occurrence of a shortage beyond the provision of normal contingency reserves, or, despite adequate provision, the occurrence of contingencies in locations different from where stocks exist, or the existence of a transportation bottleneck or any other factor – if traders have pleasant expectations of rising prices, and, therefore, tend to speculate by holding back some grain in speculative hoards, counter-speculative buffer stocks will be required to prevent a price rise.

This argument is a variant of the traditional call for a public agency to "lean against the wind." Nevertheless, it does not establish that the private speculation is irrational or even counterproductive. If prices will, in fact, be significantly higher in the future, it is rational, whether from a private or a social perspective, to be hoarding existing supplies. The rationale begs the question. Public storage is justified because private stocks are insufficient to prevent a rapid price rise. But why are these stocks insufficient in the first place?

Devarajan and Hubbard (1984, p. 188) present a variant of this argument to defend the Strategic Petroleum Reserve. They maintain that a "characteristic of disrupted oil markets is the continued increase, rather than a one-shot jump, in the spot market price," perhaps because the shortfall increases over time, or no one knows its full magnitude at first, or parties tied to long-term contracts do not use the spot market immediately. More important, they argue that the rising spot prices encourage the accumulation of private inventories. But they do not explain why this response is inappropriate; it is, after all, a feature of the welfare-maximizing stochastic steady state.

In these views one can detect an implicit assumption of a disequilibrium in the constellation of prices for different delivery dates. If spot prices are rising, why would people trade today for spot delivery at a price substantially below prices that should prevail soon when more traders are in the market? After all, spot traders know of long-term contracts or at least foresee future trading opportunities in the spot market. Devarajan and Hubbard seem to envisage a situation where spot prices are below futures prices, recorded at the same moment, by more than full carrying costs. On the contrary, the pattern characteristic of a temporary shortage is a backwardation, with prices for near-by delivery above those for later delivery. In 1973 no futures markets existed for crude oil or products. But during the disruptions of the spring of 1989 associated with the Alaskan oil spill, the constellation of futures prices moved into an "inversion" even as spot prices rose daily, as we noted in Chapter 8. That backwardation was accompanied by a reduction in private inventories. In August 1990, much comment was made about the sharp rise in the spot price caused by the Iraqi invasion of Kuwait. Little comment was made that prices moved into sharp backwardation, with oil for immediate delivery commanding a premium of some 40 percent over later delivery dates.

Nor does this style of argument, whether for grain or oil, admit that some of the seemingly perverse private behavior may be a result of public policy. As noted in Chapter 13, speculative attack is a rational response to the rigid public policy of defending a price floor. Verleger (1982) has made a convincing case that the increase in private stocks of crude oil during the supply disruption of 1979 was a rational reaction to the government's price regulations, which kept the price of crude artificially low relative to the consumption value of refined products. Such private responses should not be taken as evidence of irrational panic buying during a shortage.

Reserves to obtain a strategic advantage

A more convincing rationale for a public stockpile to supplement private storage is to reduce the probability of a disruption. Under the control of a single agency – the government – the stockpile can intimidate any exporter who is contemplating a supply disruption for political reasons. If disruptions or embargoes are part of a dominant producer's or cartel's effort to exploit consumers, the presence of stockpiles themselves may alter the frequency of this disruption, as has been pointed out by Nichols and Zeckhauser (1977) and Crawford et al. (1984).

Of course, the notion of a strategic reserve presupposes that the public interest excludes the welfare of an opposing party. Although such strategic considerations may go far in justifying the SPR for oil, they cannot justify public programs in a closed economy, like eighteenth-century France, where the social welfare encompasses all groups. In the analysis in this chapter, we concentrate on the case of a closed economy, be it an individual country or the whole world.

In passing, we would like to make three comments regarding "strategic" arguments for public storage:

1. Extractions of rents from trading partners may be possible even if disruptions are fully exogenous. (Recall the differential effects on

consumption and price in the discussion of systems with net trade in Section 9.4.)

2. It is by no means obvious that net importers are helped by stockpiles larger than otherwise. Although subsidies to storage may be a hidden trade weapon, the incidence of consumption stabilization schemes depends importantly on the curvature of consumption demand. Who knows what the parameter C is for U.S. demand for oil?

3. Although it may be comforting to have a large stockpile when dealing with a producer cartel, it is by no means obvious that a consuming country's acquisition of that stockpile is advisable. After all, the stockpile must be purchased from the cartel. Moreover, the ability to stockpile a commodity such as oil may, paradoxically, work against the strategic interests of an importer opposed by a cartel, by impeding credible commitment to a consumption plan preferred *ex ante* by both of the opposing parties. This is shown by Eaton and Eckstein (1984) for a two-period model.

Externalities

According to Hogan (1983, p. 70), discussing oil stocks, "[t]here is no doubt that a large government role is essential, the externalities are too great to rely on private stockpiles." If many small firms store oil, collectively they reduce the price during a cutoff. Because individually they will not account directly for this benefit from collective action, supposedly they will not store enough.[4] A related externality supposedly arises because they will not account for their effect on the price when putting oil into store. How the two externalities balance out supposedly determines the level of private storage compared to socially optimal storage. Only a large player, namely the government, can internalize these externalities.

This argument confuses pecuniary externalities with nonpecuniary ones. In an otherwise undistorted competitive equilibrium, the benefit to society upon release of one more unit from a small firm's stockpile is the price of that commodity. The return to the firm is none other than that price. Society and the individual firm have the same incentive. Likewise, the cost of acquisition, whether to society or to an individual firm, is the prevailing spot price. The collective storage by a competitive industry maximizes social welfare. A public stockpile can do no better. It should not store more based on vague arguments concerning externalities and public goods.

---

4   A similar argument says that individual consuming countries will rely on the stockpiles of others. This "beggar thy neighbor" policy supposedly induces too little collective storage.

Macroeconomic repercussions

The fourth broad rationale for supplemental public stockpiles parallels the externality argument. Because private storers do not consider the macroeconomic dislocations of big swings in energy prices, they store too little, or so the argument goes. Similarly, Brandow (1977) includes the relationship between food prices and industrial wage rates as one argument for public storage of grains. This style of argument is as shaky as the one based on externalities. In a flexible, competitive, undistorted, closed economy at full employment, the cost of macroeconomic change due to the shortage of one barrel of oil is the price of one barrel of oil, the private signal for storage.

Of course, the macroeconomy may not mimic the smooth adjustments of a competitive general equilibrium. The economy may have, for example, the rigidity of fixed wage contracts, or taxes tied to first-in–first-out cost accounting. If the argument for supplemental public storage rests on these rigidities, they should be modeled explicitly, as pointed out by Pindyck (1980). "Second-best" arguments cannot be evaluated unless the relevant constraints are identified. Unfortunately, the fundamental sources of macroeconomic market failures (and indeed their existence) are still the subject of fierce debate. Because second-best prescriptions are not necessarily robust to changes in the supposed constraints, macroeconomic justifications for storage interventions rest on shaky ground. This is not to deny their potential importance; but the arguments must be made more precise before it is possible to conduct the critical evaluation that could make them persuasive. Of course, if agreement were reached on the sources of any macroeconomic disequilibria, it might be possible to reach agreement on their direct elimination, in lieu of the remedy of public stockpiles.

Price ceilings

Price ceilings reduce the incentive for private storage. More precisely, a regime that will have a ceiling imposed in those periods when the market price is some specified distance above its long-run mean affects, through anticipations, the current decision to store even though the price ceiling is not in effect currently. The prospect of abrogations of private contracts under high prices, such as declarations of *force majeure,* may add to the fear of private storers that they will not receive full value for their stocks. The possibility of forced requisitions are another reason private storers may have too little incentive to store.

As Plummer (1982) has noted concerning oil, restrictions on where and to whom inventories can be sold reduce the private incentive to store. The confiscatory government actions under the Emergency Petroleum Allocation Act of 1973 will long remain in firms' memories; they will not easily be convinced to hold inventories above working levels. Countries in which hoarders are beaten or arrested for selling grain at high prices are unlikely to have optimal private stocks of food.

Thus, price ceilings and related restrictions on private exchange are reasonable justifications for supplemental public storage. The remainder of this chapter will concentrate on this rationale for public intervention, with Sections 15.2 and 15.3 devoted to a more systematic description of the distortions arising from a regime with price ceilings.

15.2   The effects of price ceilings on private storage

Political pressure for a regime of price ceilings builds up from the perception of "obscene" and "undeserved" profits from holding commodities. Because commodity prices are inherently volatile, those who produce, store, or speculate in a commodity will enjoy sporadic windfalls. Such large gains, even if only occasional, will appear to many to be "too" large in comparison to the returns to most other activities. Worse, the size of the profit will all too obviously depend on vagaries such as weather and war rather than on the wisdom and talent of the speculator. Speculative profits become an obvious political target.

Because of the collective operation of storage itself, the distribution of percentage returns to storage is skewed. Losses are more frequent but of smaller average size than the average profits in profitable years; the median percentage return is negative. (Mean profits are zero by the nature of competitive storage.) This asymmetry must have some effect on the political pressure for price ceilings. If most periods had slight positive returns and a few periods extreme losses – that is, if distribution of returns were skewed in the opposite direction – the political discussion might well emphasize bailouts of storers.

Another fact of life is that a regime of price ceilings can be self-justifying. Because price ceilings reduce the incentive to store, the frequency and extent of extreme shortages becomes higher. That is to say, the marginal valuation of consumption, whatever the constrained market price, is above the ceiling P^C a greater percentage of periods with the imposition of a ceiling. This regularity emerges clearly in Table 15.1. The table derives from simulations of storage behavior with a linear demand curve, $\eta^d = -0.2$ at the point (q^N, P^N); marginal storage costs $k = \$2.0$; and $r = 5$ percent. To isolate the effects of the price ceiling on storage, we set $\eta^s = 0.0$; $\sigma_h = 10.0$ units.[5] A commodity market with undistorted private storage and these parameters displays marginal consumption value (and market price) above $160 during 4.78 percent of the periods; yet the same system with a ceiling of $160 on the market price

[5]   This is a system examined extensively in Chapters 4–6.

Table 15.1. *Effect of price ceilings on steady-state storage*

	Regime			
	No ceiling	Ceiling of $160	Ceiling of $140	Ceiling of $120
Percent of marginal consumption values				
$\geq$ $160	4.78	4.95	5.30	5.99
$\geq$ $140	9.32	9.65	10.26	11.59
$\geq$ $120	16.47	16.94	17.88	19.84
Mean marginal consumption value	$100.00	100.00	100.00	100.00
Mean market price	$100.00	98.73	97.13	93.65
Mean storage	8.71	8.51	7.98	6.80
Percent with no storage	20.94	22.91	26.37	33.19

has the marginal consumption value above $160 during 4.95 percent of the periods. Likewise, the marginal consumption value would be above $140 during 9.32 percent of the periods without the distortion of a price ceiling, but 10.26 percent of the periods with a ceiling at that level. Whatever the ceiling, the mean steady-state marginal consumption value for this system is $100 because the consumption demand curve is linear. Thus, political supporters of a price ceiling may defend it for controlling "extremely high" prices without realizing that anticipation of the ceiling increases the number of periods that the ceiling is in effect, as well as the severity of shortages.

Part and parcel, a regime of price ceilings depresses the average amount stored privately. As can be seen in Table 15.1, this effect becomes increasingly pronounced the lower the price ceiling, such that average storage with a ceiling of $120 is merely 78 percent of average storage without any ceiling. The decline in the average amount stored derives from two related sources: First, with a price ceiling the proportion of periods without any storage is higher; second, even when storage is positive, there is less in store.

Storage rules under price ceilings

These statistics on the average amount stored and the percentage of consumption prices above a particular level are but symptoms of the effect of price ceilings. The fundamental mutation is in the storage rule. For the case of a permanent regime with a price ceiling P^C equal to $120, the reduced-form relationship for equilibrium storage is shown in Figure 15.1, along with the relationship with no distortion. (Both are for the same parameters as for the cases in Table 15.1.) The storage rule with the price ceiling is deduced in the same style as the rule with no distortions: dynamic programming and a polynomial approximation in the amount stored to the price storers expect to re-

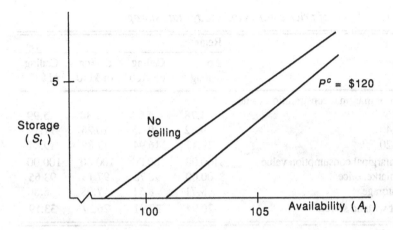

Figure 15.1. Storage rule with a regime of price ceilings.

ceive. The price ceiling affects these numerical methods only to the extent it alters the price the storers expect to receive. In other words, private competitive storage continues to follow the same complementary inequalities, although now with the distorted market price $\hat{P}_t$ rather than the marginal consumption price value P_t. Thus, the reduced-form equation for equilibrium storage, $S_t = f[A_t | P^C]$, is implicit in

$$\hat{P}_t + k = (1+r)^{-1} E_t[\hat{P}_{t+1}], \qquad S_t > 0$$
$$\hat{P}_t + k > (1+r)^{-1} E_t[\hat{P}_{t+1}], \qquad S_t = 0$$

(15.1)

The complementary inequalities in (15.1) compress an important economic argument. They presume that private storers continue to make zero profits on average. On first impression, this statement may seem to contradict the previous argument that "obscenely high" profits breed the political pressure for price ceilings. After all, by construction the average profit to storage in a system without price ceilings is zero. A truncation of the returns would seem to require negative profits. But storage behavior does not remain constant upon the introduction of a regime with a price ceiling. Indeed, it changes so that average (excess) profits remain at zero in the new equilibrium. Owners of stocks or fixed assets such as land at the time of an unanticipated imposition of a price-ceiling regime suffer losses in wealth, but the new regime does not affect the mean subsequent returns.

To understand the forces at work keeping average profits from storage at zero, imagine a situation where private storers are on the verge of committing themselves to, say, 6.0 units collectively at a price of $95.10 per unit out of an availability of 107.00 units when a public agency decrees that beginning

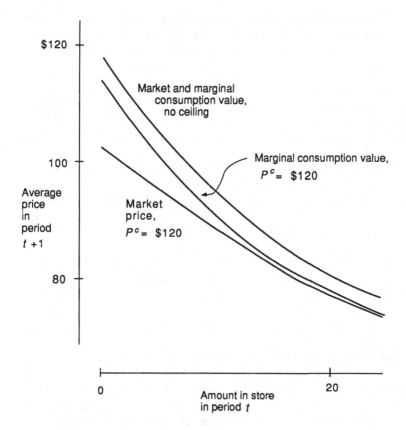

Figure 15.2. Price expected for next period as a function of current storage.

with the next period market price cannot be above $120.[6] Whereas the storers had been anticipating a price of $101.96,[7] they must recalculate the average price the next period. It would be on the lowest curve shown in Figure 15.2. Clearly, they would lose money were they to proceed with 6.0 units. Their individual bids for less to put into store have two effects in the aggregate:

1. The current price falls because of the lower demand for storage out of current availability.
2. With a smaller carryover, the average market price for the next period is higher. (True, it will not increase the expected market price

---

[6] They may have already sold any of their carryover from the previous period, or if not, the capital loss on those holdings with the announcement of the regime of price ceilings does not affect their decisions about the next carryover.

[7] $101.96 = (95.10 + 2.00) \times (1.0 + .05)$.

with the ceiling in effect as much as the same reduction in carryover would with no distortions. Note that in Figure 15.2 the curve for expected price without a ceiling is more steeply sloped than the curve for expected market price with a regime of ceilings.)

These two movements combine to restore the equilibrium, because at some amount stored the arbitrage condition (15.1) holds. For an availability of 107.00 units, the equilibrium has a current price of $89.04, an expected market price for the next period of $95.56, and storage of 4.81 units. This pair (107.00, 4.81) is one point on the storage rule with P^C = $120 in Figure 15.1. The corresponding pair (4.81, $95.56) in price–storage space is one point on the curve in Figure 15.2 marked "Market price, P^C = $120."

The two storage rules in Figure 15.1 most obviously differ in the amount stored at any given availability. The rule with a ceiling is shifted to the right. Storage under a regime of a price ceiling of $120 is typically about one unit less, in line with the difference in average storage given positive storage calculated above from Table 15.1. Also differing are the slopes of the two storage rules. The marginal propensity to store out of availability, given that storage is positive, is higher for the rule with a price ceiling. The part of the rule with positive storage is distorted more at lower availabilities, say, 103.0 units, than at, say, 114.0. This reflects the difference in the chance that the price ceiling will come into play any time soon. Figure 15.2 illustrates this in the difference between the expected marginal consumption value and the expected market price, both under the ceiling. At high current availabilities and, hence, high amounts carried out, the vagaries in the harvest are less likely to raise price to the ceiling during the next few periods. Consequently, the incentive to store is closer to the expected market price without a ceiling.

The permanence of a regime of price ceilings

The distinction between direct and indirect effects of a price ceiling deserves emphasis. The price ceiling affects consumption in the current period indirectly, via its effect on the price distribution in the next period. If storage occurs, it is at a current price far below the price ceiling. For example, with P^C = $120, storage occurs only if the price is below $95.77. Furthermore, the effect of the ceiling in the next period is not confined to those harvest outcomes that lead to a high price. Storage and by extension price in that period are depressed because the prospect of the price ceiling in yet later periods affects storage demand in that period. This cumulative effect of a permanent regime of price ceilings makes the distortion of current behavior far larger than that of a price ceiling confined to a single period.

Of course, regimes with price controls come and go with the political winds, and so the assumption of a permanent price ceiling may overstate the shift in the storage rule upon announcement of a regime change.[8] Neverthe-less, the general patterns remain even if the application of a price ceiling in a relevant period is probabilistic. The system should behave much like the one with a higher but certain price ceiling.[9]

Price ceilings, whether certain or merely possible, distort storage behavior through their effect on storers' anticipations about the future. The forward-looking nature of storage decisions is also the reason the government cannot remove fully the distortion caused by the price ceilings. Because of the many policies of price controls and forced requisitions throughout history, no gov-ernment can convince storers (and producers) that it will never in the future impose a price ceiling. By their nature governments can change laws, and cur-rent governments generally cannot commit their successors to a given course of action. On the relatively small matter of the initial imposition of a price ceiling on a particular commodity, a government may be restrained by the consequences to its reputation. But the possibility of the government's suc-cumbing to expediency cannot be excluded. And if a ceiling currently exists, reputation is a hindrance. When the ceiling is not binding, the government cannot establish its newfound good faith by some current action, such as by revoking the current price ceiling, because that action does not preclude re-imposition when the price rises. This inability discourages private storers so that they store less than is socially optimal, thus increasing the possibility of short supplies in the future and the pressure to reimpose controls. Ironically, the fundamental distortion of storage behavior and the main justification for public supplementation of private storage is the government's inability to bind itself never to confiscate or limit the profits from storage.[10]

15.3 The effect of price ceilings in a system with two locations

Private storers, worried about the prospects for price ceilings, will collectively store too little; thus, there is a role for public storage. A public agency might use the expected local marginal consumption value rather than

[8] On the other hand, the imposition of a ceiling may increase the chances of a lower ceiling in the future, offsetting the possibility that the ceiling will rise.

[9] If the caprices of politics bring to office parties with different philosophies about price ceilings, the storage rule becomes a function of two state variables, one the current availability and the other an index of the current political conditions. As with other problems with two state variables, such as serial correlation in the weather or season-ality in demand, the computation of the storage rule is possible.

[10] In modern jargon, the government's maintenance of a regime of price ceilings is "time consistent," the "closed-loop" strategy of a repeated game. A pledge never to impose a ceiling is the optimal "open-loop" strategy in an otherwise undistorted economy, but it is "time inconsistent" and not credible.

the depressed expected market price as a guide. Policy analysts can discuss the proper behavioral rule for the public agency and its interaction with existing private storage.

Yet, if the government's interest rate and physical storage costs are no greater than those of private storers, and if there is but a single commodity involved, the exercise in policy analysis is trivial. The public agency should behave exactly as undistorted private storage. With a lower expected return at all availabilities because of the distortion of the price ceiling, private storers are supplanted entirely. For this reason, Teisberg (1981) in his dynamic programming model of oil storage argues that private stockpiles can be ignored.

In reality private stocks of oil coexist with the Strategic Petroleum Reserve. A model that allows no role for private storage, such as Teisberg's or Chao and Manne's (1983), cannot hope to assess a policy of public storage of oil designed as a supplement to private storage. Each extra unit of public storage does not necessarily add a unit to total stocks.

If private storage is observed to adjust less than one-for-one to changes in public stocks, the inference is that storage costs must be different, or that the storage must be of slightly different commodities. This second possibility is likely to be the more relevant one. After all, oil in the SPR in Louisiana is subtly different from oil in Connecticut. Consequently, the model of two related commodities, developed in Chapters 9 and 10, is an appropriate tool for studying flexible public storage as a supplement to private storage.

The specific example studied

The discussion would become interminable if the many permutations of public storage were combined with every version of the model for two locations or two commodities. The approach for the rest of this chapter is to use a single interesting example, in which two locations can trade. Thus, the transportation can go from commodity (and location) a to commodity (and location) b, or, if prices warrant, the opposite direction. The two locations can be thought of as two regions of the same country (which country is a closed economy). To have some of the properties of the models of a processing industry in Chapter 10, the marginal costs of shipping are not constant over all quantities shipped. The marginal transportation costs are set at

$$z = (0.10 + 0.02|Z| + 0.003Z^2 + 0.0004|Z|^3) * sign \, [Z]$$

This function is plotted in Figure 15.3 over the typical amounts shipped.[11]

---

[11]   The resulting transport costs are usually 1 or 2 percent of value, in line with the costs of shipping gasoline, say, from one city to a neighboring city (see Spiller and Huang 1986). Were the marginal transportation costs much lower, the system would behave much like that for a single commodity. Were the transportation costs much higher, the two stockpiles would appear to represent two separate commodities.

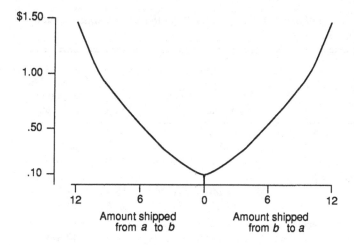

Figure 15.3. Marginal transport costs assumed.

Because the choice of location of the public stockpile is an interesting question, the example should not be symmetric. Also it is interesting to investigate the effect on planned production. For these reasons, production at location a is made perfectly inelastic, with its weather disturbance v^a having a standard deviation of 14.14 units, while location b's production has a supply elasticity $\eta^s = 1.0$, and v^b with a standard deviation of 10.00 units. The exogenous random disturbances v^a and v^b are uncorrelated. Including the endogenous variation in the planned supply of b in response to fluctuations in the producers' incentive price, the variances of the new supplies of each commodity are nearly equal when the system is undistorted by price ceilings. Of the truly exogenous uncertainty (the weather), on the other hand, location a has two-thirds of the collective variance. (The random term in the harvest at b is modeled as additive rather than multiplicative, so that the underlying uncertainty does not change with the type of public intervention.)

Aside from these differences in the variance and elasticity of production, there are no asymmetries. The demand curves at both locations are constant elasticity $\eta^d = -0.2$. Under certainty there would be no trade: Supply would equal demand in each region. Marginal physical storage costs are $2.00 at each location; the interest rate is 5 percent per period.

Thus, the chosen example is typical of the systems studied in Chapter 9 on storage and trade. But because of the relatively higher variance of weather, the roles of storage and transportation are more important. As can be seen in Table 15.2, 83.18 percent of the periods have at least some storage at one of the locations. Because its production is both more variable and less elastic, the majority of storage is at location a. Trade, however, transmits most of the

Table 15.2. *Effect of price ceilings on system with two locations (standard deviations in parentheses)*

	Regime			
	No distortions	Ceiling of $130	Ceiling of $110	Ceiling of $110, transportation undistorted
Percent of prices at *a*				
≥ $130	8.94	11.49	19.08	19.65
≥ $110	16.58	22.39	25.06	30.10
Percent of prices at *b*				
≥ $130	7.60	6.30	15.45	19.21
≥ $110	15.62	21.39	22.64	30.57
Mean consumption value at *a*	$101.52	111.14	122.67	110.61
	(26.95)	(75.22)	(104.26)	(42.32)
Mean consumption value at *b*	$100.92	102.29	109.94	111.19
	(23.65)	(25.15)	(42.45)	(39.48)
Mean planned production at *b*	100.44	99.50	97.66	97.93
	(5.34)	(4.26)	(2.95)	(3.06)
Mean amount shipped	−0.19	0.53	1.49	0.94
from *a* to *b*	(6.20)	(5.83)	(5.38)	(6.71)
Mean storage at *a*	9.56	7.06	4.77	4.98
	(9.57)	(8.33)	(7.13)	(7.36)
Mean storage at *b*	6.06	4.97	3.26	3.45
	(6.61)	(6.12)	(5.12)	(5.33)
Percent with no storage	16.82	26.43	40.55	39.81
Percent with nothing shipped	11.19	14.95	21.81	9.15

shocks in one location to the other; the standard deviation of P^a is only slightly higher than the standard deviation of P^b.

The various distortions caused by price ceilings

In this system a regime of price ceilings causes multifaceted distortions. These three effects can all be seen in Table 15.2:

1. In line with the results for a single commodity, mean storage, whether of commodity *a* or of *b*, declines with an increasing severity of the ceiling.[12]
2. Price ceilings reduce mean planned production at location *b*. As a re-

---

12 The same ceiling P^C is assumed to apply at both locations, that is, to both commodities, so that the authorities do not necessarily recognize them as distinct.

sult, on average some of commodity a is shipped to location b, the opposite of the average trade balance under no distortions.

3. Price ceilings distort and reduce overall trade. Although, for example, commodity b may be in abundance and commodity a in great shortage, shippers will act as if the shortfall is much less severe, indeed one that corresponds to the constrained market price rather than the local marginal consumption value. This distortion of shippers' incentives reduces the steady-state standard deviation of the amount shipped, and increases the percentage of periods with no trade.

In the manner of all systems with storage, the distortions feed back on one another. For example, the decline in average production reduces storage further.

Distortion of the transportation sector raises a whole host of issues. Implicitly it presumes a transportation industry fully constrained by the price ceilings; that is, no matter how much the marginal consumption value in location a is above the ceiling (i.e., no matter how far above P^C is the black market price at location a), no trade flows from location b beyond that dictated by the ceiling. There is no smuggling and no transportation by individual consumers. For highly visible bulk commodities this may be a reasonable representation.[13] The other extreme is to suppose individual consumers can transport the commodity themselves at the same cost (but cannot store). In that case the local marginal consumption values P^a and P^b are the relevant signals; the transportation industry remains undistorted, except through indirect effects by way of storage and production. These two extremes of a distorted and undistorted transportation sector will be considered here. No doubt the most realistic formulation is some mixture of the two extremes: Transportation by individual consumers is more costly than the conventional arrangement, but will be employed if the discrepancy between the market price and the marginal consumption value rises above the cost differential.

This seemingly minor issue of the effect of price ceilings on trade between the two locations leads to profound differences in variables such as mean

[13] Equivalent to the effect of price ceilings on the transportation sector would be outright restrictions on trade whenever local prices reach some level. Export prohibitions depending on the current price were a key feature of English Corn Laws, whereas in eighteenth-century France a distinct type of riot, an *entrave*, developed nearly into an institution through which peasants or small-town dwellers stopped grain convoys in order to preserve local production for local consumption (Hufton 1985). Modern versions include the zonal system in postindependence India, which imposed restrictions on movements of grain between states when there was a scarcity (Bhatia 1970). In the United States, examples include the quickly aborted soybean export embargo of President Nixon and the supplier/purchaser freeze of U.S. energy regulations of the 1970s, which allocated refined products by historical use and not current needs, much to the disadvantage of regions with above-average growth in demand (Horwich and Weimer 1984).

storage and the variances of local marginal consumption values. More to the point, a price ceiling's effect on trade strongly influences the extent public storage substitutes for private storage, as will be shown in Section 15.5, and the welfare ranking of the possible interventions, as will be shown in Section 15.6. In short, an issue assumed away in the conventional single-commodity models of public storage is one of the most crucial.

For the moment the emphasis will be on the case where the price ceilings distort trade. The deadweight loss from such a regime of price ceilings is larger and the potential gain from public intervention into storage correspondingly greater than when trade is undistorted. According to Table 15.2, distortion of trade is disproportionately harmful to consumers at location a. The mean and variance of the local marginal consumption value P^a is much higher than if trade remains (directly) undistorted. Yet with trade undistorted the proportion of marginal consumption values of either commodity a or b above the ceiling ($110 in this instance) is higher. The advantage of an undistorted transportation industry is that it alleviates extremely high prices, say, above $180. More surprising at first glance is that average S^a and S^b are both higher if trade remains undistorted. It might seem that if in the event of a shortage at one location supplies will not be shipped from the other location, the role for storage should be larger. But private storers will not make that calculation, for they receive at most the ceiling price. Moreover, one of the uses for a quantity in store is to send it to the other location, where it can be sold at the unconstrained marginal consumption value. This derived demand increases the incentive to store.

15.4   Possible public policies for supplementing private storage

An overabundance of schemes for offsetting the harmful outcomes of a regime of price ceilings can be proposed. Here three will receive scrutiny:

1.   a subsidy to private storage;
2.   public storage using the consumption price at the location of the public stockpile; and
3.   public storage maximizing social welfare and accounting for its effect on the amount of private storage and the amount transported.

Among them, the two with public storage will receive most of the attention. For the moment, both public storage schemes will operate at location a. (Commodity a, recall, is relatively more in need of storage because it has inelastic production and more variable weather.)

Each of these three candidates is more advanced than any observed public intervention designed to supplement private storage. Nevertheless, they deserve study as they are often held up as a standard for actual schemes.[14] They also illustrate well the issues of substitution of public storage for private storage and the feedback effects of a policy.

These three policies under consideration will be judged in part by their effect on the present value of current and future social welfare over the infinite horizon, given the current availabilities A_t^a and A_t^b. The expected present value of deadweight loss of a price ceiling of $110, transportation distorted, is, depending on the initial availabilities, around 14 percent of certainty revenue R^N, one period's certainty expenditure on the pair of commodities. From the perspective of a government that treats all consumers and producers as equal, such small changes in total social welfare are the sole justification for intervention in storage markets. Of course, the much larger swings in the welfare of subgroups, such as consumers at location a who may, judging from the statistics in Table 15.2, garner the lion's share of a public storage program, go far toward explaining the political pressure for the intervention. We could calculate the incidence of the various programs on producers and consumers in the two locations and on the transportation sector, but distribution is too lengthy a topic to be considered here. In any event, all these groups are included in the measure of social welfare. The social welfare is the welfare of a closed economy.

Public storage following local marginal consumption values

Among these policies with direct public storage, the one using the local marginal consumption value of commodity a is most like conventional private storage in its operation. Its storage incentive $\hat{P}^a$ is the same as the market price P^a plus the black-market price of a ration coupon. In this case the public behavioral equations for S^a are like the arbitrage equations of undistorted private storage:

$$P^a[A_t^a - Z_t - S_t^a] + k^a = (1+r)^{-1}E_t[P_{t+1}^a], \qquad S_t^a > 0$$

$$P^a[A_t^a - Z_t - S_t^a] + k^a \geq (1+r)^{-1}E_t[P_{t+1}^a], \qquad S_t^a = 0 \qquad (15.2)$$

---

[14] A price-band scheme, representative of the most common public storage program in practice, is not included for two reasons. First, price-band schemes were discussed in Chapter 14 (although there as a distortion of a first-best world). Second, a price-band scheme is known in advance not to be the best possible intervention into an already distorted market. A price-band scheme, with its purchase and release prices set from the onset, is an example of a fixed rule, one unresponsive to changes in current conditions (represented by the state variables). In the presence of uncertainty, the presumption is in favor of rules contingent on the state variables, that is, in favor of discretion (Buiter 1981, 1989). Also a particular price-band scheme is not necessarily the best intervention in the class of fixed policies. (Of course, a price-band scheme does have the advantage of simplicity. Ghosh et al. [1984] have studied the difference between simple and optimal rules.)

Although conducted by a single agency, this behavior is the same as that of a large number of decentralized agencies, each so small that it takes the local marginal consumption value P^a as given.[15]

This policy of using the expected local marginal consumption value as the storage incentive does not account for the effects on the other endogenous variables. For example, it does not account for the full social value of shipping some of the commodity that has been stored at location a to b if the marginal consumption value in b is very high in the next period. This oversight would not arise if the local consumption value at location a in that period differed from the local consumption value at b by the marginal social cost of transportation. But here the price ceilings distort that connection.

Nor does the policy using the expected next period's local marginal consumption value at a acknowledge that the social value of any commodity a stored again in the next period is not measured by the local marginal consumption value of a that period. This is because the prospect of price ceilings drives a wedge between the marginal value of consumption at location a the next period and the marginal value of consumption at a in the next more distant period. For that matter, there will be a discrepancy between the marginal value of commodity b consumed the next period and its value if stored; so that even if the price of b is below the ceiling should shipments flow from a to b in the next period, a weighting scheme should be applied.

Finally, the local marginal consumption value does not account for the effect of public storage of a on current private activities. For example, by raising the current price at a, current public storage in a reduces any incentive to ship to b currently. If the commodity in b is in great shortage currently, that policy increases future welfare at a considerable expense in current welfare. Similarly, when there is large current availability at b, a greater amount of a in storage reduces $E_t[\hat{P}^b_{t+1}]$ and thus storage at b. For all these reasons, the marginal consumption value in a is not the social shadow price.

Public storage accounting for private reactions

This logic of tracing the effects of public storage of commodity a leads to the second public storage policy under consideration. The government explicitly seeks to store the amount at location a that will maximize the present value of social welfare net of costs, given current availabilities A_t^a and A_t^b and the behavior for private storage at location b and for private transportation from a to b or from b to a. Formally, its objective is the value function:

---

[15]   In regards to oil, this is the case of many consuming countries managing their own reserves based on the local marginal value of oil.

$$J[S_t^a, S_t^b, Z_t | A_t^a, A_t^b] = \int_0^{A_t^a - S_t^a - Z_t} P^a[q^a]dq^a + \int_0^{A_t^b - S_t^b + Z_t} P^b[q^b]dq^b$$

$$- k^a S_t^a - k^b S_t^b - \int_0^{Z_t} z[Z]dZ + (1+r)^{-1}W[S_t^a, S_t^b]$$

$$(15.3)$$

The first two terms in J represent the surpluses from current consumption of commodities at locations a and b.[16] The next two terms are the total physical storage costs, while $\int z\, dZ$ is the total cost of transporting quantity Z_t. The last term, $W[S_t^a, S_t^b]$, represents the expected contribution to future welfare made by the carryovers S_t^a and S_t^b. It includes the costs H of production at b (where supply is elastic) planned for period $t+1$ associated with those amounts of storage.[17] That is,

$$W[S_t^a, S_t^b] = E_t[J[S_{t+1}^a, S_{t+1}^b, Z_{t+1} \mid \bar{h}^a + v_{t+1}^a + S_t^a, \bar{h}^b[E_t[\hat{P}_{t+1}^b]] + v_{t+1}^b + S_t^b]]$$

$$- H[E_t[\hat{P}_{t+1}^b[S_t^a, S_t^b]]]] \qquad (15.4)$$

The costs of past production and storage represented in the availabilities A_t^a and A_t^b are sunk costs irrelevant to the selection of S_t^a.

Public storage S_t^a is selected to maximize J. When $S_t^a > 0$, the public arbitrage equation is

$$\partial J / \partial S_t^a = 0 = -P^a(1 + \partial Z_t / \partial S_t^a) - P^b(\partial S_t^b / \partial S_t^a - \partial Z_t / \partial S_t^a)$$

$$- k^a - k^b(\partial S_t^b / \partial S_t^a) - z[Z_t](\partial Z_t / \partial S_t^a)$$

$$+ (1+r)^{-1}(\partial W / \partial S_t^a) + (1+r)^{-1}(\partial W / \partial S_t^b)(\partial S_t^b / \partial S_t^a)$$

$$(15.5)$$

(Were the public stockpile storing commodity b, the relevant arbitrage equation would be the corresponding first-order condition $\partial J / \partial S_t^b$.)

In (15.5) the terms involving $\partial S_t^b / \partial S_t^a$ and $\partial Z_t / \partial S_t^a$ capture the private reactions to the public storage. When private storage is constrained at zero by the nonnegativity constraint, $\partial S_t^b / \partial S_t^a = 0$. Otherwise that partial derivative must be obtained by implicit differentiation of the behavioral relationship for private storage, namely, the arbitrage equation

$$M \equiv \hat{P}_t^b[A_t^b - S_t^b + Z_t] + k^b - (1+r)^{-1}E_t[\hat{P}_{t+1}^b[S_t^a, S_t^b]] = 0 \qquad (15.6)$$

---

[16] If one group were excluded as being foreigners, the surplus could be adjusted accordingly, by $-h_t^b \hat{P}_t^b$ if they were producers at b, for example.

[17] Because the weather disturbance is additive, the producer incentive price P_t^r equals the expected market price.

(This notation for $E_t[\hat{P}^b_{t+1}]$ is used to emphasize that the current carryouts influence the price the next period.) The reaction of contemporary private storage (when positive) to public storage is then

$$\frac{dS^b_t}{dS^a_t} = \frac{-\partial M / \partial S^a_t}{\partial M / \partial S^b_t} = \frac{-(1+r)^{-1} \partial E_t[\hat{P}^b_{t+1}] / \partial S^a_t}{\partial \hat{P}^b_t / \partial q^b_t + (1+r)^{-1} \partial E_t[\hat{P}^b_{t+1}] / \partial S^b_t} \quad (15.7)$$

The reaction of the transportation industry is found by similar implicit differentiation of the equation for the equilibrium in transportation with $Z_t > 0$:

$$L \equiv \hat{P}^a_t[A^a_t - S^a_t - Z_t] \quad + z[Z_t] - \hat{P}^b_t[A^b_t - S^b_t + Z_t] = 0 \quad (15.8)$$

The reaction of the current private transportation to current public storage is

$$\frac{dZ_t}{dS^a_t} = \frac{-\partial L / \partial S^a_t}{\partial L / \partial Z_t} = \frac{\partial \hat{P}^a_t / \partial q^a_t}{-\partial \hat{P}^a_t / \partial q^a_t + \partial z[Z_t] / \partial Z_t - \partial \hat{P}^b_t / \partial q^b_t} \quad (15.9)$$

When $Z_t < 0$, the middle term in the denominator has a negative sign because of the nature of transportation costs. When $Z_t = 0$, dZ_t / dS^a_t is almost surely zero.

These private reaction functions are intricate, especially dS^b_t / dS^a_t for it includes $E_t[\hat{P}^b_{t+1}]$, which depends on all future storage. But it is possible to deduce the sign of dS^b_t / dS^a_t: It is unambiguously negative. $E_t[\hat{P}^b_{t+1}]$ falls as either S^a_t or S^b_t increases, given that the demand curves are downward sloping and the marginal transportation cost curve is upward sloping.

If there were no price ceilings to cause distortions and the government were to remain in the business of storing at location a, these private reaction functions would be immaterial. When rearranged, the public arbitrage equation (15.5) includes a set of terms $(P^b_t + k^b - (1+r)^{-1} \partial W / \partial S^b_t)(dS^b_t / dS^a_t)$. Without distortions $\partial W[S^a_t, S^b_t] / \partial S^b_t$ is $E_t[P^b_{t+1}]$. If S^b_t were greater than zero (and hence dS^b_t / dS^a_t not equal to zero), the expression in parentheses in the rearrangement would be zero because it is the arbitrage condition for storage at location b. For the same reasons, the terms in (15.5) involving Z_t, namely, $(P^a_t + z[Z_t] - P^b_t)(dZ_t / dS^a_t)$, would equal zero.

Several remarks are in order about $W[S^a_t, S^b_t]$ when there are distortions:

1. This function representing future welfare assumes that the public storage behavior determined by (15.5) is consistently followed in the future. In other words, it assumes this particular public policy for supplementing storage is permanent, just as it assumes the regime of price ceiling is permanent.

2. $\partial W / \partial S^a_t$ is not the expected marginal consumption value of commodity a, $E_t[P^a_{t+1}]$. W keeps track of all subsequent uses of S^a_t, not just consumption in location a the next period. Nor is the expected shadow price necessarily above the expected marginal local con-

sumption value. Public storage, concentrated in commodity a, shifts subsequent availabilities in that direction. Therefore, the expected social value of another unit at location a can be less than the expected marginal consumption value at location a. The expected social value of another unit at location b, in contrast, is much greater than the expected market price $E_t[\hat{P}_{t+1}^b]$.

3. $W[S_t^a, S_t^b]$ and by extension the objective function J need not be highest under the policy of maximizing the present value of social welfare given current availabilities and endogenous private sector responses. Thus, the other policies need not be dismissed out of hand and attention concentrated on this one. This counterintuitive result will be explained in Section 15.6.

Nash behavior versus Stackelberg leadership

The difference between a public storage agency's use of an expected marginal consumption value as a signal and full welfare maximization given current conditions can be characterized in the terminology of industrial organization economics. The government, which does all the storing of one of the pair of commodities, is unquestionably the major player or "dominant firm." The private storers of the other commodity and the firms in the transportation industry correspond to the "competitive fringe." The competitive fringe takes the actions of the dominant firm as given. The major player, in contrast, must decide what allowance to make for the effect of its own actions on the competitive fringe. At one extreme the dominant firm can ignore its effect on the competitive fringe; this is known as "Nash" behavior. It corresponds here to the public storage signal being the local marginal consumption value. At the other end of the spectrum is the dominant firm's full recognition of its effect; this is known as "Stackelberg leadership." It corresponds here to the effort at full welfare maximization.

The term "leadership" is sometimes used, often in the context of game theory, to indicate that one party sets policy first and the other parties follow. Here the government and private storers make their "moves" at the same time. Rather than the sequencing of decisions, here Stackelberg leadership emphasizes that the dominant party takes account of the effect of its action on the other parties when deciding on its own policy. Because a unilateral action by a single firm in the competitive fringe does not affect the other players, none of those firms takes account of the effects of its actions. Of course, collectively their actions have considerable effect. Each firm recognizes the overall effect but ignores its own contribution.

Although this terminology of "Nash" or "Stackelberg" could be used as a shorthand description of the two public storage policies, it is perhaps too

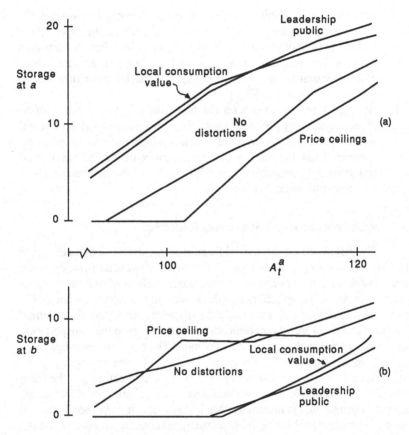

Figure 15.4. Storage rules with different public storage behavior, $A_t^b = 110$.

oblique.[18] Instead, the phrases "taking local consumption value" and "leadership behavior" will be used.

Storage rules

It remains in this section to discuss what differences these two public storage policies make to the storage and transportation rules and to the evolution of the time series of prices, storage, and production. The discussion verges on being hopelessly mystifying, because of the number of policies involved and because the rules are functions of two state variables. Because the main interest is in the government's storage behavior at location a, two slices

18 It should be stressed that the Nash behavior is found through dynamic programming, as recommended, for example, by Cohen and Michel (1988).

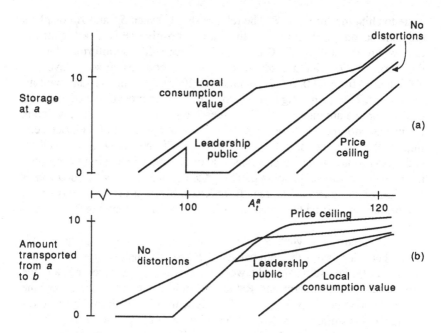

Figure 15.5. Storage and trade rules with different public storage behavior, $A_t^b = 90$.

at different levels of A_t^b through the three-dimensional diagram of the storage rules should suffice.[19] Figure 15.4 shows the amounts stored at a and b as a function of A_t^a given that $A_t^b = 110$ units. Figure 15.5 shows the relationships if A_t^b is much lower, specifically 90 units. At $A_t^b = 90$ there is no (private) storage at location b at any of the levels of A_t^a illustrated. Therefore, the rule for the amount shipped from a to b is substituted in Figure 15.5(b). All these relationships are the equilibrium amounts for the given pair of availabilities, supposing a particular regime.

In Figure 15.4 where A_t^b is large, the first reduced-form relationships to understand are those for no distortions. Those storage rules both display two kinks, which correspond to the boundaries of autarky. (Recall the discussion in Chapter 9.) Below $A_t^a = 109.5$, some of the b out of $A_t^b = 110$ is transported to location a. Trade is in the other direction if $A_t^a > 115.4$. Otherwise Z_t is 0.0.

Under a regime of price ceilings at \$110, the rule for S_t^b as a function of A_t^a, given $A_t^b = 110$, also displays two kinks corresponding to the shift from transportation of some of commodity b to location a to no trade and from no

---

[19] The storage rule for location a combines the "acquisition" and "drawdown" policies, to use the terminology of the SPR administrators.

trade to shipping from a to b. The relationship between S_t^a and A_t^a displays
only the second kink, however; the start of positive S_t^a is at a higher A_t^a
than where the shift to $Z_t = 0$ occurs. The price ceilings uniformly depress
the storage at location a at this level of A_t^b. In contrast, at some levels of
A_t^a, namely, from 98.0 to 102.7 and above 106.0, S_t^b is higher than with no
distortions. This surprising result comes from the indirect effect of the price
ceilings on the amount traded. The excessive storage at location b, which is
the private storage, is not because of the current operation of the price ceiling; at $A_t^a = 100$ and $A_t^b = 110$, both P_t^a and P_t^b are below \$110. Rather,
under conditions with no distortions, one of the uses of shipping from b to a
is to permit storage at location a. The price ceilings depress that demand at
location a and by extension trade from b to a. Some of that extra b is stored
in equilibrium, despite the prospect of the price ceilings applying the next period.

Public storage of a, whether following the local consumption price or leadership behavior, warps the split between S_t^a and S_t^b. The public rules are not
uniformly located somewhere between the private rule with ceilings and the
private rule with no distortions. Rather, the public rules differ more from the
rule with no distortions than does the rule with price ceilings. The rule for
storage at a is shifted considerably to the left, whereas private storage (at location b) becomes much less important.[20] Part and parcel the rule for the
amount transported is altered considerably. Over the whole range of A_t^a
illustrated for either public policy, some from b is shipped to a. (The kink in
the rules for S_t^a around $A_t^a = 105.00$ reflects the start of storage at location b.)
Of course, the amount of total storage, the sum of S_t^a and S_t^b, is much closer
to the amount with no distortions.

As shown in Figure 15.5, the differences between public storage following the local marginal consumption value and following "leadership" behavior are much more pronounced when $A_t^b = 90$ and not 110 – that is, when the
commodity at location b is relatively scarce rather than relatively abundant.
With no distortions, over the range of A_t^a shown, at least some a is shipped
to b to alleviate the shortage at b. With price ceilings this is true only if A_t^a is
greater than 98.5. Below that availability, both P_t^a and P_t^b are above \$110.
Constrained by the price ceilings, no trade takes place. Public storage at location a using the local marginal consumption value exacerbates this tendency.
The public storage incentive $E_t[P_{t+1}^a]$ with $S_t^b = 0$ and S_t^a as high as 6 or 7
units is above \$120. The current marginal consumption value P_t^a is above the

---

[20] That private storage (at b) under "leadership" public behavior lies for the most part to
the right of the storage rule when the government uses the local marginal consumption value of a may seem remarkable, since the leadership behavior might be expected
to mitigate the private reaction. That the private rule is driven further from its position with no distortions is due to the feedback effect of the public policy.

ceiling; none of a is shipped to b. In other words, if little is stored at location a, the expected marginal consumption value for the next period is high, on the order of $135. Consequently, the economic signals are to use the relative abundance at a for storage rather than for shipment to b, for the incentive to ship to b is merely the market price $110 because of the ceilings. But with consumption at b merely 90 units, the marginal consumption value at b is $169.35. Public storage following leadership behavior recognizes that under these circumstances a better use, in expectation, of commodity a than storage is immediate shipment to b. More precisely, the first-order condition (15.5) accounts for the immediate need in location b through the terms involving $\partial Z_t / \partial S_t^a$. Thus, over the range $99.8 < A_t^a < 104.4$, the equilibrium S_t^a is zero. Below $A_t^a = 99.8$, the equilibrium P_t^a would be above $110 even if little were stored at location a. The private transportation industry would not ship anything from a to b in any case. Given that the social value of a marginal unit at a expected for period $t+1$ is higher than the marginal value from current consumption, some amount is stored at a regardless of conditions at location b. This is the reason for the triangle at the left of the storage rule for commodity a under public leadership behavior.

The subtle differences in the operation of these two public storage policies, both storing at a, can be seen in time series of the marginal consumption values at a and b, such as those plotted in Figure 15.6. The paths evolve differently not only because of differences in the storage behavior for a given pair of A_t^a and A_t^b but because of the cumulative effect on the availabilities. Period 0 in Figure 15.6 follows one in which there was no carryout. Availabilities in period 0 are not identical, however, because of slightly different planned productions at location b (where supply is elastic).

The first noticeable difference between the two regimes is in period 2. Although P_2^b is nearly identical, P_2^a is higher under the policy of following the local marginal consumption value. As a storage incentive, $E_t[P_{t+1}^a]$ is higher than $\partial W / \partial S_t^a$. ($S_2^b$ is zero under both regimes.) Over periods 4–7, the accumulation of total storage is greater under the regime of leadership public storage, but it is disproportionately at location a. This proves unfortunate as the weather at location b is very bad in period 8 and the rising marginal transportation costs hinder the necessary shipment from location a.

The regime with leadership public behavior looks better in periods 13 and 14. The carryover from period 12 is slightly larger in total and proportionately more at location a. As events unfold in period 13, location a has the worse weather, so the inheritance from period 12 is especially well situated. In period 14, when there is a low A_t^b and relatively high A_t^a, the leadership behavior, by refraining from as much storage, keeps the market price low enough to induce some trade from a to b.

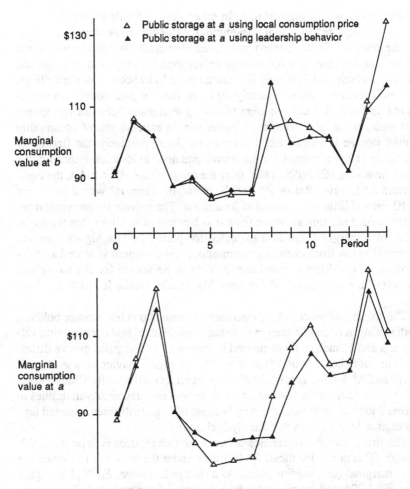

Figure 15.6. Time series of marginal consumption values with different public storage behavior.

15.5   The displacement of private storage by public storage

A frequent criticism of proposals for public storage such as the Strategic Petroleum Reserve is that much of the public storage merely replaces storage that would be undertaken privately. The supporters of public storage counter that if the program is sufficiently large, the marginal barrel in public storage is roughly a marginal barrel for the economy; it is offset by reductions in private storage only slightly, if at all.

These questions about the displacement of private storage can never be fully answered empirically, for it is difficult to estimate from the behavior of one

Table 15.3. *Substitution of public storage for private storage*

Regime	Mean total storage	Mean storage at a	at b	Percent of periods with		
				no storage	storage at a but not at b	storage at b but not at a
Undistorted private storage	15.62	9.56	6.06	16.82	16.07	5.81
Distorted private storage at both a and b	8.03	4.77	3.26	40.55	13.94	9.84
Public storage at a using consumption value at a; private storage at b	17.38	14.57	2.81	7.55	54.14	0.39
Public storage at a using leadership behavior; private storage at b	16.49	14.18	2.31	13.43	52.40	0.60

regime how the system would have evolved under another. Thus, the storage and transportation rules developed in the previous section for a system of two commodities have much to tell. They provide the controlled experiment not available in empirical data.

Displacement measured by average steady-state storage

Table 15.3 contains statistics on the stochastic steady state for the two cases with public storage developed in Section 15.4, along with purely private storage. The statistics are in line with the shifts in the storage rules discussed there, except that the feedback effects now emerge explicitly. As seen earlier in Table 15.2, the regime of price ceilings with no public intervention into storage cuts average total storage (i.e., $\bar{S}^a + \bar{S}^b$) nearly in half, from 15.62 to 8.03. Either of the public schemes raises average total storage. With public storage at location a supplementing private storage at location b, fewer periods have no storage. The storage, however, is twisted much in the favor of commodity a. In more than half the periods there is some public storage at a without any private storage at b. Rarely is there storage at b without any storage at a. In contrast, these proportions are more nearly equal under either a regime of no distortions or a regime with price ceilings and solely private storage. Under a regime of public storage at location a using the local marginal consumption value, mean private storage (now all at location b) falls from 8.03 to 2.81. Thus 35.83 percent of the average 14.57 units of public storage merely replaces private storage that would have occurred either at location a or b under a regime with price ceilings. The displacement rate for the policy of leadership public storage is slightly higher,

40.34 percent; both total storage and the remaining private storage at location b are lower.

Displacement during a string of good harvests

Another approach to the question of the displacement of private storage by public storage is to look at the accumulation of storage during a string of good harvests. The chosen string is a sequence of disturbance terms (the weather) at both locations one standard deviation above the means of zero. Because the standard deviation of v^a is greater than v^b and because planned production at location b is elastic, the availability and storage at a should become increasingly dominant. Inasmuch as the public storage is at location a, this setting should make public storage seem less inclined to replace private storage. This string might be taken as a reasonable lower bound on the extent of displacement.

In Figure 15.7 the paths of accumulation of S_t^a and S_t^b are shown for three regimes with price ceilings: solely private storage, public storage at location a using the expected marginal consumption value at a, and public storage at a using leadership behavior. Under all three regimes plotted, the amount of storage at either location converges to a level that reproduces itself, as is suggested by the declining additions to total storage. (Recall the discussion in Chapter 4.) The net addition of public storage to private storage in the regime of price ceilings is measured by the vertical distance from the triangles to the open dots.

The main insight from Figure 15.7 is that as the total accumulation grows the increase due to public storage becomes less important. The addition to total storage by either policy of public storage ranges from about 5 units in period 1 to 10 units in period 6. But total storage with solely private storage increases even faster. The marginal addition of public storage becomes less important. More of public storage merely displaces private storage. This suggests that as the SPR becomes full in a period of an oil glut it may be having its minimum effect on the total storage of oil.

The sensitivity of the displacement of private storage

Based on the schemes with public storage at location a in a system where the price ceilings distort the transportation industry, one is tempted to generalize about the displacement of private storage. Seemingly, some 35 percent of public storage replaces private storage, with this number being slightly higher if the public storage follows leadership behavior. Also public storage schemes seemingly increase average total storage beyond that with no distortions.

○ = Price ceilings, solely private storage
▲ = Public storage at *a* using local consumption value
△ = Public storage at *a* using leadership behavior

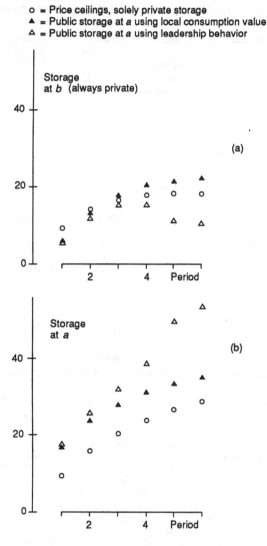

Figure 15.7. Accumulation of storage during a string of good harvests.

Not one of these generalizations holds up, even in the model under examination. Total storage would be much lower and the displacement rate much
higher if public storage were at location *b* instead of at *a*, especially if the
storage agency used the marginal consumption value at *b* as its signal. These
various statistics can be seen in Table 15.4. The displacement rates are also

Table 15.4. *Effect of location of public storage on its replacement of private storage*

Regime	Mean total storage	% of mean public out of mean total	% of public that replaces private
Price ceilings distort transportation			
Public storage at *a* using consumption value at *a*	17.38	83.83	35.83
Public storage at *b* using consumption value at *b*	11.41	65.38	54.69
Public storage at *a* using leadership behavior	16.49	85.99	40.34
Public storage at *b* using leadership behavior	14.30	74.27	40.96
Price ceilings do not distort transportation			
Public storage at *a* using consumption value at *a*	15.23	82.99	46.20
Public storage at *b* using consumption value at *b*	13.73	71.01	45.64
Public storage at *a* using leadership behavior	13.45	81.41	54.16
Public storage at *b* using leadership behavior	12.08	68.05	55.60

substantially different from one another if the price ceilings do not distort transportation along with storage and planned production.[21] The displacement

---

21   The behavior of the systems with and without transportation distorted provides an insight into "antihoarding" laws. Throughout history, a persistent and pervasive concern of public policy has been regulation of grain markets to prevent "excessive" hoarding, because, in the words of Arrow (1982, p. 24), "[w]hen situations of scarcity arise, hoarding is always blamed." For example, Ravallion (1985) believes irrationally excessive storage contributed to the famine in Bangladesh in 1974. In the English grain trade for centuries, statutes outlawed "engrossing" and "forestalling" (Gras 1915). More recently, in Pakistan and India, for example, antihoarding laws have been on the books (Patel 1965; Vyas and Bafna 1965; Chaudhary 1974; Hamid 1974). Antihoarding laws may be socially desirable when price ceilings are imposed on the grain trade, as frequently has been the case where antihoarding laws have been in force. The second distortion may alleviate the first and more fundamental distortion, which is that price ceilings can induce even competitive storers to withhold their grain during even the worst shortages (Wright and Williams 1984a).

Although the regime with the expected local marginal consumption value as the storage signal has been put forth in this chapter as a way of guiding public behavior, it can also be interpreted from the perspective of private behavior. Suppose a group of the private agents, whether consumers, storers, or producers, is not subject to the price ceiling at location *b*. For example, some of the commodity may be kept in hiding by

rate with public storage following leadership behavior is much higher than with public storage at either location following the local marginal consumption value. Thus, seemingly minor issues like the location of the public stockpile and the extent price ceilings distort the private transportation industry prove crucial in determining the contribution of a public storage agency. It is fair to say that these issues have not been given sufficient attention in the existing literature, because the existing models do not conceive of a system of related commodities. The differences and similarities among commodities need to be made explicit through formal representation of the transformation technologies.

These properties can also be seen by comparing a time series of prices with public storage at location a with a time series with public storage at location b, as done in Figure 15.8. Both storage policies follow the marginal consumption value of the publicly stored commodity. Also the private transportation industry is undistorted by the price ceilings.[22] The comparison within Figure 15.8 makes clear that the system evolves differently depending on the location of the public stockpile. Although the local marginal consumption values, whether at a or b, follow the same basic path – up, down, and up again – they do not track all that closely. Movements over periods 9–14 in particular show little similarity. With public storage at location a the marginal con-

---

the farmers at that location for their own current and future consumption. What is interesting is that those storers at b using the local marginal consumption value will be storing quite often when the marginal consumption value at a is above the price ceiling: 8.22 percent of the periods to be precise. This situation can be read as one region, the distant countryside, enjoying a surplus and storing for the future while another region, the capital city and environs, has a shortage. Amid the food riots in the capital, there will be many calls to requisition the hoarders' grain.

This "excessive" withholding of grain is perfectly rational and is consistent with nonmanipulative competitive behavior. In a system with no price ceilings, the greater the shortfall at a, the more is shipped from b. Under a regime of price ceilings that distorts trade, no matter how high is the marginal consumption value in a, the signal for shipping from b is $110. Unable to obtain the full value from a shipment of their commodity, those in region b will consume more of it, and perhaps store some of it for fear their region might have a poor harvest the next period.

The cause of seemingly excessive withholding is the distortion in the transportation incentives attributable to the price ceilings. If an antihoarding law prevents privately rational but socially excessive private holdings during scarcities, it can improve social welfare, quite apart from any public storage schemes. Suppose storers at b know their stocks will be confiscated if the marginal consumption value at location a is above the price ceiling. They will not store. The quantity they release will be partly absorbed in shipments to location a. (Of course, the amount they have available to release is also affected by the anticipation of confiscation. The net effect on social welfare from a confiscatory threat is ambiguous *a priori*.)

[22] Therefore, the series for public storage at a can be compared to the series in Figure 15.6, where trade was distorted. (The sequence of weather is the same for both figures.) This comparison of Figures 15.6 and 15.8 emphasizes that the distortion of trade causes a much higher variance in the marginal consumption value, whether at a or b.

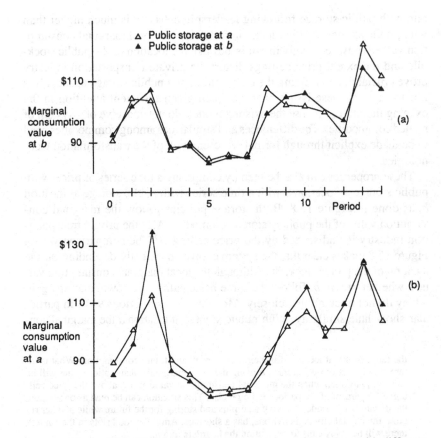

Figure 15.8. Time series of marginal consumption values with different location of public storage.

sumption value at a is sometimes lower, sometimes higher than with public storage at location b. These differences in the path for the marginal consumption value P^a, of course, reflect whether the larger carryover happened to have been at the location whose weather was relatively worse. Because the weather is inherently more volatile at location a, one might expect the series for both the consumption prices of a and b to show less variability when the public agency stores at location a. But trade conveys the variability to the other commodity. (In either case the variance of the marginal consumption value at the location of public storage is lower.)

At the heart of the differences in the effects of the various public policies is the transportation technology. If the shipping from one location to another were immediate and costless, then public storage at either location would suffice as total storage for the whole system. No private storage would remain. If transportation is costly but undistorted by the price ceilings, it can more often convey supplies where they are more useful. This property makes the location of a public stockpile less important to the behavior of the entire system.

15.6 The welfare rankings of the various public policies

The amount a public scheme contributes to total storage, just discussed, is of interest, but more fundamental is the amount it contributes to social welfare. This section presents the rankings of the various public programs by the amount that they restore, at the time of their announcement, of the present value of social welfare lost to price ceilings. It then discusses some of the counterintuitive rankings, especially the result that "leadership" public storage need not come closest to the welfare level with no distortions.

Figures 15.9 and 15.10 are a pair. The first plots the welfare measure given that the regime of price ceilings (at $P^C = \$110$) distorts shipping between the two locations, the second given that the price ceilings do not distort the transportation industry. In both figures, the welfare of the various policies is computed as the percentage recovered the deadweight loss of the regime of price ceilings with solely private storage.[23]

Strictly speaking, the present value of the welfare of a public policy depends on the availabilities A_t^a and A_t^b at the time of the introduction of the policy. Thus, a three-dimensional diagram is required for all combinations of initial conditions. In lieu of that full diagram, Figures 15.9 and 15.10 show two-dimensional combinations of A_t^a and A_t^b that have some of the largest influences on total welfare. More precisely, $A_t^b = 90$ and A_t^a ranges from 95 to 120. These are the welfare comparisons corresponding to the storage and transportation rules, illustrated in Figure 15.5, that showed the largest differences among the public policies.

A subsidy to private storage is the clear winner.[24] If such subsidies are political anathema,[25] leadership public storage at location a in the case of distorted trade and public storage at location b using the local marginal consump-

---

23 In absolute terms, the present value of the deadweight loss of the regime with distortion of the private transportation industry is some three times larger than without distortion of trade.

24 The linear subsidy has been optimized to give the highest (constrained) welfare. The best subsidy proves to be $3.90 with no distortion in transformation, and $5.00 with transformation distorted (to an accuracy of $0.10). We exclude nonlinear subsidy schemes as excessively complex, even though a flat-rate subsidy is an inflexible policy across the range of current conditions.

25 Plummer (1982) argues that, on the contrary, subsidies have the advantage of making stockpiling less political – everyone will be watching the President decide to release oil from the SPR. A subsidy may also make oil companies less fearful that the government would confiscate their oil in an emergency, which induces them to hold more in store.

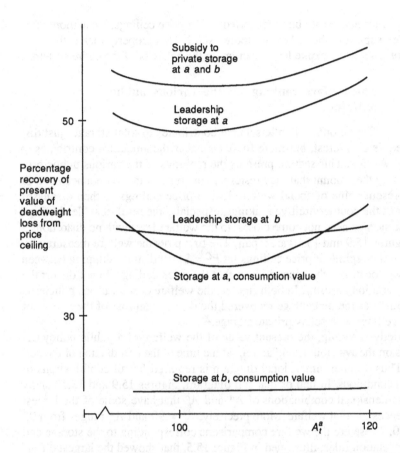

Figure 15.9. Deadweight gain of various public programs; price ceiling affects transportation, $A_t^b = 90$.

tion value in the case of undistorted trade. The relative rankings of the schemes change little over the whole set of pairs of initial availabilities, not just those in Figures 15.9 and 15.10. (They obviously differ considerably depending on whether or not the price ceilings distort the transportation industry, but that is a separate issue.) Private storers and producers can conclude that a welfare-maximizing government, choosing among the alternatives illustrated, will follow one policy (the subsidy to private storage) consistently. In short, the assumption of the public policy being permanent proves to be valid (in the context of the regime of price ceilings also being permanent).[26]

26   The further issue of the private sector's learning about the public policy upon its introduction, an issue studied by Backus and Driffill (1985), has been ignored in these welfare rankings.

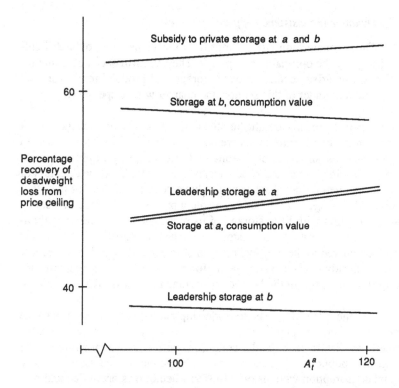

Figure 15.10. Deadweight gain of various public programs; price ceiling does not affect transportation, $A_t^b = 90$.

On the other hand, nothing ensures that one policy dominates. For example, in the comparison of two dominated policies, the rankings of leadership storage at b and storage at a guided by the local marginal consumption value cross twice in Figure 15.9. Because between this pair one policy is best in some current circumstances and another policy in other circumstances, the government would announce a new regime if new current conditions so dictated. But if such flip-flops in regime were appropriate, the welfare calculations recommending them would no longer be valid. This is because the storage rules under a particular public policy were deduced assuming that policy was followed forever. If the government found it desirable to alter its policy period to period, private storage behavior would differ from that supposed.

In comparing Figures 15.9 and 15.10 it is perhaps surprising that the simple policy of a flat-rate subsidy to private storage (at both locations) is superior. It is surely surprising that the worst policy with trade distorted, namely, public storage at location b using the marginal consumption value at b, is superior to supposedly more sophisticated policies when trade is undistorted.

Dynamic inconsistency of public policies

These counterintuitive rankings offer useful insight into the difficulties of designing the optimal public policy. They confirm once again that interesting results arise because private storage and production are forward looking. The remainder of this section and chapter will be spent trying to explain them.

In large part the results are attributable to the transportation technology. It is the reason the two commodities are not a single commodity to begin with and the reason for simultaneous public and private storage. Public storage, whether at location a or b, alters the allocation substantially in the direction of that location, even reducing what would have been the storage of the other commodity if storage of both had been solely private. In the case of a shortfall at the location with little storage of its own, some of the relative abundance of the commodity publicly stored must be transported at considerable expense, compared to the physical costs of storage at the location where it is needed. A subsidy to private storage, uniform in both locations, increases total storage without tilting the balance of storage much toward a single location.

Similarly, the main advantage to leadership public storage is its allowance for the effect of current public storage on the current amount traded when the price ceilings distort trade. Under conditions with a large availability of the location with public storage, at a for example, public storage using the local marginal consumption value is oblivious to whether its storage demand prevents some of commodity a from being transported to location b when immediate consumption at b has higher marginal social value. On the other hand, leadership public storage accounts for its own effect on current trade. When the price ceilings do not distort trade, the shortage at b is communicated to the current marginal consumption value of the publicly stored commodity. Hence, with no direct distortions to the amount traded, public behavior following the local marginal consumption value does not make the misallocation corrected by the more sophisticated leadership behavior. Consequently, as can be seen in Figure 15.10, public storage directed by the local consumption price at b dominates leadership storage at either a or b.

Whether or not the private transportation industry is distorted, the public storage following leadership behavior omits several private responses to its actions, although it ostensibly accounts for all of them. It does not recognize that A_t^a and A_t^b respond to its actions, that they are part of the "competitive fringe." Of course, A_t^a and A_t^b are unalterable at the time the public agency is selecting the level of public storage in period t. Nonetheless, those availabilities depend on the agency's actions, for the availabilities in period t depend on past decisions to store and produce. These past private actions are based in part on anticipations of future public behavior. Thus, leadership public behavior, maximizing social welfare given current availabilities, does not account for the endogenous effect on those availabilities.

The flaw in sophisticated public behavior in period t can be seen from the perspective of period $t-1$. Corresponding to (15.3), equation (15.10) is the social welfare as of $t-1$, expanded to clarify the interaction of the public agency's choices in period $t-1$ and period t:

$$J\left[S_{t-1}^a, S_{t-1}^b, Z_{t-1}, S_t^a, S_t^b, Z_t \big| A_{t-1}^a, A_{t-1}^b\right]$$

$$= \int_0^{A_{t-1}^a - S_{t-1}^a - Z_{t-1}} P^a\left[q^a\right]dq^a + \int_0^{A_{t-1}^b - S_{t-1}^b + Z_{t-1}} P^b\left[q^b\right]dq^b$$

$$- k^a S_{t-1}^a - k^b S_{t-1}^b - \int_0^{Z_{t-1}} z[Z]dZ + (1+r)^{-1}\{-H[E_{t-1}[\hat{P}_t^b]]$$

$$+ \int_0^{S_{t-1}^a + h_t^a - S_t^a - Z_t} P^a\left[q^a\right]dq^a + \int_0^{S_{t-1}^b + \bar{h}_t^b + v_t^b - S_t^b + Z_t} P^b\left[q^b\right]dq^b$$

$$- k^a S_t^a - k^b S_t^b - \int_0^{Z_t} z[Z]dZ + (1+r)^{-1} W[S_t^a, S_t^b]\} \qquad (15.10)$$

A_t^a and A_t^b have now been expanded to include S_{t-1}^a, S_{t-1}^b, and the two harvests, one of which is responsive to economic signals. S_{t-1}^a is the variable the public agency must select in period $t-1$, and S_t^a the control variable in period t. From the perspective of maximizing welfare as of period $t-1$, it should select S_{t-1}^a and S_t^a jointly (or at least decide as of period $t-1$ on the function for period t). There should be two first-order conditions: one $\partial J_{t-1} / \partial S_{t-1}^a = 0$, the other $\partial J_{t-1} / \partial S_t^a = 0$. More important, it would be apparent $\partial J_{t-1} / \partial S_t^a$ should include terms missing from $\partial J_t / \partial S_t^a$, which is equation (15.5). These are $(-P_{t-1}^b - k^b + (1+r)^{-1} E_{t-1}[P_t^b])(dS_{t-1}^b / dS_t^a)$, $(E_{t-1}[P_t^b] - \partial H / \partial \bar{h}_t^b)(d\bar{h}_t^b / dS_t^a)$, $(-P_{t-1}^a + z[Z_{t-1}] + P_{t-1}^b)(dZ_{t-1} / dS_t^a)$.[27]

The sum of these terms is almost surely positive and, if trade is undistorted, unambiguously positive. If they were added to (15.5), the equilibrium S_t^a would be higher. Clearly, as S_t^a rises, the price $\hat{P}_t^b$ also rises. As $E_{t-1}[\hat{P}_t^b]$ rises, so do S_{t-1}^b and $\bar{h}_t^b$. Hence, $dS_{t-1}^b / dS_t^a > 0$ and $d\bar{h}_t^b / dS_t^a > 0$. Private storage in period $t-1$ equates $P_{t-1}^b + k^b$ with $(1+r)^{-1} E_{t-1}[\hat{P}_t^b]$. The expected market price $E_{t-1}[\hat{P}_t^b]$ is less than the expected marginal consumption value $E_{t-1}[P_t^b]$. By the same reasoning $(E_{t-1}[P_t^b] - \partial H / \partial \bar{h}_t^b)$ can be seen to be greater than zero. On the other hand, if the expression $(-P_{t-1}^a + z[Z_{t-1}] + P_{t-1}^b)$ is not zero, it is negative. This happens only when A_{t-1}^a is much below A_{t-1}^b.

What is happening among these partial derivatives is this: If in period $t-1$ private actors anticipated that the public agency were to store more in period

---

[27] The marginal shipping cost z has the other sign if Z_{t-1} is positive. However, $Z_{t-1} < 0$ are the cases of interest.

t, the derived demand would induce more private carryover from period $t-1$ and planting for use in period t. That extra availability would help to raise welfare from period t onward. So-called leadership public storage allows for its effect on private storage in period t; but it takes availabilities in period t as given. As a result, it stores less and achieves lower social welfare than if it were to follow a policy such as using the local marginal consumption value.

Anticipations of public policies

Thus, public storage at location b using the marginal consumption value at b dominates the other policies of public storage when trade is undistorted because its greater demand for storage unintentionally induces higher availabilities. Some of this additional availability comes through more past private storage at location a. More important is its direct impetus to planned production at location b, where supply is elastic. If public storage is at a, the inducement to additional production at b is muted.

It should be clear from the logic of the effect dS^b_{t-1} / dS^a_t that similar considerations arise because the public agency in period t does not take account of its effect on private decisions in periods $t-2$, $t-3$, $t-4$, and so forth. All these could be made part of the first-order conditions for the optimization as of period t. Or to put the matter slightly differently, the additional availability from the decision to increase public storage in period t is typically not just from period $t-1$ but from previous periods. The effect feeds on itself.

Terms such as dS^b_{t-1} / dS^a_t are only part of the expressions missing from the complete first-order conditions for public storage in period t. They are all multiplied by terms like $(-P^b_{t-1} - k^b + (1+r)^{-1} E_{t-1}[P^b_t])$. If there were no distortions from price ceilings, such terms would be zero because they would correspond to the private arbitrage equations. (This is why any discussion of the welfare of undistorted private storage is solely forward looking.) The call for additional availability in period t would be equated to the marginal social costs of providing it. Price ceilings drive a wedge between the marginal social cost of future availability and its expected marginal social value. Too little is stored and produced. Hence any policy in the present that has increased carryover and production from the past helps relieve this distortion.

Of course, the government in the current period does not see that its actions have an effect on the current availability. After all, the inheritance from the past is not within its control. Even if it wanted to account for its current actions on the past, it could not. The past is unalterable. "Just as past decisions cannot be undone, allowances made in past decisions for the then expected effects of future decisions cannot be undone" (Holly and Hughes Hallett 1989, p. 167). From the government's perspective (and from the perspective of its representative citizen), it might as well do the best it can given the current conditions.

Unfortunately, a "time consistent" policy that maximizes welfare taking the past as given and expecting future policies to do the same need not actually maximize current and future welfare. That is, it is not necessarily the "optimal plan." If the current government could force future governments to follow policies it set looking far ahead from the present, it could improve welfare over the behavior where each successive government takes the past as given and reformulates its policies accordingly. Yet the current government can hardly expect future governments to be bound to its current decisions. After all, it itself is deciding on current policy taking past governments' admonitions as immaterial, and in fact can find no better approach for the current period given the current situation. The best policy, if it could be implemented, would require future administrations to behave differently from how the current government is behaving now; and the private sector must believe this will happen.

This "inconsistency" of optimal plans over time constrains the formulation of storage policies whenever market distortions are present. One must evaluate the myriad possible policies for each combination of the parameters.[28] By chance the features of oil demand and supply may be such that more sophisticated public storage of oil may lower welfare. And in just those cases where public policies have the largest effects on current private actions, and so it would seem some special attention would be needed, the effect of future policies on current forward-looking private actions is likely to be the largest.

[28] Hughes Hallett (1988) has compared the optimal intervention into the copper market of the 1970s to the time consistent but suboptimal intervention and concluded that there was no difference in practice. Although we question whether hypothetical interventions into previous historical settings can provide a valid comparison, we agree that the magnitude of the difference must be considered case by case.

PART V
Epilogue

CHAPTER 16

Lessons about commodity markets and modeling strategies

In this book, we have embodied what we consider to be the crucial stylized facts about technology in an internally consistent marketwide model of a commodity. We have used this model and its extensions to derive new insights regarding market behavior and the effects of policy interventions. Our approach differs from previous work in that it highlights dynamics. Proper consideration of storage impels a distinction between dynamics and comparative statics; all welfare effects, for example, are properly dynamic phenomena. Also the time-series behavior resulting from storage, especially the tendency for positive serial correlation, is inherently interesting.

More specifically, we have set forth and probed a multiperiod model with random weather in which storage connects the periods. The storage itself is relatively simple, the aggregate behavior of the many risk-neutral storers in a competitive industry with constant marginal costs over the whole range of positive storage. In each period, the market is in equilibrium, given the current weather. Such a formulation is firmly in the tradition of microeconomics, with an emphasis on the "whole behaving differently from the parts." We add two features to this standard industry of microeconomic theory, however. One is that the storers are forward looking – indeed, that their expectations about future prices are rational in the sense of being internally consistent. The other is that aggregate storage cannot be negative. The interaction at the level of the whole industry of this simple and obvious technical feature with the random weather, not to mention the anticipation of such interactions in the future, is sufficient to create a complex dynamic system, even without any seasonality or long-run trends. One measure of the complexity is that an analyst can only solve the model numerically.

Our modeling strategy makes possible a unified approach. All the more complicated problems considered in Parts III–IV, whether seasonality, inventories of goods in process, trade along with storage, or public price-band schemes, were extensions to our basic model. We have not tried to develop a

455

new model for each problem. Therefore, there is less worry that any particular conclusion was contrived. (Of course, the selection of the parameter set for each exercise was within our control, but we have tried to use the same parameters in most exercises and to provide a sensitivity analysis.) Storage behavior was developed in Chapters 2 and 3 from first principles without the shortcut of supposing it could be approximated, say, by a decrease in the variance of weather in a one-period model. Nor have we invoked some vague market failure to justify public interventions. In Chapter 15 on public storage designed to supplement private storage, for example, the justification was the possibility of price ceilings. This may or may not be a reasonable fear for actual storers; the point is that the condition was made explicit in our analysis. More generally, we feel that any call for public intervention on "second-best" grounds should have all the objectives, distortions, and interventions within the formal analysis, because knowledge of their precise interaction is the purpose of any analysis of public policy.

16.1   The standard of the first best

We have been largely concerned with questions such as these:

How does a market in an economy without random disturbances compare to one with disturbances?

How does an economy of the latter type without storage or lagged production responses compare to one with either of these intertemporal linkages?

What are the characteristics of the transition from one system to another?

How would an economy that could trade and store in response to random disturbances compare to one in which trade or storage alone is possible?

If there are random disturbances both to the supply of raw material and to the demand for finished goods, what should be the proportions among inventories of raw materials, goods in process, and finished goods?

We have studied these questions of storage, stochastic production, trade, and the structure of futures prices in a model in which conventional risk aversion is not included. This treatment contrasts sharply with much of the previous literature. For example, the literature on producers' decisions under uncertainty (e.g., Sandmo 1971) presupposes the importance of risk aversion with respect to profits. Similarly, the major rationale offered for stabilization through public buffer-stock schemes is usually risk aversion in the utility functions of market participants.

Our formulation of the "stabilization question" brings one issue into sharp focus: What is the first-best world against which one measures market failures, disequilibria, and policy distortions? For each of the industrywide models considered, we have offered some insights into the significance of disturbances and the technologies that ameliorate their effects. For example, if two countries can ship the commodity back and forth as a response to the vagaries of their independent harvests, one can identify a regime of unrestricted trade as the socially first-best reaction to the uncertainty. Clearly, both countries together would be yet better off if the vagaries in the weather disappeared entirely, say, by a new invention of irrigation equipment. Depending on the technically possible response, each of these is a relevant "first-best" world.

The aggregate inventories of a competitive industry of rational, risk-neutral storers achieve the first-best response to the unalterable uncertainty, given the limits of the technology of storage. It is often remarked that commodity prices seem "unduly variable." But because of physical storage costs and the nonnegativity constraint on total storage, the stabilization achieved by storage should be incomplete. Moreover, the stabilization should not be expected to be symmetric. Time series of commodity prices should be characterized by occasional steep spikes. Similarly, it should not be surprising that a particular commodity's price remains below its long-run average for a number of years on end. Most elementary but most important, *ex post* almost all storage decisions, even those that were optimal *ex ante,* look flawed to some degree.

If trade and storage are both technically possible, the first-best world is better than with either alone, as was discussed in Chapter 9. Where supply can respond to incentives (with a one-period lag), the competitive equilibrium represents the optimal dispersal of the uncertainty throughout the commodity's sector by way of adjustments in storage and planned production. In any of these cases with a closed system, the social welfare is the same as a benevolent social planner could achieve.

Thus, an advantage of our approach is that it distinguishes issues of the limits of technologies from the quite distinct issues of second-best interventions in situations with missing markets. The market stabilization literature for the most part has failed to draw this distinction. In so doing it has confused technology evaluation, such as the benefits of lower storage costs or of a reduction in weather disturbances, with arguments for government intervention.

Similar care in specifying the technical constraints reveals many implicit assumptions in the conventional analysis of the inventory behavior of an individual firm, such as the famous (S,s) model, which posits an unalterable list price and deduces an optimal reordering strategy. As we showed in Chapter 11, the requirement of a fixed list price imposes a considerable cost on a firm. Given a choice, it would much prefer to have the flexibility of adjusting prices within the period rather than having the capability to store, although better yet would be both forms of flexibility. Thus, models such as the (S,s) inventory model need to address explicitly what constrains a firm from adjusting prices. Also they need to consider more carefully the nature of the demand disturbance. If it is common to many firms, all will try to reorder at the same time. Only if the supply of the input is perfectly elastic will the models' assumption of an exogenous input price be valid.

16.2   Nonlinearities and discontinuities

The separation of the nature of technology from the nature of the utility function immediately reveals that there can be responses to risk even if all parties in the market are risk neutral with respect to fluctuations in income. Formally, risk aversion with respect to income is equivalent to a nonlinearity in the utility function. Yet storage technology also has a pronounced nonlinearity – it is physically impossible to store a negative amount. Indeed, on a "nonlinearity" scale, storage technology is more nonlinear, at least according to experimental evidence about risk aversion with respect to income. Trade is another technology with a pronounced nonlinearity, because of the discontinuity imposed by shipping costs in either direction. Likewise, an equilibrium with inventories of finished goods in addition to inventories of raw materials results from the total cost of processing not being a linear function of the amount processed in any one period. And as Pyatt (1978) has emphasized, the technology of storage can absorb highly seasonal patterns in demand or supply, which themselves are a form of nonlinearity.

It may well be that these nonlinearities in the production technologies explain much about actual commodity markets, compared to the assumption of nonlinearities in utility. More forcefully, we think it unwarranted to presume that risk aversion in the utility function is the major explanation of behavior in commodity markets. At the very least the introduction of "storability" into a system has substantial allocative effects even under risk neutrality as conventionally defined. It is also true that there can be substantial welfare effects to public stabilization programs even under risk neutrality, as we have shown in Chapters 13 and 14. Indeed, the political support for various public interventions may be well explained by the direction and magnitude of welfare effects that occur under income risk neutrality.

16.3   Endogenous responses to risk

The standard model of insurance schools one to expect no aggregate uncertainty in a first-best world. By pooling their independent risks of fire or disease, a group of many risk-averse individuals can, in the limit, remove all social risk in any given period. But if all share the same risk – weather, for instance – the situation is very different. Storage can be viewed as a method of pooling the weather across a number of periods, but because it is limited to saving for the future and not borrowing from the future, the "insurance" cannot remove all uncertainty. Moreover, it is socially useful even if everyone is risk neutral with respect to income.

The standard model of insurance also suggests that if obvious individual risks remain uninsured, some markets must not exist and the world is far from first best. The same is not necessarily the case in a situation with social risk and storage. Storage does not remove all social risk. Yet the stabilization it furnishes could be first best. For example, among risk-neutral consumers and storers, the allocative behavior of competitive storage, which would not achieve complete stability, would be the same whether or not there are markets for the "contingent claims" involving the commodity, say, 180 periods into the future.

The insurance literature, although deeply concerned with negative individual responses to the insurance (adverse selection and moral hazard), tends to neglect the capacity for positive social responses that reduce the risks in the environment. Such positive social responses are numerous. According to Rosenzweig (1988) and Rosenzweig and Stark (1989), families in a set of Indian villages in a semiarid region use marriage of their daughters to achieve a geographic dispersion of the family's fortunes; they literally send each daughter to a husband at a different point on the compass. Nomadic herding is a cultural response to local droughts, as noted by Legge (1989). McCloskey (1976) argues that spatial dispersion of a farmer's land around his locality, the open field system of the Middle Ages, eliminates a surprisingly large proportion of weather risk even though the distance between plots is modest. According to Garnsey and Morris (1989), citizenship in ancient Greek city-states and the political identity of the *polis* itself were a method of sharing risks. Thus, the very notion of government, without which there can be no thought of public intervention, is itself an endogenous response to risk. Work by Kotlikoff and Spivak (1981) indicates that intrafamily risk sharing can furnish the majority of the benefit obtainable through a complete set of markets for contingent claims, if the risks faced by the various family members are independent. And storage (or savings more generally) is an endogenous cultural response, perhaps chosen over a loss of mobility, as Rowley-Conwy and Zvelebil (1989) have pointed out was the case for prehistoric hunter-gatherers.

Endogenous responses to risk complicate considerably the analysis of any single public program. For example, a major investment in irrigation may be judged to have social benefits outweighing social costs if the benefits are appraised against consumption tied to the inherent variability of the weather. But private storage itself may have achieved half the potential social gain. Other endogenous responses, including plot dispersion, loans, and family connections, may jointly account for much of the remaining gain from the stabilizing effect of irrigation.

More complex yet are the interactions of some public programs with private responses. Clearly, a public buffer-stock scheme should not be evaluated as if there would be no private storage. Indeed, as Chapter 15 emphasized, the anticipations of future public storage policies by private parties who adjust their own responses can result in time inconsistency, a situation in which it is difficult to identify the optimal public intervention. More generally, it may be difficult to identify the best policy when the intervention is in a complex environment of private responses.

All this is not to argue that individual producers or consumers face no risk or that they are not risk averse. (Introspection, if nothing else, suggests that utility functions are nonlinear.) Rather, it is a counsel to direct attention to reactions to uncertainty in a setting of risk-neutral utility functions before the more complex analysis with risk aversion is undertaken. In addition, the multiperiod model presented here suggests that incorporating risk aversion in a realistic fashion may be very difficult, for example, because of the positive serial correlation induced by storage. Finally, risk aversion should be embodied in the price of capital assets such as land, with the result that the reduction in risk achieved by a public stabilization program affects farm owners at the time of the announcement of the scheme and not later entrants into farming, just as would happen if they were risk neutral according to their utility functions.

16.4   Multiperiod equlibrium models

A multiperiod model also brings into focus the importance of conditions in the initial period. Conventional studies in the stabilization literature contrast a one-period world with a high variance from the market disturbance to another one-period world with a lower variance achieved through some public program. The exercise is implicitly or explicitly one of comparative statics. No mention is made of the path to the new stochastic steady state. Nor is any mention made of the specific conditions at the time of the change in regime.

In a multiperiod model, it is easy to see the importance of the path from the initial circumstances. A public buffer-stock scheme, for example, must buy up some reserve before it can operate at all. Clearly, initial owners of the commodity, perhaps including producers, would prefer this sequencing of accumulations early and dispersals late. They might be in favor of the scheme even if its long-run effects are negative. Generally speaking, therefore, conventional long-run comparative statics understates the benefits to initial owners of the commodity of any public stabilization scheme. The effects on initial landowners are, as we have shown, more complex. They must balance higher near-term revenues against more negative results later. The precise "dynamic" welfare effect, however, depends very much on whether the scheme is announced in a period of scarcity or abundance. Consequently, no general propositions about welfare effects could possibly be expected.

In a multiperiod model in which decisions must be made before relevant information can be observed, the issue of how expectations are formed is crucial. It is at least plausible that market participants attempt to look into the future rather than backward into the past. In the extreme this becomes the hypothesis of rational expectations. More positively stated, if market participants do attempt to take account of the future in their current decisions, a single-period model or a model with backward-looking expectations poorly represents the dynamic equilibria in the market.

Forward-looking expectations connect the present with the future. Analysts can sometimes forget that aspects of the future that can be foreseen should already be reflected in the current price of the commodity. For example, a food policy expert might say "Because population is growing, the demand for wheat is increasing, and hence the price of wheat can be expected to be much, much higher ten years from now." (Similar statements have been made on occasion by experts in oil, copper, and almost any commodity of importance.) Such a statement reflects one of two implausible assumptions. The first assumption would be that storage costs, including interest, are prohibitive. Otherwise storers would buy the commodity today for delivery and hold it to sell at the much higher price years later (rotating stocks to maintain freshness, if necessary). The maximum price increase consistent with no opportunities for arbitrage would be one just covering, in expectation, interest and physical storage costs. The alternative assumption would be to accept the possibility of storage but to deny that anyone in the market is forward looking. Otherwise, the implications of an increasing population are imbedded in the current price.

16.5 Our model and empirical work on commodity markets

Although our focus has been on a theoretical model, with examples selected to demonstrate aspects of the theory, we can claim that the model does duplicate a number of empirical regularities. For example, the simulated time series generated by the model display the unusual but sharp spikes of time series of actual spot prices. The generated time series also display the extended "busts" typical of commodity markets. Similarly, the generated series display the positive serial correlation of actual spot prices measured each cropyear. Of course, these last two features are really one and the same, the effects of storage connecting one period with the next. The same connecting effects of storage also imply the positive serial correlation actually seen in real rents and land prices. Our model generates futures prices that have many of the patterns of actual futures prices, notably backwardations in which the price for a more distant delivery date is below the price for earlier delivery. Either the extension of our model to storage in two locations or the extension with goods in process creates relationships between price spreads and total storage that look like so-called supply-of-storage curves.

By claiming that our model duplicates several empirical regularities, we are also accepting that it can be used to derive "testable hypotheses" and to narrow the search for other empirical regularities. The model indicates that the sharp spikes in price should correspond to periods with minimal stocks. Another testable implication is that time series of prices by cropyear should be heteroskedastic, since large price changes are more likely when stockpiles are low than when they are high. For the same reason, the degree of skewness should be related to the size of stocks. These relations should hold even in a situation with considerable seasonality in excess demand. Seasonality, moreover, should be much more manifest in the level of stocks than in prices. The model also indicates that, if supply is adjustable with a one-period lag, there should be negative correlation between acres planted and stocks as of that point in the crop year. For the same reasons that price is serially correlated, carryovers between cropyears should be positively serially correlated. Quantities traded between regions or countries should likewise be positively correlated production period to production period, apart from any long-term growth.

The relationships revealed by our theoretical model lead to several suggestions for improving econometric practice involving commodities. Because of the way storage connects periods, current right-hand-side variables in regressions, such as futures prices or acres planted, are likely to be correlated with previous error terms in that regression. This statistical connection causes biased estimates of coefficients when samples are of the size normally used in studying commodity markets. Perhaps most important for econometric practice, the demand for inventories as a function of current conditions should not be written as a structural equation. Rather it is a functional of the true structural consumption demand function, supply function, and storage cost function. Admittedly, this is not analytically convenient: Without an explicit equation for a demand for inventories, sectoral models cannot be closed. But the procedure should not be to make an arbitrary specification of the missing relationship.

More boldly, we propose that our model could be used to vet econometric techniques. It can generate many time series of a desired length, with the true values of important parameters known. An econometric technique should perform reasonably well in these controlled conditions, it would seem; yet by that minimal standard, a number of accepted empirical techniques perform poorly on average. For example, the accepted techniques for testing for bias in futures prices find bias in the model's futures prices, which are unbiased by construction. Similarly, the standard ARMA representations of commodity prices appear to work on our generated time series yet are subtly wrong.

The econometric implications of our model also call into question the interpretation of many empirical regularities. For example, the observed positive serial correlation in the quantity of inventories has lead many to fit partial-adjustment or accelerator equations with apparent success. Our model has this empirical regularity in inventories but no adjustment costs nor accelerator-style expectations. Similarly, econometric techniques of supply estimation, such as cobweb or adaptive expectations, appear to work reasonably well in practice. They also appear to work reasonably well on data generated by our model, in which the supply response in fact follows neither form and is much more elastic than estimated. It falls to those who use these econometric formulations to demonstrate that their results are not due to the hidden effects of storage.

16.6   For the future

Our approach, based on the stylized microeconomic fundamentals of commodity markets, can form the basis of a new econometric methodology for the analysis of time series of commodity prices. A first and very encouraging example of this potential is the methods of moments estimation by Deaton and Laroque (1990). A generated time series from storage behavior derived through a dynamic programming algorithm for a particular set of parameters is compared to an observed series, this comparison suggesting a refinement in the parameter set, a new generated time series, and so on. In such a technique, the speed of the dynamic programming algorithm is especially important; the fast algorithm described in the Appendix to Chapter 3 should be useful. We also expect to see soon maximum-likelihood methods incorporating the relationships identified in our model.

In making commodity policy, future economic analysis should explicitly recognize the role of storage. The result of such common analytical conveniences as ignoring private storage, assuming backward-looking expectations, or positing a self-liquidating stockpile can be seriously flawed commodity policy. Likewise, the discussion of trade policy should not ignore storage, because impressions formed in a single-period model of the importance of trade or of the indications of self-sufficiency can be markedly wrong if the traded good is in fact storable. The models we have used to show the dangers of these conveniences also indicate the increasing practicality of more realistic, numerical modeling techniques and the corresponding weakening of the need to sacrifice relevance in the name of analytical tractability.

There should be no need to remind the reader that our chapters on trade and storage, to name one subject, are hardly the last word on the potential of our approach. Integration of production, consumption, costly transport, and inventories in an internally consistent model opens up a whole new set of questions. Similarly, our model of raw material, goods in process, and finished goods or our model of firms with list prices raises many questions about the behavior of macroeconomic aggregates.

Thus, at the end of this book, we leave a wealth of areas for further research. We hope that those who pursue the modeling approach we have presented here find the work as stimulating and the results as interesting as we have thus far.

References

Abel, Andrew B. 1985. "Inventories, Stock-Outs and Production Smoothing." *Review of Economic Studies* 52: 283–93.

Adams, F. Gerald. 1978. "Implementation of Commodity Market Theory in Empirical Econometric Models." In F. Gerald Adams and Jere R. Behrman (eds.), *Econometric Modeling of World Commodity Policy*, 47–70. Lexington, Mass.: Lexington Books.

Adams, Richard H., Jr. 1983. "The Role of Research in Policy Development: The Creation of the IMF Cereal Import Facility." *World Development* 7: 549–63.

Ahmed, Raisuddin, and Bernard, Andrew. 1989. "Rice Price Fluctuation and an Approach to Price Stabilization in Bangladesh." International Food Policy Research Institute, Research Report 72.

Aiyagari, S. Rao; Eckstein, Zvi; and Eichenbaum, Martin. 1989. "Inventories and Price Fluctuations under Perfect Competition and Monopoly." In Tryphon Kollintzas (ed.), *The Rational Expectations Equilibrium Inventory Model*, 34–68. New York: Springer-Verlag.

Aiyagari, S. Rao, and Riezman, Raymond G. 1985. "Embargoes and Supply Shocks in a Market with a Dominant Seller." In Thomas J. Sargent (ed.), *Energy, Foresight, and Strategy*, 14–40. Washington, D.C.: Resources for the Future.

Alaouze, Chris M.; Sturgess, N. H.; and Watson, A. S. 1978. "Australian Wheat Storage: A Dynamic Programming Approach." *Australian Journal of Agricultural Economics* 22: 158–74.

1979. "Australian Wheat Storage: A Dynamic Programming Approach – A Correction." *Australian Journal of Agricultural Economics* 23: 231–2.

Alchian, Armen A. 1974. "Information, Martingales and Prices." *Swedish Journal of Economics* 76: 3–11.

Allen, S. G. 1954. "Inventory Fluctuations in Flaxseed and Linseed Oil, 1926–1939." *Econometrica* 22: 310–27.

Amihud, Yakov, and Mendelson, Haim. 1982. "The Output–Inflation Relationship: An Inventory-Adjustment Approach." *Journal of Monetary Economics* 9: 163–84.

465

1983. "Price Smoothing and Inventory." *Review of Economic Studies* 50: 87–98.

Anderson, Ronald W. 1985. "Some Determinants of the Volatility of Futures Prices." *Journal of Futures Markets* 5: 331–48.

Ardeni, Pier Giorgio. 1989. "Does the Law of One Price Really Hold for Commodity Prices?" *American Journal of Agricultural Economics* 71: 661–9.

Arrow, Kenneth J. 1978. "The Future and the Present in Economic Life." *Economic Inquiry* 16: 157–69.

1982. "Why People Go Hungry." *New York Times Review of Books* 15 July: 24–6.

Arrow, Kenneth J.; Harris, Theodore; and Marschak, Jacob. 1951. "Optimal Inventory Policy." *Econometrica* 19: 250–72.

Arzac, Enrique R., and Wilkinson, Maurice. 1979. "Stabilization Policies for United States Feed Grain and Livestock Markets." *Journal of Economic Dynamics and Control* 1: 39–58.

Ashley, Richard A., and Orr, Daniel. 1985. "Further Results on Inventories and Price Stickiness." *American Economic Review* 75: 964–75.

Backus, David, and Driffill, John. 1985. "Rational Expectations and Policy Credibility Following a Change in Regime." *Review of Economic Studies* 52: 211–21.

Baillie, Richard T.; Lippens, Robert E.; and McMahon, Patrick C. 1983. "Testing Rational Expectations and Efficiency in the Foreign Exchange Market." *Econometrica* 51: 553–63.

Bale, Malcolm D., and Lutz, Ernst. 1978. "Trade Restrictions and International Price Instability." World Bank Staff Working Paper No. 303.

1979. "The Effects of Trade Intervention on International Price Instability." *American Journal of Agricultural Economics* 61: 512–16.

Ball, Laurence, and Romer, David. 1989. "The Equilibrium and Optimal Timing of Price Changes." *Review of Economic Studies* 56: 179–98.

Basar, Tamer, and Olsder, Geert Jan. 1982. *Dynamic Noncooperative Game Theory*. London: Academic Press.

Bateman, D. I. 1965. "Buffer Stocks and Producers' Incomes." *Journal of Agricultural Economics* 16: 573–5.

Baxter, Jennefer; Conine, Thomas E., Jr.; and Tamarkin, Maurry. 1985. "On Commodity Market Risk Premiums: Additional Evidence." *Journal of Futures Markets* 5: 121–5.

Behrman, Jere R. 1968. *Supply Response in Underdeveloped Agriculture*. Amsterdam: North Holland.

1979. "International Commodity Agreements: An Evaluation of the UNCTAD Integrated Commodity Programme." In William R. Cline (ed.), *Policy Alternatives for a New International Order*, 63–153. New York: Praeger.

Behrman, Jere R., and Tinakorn-Ramangkura, Pranee. 1978. "Evaluating Integrated Schemes for Commodity Market Stabilization." In F. Gerald Adams and Jere R. Behrman (eds.), *Econometric Modeling of World Commodity Policy*, 147–85. Lexington, Mass.: Lexington Books.

Bellman, Richard. 1957. *Dynamic Programming*. Princeton, N.J.: Princeton University Press.

Bertsekas, Dimitri P. 1987. *Dynamic Programming: Deterministic and Stochastic Models*. Englewood Cliffs, N.J.: Prentice-Hall.

Bhatia, B. M. 1970. *India's Food Problem and Policy since Independence*. Bombay: Somaiya Publications.

Bieri, Jurg, and Schmitz, Andrew. 1973. "Export Instability, Monopoly Power, and Welfare." *Journal of International Economics* 3: 389–96.

1974. "Market Intermediaries and Price Instability: Some Welfare Implications." *American Journal of Agricultural Economics* 56: 280–5.

Bigman, David. 1985a. *Food Policies and Food Security under Instability*. Lexington, Mass.: Lexington Books.

1985b. "International Trade and Trade Creation under Instability. *European Economic Review* 28: 309–30.

Bigman, David; Goldfarb, David; and Schechtman, Edna. 1983. "Futures Market Efficiency and the Time Content of the Information Sets." *Journal of Futures Markets* 3: 321–34.

Binswanger, Hans P. 1980. "Attitudes Toward Risk: Experimental Measurement in Rural India." *American Journal of Agricultural Economics* 62: 395–402.

1981. Attitudes Toward Risk: Theoretical Implications of an Experiment in India." *Economic Journal* 91: 867–90.

Bivin, David G. 1986. "Inventories and Interest Rates: A Critique of the Buffer Stock Model." *American Economic Review* 76: 168–76.

Bizer, David S., and Judd, Kenneth L. 1989. "Taxation and Uncertainty." *American Economic Review Papers and Proceedings* 79: 331–6.

Black, J. Roy, and Thompson, Stanley R. 1978. "Some Evidence on Weather–Crop-Yield Interaction." *American Journal of Agricultural Economics* 60: 540–3.

Blackorby, Charles, and Donaldson, David. 1984. "Consumer's Surplus and Welfare Change in a Simple Dynamic Model." *Review of Economic Studies* 51: 171–6.

Blinder, Alan S. 1980. "Inventories in the Keynesian Macro Model." *Kyklos* 33: 585–614.

1981. "Retail Inventory Behavior and Business Fluctuations." *Brookings Papers on Economic Activity*, 443–505.

1982. "Inventories and Sticky Prices: More on the Microfoundations of Macroeconomics." *American Economic Review* 72: 334–48.

1986. "Can the Production Smoothing Model of Inventory Behavior Be Saved?" *Quarterly Journal of Economics* 101: 431–53.

Blinder, Alan S., and Fischer, Stanley. 1981. "Inventories, Rational Expectations, and the Business Cycle." *Journal of Monetary Economics* 8: 277–304.

Blume, Lawrence E., and Easley, David. 1982. "Learning to be Rational." *Journal of Economic Theory* 26: 340–51.

Bollerslev, Tim. 1986. "Generalized Autoregressive Conditional Heteroskedasticity." *Journal of Econometrics* 31: 307–27.

Bopp, Anthony E., and Sitzer, Scott. 1987. "Are Petroleum Futures Prices Good Predictors of Cash Value?" *Journal of Futures Markets* 7: 705–19.

1988. "On the 'Efficiency' of Futures Markets: Another View." *Energy Economics* 10: 199–205.

Bosworth, Barry P., and Lawrence, Robert Z. 1982. *Commodity Prices and the New Inflation.* Washington, D.C.: Brookings.

Brandow, G. E. 1977. "Policy for Commercial Agriculture, 1945–1971." In Lee R. Martin (ed.), *A Survey of Agricultural Economics Literature,* Vol. 1, 209–94. Minneapolis: University of Minnesota Press.

Bray, Margaret. 1982. "Learning, Estimation, and the Stability of Rational Expectations." *Journal of Economic Theory* 26: 318–39.

Brennan, Michael J. 1958. "The Supply of Storage." *American Economic Review* 47: 50–72.

  1959. "A Model of Seasonal Inventories." *Econometrica* 27: 228–44.

Bresnahan, Timothy F., and Spiller, Pablo T. 1986. "Futures Market Backwardation under Risk Neutrality." *Economic Inquiry* 24: 429–41.

Bresnahan, Timothy F., and Suslow, Valerie Y. 1985. "Inventories as an Asset: The Volatility of Copper Prices." *International Economic Review* 26: 409–24.

  1989. "Short-run Supply with Capacity Constraints." *Journal of Law and Economics* 32: S11-S46.

Brockwell, Peter J., and Davis, Richard A. 1987. *Time Series: Theory and Methods.* New York: Springer-Verlag.

Brown, Christopher P. 1975. *Primary Commodity Control.* Kuala Lampur: Oxford University Press.

  1980. *The Political and Social Economy of Commodity Control.* New York: Praeger.

Buccola, Steven T., and Sukume, Chrispen. 1988. "Optimal Grain Pricing and Storage Policy in Controlled Agricultural Economies: Application to Zimbabwe." *World Development* 16: 361–71.

Buiter, Willem H. 1981. "The Superiority of Contingent Rules over Fixed Rules in Models with Rational Expectations." *Economic Journal* 91: 647–70.

  1989. "A Viable Gold Standard Requires Flexible Monetary and Fiscal Policy." *Review of Economic Studies* 56: 101–18.

Burmeister, Edwin. 1978. "Is Price Stabilization Theoretically Desirable?" In F. Gerald Adams and Sonia A Klein (eds.), *Stabilizing World Commodity Markets,* 189–91. Lexington, Mass.: Lexington Books.

Burt, Oscar R. 1986. "Econometric Modeling of the Capitalization Formula for Farmland Prices." *American Journal of Agricultural Economics* 68: 10–26.

Burt, Oscar R., and Cummings, Ronald G. 1977. "Natural Resource Management, the Steady State, and Approximately Optimal Decision Rules." *Land Economics* 53: 1–22.

Burt, Oscar R.; Koo, Won W.; and Dudley, Norman J. 1982. "Optimal Stochastic Control of United States Wheat Stocks." In Gordon C. Rausser (ed.), *New Directions in Econometric Modeling and Forecasting in U. S. Agriculture,* 407–42. New York: North-Holland.

Campbell, John Y., and Mankiw, N. Gregory. 1987. "Are Output Fluctuations Transitory?" *Quarterly Journal of Economics* 102: 857–80.

Campbell, John Y., and Shiller, Robert J. 1989. "The Dividend Ratio Model and Small Sample Bias." *Economics Letters* 29: 325–31.

Campbell, R.; Gardiner, B.; and Haszler, H. 1980. "On the Hidden Revenue Effects of Wool Price Stabilization in Australia: Initial Results." *Australian Journal of Agricultural Economics* 24: 1–15.

Canarella, Giorgio, and Pollard, Stephen K. 1986. "The 'Efficiency' of the London Metal Exchange." *Journal of Banking and Finance* 10: 575–93.

Caplin, Andrew S. 1985. "The Variability of Aggregate Demand with (S, s) Inventory Policies." *Econometrica* 53: 1395–409.

Carlton, Dennis W. 1979. "Vertical Integration in Competitive Markets under Uncertainty." *Journal of Industrial Economics* 27: 189–209.

Carter, Colin A.; Rausser, Gordon C.; and Schmitz, Andrew. 1983. "Efficient Asset Portfolios and the Theory of Normal Backwardation." *Journal of Political Economy* 91: 319–31.

Chaipravat, Olarn. 1978. "International Rice Buffer Stock Operations: A Simulation Study." In F. Gerald Adams and Sonia A Klein (eds.), *Stabilizing World Commodity Markets*, 63–81. Lexington, Mass.: Lexington Books.

Chamley, Christophe, and Wright, Brian D. 1987. "Fiscal Incidence in an Overlapping Generations Model with a Fixed Asset." *Journal of Public Economics* 32: 3–24.

Chao, Hung-Po, and Manne, Alan S. 1983. "Oil Stockpiles and Import Reductions: A Dynamic Programming Approach." *Operations Research* 31: 632–51.

Chaudhary, Zafar Hussain. 1974. *Food Laws of Pakistan*. Lahore: National Law Publications.

Chopra, R. N. 1981. *Evolution of Food Policy in India*. Dehli: Macmillan.

Christiano, Lawrence J. 1988. "Why Does Inventory Investment Fluctuate So Much?" *Journal of Monetary Economics* 21: 247–80.

——— 1990. "Solving the Stochastic Growth Model by Linear-Quadratic Approximation and by Value-Function Iteration." *Journal of Business and Economic Statistics* 8: 23–6.

Christiano, Lawrence J., and Eichenbaum, Martin. 1989. "Temporal Aggregation and the Stock Adjustment Model of Inventories." In Tryphon Kollintzas (ed.), *The Rational Expectations Equilibrium Inventory Model*, 70–108. New York: Springer-Verlag.

Clark, Colin W. 1990. *Mathematical Bioeconomics: The Optimal Management of Renewable Resources*, 2nd ed. New York: Wiley.

Clark, Peter K. 1988. "Nearly Redundant Parameters and Measures of Persistence in Economic Time Series." *Journal of Economic Dynamics and Control* 12: 447–61.

Clower, R. W., and Bushaw, D. W. 1954. "Price Determination in a Stock-Flow Economy." *Econometrica* 22: 328–43.

Cochrane, John H. 1988. "How Big Is the Random Walk in GNP?" *Journal of Political Economy* 96: 893–920.

Cochrane, John H., and Sbordone, Argia M. 1988. "Multivariate Estimates of the Permanent Components of GNP and Stock Prices." *Journal of Economic Dynamics and Control* 12: 255–96.

Cochrane, Willard W. 1980. "Some Nonconformist Thoughts on Welfare Economics and Commodity Stabilization Policy." *American Journal of Agricultural Economics* 62: 508–11.

Cohen, Daniel, and Michel, Philippe. 1988. "How Should Control Theory Be Used to Calculate a Time-consistent Government Policy?" *Review of Economic Studies* 55: 263–74.

Coleman, Wilbur John, II. 1990. "Solving the Stochastic Growth Model by Policy-Function Iteration." *Journal of Business and Economic Statistics* 8: 27–30.

Cooper, Leon, and Cooper, Mary W. 1981. *Introduction to Dynamic Programming.* Oxford: Pergamon.

Cooper, Richard N., and Lawrence, Robert Z. 1975. "The 1972–75 Commodity Boom." *Brookings Papers on Economic Activity* 3: 671–715.

Cootner, Paul H. 1967. "Speculation and Hedging." *Food Research Institute Studies* 7: S65-S105.

Cox, Charles C. 1976. "Futures Trading and Market Information." *Journal of Political Economy* 84: 1215–37.

Crawford, Vincent P.; Sobel, Joel; and Takahashi, Ichiro. 1984. "Bargaining, Strategic Reserves, and International Trade in Exhaustible Resources." *American Journal of Agricultural Economics* 66: 472–80.

Cuddington, John T., and Urzúa, Carlos M. 1989. "Trends and Cycles in the Net Barter Terms of Trade: A New Approach." *Economic Journal* 99: 426–42.

Danielson, Albert L., and Cartwright, Phillip A. 1987. "Inventory Theory in Cartelized Markets." *Energy Economics* 9: 167–75.

Danthine, Jean-Pierre. 1977. "Martingale, Market Efficiency and Commodity Prices." *European Economic Review* 10: 1–17.

Day, Richard H. 1965. "Probability Distributions of Field Crop Yields." *Journal of Farm Economics* 47: 713–41.

Deaton, Angus, and Laroque, Guy. 1990. "On the Behavior of Commodity Prices." Mimeo, Princeton University.

DeCanio, Stephen J. 1979. "Rational Expectations and Learning from Experience." *Quarterly Journal of Economics* 93: 47–57.

Devarajan, Shantayanan, and Hubbard, R. Glenn. 1984. "Drawing Down the Strategic Petroleum Reserve." In Alvin L. Alm and Robert J. Weiner (eds.), *Oil Shock: Policy Response and Implementation.* Cambridge, Mass.: Ballinger.

Dickey, David A., and Fuller, Wayne A. 1981. "Likelihood Ratio Statistics for Autoregressive Time Series with a Unit Root." *Econometrica* 49: 1057–72.

Diebold, Francis X., and Rudebusch, Glenn D. 1989. "Long Memory and Persistence in Aggregate Output." *Journal of Monetary Economics* 24: 189–209.

Dixon, Bruce L., and Chen, Wu-Hsiung. 1982. "A Stochastic Control Approach to Buffer Stock Management in the Taiwan Rice Market." *Journal of Development Economics* 10: 187–207.

Dow, J. C. R. 1941. "The Inaccuracy of Expectations." *Economica* 8: 162–75.

Duddy, Edward A., and Revzan, David A. 1933. "Profits and Losses in the Storage of Butter." *Journal of Business* 6: 293–317.

Dusak, Katherine. 1973. "Futures Trading and Investor Returns: An Investigation of Commodity Market Risk Premiums." *Journal of Political Economy* 81: 1387–406.

Dvoretzky, A.; Kiefer, J.; and Wolfowitz, J. 1952a. "The Inventory Problem: I. Case of Known Distributions of Demand." *Econometrica* 20: 187–222.

1952b. "The Inventory Problem: II. Case of Unknown Distributions of Demand." *Econometrica* 20: 450–66.

Eaton, Jonathan, and Eckstein, Zvi. 1984. "The U.S. Strategic Petroleum Reserve: An Analytical Framework." In Robert E. Baldwin and Anne O. Krueger (eds.), *The Structure and Evolution of Recent U.S. Trade Policy*, 237–72. Chicago: University of Chicago Press.

Eckalbar, John C. 1985a. "Inventories in a Dynamic Macro Model with Flexible Prices." *European Economic Review* 27: 201–19.

1985b. "Inventory Fluctuations in a Disequilibrium Macro Model." *Economic Journal* 95: 976–91.

Eckstein, Zvi. 1984. "A Rational Expectations Model of Agricultural Supply." *Journal of Political Economy* 92: 1–19.

1985. "The Dynamics of Agricultural Supply: A Reconsideration." *American Journal of Agricultural Economics* 67: 204–14.

Eckstein, Zvi, and Eichenbaum, Martin S. 1985. "Oil Supply Disruptions and the Optimal Tariff in a Dynamic Stochastic Equilibrium Model." In Thomas J. Sargent (ed.), *Energy, Foresight, and Strategy*, 40–69. Washington, D.C.: Resources for the Future.

Eichenbaum, Martin S. 1984. "Rational Expectations and the Smoothing Properties of Finished Goods." *Journal of Monetary Economics* 14: 71–96.

1989. "Some Empirical Evidence on the Production Level and Production Cost Smoothing Models of Inventory Investment." *American Economic Review* 79: 853–64.

Elam, Emmett, and Dixon, Bruce L. 1988. "Examining the Validity of a Test of Futures Market Efficiency." *Journal of Futures Markets* 8: 365–72.

Engle, Robert F.; Lilien, David M.; and Robins, Russell P. 1987. "Estimating Time Varying Risk Premia in the Term Structure: The ARCH-M Model." *Econometrica* 55: 391–407.

Epps, T. W., and Kukanza, Michael J. 1985. "Predictions of Returns to Commodities Speculation: Some Evidence of Informational Inefficiency in Futures Markets." *Review of Research in Futures Markets* 4: 366–82.

Evans, G. B. A., and Savin, N. E. 1984. "Testing for Unit Roots: 2." *Econometrica* 52: 1241–71.

Ezekiel, Mordecai. 1938. "The Cobweb Theorem." *Quarterly Journal of Economics* 52: 255–80.

Fafchamps, Marcel. 1989. "Sequential Decisions under Uncertainty and Labor Market Failure: A Model of Household Behavior in the African Semi-Arid Tropics." Ph.D. dissertation, University of California, Berkeley.

Fair, Ray C. 1989. "The Production-Smoothing Model Is Alive and Well." *Journal of Monetary Economics* 24: 353–70.

Fama, Eugene F., and French, Kenneth, R. 1987. "Commodity Futures Prices: Some Evidence on Forecast Power, Premiums, and the Theory of Storage." *Journal of Business* 60: 55–73.

472   References

1988. "Business Cycles and the Behavior of Metals Prices." *Journal of Finance* 43: 1075–93.
Farmer, Roger E. A. 1990. "Rince Preferences." *Quarterly Journal of Economics* 105: 43–60.
Feder, Gershon; Just, Richard E.; and Schmitz, Andrew. 1977. "Storage with Price Uncertainty in International Trade." *International Economic Review* 18: 553–68.
1980. "Futures Markets and the Theory of the Firm Under Price Uncertainty." *Quarterly Journal of Economics* 94: 317–28.
Feldman, Mark. 1987. "An Example of Convergence to Rational Expectations with Heterogeneous Beliefs." *International Economic Review* 28: 635–50.
Feldstein, Martin. 1977. "The Surprising Incidence of a Tax on Pure Rent: A New Answer to an Old Question." *Journal of Political Economy* 85: 349–60.
Flavin, Marjorie A. 1983. "Excess Volatility in the Financial Markets: A Reassessment of the Empirical Evidence." *Journal of Political Economy* 91: 929–56.
Flood, Robert P., and Hodrick, Robert J. 1985. "Optimal Price and Inventory Adjustment in an Open-Economy Model of the Business Cycle." *Quarterly Journal of Economics* 100: 887–914.
Floyd, John E. 1965. "The Effects of Farm Price Supports on the Returns to Land and Labor in Agriculture." *Journal of Political Economy* 73: 148–58.
Ford, Derek J.. 1978. "Simulation Analyses of Stabilization Policies in the International Coffee Market." In F. Gerald Adams and Jere R. Behrman (eds.), *Econometric Modeling of World Commodity Policy*, 117–45. Lexington, Mass.: Lexington Books.
Frankel, Jeffrey A. 1986. "Expectations and Commodity Price Dynamics." *American Journal of Agricultural Economics* 68: 344–48.
French, Kenneth R. 1986. "Detecting Spot Price Forecasts in Futures Prices." *Journal of Business* 59: S39–S54.
Fuller, Wayne A. 1976. *Introduction to Statistical Time Series*. New York: Wiley.
Gal, Shmuel. 1989. "The Parameter Iteration Method of Dynamic Programming." *Management Science* 35: 675–84.
Gallagher, Paul. 1987. "U.S. Soybean Yields: Estimation and Forecasting with Nonsymmetric Disturbances." *American Journal of Agricultural Economics* 69: 796–803.
Gardner, Bruce L. 1975. "The Farm–Retail Price Spread in a Competitive Food Industry." *American Journal of Agricultural Economics* 57: 399–409.
1979. *Optimal Stockpiling of Grain*. Lexington, Mass.: Lexington Books.
1981. "Farmer-Owned Grain Reserve Program Needs Modification: Consequences of USDA's Farmer-Owned Reserve Program for Grain Stocks and Prices." Vol. 2 of Report to the Congress, U.S. General Accounting Office, June 26, 1981.
1982. "Public Stocks of Grain and the Market for Grain Storage." In Gordon C. Rausser (ed.), *New Directions in Econometric Modeling and Forecasting in U. S. Agriculture*, 443–69. New York: North-Holland.
1983. "Efficient Redistribution through Commodity Markets." *American Journal of Agricultural Economics* 65: 225–34.

1985. "International Commodity Agreements." Mimeo.

1987. "Causes of U.S. Farm Commodity Programs." *Journal of Political Economy* 95: 290–310.

Garnsey, P., and Morris, I. 1989. "Risk and the *Polis:* The Evolution of Institutionalized Responses to Food Supply Problems in the Ancient Greek State." In Paul Halstead and John O'Shea (eds.), *Bad Year Economics: Cultural Responses to Risk and Uncertainty*, 98–105. Cambridge, U.K.: Cambridge University Press.

Gavish, Bezalel, and Johnson, Robert E. 1990. "A Fully Polynomial Approximation Scheme for Single-Product Scheduling in a Finite Capacity Facility." *Operations Research* 38: 70–83.

Gelb, Alan H. 1979. "On the Definition and Measurement of Instability and the Costs of Buffering Export Fluctuations." *Review of Economic Studies* 46: 149–62.

Gemmill, Gordon. 1985. "Forward Contracts or International Buffer Stocks? A Study of Their Relative Efficiencies in Stabilising Commodity Export Earnings." *Economic Journal* 95: 400–17.

Ghali, Moheb A. 1987. "Seasonality, Aggregation and the Testing of the Production Smoothing Hypothesis." *American Economic Review* 77: 464–9.

Ghosh, S.; Gilbert, C. L.; and Hughes Hallett, A. J. 1984. "Simple and Optimal Control Rules for Stabilizing Commodity Markets." In A. J. Hughes Hallett (ed.), *Applied Decision Analysis and Economic Behavior*, 209– 48. Dordrecht: Martinus Nijhoff.

1987. *Stabilizing Speculative Commodity Markets*. Oxford: Clarendon.

Gilbert, Christopher L. 1986. "Commodity Price Stabilization: The Masell Model and Multiplicative Disturbances." *Quarterly Journal of Economics* 101: 635–40.

1987. "International Commodity Agreements: Design and Performance." *World Development* 15: 591–616.

1988. "Optimal and Competitive Storage Rules: The Gustafson Problem Revisited." In O. Guvenen (ed.), *International Commodity Market Models and Policy Analysis*, 27–52. Dordrecht: Kluwer.

Gislason, Conrad. 1960. "Grain Storage Rules." *Journal of Farm Economics* 42: 576–95.

Glauber, Joseph; Helmberger, Peter; and Miranda, Mario. 1989. "Four Approaches to Commodity Market Stabilization: A Comparative Analysis." *American Journal of Agricultural Economics* 71: 326–37.

Godden, D. P., and Helyar, K. R. 1980. "An Alternative Method for Deriving Optimal Fertilizer Rates." *Review of Marketing and Agricultural Economics* 48: 83–97.

Goss, Barry A. 1981. "The Forward Pricing Function of the London Metal Exchange." *Applied Economics* 13: 133–50.

1983. "The Semi-Strong Form Efficiency of the London Metal Exchange." *Applied Economics* 15: 681–98.

Gould, John P. 1978. "Inventories and Stochastic Demand: Equilibrium Models of the Firm and Industry." *Journal of Business* 51: 1–42.

Grandmont, Jean Michel. 1977. "Temporary General Equilibrium Theory." *Econometrica* 45: 535–72.

Gras, Norman S. B. 1915. *The Evolution of the English Corn Market from the Twelfth to the Eighteenth Century*. Cambridge, Mass.: Harvard University Press.

Gray, Roger W., and Peck, Anne E. 1981. "The Chicago Wheat Futures Market: Recent Problems in Historical Perspective." *Food Research Institute Studies* 44: 431–49.

Gray, Roger W., and Tomek, William G. 1971. "Temporal Relationships among Futures Prices: Reply." *American Journal of Agricultural Economics* 53: 362–6.

Green, Jerry, and Laffont, Jean-Jacques. 1981. "Disequilibrium Dynamics with Inventories and Anticipatory Price-Setting." *European Economic Review* 16: 199–221.

Gregory, Allan W., and McCurdy, Thomas H. 1984. "Testing the Unbiasedness Hypothesis in the Forward Foreign Exchange Market: A Specification Analysis." *Journal of International Money and Finance* 3: 357–68.

Grennes, Thomas; Johnson, Paul R.; and Thursby, Marie. 1978. "Insulating Trade Policies, Inventories, and Wheat Price Stability." *American Journal of Agricultural Economics* 60: 132–4.

Gustafson, Robert L. 1958a. "Carryover Levels for Grains: A Method for Determining Amounts That Are Optimal under Specified Conditions." USDA Technical Bulletin 1178.

1958b. "Implications of Recent Research on Optimal Storage Rules." *Journal of Farm Economics* 40: 290–300.

Hakkio, Craig S. 1986. "Does the Exchange Rate Follow a Random Walk? A Monte Carlo Study of Four Tests for a Random Walk." *Journal of International Money and Finance* 5: 221–9.

Hallwood, Paul. 1977. "Interactions between Private Speculation and Buffer Stock Agencies in Commodity Stabilization." *World Development* 5(4): 349–53.

1979. *Stabilization of International Commodity Markets*. Greenwich, Conn.: JAI Press.

Haltiwanger, John C., and Maccini, Louis J. 1988. "A Model of Inventory and Layoff Behavior under Uncertainty." *Economic Journal* 98: 731–45.

Hamid, Mian Abdul. 1974. *Hoarding and Black Market Act*. Lahore, Pakistan: Khyber Law Publishers.

Hart, Albert Gailord. 1942. "Risk, Uncertainty, and the Unprofitability of Compounding Probabilities." In Oscar Lange, Francis McIntyre, and Theodore O. Yntema (eds.), *Studies in Mathematical Economics and Econometrics*, 110–18. Chicago: University of Chicago Press.

Hartman, Richard. 1976. "Factor Demand with Output Price Uncertainty." *American Economic Review* 66: 675–81.

Hartzmark, Michael L. 1987. "Returns to Individual Traders of Futures: Aggregate Results." *Journal of Political Economy* 95: 1292–306.

Harvey, Roy. 1974. "Dygam: A Computer System for the Solution of Dynamic Programs." Mimeo, Control Analysis Corporation, Palo Alto, Calif.

Hausman, Jerry A. 1981. "Exact Consumer's Surplus and Deadweight Loss." *American Economic Review* 71: 662–76.

Hay, George A. 1970. "Production, Price, and Inventory." *American Economic Review* 60: 531–45.

Helmberger, Peter G., and Akinyosoye, Vincent. 1984. "Competitive Pricing and Storage under Uncertainty with an Application to the U.S. Soybean Market." *American Journal of Agricultural Economics* 66: 119–30.

Helmberger, Peter G., and Weaver, Robert D. 1977. "Welfare Implications of Commodity Storage under Uncertainty." *American Journal of Agricultural Economics* 59: 639–51.

Helmberger, Peter G.; Weaver, Robert D.; and Haygood, Kathleen T. 1982. "Rational Expectations and Competitive Pricing and Storage." *American Journal of Agricultural Economics* 64: 266–70.

Helpman, Elhanan. 1988. "Trade Patterns under Uncertainty with Country Specific Shocks." *Econometrica* 56: 645–59.

Higginbotham, Harlow N. 1976. "The Demand for Hedging in Grain Futures Markets." Ph.D. dissertation, University of Chicago.

Hillman, Jimmye; Johnson, D. Gale; and Gray, Roger. 1975. "Food Reserve Policies for World Food Security: A Consultant Study for Alternative Approaches." Publication No. CSP/75/2, Food and Agriculture Organization, United Nations.

Hinchy, Mike, and Fisher, Brian S. 1988. "Benefits from Price Stabilization to Producers and Processors: The Australian Buffer-Stock Scheme for Wool." *American Journal of Agricultural Economics* 70: 604–15.

Hogan, William W. 1983. "Oil Stockpiling: Help Thy Neighbor." *Energy Journal* 4: 49–71.

Holly, Sean, and Hughes Hallett, Andrew. 1989. *Optimal Control, Expectations and Uncertainty.* Cambridge, U.K.: Cambridge University Press.

Holt, Matthew T., and Johnson, Stanley R. 1989. "Bounded Price Variation and Rational Expectations in an Endogenous Switching Model of the U.S. Corn Market." *Review of Economics and Statistics* 71: 605–13.

Holthausen, Duncan M. 1979. "Hedging and the Competitive Firm under Price Uncertainty." *American Economic Review* 69: 989–95.

Honkapohja, Seppo, and Ito, Takatoshi. 1980. "Inventory Dynamics in a Simple Disequilibrium Macroeconomic Model." *Scandinavian Journal of Economics* 82: 184–98.

Horwich, George, and Weimer, David Leo. 1984. *Oil Price Stocks, Market Response, and Contingency Planning.* Washington, D.C.: American Enterprise Institute.

Houthakker, Hendrik S. 1959. "The Scope and Limits of Futures Trading." In *The Allocation of Economic Resources: Essays in Honor of Francis Haley*, 134 – 59. Stanford: Stanford University Press.

Howell, L. D. 1956. "Influence of Certified Stocks on Spot-Futures Price Relationships for Cotton." USDA Technical Bulletin 1151.

Hsieh, David A., and Kulatilaka, Nalin. 1982. "Rational Expectations and Risk Premia in Forward Markets: Primary Metals at the London Metals Exchange." *Journal of Finance* 37: 1199–207.

Hubbard, R. Glenn. 1986. "Supply Shocks and Price Adjustment in the World Oil Market." *Quarterly Journal of Economics* 101: 85–102.

Hubbard, R. Glenn, and Weiner, Robert J. 1984. "Government Stockpiles in a Multicountry World." In Alvin L. Alm and Robert J. Weiner (eds.), *Oil Shock: Policy Response and Implementation*, 197–218. Cambridge, Mass.: Ballinger.

Hufton, Olwen. 1985. "Social Conflict and the Grain Supply in Eighteenth-Century France." in Robert I. Rotberg and Theodore K. Rabb (eds.), *Hunger and History: The Impact of Changing Food Production and Consumption Patterns on Society*, 105–33. Cambridge, U.K.: Cambridge University Press.

Hughes Hallett, A. J. 1984. "Optimal Stockpiling in a High-Risk Commodity Market: The Case of Copper." *Journal of Economic Dynamics and Control* 8: 211–38.

1986. "Commodity Market Stabilization and 'North–South' Income Transfers." *Journal of Development Economics* 24: 293–316.

1988. "Commodity Market Stabilization with Speculative Activity: An Example from the World Copper Market." In O. Guvenen (ed.), *International Commodity Market Models and Policy Analysis*, 185–204. Dordrecht: Kluwer.

Imrohoroglu, Ayse. 1989. "Cost of Business Cycles with Indivisibilities and Liquidity Constraints." *Journal of Political Economy* 97: 1364–83.

Innes, Robert D. 1990a. "Government Target Price Intervention in Economies with Incomplete Markets." *Quarterly Journal of Economics*.

1990b. "Limited Liability and Incentive Contracting with Ex Ante Action Choices." *Journal of Economic Theory* 52: 45–67.

Irvine, F. Owen, Jr. 1981. "An Optimal Middleman Firm Price Adjustment Policy: The 'Short-Run Inventory-Based Pricing Policy'." *Economic Inquiry* 19: 245–69.

Jacobs, O. L. R. 1967. *An Introduction to Dynamic Programming*. London: Chapman and Hall.

James, Robert G., and Perelman, Michael. 1986. "Large Biases in Small Sample Tests of Random Walk Behavior." California State University, Behavior and Social Sciences Paper No. 86–8.

Johnson, D. Gale. 1975. "World Agriculture, Commodity Policy, and Price Variability." *American Journal of Agricultural Economics* 57: 823–8.

Johnson, D. Gale, and Sumner, Dan. 1976. "An Optimization Approach to Grain Reserves for Developing Countries." In David J. Eaton and W. Scott Steele (eds.), *Analysis of Grain Reserves*, 56–75. USDA, Economic Research Service Report No. 634.

Jones, Robert A., and Ostroy, Joseph M. 1984. "Flexibility and Uncertainty." *Review of Economic Studies* 51: 13–32.

Jongman, Willem, and Dekker, Rudolf. 1989. "Public Intervention in the Food Supply in Pre-Industrial Europe." In Paul Halstead and John O'Shea (eds.), *Bad Year Economics: Cultural Responses to Risk and Uncertainty*, 114–22. Cambridge, U.K.: Cambridge University Press.

Josling, Timothy E. 1974. "Agricultural Policies in Developing Countries: A Review." *Journal of Agricultural Economics* 25: 220–64.

1976. "Role of Grain Reserves in an International Food Strategy." In Brian

Davey, Timothy E. Josling, and Alister McFarquhar (eds.), *Agriculture and the State: British Policy in a World Context*, 237–47. London: Macmillan.

1977a. "Government Price Policies and the Structure of International Agricultural Trade." *Journal of Agricultural Economics* 28: 261–77.

1977b. "Grain Reserves and Government Agricultural Policies." *World Development* 5: 603–11.

Josling, Timothy E., and Barichello, Richard. 1984. "International Trade and World Food Security: The Role of Developed Countries since the World Food Conference." *Food Policy* 9(4): 317–27.

Judd, Kenneth L. 1990. "Minimum Weighted Residual Methods for Solving Dynamic Economic Models." Mimeo, Hoover Institution.

Just, Richard E. 1981. "Farmer-Owned Grain Reserve Program Needs Modification to Improve Effectiveness: Theoretical and Empirical Considerations in Agricultural Buffer Stock Policy under the Food Aid Agricultural Act of 1977." Vol. 3 of Report to the Congress, U.S. General Accounting Office, June 26, 1981.

Just, Richard E., and Hallam, J. Arne. 1978. "Functional Flexibility in Commodity Price Stabilization Policy." *Proceedings, Journal of the American Statistical Association*, Business and Economics Section, 177–86.

Just, Richard E., and Rausser, Gordon C. 1981. "Commodity Price Forecasting with Large-Scale Econometric Models and the Futures Market." *American Journal of Agricultural Economics* 63: 197–208.

Just, Richard; Lutz, Ernst; Schmitz, Andrew; and Turnovsky, Stephen. 1978. "The Distribution of Welfare Gains from Price Stabilization: An International Perspective." *Journal of International Economics* 8: 551–63.

Kahl, Kandice H., and Tomek, William G. 1986. "Forward-Pricing Models for Futures Markets: Some Statistical and Interpretative Issues." *Food Research Institute Studies* 20: 71–85.

Kahn, James A. 1987. "Inventories and the Volatility of Production." *American Economic Review* 77: 667–79.

Kahneman, Daniel, and Tversky, Amos. 1979. "Prospect Theory: An Analysis of Decision Under Risk." *Econometrica* 47: 263–91.

Kaldor, Nicholas. 1939. "Speculation and Economic Stability." *Review of Economic Studies* 7: 1–27.

Kaplan, Steven L. 1976. *Bread, Politics and Political Economy in the Reign of Louis XV*, 2 vols. The Hague: Martinus Nijhoff.

1977. "Lean Years, Fat Years: The 'Community' Granary System and the Search for Abundance in Eighteenth-Century Paris." *French Historical Studies* 10: 197–230.

Karp, Larry, and Newbery, David M. G. In press. "Intertemporal Consistency Issues in Depletable Resources." In Allen V. Kneese and James L. Sweeney (eds.), *Handbook of Natural Resource and Energy Economics*, Vol 3. New York: North-Holland.

Kennedy, John O. S. 1979. "Optimal Buffer Stock Policies for Wheat at the World Level." *Australian Journal of Agricultural Economics* 23: 163–75.

1981. "An Alternative Method for Deriving Optimal Fertilizer Rates: Comment and Extension." *Review of Marketing and Agricultural Economics* 49: 203–11.

1986. *Dynamic Programming: Applications to Agriculture and Natural Resources.* London: Elsevier.

Kennedy, John O. S.; Whan, I. F.; Jackson, R.; and Dillon, J. L. 1973. "Optimal Fertilizer Carryover and Crop Recycling Policies for a Tropical Grain Crop." *Australian Journal of Agricultural Economics* 17: 104–13.

Kenyon, David; Kling, Kenneth; Jordan, Jim; Seale, William; and McCabe, Nancy. 1987. "Factors Affecting Agricultural Futures Price Variance." *Journal of Futures Markets* 7: 73–91.

Keynes, John Maynard. 1930. *A Treatise on Money: Volume II: The Applied Theory of Money.* London: Macmillan.

1938. "The Policy of Government Storage of Foodstuffs and Raw Materials." *Economic Journal* 48: 449–60.

1974 [1942]. "The International Control of Raw Materials." *Journal of International Economics* 4: 299–315.

Khusro, A. M. 1973. *Buffer Stocks and Storage of Foodgrains in India.* Bombay: Tata McGraw-Hill.

Kimball, M. S. 1990. "Precautionary Saving in the Small and in the Large." *Econometrica* 58: 53–73.

Kleidon, Allan W. 1986a. "Bias in Small Sample Tests of Stock Price Rationality." *Journal of Business* 59: 237–61.

1986b. "Variance Bounds Tests and Stock Price Valuation Models." *Journal of Political Economy* 94: 953–1001.

Knapp, Keith C. 1982. "Optimal Grain Carryovers in Open Economies: A Graphical Analysis." *American Journal of Agricultural Economics* 64: 198–204.

Kofi, Tetteh A. 1973. "A Framework for Comparing the Efficiency of Futures Markets." *American Journal of Agricultural Economics* 55: 584–94.

Kollintzas, Tryphon. 1989. "The Linear Rational Expectations Equilibrium Inventory Model: An Introduction." In Tryphon Kollintzas (ed.), *The Rational Expectations Equilibrium Inventory Model,* 1–32. New York: Springer-Verlag.

Kotlikoff, Lawrence J., and Spivak, Avia. 1981. "The Family as an Incomplete Annuities Market." *Journal of Political Economy* 89: 372–91.

Krapels, Edward N. 1980. *Oil Crisis Management: Strategic Stockpiling for International Security.* Baltimore: Johns Hopkins University Press.

Krol, Robert, and Svorny, Shirley. 1987. "A Time-Series Analysis of U.S. Petroleum Industry Inventory Behavior." *Energy Journal* 8: 65–78.

Kydland, Finn E., and Prescott, Edward C. 1977. "Rules Rather than Discretion: The Inconsistency of Optimal Plans." *Journal of Political Economy* 83: 473–91.

Labys, Walter C. 1980. "Commodity Price Stabilization Models: A Review and Appraisal." *Journal of Policy Modeling* 2: 121–36.

1987. *Primary Commodity Markets and Models: An International Bibliography.* Aldershot, U.K.: Gower.

Langemeier, Michael R., and Patrick, George F. 1990. "Farmers' Marginal Propensity to Consume: An Application to Illinois Grain Farms." *American Journal of Agricultural Economics* 72: 309–16.

Langley, James A.; Reinsel, Robert D.; Craven, John A.; Zellner, James A.; and

Nelson, Frederick J. 1985. "Commodity Price and Income Support Policies in Perspective." USDA *Agricultural Food Policy Review* Report 530, 122–65.

Laroque, Guy. 1989. "On the Inventory Cycle and the Instability of the Competitive Mechanism." *Econometrica* 57: 911–35.

Lee, Seon, and Blandford, David. 1980. "An Analysis of International Buffer Stocks for Cocoa and Copper Through Dynamic Optimization." *Journal of Policy Modeling* 2: 371–88.

Legge, Karen. 1989. "Changing Responses to Drought among the Wodaabe of Niger." In Paul Halstead and John O'Shea (eds.), *Bad Year Economics: Cultural Responses to Risk and Uncertainty*, 81–6. Cambridge, U.K.: Cambridge University Press.

LeRoy, Stephen F., and Porter, Richard D. 1981. "The Present-Value Relation: Tests Based on Implied Variance Bounds." *Econometrica* 49: 555–74.

Leuthold, Raymond. 1974. "The Price Performance on the Futures Market of a Nonstorable Commodity: Live Beef Cattle." *American Journal of Agricultural Economics* 56: 271–9.

Lichtenberg, A. J., and Ujihara, A. 1989. "Application of Nonlinear Mapping Theory to Commodity Price Fluctuations." *Journal of Economic Dynamics and Control* 13: 225–46.

Lin, Ying-shiang; Hildreth, R. J.; and Tefertiller, K. R. 1963. "Non-Parametric Statistical Tests for Bunchiness of Dryland Crop Yields and Reinvestment Income." *Journal of Farm Economics* 45: 592–8.

Liu, Ts'ui-jung. 1985. "A Reappraisal of the Functions of the Granary System in Ch'ing China (1644–1911)." *Les techniques de conservation des grains à long terme* 3: 305–21.

Lovell, Michael. 1961. "Manufacturers' Inventories, Sales Expectations, and the Acceleration Principle." *Econometrica* 29: 293–314.

Lowry, Mark Newton. 1989. "Competitive Speculative Storage and the Cost of Refinery Product Supply." *Energy Journal* 10: 187–93.

Lowry, Mark; Glauber, Joseph; Miranda, Mario; and Helmberger, Peter. 1987. "Pricing and Storage of Field Crops: A Quarterly Model Applied to Soybeans." *American Journal of Agricultural Economics* 69: 740–9.

Luttrell, Clifton B., and Gilbert, R. Alton. 1976. "Crop Yields: Random, Cyclical, or Bunchy?" *American Journal of Agricultural Economics* 58: 521–31.

Ma, Cindy W. 1989. "Forecasting Efficiency of Energy Futures Prices." *Journal of Futures Markets* 9: 393–419.

Maberly, Edwin D. 1985. "Testing Futures Market Efficiency – A Restatement." *Journal of Futures Markets* 5: 425–432.

MacAvoy, Paul W. 1988. *Explaining Metals Prices*. Boston: Kluwer.

MacBean, Alasdair, and Nguyen, Duc Tin. 1987. "International Commodity Agreements: Shadow and Substance." *World Development* 15: 575–90.

McCallum, B. T. 1976. "Rational Expectations and the Natural Rate Hypothesis: Some Consistent Estimates." *Econometrica* 44: 43–52.

McCloskey, Donald N. 1976. "English Open Fields as Behavior Towards Risk." In Paul Uselding (ed.), *Research in Economic History*, Vol. 1, 124–70. Greenwich, Conn.: JAI Press.

McCloskey, Donald N., and Nash, John. 1984. "Corn at Interest: The Extent and Cost of Grain Storage in Medieval England." *American Economic Review* 74: 174–87.

MacDonald, Ronald, and Taylor, Mark P. 1988a. "Metals Prices, Efficiency and Cointegration: Some Evidence from the London Metal Exchange." *Bulletin of Economic Research* 40: 235–9.

1988b. "Testing Rational Expectations and Efficiency in the London Metal Exchange." *Oxford Bulletin of Economics and Statistics* 50: 41–52.

Machina, Mark J. 1984. "Temporal Risk and the Nature of Induced Preferences." *Journal of Economic Theory* 33: 231–8.

Machina, Mark J. 1987. "Choice under Uncertainty: Problems Solved and Unsolved." *Economic Perspectives* 1: 121–54.

McNicol, David L. 1978. *Commodity Agreements and Price Stabilization.* Lexington, Mass.: Lexington Books.

Mangel, Marc. 1985. *Decision and Control in Uncertain Resource Systems.* Orlando, Fla.: Academic Press.

Marcus, Alan J. 1984. "Efficient Asset Portfolios and the Theory of Normal Backwardation: A Comment." *Journal of Political Economy* 92: 162–4.

Marcus, Alan J., and Modest, David M. 1984. "Futures Markets and Production Decisions." *Journal of Political Economy* 92: 409–26.

Martin, Larry, and Garcia, Philip. 1981. "The Price-Forecasting Performance of Futures Markets for Live Cattle and Hogs: A Disaggregated Analysis." *American Journal of Agricultural Economics* 63: 209–15.

Maskin, Eric, and Newbery, David. 1990. "Disadvantageous Oil Tariffs and Dynamic Consistency." *American Economic Review* 80: 143–56.

Massell, Benton F. 1969. "Price Stabilization and Welfare." *Quarterly Journal of Economics* 83: 284–98.

Meade, J. E. 1950. "Degrees of Competitive Speculation." *Review of Economic Studies* 17: 159–67.

Miranda, Mario J. 1985. "Analysis of Rational Expectation Models for Storable Commodities under Government Regulation." Ph.D. dissertation, University of Wisconsin – Madison.

Miranda, Mario J., and Glauber, Joseph W. 1989. "Competitive Spatial-Temporal Price Equilibrium under Uncertainty." Mimeo.

Miranda, Mario J., and Helmberger, Peter G. 1988. "The Effects of Commodity Price Stabilization Programs." *American Economic Review* 78: 46–58.

Miron, Jeffrey A., and Zeldes, Stephen P. 1988. "Seasonality, Cost Shocks, and the Production Smoothing Model of Inventories." *Econometrica* 56: 877–908.

Miron, Jeffrey A., and Zeldes, Stephen P. 1989a. "Production, Sales, and the Change in Inventory: An Identity that Doesn't Add Up." *Journal of Monetary Economics* 24: 31–51.

1989b. "Seasonality, Cost Shocks, and the Production Smoothing Model of Inventories." In Tryphon Kollintzas (ed.), *The Rational Expectations Equilibrium Inventory Model,* 246–69. New York: Springer-Verlag.

Moalla-Fetini, Rakia. 1990. "Storage Arbitrage Condition and Overshooting: An Impossibility Theorem." Ph.D. dissertation, University of California, Berkeley.

Monke, Eric A.; Cory, Dennis C.; and Heckerman, Donald G. 1987. "Surplus Disposal in World Markets: An Application to Egyptian Cotton." *American Journal of Agricultural Economics* 69: 570–9.

Moore, Michael J. 1989. "Inventories in the Open Economy Macro Model: A Disequilibrium Analysis." *Review of Economic Studies* 56: 157–62.

Murphy, Frederic H., Toman, Michael A., and Weiss, Howard J. 1986. "An Integrated Analysis of U.S. Oil Security Policies." *Energy Journal* 7(3): 67–82.

Muth, John F. 1961. "Rational Expectations and the Theory of Price Movements." *Econometrica* 29: 315–35.

Nankervis, J. C., and Savin, N. E. 1985. "Testing the Autoregressive Parameter with the *t* Statistic." *Journal of Econometrics* 27: 143–61.

Nelson, Charles R., and Plosser, Charles I. 1982. "Trends and Random Walks in Macroeconomic Time Series." *Journal of Monetary Economics* 10: 139–62.

Nerlove, Marc. 1958. *The Dynamics of Supply: Estimation of Farmers' Response to Price.* Baltimore: Johns Hopkins University Press.

Newbery, David M. G. 1981. "Oil Prices, Cartels, and the Problem of Dynamic Inconsistency." *Economic Journal* 91: 617–46.

1984. "Commodity Price Stabilization in Imperfect or Cartelized Markets." *Econometrica* 52: 563–78.

1989. "The Theory of Food Price Stabilization." *Economic Journal* 99: 1065–82.

Newbery, David M. G., and Stiglitz, Joseph E. 1979. "The Theory of Commodity Price Stabilization Rules: Welfare Impacts and Supply Responses." *Economic Journal* 89: 799–817.

1981. *The Theory of Commodity Price Stabilization: A Study in the Economics of Risk.* Oxford: Clarendon.

1982. "Optimal Commodity Stock-Piling Rules." *Oxford Economic Papers* 34: 403–27.

Nichols, Albert L., and Zeckhauser, Richard J. 1977. "Stockpiling Strategies and Cartel Prices." *Bell Journal of Economics* 8: 66–96.

Obstfeld, Maurice. 1986. "Rational and Self-Fulfilling Balance of Payments Crises." *American Economic Review* 76: 72–81.

Oi, Walter Y. 1961. "The Desirability of Price Instability under Perfect Competition." *Econometrica* 29: 58–64.

Owen, A. D. 1985. "Short-Term Price Formation in the U.S. Uranium Market." *Energy Journal* 6: 37–49.

Patel, Maneklal D. 1965. *Essential Commodities Act,* Bhadra, India: Gujarat Law House.

Paul, Allen B. 1970. "The Pricing of Binspace – A Contribution to the Theory of Storage." *American Journal of Agricultural Economics* 52: 1–12.

Paxson, Christina H. 1989. "Household Savings in Thailand: Responses to Income Shocks." Discussion Paper No. 137, Research Program in Development Studies, Woodrow Wilson School, Princeton University.

Peck, Anne E. 1976. "Futures Markets, Supply Response, and Price Stability." *Quarterly Journal of Economics* 90: 407–23.

1989. "Futures Markets Forecasting Performance and Carrying Charge Relations." Mimeo, Stanford University.

Peck, Anne E., and Gray, Roger W. 1980. "Grain Reserves – Unresolved Issues." *Food Policy* 5: 26–37.

Perron, Pierre. 1988. "Trends and Random Walks in Macroeconomic Time Series: Further Evidence from a New Approach." *Journal of Economic Dynamics and Control* 12: 297–332.

Pesaran, M. Hashem. 1987. *The Limits to Rational Expectations*. Oxford: Basil Blackwell.

Phillips, P. C. B. 1987. "Time Series Regression with a Unit Root." *Econometrica* 55: 277–301.

Phlips, Louis. 1983. *The Economics of Price Discrimination*. Cambridge, U.K.: Cambridge University Press.

Phlips, P. J., and Phlips, L. 1981. "Price Variability, Changes in Demand and the Rate of Interest." *Economic Letters* 7: 7–10.

Pinckney, Thomas C. 1988. "Storage, Trade, and Price Policy under Production Instability: Maize in Kenya." International Food Policy Research Institute, Research Report 71.

1989. "The Demand for Public Storage of Wheat in Pakistan." International Food Policy Research Institute, Research Report 77.

Pindyck, Robert S. 1980. "Energy Price Increases and Macroeconomic Policy." *Energy Journal* 1(4): 1–20.

1990. "Inventories and the Short-Run Dynamics of Commodity Prices." Mimeo, MIT.

Plato, Gerald, and Gordon, Douglas. 1983. "Dynamic Programming and the Economics of Optimal Grain Storage." USDA *Agricultural Economics Research* 35: 10–22.

1984. "Stockpiling U.S. Agricultural Commodities with Volatile World Markets: The Case of Soybeans." USDA *Agricultural Economics Research* 36: 1–9.

Plosser, Charles I. 1989. "Understanding Real Business Cycles." *Journal of Economic Perspectives* 3: 51–77.

Plummer, James L. 1982. "U.S. Stockpiling Policy." In James L. Plummer (ed.), *Energy Vulnerability*. Cambridge, Mass.: Ballinger.

Pope, Rulon D. 1987. "An Analogy between Risk Aversion and Homethetic Production under Certainty." *American Journal of Agricultural Economics* 69: 378–81.

Pratt, John W. 1964. "Risk Aversion in the Small and in the Large." *Econometrica* 32: 122–36.

Protopapadakis, Aris, and Stoll, Hans R. 1983. "Spot and Futures Prices and the Law of One Price." *Journal of Finance* 38: 1431–55.

Pyatt, Graham. 1978. "Marginal Costs, Prices and Storage." *Economic Journal* 88: 749–62.

Quizon, J. B.; Binswanger, Hans P.; and Machina, Mark J. 1984. "Attitudes Toward Risk: Further Remarks." *Economic Journal* 94: 144–8.

Rajaraman, Indira. 1986. "Testing the Rationality of Futures Prices for Selected LDC Agricultural Exports." *Journal of Futures Markets* 6: 523–40.

Ramey, Valerie A. 1989. "Inventories as Factors of Production and Economic Fluctuations." *American Economic Review* 79: 338–54.

Rashid, Salim. 1980. "The Policy of Laissez-Faire during Scarcities." *Economic Journal* 90: 493–503.

Rausser, Gordon C., and Carter, Colin. 1983. "Futures Market Efficiency in the Soybean Complex." *Review of Economics and Statistics* 65: 469–78.

Rausser, Gordon C., and Hochman, Eithan. 1979. *Dynamic Agricultural Systems: Economic Prediction and Control.* New York: North Holland.

Ravallion, Martin. 1985. "The Performance of Rice Markets in Bangladesh During the 1974 Famine." *Economic Journal* 95: 15–29.

Raynauld, Jacques, and Tessier, Jacques. 1984. "Risk Premiums in Futures Markets: An Empirical Investigation." *Journal of Futures Markets* 4: 189–211.

Raynor, A. J., and Reed, G. V. 1978. "Domestic Price Stabilization, Trade Restrictions and Buffer Stock Policy: A Theoretical Policy Analysis with Reference to EEC Agriculture." *European Review of Agricultural Economics* 5: 101–18.

Reagan, Patricia B. 1982. "Inventory and Price Behavior." *Review of Economic Studies* 49: 137–42.

Reagan, Patricia B., and Sheehan, Dennis P. 1985. "The Stylized Facts about the Behavior of Manufacturers' Inventories and Backorders over the Business Cycle: 1959–1980." *Journal of Monetary Economics* 15: 217–46.

Reagan, Patricia B., and Weitzman, Martin L. 1982. "Asymmetries in the Price and Quantity Adjustments by the Competitive Industry." *Journal of Economic Theory* 27: 410–20.

Reutlinger, Shlomo. 1976. "A Simulation Model for Evaluating Worldwide Buffer Stocks of Wheat." *American Journal of Agricultural Economics* 58: 1–12.

1982. "Policies for Food Security in Food-Importing Developing Countries." In Anthony H. Chisholm and Rodney Tyers (eds.), *Food Security: Theory, Policy, and Perspectives from Asia and the Pacific Rim*, 21–44. Lexington, Mass.: Lexington Books.

Reutlinger, Shlomo; Eaton, David; and Bigman, David. 1976. "Should Developing Countries Carry Grain Reserves?" In David J. Eaton and W. Scott Steele (eds.), *Analysis of Grain Reserves*, 12–38. USDA, Economic Research Service Report No. 634.

Rojko, Anthony S. 1975. "The Economics of Food Reserve Systems." *American Journal of Agricultural Economics* 57: 866–72.

Rosenblatt, Murray. 1954. "An Inventory Problem." *Econometrica* 22: 244–7.

Rosenzweig, Mark R. 1988. "Risk, Implicit Contracts and the Family in Rural Areas of Low-Income Countries." *Economic Journal* 98: 1148–70.

Rosenzweig, Mark R., and Stark, Oded. 1989. "Consumption Smoothing, Migration, and Marriage: Evidence from Rural India." *Journal of Political Economy* 97: 905–26.

Ross, Stephen A. 1989. "Information and Volatility: The No-Arbitrage Martingale Approach to Timing and Resolution Irrelevancy." *Journal of Finance* 44: 1–17.

Rotemberg, Julio J., and Saloner, Garth. 1989. "The Cyclical Behavior of Strategic Inventories." *Quarterly Journal of Economics* 104: 73–97.

Rothschild, Michael, and Stiglitz, Joseph E. 1970. "Increasing Risk: I. A Definition." *Journal of Economic Theory* 2: 225–43.

Rowley-Conwy, Peter, and Zvelebil, Marek. 1989. "Saving It for Later: Storage by

Prehistoric Hunter-Gatherers in Europe." In Paul Halstead and John O'Shea (eds.), *Bad Year Economics: Cultural Responses to Risk and Uncertainty*, 40–56. Cambridge, U.K.: Cambridge University Press.

Rutledge, David J. S. 1976. "A Note on the Variability of Futures Prices." *Review of Economics and Statistics* 58: 118–20.

Salant, Stephen W. 1983. "The Vulnerability of Price Stabilization Schemes to Speculative Attack." *Journal of Political Economy* 91: 1–38.

Salant, Stephen W., and Henderson, Dale W. 1978. "Market Anticipations of Government Policies and the Price of Gold." *Journal of Political Economy* 86: 627–48.

Samuelson, Paul A. 1957. "Intertemporal Price Equilibrium: A Prologue to the Theory of Speculation." *Weltwirtschafliches Archiv* 79: 181–219.

1965. "Proof that Properly Anticipated Prices Fluctuate Randomly." *Industrial Management Review* 6: 41–50.

1971. "Stochastic Speculative Price." *Proceedings of the National Academy of Sciences* 68: 335–7.

1972. "The Consumer Does Benefit from Feasible Price Stability." *Quarterly Journal of Economics* 86: 476–93.

1976. "Is Real-World Price a Tale Told by the Idiot of Chance?" *Review of Economics and Statistics* 58: 120–3.

Sandmo, Agnar. 1971. "On the Theory of the Competitive Firm under Price Uncertainty." *American Economic Review* 61: 65–73.

Sarris, Alexander H. 1982. "Commodity-Price Theory and Public Stabilization Stocks." In Anthony H. Chisholm and Rodney Tyers (eds.), *Food Security: Theory, Policy, and Perspectives from Asia and the Pacific Rim*, 105–28. Lexington, Mass.: Lexington Books.

1984. "Speculative Storage, Futures Markets, and the Stability of Agricultural Prices." In Gary G. Storey, Andrew Schmitz, and Alexander H. Sarris (eds.), *International Agricultural Trade: Advanced Readings in Price Formation, Market Structure, and Price Instability*, 65–97. Boulder, Colo.: Westview.

Sarris, Alexander H.; Abbott, Philip C.; and Taylor, Lance. 1979. "Grain Reserves, Emergency Relief, and Food Aid." In William R. Cline (ed.), *Policy Alternatives for a New International Order*, 157–214. New York: Praeger.

Scandizzo, Pasquale; Hazell, Peter; and Anderson, Jock. 1984. *Risky Agricultural Markets: Price Forecasting and the Need for Intervention Policies*. Boulder, Colo.: Westview.

Scarf, Herbert. 1959. "The Optimality of (S, s) Policies in the Dynamic Inventory Problem." In Kenneth J. Arrow; Samuel Karlin; and Patrick Supples (eds.), *Stanford Symposium on Mathematical Methods in the Social Sciences, 1959*, 196–202. Stanford, Calif.: Stanford University Press.

Schechtman, Jack, and Escudero, Vera L. S. 1977. "Some Results on 'An Income Fluctuation Problem.'" *Journal of Economic Theory* 16: 151–66.

Scheinkman, José A., and Schechtman, Jack. 1983. "A Simple Competitive Model with Production and Storage." *Review of Economic Studies* 50: 427–41.

Schmitz, Andrew. 1984. *Commodity Price Stabilization: The Theory and Its Application.* World Bank Staff Working Papers No. 668.

Schmitz, Andrew; McCalla, Alex F.; Mitchell, Donald O.; and Carter, Colin. 1981. *Grain Export Cartels.* Cambridge, Mass.: Ballinger.

Schutte, David P. 1983. "Inventories and Sticky Prices: Note." *American Economic Review* 73: 815–16.

————. 1984. "Optimal Inventories and Equilibrium Price Behavior." *Journal of Economic Theory* 33: 46–58.

Seidmann, Daniel J. 1985. "Target Buffer Stocks." *European Economic Review* 27: 165–82.

Sengupta, Jati K. 1988. "Asymmetry and Robustness in Stabilization Policy for Imperfect Commodity Markets." In O. Guvenen (ed.), *International Commodity Market Models and Policy Analysis*, 167–84. Dordrecht: Kluwer.

Sharples, Jerry A., and Holland, Forrest D. 1981. "Impact of the Farmer-Owned Reserve on Privately Owned Wheat Stocks." *American Journal of Agricultural Economics* 63: 538–43.

Shaw, E. S. 1940. "Elements of a Theory of Inventory." *Journal of Political Economy* 48: 465–85.

Sheffrin, Steven M. 1983. *Rational Expectations.* New York: Cambridge University Press.

Shei, Shun-Yi, and Thompson, Robert L. 1977. "The Impact of Trade Restrictions on Price Stability in the World Wheat Market." *American Journal of Agricultural Economics* 59: 628–38.

Shepherd, Geoffrey S. 1945. *Agricultural Price Control.* Ames, Iowa: Collegiate Press.

Shiller, Robert J. 1981. "Do Stock Prices Move Too Much to Be Justified by Subsequent Changes in Dividends?" *American Economic Review* 71: 421–36.

Shonkwiler, J. S., and Maddala, G. S. 1985. "Modeling Expectations of Bounded Prices: An Application to the Market for Corn." *Review of Economics and Statistics* 67: 697–702.

Smith, Adam. 1784. *Wealth of Nations.* London: Strahan and Cadell.

Smith, Gordon W. 1978a. "Commodity Instability and Market Failure: A Survey of Issues." In F. Gerald Adams and Sonia A Klein (eds.), *Stabilizing World Commodity Markets*, 161–88. Lexington, Mass.: Lexington Books.

————. 1978b. "Modeling Commodity Policy: Issues and Objectives." In F. Gerald Adams and Jere R. Behrman (eds.), *Econometric Modeling of World Commodity Policy*, 99–116. Lexington, Mass.: Lexington Books.

Smith, Rodney T. 1988. "International Energy Cooperation: The Mismatch between IEA Policy Actions and Policy Goals." in George Horwich and David Leo Weimer (eds.), *Responding to International Oil Crises*, 17–103. Washington, D.C.: American Enterprise Institute.

Smithies, A. 1939. "The Maximization of Profits over Time with Changing Cost and Demand Functions." *Econometrica* 7: 312–18.

Spiller, Pablo T., and Huang, Cliff J. 1986. "On the Extent of the Market: Wholesale Gasoline in the Northeastern United States." *Journal of Industrial Economics* 35: 131–45.

Stauber, M. S.; Burt, Oscar R.; Linse, Fred. 1975. "An Economic Evaluation of Nitrogen Fertilization of Grasses When Carry-over Is Significant." *American Journal of Agricultural Economics* 57: 463–71.

Stein, Jerome L. 1981. "Speculative Price: Economic Welfare and the Idiot of Chance." *Review of Economics and Statistics* 36: 223–32.

Stigler, George. 1939. "Production and Distribution in the Short Run." *Journal of Political Economy* 47: 305–27.

Stokey, Nancy L. 1981. "Rational Expectations and Durable Goods Pricing." *Bell Journal of Economics* 12: 112–28.

Stokey, Nancy L., and Lucas, Robert E., Jr. 1989. *Recursive Methods in Economic Dynamics.* Cambridge, Mass.: Harvard University Press.

Summers, Lawrence H. 1981. "Comments on Blinder." *Brookings Papers on Economic Activity,* 513–17.

Takayama, T., and Judge, G. G. 1964. "An Intertemporal Price Equilibrium Model." *Journal of Farm Economics* 46: 477–84.

1971. *Spatial and Temporal Price and Allocation Models.* Amsterdam: North-Holland.

Taub, B. 1987. "A Model of Medieval Grain Prices: Comment." *American Economic Review* 77: 1048–53.

Taylor, C. Robert. 1983. "Certainty Equivalence for Determination of Optimal Fertilizer Application Rates with Carry-over." *Western Journal of Agricultural Economics* 8: 64–7.

Taylor, C. Robert, and Talpaz, Hovav. 1979. "Approximately Optimal Carryover Levels for Wheat in the United States." *American Journal of Agricultural Economics* 61: 33–40.

Taylor, John B., and Uhlig, Harold. 1990. "Solving Nonlinear Stochastic Growth Models: A Comparison of Alternative Solution Methods." *Journal of Business and Economic Statistics* 8: 1–18.

Teisberg, T. J. 1981. "A Dynamic Programming Model of the U.S. Strategic Petroleum Reserve." *Bell Journal of Economics* 12: 526–46.

Telser, Lester G. 1958. "Futures Trading and the Storage of Cotton and Wheat." *Journal of Political Economy* 66: 233–55.

1978. *Economic Theory and the Core.* Chicago: University of Chicago Press.

Theil, H. 1957. "A Note on Certainty Equivalence in Dynamic Planning." *Econometrica* 25: 346–9.

Thompson, Sarahelen. 1986. "Returns to Storage in Coffee and Cocoa Futures Markets." *Journal of Futures Markets* 6: 541–64.

Thurman, Walter N. 1988. "Speculative Carryover: An Empirical Examination of the U.S. Refined Copper Market." *Rand Journal of Economics* 19: 420–37.

Tilley, Daniel S., and Campbell, Steven K. 1988, "Performance of the Weekly Gulf–Kansas City Hard-Red Winter Wheat Basis." *American Journal of Agricultural Economics* 70: 929–35.

Tilly, Louise A. 1971. "The Food Riot as a Form of Political Conflict in France." *Journal of Interdisciplinary History* 2: 23–57.

Timmer, C. Peter. 1989. "Food Price Policy: The Rationale for Government Intervention." *Food Policy* 14: 17–27.

Timoshenko, Vladimir P. 1942. "Variability in Wheat Yields and Outputs: Part I. Cycles or Random Fluctuations." Food Research Institute *Wheat Studies* 18: 291–330.

——— 1943. "Variability in Wheat Yields and Outputs: Part II. Regional Aspects of Variability." Food Research Institute *Wheat Studies* 19: 151–200.

Tisdell, Clem. 1963. "Uncertainty, Instability, and Expected Profit." *Econometrica* 31: 243–7.

Tomek, William G., and Gray, Roger W. 1970. "Temporal Relationships among Prices on Commodity Futures Markets." *American Journal of Agricultural Economics* 52: 372–80.

Townsend, Robert M. 1977. "The Eventual Failure of Price Fixing Schemes." *Journal of Economic Theory* 14: 190–9.

——— 1983. "Equilibrium Theory with Learning and Disparate Expectations: Some Issues and Methods." In Roman Frydman and Edmund S. Phelps (eds.), *Individual Forecasting and Aggregate Outcomes: "Rational Expectations" Examined*, 169–98. New York: Cambridge University Press.

Turnovsky, Stephen J. 1976. "The Distribution of Welfare Gains from Price Stabilization: The Case of Multiplicative Disturbances." *International Economic Review* 17: 133–48.

——— 1978. "The Distribution of Welfare Gains from Price Stabilization: A Survey of Some Theoretical Issues." In F. Gerald Adams and Sonia A Klein (eds.), *Stabilizing World Commodity Markets*, 119–48. Lexington, Mass.: Lexington Books.

Turnovsky, S.; Shalit, H.; and Schmitz, A. 1980. "Consumer's Surplus, Price Instability, and Consumer Welfare." *Econometrica* 48: 135–52.

Tyers, Rodney, and Chisholm, Anthony H. 1982. "Agricultural Policies in Industrialized and Developing Countries and International Food Security." In Anthony H. Chisholm and Rodney Tyers (eds.), *Food Security: Theory, Policy, and Perspectives from Asia and the Pacific Rim*, 307–53. Lexington, Mass.: Lexington Books.

United Nations FAO. 1983. *Approaches to World Food Security*. Rome: Food and Agricultural Organization of the United Nations.

Vaile, Roland S. 1944. "Cash and Future Prices of Corn." *Journal of Marketing* 9: 53–4.

Vance, Lawrence L. 1946. "Grain Market Forces in the Light of Inverse Carrying Charges." *Journal of Farm Economics* 28: 1036–40.

Varian, Hal R. 1984. *Microeconomic Analysis*, 2nd ed. New York: W. W. Norton.

Vartia, Yrjö. 1983. "Efficient Methods of Measuring Welfare Change and Compensated Income in Terms of Ordinary Demand Functions." *Econometrica* 51: 79–98.

Verleger, Philip K., Jr. 1982. *Oil Markets in Turmoil: An Economic Analysis*. Cambridge, Mass.: Ballinger.

——— 1989. Prepared Statement before the Energy Resources Conservation and Development Commission of the State of California, November 13.

Vyas, Nawal Kishore B., and Bafna, Champa Lal M. 1965. *Law of Foodstuffs in Rajasthan*. Pali, Rajasthan: BSV Publishing House.

Wallace, T. D. 1962. "Measures of Social Costs of Agricultural Programs." *Journal of Farm Economics* 44: 580–97.

Waugh, Frederick V. 1944. "Does the Consumer Benefit from Price Instability?" *Quarterly Journal of Economics* 58: 602–14.

Weaver, Robert, and Helmberger, Peter. 1977. "Welfare Implications of Stabilizing Consumption and Production: Comment." *American Journal of Agricultural Economics* 59: 397.

Weckstein, Richard S. 1977. "Food Security: Storage vs Exchange." *World Development* 5: 613–21.

Weil, Philippe. 1990. "Nonexpected Utility in Macroeconomics." *Quarterly Journal of Economics* 105: 29–41.

Weimer, David Leo. 1982. *The Strategic Petroleum Reserve: Planning, Implementation, and Analysis.* Westport, Conn.: Greenwood.

Weitzman, Martin L. 1974. "Prices vs. Quantities." *Review of Economic Studies* 41: 477–91.

West, Kenneth D. 1986. "A Variance Bounds Test of the Linear Quadratic Inventory Model." *Journal of Political Economy* 94: 374–401.

Weyant, John P. 1988. "Coordinated Stock Drawdown: Pros and Cons." In George Horwich and David Leo Weimer (eds.), *Responding to International Oil Crises,* 179–99. Washington, D.C.: American Enterprise Institute.

Weymar, F. Helmut. 1968. *The Dynamics of the World Cocoa Market.* Cambridge, Mass.: MIT Press.

1974. "The Effects of Cocoa Inventories on Price Forecasting." In R. A. Kotey, C. Okali, and B. E. Rourke (eds.), *The Economics of Cocoa Production and Marketing,* 432–49. Legon: University of Ghana Press.

Williams, Jeffrey. 1986. *The Economic Function of Futures Markets.* New York: Cambridge University Press.

Wolff, Christian D. 1987 "Forward Foreign Exchange Rates, Expected Spot Rates, and Premia: A Signal-Extraction Approach." *Journal of Finance* 42: 395–406.

Wong, Chung Ming. 1989. "Welfare Implications of Price Stabilization with Monopolistic Trade." *American Journal of Agricultural Economics* 71: 43–54.

Working, Holbrook. 1934. "Price Relations between May and New-Crop Wheat Futures at Chicago since 1885." Food Research Institute *Wheat Studies* 10: 183–228.

1942. "Quotations on Commodity Futures as Price Forecasts." *Econometrica* 11: 39–52.

1948. "Theory of the Inverse Carrying Charge in Futures Markets." *Journal of Farm Economics* 30: 1–28.

1949. "The Theory of Price of Storage." *American Economic Review* 39: 1254–62.

1953. "Hedging Reconsidered." *Journal of Farm Economics* 35: 544–61.

1962. ""New Concepts Concerning Futures Markets and Prices." *American Economic Review* 52: 431–59.

World Bank. 1989. *Price Prospects for Major Primary Commodities, 1988–2000.* Washington, D.C.: World Bank.

Wright, Brian D. 1979. "The Effects of Ideal Production Stabilization: A Welfare

Analysis under Rational Expectations." *Journal of Political Economy* 87: 1011–33.

1984. "The Effects of Price Uncertainty on the Factor Choices of the Competitive Firm." *Southern Economic Journal* 51: 443–55.

1985. "Commodity Market Stabilization in Farm Programs." In Bruce L. Gardner (ed.), *U.S. Agricultural Policies: The 1985 Farm Legislation*, 257–82. Washington, D.C.: American Enterprise Institute.

Wright, Brian D., and Williams, Jeffrey C. 1982a. "The Economic Role of Commodity Storage." *Economic Journal* 92: 59 6–614.

1982b. "The Roles of Public and Private Storage in Managing Oil Import Disruptions." *Bell Journal of Economics* 13: 341–53.

1984a. "Anti-hoarding Laws: A Stock Condemnation Reconsidered." *American Journal of Agricultural Economics* 66: 447–55.

1984b. "The Welfare Effects of the Introduction of Storage." *Quarterly Journal of Economics* 99: 169–82.

1988a. "The Incidence of Market-Stabilising Price Support Schemes." *Economic Journal* 98: 1183–98.

1988b. "Measurement of Consumer Gains from Market Stabilization." *American Journal of Agricultural Economics* 70: 616–27.

1988c. "Speculative Attack and Market Stabilization." Mimeo, University of California at Berkeley.

1989. "A Theory of Negative Prices for Storage." *Journal of Futures Markets* 9: 1–13.

Young, Leslie, and Schmitz, Andrew. 1984. "Storage under a Cartel." In Gary G. Storey, Andrew Schmitz, and Alexander H. Sarris (eds.), *International Agricultural Trade: Advanced Readings in Price Formation, Market Structure, and Price Instability*, 285–303. Boulder, Colo.: Westview Press.

Zeldes, Stephen P. 1989. "Optimal Consumption with Stochastic Income Deviations from Certainty Equivalence." *Quarterly Journal of Economics* 104: 275–98.

Zwart, A. C., and Meilke, K. D. 1979. "The Influence of Domestic Pricing Policies and Buffer Stocks on Price Stability in the World Wheat Industry." *American Journal of Agricultural Economics* 61: 434–47.

Author index

491

Subject index